JESUS AND THE LAST SUPPER

Jesus and the Last Supper

Brant Pitre

William B. Eerdmans Publishing Company
Grand Rapids, Michigan

Wm. B. Eerdmans Publishing Co.
2140 Oak Industrial Drive N.E., Grand Rapids, Michigan 49505
www.eerdmans.com

Hardcover edition 2015
Paperback edition 2017
Printed in the United States of America

23 22 21 20 19 18 17 1 2 3 4 5 6 7

Library of Congress Cataloging-in-Publication Data

Pitre, Brant James.
Jesus and the Last Supper / Brant Pitre.
pages cm
Includes bibliographical references and index.
ISBN 978-0-8028-7533-4 (pbk.: alk. paper)
1. Lord's Supper. 2. Lord's Supper — Biblical teaching.
3. Jesus Christ — Historicity. 4. Jesus Christ — Jewishness.
5. Church history — Primitive and early church, ca. 30-600.
6. Judaism — History — Post-exilic period, 586 B.C.–210 A.D.
7. Christianity and other religions — Judaism.
8. Judaism — Relations — Christianity.
9. Christianity —Origin. I. Title.

BV823.P58 2015
232.9′57 — dc23

2015018063

For

David Aune,

Delbert Burkett,

Amy-Jill Levine,

John Meier, and

James VanderKam,

my teachers

Contents

Preface

The gestation period of this book has been unusually long. To put it in perspective: when I first began research on *Jesus and the Last Supper,* I was on the verge of publishing my doctoral dissertation as a book; my wife and I were anxiously awaiting the birth of our third child; and the name "Katrina" had absolutely no significance to me whatsoever. As I write the words of this Preface, my daughter Hannah is fast approaching her tenth birthday; New Orleans (the city where I teach) is coming up on the tenth anniversary of Hurricane Katrina; and *Jesus, the Tribulation, and the End of the Exile* (my first book) seems like it was written a lifetime ago.

In part, the delay was due to the explosion that has taken place in historical Jesus research in the last decade. Anyone familiar with the field is well aware that it is undergoing a remarkable period of both prolific output and rapid flux. Much of what was once deemed settled — such as the use of the form-critical criteria of authenticity — is now considered up for grabs. In particular, the sands of methodology seem to be shifting so rapidly that it can be somewhat difficult to find and maintain one's footing. I for one found myself delayed time and time again in my specific work on the topic of the Last Supper simply by trying to keep up with the torrent of recent publications on the historical Jesus, early Judaism (especially studies of Temple and cult), the criteria of authenticity, historical methodology, first-century archaeology, as well as the related field of Gospel studies, which is undergoing its own explosion of fresh research (the debate over Q and the Synoptic problem, eyewitness testimony, and memory studies come to mind). And that is to say nothing of the dreadful abyss of secondary literature that has grown up around the question of the date of the Last Supper, into which I willingly descended and found myself unable to emerge until I had come to peace with what I hope readers will consider to be a fresh and compelling solution to the problem. When I started, if I had known how long that particular chapter would take, I suspect I would be writing the Preface to some other, much shorter, book.

With that said, the journey has been unbelievably worthwhile. I hope it has resulted in a much better book. With that hope in mind, there are a number of people who deserve special thanks for helping me along the way. First and foremost, I wish to express my deepest gratitude to Michael Thomson of Eerdmans not only for agreeing to publish my second academic monograph but for his extraordinary patience during the two new jobs, three moves, and two major (and unexpected) illnesses in my family — all of which played no little role in the expanded time frame it took for the book to be written. Thank you, Michael, for your professionalism and your friendship over these ten years. Second, I am extremely grateful to scholarly colleagues and friends who have read through various drafts or parts of the manuscript and offered me all kinds of critical feedback, especially Dale Allison, Michael Barber, John Bergsma, Michael Bird, Nathan Eubank, Craig Keener, Matthew Levering, Curtis Mitch, Br. Isaac Morales, Nicholas Perrin, and Jim Seghers. In a special way, I want to thank Dale Allison and Craig Keener for taking precious time out of their undoubtedly busy and unbelievably prolific writing schedules to give invaluable feedback and encouragement to a younger scholar who cut his teeth reading their writings and who continues to buy everything they publish and (at least try!) to read everything they write (though whether this is humanly possible with Craig's commentary on Acts is open to debate). Third, the research for this book would not have been possible without the generous grant provided to me by the St. Paul Center for Biblical Theology while I was still reeling from the upheaval that Hurricane Katrina wrought in the city of New Orleans and unsure of exactly where my next paycheck would come from. I am especially grateful to Scott Hahn for his abundant patience and unflagging support for this project. I hope that it makes some small contribution to the St. Paul Center's mission of fostering biblical studies. Fourth, it should go without saying (but must yet be said) that I could not have written this book without the support and encouragement of my wife, Elizabeth, and our children: Morgen, Aidan, Hannah, Marybeth, and Lillia. I would promise never again to write a book this long and involved, but I suspect you know me too well to believe me.

Last, but certainly not least, I wish to thank my teachers over the years: Delbert Burkett, for opening the door to historical Jesus research for me; John Meier, for inspiring me to actually become a New Testament scholar; James VanderKam, for immersing me in the amazing universe of the Dead

Sea Scrolls and Second Temple Judaism; Amy-Jill Levine, for pretty much *everything;* and David Aune, for being a truly humble and enviously learned *Doktorvater* and, even more, my friend. I'm certain that you all will see the deficiencies in this book much more clearly than I do (though I am, of course, the only one responsible for them). Nevertheless, whatever strengths it may possess and whatever contribution it makes to the study of Jesus, Judaism, and Christian origins would not have been possible without all that you taught me. With deepest gratitude, then, I dedicate its pages to you.

BRANT PITRE
July 16, 2015
Our Lady of Mount Carmel

Abbreviations

ABD	*Anchor Bible Dictionary*
ABRL	Anchor Bible Reference Library
AGJU	Arbeiten zur Geschichte des antiken Judentums und des Urchristentums
AnBib	Analecta biblica
ArBib	Aramaic Bible
AYB	Anchor Yale Bible
AYBRL	Anchor Yale Bible Reference Library
BADG	Bauer, Arndt, Gingrich, and Danker, *Greek-English Lexicon of the New Testament and Other Early Christian Literature,* 2nd ed.
BBR	*Bulletin of Biblical Research*
BDB	Brown, Driver, and Briggs, *A Hebrew and English Lexicon of the Old Testament*
BECNT	Baker Exegetical Commentary on the New Testament
BETL	Bibliotheca ephemeridum theologicarum lovaniensium
Bib	*Biblica*
BibInt	Biblical Interpretation
BibRev	*Bible Review*
BRev	*Bible Review*
BTB	*Biblical Theology Bulletin*
BZ	*Biblische Zeitschrift*
BZNW	Beihefte zur Zeitschrift für die neutestamentliche Wissenschaft
CBQ	*Catholic Biblical Quarterly*
CBQMS	Catholic Biblical Quarterly Monograph Series
ConBNT	Coniectanea neotestamentica
CQR	*Church Quarterly Review*
CRINT	Compendia rerum iudaicarum ad Novum Testamentum

CTM	Calwer Theologische Monographien
EdF	Erträge der Forschung
EncJud	*Encyclopaedia Judaica*
EvQ	*Evangelical Quarterly*
ExpTim	*Expository Times*
FAT	Forschungen zum Alten Testament
FBBS	Facet Books, Biblical Series
Greg	*Gregorianum*
HAR	*Hebrew Annual Review*
HDR	Harvard Dissertations in Religion
HSS	Harvard Semitic Studies
HTKNT	Herders theologischer Kommentar zum Neuen Testament
JBL	*Journal of Biblical Literature*
JCT	Jewish and Christian Texts
JJS	*Journal of Jewish Studies*
JQR	*Jewish Quarterly Review*
JSHJ	*Journal for the Study of the Historical Jesus*
JSJSup	Journal for the Study of Judaism Supplements
JSNT	*Journal for the Study of the New Testament*
JSNTSup	Journal for the Study of the New Testament Supplements
JSOTSup	Journal for the Study of the Old Testament Supplements
JSP	*Journal for the Study of the Pseudepigrapha*
JTS	*Journal of Theological Studies*
L&S	*Letter & Spirit*
LCL	Loeb Classical Library
LHJS	Library of Historical Jesus Studies
LNTS	Library of New Testament Studies
LO	Liturgica Oeninpontana
LS	*Louvain Studies*
NACSBT	NAC Studies in Bible and Theology
NGS	New Gospel Studies
NICNT	New International Commentary on the New Testament
NICOT	New International Commentary on the Old Testament
NIGTC	New International Greek Testament Commentary
NovT	*Novum Testamentum*
NovTSup	Novum Testamentum Supplements
NTAb	Neutestamentliche Abhandlungen
NTS	*New Testament Studies*
NTTS	New Testament Tools and Studies

OJC	Orientalia Judaica Christianica
OTL	Old Testament Library
OTP	*Old Testament Pseudepigrapha*
QD	Quaestiones disputatae
RB	*Revue biblique*
SANT	Studien zum Alten und Neuen Testaments
SBAB	Stuttgarter biblische Aufsatzbände
SBF.CMa	Studium biblicum Franciscanum — Collection Major
SBLABS	Society of Biblical Literature Archaeology and Biblical Studies
SBLMS	Society of Biblical Literature Monograph Series
SBS	Stuttgarter Bibelstudien
SBT	Studies in Biblical Theology
SJ	Studia Judaica
SJT	*Scottish Journal of Theology*
SNTSMS	Society of New Testament Studies Monograph Series
SP	Sacra Pagina
TANZ	Texte und Arbeiten zum neutestamentlichen Zeitalter
TDNT	*Theological Dictionary of the New Testament*
TGl	*Theologie und Glaube*
TRENT	Traditions of the Rabbis in the Era of the New Testament
TS	*Theological Studies*
TSAJ	Texts and Studies in Ancient Judaism
TynBul	*Tyndale Bulletin*
VT	*Vetus Testamentum*
VTSup	Vetus Testamentum Supplements
WBC	Word Biblical Commentary
WTJ	*Westminster Theological Journal*
WUNT	Wissenschaftliche Untersuchungen zum Neue Testament
ZAW	*Zeitschrift für die alttestamentliche Wissenschaft*
ZDPV	*Zeitschrift des Deutschen Palästina-Vereins*
ZNT	*Zeitschrift für Neues Testament*
ZNW	*Zeitschrift für die neutestamentliche Wissenschaft*

CHAPTER 1

The Problem of the Last Supper

The problem of the Lord's Supper is the problem of the life of Jesus!

ALBERT SCHWEITZER[1]

Pick up any major historical study of the life of Jesus, read it carefully from cover to cover, and you will probably find at least four key questions operative in it:

1. What is the relationship between Jesus and Judaism? This is the question of *historical context.*
2. Who did Jesus think he was? This is the question of Jesus' self-identification — or, more commonly, his *self-understanding.*
3. What did Jesus expect to happen in the future? This is the question of Jesus' *eschatology,* the discussion of which has tended to revolve around how and when he thought the kingdom of God would come.
4. What is the relationship between Jesus and the early church? This is the question of Jesus' *intentions,* the discussion of which has often revolved around whether or not his aims were fulfilled, abandoned, or distorted by the emerging church.[2]

1. Albert Schweitzer, *The Problem of the Lord's Supper* (trans. A. J. Mattill Jr.; ed. John Reumann; Macon, GA: Mercer University Press, 1982 [orig. 1901]), 137.

2. Significantly, this last question dates back to the work of Hermann Samuel Reimarus, at the very beginnings of the modern historical quest for the historical Jesus. See Hermann Samuel Reimarus, "The Aims of Jesus and His Disciples," in his *Fragments* (ed. Charles H. Talbert; trans. Ralph Fraser; Philadelphia: Fortress, 1970 [orig. 1774-78]). More recently, see Ben F. Meyer, *The Aims of Jesus* (London: SCM, 1979).

At least since the eighteenth century, these four questions have dominated the historical study of Jesus and continue to play a central role in major works on the man from Nazareth.[3] Moreover, as a close study of competing hypotheses reveals, the way in which any given scholar answers these questions will to a large degree constitute some of the starkest dividing lines between their overall proposals about who Jesus was and the meaning of what he did and said.

In this book, I will examine these questions with a particular focus on the words and deeds of Jesus at the Last Supper. Specifically, I wish to ask and answer, in a thoroughgoing way, the following:

1. *Are the words and deeds of Jesus at the Last Supper historically plausible in a Jewish context? If so, what did Jesus mean by them?* For example, as a first-century Jew, how could Jesus have ever uttered the words "This is my body" or "This is my blood," and then commanded his disciples to consume them? If the substance of the words of institution is historical, what did Jesus himself mean by them?
2. *What does the Last Supper reveal about Jesus' self-understanding?* For example, if the Last Supper was a prophetic sign of the messianic banquet, what is the implication of his acting as host of the meal? If his words at the Last Supper do in fact allude to the covenant sacrifice of Moses and the Suffering Servant of Isaiah, what are the implications for how he viewed his own death?
3. *How does the Last Supper fit in Jesus' overall eschatological outlook?* For example, what do his words and actions imply about the relationship between the Last Supper and the coming of the eschatological kingdom of God? If historical, how does Jesus' command for the disciples to repeat his actions fit into his eschatology?
4. *What does the Last Supper reveal about Jesus' intentions toward the community of his disciples?* For example, if the Twelve disciples are a prophetic sign of the restoration of Israel, what is the significance of their presence at the Last Supper? And if historically plausible, what would it mean for Jesus to have linked his own blood with the establishment of a "covenant"?

3. For similar lists, see N. T. Wright, *Jesus and the Victory of God* (*Christian Origins and the Question of God*, vol. 1; Minneapolis: Fortress, 1996), 89-116; E. P. Sanders, *Jesus and Judaism* (Philadelphia: Fortress, 1985), 1.

In order to answer these questions adequately, over the course of this book, we will not only need to examine the so-called "words of institution," but also other words and deeds attributed to Jesus that seem to be directly related to or shed significant light on the Last Supper (e.g., feeding of the multitude, teachings about the eschatological manna, the messianic banquet, etc.).

As I hope to show, when the Last Supper is properly situated in the context of early Jewish practice and belief — especially its hopes for the future — it has the power to provide important and sometimes unexpected answers to each of these questions. Indeed, I would contend that to the extent that contemporary Jesus research has failed to integrate the Last Supper into its overall reconstruction of Jesus' life and teaching — which it often has — it has also failed to answer adequately the four guiding questions in the historical quest for Jesus. By contrast, when the Last Supper and Jesus' related words and deeds are situated within the triple contexts of ancient Judaism, his public life and ministry, and the rise of the early church, they strongly suggest that Jesus saw himself as the new Moses who would inaugurate the long-awaited new exodus, set in motion by a new Passover, bring back the miracle of the manna from heaven, and gather the twelve tribes of Israel into the heavenly and eschatological kingdom of God — all by means of his sacrificial death and the prophetic sign of his death that he performed at the Last Supper.

Before going into all of this, however, in this first chapter, we will take a few moments to lay out in somewhat more detail how the Last Supper is related to the four questions of Jesus' Jewish context, self-understanding, eschatological outlook, and intentions.

Jesus and Judaism

The first question that presents itself to us is that of Jesus' Jewish context. How do the accounts of the Last Supper fit into the context of first-century Judaism? Are their basic contents historically plausible? If so, what might they have meant in Jesus' Jewish context? When we examine such questions in light of recent scholarship on Jesus, something of a paradox emerges.

The Jewish Jesus

On the one hand, nowadays it is all but universally recognized by scholars that Jesus of Nazareth was born, lived, and died a Jew. Perhaps more than any other tenet of contemporary Jesus research, the Jewish identity of Jesus has commanded a widespread acceptance, and represents a virtual consensus. Consider, for example, the remarkably categorical statements of several prominent scholars:

> It is with . . . Judaism, the Judaism of the first century CE, that we must carry through the task of finding the historical Jesus.[4]

> Virtually no one today disputes or has any reason to dispute that Jesus was a Jew from Galilee.[5]

> One of the characteristic pursuits of the latest phase of Jesus-of-history research, namely the so-called Third Quest, has been the serious attempt to locate Jesus within first-century AD Judaism, to seek a Jesus who would be plausible within his Jewish context.[6]

> Jesus had to have made sense in his own context, and his context is that of Galilee and Judea. Jesus cannot be fully understood unless he is understood through first-century Jewish eyes and heard through first-century Jewish ears. . . . To understand Jesus' impact in his own setting — why some chose to follow him, others to dismiss him, and still others to seek his death — requires an understanding of that setting.[7]

> [A]ny attempt to build up a historical picture of Jesus of Nazareth should and must begin from the fact that he was a first-century Jew operating in a first-century milieu.[8]

> [I]f there is any enduring gain from the so-called third quest, it is the one hammered home by scholars like Geza Vermes and E. P. Sanders: Jesus first, last, and only a Jew.[9]

4. Maurice Casey, *Jesus of Nazareth: An Independent Historian's Account of His Life and Teaching* (London: T. & T. Clark, 2010), 59.

5. Craig S. Keener, *The Historical Jesus of the Gospels* (Grand Rapids: Eerdmans, 2009), 178.

6. Tom Holmén, *Jesus from Judaism to Christianity: Continuum Approaches to the Historical Jesus* (ed. Tom Holmén; LNTS 352; Edinburgh: T. & T. Clark, 2007), 1.

7. Amy-Jill Levine, *The Misunderstood Jew: The Church and the Scandal of the Jewish Jesus* (San Francisco: HarperCollins, 2006), 20-21.

8. James D. G. Dunn, *Jesus Remembered (Christianity in the Making,* vol. 1; Grand Rapids: Eerdmans, 2003), 86.

9. John P. Meier, *A Marginal Jew: Rethinking the Historical Jesus* (4 vols. [5th vol. forthcoming]; AYBRL; New Haven & London: Yale University Press, 1991, 1994, 2001, 2009), 4:7.

> If [Jesus] belongs anywhere in history, it is within the history of first-century Judaism."[10]

Of course, scholars continue to debate exactly what it *means* to say that Jesus was "Jewish" and what Judaism was like at the time of Jesus.[11] Nevertheless, the same general point is made by many recent titles, which go out of their way to emphasize that the Jesus of history is unequivocally a Jewish Jesus.[12] In short, the importance of Jesus' Jewish identity and context has become one of those extremely rare occasions where virtually everyone in the scholarly realm agrees upon a basic conclusion and treats it as settled.

The Problem of the Last Supper

With that said, it is by no means immediately evident how the Jewish Jesus of scholarly consensus can be reconciled with what might be called the "eucharistic Jesus" — that is, the Jesus depicted in the words of institution recorded in the Synoptic Gospels and Paul, as well as the arguably eucharistic elements of the discourse in the synagogue at Capernaum attributed to Jesus in the Gospel of John.

As is well known, according to all four accounts of Jesus' words and deeds at the Last Supper — including what is commonly regarded as the most ancient account in 1 Corinthians — Jesus identified the bread and wine of his final meal with his own body and blood, but also commanded his disciples to eat and drink them (Matt 26:26-28; Mark 14:22-25; Luke 22:19-20; 1 Cor 11:23-25). According to the Gospel of John, Jesus said something very similar to this while teaching in the Jewish synagogue at Capernaum, when he declared it necessary to eat the flesh and drink the blood of the Son of Man — which he identifies as real food and drink — in order to participate in the resurrection of the dead and eternal life (John 6:53-54).

10. N. T. Wright, *Jesus and the Victory of God*, 91.

11. See William Arnal, *The Symbolic Jesus: Historical Scholarship, Judaism and the Construction of Contemporary Identity* (Sheffield: Equinox, 2005).

12. E.g., Martin Hengel and Anna Maria Schwemer, *Jesus und das Judentum* (*Geschichte des frühen Christentums*, vol. 1; Tübingen: Mohr-Siebeck, 2007); John Dominic Crossan, *The Historical Jesus: The Life of a Mediterranean Jewish Peasant* (San Francisco: HarperCollins, 1991); James H. Charlesworth, *Jesus within Judaism: New Light from Exciting Archaeological Discoveries* (ABRL; New York: Doubleday, 1990); Geza Vermes, *Jesus the Jew: A Historian's Reading of the Gospels* (Philadelphia: Fortress, 1973).

The problem with this evidence is that it stands in stark contrast to the express directives of Jewish Scripture. Indeed, according to the Torah of Moses, it was absolutely forbidden for anyone to consume blood:

> Every moving thing that lives shall be food for you. . . . Only *you shall not eat flesh with its life, that is, its blood.* (Gen 9:3-4)[13]

> If any man among the house of Israel or of the stranger that sojourns among them eats any blood, *I will set my face against that person who eats blood, and I will cut him off from among his people. For the life of the flesh is in the blood; and I have given it for you upon the altar to make atonement for your souls;* for it is the blood that makes atonement, by reason of its life. Therefore I have said to the people of Israel, *No person among you shall eat blood, neither shall any stranger who sojourns among you eat blood.* (Lev 17:10-12)

> You may slaughter and eat flesh within any of your towns, as much as you desire. . . . *Only you shall not eat the blood;* you shall pour it out upon the earth like water. (Deut 12:15-16)

Clearly, the biblical commandment against drinking blood was grave. Any transgression of this law would mean being "cut off" from God and from the people of Israel. Notice also that the law is universal in scope: the Torah commands that not only Israelites avoid the consumption of blood, but any Gentile "strangers" living among them.

In light of such evidence, a fundamental problem arises. If, for the sake of argument, we assume that the substance of Jesus' words regarding eating his body and drinking blood is historical, then how could he as a first-century Jew have ever commanded his disciples to eat his flesh and drink his blood? If he did, would this not entail explicitly breaking the Torah's repeated commandments against consuming blood? It is precisely this tension between the Jewish Torah and the eucharistic words attributed to Jesus that leads Geza Vermes to contend:

> [T]he imagery of eating a man's body and especially drinking his blood . . . , even after allowance is made for metaphorical language, strikes a totally

13. Unless otherwise noted, all translations of Scripture herein are from the Revised Standard Version (RSV).

> foreign note in a Palestinian Jewish cultural setting (cf. John 6.52). With their profoundly rooted blood taboo, Jesus' listeners would have been overcome with nausea at hearing such words.[14]

Along similar lines, another major Jewish scholar, Joseph Klausner, writes:

> [I]t is quite impossible to admit that Jesus would have said to his disciples that they should eat of his body and drink of his blood, "the blood of the new covenant which was shed for many." The drinking of blood, even if it was meant symbolically, could only have aroused horror in the minds of such simple Galilean Jews.[15]

Note two points about the views of both Vermes and Klausner. First, both agree that there is simply no way to reconcile the Jewish taboo against blood consumption with Jesus' command for his disciples to eat his flesh and drink his blood at the Last Supper. The words of institution are thus historically "impossible." Second — and this is significant — both also agree that even if Jesus only meant these words *metaphorically,* as many Christian interpreters since the Protestant Reformation have contended, in an ancient Jewish context, such a command would have been completely repugnant. From this point of view, there is no way to reconcile the Jewish Jesus and the Jesus of the Last Supper accounts. Therefore, since the Jewishness of Jesus cannot be called into question, it is the words of institution that must be rejected as unhistorical.

It is worth noting that this tension between the Jewish Jesus and the eucharistic Jesus has been felt since the very beginning of the modern quest, and continues to be present in studies of Jesus and the Last Supper. For example, already in the eighteenth century, Hermann Samuel Reimarus found it impossible to reconcile the accounts of the Last Supper with his portrait of Jesus as a Jewish revolutionary. As a result, Reimarus was forced to insist — against the testimony of all the extant evidence — that Jesus celebrated the Last Supper "without the least alteration" from the ordinary Jewish Passover meal. Indeed, Reimarus claims that "one cannot see that he omitted or changed anything that was customary for this meal."[16] To say the least, this is a questionable

14. Geza Vermes, *The Religion of Jesus the Jew* (Minneapolis: Fortress, 1993), 16.

15. Joseph Klausner, *Jesus of Nazareth: His Life, Times, and Teaching* (trans. Herbert Danby; New York: Macmillan, 1925), 329.

16. Reimarus, *Fragments,* 118-19.

interpretation of the data. To the contrary, if anything is certain, it is that all four accounts of the Last Supper agree that Jesus identified the bread and wine of the meal with his own body and blood, and that such an identification was certainly *not* customary Jewish Passover practice (cf. Matt 26:26-28; Mark 14:22-24; Luke 22:19-20; 1 Cor 11:23-25). However, Reimarus's assertion helps to make an important point: from the earliest days of the modern quest, in order to maintain the hypothesis that Jesus was thoroughly Jewish, scholars were forced to explain away the eucharistic words. In the figure of Reimarus, the quest begins with a tendency to dismiss the startling words of Jesus at the Last Supper as "incidental."[17]

Much more recently, this tension between the Jewish Jesus and the eucharistic Jesus manifests itself in another way: entire studies of the Last Supper that pay almost no attention to the Old Testament and Second Temple Judaism.[18] For example, one searches Jens Schröter's recent monograph on the Last Supper in vain for any detailed discussion of the early Jewish context of the images of blood, covenant, Passover, sacrifice, kingdom of God, etc.[19] Perhaps unsurprisingly, Schröter ends up concluding that the words of institution, with the sole exception of Jesus' vow about not drinking in the kingdom (Mark 14:25), in all probability do not stem from Jesus, but from the early church (to which he has devoted all his attention).[20]

In sum, there remains an undeniable tension between Jesus the Jew and the Jesus of the Last Supper accounts — a tension that is sometimes not faced head-on. If the substance of the eucharistic words recorded in the Gospels and Paul is historical, then how could Jesus have ever commanded his disciples to eat his body and drink his blood — even if he only meant it symbolically? In a word, how does one reconcile the Jewish Jesus and the eucharistic Jesus?

17. Cf. Reimarus, *Fragments*, 118.

18. For example, there is a stunning dearth of discussion of Old Testament and early Jewish sources in Rudolf Pesch, *Das Abendmahl und Jesu Todesverständnis* (QD 80; Freiburg: Herder, 1978), and Helmut Feld, *Das Verständnis des Abendmahls* (EdF 50; Darmstadt: Wissenschaftliche Buchgesellschaft, 1976). By contrast, Hermann Patsch, *Abendmahl und historischer Jesus* (CTM 1; Stuttgart: Calwer, 1972), 17-39, devotes substantial attention to the Old Testament and early Jewish parallels.

19. Jens Schröter, *Das Abendmahl: Frühchristliche Deutungen und Impulse für die Gegenwart* (SBS 210; Stuttgart: Katholisches Bibelwerk, 2006).

20. Schröter, *Das Abendmahl*, 132-33.

The Self-Understanding of Jesus

When we turn from the question of Jesus' context to the question of his self-understanding, the Last Supper presents us with yet another paradox. On the one hand, much of modern biblical scholarship on Jesus concludes that we lack solid evidence that he saw himself as or ever claimed to be the messiah. On the other hand, if the words of institution at the Last Supper are basically historical, then it is rather hard to square them with a Jesus who did not see himself as anything more than just a Jewish teacher or prophet.

The Dogma of the Non-Messianic Jesus

In his massive study of the death of Jesus, Raymond Brown once described the idea that "neither Jesus nor his followers thought he was the Messiah" as a "'dogma' of modern critical scholarship."[21] Roughly around the same time, Martin Hengel used equally strong language: "Today the unmessianic Jesus has almost become a dogma among many New Testament scholars."[22]

To be sure, there are numerous scholars who have levied arguments in favor of some kind of messianic self-understanding on the part of the historical Jesus.[23] Indeed, at the end of his life, even Rudolf Bultmann retracted his earlier assertion that Jesus saw himself merely as a rabbi and concluded instead that Jesus appeared as a messianic prophet whose proclamation "implies a christology."[24] Nevertheless, it remains true that many scholarly works and introductions to the New Testament reflect the assumption no historically reliable evidence exists that Jesus saw himself as the Jewish messiah.

21. Raymond E. Brown, *The Death of the Messiah* (2 vols.; ABRL; New York: Doubleday, 1993), 1:478.

22. Martin Hengel, "Jesus, the Messiah of Israel," in *Studies in Early Christology* (Edinburgh: T. & T. Clark, 1995), 16.

23. Most recently, see Dale C. Allison Jr., *Constructing Jesus: Memory, Imagination, and History* (Grand Rapids: Baker Academic, 2010), 221-304; Michael F. Bird, *Are You the One Who Is to Come? The Historical Jesus and the Messianic Question* (Grand Rapids: Baker Academic, 2009). I too have made the case for Jesus' messianic self-understanding in Brant Pitre, *Jesus, the Tribulation, and the End of the Exile* (WUNT 2.204; Tübingen: Mohr Siebeck; Grand Rapids: Baker Academic, 2005), 455-514. See also Wright, *Jesus and the Victory of God*, 477-539; Meyer, *The Aims of Jesus*, 178-80.

24. Rudolf Bultmann, "The Primitive Christian Kerygma and the Historical Jesus," in *The Historical Jesus and the Kerygmatic Christ: Essays on the New Quest for the Historical Jesus* (ed. Carl E. Braaten and Roy A. Harrisville; Nashville: Abingdon, 1964), 28-29.

For our purposes in this book, one key feature of this dogma is the conviction that Jesus did not attribute any redemptive or saving significance to his death.[25] Consider the following remarks from recent works on Jesus:

> The inauthenticity [of Jesus' description of his death as a "ransom for many"] follows from the fact that it is the "risen Christ" speaking.[26]

> It's not clear why, exactly, Jesus went with his disciples to Jerusalem. A theologian, of course, might say that it was in order to die for the sins of the world. This view, though, is based on Gospel sayings . . . that cannot pass the criterion of dissimilarity, in that they portray Jesus as being fully cognizant of the details of his own fate.[27]

> It is not historically impossible that Jesus was weird. . . . But the view that he plotted his own redemptive death makes him strange in any century and thrusts the entire drama into his peculiar inner psyche. The other things that we know about him make him a *reasonable* first-century visionary. We should be guided by them.[28]

Perhaps the most influential articulation of this view comes from Rudolf Bultmann, who famously wrote:

> The greatest embarrassment to the attempt to reconstruct a portrait of Jesus is the fact that we cannot know how Jesus understood his end, his death. It is symptomatic that it is practically universally assumed that he understood this as the organic or necessary conclusion to his activity. But how do we know this, when prophecies of the passion must be understood by critical research as *vaticinia ex eventu?* . . . What is certain is that he was merely crucified by the Romans, and thus suffered the death of a political criminal. This death can scarcely be understood as an inherent and necessary consequence of his activity; rather it took place because his

25. For discussion, see Scot McKnight, *Jesus and His Death: Historiography, the Historical Jesus, and Atonement Theory* (Waco, TX: Baylor University Press, 2005), 47-75; Dunn, *Jesus Remembered,* 805-18; Brown, *The Death of the Messiah,* 2:1468-91 (with bibliography).

26. Gerd Lüdemann, *Jesus After 2000 Years: What He Really Did and Said* (trans. John Bowden; London: SCM; Amherst, MA: Prometheus, 2001), 72.

27. Bart Ehrman, *Jesus: Apocalyptic Prophet of the New Millennium* (New York: Oxford University Press, 1999), 209-10.

28. Sanders, *Jesus and Judaism,* 332-33 (emphasis original).

> activity was misconstrued as political activity. In that case it would have been — historically speaking — a meaningless fate. We may not veil from ourselves the possibility that he suffered a collapse.[29]

The impact of Bultmann's point of view on the historical question of Jesus' self-understanding is hard to overestimate. As I have shown elsewhere, such sentiments have led to a situation in which many influential scholars on Jesus do not consider it necessary even to discuss the evidence that Jesus saw his death as redemptive, much less to provide arguments for why this evidence should be regarded as unhistorical.[30] As I stated above, while this is certainly not true of all studies on Jesus, it is widespread enough for the most recent full-length study of Jesus and his death to draw the following conclusion: "Many scholars, perhaps a majority today, think Jesus was innocent, that he was righteous, that his death was splendidly exemplary, and/or that he died as a result of his self-claim and his mission, but that his death was not undertaken (consciously and deliberately) as an atonement."[31]

It seems, then, that the "dogma" of the non-messianic Jesus — and its corollary, the dogma of the non-redemptive Jesus — has become something of an assumption in the minds of many contemporary scholars.

The Problem of the Words of Interpretation

One major problem with this dogma is that if the words of interpretation attributed to Jesus at the Last Supper are basically historical, then it is rather difficult to square them with the non-messianic Jesus.

Once again, in all three Synoptic accounts of Jesus' words at the Last Supper, he specifically identifies himself with "the Son of Man" whose death is

29. Bultmann, "The Primitive Christian Kerygma and the Historical Jesus," 22-23.

30. For example, the evidence that Jesus saw his death as Son of Man as redemptive (Matt 20:28; Mark 10:45) is ignored in the following reconstructions: Karl Jaros, *Jesus von Nazareth: Geschichte und Deutung* (Mainz: Verlag Philipp von Zabern, 2000); Paula Fredriksen, *Jesus of Nazareth, King of the Jews* (New York: Vintage, 2000); Ehrman, *Jesus: Apocalyptic Prophet;* Joachim Gnilka, *Jesus of Nazareth: Message and History* (trans. Siegfried S. Schatzmann; Peabody, MA: Hendrickson, 1997); Crossan, *The Historical Jesus;* Vermes, *Jesus the Jew;* Norman Perrin, *Rediscovering the Teaching of Jesus* (New York: Harper & Row, 1967); Günther Bornkamm, *Jesus of Nazareth* (trans. Irene and Fraser McLuskey with James Robinson; New York: Harper, 1960). See Pitre, *Jesus, the Tribulation, and the End of the Exile,* 419.

31. McKnight, *Jesus and His Death,* 71.

prophesied in Jewish Scripture (Matt 26:24; Mark 14:21; Luke 22:22). Although the exact meaning of Jesus' usage of the "Son of Man" continues to be debated, the expression itself continues to be widely regarded as a positive indicator of historicity. If, as some scholars hold (and I have argued elsewhere), the Son of Man is in fact a messianic figure in Daniel and Jesus saw himself as this figure, then this strong linkage between the Last Supper and Jesus' self-understanding as Son of Man poses a serious problem for the dogma of the non-messianic Jesus.[32] Perhaps even more striking, in all four accounts of the Last Supper, Jesus identifies the wine of the meal with his own "blood" that will establish a new "covenant" between God and his people (Matt 26:28; Mark 14:24; Luke 22:20; 1 Cor 11:25). Despite important differences in vocabulary, likewise, in all four accounts, Jesus uses the language of sacrifice to describe his blood as being offered for others (Matt 26:28; Mark 14:24; Luke 22:20; 1 Cor 11:25). As we will see in subsequent chapters, numerous scholars have identified in these accounts allusions to the "blood of the covenant" established by Moses (Exod 24:8), the "new covenant" spoken of by the prophets (Jer 31:31), as well as the sacrificial death of the suffering servant who offers himself for "many" (Isa 53:12).[33]

Now, if Jesus only saw himself as a rabbi, prophet, or anything less than the messianic redeemer (whether he saw himself as *more* than a messiah is yet another question), then we should not expect to find him saying and doing the kinds of things the evidence claims he said and did at his final meal. Conversely, if the eucharistic words of interpretation are basically historical, then they make good sense on the lips of a Jesus who saw himself as the messianic deliverer of Israel, one whose death would somehow usher in the age of redemption awaited by many Jews and spoken of by the prophets.

This tension between the dogma of the non-messianic Jesus and the evidence in the accounts of the Last Supper is manifest in the work of scholars who deny that Jesus saw himself as messiah and/or that he attributed any redemptive significance to his death.[34] Consider the following conclusions of various scholars:

32. Cf. Allison, *Constructing Jesus,* 293-303; Bird, *Are You the One Who Is to Come?,* 78-98; Pitre, *Jesus, the Tribulation, and the End of the Exile,* 54-55; Delbert Burkett, *The Son of Man Debate: A History and Evaluation* (SNTSMS 107; Cambridge: Cambridge University Press, 1999). In light of these connections, Seyoon Kim holds that the words of institution may be aptly described as "the eucharistic words of the Son of Man." Seyoon Kim, *The Son of Man as the Son of God* (WUNT 30; Tübingen: Mohr Siebeck, 1983).

33. Cf. McKnight, *Jesus and His Death,* 275-92.

34. See, e.g., Jürgen Becker, *Jesus of Nazareth* (trans. James E. Crouch; New York/Berlin: Walter de Gruyter, 1998), 187-97, for an emphatic denial of Jesus' messianic self-understanding.

> All of the texts which deal with the last supper of Jesus reflect the liturgical concerns of the meal celebrations of the various churches. No text reports the historical event. . . . The words of institution . . . [are] reminiscent of Isa 53:12, but Jesus cannot have spoken that way. . . . [W]hen we examine Jesus' message elsewhere, we find nowhere the suggestion that God's gracious acceptance of the lost was dependent in any way on the sacrifice of Jesus' own life.[35]

> If it is certain that according to the accounts of Paul and Mark (the same is probably true of the accounts of Matthew and Luke) Jesus celebrated the first Lord's Supper with his disciples, at which he distributed to them his body and blood and at which they ate his body and drank his blood symbolically, really, or in whatever way, then it is equally certain that the institution of the supper thus described is not historical. . . . [For] he had said nothing about a saving effect of his death or even his resurrection. . . . Only Jesus' expectation of the future kingdom of God stands at the centre, not Jesus as savior. . . .[36]

> According to these accounts [of the Last Supper], he told his disciples that the unleavened bread was (or represented) his body that would be broken, and the cup of wine was (or represented) his blood that would be shed (Mark 14:22-25; Matt. 26:26-29; Luke 22:15-20; 1 Cor. 11:23-26). It's very difficult to know whether this "institution" of the Lord's Supper is historical. On the one hand, it is multiply attested in independent sources, even though they disagree concerning the precise words that were spoken. And one of these sources, Paul, who claimed to know people who had been there at the time, was writing just twenty years after the event. On the other hand, the accounts seems so heavily "Christianized" with the doctrine of the saving effect of Jesus' death (a doctrine that developed, of course, after he had died), that it is hard to know here what is history and what is later theology.[37]

Although much could be said about the arguments used here, for our purposes, the main point is this: in all three quotations, the historicity of the words of interpretation at the Last Supper is rejected, not because of any evidence to

35. Becker, *Jesus of Nazareth*, 340-42.
36. Lüdemann, *Jesus After 2000 Years*, 96-97.
37. Ehrman, *Jesus: Apocalyptic Prophet*, 215.

the contrary, but because of the assumption that Jesus did not see his death as redemptive. In this regard, the final quotation from Bart Erhman is particularly revealing. On the one hand, according to his own criteria of historicity, the words of interpretation should pass with flying colors, since they are quadruply attested, and since he regards Paul's account as the earliest recorded words of Jesus.[38] On the other hand, when Ehrman is faced with the evidence in the Last Supper accounts that Jesus saw his death as redemptive, he quickly jettisons the very criteria of authenticity that in other cases he utilizes to establish the historicity of a given saying or deed, thus casting doubt on the words of interpretation. Indeed, he does not seem to consider the possibility that the reason why the words of interpretation are so solidly attested may be that the idea that Jesus' death had "saving significance" goes back to the man himself.

In sum, it is quite common nowadays to assume that Jesus did not see himself as the messiah and, *a fortiori,* did not see his death as redemptive. However, it is very difficult to see how such conclusions can be reconciled with the words and deeds of Jesus at the Last Supper. In light of this situation, we find ourselves on the horns of yet another historical dilemma: Is it possible to reconcile the non-messianic Jesus and the Jesus of the Last Supper? Or is one of them in error? If so, which?

The Eschatology of Jesus

A third issue regards the relationship between the accounts of the Last Supper and Jesus' eschatological expectations. On the one hand, one of the most influential theses of the twentieth century is that Jesus' proclamation of the kingdom of God should be understood in light of ancient Jewish beliefs about the end of history, the final judgment, and the destruction and renewal of creation. On the other hand, what often goes unnoted is how difficult it has proven to integrate the words of institution into the portrait of Jesus as an apocalyptic prophet of the end of history.[39]

38. Cf. Ehrman, *Jesus: Apocalyptic Prophet,* 85-96.

39. See Brant J. Pitre, "Apocalypticism and Apocalyptic Teaching," in *Dictionary of Jesus and the Gospels* (2nd ed.; ed. Joel B. Green, Jeannine K. Brown, and Nicholas Perrin; Downers Grove: IVP Academic, 2013), 23-33.

The Apocalyptic Jesus and the End of History

The pervasive influence of an apocalyptic view of Jesus is commonly credited to Albert Schweitzer's famous book, *The Quest of the Historical Jesus* (1906).[40] In the wake of Schweitzer's work, it became widely accepted that Jesus' expectations were characterized by what Schweitzer referred to as "thoroughgoing eschatology" (German *konsequente Eschatologie*).[41] From this perspective, Jesus acted on the conviction that the end of the present world was imminent and would coincide with the advent of the kingdom of God. In Schweitzer's own words, Jesus "thought the end at hand."[42] Therefore, he expected "the immediate coming of the last things" — i.e., the final tribulation, the last judgment, the resurrection of the dead, etc. — along with "the coming of the new supernatural world."[43]

Indeed, for Schweitzer, Jesus not only expected the end to take place soon, he also acted on this expectation by going to Jerusalem to die and thereby force the coming of the kingdom to take place. Consider Schweitzer's famous description of how Jesus understood his death with the accounts of the Last Supper in mind:

> There is silence all around. The Baptist appears, and cries: "Repent, for the Kingdom of Heaven is at hand." Soon after that comes Jesus, and in the knowledge that he is the coming Son of Man lays hold of the wheel of the world to set it moving on that last revolution which is to bring all ordinary history to a close. It refuses to turn, and He throws himself upon it. Then it does turn; and crushes Him. Instead of bringing in the eschatological conditions, He has destroyed them. The wheel rolls onward, and the mangled body of the one immeasurably great Man, who was strong enough to think of Himself as the spiritual ruler of mankind and to bend history to His purpose, is hanging upon it still. That is His victory and His reign.[44]

40. Albert Schweitzer, *The Quest of the Historical Jesus: A Critical Study of Its Progress from Reimarus to Wrede* (trans. William Montgomery; rev. ed.; New York: Macmillan, 1968 [orig. 1906]). The English translation was recently revised and expanded in Albert Schweitzer, *The Quest of the Historical Jesus: First Complete Edition* (trans. William Montgomery, J. R. Coates, Susan Cupitt, and John Bowden; Minneapolis: Fortress, 2001). Given the impact of the first edition on English-speaking scholarship, in what follows, the page references (unless otherwise noted) are to the first English edition.

41. Schweitzer, *The Quest of the Historical Jesus*, 330-97.

42. Schweitzer, *The Quest of the Historical Jesus*, 395.

43. Schweitzer, *The Quest of the Historical Jesus*, 365.

44. Schweitzer, *The Quest of the Historical Jesus*, 371.

For our purposes here, what is significant about this quotation is that Schweitzer's Jesus does not look beyond his own death precisely because he saw it as the event that would "bring all ordinary history to a close." Consequently, for Schweitzer, Jesus did not expect his disciples to continue the work of his public ministry after his death: "[The disciples] are not [Jesus'] helpers in the work of teaching; we never see them in that capacity, and He did not prepare them to carry on that work after His death."[45] For Schweitzer, then, Jesus was an eschatological prophet in the strictest sense of the word: he proclaimed and expected the end of ordinary history to coincide with his own demise.

In the wake of Schweitzer's work, the view of Jesus as an apocalyptic prophet of the imminent end of the world soon became widely accepted by a large sector of New Testament studies.[46] Over and over again in influential books on Jesus, we find conclusions such as the following:

> Jesus' generation . . . passed away. They all tasted death. And it is not the kingdom of God that has come but the scoffers who ask, Where is the promise of his coming? For all things continue as they were from the beginning of creation. Jesus the millenarian prophet, like all millenarian prophets, was wrong.[47]

> Jesus appears to have anticipated that the coming of judgment of God, to be brought by the Son of Man in a cosmic act of destruction and salvation, was imminent. It could happen at any time. But it would certainly happen within his own generation.[48]

> [T]he great event which Jesus was convinced would happen in his lifetime failed to materialize. . . .[49]

> We have no saying of Jesus that postpones the end into the distant future. . . . That raises an extremely serious question: must we not concede that Jesus' expectation of an imminent end was one that remained un-

45. Schweitzer, *The Quest of the Historical Jesus,* 371.

46. On the influence of Schweitzer, see Wright, *Jesus and the Victory of God,* 83-124.

47. Dale C. Allison Jr., *Jesus of Nazareth: Millenarian Prophet* (Minneapolis: Fortress, 1998), 218.

48. Ehrman, *Jesus: Apocalyptic Prophet,* 161.

49. Geza Vermes, *The Religion of Jesus the Jew* (Minneapolis: Fortress, 1993), 211.

> fulfilled? Honesty and the demand for truthfulness compel us to answer "Yes." Jesus expected the end would come soon.[50]

> [Jesus expected] salvation not from a miraculous change in historical (i.e., political and social) conditions, but from a cosmic catastrophe which will do away with all conditions of the present world as it is.[51]

Such examples could be easily multiplied. To be sure, there are voices to the contrary.[52] Nevertheless, when modern scholarship is taken as a whole, it seems as if the Jesus of Schweitzer — the apocalyptic Jesus of the imminent end of history — has convinced many and left an indelible mark on the way in which Jesus' eschatological outlook is conceived.

The Problem of the Words of Institution

One serious problem with the hypothesis of Jesus as an apocalyptic prophet of the imminent end of history is that scholars who adopt this point of view have substantial difficulty making sense of the words of institution recorded in our earliest accounts of the Last Supper. In these words, Jesus apparently looks *beyond* his own imminent suffering and death, in at least two ways. First, as we have already mentioned, in all four accounts of the Last Supper, he speaks of his own "blood" as establishing a new "covenant" between God and his people (Matt 26:28; Mark 14:24; Luke 22:20; 1 Cor 11:25). Second, and equally important, he commands the disciples to repeat his actions in "remembrance" of him (Luke 22:19-20; 1 Cor 11:23-25).[53] Taken together, these passages can be

50. Joachim Jeremias, *New Testament Theology I. The Proclamation of Jesus* (trans. John Bowden; New York: Charles Scribner's Sons; London: SCM, 1971), 139.

51. Rudolf Bultmann, *Theology of the New Testament* (2 vols.; New York: Charles Scribner's Sons, 1951-55), 1:4.

52. See Robert J. Millar, ed., *The Apocalyptic Jesus: A Debate* (Santa Rosa: Polebridge, 2001); John Dominic Crossan, *The Historical Jesus: The Life of a Mediterranean Jewish Peasant.* For a very helpful analysis, see also Ben Witherington III, *Jesus the Seer: The Progress of Prophecy* (Peabody, MA: Hendrickson, 1999), 246-92. In recent times a number of scholars differ from Schweitzer in rejecting as unhistorical the three key passages in which Jesus seems to speak of the imminent advent of the kingdom of God (Matt 10:23; Mark 9:1; 13:30 et par.). With this solution, the difficulty of the imminent end of history disappears, though the problem of exactly what the coming of the kingdom means remains. See, e.g., Meier, *A Marginal Jew,* 2:336-48; Gnilka *Jesus of Nazareth,* 147-49; Perrin, *Rediscovering the Teaching of Jesus,* 199-202.

53. In treating the longer version of the words of institution in Luke's Gospel as text-

accurately described as words of institution, in which Jesus is commanding the disciples to repeat a particular ritual in his absence and after his death.

In light of such texts, T. Francis Glasson, one of the twentieth century's most vocal critics of Schweitzer's reconstruction, makes a case against the apocalyptic Jesus of the immediate end in his small but significant book, *Jesus and the End of the World*.[54] First, Glasson argues that the command to repeat his actions at the Last Supper implies that Jesus did not expect the end of history to coincide with his death:

> For seventy years we have been told that Jesus could not have envisaged the Church because his view of the future left no interval of time in which such a community could operate. Yet the evidence . . . surely shows that he did count on the continuance of human history after his death. . . . The words "This do in remembrance of me" occur twice in the oldest account we have, *1 Corinthians* 11:24 and 25. . . . However the words are interpreted, they are inconsistent with the view that Jesus expected the world to end immediately after his crucifixion. . . .[55]

Second, and perhaps even more important, Glasson also points out that Jesus' words about establishing a new "covenant" in his blood not only shows that he did not think the world would end immediately. When interpreted in the light of Jewish Scripture, such a statement presupposes that the era of Jesus' new covenant would endure for some time, and not just a short period:

---

critically authentic, I am following the most recent and exhaustive work on the subject by Bradly S. Billings, *Do This in Remembrance of Me: The Disputed Words in the Lukan Institution Narrative (Luke 22:19b-20): An Historico-Exegetical, Theological, and Sociological Analysis* (Library of New Testament Studies; London: T. & T. Clark, 2006), as well as François Bovon, *Luke 3* (trans. James Crouch; Hermeneia; Minneapolis: Fortress, 2012), 154-55. See also Eldon Jay Epp, "The Disputed Words of the Eucharistic Institution (Luke 22, 19b-20): The Long and Short of the Matter," *Bib* 90 (2009): 407-16; I. Howard Marshall, "The Last Supper," in *Key Events in the Life of the Historical Jesus* (ed. Darrell L. Bock and Robert L. Webb; WUNT 247; Tübingen: Mohr Siebeck, 2009), 529-41; Joseph A. Fitzmyer, S.J., *The Gospel according to Luke* (AB; New York: Doubleday, 1983, 1985), 2:1387-89. Given the strength and diversity of the mss of Luke that contain the longer form and the circularity of arguments in favor of the shorter version, this seems to be the strongest position.

54. T. F. Glasson, *Jesus and the End of the World* (Edinburgh: St. Andrew, 1980). See also the important essay, T. Francis Glasson, "Schweitzer's Influence — Blessing or Bane?" *JTS* 28 (1977): 289-302; idem, *The Second Advent: The Origin of the New Testament Doctrine* (London: Epworth, 1963).

55. Glasson, *Jesus and the End of the World*, 65-66.

> [Even a] "short interval" does not appear to do justice to the conception of a new covenant and a period in which it would operate. . . . The words "my blood of the covenant" (Mark 14:24) and "This cup is the new covenant in my blood" (1 Corinthians 11:25) look back, as the commentators remind us, to Exodus 24. . . . Jesus knew that the covenant at Sinai had been instituted many centuries before. Is it conceivable that he envisaged only a "short interval" before the Last Judgment and a supernatural new world? . . . When Jesus in the upper room referred to this [the covenant], surely he cannot at the same time have thought that a catastrophic kingdom was imminent, bringing history to an end, and touching off the resurrection of the dead, the last judgment, a new heaven and earth. This just does not make sense. Judas had departed, and Jesus knew that in all probability he had not many hours to live. Was the new covenant to operate for merely a few hours, or a few days, or a "short interval"?[56]

This is a powerful argument, one that to my knowledge has never been rebutted by advocates of Schweitzer's reconstruction. If Jesus did indeed think that the end of the world would coincide with his death, or even that it would take place a few days thereafter, then it would be nonsense — especially in a Jewish context — for him to compare his actions to the covenant established by Moses at Sinai, which had lasted for well over a thousand years. By contrast, once we dispense with the idea that Jesus expected the immediate end of the world and entertain the possibility that he expected history to continue after his death — however long that may be — then both his commands to repeat his actions in memory of him and his establishment of a new covenant make good sense. Should there be any doubt about the problems caused by the words of institution for the hypothesis of Jesus as an apocalyptic prophet of the immediate end, it is striking to note how, over the course of the last century, scholarly advocates of Schweitzer's hypothesis consistently ignore the words of institution in their reconstruction of Jesus' eschatology.[57] For example, in

56. Glasson, *Jesus and the End of the World*, 67-68.

57. This tendency to downplay the words of institution can already be found in the seminal work of Johannes Weiss, *Jesus' Proclamation of the Kingdom of God* (trans. R. H. Hiers and D. L. Holland; Philadelphia: Fortress, 1971 [orig. 1892]), 83-84. To be fair, there are some scholars indebted to Schweitzer's outlook who give attention to the Last Supper, such as Wright, *Jesus and the Victory of God*, 553-63; Jeremias, *New Testament Theology I*, 288-92; idem, *The Eucharistic Words of Jesus* (trans. Norman Perrin; London: SCM; New York: Charles Scribner's Sons, 1966). That said, even these scholars do not often make clear how the command to repeat Jesus' actions and the imagery of a new covenant fit into the overall picture of Jesus' eschatology.

Schweitzer's famous work, *The Quest of the Historical Jesus,* he dismisses the words of institution with a single sentence.

> The mysterious images which He used at the time of the distribution concerning the atoning significance of His death do not touch the essence of the celebration, they are only discourses accompanying it.[58]

Notice here that Schweitzer does not argue that the words of institution are unhistorical — the evidence for them is too strong for that — he just dismisses them as insignificant, not touching the "essence" of the Last Supper.

Along similar lines is the work of E. P. Sanders, who follows Schweitzer's basic reconstruction of Jesus as a Jewish eschatological prophet for whom "the end was at hand."[59] Remarkably, when it comes to the Last Supper, Sanders concludes it is "almost equally certain" in historical plausibility to Jesus' act of cleansing of the Temple, which he considers certain.[60] However, while Sanders devotes two long chapters to Jesus' words and deeds regarding the Temple, *he completely ignores the Last Supper* and never explains how the words of institution can be reconciled with his overall reconstruction of Jesus' eschatology.[61]

Last, but certainly not least, there is the work Dale Allison, one of the most brilliant and persistent advocates for Schweitzer's apocalyptic Jesus. In his most comprehensive study to date, Allison makes a powerful case for Jesus as an apocalyptic prophet of the immediate end of the world.[62] Nevertheless, despite the fact that eschatological concepts such as the kingdom of God and the Son of Man are front and center in the accounts of the Last Supper (Matt 26:24-29; Mark 14:21-25; Luke 22:14-22), the reader will search Allison's reconstruction in vain for any detailed discussion of the words of institution.[63] Indeed, in his many writings on Jesus and eschatology, Allison never explains how the words of institution do or do not fit into his overall reconstruction of Jesus' eschatology.[64]

58. Schweitzer, *The Quest of the Historical Jesus,* 380.

59. Sanders, *Jesus and Judaism,* 334. (For his differences with Schweitzer, see idem, 327-30.)

60. Sanders, *Jesus and Judaism,* 307.

61. Sanders, *Jesus and Judaism,* 131-33.

62. Allison, *Constructing Jesus,* 31-220.

63. He does devote a brief paragraph to the Last Supper in Allison, *Constructing Jesus,* 272.

64. See e.g., Dale C. Allison Jr., *The Historical Christ and the Theological Jesus* (Grand Rapids: Eerdmans, 2009); idem, "Jesus and the Victory of Apocalyptic," in *Jesus & the Res-*

In short, it seems that the apocalyptic Jesus of the immediate end of history has proven very hard to square with the Jesus of the Last Supper. This is an interesting situation. Given the importance in Jesus research of the question of his eschatological expectations, it seems that any worthwhile reconstruction of Jesus' eschatology must not fail to take into account his words and deeds at the Last Supper. To be sure, the words of institution can be dismissed as unhistorical; they can be reinterpreted so as to accommodate an imminent eschatology; but they should not simply be ignored.

As a result, exploring the relationship between the Last Supper and the eschatology of Jesus will be one of the primary goals of this book. Indeed, almost every one of the following chapters will in some way be tied to a particular Jewish hope for the future: the expectation of a new Moses, a new covenant, an eschatological Passover, the messianic banquet, the ingathering of the lost tribes of Israel, and the coming of the kingdom of God. As I hope to demonstrate, a close study of ancient Jewish eschatology, far from justifying the dismissal of the words of institution, has the power to offer some important correctives to Schweitzer's influential portrait, as well as some important answers to the vexed question of what exactly were Jesus' hopes for the future.

Jesus and the Early Church

The fourth and final issue has to do with the question of Jesus' intentions and the origin of the early church. On the one hand, in contrast to popular Christian belief, many scholars conclude that Jesus himself did *not* intend to found a church. Indeed, any talk of such an intention on his part is commonly viewed as anachronistic. For example, the famous text in which Jesus speaks of building his "assembly" or "church" on Peter (Matt 16:18-19) is widely ignored or regarded as unhistorical by most works on Jesus.

On the other hand, several scholars have argued the eucharistic words of institution, when situated in the context of ancient Jewish hopes for the restoration of Israel, *do* reveal an intention on Jesus' part both to replace the Jerusalem Temple cult with his own sacrificial meal and, in this way, to begin a new community. From this perspective, a case can be

---

toration of Israel: A Critical Assessment of N. T. Wright's Jesus and the Victory of God (ed. Carey C. Newman; Downers Grove: IVP, 1999), 126-41; idem, *Jesus of Nazareth: Millenarian Prophet;* idem, "The Eschatology of Jesus," in *The Encyclopedia of Apocalypticism,* vol. 1: *The Origins of Apocalypticism in Judaism and Christianity* (ed. John J. Collins; New York: Continuum, 1998), 267-302; idem, "A Plea for Thoroughgoing Eschatology," *JBL* (1994): 651-68.

made that at the Last Supper, Jesus saw himself as founding a new cult, one focused on the sacrifice of his own body and blood that would establish a new "covenant."

The Question of Jesus and the Church

The first of these two positions — that Jesus did not intend to found any kind of enduring community and that it is anachronistic to speak of him instituting the church — is widely attested. In 1902, it found its classic formulation in the work of the French biblical scholar Alfred Loisy, who famously concluded:

> It is certain, for instance, that Jesus did not systematize beforehand the constitution of the Church as that of a government established on earth and destined to endure for a long series of centuries. . . . *Jesus foretold the kingdom, and it was the Church that came.*[65]

Although this last line has been often been taken out of context, it became over the course of the twentieth century an influential way of summing up the discontinuity between the intentions of the historical Jesus and the actual effects of his ministry. Indeed, many recent studies, if they take up the question of Jesus and the church at all, often declare — usually in no uncertain terms — that he did not intend to found any kind of community that would live on after his death. Consider, for example, the following statements regarding Jesus and the institution of an *ekklēsia:*

> [T]here arise most serious doubts as to whether the historical Jesus himself really did speak these words [to Peter about the building of the church]. This is not only because they have no parallel in the other Gospels, and because this is the only place in the whole synoptic tradition where the word *"ekklēsia"* appears in the sense of the church as a whole. . . . But the authenticity of the passage in Matthew xvi is questioned chiefly because it is not easily compatible with Jesus' proclamation of the imminent coming of the kingdom of God.[66]

65. Alfred Loisy, *The Gospel and the Church* (trans. Christopher Home; London: Isbister & Co., 1903), 166.

66. Bornkamm, *Jesus of Nazareth,* 187.

> [L]et it be re-stated for a last time, if [Jesus] meant and believed what he preached . . . namely, that the eternal Kingdom of God was truly at hand, he simply could not have entertained the idea of founding and setting in motion an organized society intended to endure for ages to come.[67]

> [*E*]*kklēsia* in Matt 16:18 comes from the usage of the early church, and not from the historical Jesus. . . . It is difficult to imagine such a usage in the mouth of the historical Jesus.[68]

> Jesus cannot have spoken these words [in Matt 16:18-19] as he did not found a church.[69]

> In two famous passages in Matthew, Jesus is reported as speaking of his *ekklēsia*. . . . Both passages are probably redactional and indicative of later developments.[70]

It should be clear from statements such as these that many modern biblical scholars, even those who are otherwise disposed to affirm many of the sayings of Jesus in the Synoptic Gospels as historically reliable, reject the historicity of the evidence that Jesus intended to found a church of any kind. Note in particular the last two quotes, in which the rejection of the idea that Jesus instituted any kind of community is directly based on the idea that he expected the imminent coming of the kingdom of God (*à la* Loisy).

Indeed, many recent books on the historical Jesus show their allegiance to the idea that Jesus did not intend to found a church by simply ignoring the question altogether. One searches the indexes of a remarkable number of major works on Jesus in vain for any discussion of whether or not he intended to found a community in the wake of his death.[71] As always, there are excep-

67. Vermes, *The Religion of Jesus the Jew,* 214.

68. Meier, *A Marginal Jew,* 232, 233.

69. Lüdemann, *Jesus After 2000 Years,* 198.

70. Dunn, *Jesus Remembered,* 513.

71. For example, in many reconstructions of Jesus' life, the famous passage in which Jesus speaks of "building" the "church" *(ekklēsia)* on the disciple Peter (Matt 16:16-19) is treated almost as if it did not exist. The following major works on Jesus simply ignore the evidence that Jesus intended to "build" his *ekklēsia* on Peter and his disciples, leaving the reader to come to his or her own (negative) conclusion: Allison, *Constructing Jesus;* David R. Flusser, with R. Steven Notley, *The Sage from Galilee: Rediscovering Jesus' Genius* (Grand Rapids: Eerdmans, 2007); Fredriksen, *Jesus of Nazareth, King of the Jews;* Ehrman, *Jesus: Apocalyptic Prophet;* Sanders, *The Historical Figure of Jesus;* Becker, *Jesus of Nazareth;* Allison, *Jesus of Nazareth;*

tions;[72] but there remains a remarkable lack of conversation about the topic in most works. The implication of this lacuna is that there is no need to discuss the evidence that Jesus may have intended to found a church because the assumption that he did not need not be defended or explained. Hand in hand with the apocalyptic Jesus of the imminent end of history, the non-ecclesial Jesus also seems to have largely won the day.

The Problem of the Cultic Words of Jesus

One problem with this view is that it fails to take seriously the evidence for Jesus' intentions implicit in the accounts of the Last Supper. For example, in all four accounts, Jesus explicitly speaks of a "covenant" that is centered on the sacrifice of his own blood, not the covenant sacrifices of the Jerusalem Temple (Matt 26:28; Mark 14:24; Luke 22:20; 1 Cor 11:25). Moreover, in the Synoptic accounts, this covenant is not established with just anyone, but with "the twelve" disciples, who represent the nucleus of a new Israel that is bound together by the blood of Jesus, rather than the blood of Jacob the patriarch (Matt 26:20; Mark 14:17; Luke 22:14, 28-30).[73]

In light of this evidence, a number of studies over the course of the last century have concluded that Jesus did in fact intend to establish a new covenant in his own blood and a new community in the persons of the twelve disciples. Although the following articulations are lengthy, they are worth citing in full:

> If Jesus understood his Messiah-ship in the sense of Daniel 7, this will open up new vistas when we are considering the nature and the impor-

Crossan, *The Historical Jesus;* Vermes, *Jesus the Jew;* Perrin, *Rediscovering the Teaching of Jesus,* etc. Other scholars will briefly mention Matt 16:16-19 as the source of Simon's being renamed "Peter," but either dismiss or ignore Jesus' express statements about building his *ekklēsia* on Peter. See, e.g., Gnilka, *Jesus of Nazareth,* 186-87; Sanders, *Jesus and Judaism,* 146-47; Bornkamm, *Jesus of Nazareth,* 186-87.

72. See Michael J. Wilkins, "Peter's Declaration concerning Jesus' Identity at Caesarea Philippi," in *Key Events in the Life of the Historical Jesus* (ed. Darrell L. Bock and Robert L. Webb; WUNT 247; Tübingen: Mohr Siebeck, 2009), 292-381; Michael F. Bird, *Jesus and the Origins of the Gentile Mission* (LNTS 331; Edinburgh: T. & T. Clark, 2007), 155-61.

73. On Jesus and the restoration of the twelve tribes of Israel, see Meier, *A Marginal Jew,* 3:153; Allison, *Jesus of Nazareth,* 101-2; Wright, *Jesus and the Victory of God,* 300; Sanders, *Jesus and Judaism,* 97; Jeremias, *New Testament Theology,* 234. See also Pitre, *Jesus, the Tribulation, and the End of the Exile,* throughout.

tance of his founding of the church. For the Son of Man in Daniel is not a mere individual: he is the representative of "the people of the saints of the Most High" and has set himself the task of making this people of God, the *ekklēsia*, a reality. From this point of view, the so-called institution of the Lord's Supper can be shown to be the formal founding of the church.[74]

The decisive saying for the connection of the message of a crucified Messiah with the reconstituted People of God is to be found in the words of institution at the Last Supper, and particularly in the use of the word *diathēkē* ["covenant"]. . . . If we may look for any one moment wherein the new Israel was constituted, it would be in the act of Jesus at the Last Supper.[75]

In the time of Jesus the sectaries of Qumran regarded themselves as the people of the new covenant. The idea, therefore, of a covenant as the foundation charter (so to speak) of the people of God was very much alive at the time, and there can be no doubt what Jesus had in mind when he invited his followers to drink of the cup of the covenant: he was formally installing them as foundation members of the new people of God.[76]

By the command "Do this" (Luke 22.19; cf. 1 Cor 11:25) he enjoined the continuation of this fellowship in his absence and endowed it with a distinctive social and cultic act. This was to be the visible unifying factor of a community otherwise remaining scattered throughout Israel. . . . Until the definitive gathering of the saved at the end of time the aims of Jesus would be incarnated in this community, at once the remnant and the first fruits of messianic Israel.[77]

[T]he twelve disciples were probably looked upon by Jesus as the nucleus of the restored people of God in an eschatological sense. The choosing of the twelve took place during Jesus' Galilean ministry. The interesting point

74. Karl Ludwig Schmidt, *The Church* (trans. J. R. Coates; London: SCM, 1950 [orig. 1935]), 39-40. Here Schmidt is following F. Kattenbusch, "Der Quellort der Kirchenidee," in *Festgabe von Fachgenossen und Freunden A. von Harnack zum siebzigsten geburtstag dargebracht* (Tübingen: Mohr-Siebeck, 1921), 143-72 (esp. 171).

75. R. Newton Flew, *Jesus and His Church* (London: Epworth, 1938), 71, 76.

76. C. H. Dodd, *The Founder of Christianity* (London: Macmillan, 1970), 96.

77. Ben F. Meyer, *The Aims of Jesus* (London: SCM, 1979), 219.

> now to note is that the *definitive* constitution of this new people of God *in nuce* was done in proleptic manner *at the Last Supper.*[78]

> The symbolic action against the temple cult was complemented by Jesus' symbolic action at the last supper in founding a cult, though he did not intend to found a cult which would last through time. He simply wanted to replace provisionally the temple cult which had become obsolete: Jesus offers the disciples a replacement for the official cult in which they could either no longer take part, or which would not bring them salvation — until a new temple came. This "substitute" was a simple meal. By a new interpretation, the last supper becomes a substitute for the temple cult — a pledge of the eating and drinking in the kingdom of God which is soon to dawn.[79]

Three aspects of these proposals are worth highlighting.

First, the question of Jesus' self-understanding and the question of his intentions are inextricably bound up with one another.[80] For if Jesus saw himself as the messianic head of Israel, then one of his key tasks will be to gather the eschatological community. Second, insofar as the Last Supper was intended to function as a unifying factor among the twelve disciples, it would have the effect of creating an eschatological community. In other words, the Last Supper is not just a sign of the restoration of Israel, but to a certain extent, the very *means* by which Jesus unifies the community of followers that would exist in his absence.[81] Third, the presence of the language of a "covenant" at the Last Supper is implicitly but undeniably cultic. In a Jewish context, such language would have enormous implications. Indeed, as a number of scholars have suggested recently, when Jesus' demonstration in the Temple and the Last Supper are taken together, they may suggest that he intended to replace the atoning cult of the Jerusalem Temple with the atoning cult of his own sacrifice, embodied in the eucharist.[82] In short, the messianic Jesus, as head of a com-

78. Kim Huat Tan, *The Zion Traditions and the Aims of Jesus* (SNTSMS 91; Cambridge: Cambridge University Press, 1997), 217.

79. Gerd Theissen and Annette Merz, *The Historical Jesus: A Comprehensive Guide* (trans. John Bowden; Minneapolis: Fortress, 1998), 434.

80. As Schmidt says elsewhere: "The question whether Jesus himself founded the Church is really the question concerning his Messiah-ship." Schmidt, *The Church,* 41.

81. See also Gerhard Lohfink, *Jesus and Community* (trans. John P. Galvin; Philadelphia: Fortress; New York: Paulist, 1984), 9-12, 23-26; Jeremias, *New Testament Theology,* 167-70.

82. See, e.g., Brant Pitre, "Jesus, the New Temple, and the New Priesthood," *Letter & Spirit* 4 (2008): 47-83 (esp. 63-82); McKnight, *Jesus and His Death,* 325-28; Jostein Ådna, *Jesu*

munity, and the eucharistic Jesus, as the founder of a cultic rite, lead directly to the ecclesial Jesus, the founder of a community unified by his leadership and his covenant.

Indeed, if any of the suggestions listed above are correct, then Jesus' actions at the Last Supper do not cohere well with the overly simplistic (but quite common) picture of an eschatological prophet who had no intentions of establishing any community that would survive him. To the contrary, when the words and deeds of Jesus are interpreted within the context of ancient Judaism, a case can be made that he not only awaited the eschatological restoration of the people of Israel, he deliberately established the nucleus of a new Israel precisely by means of the Last Supper. At the very least, the question of Jesus' intentions cannot simply be decided on the basis of an evaluation of Jesus' words to Peter at Caesarea Philippi; the accounts of the Last Supper must be taken into account. As A. J. B. Higgins put it in his study of the Lord's Supper:

> *The cleavage of opinion as to whether Jesus did or did not "found" the Church has its counterpart in the debate on the origin of the Eucharist.* Was it deliberately "instituted" by Jesus himself, or is it a natural and perhaps inevitable development which began in the earliest days of the Church, but which Jesus had neither foreseen nor intended? These two questions of the Church and the Eucharist are inseparably connected, just as it is impossible to isolate Israel and the Passover from one another.[83]

In other words, if Jesus did indeed institute a new cultic ritual to be performed after his death, by his twelve disciples, as the sign of a new covenant with the new Israel, then on some level, he has to have likewise envisioned a commu-

---

Stellung zum Tempel (WUNT 2.119; Tübingen: Mohr-Siebeck, 2000); idem, "Jesus' Symbolic Action in the Temple (Mark 11:15-17): The Replacement of the Sacrificial Cult by His Atoning Death," in *Gemeinde ohne Tempel* (ed. Beate Ego, Armin Lange, and Peter Pilhofer; Tübingen: Mohr Siebeck, 1999), 461-73; Bruce D. Chilton, *Rabbi Jesus* (New York: Doubleday, 2000), 248-57; Wright, *Jesus and the Victory of God*, 557-63; Bruce Chilton, *The Temple of Jesus* (University Park: Pennsylvania State University Press, 1992); Jacob Neusner, "Money-Changers in the Temple: The Mishnah's Explanation," *NTS* 35 (1989): 287-90 (here 290).

83. A. J. B. Higgins, *The Lord's Supper in the New Testament* (Chicago: Alec R. Allenson; Alva: Robert Cunningham and Sons, 1952), 9. For similar sentiments, see Vermes, *The Religion of Jesus the Jew*, 15: "[T]he historical authenticity of the establishment of the eucharist as a permanent institution depends not only on whether the meal was really a Passover supper celebrated on the correct date . . . , but also on whether [Jesus] ever envisaged the creation of an enduring church." See also Rudolf Pesch, "Das Abendmahl, Jesu Todesverständnis und die Konstitution der Kirche," in *Das Abendmahl und Jesu Todesverständnis*, 112-25.

nity that would perform the ritual. And if he did indeed intend to replace the Jerusalem Temple cult with the sacrificial banquet of the coming kingdom of God, then the whole question of the opposition between the kingdom and the church posed by Loisy at the start of the century needs to be reexamined. In short, if what Jesus intended for his followers is important, then the quest for the historical Jesus must pay serious attention to the question of what he did and said — and hence, what he intended — at the Last Supper. In the words of Albert Schweitzer: "The problem of the Lord's Supper is the problem of the life of Jesus!"[84]

Method of Proceeding

If there is any aspect of the historical quest for Jesus that is currently in a remarkable state of flux, it is the question of method. In recent decades, methodology in Jesus research has become a field of study in its own right, with the number of publications on this topic showing no signs of abating.[85] Indeed, a whole host of issues that are fundamental to methodology in Jesus research — such as the literary genre of the Gospels,[86] their relationship to the living memory and testimony of eyewitnesses,[87] the Synoptic problem and the existence of

84. Schweitzer, *The Problem of the Lord's Supper,* 137.

85. See esp. Tom Holmén and Stanley E. Porter, eds., *Handbook for the Study of the Historical Jesus* (4 vols.; Leiden: Brill, 2011). The first 1,000 pages of this 3,500-page collection are devoted entirely to questions of methodology.

86. See esp. Richard A. Burridge, "*What Are the Gospels? A Comparison with Graeco-Roman Biography* (2nd ed.; Grand Rapids: Eerdmans, 2004). See also Richard Burridge, "Gospel: Genre," in *Dictionary of Jesus and the Gospels* (2nd ed.; ed. Joel B. Green, Jeannine K. Brown, and Nicholas Perrin; Downers Grove: IVP Academic, 2013), 335-42; E. W. Klink, *The Audience of the Gospels: The Origin and Function of the Gospels in Early Christianity* (LNTS 353; London: T. & T. Clark, 2010); Craig S. Keener, *The Historical Jesus of the Gospels* (Grand Rapids: Eerdmans, 2009), 71-83; Graham Stanton, *Jesus and Gospel* (Cambridge: Cambridge University Press, 2004); Craig S. Keener, *The Gospel of John: A Commentary* (2 vols.; Peabody, MA: Hendrickson, 2003), 3-52; Samuel Byrskog, *Story as History — History as Story: The Gospel Tradition in the Context of Ancient Oral History* (Boston/Leiden: Brill, 2002); L. M. Wills, *The Quest of the Historical Gospel: Mark, John, and the Origins of the Gospel Genre* (London: Routledge, 1997); Dirk Frickenschmidt, *Evangelium als Biographie: Die vier Evangelien im Rahmen antiker Erzählkunst* (TANZ 22; Tübingen: Francke, 1997).

87. See Chris Keith, *Jesus' Literacy: Scribal Culture and the Teacher from Galilee* (LNTS 413; LHJS 8; London: Bloomsbury T. & T. Clark, 2011), 27-70; Alan Kirk, "Memory Theory and Jesus Research," in *Handbook for the Study of the Historical Jesus* (4 vols.; ed. Tom Holmén and Stanley E. Porter; Leiden: Brill, 2011), 809-43; Robert McKiver, *Jesus, Memory, and the Synoptic*

"Q,"[88] the question of whether the Gospel of John should be used as a source,[89] just to mention a few — can no longer be treated as settled, but are the subject of lively debate and a growing number of competing scholarly viewpoints.

Above all, there is the current debate over the validity of the form-critical criteria of historical authenticity. On the one hand, many scholars within the

---

Gospels (Atlanta: Society of Biblical Literature, 2011); Robert B. Stewart and Gary R. Habermas, eds., *Memories of Jesus: A Critical Appraisal of James D. G. Dunn's* Jesus Remembered (Nashville: B&H Academic, 2010); Anthony Le Donne, *The Historiographical Jesus: Memory, Typology, and the Son of David* (Waco, TX: Baylor University Press, 2009), 1-64; Alan Kirk and Tom Thatcher, eds., *Memory, Tradition, and Text: Use of the Past in Early Christianity* (SBLMS; Atlanta: Society of Biblical Literature, 2005); Martin Hengel, "Eye-witness Memory and the Writing of the Gospels: Form Criticism, Community Tradition, and the Authority of the Authors," in *The Written Gospel* (ed. Markus Bockmuehl and Donald Hagner; Cambridge: Cambridge University Press, 2005), 70-96; Paul Rhodes Eddy and Gregory A. Boyd, *The Jesus Legend: A Case for the Historical Reliability of the Synoptic Jesus Tradition* (Grand Rapids: Baker Academic, 2007), 269-454; Richard Bauckham, *Jesus and the Eyewitnesses: The Gospels as Eyewitness Testimony* (Grand Rapids: Eerdmans, 2006); Keener, *The Gospel of John,* 3-52.

88. See Paul Foster, A. Gregory, J. S. Kloppenborg, and J. Verheyden, eds., *New Studies in the Synoptic Problem: Oxford Conference, April 2008; Essays in Honor of Christopher M. Tuckett* (BETL 239; Leuven: Peeters, 2011); Mark Goodacre and Nicholas Perrin, eds., *Questioning Q: A Multidimensional Critique* (Downers Grove: IVP, 2005); Mark Goodacre, *The Case Against Q: Studies in Markan Priority and the Synoptic Problem* (Harrisburg, PA: Trinity Press International, 2002); E. P. Sanders and Margaret Davies, *Studying the Synoptic Gospels* (London: SCM; Philadelphia: Trinity Press International, 1989).

89. See Paul Foster, "Memory, Orality, and the Fourth Gospel: Three Dead Ends in Historical Jesus Research," *JSHJ* 10 (2012): 191-227; Paul N. Anderson, Felix Just, S.J., and Tom Thatcher, eds., *John, Jesus, and History,* vol. 1: *Critical Appraisals of Critical Views* (Atlanta: Society of Biblical Literature, 2007); idem, *John, Jesus, and History,* vol. 2: *Aspects of Historicity in the Fourth Gospel* (ed. Paul N. Anderson, Felix Just, S.J., and Tom Thatcher; Atlanta: Society of Biblical Literature, 2009). See also James D. G. Dunn, *The Oral Gospel Tradition* (Grand Rapids: Eerdmans, 2013), 138-95; Richard Horsley and Tom Thatcher, *John, Jesus, and the Renewal of Israel* (Grand Rapids: Eerdmans, 2013); Anthony Le Donne and Tom Thatcher, eds., *The Fourth Gospel in First-Century Media Culture* (LNTS 426; London: T. & T. Clark, 2011); Dwight Moody Smith, "Jesus Tradition in the Gospel of John," in *Handbook for the Study of the Historical Jesus* (4 vols.; Leiden: Brill, 2011), 3:1997-2040; Richard Bauckham, *The Testimony of the Beloved Disciple: Narrative, History, and Theology in the Gospel of John* (Grand Rapids: Baker Academic, 2007); idem, *Jesus and the Eyewitnesses* (Grand Rapids: Eerdmans, 2008), 358-411; Paul N. Anderson, *The Fourth Gospel and the Quest for Jesus: Modern Foundations Reconsidered* (LNTS 321; New York: T. & T. Clark, 2006); Craig L. Blomberg, "John and Jesus," in *The Face of New Testament Studies: A Survey of Recent Research* (ed. Scot McKnight and Grant R. Osborne; Grand Rapids: Baker Academic, 2004), 209-26; idem, *The Historical Reliability of John's Gospel: Issues & Commentary* (Downers Grove: IVP, 2001); John P. Meier, *A Marginal Jew: Rethinking the Historical Jesus* (3 vols.; ABRL; New York: Doubleday, 1991, 1994, 2001), 1:44-45.

field of Jesus research continue to employ the criteria of historical authenticity that grew out of twentieth-century form, source, and redaction criticism — i.e., multiple attestation, embarrassment, coherence, and dissimilarity — in their reconstructions of the life and mission of Jesus.[90] On the other hand, one recognizes a rising tide (whether it will crest or not remains to be seen) of other scholars levying serious critiques of some or all of the "traditional" criteria of authenticity.[91] These studies call for the now-standard methods of historical authentication to be either radically revised or, in some cases, abandoned altogether. Still other scholars go about their work trying to keep somewhat out of the methodological fray, whether by devising their own distinctive criteria of historical authentication — such as "double similarity"[92] or "characteristic and distinctive tradition"[93] — or by preferring to take a more pragmatic approach and avoid restricting research by "strict predetermined rules."[94]

In the midst of so much disagreement about fundamentals, modesty and caution seem called for, on several counts. First, given the powerful critiques of the traditional form-criteria of authenticity in recent discussion, it seems unwise to simply continue using them as if there were no serious problems.[95] Second, given the recent debates over the Synoptic problem and the existence

90. E.g., John P. Meier, "Basic Methodology in the Quest for the Historical Jesus," in *Handbook for the Study of the Historical Jesus* (4 vols.; ed. Tom Holmén and Stanley E. Porter; Leiden: Brill, 2011), 1:291-331; Keener, *The Historical Jesus of the Gospels*, 155-58; the scholars assembled in *Key Events in the Life of the Historical Jesus* (ed. Darrell L. Bock and Robert L. Webb; WUNT 247; Tübingen: Mohr Siebeck, 2009); Meier, *A Marginal Jew*, 1:167-96. For a defense of the traditional criteria, see Gerd Häfner, "Das Ende der Kriterien? Jesusforschung angesichts der geschichtstheoretischen Diskussion," in *Historiographie und fiktionales Erzählen: Zur Konstrucktivität in Geschichtstheorie und Exegese* (ed. Knut Backhaus and Gerd Häfner; Neukirchen-Vluyn: Neukirchener Verlag, 2008), 97-103. For a history and overview, see Stanley E. Porter, *The Criteria for Authenticity in Historical-Jesus Research: Previous Discussion and New Proposals* (JSNTSup 191; Sheffield: Sheffield Academic Press, 2000).

91. Above all, see the essays in *Jesus, Criteria, and the Demise of Authenticity* (ed. Chris Keith and Anthony Le Donne; London: T. & T. Clark, 2012). See also Dale C. Allison, "How to Marginalize the Traditional Criteria of Authenticity," in *The Handbook for the Study of the Historical Jesus* (ed. Tom Holmén and Stanley E. Porter, 4 vols.; Leiden: Brill, 2009), 1:3-30; Rafael Rodríguez, "Authenticating Criteria: The Use and Misuse of a Critical Method," *JSHJ* 7 (2009): 152-67; Klaus Berger, "Kriterien für echte Jesuworte?" *ZNT* 1 (1998): 52-58; Allison, *Jesus of Nazareth*, 1-77. The classic formulation of this critique of the criteria goes back to Morna Hooker, "On Using the Wrong Tool," *Theology* 75 (1972): 570-81.

92. Wright, *Jesus and the Victory of God*, 131-33.

93. Dunn, *Jesus Remembered*, 333.

94. Vermes, *The Religion of Jesus the Jew*, 7.

95. Cf. Keener, *The Historical Jesus of the Gospels*, 155.

of the "Q" source, it also seems highly imprudent to base any historical conclusions about Jesus on a particular source-critical solution to the question of the literary relationship between the Gospels. This is especially true when we consider that scholars such as Joseph Fitzmyer deem the Synoptic problem "practically insoluble"[96] and E. P. Sanders draws the somewhat shocking conclusion that the Two-Source hypothesis is not only problematic but "the least satisfactory" of "all the solutions."[97] Third, as Albert Schweitzer pointed out over a hundred years ago, the Synoptic problem is of course "a *literary* question" about the relationships between the Gospels, one that is methodologically incapable of answering "the *historical* problem" of whether Jesus did or said any of the things reported in the Gospels.[98] In other words, whatever literary solution one adopts to the problem, we are still left with the historical question of the plausibility or implausibility of the evidence, which simply cannot be answered by recourse to theories about the literary relationships between the documents. Finally, given the growing skepticism about the possibility of reconstructing the "original form" of a saying or deed of Jesus, it seems illogical to base any historical conclusions on scholarly reconstructions of the words and deeds of Jesus rather than the extant evidence in the Gospels.[99] Such reconstructions, however brilliantly argued, are always hypothetical and only exist in the imagination of the scholar who proposes them. By contrast, the evidence in the Gospels, however complex and difficult to assess, is the only truly historical data we possess.

The Method of E. P. Sanders

With all these caveats in mind, how then should one proceed? Given the current state of affairs, I have chosen to model my approach herein on the method laid out by E. P. Sanders in his rightly famous work, *Jesus and Judaism.* Although Sanders's study is not without its own problems and methodological inconsistencies, it remains to my mind (and in the opinion of many others) one of the most brilliant and enduring contributions to the historical

96. Joseph A. Fitzmyer, S.J., "The Priority of Mark and the 'Q' Source in Luke," in *Jesus and Man's Hope* (Pittsburgh: Pittsburgh Theological Seminary, 1970), 131-70 (here 132).

97. Sanders and Davies, *Studying the Synoptic Gospels,* 117.

98. See Albert Schweitzer, *The Quest of the Historical Jesus: First Complete Edition* (trans. William Montgomery, J. R. Coates, Susan Cupitt, and John Bowden; Minneapolis: Fortress, 2001), xli.

99. See Wright, *Jesus and the Victory of God,* 133.

study of Jesus. In his section on the "Method of Proceeding," Sanders not only anticipates many of the recent criticisms of the form-critical criteria of authenticity, but, unlike some recent studies, suggests a reasonable alternative approach:

> No matter what criteria for testing the sayings are used, scholars still need to move beyond the sayings themselves to a broader *context* than a summary of their contents if they are to address historical questions about Jesus. Since historical reconstruction requires that data be fitted into a context, the establishment of a secure context, or framework of interpretation, becomes crucial. There are basically three kinds of information which provide help in this endeavor: (1) such *facts about Jesus as those outlined above;* (2) *knowledge about the outcome of his life and teaching;* (3) *knowledge of first-century Judaism.*[100]

Notice that for Sanders, unlike the traditional form-critical criteria, these three sets of information do not work in isolation. Instead, each of them constitutes important indicators that must be used in tandem with the others.

Later on in the book, Sanders sharpens this insight into an important statement of historical method in Jesus research (which I have taken the liberty to enumerate):

> [T]he only way to proceed in the search for the historical Jesus is to offer hypotheses based on the evidence and to evaluate them in light of how satisfactorily they account for [1] the material in the Gospels, while also making Jesus [2] a believable figure in first-century Palestine and [3] the founder of a movement that eventuated in the Church.[101]

There are three implicit arguments for historicity embedded in these lines. This triple-context approach is, in my opinion, one of the main reasons that Sanders's study has been so influential as a historical hypothesis about Jesus and, on many points, has stood the test of time. Although this is not a book on methodology, one of the conclusions I hope to demonstrate over the course of this book as we weigh the various scholarly arguments for and against the historicity of various words and deeds of Jesus is that Sanders's three kinds of arguments — unlike some of the traditional form-critical criteria of authentic-

100. Sanders, *Jesus and Judaism,* 17 (enumeration and emphasis added).
101. Sanders, *Jesus and Judaism,* 166-67.

ity — are implicitly at work in virtually *all* historical studies of Jesus. Indeed, as I will document over the course of our study, these three arguments are often the actual *reasons* scholars conclude for or against the historicity of particular sayings or deeds.

Indeed, given the recent (and trenchant) criticisms of the form-critical criteria of multiple attestation, embarrassment, dissimilarity, and the like, it is worth highlighting here that historical arguments from Jewish contextual plausibility, coherence with the overall evidence in the Gospels, and effects within the early church are even employed by the most vocal critics of the traditional "criteria of authenticity" — such as Dale Allison, Chris Keith, and Anthony Le Donne — when they draw historical conclusions about Jesus.[102] However, in order to see this clearly, we will need to take a few moments to examine each of Sanders's implicit arguments, flesh out their implications, and see how they are already materially (if not formally) in use in a remarkably diverse body of Jesus scholarship.

102. For example, Dale Allison, in his recent essay "How to Marginalize the Traditional Criteria of Authenticity," appeals to all three of the arguments I propose above when he finally attempts to make positive historical arguments about Jesus. He argues that Jesus should be regarded as an eschatological prophet precisely because this reconstruction is (1) compatible with "whatever knowledge we have of his first-century Jewish world," (2) coheres with "whatever circumstances about his life we can recover with assurance," and (3) because a non-eschatological Jesus entails "discontinuity with the movement out of which he came as well as with the movement that came out of him." See Allison, "How to Marginalize the Traditional Criteria of Authenticity," 26-27. Along similar lines, Chris Keith concludes that Jesus was not a scribal-literate teacher (though some of his contemporaries thought he was), among other reasons, because (1) "a Second Temple Palestinian context favors the theory that Jesus was a scribal-illiterate teacher . . . ," (2) because it coheres with the broad impression of the Gospels that "Jesus often engaged in activity that invited assessment of him vis-à-vis known scribal literate authorities" (citing a number of Gospel texts in which Jesus engages the scribal-literature authorities), on which basis Keith assumes that "Jesus did at least some of these things in his ministry," and (3) because "this proposed historical reality best explains the existence and development of the diverse Jesus-memories of his scribal literate status." Keith, *Jesus' Literacy,* 168-69, 177-79. Le Donne explicitly engages Sanders's method in Le Donne, *The Historiographical Jesus,* 74-76, though he describes it as a "two context" approach rather than three. By making explicit their implicit appeal to contextual plausibility, coherence with other evidence about Jesus, and continuity with the early church more explicit, critics of the criteria could avoid the (unjustified) accusation that they are jettisoning historical argumentation altogether.

1. Contextual Plausibility

First and foremost, according to Sanders, any hypothesis must make Jesus *"a believable figure in first century Palestine."*[103] Implicit in these words is what we might call an argument from *contextual plausibility*, with a particular emphasis on his Jewish context. It can be formulated as follows: If evidence about Jesus is compatible or believable within his first-century Jewish context, then this is an important argument in favor of its historicity.

Although I am following Sanders in my formulation, it should go without saying that the argument from contextual plausibility is operative in almost all recent works on Jesus, although it takes different forms. To take but a few examples, consider the following statements:

> Our early primary sources are unanimous and unambiguous in placing Jesus within a context of first-century Judaism. It follows that our picture of Jesus should be comprehensible within that cultural framework, and, further, when a piece of information about Jesus or those present during the historic ministry fits *only* there, that is a strong argument in favour of its historicity.[104]

> I concur [with Sanders] that we should proceed by abduction — that is, by inference to the best explanation, always looking for a Jesus who makes the most sense of the available facts and what we otherwise know of Judaism and nascent Christianity.[105]

> A more general consideration, known as "historical plausibility" is particularly important. . . . Our knowledge of first-century Judaism has increased rapidly in recent decades. Since it is now possible to place Jesus within that context with much more confidence, Jesus traditions which can plausibly be linked to that context may be accepted.[106]

> What is plausibly "Jewish" enjoys a high degree of historical plausibility in being traced back to the historical Jesus. At the least, "authentic" Jesus

103. Sanders, *Jesus and Judaism*, 167.

104. Casey, *Jesus of Nazareth*, 106.

105. Allison, *Constructing Jesus*, 22. Note here that Allison is directly engaging Sanders, *Jesus and Judaism*, 18-22, and explicitly states that his approach "corresponds in part to the notion of 'historical plausibility' in Theissen and Winter, *Quest*."

106. Graham Stanton, *The Gospels and Jesus* (2nd ed.; Oxford: Oxford University Press, 2002), 175.

> material must be material that in the broadest sense can be integrated into the multi-sided picture of the Judaism of his time. That is what we call "Jewish contextual plausibility."[107]

> When something can be seen to be credible (though perhaps deeply subversive) within first-century Judaism . . . there is a strong possibility of our being in touch with the genuine history of Jesus.[108]

> Material that coheres with what we know of Jesus' historical circumstances . . . should be given priority.[109]

Such scholarly sentiments could be multiplied.[110] For our purposes, what matters is that the argument from contextual plausibility, even though sometimes not explicitly formulated, is in fact a major determining factor in the way much contemporary scholarship on Jesus evaluates the historical plausibility of the evidence in the Gospels. Indeed, it was precisely the fact that Sanders's reconstruction of Jesus' views of the Jerusalem Temple was viewed as compatible with early Jewish restoration eschatology that made his hypothesis a convincing and lasting contribution to the field of Jesus research.

With that said, this argument does suffer from several weaknesses. For one thing, its helpfulness as a tool is constrained by the fact that the evidence we have for what Judaism was like at the time of Jesus is limited. We do not know everything there is to know about Judaism at the time of Jesus, and there are now and will always be major gaps in our knowledge. For example, the discovery of the Dead Sea Scrolls in the 1940s has had a direct effect on scholarly judgments about the historical plausibility of Jesus' criticisms of the Temple, establishment of a community of disciples united by a new "covenant," and gathering of twelve disciples around himself to symbolize the restoration of Israel.[111] Before the Scrolls were discovered, the historical plausibility of

107. Gerd Theissen and Dagmar Winter, *The Quest for the Plausible Jesus: The Question of Criteria* (trans. M. Eugene Boring; Louisville: Westminster, 2002), 206; cf. also 180-84, 211.

108. Wright, *Jesus and the Victory of God*, 132. This is, of course, only half of Wright's criterion of "double similarity"; the other half is given below.

109. Craig A. Evans, *Jesus and His Contemporaries: Comparative Studies* (AGJU 25: Leiden: Brill, 1995), 13.

110. See Keith, *Jesus' Literacy*, 175 n. 31, who cites Allison positively on this point. See also Sean Freyne, *Jesus, a Jewish Galilean: A New Reading of the Jesus-Story* (repr.; London: T. & T. Clark, 2005), 22-23, 171.

111. See, Heinz-Wolfgang Kuhn, "Jesus im Licht der Qumrangemeinde," in *Handbook*

such elements in the Gospels was much easier to reject because we lacked evidence for such strikingly similar currents in first-century Judaism as the Scrolls provided.

Moreover, although seldom noted, the argument from Jewish contextual plausibility is also extremely dependent on *how familiar any given scholar actually is with the ancient Jewish evidence.* What seems implausible to one scholar who is ignorant of some aspect of ancient Jewish practice and belief may appear eminently plausible to another who is more familiar with the Jewish evidence, or vice versa. Indeed, even this familiarity itself will be contingent upon scholarly judgments about which Jewish sources are relevant and/or admissible to the study of Jesus, and which sources are too far removed to be helpful. Because of this, in the following pages, we will have to spend a great deal of time quoting ancient Jewish sources in order to see how and whether the words and deeds of Jesus in the Gospels can be plausibly situated in an ancient Jewish setting. (This will make for a longer, but hopefully, more informative and interesting book.)

Also, as we will see, this argument needs to be balanced out by the fact that Jesus was an individual figure within his contemporary landscape, who did and said things that, while they would have made sense in a Jewish context, were at the same time unusual and even shocking.[112] If the Gospels are any indicator, he said and did things that were distinctive enough to set him apart as a major and memorable figure and dangerous enough to get him crucified in the process.

Finally, as noted above, in Sanders's work and others', contextual plausibility does not function as a "criterion" that can be used in isolation (e.g., "if it's Jewish, then it's from Jesus"). Rather, it should be used in tandem with the other two sets of information: other evidence about Jesus and the effects within the early church.

2. *Coherence with Other Evidence about Jesus*

Second, according to Sanders, any hypothesis about Jesus must provide a *"satisfactory account of the material in the Gospels."*[113] Implicit in these words is a

for the Study of the Historical Jesus (4 vols.; ed. Tom Holmén and Stanley E. Porter; Leiden: Brill, 2011), 3:1245-86; Meier, *A Marginal Jew,* 3:488-614; James H. Charlesworth, ed., *Jesus and the Dead Sea Scrolls* (ABRL; New York: Doubleday, 1992).

112. See Dunn, *Jesus Remembered,* 333 (regarding what is "distinctive" of Jesus).

113. Sanders, *Jesus and Judaism,* 167.

second argument — the argument from *coherence with other evidence about Jesus*. This argument can be formulated as follows: If a particular saying or deed attributed to Jesus is both contextually plausible and coheres with or illuminates other first-century evidence about Jesus, then this too is an important argument in favor of its historicity.

It is, of course, a standard principle of historiography to aim at constructing a basically coherent account of the words and deeds of any given historical figure. Consequently, the argument from coherence is easily documented in the works of scholars besides Sanders, both as an explicit working principle and, more commonly, as an implicit principle of evaluation. To cite but a few examples:

> The criterion of coherence: All that is repeated in different forms of Jesus' words and, moreover, is illustrated through the acts of Jesus, must be historical.[114]

> Historical plausibility demands that we take seriously *the whole of Jesus' life* in first-century Judaism. . . .[115]

> Certain themes, motifs, and rhetorical strategies recur again and again throughout the primary sources; and it must be in those themes and motifs and rhetorical strategies — which taken together, leave some distinct impressions — if it is anywhere, that we will find memory.[116]

> The question again and again will be not simply "Is this detail or that detail historically plausible/reliable?" but "Does this particular story or teaching build into a coherent and consistent picture of the person who made the impact evident in the broader picture?"[117]

> Elements which recur and correspond to one another in different independent currents of tradition and forms (and are thus numerously attested), may be due to an effect made by the historical Jesus.[118]

114. Ernst Baasland, "Fourth Quest? What Did Jesus Really Want?" in *Handbook for the Study of the Historical Jesus* (ed. Tom Holmén and Stanley E. Porter; 4 vols.; Leiden: Brill, 2011), 31-56 (here 49).

115. Casey, *Jesus of Nazareth*, 107 (emphasis added).

116. Allison, *Constructing Jesus*, 15.

117. Dunn, *Jesus Remembered*, 334.

118. Gerd Theissen and Annette Merz, "The Delay of the Parousia as a Test Case for

> Material that coheres with what we know of . . . the principal features of his [Jesus'] life should be given priority.[119]

Once again, more examples could be given.[120] For now, I only wish to highlight two important and distinctive features of my use of the argument from coherence.

First, unlike some of the scholars cited above, I believe it is reasonable to apply the argument from coherence to the question of the historical plausibility of individual teachings and actions of Jesus (always keeping in mind that we are not seeking the *ipsissima verba;* see discussion below). Some scholars, such as E. P. Sanders himself, are of the opinion that as a general rule it is difficult if not impossible to draw firm conclusions about the historicity of any single teaching or action of Jesus; we can only really know about the big picture.[121] While such caution is understandable if one accepts the form-critical hypothesis that the Gospels are the products of long periods of anonymous oral traditioning processes, it is also possible to turn this point around. If Dale Allison is right and the Gospels provide us with substantially reliable "broad impressions" of Jesus, then it is also reasonable to explore whether they might also provide us with "substantially reliable" accounts of *particular* teachings or actions of Jesus.[122] One does not have to subscribe to the simplistic view that we can "peel away" the unhistorical "layers" in the Gospels to find the "authentic" core to hold that scholars can (and do) make judgments about the historical truth or falsity of particular events or teachings from the life of Jesus.[123]

Second, as I have argued elsewhere, unlike those scholars who see the argument from coherence as "secondary" or supplementary, in my view, coherence is actually one of the most significant factors in making judgments about the historicity of any given teaching or action of Jesus.[124] Even a cursory

---

the Criterion of Coherence," *LS* 32 (2007): 49-66 (here 54). See also Theissen and Winter, *The Quest for the Plausible Jesus,* 234-39.

119. Evans, *Jesus and His Contemporaries,* 13.

120. E.g., Lüdemann, *Jesus After 2000 Years,* 5; Allison, *Jesus of Nazareth,* 27.

121. See Sanders, *Jesus and Judaism,* 4-5.

122. Cf. Allison, *Constructing Jesus,* 17.

123. Cf. Richard Bauckham, "Eyewitnesses and Critical History: A Response to Jens Schröter and Craig Evans," *JSNT* 31 (2008): 221-35.

124. Cf. John P. Meier, "Basic Methodology in the Quest for the Historical Jesus," in *Handbook for the Study of the Historical Jesus* (4 vols.; ed. Tom Holmén and Stanley E. Porter; Leiden: Brill, 2011), 1:320-22.

examination of Jesus research reveals that scholars consistently accept or reject a given piece of evidence based on whether it coheres with other data about Jesus that they accept as historically accurate. (Once again, I will document this as we move through our study.) In this book, I will treat the argument from coherence as particularly forceful when a datum not only displays consistency or coherence with other evidence about Jesus, but *explanatory power* with reference to data that may seem obscure or difficult.[125] As we will see over the course of this study, such "intertextual linkage" is often one of the most helpful ways of deepening our understanding of the meaning Jesus' words and deeds might have had in the overall context of his public ministry.

The argument from coherence, of course, also has its weaknesses.[126] First, depending on how one employs it, it is more or less contingent on the historical truth of the other evidence about Jesus that is brought to bear on any given question. If the corroborative evidence cited is substantially unhistorical or distorted enough to be misleading, then the argument obviously loses its force. In light of this situation, if one were to take a strictly inductive approach, one would be forced into the difficult position of having to argue for the historical plausibility of every single piece of data about Jesus before being able to draw any conclusions about whether or not any other single piece of evidence is coherent. Needless to say, such an approach would not only be tedious, but would ultimately fail to reckon with the fact that in historical research, such strictly inductive logic is not only unnecessary, but probably impossible.[127] Moreover, as with Jewish contextual plausibility, the argument from coherence is, of course, inescapably subjective in its application. What seems coherent to one interpreter based on one's evaluation of the overall evidence about Jesus, may appear to be incompatible to another, who has a different overall picture.[128] However, this subjective element is simply part of the tentative nature of all historical argumentation and once again serves to remind us of the limits of what human reason can demonstrate and the fact that historical argumentation is about various levels of probability. In some ways, the subjective dimension of coherence can even be beneficial, and serve as a check against historical

125. Pitre, *Jesus, the Tribulation, and the End of the Exile*, 27.

126. See Anthony Le Donne, "The Criterion of Coherence: Its Development, Inevitability, and Historiographical Limitations," in *Jesus, Criteria, and the Demise of Authenticity* (ed. Chris Keith and Anthony Le Donne; London: T. & T. Clark, 2012), 95-114.

127. Pitre, *Jesus, the Tribulation, and the End of the Exile*, 27 n. 112; Meyer, *The Aims of Jesus*, 83-84.

128. Allison, *Jesus of Nazareth*, 2-3.

positivism.[129] Once again, even certain critics of the criteria of authenticity admit that "coherence is *a necessary and inevitable principle*" of historical argumentation and that some form of it provides "a useful tool to guide us toward the construction of the most plausible narrative."[130] Indeed, in spite of these problems, there is arguably no study of Jesus — and perhaps, no work of good historiography — that does *not* utilize some form of argument from coherence as a tool for drawing conclusions about the data.

Nevertheless, in order to offset these weaknesses as much as possible, in what follows, I will always try to give a judicious sampling of evidence about Jesus when making the case for coherence, so that it does not hang upon the historicity of any one word or deed. As Sanders says:

> The method which is being followed more and more, and the one which it seems necessary to follow in writing about Jesus, is to construct hypotheses which, on the one hand, do rest on material generally considered reliable without, on the other hand, being totally dependent on the authenticity of any given pericope.[131]

Moreover, when treating the question of coherence, I will try to always explain exactly *how* I think the one piece of evidence coheres with another, rather than just asserting that it does. Again, this will make for somewhat longer discussions of historical plausibility than is found in other works on Jesus. However, in this way, the reader will be free to evaluate the explanations given. In the final analysis, when it comes to the argument from coherence, as Sanders points out, "The reader will have to judge how good the evidence is."[132]

3. *Plausibility of Effects in Early Christianity*

Third and finally, according to Sanders, any sound historical hypothesis must also depict Jesus as *"the founder of a movement that eventuated in the*

129. Le Donne, "The Criterion of Coherence," 109, even goes so far as to say that "Not only is subjectivity not a detriment to historiographical rigor, it is necessary and even beneficial."

130. Le Donne, "The Criterion of Coherence," 113 (emphasis added; though he thinks it must be situated in "a world of mnemonic cross-pollination and overlapping social sets").

131. Sanders, *Jesus and Judaism,* 3.

132. Sanders, *Jesus and Judaism,* 22.

Church."[133] Implicit in these words is a third argument — the argument from the *plausibility of effects within the early church*. It can be formulated as follows: If a saying or deed attributed to Jesus is contextually plausible, coherent with other evidence about Jesus, and continuous with or provides a plausible cause for the practice and belief of the early church, then it is reasonable to conclude that the evidence in question is historical. In other words, if a saying or deed of Jesus not only fits with his historical context and other evidence about him, but also has the power to explain why the early church acted and believed the way they did, then it is reasonable to conclude that the saying or deed can be traced back to Jesus.

In contrast to the two previous arguments, this one is somewhat more controversial, since it stands in direct opposition to the form-critical criterion of authenticity based on dissimilarity with the early church.[134] In principle, the criterion of dissimilarity was only supposed to be used to argue *for* the historicity of evidence unlikely to have been created by the early church. However, in practice, it has often been used as a criterion of inauthenticity: any evidence that was even remotely similar to the practice and belief of the early church was often deemed unhistorical or at least too suspect to be treated as evidence for Jesus.[135] However, in more recent scholarship, it has been recognized that this negative use of the criterion of dissimilarity with the early church drives too strong of a wedge between Jesus and the movement that followed him.[136] In contrast to this form-critical approach, an argument from plausibility of

133. Sanders, *Jesus and Judaism*, 167.

134. See Chris Keith, "The Indebtedness of the Criteria Approach to Form Criticism and Recent Attempts to Rehabilitate the Search for an Authentic Jesus," in *Jesus, Criteria, and the Demise of Authenticity* (ed. Chris Keith and Anthony Le Donne; London: T. & T. Clark, 2012), 25-48.

135. See Theissen and Winter, *The Quest for the Plausible Jesus*, 1-171. For an example of dissimilarity as a "criterion of inauthenticity," see Lüdemann, *Jesus After 2000 Years*, 4.

136. See Dagmar Winter, "Saving the Quest for Authenticity from the Criterion of Dissimilarity: History and Plausibility," in *Jesus, Criteria, and the Demise of Authenticity* (ed. Chris Keith and Anthony Le Donne; London: T. & T. Clark, 2012), 115-31; Craig A. Evans, "Jesus' Dissimilarity from Second Temple Judaism and the Early Church," in *Memories of Jesus: A Critical Appraisal of James D. G. Dunn's* Jesus Remembered (ed. Robert B. Stewart and Gary R. Habermas; Nashville: B&H Academic, 2010), 145-58 (esp. 145-46); Keener, *The Historical Jesus of the Gospels*, 144; Dunn, *Jesus Remembered*, 92-97, 191-92; Porter, *The Criteria for Authenticity in Historical-Jesus Research*, 70-89, 126; Theissen and Winter, *The Quest for the Plausible Jesus*, 19-24; Tom Holmén, "Doubts About Double Dissimilarity: Restructuring the Main Criterion of Jesus-of-History Research," in *Authenticating the Words of Jesus* (ed. Bruce Chilton and Craig A. Evans; Leiden: Brill, 1999), 47-80. See also Meyer, *The Aims of Jesus*, 83.

effects within (or continuity with) the early church has begun to be iterated with more frequency:

> The criterion of consequence: All that explains the emergence of the Jesus tradition, that Jesus is the only teacher, Jesus' death, as well as the emergence of the ancient congregation and the first Christian mission, must be historical.[137]

> It is more difficult to ensure that a picture of Jesus is "compatible with the Christian . . . history of his effects," because tracking these out is a complex task in itself. It is however a very important task. . . . [W]e must be able to see the connections between the historical Jesus and the subsequent movement that regarded him as its central figure.[138]

> A sort of "similarity" criterion is thus more in vogue today: whatever situates Jesus in the continuum between contemporary Judaism and the movement that emerged from him offers the likeliest portrait of Jesus.[139]

> A Jesus who can be placed within early Judaism but who cannot be understood in relation to early Christianity is no more historically plausible than a Jesus who can be combined with nascent Christianity while remaining an enigma to a Jew of his time. Both dimensions should receive enough attention and be explained satisfactorily.[140]

> The final and perhaps most important consideration of all is the *aftermath* of Jesus. It is greatly to the credit of E. P. Sanders to have drawn attention to the question posed in 1925 by the distinguished Jewish scholar Joseph Klausner: "How was it that Jesus lived totally within Judaism, and yet was

137. Baasland, "Fourth Quest? What Did Jesus Really Want?" 49.

138. Casey, *Jesus of Nazareth*, 107, citing Theissen and Winter, *The Quest for the Plausible Jesus*, 211.

139. Keener, *The Historical Jesus of the Gospels*, 157. Keener goes on to point out that this recent development distinguishes it somewhat from the so-called "Third Quest": "The Third Quest tends to highlight Jesus' Jewish environment, but sometimes to the neglect of the movement that emerged from his teaching; a 'continuum' approach seeks to integrate both contexts" (157). Here Keener is following Tom Holmén (see footnote below).

140. Tom Holmén, "An Introduction to the Continuum Approach," in *Jesus from Judaism to Christianity: Continuum Approaches to the Historical Jesus* (ed. Tom Holmén; LNTS 352; London: T. & T. Clark, 2007), 1-16 (here 4).

the origin of a movement that separated from Judaism, since *ex nihilo nihil fit,* nothing comes from nothing, or more idiomatically, where there is smoke there is fire."[141]

> What we know of Jesus as a whole must allow him to be recognized within his contemporary Jewish context and must be compatible with the Christian (canonical and noncanonical) history of his effects.[142]

> [The] goal is to find an unmistakable nucleus of Jesus material that is at one and the same time an expression of his Jewish context and an antecedent that stands in continuity with Primitive Christianity.[143]

> [W]hen something can be seen to be . . . credible as the implied starting-point (though not the exact replica) of something in later Christianity, there is a strong possibility of our being in touch with the genuine history of Jesus.[144]

> [I]t must be inferred in any case that, if authentic materials contrary to church tendencies were conserved, authentic materials in accord with church tendencies were *a fortiori* conserved.[145]

Perhaps the strongest formulation comes from Sanders himself:

> In the first place, a good hypothesis with regard to Jesus' intention and his relationship to Judaism should meet [Joseph] Klausner's test: it should situate Jesus believably in Judaism and yet explain why the movement initiated by him eventually broke with Judaism. . . . I propose that a hypothesis which does offer a reasonable and well-grounded connection between Jesus and the Christian movement is better than one which offers no connection, but which appeals, finally, to accident. . . .[146]

141. Stanton, *Jesus and the Gospels,* 176.

142. Theissen and Winter, *The Quest for the Plausible Jesus,* 211-12.

143. Becker, *Jesus of Nazareth,* 14 (here speaking of correct application of dissimilarity).

144. Wright, *Jesus and the Victory of God,* 132. This is the second half of Wright's "double similarity."

145. Meyer, *The Aims of Jesus,* 83.

146. Sanders, *Jesus and Judaism,* 18, 22. Sanders iterates this criterion at the very beginning of his study: "It has proved difficult to do justice to the question posed by Joseph Klausner: how was it that Jesus lived totally within Judaism, and yet was the origin of a movement

These are a remarkable series of quotations, since they cut against the grain of the way in which much of the quest for the historical Jesus has evaluated evidence in the Gospels. And yet, as these scholars point out, it makes good historical sense to demand that any reasonable portrait of Jesus must do its best not only to explain how he fit into the Judaism of his day, but how his teachings and actions gave rise to the early Christian movement. Otherwise, one is forced into the historically dubious position of positing an implausible (or even nonexistent) cause-effect relationship between Jesus and his followers. As Sanders puts it: "[T]hat there is no causal thread between his [i.e., Jesus'] life, his death, and the Christian movement . . . is possible, but is not satisfying historically."[147] In other words, the argument from plausibility of effects within the early church forces us to remember that Jesus not only stood within the Judaism of his day, he also stood at the origins of early Christianity. Consequently, *both* contexts should be part of any plausible historical portrait.

On the other hand, the argument, like all others, suffers from several weaknesses. Once again, it is limited by the fact that we do not know everything there is to know about the early church.[148] Not only was it characterized by a remarkable diversity, but many of its practices and beliefs are shrouded in mystery. (Think here of how little we know about the exact forms that baptism and the eucharist took in the earliest communities.) Consequently, we will often have to work with very limited data, and therefore constantly call to mind that all our conclusions are tentative and subject to revision. Moreover, in any given case, exactly what constitutes plausible "effects" within the early church will not always be immediately clear. As a result, this approach will demand that we take time (once again, within reasonable limits) to carefully compare and contrast the evidence in the Gospels with what we do know about the early church and attempt to plot (insofar as possible) a plausible trajectory of *development.*[149]

Finally, it should go without saying that this argument, like contextual plausibility and coherence with other evidence about Jesus, should not be used in isolation. In this way, the danger of attributing to Jesus what was in fact created by the early church can be offset by paying close attention to an-

---

that separated from Judaism, since *ex nihilo nihil fit,* nothing comes from nothing, or, more idiomatically, where there is smoke there is fire." Sanders, *Jesus and Judaism,* 3. He is following Klausner, *Jesus of Nazareth,* 369.

147. Sanders, *Jesus and Judaism,* 22.

148. Allison, *Jesus of Nazareth,* 5, following F. Gerald Downing, *The Church and Jesus: A Study in History, Philosophy, and Theology* (London: SCM, 1968), 51.

149. See Holmén, "An Introduction to the Continuum Approach," 2-3.

cient Jewish practices and belief. Indeed, as we will see, in several cases where critics have alleged that the early church must have created a saying or deed of Jesus or distorted it to the point that it should be deemed inauthentic, a closer examination of Jewish parallels and Jesus material strongly suggests that the evidence in question is in fact both plausible in an ancient Jewish context and coherent with other first-century evidence about Jesus.[150]

For example, Sanders's use of the argument from continuity with the early church is one of the primary reasons his basic hypothesis about Jesus' eschatological outlook has been widely regarded as convincing. In the final analysis, the portrait of a Jesus who awaited and sought the eschatological restoration of Israel not only makes sense within a first-century Jewish context, it also provides a good explanation for the eschatological beliefs and activities of the early church. This is especially true of the church's missionary activity among both Jews and Gentiles. As an eschatological prophet, Jesus founded a movement that was focused on eschatological fulfillment. The eschatological smoke of the early church had its origin in the eschatological "fire" of Jesus himself.[151]

Finally, it is important here to point out that, in contrast to the traditional form-critical criteria, the triple-context approach of E. P. Sanders also works in reverse. Taken together, these three arguments can also be inverted and used as reasons *against* the historicity of a given piece evidence: If evidence about Jesus (1) cannot be plausibly situated within the ancient Jewish context in which he lived (contextual implausibility); (2) is irreconcilable with other data about him (incoherence); and (3) cannot be plausibly situated at the origins of the movement to which his life and death gave rise (implausibility of effects), then it is reasonable to conclude that the evidence in question is substantially unhistorical. Once again, even a brief glance at the scholarly literature shows that it is precisely these kinds of arguments that are used all the time to reject the historicity of certain events and teachings recorded in the Gospels and other early-first-century literature about Jesus. It is important to stress that the arguments I am employing in this study actually work in reverse, since one of the most important criticisms of the form-critical criteria of multiple attestation, embarrassment, and dissimilarity is that they only work in *one direction* — to authenticate evidence.[152] More sound historical tools,

150. See Theissen and Winter, *The Quest for the Plausible Jesus,* 207.

151. On criteria of inauthenticity, see Casey, *Jesus of Nazareth,* 107-8; Keener, *The Historical Jesus of the Gospels,* 157; Lüdemann, *Jesus After 2000 Years,* 4; Sanders, *Jesus and Judaism,* 22. For the whole issue, see Allison, "How to Marginalize the Criteria of Authenticity," 3-30.

152. See Robert L. Webb, "The Historical Enterprise and Historical Jesus Research," in

by contrast, should be able to be used both for and against any given piece of evidence, as do these three indexes.

With that said, there are a couple of final points of method that need to be explained before we turn to the evidence itself.

Historicity and the Substantia Verba Jesu

First, with reference in particular to the sayings of Jesus, it is important to be precise about what I mean when I speak about the "historicity" or "historical plausibility."

On the one hand, there are some readers of the Gospels who come to them looking for the *ipsissima verba Jesu* (the "exact words of Jesus"). As contemporary scholarship rightly insists, rarely, if ever, is it possible for us to reconstruct the exact words of Jesus.[153] Indeed, as even a cursory comparison of the sayings of Jesus in a Gospel synopsis shows, on many occasions, the evangelists themselves do not seem bent on giving us anything like the exact words of Jesus. The most obvious example of this is none other than the accounts of *the Last Supper itself,* in which the words of institution contain obvious differences in form, order, detail, and vocabulary (see Matt 26:28; Mark 14:24; Luke 22:19-20; 1 Cor 11:23-25). In light of such differences, it should go without saying that the four Gospels should not be treated as stenographs of Jesus' teachings but as ancient Greco-Roman biographies, in which the historical truth of Jesus' sayings should not be equated with exactitude in form and detail. It would be the height of irony if a book on the Last Supper proceeded by trying to recover the *ipsissima verba* when this is incontrovertibly *not* what the Gospel authors (or, in this case, the apostle Paul) ever intended to provide us.

On the other hand, it is much more popular in the scholarly realm to come to the Gospels seeking the *ipsissima vox Jesu,* an expression sometimes used to refer to "the basic message of Jesus" or "the 'kind of thing' he usually or typically said."[154] Although at first glance this may seem like a more helpful formulation, upon further reflection, there are several problems with it. For one thing, "the exact voice of Jesus" *(ipsissima vox Jesu)* reflects the peculiarly

---

Key Events in the Life of the Historical Jesus (ed. Darrell L. Bock and Robert L. Webb; WUNT 247; Tübingen: Mohr Siebeck, 2009), 54-75.

153. E.g., Geza Vermes, *Jesus in His Jewish Context* (Minneapolis: Fortress, 2003), 74.

154. Meier, *A Marginal Jew,* 1:174, following Robert H. Stein, "The Criteria of Authenticity," in *Gospel Perspectives: Studies of History and Tradition in the Four Gospels,* vol. 1 (ed. R. T. France and D. Wenham; Sheffield: JSOT, 1980), 228-29.

modern preoccupation with *exactitude (ipse),* and hence smacks both of historical positivism and philosophical foundationalism. Moreover, the emphasis on the exact "voice" *(vox)* of Jesus is precisely the wrong emphasis. The image of a "voice" lends itself to a focus on how someone sounds (form), rather than what someone says (content), for a "voice" can be completely without substance or meaning. This can result in placing too much emphasis on the *form* of Jesus' words rather than the *content.* Indeed, this may explain why so many studies that claim to be seeking the *ipsissima vox* pour so much effort into reconstructing the exact primitive or original "form" of any given saying (e.g., reconstructions of the "original" Lord's Prayer).[155] However, for historical research, a case can be made that it is not so much the form of Jesus' teaching that is most important, but the content or substance. (To make this point is not, of course, to completely separate the two, but to distinguish between them.) Once again, even a quick glance at any Synopsis of the Gospels should show us that a representation of the exact forms of Jesus' sayings does not seem to have been a primary goal of the evangelists. By contrast, the parallel traditions in the Gospels are identified as such precisely because there is often a substantial amount of overlap in the substance of the words *(verba).*[156] This is of course because in human discourse, for better or for worse, content is inextricably tied to words.

In light of such considerations, I suggest a third way. In this study, I will be pursuing what I would like to refer to as the *substantia verba Jesu* — i.e., the substance of the words of Jesus.[157] In other words, I am interested in *what* he said and did and what it might have meant in a first-century Jewish context. Hence, whenever I conclude that a particular saying or action is historical or historically plausible, I am not saying that Jesus said exactly these words *(ipsissima verba),* nor am I just saying the text "sounds exactly like Jesus" *(ipsissima vox).* Instead, I am claiming that the basic *substance* or content of the teaching or action can be reasonably concluded as having originated with him. That is what I mean by historical — no more, and no less.[158] This

155. E.g., Meier, *A Marginal Jew,* 2:291-94; Jeremias, *New Testament Theology,* 193-96.

156. See, e.g., the synoptic charts throughout Dunn, *Jesus Remembered.*

157. This is my own formulation, and is quite similar to the idea of the *sensus verba Jesu* found in the Pontifical Biblical Commission, Instruction on the Historical Truth of the Gospels, *Sancta Mater Ecclesia,* which states that "The truth of the Gospel account is not compromised because the Evangelists report the Lord's words and deeds in different order. Nor is it hurt because they report his words (Latin *verba*), not literally, but in a variety of ways, while retaining the same meaning (Latin *sensus*)." See also Augustine, *Harmony of the Gospels* 2.12.28.

158. See Theissen and Winter, *The Quest for the Plausible Jesus,* 197-99.

focus on substance of the sayings of Jesus in the Gospels has several important practical implications.

First, a focus on the *substantia verba Jesu* means that I will not attempt to reconstruct an "original form" of any of Jesus' sayings.[159] Modern scholarly reconstructions of such primitive forms, for all their ingenuity and display of learning, manifest precisely the concern for exactitude and detail that the first-century evangelists do not seem concerned about and that I wish to avoid. Indeed, even though such reconstructions are often posited by scholars who claim that they are only looking for the kind of thing Jesus said, they ironically often seem to manifest an actual desire to discover the *ipsissima verba.*

Second, it also means that I will not spend much time evaluating differences in form and detail between various accounts of Jesus' words or actions in the Gospels — except when they have a direct bearing on the substance of the text. Such differences, which may be quite significant for redaction-critical analyses of the Gospels, are of far less importance for Jesus research. In contrast to the *ipsissima verba* and *ipsissima vox* approaches outlined above, *I am not looking for the* ipsissima *anything.* Instead, I will focus on the basic substance of any given saying and attempt to ascertain what it might have meant in the historical context of first-century Judaism and the life of Jesus. Obviously, this will entail a certain amount of reductionism, as well as judgments about what is substantive and major and what is incidental and minor with reference to any given data. I leave it to the reader to decide to what extent I have succeeded in keeping the discussion focused on the substance of Jesus' words and deeds.

Third and finally, along similar lines, this focus on the substance of Jesus' sayings will require us to pay due attention to the first-century account of Jesus' words and deeds given to us in the Gospel of John (e.g., the manna discourse in the synagogue at Capernaum).[160] Once again, this is in accord with a rising tide of scholarship that is emphasizing with ever-increasing urgency the need for Jesus research to give adequate attention to the evidence about Jesus in the Fourth Gospel.[161] Consider, for example, the words of Mark Alan Powell:

159. Cf. Dunn, *Jesus Remembered,* 332.

160. Cf. Keener, *The Gospel of John,* 53-80 on the historical use of the discourses in John.

161. See the essays in Paul N. Anderson, Felix Just, S.J., and Tom Thatcher, eds., *John, Jesus, and History,* vol. 1: *Critical Appraisals of Critical Views* (Atlanta: Society of Biblical Literature, 2007); idem, *John, Jesus, and History,* vol. 2: *Aspects of Historicity in the Fourth Gospel* (ed. Paul N. Anderson, Felix Just, S.J., and Tom Thatcher; Atlanta: Society of Biblical Literature, 2009), and Craig L. Blomberg, *The Historical Reliability of John's Gospel* (Downers Grove: IVP Academic, 2001). I would note here that I agree with several of Paul Foster's criticisms of the use of John's Gospel in recent research as problematic. See Foster, "Memory, Orality, and the

> We are not even close to an "emerging consensus" but we may at least say that there is a "growing trend" in Jesus studies toward recognition of the Fourth Gospel as a "dissonant tradition" that not only *can* be utilized but *must* be, if the Synoptic tradition is not to be accorded free rein in a manner that increasingly seems uncritical. If John's Gospel had not made it into the canon, if it had been lost to history only to be discovered now, the impact on historical Jesus studies would be revolutionary. Imagine! A book on the life and teachings of Jesus that is almost as early as the Synoptic Gospels, that claims to be based in part on eyewitness testimony, that contains some material that is almost certainly very primitive, that may very well be independent of the other Gospels while corroborating what they say at many points, and that offers what is ultimately a rather different (although not wholly incompatible) spin on the Jesus story. The implications of such a discovery would be *phenomenal:* every work previously written on the historical Jesus would be deemed obsolete and the full attention of scholarship would turn toward discovering what this alternative tradition had to offer. Of course, nothing like this has occurred, but many scholars seem to be saying, "we *do* have such a book; perhaps we should not ignore it."[162]

With this said, I must emphasize here that by being willing to examine some of the sayings of Jesus in John's Gospel, *I am not implying that it provides us* the *ipsissima verba Jesu,* or even the *ipsissima vox Jesu* — although I anticipate some readers will assume I am doing just that. Rather, what I am saying is that if scholars are going to be methodologically consistent, then we need to be able to apply the same arguments for historical plausibility to the words and deeds of Jesus in the Gospel of John as we do to the Synoptics, Paul, or any other source of material about Jesus. In other words, despite their obviously unique *form,* if in their *substance* Jesus' teachings and actions in John's Gospel

---

Fourth Gospel," 212-25. At the same time, given the fact that these developments are recent, weaknesses and methodological difficulties are to be expected. I hope to offer in this volume a more compelling approach by focusing attention on the substance of Jesus' teachings and by carefully evaluating these data methodically according to their contextual plausibility, coherence with other evidence about Jesus, and plausible effects within the early church. My approach also differs from Blomberg, *The Historical Reliability of John's Gospel,* insofar as I am not having recourse to the form-critical criteria of multiple attestation, embarrassment, and dissimilarity.

162. Mark Alan Powell, "The De-Johannification of Jesus: The Twentieth Century and Beyond," in *John, Jesus, and History,* vol. 1: *Critical Appraisals of Critical Views* (ed. Paul N. Anderson, Felix Just, S.J., and Tom Thatcher; Atlanta: Society of Biblical Literature, 2007), 132.

are (1) contextually plausible within a first-century Jewish context, (2) coherent with other reliable evidence about Jesus, and (3) provide a plausible origin for the beliefs of the early church, then it is reasonable to conclude that they originated with Jesus. Likewise, if they are not contextually plausible, coherent with other words and deeds of Jesus, or plausibly continuous with the early church, then it is reasonable to reject them as unhistorical. Ironically, by having a somewhat less exact measure of historicity and focusing on the *substantia verba Jesu,* we will be able to cast the historical net somewhat more widely than was often the case in Synoptic-only Jesus research. This will open the door to examining sayings material frequently excluded by scholars who tend to confuse exactitude *(ipse)* with historicity. In this way, I hope to offer an important corrective to the widespread tendency of Jesus research to ignore the Gospel of John, a tendency that John Meier has rightly referred to as "the tyranny of the Synoptic Jesus."[163] Indeed, one cannot help but wonder if this tyranny of the Synoptics in Jesus research is because, in the final analysis, many scholars really *are* after the exact words of Jesus, and, as a result, they continue to focus almost exclusively on the form they take in the Synoptic Gospels.[164]

Interpretation and Historical Plausibility

Finally, in contrast to some studies on Jesus, I contend that a scholar must first *interpret* the evidence in the Gospels *before* drawing any conclusions about the historical plausibility of a saying or deed of Jesus.[165] A similar approach is supported by the recent work of Gerd Theissen and Dagmar Winter. On several occasions, they make the important observation that the "interpretation" of a saying or deed of Jesus and one's conclusions about the historicity of a saying "mutually condition each other."[166]

Although the point is often overlooked, interpretation and historical plausibility are not separate issues, but rather are inextricably tied to one another:

163. Meier, *A Marginal Jew,* 1:45.

164. Consider, for example, Paul Foster's repeated emphasis on the "distinctive language," the "distinctive voice of Jesus," and "Jesus' language" in John's Gospel as decisive in declaring the attention being given to this Gospel a "dead-end in historical Jesus research." See Foster, "Memory, Orality, and the Fourth Gospel," 224-25.

165. See Pitre, *Jesus, the Tribulation, and the End of the Exile,* passim. See also Rodríguez, "Authenticating Criteria," 166.

166. Theissen and Winter, *The Quest for the Plausible Jesus,* 194.

> [T]he question of the authenticity is bound up with the understanding of the meaning of the saying, and vice versa.[167]

> Since the time that the historicity of the Jesus traditions has been disputed, whether or not they have been considered historical has depended largely on their interpretation.[168]

> Also in the case of an "event," the question is not exclusively whether it is historical or unhistorical but in what sense it must be understood in order to consider it either historical or unhistorical. The interpretation of its meaning decides the issue of its facticity.[169]

It is difficult to overestimate the significance of these insights for how Jesus research should proceed. This approach stands in stark contrast to scholars who *begin* by applying form-critical criteria of historical authenticity and *then* proceed to interpret whatever data are left over. Instead, in this work, my first step will be to at least attempt to offer a historically plausible interpretation of any given saying or deed of Jesus before rendering any judgments about its historicity. Indeed, how can a scholar decide whether or not an episode from the Gospels is historically plausible without actually having attempted to situate it in Jesus' historical context to see whether it fits?

Yet, as we will see over and over again in the course of this study, on numerous occasions, many Jesus scholars will reject a particular episode from the Gospels as unhistorical or implausible *before they have even interpreted the evidence in its context.* In this way, historical conclusions are drawn based on presuppositions and prejudgments that are often unstated, apart from any detailed analysis of the passage in question. This is to put the historical "cart" before the exegetical "horse," and, in my opinion, is one of the most serious weaknesses of many scholarly works on Jesus. Along similar lines, scholars often conclude that simply because a passage from the Gospels can be given plausible interpretation within an early Christian context (or *Sitz im Leben*), then the text must not have originated with Jesus. However, as Theissen and Winter point out:

> It is possible for a saying that has a plausible Christian sense to receive a different plausible meaning if it can be traced back to Jesus. Thus, in

167. Theissen and Winter, *The Quest for the Plausible Jesus*, 193.
168. Theissen and Winter, *The Quest for the Plausible Jesus*, 195.
169. Theissen and Winter, *The Quest for the Plausible Jesus*, 197.

> declaring a tradition to be inauthentic, we must always also test whether the saying, in a different meaning, cannot also be understood as a saying of the historical Jesus. Fitting well into the context of post-Easter Christianity *does not exclude* the possibility that it also fits well into the context of Jesus' ministry.[170]

This is quite true, and why it is so important that historical exegesis must be carried out prior to any conclusions being drawn about historicity. And when these conclusions are drawn, we must always remember that historical plausibility is a limited conclusion, contingent on our knowledge at the current time, and not an incontrovertible "proof."

With all of this in mind, let us now turn to the evidence, keeping our four overarching questions about Jesus and the Last Supper firmly in mind.

170. Theissen and Winter, *The Quest for the Plausible Jesus*, 207.

CHAPTER 2

The New Moses

> Just as the prophet of Deuteronomy 18:15-18 becomes an eschatological expectation, so Jesus, by claiming his actions are like those of Moses at the time of the exodus, can infer that the kingdom of God has been inaugurated. . . . Jesus, in some senses, modeled his own mission and identity on that of Moses — in particular, the expectation of an eschatological Moses.
>
> SCOT MCKNIGHT[1]

If there is anything that is virtually uncontested in the highly contested world of Jesus scholarship, it is the conclusion that Jesus likely spoke and acted in ways that identified him as a prophet. Indeed, the idea that Jesus saw himself as a man sent by God to speak the word of God to the people of God has become a staple of historical Jesus research. As a result, it is relatively easy to list numerous examples of studies on Jesus that contain the now-requisite (and often lengthy) chapter exploring his identity and message as a Jewish prophet.[2] This widespread agreement has been greatly bolstered by the work

1. Scot McKnight, *Jesus and His Death: Historiography, the Historical Jesus, and Atonement Theory* (Waco: Baylor University Press, 2005), 198, 200.

2. E.g., Craig A. Evans, "Prophet, Sage, Healer, Messiah, and Martyr: Types and Identities of Jesus," in *Handbook for the Study of the Historical Jesus* (4 vols.; ed. Tom Holmén and Stanley E. Porter; Leiden: Brill, 2011), 3:1217-44; W. R. Herzog II, *Prophet and Teacher: An Introduction to the Historical Jesus* (Louisville: Westminster John Knox, 2005), 99-124; James D. G. Dunn, *Jesus Remembered* (*Christianity in the Making*, vol. 1; Grand Rapids: Eerdmans, 2003), 655-66; Bart D. Ehrman, *Jesus: Apocalyptic Prophet of the New Millennium* (Oxford: Oxford University Press, 1999) 125-40; Ben Witherington III, *Jesus the Seer* (Peabody: Hendrickson,

of E. P. Sanders, whose influential study *Jesus and Judaism* focused its attention on the prophetic actions of Jesus as clues to understanding his prophetic proclamation of the coming kingdom of God.[3]

However, in recent years, there has also been a growing recognition among various scholars that Jesus did not view himself as just any kind of prophet. Rather, when certain of his words and deeds are situated in their ancient Jewish context, especially against the background of Jewish Scripture and eschatology, a strong case can be made that Jesus spoke and acted in ways that hearkened back to the prophet Moses and the exodus from Egypt. Consider some of the key data that have led scholars to this conclusion:[4]

1. Jesus claims to cast out demons by *"the finger of God"* (Luke 11:20), just as Moses worked marvels during the exodus by "the finger of God" (Exod 8:19).
2. Jesus chooses *twelve disciples* to act as leaders of the "twelve tribes of Israel" (Matt 19:28; Luke 22:30), just as Moses chooses twelve young men to act as "leaders of their ancestral tribes" during the wilderness wandering (Num 1:1-16).[5] Jesus also chooses *seventy* (or seventy-two) *disciples* (Luke 10:1), just as Moses chose seventy (or seventy-two) elders to assist him in leading the people of Israel (Num 11:16-30; cf. Exod 24:1-11).
3. During his public ministry, Jesus repeatedly describes his contemporaries who rejected his message as *"this [evil] generation"* (Matt 12:39-42;

1999), passim; Gerd Theissen and Annette Merz, "Jesus the Prophet: Jesus' Eschatology," in *The Historical Jesus: A Comprehensive Guide* (Minneapolis: Fortress, 1998), 240-80; Jürgen Becker, "Jesus as Mediator of Salvation and Eschatological Prophet of the Kingdom of God," in *Jesus of Nazareth* (trans. James E. Crouch; New York/Berlin: Walter de Gruyter, 1998), 186-224; Morna D. Hooker, *The Signs of a Prophet: The Prophetic Actions of Jesus* (Harrisburg: Trinity Press International, 1997); N. T. Wright, "The Praxis of a Prophet," in *Jesus and the Victory of God* (*Christian Origins and the Question of God,* vol. 2; Minneapolis: Fortress, 1996), 147-97; David E. Aune, "The Prophetic Role of Jesus," in *Prophecy in Early Christianity and the Ancient Mediterranean World* (Grand Rapids: Eerdmans, 1983), 153-69; Geza Vermes, "Jesus the Prophet," in *Jesus the Jew: A Historian's Reading of the Gospels* (Philadelphia: Fortress, 1973), 86-102.

3. E. P. Sanders, *Jesus and Judaism* (Minneapolis: Fortress, 1985).

4. See especially Dale C. Allison, *Constructing Jesus: Memory, Imagination, and History* (Grand Rapids: Baker Academic, 2010), 270-73; Craig S. Keener, *The Historical Jesus of the Gospels* (Grand Rapids: Eerdmans, 2009), 244-45; McKnight, *Jesus and His Death,* 197-200; R. F. O'Toole, "The Parallels between Jesus and Moses," *BTB* 20 (1990): 22-29.

5. See William Horbury, "The Twelve and the Phylarchs," *NTS* (1986): 503-27.

Luke 11:29-32; Mark 8:12) just as Moses repeatedly described the wilderness generation as "this evil generation" (Deut 1:35).[6]

4. Jesus performs a sign in which he *feeds thousands in the wilderness with bread* (Matt 14:13-21; Mark 6:30-44; Luke 9:10-17; John 6:1-15), just as Moses had fed thousands with manna during the exodus from Egypt (Exod 16:1-31). According to the Gospel of John, the response of the crowd to this sign in the desert was to hail Jesus as "the prophet" (John 6:14), referring to "the prophet like Moses" from Jewish Scripture (Deut 18:15-18).
5. Jesus performs a sign of the *"blood" of a "covenant"* with the twelve disciples (Matt 26:27-28; Mark 14:23-24; Luke 22:20; 1 Cor 11:25), just as Moses poured out "the blood of the covenant" at Sinai with the twelve tribes of Israel (Exod 24:1-11).

Whether or not one accepts the historicity of each one of these episodes, they more than suffice to show that "the general impression"[7] produced by our primary sources is that Jesus spoke and acted in ways that hearkened back to the words and deeds of Moses in the Pentateuch.

In light of such data, more than one scholar has come to the conclusion that Jesus understood himself as not just any eschatological prophet, but as the long-awaited prophet like Moses:

> Taken together, these several units[8] strongly suggest that the eschatological Jesus, like Deutero-Isaiah long before him, conceived of the coming of the kingdom in his own day as a sort of new exodus. One might even speculate . . . that Jesus, who surely conceived of himself as an eschatological prophet . . . found the fulfillment of Deut 18:15, 18 (God will raise up a prophet like Moses) in his own ministry.[9]

> Jesus, in some senses, modeled his own mission and identity on that of Moses — in particular, the expectation of an eschatological Moses.[10]

6. See also Matt 11:16; 16:4; 17:17; 23:36; Mark 8:38; 9:19; Luke 7:31; 9:41; 11:50-51; 17:25; Evald Lövestam, *Jesus and 'This Generation': A New Testament Study* (ConBNT 25; Stockholm: Almqvist & Wiksell, 1995).

7. Cf. Allison, *Constructing Jesus,* 15-16.

8. Luke 11:3; 11:20; 11:29-30.

9. Dale C. Allison Jr., *The Intertextual Jesus: Scripture in Q* (Harrisburg: Trinity Press International, 2000), 218.

10. McKnight, *Jesus and His Death,* 200.

> If we can combine the new Moses as reconstituting the covenantal people (as leader of the new exodus) evident in the Righteous Teacher of the Qumran Movement with the new Moses as leader of the new exodus evident in the popular prophetic movements, then we have a more complete sense of the popular prophetic script that may have been followed by the historical Jesus.[11]

> [I]t is highly probable that, like his contemporaries, Jesus took the promise of a prophet like Moses (Deut 18:15, 18) to await its fulfillment in the end-time — and concretely to find this fulfillment in his own act of bringing to completion the last measure, the fullness, of revealed truth.[12]

> Jesus may well have seen himself as the Mosaic prophet of the eschatological age. . . .[13]

To be sure, some scholars disagree.[14] Others are hesitant to draw any firm conclusions about Jesus' Mosaic self-understanding.[15] Nevertheless, as I will argue in this chapter, there are solid grounds for concluding that Jesus did in fact speak and act in ways that deliberately hearkened back to the prophet Moses and the exodus from Egypt and that this Mosaic self-understanding provides a critical framework for understanding the feeding of the multitude in the desert (Matt 14:13-21; Mark 6:32-44; Luke 9:11-17; John 6:1-15) and why Jesus describes his actions at the Last Supper as inaugurating a new "covenant" in his blood (Matt 26:27-28; Mark 14:23-24; Luke 22:20; 1 Cor 11:25).[16] Specifically I will contend that Jesus saw himself as *the new Moses* whose advent and

11. Richard A. Horsley, "The Dead Sea Scrolls and the Historical Jesus," in *The Bible and the Dead Sea Scrolls*, vol. 3: *The Scrolls and Christian Origins* (ed. James H. Charlesworth; Waco: Baylor University Press, 2006), 36-60 (here 59).

12. Ben F. Meyer, "Appointed Deed, Appointed Doer: Jesus and the Scriptures," in *Authenticating the Activities of Jesus* (ed. Bruce Chilton and Craig A. Evans; NTTS 28.2; Leiden: Brill, 1999), 171.

13. Ben Witherington III, *The Christology of Jesus* (Minneapolis: Fortress, 1990), 101.

14. E.g., James D. G. Dunn, *Jesus Remembered* (Grand Rapids: Eerdmans, 2003), 656; Wright, *Jesus and the Victory of God*, 163; Martin Hengel, "Jesus, the Messiah of Israel," *Studies in Early Christology* (Edinburgh: T. & T. Clark, 1995), 1-72 (here 27); Howard M. Teeple, *The Mosaic Eschatological Prophet* (SBLMS 10; Philadelphia: Society of Biblical Literature, 1957), 115-18.

15. E.g., Keener, *The Historical Jesus of the Gospels*, 255; Vermes, *Jesus the Jew*, 95-99.

16. Dale C. Allison, "The Allusive Jesus," in *The Historical Jesus in Recent Research* (ed. James D. G. Dunn and Scot McKnight; Winona Lake: Eisenbrauns, 2005), 238-48.

actions would inaugurate the new exodus spoken of by the prophets, and that Jesus saw his actions at the Last Supper as the culmination of the new exodus, through the establishment of a new covenant sacrifice that would be sealed in his own blood.

However, in order to situate his words and deeds at the Last Supper in their historical context, we will have to first briefly survey the ancient Jewish expectation of a prophet like Moses who would one day come and inaugurate a new exodus.

The New Moses in Early Judaism[17]

As numerous studies have shown, a substantial body of evidence exists showing that in ancient Jewish practice and belief, there was a remarkably widespread expectation that the future age of salvation would be heralded by the coming of a new Moses, whose advent would initiate the new exodus spoken of by the prophets.

The New Moses in the Old Testament

In the Jewish Scripture, there are two key sources of the later expectation of a Mosaic eschatological figure: first, the biblical oracle of a "prophet-like-Moses" from the Pentateuch; and second, the widespread prophetic depictions of the future age of salvation in terms of a new exodus.[18]

17. See Daniel K. Falk, "Moses," in *The Eerdmans Dictionary of Early Judaism* (ed. John J. Collins and Daniel C. Harlow; Grand Rapids: Eerdmans, 2010), 967-70; Axel Graupner and Michael Wolpner, eds., *Moses in Biblical and Extrabiblical Traditions* (BZAW 372; Berlin: De Gruyter, 2007); J. Bowley, "Moses in the Dead Sea Scrolls: Living in the Shadow of God's Anointed," in *The Bible at Qumran: Text, Shape, and Interpretation* (Grand Rapids: Eerdmans, 2001), 159-81; Daniel K. Falk, "Moses," in *Encyclopedia of the Dead Sea Scrolls* (2 vols.; ed. Lawrence H. Schiffman and James C. VanderKam; Oxford: Oxford University Press, 2000), 576-77; Dale C. Allison, *The New Moses: A Matthean Typology* (Minneapolis: Fortress, 1993), 73-84; Israel Abrahams, "Moses," in *Encyclopedia Judaica* (16 vols.; ed. Cecil Roth; Jerusalem: Keter, 1972), 12:371-411; Wayne A. Meeks, *The Prophet King: Moses Traditions and the Johannine Christology* (NovTSup 14; Leiden: Brill, 1967); Howard M. Teeple, *The Mosaic Eschatological Prophet* (SBLMS 10; Philadelphia: Society of Biblical Literature, 1957), 29-73; Joachim Jeremias, *"Mōüsēs,"* in *Theological Dictionary of the New Testament* (ed. G. Kittel and G. Friedrich; trans. G. W. Bromiley; 10 vols.; Grand Rapids: Eerdmans, 1964-1976 [orig. 1933]), 4:848-73 (hereafter cited as *TDNT*).

18. Teeple, *The Mosaic Eschatological Prophet*, 48.

The first of these two foundations comes from the book of Deuteronomy, which is cast as the last prophetic will and testament of Moses, given to the Israelites just before his death and their entry into the promised land of Canaan. In the context of describing their future fate in the land, Moses says these words to the people:

> *The* LORD *your God will raise up for you a prophet like me* from among you, from your brethren — him you shall heed — just as you desired of the LORD your God at Horeb on the day of the assembly, when you said, "Let me not hear again the voice of the LORD my God, or see this great fire any more, lest I die." And the LORD said to me [Moses], "They have rightly said all that they have spoken. *I will raise up for them a prophet like you from among their brethren; and I will put my words in his mouth, and he shall speak to them all that I command him.*" (Deut 18:15-18)

According to this text, the people of Israel are to expect that God will one day raise up a "prophet" *(nābî')* who will speak the word of the Lord to the people as Moses did during his lifetime. Given the future outlook of the text, it is not surprising that it gave rise to the expectation of a coming redeemer who would recapitulate the saving actions of Moses in the exodus from Egypt.[19] Although some interpreters would suggest the oracle points to Joshua, whose actions parallel those of Moses, the ending of Deuteronomy closes off this possibility, declaring that "there has not arisen a prophet since in Israel like Moses, whom the LORD knew face to face, none like him for all the signs and wonders which the LORD sent him to do in the land of Egypt" (Deut 34:10-11). Significantly, the Mosaic Torah therefore ends with the assertion that the promise of the new Moses has not yet been fulfilled.[20] Given the importance of the Pentateuch for ancient Judaism, these final verses of Deuteronomy would give the unfulfilled expectation of the prophet like Moses a prominence that would ensure it was widely known.

The second foundation is the biblical hope for a new exodus, a hope so widely attested that it almost hardly needs recounting.[21] Over and over again, in the books of the prophets, the future age of salvation is modeled on and

19. See Allison, *The New Moses*, 73-84.

20. Aune, *Prophecy in Early Christianity*, 125.

21. Cf. F. Ninow, *Indicators of Typology within the Old Testament: The Exodus Motif* (New York: Peter Lang, 2001); Bernhard Anderson, "Exodus Typology in Second Isaiah," in *Israel's Prophetic Heritage: Essays in Honor of James Muilenberg* (New York: Harper, 1962), 177-95; Teeple, *The Mosaic Eschatological Prophet*, 29-31.

described in terms of the deliverance of Israel from Egypt at the time of Moses and the exodus. For example, in the book of Hosea, God promises to restore the covenant with Israel by bringing her out "into the desert" so that she will return to him "as at the time when she came out of the land of Egypt" (Hos 2:14-15). Likewise, according to the prophet Micah, the restoration from exile and the rebuilding of Jerusalem will recapitulate the exodus at the time of Moses: "As in the days when you came out of the land of Egypt, I will show them marvelous things" (Mic 7:11-15). The prophet Jeremiah goes further, declaring that this new exodus will so outshine the first exodus from Egypt that people will forget the former because of the latter. Indeed, when the messianic "king" comes, "men shall no longer say 'As the LORD lives who brought up the people of Israel out of the land of Egypt,' but 'As the LORD lives who brought up and led the descendants of the house of Israel out of the north country and out of all the countries where he had driven them.' Then they shall dwell in their own land" (Jer 23:5-8).

Above all of these stands the book of Isaiah, which may well be the prophetic book of the new exodus *par excellence.* Numerous oracles could be cited from Isaiah that depict the age of salvation in terms of a new exodus.[22] For our purposes here, one in particular stands out:

> "I am the LORD, your Holy One, the Creator of Israel, your King."
> Thus says the LORD, who makes a way in the sea, a path in the mighty waters,
> who brings forth chariot and horse, army and warrior;
> they lie down, they cannot rise, they are extinguished, quenched like a wick:
> *"Remember not the former things, nor consider the things of old.*
> *Behold, I am doing a new thing; now it springs forth, do you not perceive it?*
> *I will make a way in the wilderness and rivers in the desert. . . ."* (Isa 43:15-19)

Notice here that in Isaiah the future exodus is expected to be both similar to the first and "new." In light of this and similar texts, some scholars have

22. E.g., Isaiah 2, 11, 40, 43, 49, 52–53. See also David W. Pao, *Acts and the Isaianic New Exodus* (WUNT 2:130; Tübingen: Mohr Siebeck: 2000; repr. Grand Rapids: Baker Academic, 2002); Rikki E. Watts, *Isaiah's New Exodus in Mark* (WUNT 2:88; Tübingen: Mohr Siebeck, 1997; repr. Grand Rapids: Baker Academic, 2000); H. M. Barstad, *A Way in the Wilderness: The 'Second Exodus' in the Message of Second Isaiah* (Manchester: University of Manchester Press, 1989).

concluded that the biblical hope for a new exodus, like no other expectation, "comprehensively determined at an early period the shape of the teaching concerning the final redemption."[23] Whether or not this is somewhat overstated, it cannot be denied that in Jewish Scripture, there is a powerful emphasis on the idea that in the latter days, God would deliver the scattered children of Israel by means of a new exodus, making a new "way" in the desert in order to bring them home to the promised land.

With these undisputed texts in mind, it is also worth noting that several scholars have also argued that one other figure in Jewish Scripture is crafted according to the expectation of a new Moses: the famous (and mysterious) "Servant" in the book of Isaiah. According to this position, the suffering Servant in Isaiah is in fact a Mosaic figure, insofar as he is modeled deliberately on the figure of Moses and because his appearance inaugurates the new exodus.[24] When the characteristics of Moses in the Torah and the Servant in Isaiah are placed side-by-side, a number of striking parallels emerge:

Moses	**The Servant in Isaiah**
1. He is called "servant" *('ebed)* (Exod 14:31; Num 12:7-8; Deut 34:5; Josh 1:1-7; 1 Kings 8:56; 2 Kings 18:12; 1 Chron 6:49; 2 Chron 1:3; Ps 105:26; Dan 9:11; Mal 4:4; Bar 1:20; 2:28)	1. He is called "servant" *('ebed)* (Isa 42:1-9; 49:1-13; 50:4-11; Isa 52:13–53:12)
2. He is chosen from birth. (Exod 1-2)	2. He is chosen from birth. (Isa 49:1)
3. God's "spirit" is "upon" him. (Num 11:17)	3. God's "spirit" is "upon" him. (Isa 42:1)
4. He gives the *torah.* (Deut 31:24-26)	4. He gives a new *torah.* (Isa 42:4)
5. He establishes a "covenant" *(berith).* (Exod 24:3-8)	5. He establishes a new "covenant" *(berith).* (Isa 42:6; 49:8)

23. Jeremias, *"Mōüsēs,"* 859-60.

24. See R. E. Clements, "Isaiah 53 and the Restoration of Israel," in *Jesus and the Suffering Servant: Isaiah 53 and Christian Origins* (ed. William H. Bellinger Jr. and William R. Farmer; Harrisburg: Trinity Press International, 1998), 47-54; H. P. Hugenberger, "The Servant of the Lord in the 'Servant Songs' of Isaiah: A Second Moses Figure," in *The Lord's Anointed* (ed. P. E. Satterthwaite, R. S. Hess, and G. J. Wenham; Grand Rapids: Baker, 1995), 105-40; Allison, *The New Moses,* 68-71; Aune, *Prophecy in Early Christianity,* 125; H. J. Krause, *Worship in Israel: A Cultic History of the Old Testament* (Oxford: Basil Blackwell, 1966), 231; C. R. North, *The Second Isaiah* (Oxford: Clarendon, 1964), 21-22; Jeremias, *"Mōüsēs,"* 863-64.

6. He leads the people in the desert to "springs of water." (Exod 15:27; cf. 15:22-25; 17:1-7)	6. He leads the people in the desert by "springs of water." (Isa 49:10)
7. He is exceedingly meek. (Num 12:3)	8. He is exceedingly meek. (Isa 42:2-3; 50:5-6; 53:3-4)
9. He is God's "chosen one." (Ps 106:23)	9. He is God's "chosen one." (Isa 42:1)
10. He offers his life for others. (Exod 32:30-34; cf. Exod 17:4; Numbers 11-14; Deut 1:37-40; 3:26; 4:21-22).	10. He offers his life for others. (Isa 53:4-12)
11. He "sprinkles" *(nāzāh)* blood upon the people. (Exod 24:8)	11. He "sprinkles" *(nāzāh)* the peoples. (Isa 52:15)
12. He inaugurates the first exodus. (Exod, Num, Lev, Deut)	12. He inaugurates the "new" exodus. (Isa 52:7-15; cf. Isa 40:1-11; 42:1-9; 51:10-11)

These are not the only parallels offered by commentators, but they should suffice to establish the basic point.[25] On the basis of such evidence, no less an authority than Gerhard von Rad, in his famous *Old Testament Theology,* identified the Isaianic Servant with the prophet like Moses:

> There is . . . one strand of tradition which we must recognize as particularly important for the origin of these [Servant] songs: this is that of Moses, especially as he is represented in Deuteronomy. Moses is there designated as the Servant of God . . . he too acts as a mediator between Jahweh and Israel, he suffers, and raises his voice in complaint to Jahweh, and at the last dies vicariously for the sins of his people. "Chastisement was laid upon him" — are not these the traits which all recur in the Servant? And now consider further that the Servant is given the task of raising up the tribes of Jacob. . . . Here is struck up the message of the new Exodus, which is of course one of Deutero-Isaiah's main topics. Does not this message actually demand the foretelling — as antitype — of a prophetic mediator who is to be greater than Moses in the same degree as the new Exodus is to outdo the old? He ought not, of course, to be spoken of as a "second Moses" or a *Moses redivivus,* but as a prophet "like Moses." In my opinion, it is very probable that, as with Deuteron-

25. For more, see Allison, *The New Moses,* 68-71.

> omy, Deutero-Isaiah stood within a tradition which looked for a prophet like Moses.[26]

Von Rad was not alone in drawing this conclusion. Along similar lines, Sigmund Mowinckel also concluded in his equally famous study of the Messiah that the memory of Moses as the "prophet *par excellence*" who was "ready to die" for the people "helped to form the portrait of the Servant" in the later chapters of Isaiah.[27] In short, according to several major Old Testament scholars, there are good reasons to conclude that Moses, as the preeminent servant of the LORD, provided the book of Isaiah with a fundamental prototype of the suffering Servant of the new exodus.[28]

In sum, although the imagery of a new Moses or the prophet like Moses is certainly not the most abundantly attested idea in Jewish Scripture, it does occur in two of the most popular and widely read biblical books in ancient Judaism: the book of Deuteronomy and the book of Isaiah.[29] This seems to have led the notion to become rather influential in the development of early Jewish hopes for the future.

The New Moses in Early Jewish Literature

When we turn from the Jewish scriptures to early Jewish writing outside the Bible, we find several further pieces of evidence pointing to the hope for the coming of a Mosaic deliverer.

The first is from the Dead Sea Scroll known as *4QTestimonia*. The name of this brief scroll derives from the fact it appears to be a collection of biblical "testimonies" to various eschatological figures. The first figure described in the list appears to be none other than the biblical prophet like Moses:

26. Gerhard von Rad, *Old Testament Theology* (2 vols.; trans. D. M. G. Stalker; New York: Harper & Row, 1965), 2:260-61 (emphasis omitted).

27. Sigmund Mowinckel, *He That Cometh: The Messiah Concept in the Old Testament and Later Judaism* (trans. G. W. Anderson; New York: Abingdon, 1956; repr. Grand Rapids: Eerdmans, 2005), 232.

28. Cf. Allison, *The New Moses*, 70.

29. On the abundance of manuscripts of Deuteronomy (thirty mss recovered) and Isaiah (twenty-one mss recovered) at Qumran, see Martin Abegg Jr., Peter Flint, and Eugene Ulrich, *The Dead Sea Scrolls Bible* (San Francisco: HarperOne, 1999), 145-47, 267-71, characterizing the latter as "one of the three most popular books at Qumran."

> And the LORD spoke to Moses, saying: "You have heard the sound of the words of this people, what they said to you: all they have said is right. If (only) it were given that they had /this/ heart to fear me and keep all my precepts all the days, so that it might go well with them and their sons for ever!" (Deut 5:28-29) "*I would raise up for them a prophet from among their brothers, like you, and place my words in his mouth, and he would tell them all that I command him.* And it will happen that /the/ man who does not listen to my words which the prophet will speak in my name, I shall require a reckoning from him" (Deut 18:18-19). (*4QTestimonia* [4Q175] 1-8)[30]

The reason we know that the prophet like Moses here is an eschatological figure is that the passage quoted above is followed immediately in *4QTestimonia* by two other biblical oracles: the coming of the "Scepter" (Num 24:15-17), which was widely interpreted among ancient Jews as a prophecy of the royal messiah; and the Mosaic blessing of the patriarch Levi, which was likewise interpreted by some as a prophecy of a priestly messiah (Deut 33:8-11).[31] Hence, when read as a whole, *4QTestimonia* is clear evidence for an early Jewish hope for a future prophet like Moses, who, in context, is an eschatological figure associated with the coming of the messiahs of Aaron and Israel.[32]

This conclusion finds support elsewhere in the Dead Sea Scrolls. Indeed, the three biblical texts cited in *4QTestimonia* seem to correspond to the three eschatological figures — prophetic, priestly, and royal — that are mentioned in *1QRule of the Community*. In this scroll, which is widely regarded as the charter for the community that produced the Dead Sea Scrolls, we find the following statement:

30. Unless otherwise noted, all translations of the Dead Sea Scrolls contained herein are from Florentino García Martínez and Eibert J. C. Tigchelaar, *The Dead Sea Scrolls Study Edition* (2 vols.; Grand Rapids: Eerdmans, 2000). The translation here is slightly adapted.

31. See CD[a] 7:19; 1QM 11:6-7; Philo, *Rewards* 95 (cf. Num 24:17 LXX); *T. Jud.* 24:1-6; etc. The most famous interpretation of Numbers 24 is Rabbi Akiba's application of the text to the failed messianic claimant Simeon Bar Kochba [a.k.a. Kosiba], who led the second Jewish revolt against Rome in A.D. 135. See Jerusalem Talmud, *Ta'anith* 68d.

32. See Falk, "Moses," 968; John J. Collins, *The Scepter and the Star: The Messiahs of the Dead Sea Scrolls and Other Ancient Literature* (ABRL; New York: Doubleday, 1995), 74-75; Craig A. Evans, *Jesus and His Contemporaries: Comparative Studies* (Leiden: Brill, 1995), 113-16; Frank Moore Cross, *The Ancient Library at Qumran* (3rd ed.; Minneapolis: Fortress, 1995), 158. For a full study, see George J. Brooke, *Exegesis at Qumran: 4QFlorilegium in Its Jewish Context* (JSOTSup 29; Sheffield: Journal for the Study of the Old Testament, 1985).

> They should not depart from any counsel of the law in order to walk in complete stubbornness of their heart, but instead shall be ruled by the first directives which the men of the Community began to be taught, *until a Prophet arrives, and the Messiahs of Aaron and Israel.* (*1QRule of the Community* [1QS] 9:11)

Although the question of multiple messiahs in this passage has been hotly debated, for our purposes, its main significance lies in the fact that it gives the advent of the "prophet" like Moses a central place. According to this Dead Sea Scroll, the coming of this eschatological prophet will coincide with that of an eschatological priest (the Messiah of Aaron) and an eschatological king (the Messiah of Israel).[33] If *1QRule of the Community* was indeed the charter for the Qumran community, then the expectation of the Mosaic eschatological prophet seems to have been a constitutive part of their messianic hopes for the future.

In addition to this evidence from the Scrolls, there is also evidence that other Second Temple Jews were waiting for an eschatological prophet like Moses. In the first century A.D., Josephus records the activities of several Jewish messianic claimants who seem to have modeled their actions on the biblical accounts of the exodus from Egypt.[34] According to his history of the Jewish people, during the first century A.D., there were certain anonymous Jewish figures who led crowds of people "into the desert" *(eis tēn erēmian),* with the apparent intention of recapitulating Moses' act of leading the Israelites into the desert.[35] For our purposes here, let the following two examples suffice:

> During the period when Fadus was procurator of Judaea, a certain impostor named Theudas persuaded the majority of the masses to take up their possessions and follow him to the Jordan River. *He stated that he was a prophet and that at his command the river would be parted and would provide them an easy passage.* (Josephus, *Antiquities* 20.97-98)[36]

33. So Evans, *Jesus and His Contemporaries,* 94; Collins, *The Scepter and the Star,* 74-75; Cross, *The Ancient Library at Qumran,* 158-59.

34. See Evans, *Jesus and His Contemporaries,* 53-81; Rebecca Gray, *Prophetic Figures in Late Second Temple Jewish Palestine: The Evidence from Josephus* (New York: Oxford University Press, 1993).

35. Josephus, *War* 2.259; paralleled in *Ant.* 20.167.

36. Unless otherwise noted, all translations of Josephus contained herein are from Josephus, *Works* (10 vols.; trans. and ed. H. St. J. Thackeray, R. Marcus, and L. Feldman; Loeb Classical Library; Cambridge: Harvard University Press, 1926-1965).

> *At this time there came to Jerusalem from Egypt a man who declared that he was a prophet* and advised the masses of the common people to go out with him to the mountain called the Mount of Olives, which lies opposite the city at a distance of five furlongs. *For he asserted that he wished to demonstrate from there that at his command Jerusalem's walls would fall down,* through which he promised to provide them an entrance into the city. (Josephus, *Antiquities* 20.169-70)

The two figures of Theudas and the Egyptian — now commonly referred to as "sign prophets" — were clearly modeling themselves on the famous leaders of the exodus from Egypt: Moses, who miraculously parted the waters of the Red Sea (Exodus 15); and Joshua, his successor, who miraculously overthrew the walls of the city of Jericho (Joshua 6).[37] As Dale Allison puts it: "To cross the Jordan once again was to repeat the exodus again, and to be like Joshua was to be like Moses."[38] Significantly, according to Josephus, both figures explicitly claimed to be "a prophet" *(prophētēs),* which strongly suggests that they were deliberately tapping into the expectation, based on Jewish Scripture, of a prophet like Moses (which Joshua himself was) and a new exodus.[39] Moreover, for any first-century Jew familiar with the book of Exodus, "the Egyptian" would be a name that would be easily connected with Moses the Egyptian (cf. Exod 2:1-10)!

In addition to this evidence, scholars have suggested that other texts from early Jewish writers such as Philo, as well as other Jewish figures — such as the "Samaritan" and the "Teacher of Righteousness" described in the Dead Sea Scrolls — may also have drawn directly on the eschatological expectation of a prophet like Moses.[40] Whether that be so or not, for our purposes, what matters is that both Theudas and the Egyptian were such well-known prophetic claimants that, according to the Acts of the Apostles, they were known by both Rabbi Gamaliel and a Roman tribune in the city of Jerusalem (see Acts 5:33-39; 21:38). In this way, they provide us with important evidence for

37. See Paul W. Barnett, "The Jewish Sign Prophets — A.D. 40-70 — Their Intentions and Origin," *NTS* 27 (1981): 679-97 (here 682-83).

38. Allison, *The New Moses,* 79; cf. 23-28.

39. Cf. Artapanus frg. 3, where Moses is described as the founder of Egyptian culture. See S. Schapdick, "Moses," in *Dictionary of Jesus and the Gospels* (2nd ed.; ed. Joel B. Green, Jeannine K. Brown, and Nicholas Perrin; Downers Grove: IVP Academic, 2013), 610-15 (here 610). Jeremias, *"Mōüsēs,"* 862.

40. See Philo, *Special Laws* 1.65; Josephus, *Ant.* 18.85-87; Allison, *The New Moses,* 84 n. 196; Teeple, *The Mosaic Eschatological Prophet,* 63-68.

the conclusion that the Jewish hope for a prophet like Moses, in the words of Dale Allison, "was very much in the air in first-century Palestine."[41]

In order to see more clearly how these early Jewish traditions shed light on the words and deeds of Jesus, we need now to turn to Jesus' own prophetic actions, and attempt to interpret them in light of the early Jewish hope for a new Moses and a new exodus.

The Feeding of the Multitude[42]

If there is any testimony that suggests that Jesus saw himself as the long-awaited prophet like Moses, it is the testimony regarding the famous feeding

41. Allison, *The New Moses,* 83. This at the very least would provide a plausible explanation for the veritable explosion of texts regarding the prophet like Moses in later rabbinic literature. See esp. *Targum Neofiti* on Exodus 12:42; *Ecclesiastes Rabbah* 1:9 §1; *Deuteronomy Rabbah* 3:17. See also Keener, *The Historical Jesus of the Gospels,* 527-28 n. 99, citing *Pesiq. Rab Kah.* 27:5; *b. Ber.* 12b; *j. Ber.* 1:5, §8; *Exod. Rab.* 1:5; 3:4; 15:11; 19:5; 32:9; *Lev. Rab.* 27:4; *Pesiq. Rab.* 52:8; cf. *t. Ber.* 1:10; *Eccl. Rab.* 21:15, §2, as well as *Pesiq. Rab Kah.* 5:8; *Num. Rab.* 11:2; *Ruth Rab.* 5:6; *Eccl. Rab.* 1:9 §1; cf. *Pes. Rab Kah.* 27:5; *Eccl. Rab.* 3:15, §1; *Tg. Neof.* on Exod 12:42. See also Jeremias, "*Mōüsēs,*" 857-62. Intriguingly, in *Pes. Rab.* 31:10, the Messiah leads the exiles home to the promised land in a new exodus.

42. For discussion and bibliography, see esp. Meier, *A Marginal Jew,* 3:950-67 (extensive bibliography on 1023-24 n. 257). See also Adela Yarbro Collins, *Mark: A Commentary* (Hermeneia; Minneapolis: Fortress, 2007), 316-26; Dunn, *Jesus Remembered,* 645-48, 683-88; Craig S. Keener, *The Gospel of John: A Commentary* (2 vols.; Peabody: Hendrickson, 2003), 1:663-71; Craig L. Blomberg, *The Historical Reliability of John's Gospel* (Downers Grove: IVP, 2001), 118-21; Joel Marcus, *Mark* (2 vols.; AYB 27-27A; New Haven: Yale University Press, 2000, 2009), 1:404-21; Graham H. Twelftree, *Jesus the Miracle Worker: A Historical & Theological Study* (Downers Grove: IVP, 1999), 76-77, 128-30, 158-59, 204-8, 318-20; Davies and Allison, *Saint Matthew,* 2:471-95; Theissen and Merz, *The Historical Jesus,* 294-96; Robert W. Funk and the Jesus Seminar, *The Acts of Jesus: The Search for the Authentic Deeds of Jesus* (San Francisco: HarperSanFrancisco/Polebridge, 1998), 89-91; Witherington, *The Christology of Jesus,* 98-101; René Latourelle, *The Miracles of Jesus and the Theology of Miracles* (trans. Matthew J. O'Connell; New York: Paulist, 1988), 72-79; John A. T. Robinson, *The Priority of John* (London: SCM, 1985), 190-211; P. W. Barnett, "The Feeding of the Multitude in Mark 6/John 6," in *Gospel Perspectives: The Miracles of Jesus,* vol. 6 (ed. David Wenham and Craig Blomberg; Sheffield: JSOT, 1986), 273-93; Joseph A. Fitzmyer, *The Gospel according to Luke* (2 vols.; AB 28-28A; New York: Doubleday, 1983, 1985), 761-69; Raymond E. Brown, *The Gospel according to John* (2 vols.; Anchor Bible 29-29A; New York: Doubleday, 1966, 1970), 1:231-50; H. van der Loos, *The Miracles of Jesus* (NovTSup 9; Leiden: E. J. Brill, 1965), 619-31; T. Francis Glasson, *Moses in the Fourth Gospel* (SBT 40; London: SCM, 1963), 45-47; C. H. Dodd, *Historical Tradition in the Fourth Gospel* (Cambridge: Cambridge University Press, 1963), 196-222; H. W. Montefiore, "Revolt in the Desert," *NTS* 8 (1962): 135-41; Rudolf Bultmann, *The History of the Synoptic Tradition* (trans. J. H. Marsh; rev. ed.; Oxford: Basil Blackwell, 1972 [orig. 1931], 217.

of the five thousand, the only miracle of Jesus recorded in all four Gospels. Despite the length of these accounts, I will reproduce them here in full with key elements highlighted, so that all of the data in question can be examined carefully, with Moses, the exodus from Egypt, and the Jewish hope for a prophet like Moses in mind:

> Now when Jesus heard [of John the Baptist's death], he withdrew from there in a boat to a deserted place apart *(eis erēmon topon kat' idian)*. But when the crowds heard it, they followed him on foot from the towns. As he went ashore he saw a great throng; and he had compassion on them, and healed their sick. When it was evening, the disciples came to him and said, "This is a wilderness *(erēmos)* and the day is now over; send the crowds away to go into the villages and buy food for themselves." Jesus said, "They need not go away; you give them something to eat." They said to him, "We have only five loaves here and two fish." And he said, "Bring them here to me." Then he ordered the crowds to sit down on the grass; and taking the five loaves and the two fish he looked up to heaven, and blessed, and broke and gave the loaves to the disciples, and the disciples gave them to the crowds. And they all ate and were satisfied. And they took up twelve baskets full of the broken pieces left over. And those who ate were about five thousand men, besides women and children. Then he made the disciples get into the boat and go before him to the other side, while he dismissed the crowds. After he had dismissed the crowd, he went up the mountain by himself to pray. (Matt 14:13-23)[43]

> And they [Jesus and the disciples] went away in the boat to a deserted place by themselves *(eis erēmon topon kat' idian)*. Now many saw them going, and knew them, and they ran there on foot from all the towns, and got there ahead of them. As he landed he saw a great throng, and he had compassion on them, because they were like sheep without a shepherd; and he began to teach them many things. And when it grew late, his disciples came to him and said, "This is a wild place *(erēmos)*, and the hour is now late; send them away, to go into the country and villages round about and buy themselves something to eat." But he answered them, "You give them something to eat." And they said to him, "Shall we go and buy two

43. I have slightly adapted the RSV in each of the quotations to bring out the imagery of the "desert" or "wilderness" *(erēmos)* and the "mountain" *(to oros)* which is clear in Greek but lost in the English translations.

hundred denarii worth of bread, and give it to them to eat?" And he said to them, "How many loaves have you? Go and see." And when they had found out, they said, "Five, and two fish." Then he commanded them all to recline by companies upon the green grass. So they sat down in groups, by hundreds and by fifties. And taking the five loaves and the two fish he looked up to heaven, and blessed, and broke the loaves, and gave them to the disciples to set before the people; and he divided the two fish among them all. And they all ate and were satisfied. And they took up twelve baskets full of broken pieces and of the fish. And those who ate the loaves were five thousand men. Immediately he made his disciples get into the boat and go before him to the other side, to Bethsaida, while he dismissed the crowd. (Mark 6:32-45)

When the crowds learned it, they followed him; and he welcomed them and spoke to them of the kingdom of God, and cured those who had need of healing. Now the day began to wear away; and the twelve came and said to him, "Send the crowd away, to go into the villages and country round about, to lodge and get provisions; for we are here in a wilderness *(en erēmō topō)*." But he said to them, "You give them something to eat." They said, "We have no more than five loaves and two fish — unless we are to go and buy food for all these people." For there were about five thousand men. And he said to his disciples, "Make them sit down in companies, about fifty each." And they did so, and made them all sit down. And taking the five loaves and the two fish he looked up to heaven, and blessed and broke them, and gave them to the disciples to set before the crowd. And all ate and were satisfied. And they took up what was left over, twelve baskets of broken pieces. (Luke 9:11-17)

After this Jesus went to the other side of the Sea of Galilee, which is the Sea of Tiberias. And a multitude followed him, because they saw the signs which he did on those who were diseased. Jesus went up the mountain, and there sat down with his disciples. Now the Passover, the feast of the Jews, was at hand. Lifting up his eyes, then, and seeing that a multitude was coming to him, Jesus said to Philip, "How are we to buy bread, so that these people may eat?" This he said to test him, for he himself knew what he would do. Philip answered him, "Two hundred denarii would not buy enough bread for each of them to get a little." One of his disciples, Andrew, Simon Peter's brother, said to him, "There is a lad here who has five barley loaves and two fish; but what are they among so many?" Jesus said, "Make

> the people sit down." Now there was much grass in the place; so the men sat down, in number about five thousand. Jesus then took the loaves, and when he had given thanks, he distributed them to those who were seated; so also the fish, as much as they wanted. And when they had eaten their fill, he told his disciples, "Gather up the fragments left over, that nothing may be lost." So they gathered them up and filled twelve baskets with fragments from the five barley loaves, left by those who had eaten. When the people saw the sign which he had done, they said, "This is indeed the prophet who is to come into the world!" Perceiving then that they were about to come and take him by force to make him king, Jesus withdrew again to the mountain by himself. (John 6:1-15)

Much could be said about this extensive body of data; for our purposes here, three main questions of interpretation demand our attention. First, what kind of action is Jesus engaged in here? Second, what is the basic meaning of the action? How do the Jewish crowds react? Third, in two of the four accounts, why does Jesus go to the trouble of sorting the crowds into specific "companies" of "fifties" or "fifties and hundreds" before performing the sign and feeding the multitude? Finally, what are the scholarly arguments for and against the historicity of this event? Are these accounts historically plausible given what we know of Jesus, first-century Judaism, and the early church?

A Prophetic Sign of the New Moses

The first thing that should be said here is that Jesus' act of feeding the multitude, when viewed in light of ancient Jewish Scripture, is best explained as a prophetic sign meant to signal Jesus' identity as the long-awaited "prophet-like-Moses."

For one thing, Jesus' actions in the wilderness point back to Moses and the exodus from Egypt. For anyone familiar with the Jewish Torah, a miraculous provision of bread, given to a hungry multitude in the wilderness, could not help but recall one of the most memorable acts of Moses in the exodus from Egypt — the provision of the manna for the thousands of Israelites who had gone out into the desert. Compare the following account, taken from the Pentateuch:

> They set out from Elim, and all the congregation of the people of Israel came to the *wilderness* of Sin, which is between Elim and Sinai, on the

> fifteenth day of the second month after they had departed from the land of Egypt. And the whole congregation of the people of Israel murmured against Moses and Aaron *in the wilderness,* and said to them, "Would that we had died by the hand of the LORD in the land of Egypt, when we sat by the fleshpots and *ate bread to the full;* for you have brought us out into this *wilderness* to kill this whole assembly with hunger." Then the LORD said to Moses, "Behold, *I will rain down bread from heaven for you;* and the people shall go out and gather a day's portion every day. . . ." (Exod 16:1-4)

In addition to these basic parallels, there is a brief but important indicator in John's Gospel, which notes that Jesus performs the sign in the spring, "near" the time of "the Passover" feast (John 6:4). Hence, according to John, Jesus not only feeds the five thousand in the wilderness at the very same time in the year when the original miracle of the manna is purported to have taken place (the "second month") (Exod 16:1), he also does so at a time during the Jewish calendar when the scriptural readings in the synagogue would in all likelihood have been recalling the exodus from Egypt and its miracles.[44] In light of such parallels, commentators both ancient and modern have regularly seen Jesus' act of multiplying the loaves in the wilderness as a recapitulation of one of the signs and wonders performed by Moses in the exodus from Egypt.[45] Indeed, even the multiplication of fishes along with bread may hearken back to the Mosaic exodus, since in the Pentateuch, Moses mentions the Israelites being given fish to eat precisely in the context of appeasing their hunger:

> Moses said, "The people among whom I am number six hundred thousand on foot; and you [God] have said, 'I will give them meat, that they may eat for a whole month! Shall flocks and herds be slaughtered for them, to suffice them? *Shall all the fish of the sea be gathered together for them, to suffice them?*" And the LORD said to Moses, "Is the Lord's hand shortened?

44. So Brown, *The Gospel According to John,* 245, 278-79, following Aileen Guilding, *The Fourth Gospel and Jewish Worship: A Study of the Relation of St. John's Gospel to the Ancient Jewish Lectionary System* (Oxford: Clarendon, 1960), 58-68.

45. Among moderns, see Collins, *Mark,* 322; Keener, *The Gospel of John,* 670; Marcus, *Mark,* 1:417; Twelftree, *Jesus the Miracle Worker,* 77; Allison, *The New Moses,* 238-42; Witherington, *The Christology of Jesus,* 100; van der Loos, *The Miracles of Jesus,* 624. Among ancients, see Eusebius, *Demonstratio evangelica* 3.2; Cyril of Alexandria, *Commentary on Luke* 48; *Fragment* 178; Ephrem the Syrian, *Commentary on Tatian's Diatesseron* 12.5. However, these connections are rejected by some: e.g., Meier, *A Marginal Jew,* 2:1030 n. 298.

Now you will see whether my word will come true for you or not." (Num 11:21-23)[46]

In addition, Jesus' sign in the wilderness not only points back to the exodus from Egypt; it also points forward to the eschatological exodus spoken of by the prophets and awaited by many Jews. In addition to the hope for a new exodus and the new Moses that we surveyed above, there also appears to have been some expectation that in the coming age of salvation, God would recapitulate the miracle of the manna in the desert.[47] We will examine this expectation in some depth in a later chapter; for now, consider only the following early Jewish witness to the hope for the return of the manna from heaven:

> And it will happen that when all that which should come to pass in these parts has been accomplished, *the Messiah will begin to be revealed*. . . . The earth will also yield fruits ten thousandfold. And on one vine will be a thousand branches, and one branch will produce a thousand clusters, and one cluster will produce a thousand grapes, and one grape will produce a cor of wine. *And those who are hungry will enjoy themselves and they will, moreover, see marvels every day. . . . And it will happen at that time that the treasury of manna will come down again from on high, and they will eat of it in those years* because these are they who will have arrived at the consummation of time. (2 *Bar* 29:3-8)[48]

Notice there that the return of the manna from heaven is not just linked to the eschatological age of salvation in a general way, but specifically to Messiah, whose advent is to be heralded by miracles (something for which Moses, among others, was remembered as having performed). When such Jewish parallels are taken into account, it seems clear that Jesus' act of giving miraculous bread to a multitude in the wilderness not only points back to the biblical accounts of the exodus from Egypt, it also points forward to one of the signs that was expected by some Jews to accompany the arrival of the long-awaited Messiah.[49]

46. Intriguingly, in later rabbinic literature, this text gave rise to the belief that Miriam's well also fed the people with fish to eat during their wanderings in the wilderness. See *Sifre* on Numbers 11:22 (95); cited in Marcus, *Mark,* 1:411.

47. See R. Meyer, "manna," *TDNT* 4:462-66. For a full study, see Bruce J. Malina, *The Palestinian Manna Tradition: The Manna Tradition in the Palestinian Targums and Its Relationship to the New Testament Writings* (Leiden: E. J. Brill, 1968).

48. Trans. in Charlesworth, *OTP.*

49. Keener, *The Gospel of John,* 667-69; Marcus, *Mark,* 408.

A Prophetic Sign of the New Exodus

A second Mosaic aspect of the feeding of the five thousand is Jesus' act of not only feeding the crowds, but instructing the disciples to organize the multitude in the wilderness into "companies" of "hundreds" and "fifties" before performing the sign (Mark 6:40-41; Luke 9:14). In an ancient Jewish context, what might be the meaning of such an elaborate and involved action? Why not just feed the multitudes in a haphazard manner (as in modern-day "Jesus films")?

As a number of scholars have noted, this deliberate arrangement of the hungry crowd into companies under the leadership of the twelve disciples appears to be directly evocative of the arrangement of the Israelites in the desert during the exodus from Egypt.[50] Jesus' actions echo the following accounts from the Jewish Torah:

> Moses chose able men out of all Israel, and made them heads over the people, rulers of *thousands, of hundreds, of fifties, and of tens.* And they judged the people at all times. . . . (Exod 18:25-26)

> [Moses said:] "Choose wise, understanding, and experienced men, *according to your tribes,* and I will appoint them as your heads." And you answered me, "The thing that you have spoken is good for us to do." So *I took the heads of your tribes,* wise and experienced men, and *set them as heads over you, commanders of thousands, commanders of hundreds, commanders of fifties,* commanders of tens, and officers, throughout your tribes. (Deut 1:13-15)

In light of such parallels, a case can be made that Jesus is deliberately (and painstakingly) organizing the crowd of thousands into groups that would call to mind the exodus from Egypt. If this is correct, then the twelve disciples may be taking the role of the "twelve phylarchs" who acted as leaders of the military camps in the exodus.[51]

In support of this suggestion, it is important to point out that the two "charter documents" of the Dead Sea Scroll communities also describe the

50. Collins, *Mark,* 324-25; Marcus, *Mark,* 408-9; Twelftree, *Jesus the Miracle Worker,* 77, 318-20; Robinson, *The Priority of John,* 203; Dodd, *Historical Tradition in the Fourth Gospel,* 214; Montefiore, "Revolt in the Desert," 135-41.

51. See Horbury, "The Twelve and the Phylarchs," 503-27.

organization of the end-time community into thousands, hundreds, fifties, and tens with the eschatological age — apparently envisioned as a second exodus:[52]

> And in accordance with this regulation shall the seed of Israel walk. . . . And this is the rule of the assembly of the cam[ps]. Those who walk in them, in the time of wickedness *until there arises the Messiah of Aaron and Israel,* shall be ten in number as a minimum *to (form) thousands, hundreds, fifties, and tens.* (*Damascus Document*[a] 12:21–13:2)

> These are the men who are to be summoned to the community council from . . . all the wi[se men] of the congregation . . . together with [the chiefs of the tri]bes and all their judges, their officials, *the chiefs of thousands, the chiefs of [hundreds,] of fifties* and of tens, and the Levites, (each one) in the mid[st of his divi]sion of service. These are the men of renown, those summoned to the assembly, those gathered for the community council in Israel. . . . At [a ses]sion of the men of renown, [those summoned to] the gathering of the community council, when [God] begets the Messiah with them . . . the men of renown, and they shall sit be[fore him, each one] according to his dignity. *After, [the Mess]iah of Israel shall [enter] and before him shall sit the heads of the th[ousands of Israel, each] one according to his dignity, according to [his] po[sition] in their camps and according to their marches.* . . . And [when] they gather [at the tab]le of community [or to drink the n]ew wine, and the table of the community is prepared [and the] new wine [is mixed] for drinking, [no-one should stretch out] his hand to the first-fruit of the bread and of [the new wine] before the priest, for [he is the one who bl]esses the first-fruit of the bread and of the new win[e and stretches out] his hand towards the bread before them. *Afterwar[ds,] the Messiah of Israel [shall str]etch out his hands toward the bread.* (*1QRule of the Congregation* [1QSa] 1:27–2:21)

These ancient Jewish parallels with Jesus' organization of the multitudes are astonishing. On the basis of this evidence, various scholars have interpreted these numerical organizations of the Dead Sea Scroll community as a recapitulation of the exodus from Egypt and an anticipation of the new exodus.[53]

52. See 1QS 2:21; CD[a] 13:1; 1QSa 1:14-15; 1QM 4:1-5.

53. E.g., Marcus, *Mark,* 1:408-9; Allison, *The New Moses,* 239; Teeple, *The Mosaic Eschatological Prophet,* 30-31.

This is especially clear when the numerical orders in the Scrolls are combined with the explicit testimony elsewhere that the community has been chosen by God to fulfill Isaiah's prophecies of a new exodus: the covenant community shall "walk in the desert in order to open there His path. As it is written, 'In the desert, prepare the way of the LORD, straighten in the steppe a roadway for our God (Isa 40:3)'" (*1QRule of the Community* [1QS] 8:13-14). In light of such passages, Frank Moore Cross's influential work on the Dead Sea Scrolls interprets the numerical organizations as indicative of a "typology of the second Exodus."[54]

If Cross is correct — and I think he is — then the full force of these parallels needs to be brought to bear on the interpretation of Jesus' actions with the multitudes.[55] For in the Scrolls, it is critical to note that the division of the community into thousands, hundreds, fifties, and tens not only calls to mind the exodus from Egypt; these divisions are explicitly linked in the Scrolls to the coming of the messiah. Indeed, in the second Scroll cited above, the division of the Israelites into thousands, hundreds, fifties, and tens is explicitly set in the context of the banquet of the messiah. We will examine the Jewish hope for the eschatological banquet in detail later in our study; for now, we need only note that there was a widespread expectation, based on Jewish scripture, that when the messiah finally came, he would host a great eschatological feast.[56] We have already seen one witness to this, cited above, in which the messiah was expected to give the manna itself as the food of the eschatological feast.[57] Now, if Jesus' act of feeding the multitude is not just a sign of the new exodus, but of the messianic banquet as well, and the twelve disciples are being given the role of the twelve phylarchs, then Jesus, by acting as host who "blesses" the bread to be distributed, is quite arguably not just

54. See Cross, *The Ancient Library at Qumran,* 70 n. 1: "In the War scroll (1QM), the camp of the Sons of Light . . . is ordered precisely after the prescriptions for the priestly arrangement of the Mosaic camp of the desert in Num. 2.1–5.4; 10.17-28, etc. (1QM 3.12–4.11). The law of the camp (Num. 5.1-4) is kept (1QM 7.3-7). The victory of God in the final war is compared with the first Exodus (1QM 11.8). The typology of the Mosaic camp lies close to the surface in CD[a] (20.26 quotes Deut. 2.14 of the Mosaic camp) and 1QS and 1QSa. The typology of the second Exodus appears in the use of Isa. 40 (1QS 8.12-14) and Ezek. 20 (1QS 6.2. *mgwryhm;* cf. Ezek. 20.38, 1QM 1.3 *mdbr h'mym;* cf. Ezek. 20.35)."

55. Cf. Marcus, *Mark,* 1:409, and Twelftree, *Jesus the Miracle Worker,* 77, 318-20, neither of whom draws out the messianic implications of the parallels. Others, such as Fitzmyer, *The Gospel according to Luke,* 1:767, simply dismiss them.

56. E.g., Isaiah 25:6-9; *1 En.* 62:14; *m. 'Abot* 3:16; 4:16; *b. Ber.* 34b; *Sanh.* 98b. D. Smith, "Messianic banquet," *Anchor Bible Dictionary* 4.788-91; Keener, *The Gospel of John,* 1:682 n. 184.

57. *2 Baruch* 29:3-8.

playing the role of the prophet like Moses, but also of the messiah who will host the eschatological feast.[58]

This is, of course, exactly how the crowd in John's Gospel responds to the prophetic sign. In this account, *the crowds recognize Jesus' actions for what they are* — a sign of the new Moses, the new exodus, and the messianic banquet — and therefore acclaim him both the prophet like Moses and a royal Messiah:

> When the people saw the sign which he had done, they said, "This is indeed the prophet [=*new Moses*] who is to come into the world"! Perceiving then that they were about to come and take him by force and make him king [= *messiah*], Jesus withdrew again to the mountain by himself. (John 6:14-15)

In short, when Jesus' act of feeding the five thousand in the wilderness is interpreted in light of the Old Testament background and ancient Jewish parallels, there are good reasons to conclude that his actions are both recapitulating the events of the exodus from Egypt and anticipating the new exodus spoken of by the prophets and associated in some Jewish circles with the coming of the messiah.

A Miraculous Prophetic Sign

Before bringing this section to a close, it is perhaps important to note that in all four accounts, Jesus' act of feeding the multitude is implicitly described as a miraculous prophetic sign, and not merely an ordinary act of feeding.[59]

The only reason this is even necessary to point out is the surprising popularity of a non-miraculous interpretation of the feeding of the multitude in recent times.[60] This approach is commonly traced back to the work of H. E. G. Paulus who, from the perspective of post-Enlightenment rationalism, proposed in 1828 that the evangelists themselves did not view the feeding of the

58. On the feeding of the multitude as a sign of the banquet, see Dunn, *Jesus Remembered,* 645-46; Twelftree, *Jesus the Miracle Worker,* 129; Witherington, *The Christology of Jesus,* 100; Vincent Taylor, *The Gospel according to St. Mark* (2nd ed.; London: Macmillan, 1966), 321; Schweitzer, *The Quest of the Historical Jesus,* 376-77.

59. Davies and Allison, *Saint Matthew,* 2:483-85.

60. See van der Loos, *The Miracles of Jesus,* 627-31.

five thousand as miraculous.[61] In his famous book on Jesus, Albert Schweitzer summarized Paulus's interpretation as follows:

> When Jesus saw the multitude an hungered [sic], He said to His disciples, "We will set the rich people among them a good example, that they may share their supplies with the others," and He began to distribute His own provisions, and those of the disciples, to the people who were sitting near them. The example had its effect, and soon there was plenty for everyone.[62]

According to Paulus, then, the feeding of the five thousand, though tied to the actions of Jesus, is a purely natural event, in which the catalyst is not the prophetic power of Jesus over the elements of bread and fish, but the moral example of Jesus in inducing the crowds to share. Obviously, all of this is without any exegetical foundation whatsoever. Such an interpretation seems to have been driven purely by the rationalistic antipathy toward miracles that characterized much nineteenth-century scholarship.[63] As John Meier catalogues in his analysis, there are other non-miraculous interpretations that are even more fanciful: these range from the suggestion that Jesus stood near the "secret entrance to a cave" from which he distributed the stored bread, to the theory that "devout rich ladies" provided the loaves and fish for the multitudes.[64]

It should go without saying that such interpretations are indefensible. However, we might note here that Paulus has one point in his favor: in the Gospel accounts, the direct cause of the multiplication of the loaves is not explicitly narrated. Nevertheless, a miraculous event is still clearly being described. For one thing, in all four accounts the five thousand people are able to eat enough bread to be "satisfied," consuming "as much as they wanted" — something that would necessitate the distribution of literally thousands of loaves and fishes (Matt 14:20; Mark 6:42; Luke 9:17; John 6:11). Moreover, in all four accounts, there are still twelve baskets of loaves left over after everyone has eaten their fill (Matt 14:20; Mark 6:43; Luke 9:17). This clearly necessitates some kind of supernatural multiplication of the original elements, which the evangelists

61. Heinrich Eberhard Gottlieb Paulus, *Das Leben Jesu als Grundlage einer reinen Geschichte des Urchristentums* (2 vols.; Heidelberg: C. F. Winter, 1828).

62. Albert Schweitzer, *The Quest of the Historical Jesus: A Critical Study of Its Progress from Reimarus to Wrede* (trans. James M. Montgomery; New York: Macmillan, 1968 [orig. 1906]), 52.

63. For a scathing critique of Paulus's interpretation see David Friedrich Strauss, *The Life of Jesus Critically Examined* (trans. G. Elliot; Philadelphia: Fortress, 1972 [orig. 1840]), 507-19.

64. See Meier, *A Marginal Jew,* 2:1037 n. 319; van der Loos, *The Miracles of Jesus,* 627-31.

remarkably agree consisted of precisely five loaves and two fish (Matt 14:17; Mark 6:38; Luke 9:13; John 6:9). Lest there be any doubt about this, however, John's account makes explicit what is implicit in the Synoptics: the disciples "filled twelve baskets with fragments *from the five barley loaves,* left by those who had eaten" (John 6:13). It does not take a mathematician to deduce that twelve baskets could not be filled with fragments from a mere five loaves, unless there be some concomitant miracle of multiplication. As R. T. France wryly notes: "However small the pieces, to get five thousand out of five small loaves and two fish would surely be in itself a miracle."[65]

In support of the miraculous interpretation of the sign, it is worth noting that a similar wonder is attributed to the prophet Elisha in the Old Testament:

> A man came from Baal-shalish, bringing the man of God [Elisha] bread of the first fruits, twenty loaves of barley, and fresh ears of grain in his sack. And Elisha said, "Give to the men, that they may eat." But his servant said, "How am I to set this before a hundred men?" So he repeated, "Give them to the men, that they may eat, for thus says the LORD, 'They shall eat and have some left.' " So he set it before them. And they ate, and had some left, according to the word of the LORD. (2 Kings 4:42-44)

As is widely recognized, this episode is one of a series of miraculous signs and wonders performed by Elisha the prophet, who in doing so surpasses even those of his master, Elijah (see 2 Kings 1–13). Indeed, Josephus would later go on to refer to Elisha as one who "worked . . . startling deeds" *(paradoxa . . . erga),* almost the exact same usage he uses elsewhere to describe Jesus of Nazareth, "a doer of startling deeds" *(paradoxōn ergōn poiētēs)* (*Antiquities* 9.182, 18.63).[66] In light of such background, it should go without saying that at the level of exegesis, the non-miraculous interpretation of the feeding of the five thousand that has become popular in some quarters in the wake of the Enlightenment fails to pass exegetical muster. (One hopes that it will finally be consigned to the graveyard of bad exegetical hypotheses, where it belongs.)

To sum up what we have seen so far: according to the data in all four Gospels, Jesus appears to have enacted a miraculous prophetic sign by feeding a crowd of five thousand people. When interpreted in light of its Old Testament and ancient Jewish parallels, Jesus' act of feeding a multitude in the wilderness seems to function as a miraculous prophetic sign that points

65. R. T. France, *The Gospel of Matthew* (NICNT; Grand Rapids: Eerdmans, 2007), 563.
66. See Meier, *A Marginal Jew,* 2:199-200 n. 92.

back to the exodus from Egypt as well as forward to the new exodus. The Mosaic shape of his actions is magnified by the deliberate arrangement of the multitudes into groups of thousands, fifties, and hundreds, which would have called to mind the numerical divisions of the twelve tribes during the exodus from Egypt and which, in the Dead Sea Scrolls, the people of Israel would be arranged into at the time of the second exodus. Significantly, in John's Gospel, the Jewish crowds get the point: their interpretation of Jesus' action is not only that he is the prophet like Moses, but that he is none other than the messiah, and so they seek to make him king.[67]

This is the basic thrust of the evidence as it stands in the Gospels. Now that we have situated this evidence in its ancient context, we can ask the question: Can this event be reasonably attributed to the impact made by the historical Jesus himself or should it rather be seen as a later creation? Is the substance of Jesus' act of feeding the five thousand as it is presented in the four Gospels historically plausible?

Arguments against Historical Plausibility

When we turn from interpretation to the question of historicity, the first thing important to note is that many major works on Jesus do not actually give arguments against the historicity of the feeding of the multitude. When reasons are given, the historical argumentation is not always clearly explicated.

Indeed — despite the fact that this event is the only miracle given extensive coverage in all four first-century Gospels — there is a remarkably widespread tendency to simply ignore the feeding of the five thousand in historical reconstructions of Jesus' life, almost as if the evidence for it did not exist.[68] The most plausible explanation for why so many scholars ignore an event that the four evangelists consider a major occurrence in the life of Jesus — think here of the length of the Gospel material cited given above — is simple: there is no need to discuss the feeding of the multitude, because it likely did not take place.

To be fair, some historical studies of Jesus do mention the feeding of the

67. Dunn, *Jesus Remembered,* 647; Witherington, *The Christology of Jesus,* 100.

68. For example, the feeding of the five thousand is completely ignored in Casey, *Jesus of Nazareth;* Becker, *Jesus of Nazareth;* Sanders, *Jesus and Judaism;* Meyer, *The Aims of Jesus;* Vermes, *Jesus the Jew.* It receives only a passing mention (and no historical verdict) in Keener, *The Historical Jesus of the Gospels,* 261; Theissen and Merz, *The Historical Jesus,* 302; Wright, *Jesus and the Victory of God,* 193, 533 n. 202.

multitude, but they seem somewhat embarrassed by the data. These works are deliberately ambiguous when it comes to the question of historicity — sometimes speaking rather vaguely about the importance of "Easter faith,"[69] sometimes mentioning the accounts but withholding historical judgment,[70] and still other times affirming a basic event but pleading agnosticism about its miraculous character.[71]

Nevertheless, one can find a few explicit arguments used on occasion against the historicity of the feeding of the five thousand. Of these, three in particular stand out.

First and foremost, some scholars argue that the literary parallels between Jesus' actions with the multitude and similar miracles in Jewish Scripture raise doubts about the historicity of the feeding of the five thousand. From this perspective, the parallels between Jesus' actions and Moses' provision of the manna for the Israelites in the desert (Exod 16:1-36), as well as Elisha's miraculous provision of bread for a hundred men in the book of Kings (2 Kings 4:42-44), strongly suggest that the early church simply created the story of the feeding of the five thousand out of a desire to make Jesus look like Moses and/or Elijah.[72] For such scholars, the feeding of the five thousand is "understandable as *poetry,*" fueled by the creative (but misguided) imagination of Jesus' followers, but is not a historical event.[73] Although the scholars who make this argument do not make the reasoning explicit, this appears to be an argument from incoherence with other evidence about Jesus. The assumption seems to be that Jesus never drew connections between himself and figures in Jewish Scripture such as Moses and Elijah. Therefore, when we come across parallels between Jesus and Old Testament figures in the Gospels, they should be regarded as the unhistorical creations of the church.

Second, other scholars argue that the liturgical parallels between the feeding of the five thousand and the celebration of the early Christian eucharist cast doubt on the historical truth of Jesus' actions. From this point of view, the

69. Joachim Gnilka, *Jesus of Nazareth: Message and History* (trans. Siegfried S. Schatzmann; Peabody: Hendrickson, 1997), 132-33.

70. E. P. Sanders, *The Historical Figure of Jesus* (London: Penguin, 1994), 156-57.

71. Twelftree, *Jesus the Miracle Worker,* 320. Cf. van der Loos, *The Miracles of Jesus,* 636, who affirms the historicity of the event yet concludes that "how this food was provided was a mystery to those present," though the evangelists and the crowds do not seem in the dark in this regard.

72. Funk and the Jesus Seminar, *The Acts of Jesus,* 89-90; Rudolf Pesch, *Das Markusevangelium* (2 vols.; HTKNT; Freiburg: Herder, 1977), 1:353-56.

73. Theissen and Merz, *The Historical Jesus,* 295 (emphasis added).

feeding of the five thousand was created by the early church from accounts of the Last Supper and the influence of the early Christian practice of the eucharist, which realities are being read back into the life of Jesus.[74] Again, the working assumption behind this argument seems to be from a lack of coherence: since we know that Jesus himself did not engage in any cultic acts, any such actions must be regarded as unhistorical and the creation of early Christians.

Third and finally — and here we come to what seems to me to be the primary reason many modern scholars reject (or at least shy away from) the feeding of the multitude — others deny the historicity of Jesus' action based on the impossibility of so-called "nature" miracles.[75] In the words of Gerd Lüdemann: whenever any act of Jesus described in the Gospels presumes that "the laws of nature are broken," one can only conclude that "the historical value is nil."[76] Even more forthrightly, the Jesus Seminar concludes:

> The multiplication of the loaves and fish is magic: it is the equivalent of changing base metals into gold, if taken literally.[77]

The logic of this position is straightforward: because miracles *per se* are impossible, the Gospel accounts of Jesus' miraculous prophetic sign, in which he feeds five thousand people from just five loaves and two fish, did not take place. For such scholars, there is sometimes no need to even raise the question of historicity: it can be assumed that the "miracle stories" are not truly "historical reports."[78] The presence of the miracle itself changes the genre, so to speak, from *bios* to "poetry."

In sum, arguments such as these have led numerous scholars either to reject the feeding of the five thousand in its entirety as unhistorical or to affirm as historical only the smallest "core" of the event. From this perspective, either nothing like the feeding of the five thousand ever happened, or all we can say is that Jesus celebrated some kind of "especially memorable meal" with his followers.[79] Beyond that, there lies only the shadow of doubt.

74. John Dominic Crossan, *The Historical Jesus: The Life of a Mediterranean Jewish Peasant* (San Francisco: HarperCollins, 1991), 398-402.

75. Theissen and Merz, *The Historical Jesus*, 296, 301; cf. Jeremias, *New Testament Theology*, 88.

76. Lüdemann, *Jesus after 2000 Years*, 4, 45.

77. Funk and the Jesus Seminar, *The Acts of Jesus*, 91.

78. Bultmann, *The History of the Synoptic Tradition*, 228 (cf. 217).

79. Meier, *A Marginal Jew*, 2:966, whose minimalist conclusion in this regard seems to be based on something other than the excellent arguments for historicity that precede it.

Context: Jewish Sign Prophets and the Exodus in the Scrolls

On the other side of the historical ledger, there are also several positive arguments that support the historical plausibility of the feeding of the five thousand. The first of these is that the prophetic sign of feeding the multitude in the desert is contextually plausible within a first-century Jewish setting, in a couple of ways.

First and foremost, if Jesus' act of feeding the five thousand in the wilderness was in fact a prophetic sign of the new exodus, then it fits remarkably well with the actions of other Jewish "sign prophets" in the first century A.D., such as Theudas and the Egyptian.[80] As we saw above in our survey of the Jewish hope for a new Moses, there is ample evidence that figures such as the Egyptian and Theudas performed prophetic signs of the long-awaited eschatological exodus. In addition to the mere attempt to perform miraculous signs, it is worth noting here that both Theudas and the Egyptian eventually garnered not only the attention of the Jewish crowds, but the wrath of the Roman authorities:

> [Theudas] stated that he was a prophet and that at his command the river would be parted and would provide them with easy passage. . . . Fadus, however, did not permit them to reap the fruit of their folly, but sent against them a squadron of cavalry. These fell upon them unexpectedly, slew many of them, and took many prisoners. *Theudas himself was captured, whereupon they cut off his head and brought it to Jerusalem.* (Josephus, *Antiquities* 20.97-99)

> When Felix heard of this [the Egyptian's promise that the walls of Jerusalem would miraculously fall down] he ordered his soldiers to take up their arms. Setting out from Jerusalem with a large force of cavalry and infantry, he fell upon the Egyptian and his followers, *slaying four hundred of them and taking two hundred prisoners.* The Egyptian himself escaped from the battle and disappeared. (Josephus, *Antiquities* 20.171-72)

Four aspects of these parallels are important for us. First, if both Theudas and the Egyptian could attempt miraculous signs modeled on the exodus and conquest for their first-century contemporaries, then it is contextually quite

80. On this, see especially Eric Eve, *The Jewish Context of Jesus' Miracles* (JSNTSup 231; London: Sheffield Academic Press, 2002); McKnight, *Jesus and His Death,* 177-87; Barnett, "Jewish Sign Prophets," 679-97; Craig A. Evans, "Messianic Claimants of the First and Second Centuries," in his *Noncanonical Writings and New Testament Interpretation* (Peabody: Hendrickson, 1992), 239-52.

plausible to suggest that Jesus of Nazareth, as a first-century Jewish prophet, also performed a sign hearkening back to another miracle of the exodus: the miracle of the manna (see Exodus 16). As James Dunn points out, these ancient Jewish parallels from Josephus strongly suggest that Jesus' actions with the crowds were simply tapping into "a popular conception of the royal Messiah, who would echo the great events of Israel's first liberation of Canaan."[81] And Theudas and the Egyptian are by no means the only such examples, just the most famous.[82] Second, if Theudas' and the Egyptian's actions garnered crowds of "common people" large enough to draw the attention of the Roman authorities, then it is equally reasonable to accept the historical evidence that Jesus' Moses-like actions in the wilderness of Galilee would have likewise drawn crowds of his fellow Jews. Third, it is important to stress that both Theudas and the Egyptian not only performed prophetic signs modeled on the exodus from Egypt; they also apparently expected these public actions to be accompanied by *miracles akin to those of the exodus* (cf. Psalm 78). Hence, even the miraculous character of Jesus' sign with the multitude fits quite squarely into a first-century Jewish historical context. Fourth and finally, it is intriguing to note that Theudas and Jesus share the same fate: after garnering the attention of Jewish crowds and followers with their signs hearkening back to the exodus, both are executed at the hands of the Roman authorities. The Egyptian prophet only narrowly escaped suffering the same fate.

Second, as we also saw in our interpretation of the event, Jesus' act of organizing the crowds into groups of hundreds and fifties is also historically compatible with similar arrangements of the "new exodus" community in the Dead Sea Scrolls. Although we examined some of the evidence above, consider yet one more text from the scrolls:

> And all those who enter the covenant shall respond and say after them, "Amen, amen." *Blank* They shall act in this way year after year, all the days of Belial's dominion. The priests shall enter in order foremost, one behind the other, according to their spirits. And the levites shall enter after them. *In third place all the people shall enter in order, one after another, in thousands, hundreds, fifties, and tens, so that each Israelite may know his standing in God's Community, in conformity with an eternal plan.* (*1QRule of the Community* 2:18-23)

81. Dunn, *Jesus Remembered*, 647.

82. Cf. McKnight, *Jesus and His Death*, 177-87; Evans, *Jesus and His Contemporaries*, 54-81.

Once again, if the new covenant community envisioned in the Dead Sea Scrolls could consciously and deliberately model itself on the exodus generation in anticipation of the eschatological age, then it is plausible to suggest that Jesus himself did the same, when performing a memorable and striking prophetic sign of the new exodus.

Coherence: Miraculous Signs, Table Fellowship, and Figures from Jewish Scripture

In addition to the argument from Jewish contextual plausibility, the feeding of the five thousand also coheres with other evidence we possess about the words and deeds of Jesus, in several ways.

First and foremost, the description of Jesus' act of feeding the multitude as a miraculous prophetic sign coheres perfectly with the abundant first-century evidence that Jesus — in stark contrast to, say, his predecessor John the Baptist — was known for performing miraculous and wondrous acts, such as the casting out of demons (Mark 1:23-28; Luke 4:33-37; Matt 12:22-23; Luke 11:14), the healing of the paralyzed and crippled (Matt 9:2-8; Mark 2:3-12; Luke 5:18-26; 13:10-17; John 5:1-9), the blind (Matt 11:5; Luke 7:22; Mark 8:22-26; John 9:1-41), lepers (Matt 8:2-4; Mark 1:40-45; Luke 5:12-16), the raising of the dead (Matt 9:18-26; Mark 5:21-43; Luke 8:40-56; Luke 7:11-17; John 11:1-45), just to name a few.[83] Indeed, it is worth noting in this regard that even Josephus apparently claims that Jesus of Nazareth performed "startling deeds" *(paradoxa)* (*Antiquities* 18.63).[84] Now, as John Meier has rightly pointed out, one's judgment about whether or not the events in the Gospels described as miracles can be explained as acts of God, in some other way (e.g., as fraud), or as having no reasonable explanation, will depend upon philosophical and theological arguments and assumptions that go beyond the bounds of this particular study.[85] For our purposes here, we restrict ourselves to the basic (and incontrovertible) historical point that the miraculous feeding of the multitude presents a strong case of coherence with the many other accounts of miracles and wonders that are ascribed to Jesus. There is nothing here at odds with the overall data we possess about the man from Nazareth. Indeed, if there is any one miracle that

83. See esp. Craig S. Keener, *Miracles: The Credibility of the New Testament Accounts* (2 vols.; Grand Rapids: Baker Academic, 2011), 1:22-29.

84. Keener, *Miracles,* 1:25. For discussion of Josephus on Jesus, see Meier, *A Marginal Jew,* 1:56-88.

85. See Meier, *A Marginal Jew,* 2:509-21.

should be considered representative of the evidence we possess about Jesus, it is the feeding of the five thousand, the only "startling deed" of Jesus recorded in all four first-century Gospels.

Second, Jesus' act of feeding the five thousand is congruent with the evidence for Jesus' practice of "table fellowship" and frequenting banquets.[86] As is widely known, this evidence is not limited to a single text, but consists of a broad swath of data in the Gospels. Think here of the critique of Jesus' eating with tax collectors and sinners, a critique that was apparently leveled against him on more than one occasion (Mark 2:15-16; Matt 9:9-13; Luke 5:27-32; Matt 11:18-19; Luke 7:33-34). As John Meier points out:

> In both parables and other sayings, Jesus regularly spoke of the coming kingdom of God under the image of a banquet. The intriguing thing here is that this emphasis on a banquet or a festive meal as an image of the kingdom was not simply a matter of words Jesus spoke; banquets and festive meals played an important part in Jesus' actions as well. Quite apart from the feeding miracle, Jesus is attested in both Gospel sayings and non-miraculous Gospel stories to have been noteworthy for his presence at festive meals and banquets, a remarkably non-ascetic habit considered scandalous by some (Mark 2:15-17 par.; cf. Luke 15:1-2; 19:1-10; Matt 11:18-19//Luke 7:33-34). His offer of table fellowship to all, including social and religious "lowlifes" like toll collectors and "sinners," was meant to foreshadow the final eschatological banquet and give a foretaste of that banquet even during his public ministry (cf. Matt 8:11-12//Luke 13:28-29; Mark 14:25 par.). It is within this greater context and regular habit of Jesus' public ministry, a habit that culminated in what was literally the *Last* Supper among a great number of "suppers," that one may try to understand the origin of the story of the feeding miracle.[87]

86. Perrin, "The Last Supper," 493. On table fellowship, see Mark Alan Powell, "Table Fellowship," in *Dictionary of Jesus and the Gospels* (2nd ed.; ed. Joel B. Green, Jeannine K. Brown, and Nicholas Perrin; Downers Grove: IVP Academic, 2013), 925-31; Tom Holmén, "Jesus and the Purity Paradigm," in *The Handbook for the Study of the Historical Jesus* (ed. Tom Holmén and Stanley E. Porter; 4 vols.; Leiden: Brill, 2011), 3:2709-44; Craig L. Blomberg, "The Authenticity and Significance of Jesus' Table Fellowship with Sinners," in *Key Events in the Life of the Historical Jesus* (ed. Darrell L. Bock and Robert L. Webb; WUNT 247; Tübingen: Mohr Siebeck, 2009), 215-50; Dunn, *Jesus Remembered*, 599-607; Crossan, *The Historical Jesus*, 344; Sanders, *Jesus and Judaism*, 20.

87. Meier, *A Marginal Jew*, 2:965-66.

If Meier's observations are correct, and if Jesus' practice of eschatological "table fellowship" is historical, then these data cohere quite nicely with the evidence for Jesus' act of feeding the multitude.[88] Such evidence also highlights the fact that the primary reason for disputing the historicity of the feeding of the five thousand seems to stem primarily from its miraculous nature, and not from it being in any way out of character for Jesus as he is portrayed in the Gospels.

Third, Jesus' implicit modeling of his actions on the figure of Moses also coheres with other evidence in which Jesus speaks and acts like figures from Jewish Scripture, such as Moses and Solomon.[89] As I summarized at the beginning of the chapter, there is evidence that Jesus: (1) claimed to cast out demons by "the finger of God" (Luke 11:20), just as Moses worked marvels during the exodus by "the finger of God" (Exod 8:19); (2) chose twelve young men to act as leaders of the "twelve tribes of Israel" (Matt 19:28; Luke 22:30), just as Moses had chosen twelve young men to act as "leaders of their ancestral tribes" during the wilderness wandering (Num 1:1-16); (3) repeatedly described his contemporaries who rejected his message as "this [evil] generation" (Matt 12:39-42; Luke 11:29-32; Mark 8:12) just as Moses repeatedly described the wilderness generation as "this evil generation" (Deut 1:35); (4) and spoke of a heavenly ascent as Son of Man (Matt 26:64; Mark 14:62; Luke 22:69), just as Moses was believed by some Jews to have ascended into heaven at the end of his life (Philo, *Life of Moses* 2.288, 291-92; Josephus, *Antiquities* 4.323-25). Moreover, the Gospels even testify that Jesus explicitly compared himself to famous figures from Jewish Scripture:

> But he answered them, "An evil and adulterous generation seeks for a sign; but no sign shall be given to it except the sign of the prophet Jonah. For as Jonah was three days and three nights in the belly of the whale, so will the Son of Man be three days and three nights in the heart of the earth. The men of Nineveh will arise at the judgment with this generation and condemn it; for they repented at the preaching of Jonah, and *behold, something greater than Jonah is here.* The queen of the South will arise at

88. Twelftree, *Jesus the Miracle Worker,* 319.

89. See esp. Anthony Le Donne, *The Historiographical Jesus: Memory, Typology, and the Son of David* (Waco: Baylor University Press, 2009), 93-220; Craig A. Evans and L. Novakovic, "Typology," in *Dictionary of Jesus and the Gospels* (2nd ed.; ed. Joel B. Green, Jeannine K. Brown, and Nicholas Perrin; Downers Grove: IVP Academic, 2013), 986-90; Allison, *Constructing Jesus,* 263-303; Thomas Hatina, "Moses," in *The Routledge Encyclopedia of the Historical Jesus* (ed. Craig A. Evans; London: Routledge, 2008), 421-22.

> the judgment with this generation and condemn it; for she came from the ends of the earth to hear the wisdom of Solomon, and *behold, something greater than Solomon is here.* (Matt 12:39-42)
>
> When the crowds were increasing, he began to say, "This generation is an evil generation; it seeks a sign, but no sign shall be given to it except the sign of Jonah. For as Jonah became a sign to the men of Nineveh, so will the Son of Man be to this generation. The queen of the South will arise at the judgment with the men of this generation and condemn them; for she came from the ends of the earth to hear the wisdom of Solomon, *and behold, something greater than Solomon is here.* The men of Nineveh will arise at the judgment with this generation and condemn it; for they repented at the preaching of Jonah, and *behold, something greater than Jonah is here.* (Luke 11:29-32)

Now, if Jesus could explicitly compare himself to Solomon and Jonah by means of his words, there is no reason to deny *a priori* that he could compare himself to Moses by means of his actions. Indeed, according to other evidence in the Gospels, his first-century Jewish contemporaries took the liberty of comparing him with several figures from the Old Testament: "some say . . . Elijah, and others Jeremiah, or one of the prophets" (Matt 16:14; Mark 8:28). Moses would no doubt be included among the latter list, as the "prophet" *par excellence* (Deut 34:10).

In short: if the evidence in the Gospels regarding Jesus' words and deeds with reference to figures in Jewish Scripture is historically reliable, even in its broad contours, then this evidence coheres quite well with the idea that he performed actions that were strikingly similar to (though not identical with) famous biblical prophets such as Moses.

Effects: The Prophet Like Moses in the Early Church

The final argument in favor of the historical plausibility of the feeding of the five thousand is based on the argument from plausibility of effects within the early church. Indeed, if this event is historical, it has the power to explain at least two aspects of life in the early church.

First, if the feeding of the five thousand was indeed a prophetic sign of the new exodus in which Jesus modeled his actions on Moses, then it would provide a plausible explanation for why the early church elsewhere described

Jesus as the long-awaited prophet like Moses of Deuteronomy 18.[90] Particularly important here are Peter's speech to the Jews in Jerusalem and Stephen's speech before the high priest and Jewish leaders, both of which explicitly identify Jesus as such:

> [Peter said:] Repent therefore, and turn again, that your sins may be blotted out, that times of refreshing may come from the presence of the Lord, and *that he may send the Messiah appointed for you, Jesus,* whom heaven must receive until the time for establishing all that God spoke by the mouth of his holy prophets from of old. *Moses said, "The Lord God will raise up for you a prophet from your own brethren as he raised me up.* You shall listen to him in whatever he tells you. And it shall be that every soul that does not listen to that prophet shall be destroyed from the people." (Acts 3:19-23)

> [Stephen said:] "This is the Moses who said to the Israelites, '*God will raise up for you a prophet from your brethren as he raised me up.*' . . . As your fathers did, so do you. Which of the prophets did not your fathers persecute? And they killed those who announced beforehand *the coming of the Righteous One,* whom you have now betrayed and murdered. . . ." (Acts 7:37, 51-52)

Given the fact that the early church clearly regarded Jesus as more than a prophet, and given the multiple convergences we have seen with an ancient Jewish context, a plausible explanation for the early Christian identification of Jesus with the "prophet like Moses" of Deuteronomy 18 is that Jesus himself performed signs of the coming of the new Moses and the new exodus. Notice here that if this is correct, then we have both continuity and development: while Jesus' act of feeding the multitude implicitly identifies him as the new Moses, Peter's and Stephen's speeches in the book of Acts make this implicit identification explicit, by citing the fulfillment of the prophecy from the Jewish Torah and applying it directly to Jesus.

Second, the feeding of the five thousand also presents a strong case of plausibility of effects with the eucharistic practice of the early church. On

90. For discussion, see Craig S. Keener, *Acts: An Exegetical Commentary* (3 vols.; Grand Rapids: Baker Academic, 2012, 2013, vol. 3 forthcoming); John Lierman, *The New Testament Moses: Christian Perceptions of Moses and Israel in the Setting of Jewish Religion* (WUNT 2.173; Tübingen: Mohr Siebeck, 2004); Teeple, *The Mosaic Eschatological Prophet*, 74-99.

the one hand, the feeding of the multitude provides a plausible origin for the early church's practice of "breaking bread" with one another, in continuity with Jesus' own table fellowship (Acts 2:42). On the other hand, there are once again both continuity and development: whereas Jesus celebrates the meal with bread and fish, as far as we know, the early Christian eucharist is celebrated with bread and wine (e.g., 1 Cor 11:23-25). There is no evidence for fish being utilized in these meals. Hence, the argument against historicity mentioned above based on the supposed "liturgical parallels" with the Christian eucharist fails to explain the very elements of the meal that supposedly gave rise to the stories about Jesus. Even Gerd Theissen and Annette Merz, who do not accept the historicity of the feeding of the five thousand, point out:

> [I]t is impossible for the miraculous feeding to be derived completely from the experience of the celebration of the eucharist: not bread and wine but *bread and fish* stand at the centre of Mark 6.35ff.[91]

I agree, but I would add that the connections between this prophetic sign and the Last Supper can actually function as an argument from coherence. In other words, if, as I will argue later, the Last Supper *itself* was a Mosaic action and a prophetic sign that Jesus performed in order to recapitulate the events at Mount Sinai and inaugurate the new exodus, then one would expect there to be parallels between it and other signs of the new exodus that he had performed during his public ministry.[92] From this perspective, the feeding of the five thousand would function as a kind of preparation or anticipation of what Jesus was ultimately going to accomplish in the Upper Room.

To be sure, other arguments for historicity could be mounted, but these should be enough.[93] For our purposes here, suffice it to say that there are good historical reasons to conclude that Jesus likely performed a prophetic sign of feeding five thousand people in the wilderness sometime during his ministry in Galilee.[94] Like other prophets of his day, this sign functioned both to reveal himself as a new Moses figure and to anticipate the advent of the long-awaited new exodus. Even scholars who are very hesitant to conclude positively about

91. Theissen and Merz, *The Historical Jesus,* 303.

92. For these arguments, see below, as well as chapter 3.

93. For further arguments, see Blomberg, *The Historical Reliability of John's Gospel,* 118-21.

94. Cf. Dunn, *Jesus Remembered,* 664: "That Jesus every so often acted, not like the sign-prophets of whom Josephus speaks, but in the mode of the great prophets must be judged very likely."

this particular event feel the force of some of these arguments. Consider the comments of Dale Allison:

> The Gospels report that Jesus, on at least one occasion, fed a large crowd in the wilderness (Matt 14:13-21; 15:32-39; Mark 6:30-44; 8:1-10; Luke 9:10-17; John 6:1-15). One can hardly demonstrate that these texts preserve memory, just as one can hardly establish the opposite. All we can say is this: given what we know of the so-called sign prophets of Jesus' day, it is not implausible that he too once retreated into the wilderness in order to stir up memories of the exodus.[95]

I largely concur with Allison, though I think we can be more confident about the historical plausibility of this particular prophetic sign. If the broad impression of the Gospels is correct, and Jesus was like the sign prophets of his day who performed marvelous signs hearkening back to the exodus for large crowds, and if he spoke and acted in ways that echoed the figure of Moses in Jewish Scripture, then it is quite reasonable to conclude that the accounts of the feeding of the multitude in the desert are substantially historical. From this point of view, the explicit identification of Jesus with the prophet like Moses in the early church has its origin in his own implicit prophetic signs and actions.

If this is correct, then Jesus seems to have both deliberately *modeled* his words and deeds on events from biblical history and *anticipated* what he would ultimately accomplish at the Last Supper. Indeed, the Janus-like quality of the feeding of the multitude would provide a powerful explanation for both the similarities and the dissimilarities between Jesus' actions and both the biblical miracles and the Last Supper. If the early church had simply created the accounts of Jesus' feeding the multitudes to root their celebration of the eucharist more deeply in his public ministry, then we would not expect to find such significant differences between Jesus' miracle and the Last Supper, as, for example, in the presence of bread and fish rather than bread and wine. Likewise, if the early church had created the parallels between Jesus and the Jewish Scripture, then one would expect them to be identical. By contrast, Jesus would have had to perform his signs within the real historical, geographical, and political limitations of his time and place. Hence, such signs — like those of other first-century Jewish sign prophets, such as Theudas and the Egyptian — would be characterized by both similarities and dissimilarities with their

95. Allison, *Constructing Jesus*, 273.

scriptural prototypes. And that is exactly what we find in the Gospel accounts of the feeding of the five thousand.

With all this in mind, we can now turn to what is arguably the most explicit prophetic sign of Jesus' identification with the new Moses: his inauguration of a new "covenant" in "blood" during his actions at the Last Supper.

The Blood of the Covenant[96]

Now that we have examined the widespread scholarly agreement that Jesus saw himself as a new Moses, as well as the principal prophetic sign from his prophetic ministry in which Jesus appears to have deliberately acted like Moses,

96. In what follows, I am heavily indebted to the excellent study of Jesus, the Last Supper, and the Covenant in Michael Barber, "The Historical Jesus and Cultic Restoration Eschatology: The New Temple, the New Priesthood, and the New Cult" (Ph.D. dissertation; Fuller Theological Seminary, 2010). See also Nicholas Perrin, "Last Supper," *Dictionary of Jesus and the Gospels* (2nd ed.; ed. Joel B. Green, Jeannine K. Brown, and Nicholas Perrin; Downers Grove: IVP Academic, 2013), 492-501; Allison, *Constructing Jesus,* 272; Keener, *The Historical Jesus of the Gospels,* 298-302; Marcus, *Mark,* 2:956-67; Jens Schröter, *Das Abendmahl: Frühchristliche Deutungen und Impulse für die Gegenwart* (SBS 210; Stuttgart: Katholisches Bibelwerk, 2006), 25-52, 132-34; McKnight, *Jesus and His Death,* 303-21; Tom Holmén, "Jesus, Judaism, and the Covenant," *JSHJ* 2, no. 1 (2004): 3-27; Dunn, *Jesus Remembered,* 512-13, 815-18; Tom Holmén, *Jesus and Jewish Covenant Thinking* (BibInt 55; Leiden: Brill, 2001); Davies and Allison, *Saint Matthew,* 3:464-81 (with bibliography); Theissen and Merz, *The Historical Jesus,* 414-23; Becker, *Jesus of Nazareth,* 340-42; Kim Huat Tan, *The Zion Traditions and the Aims of Jesus* (SNTSMS 91; Cambridge: Cambridge University Press, 1997), 197-226; Gnilka, *Jesus of Nazareth,* 285-87; H. Lichtenberger, "'Bund' in Abendmahlüberlieferung," in *Bund und Tora: Zur theologischen Begriffsgeschichte in alttestamentlicher, frühjüdischer und urchristlicher Tradition* (WUNT 92; ed. F. Avemarie and H. Lichtenberger; Tübingen: Mohr-Siebeck, 1996), 217-28; Wright, *Jesus and the Victory of God,* 560-63; K. Backhaus, "Hat Jesus vom Gottesbund gesprochen?" *TGl* 86 (1996): 343-56; Dale C. Allison Jr., *The New Moses,* 256-61; idem, "Jesus and the Covenant: A Response to E. P. Sanders," *JSNT* 29 (1987): 57-78; Xavier Léon-Dufour, *Sharing the Eucharistic Bread: The Witness of the New Testament* (trans. Matthew J. O'Connell; New York/Mahwah: Paulist, 1987 [orig. 1982]), 137-56; G. R. Beasley-Murray, *Jesus and the Kingdom of God,* 264-67; Ben F. Meyer, *The Aims of Jesus* (London: SCM, 1979), 216-19; Pesch, *Das Abendmahl und Jesu Todesverständnis,* 93-101; Patsch, *Abendmahl und historischer Jesus,* 71-73, 80-87, 151-225; Joachim Jeremias, *New Testament Theology I. The Proclamation of Jesus* (trans. John Bowden; New York: SCM; London: Charles Scribner's Sons, 1971), 286-99; idem, *The Eucharistic Words of Jesus* (trans. Norman Perrin; Philadelphia: Fortress, 1977), 225-31; Bernard Cooke, "Synoptic Presentation of the Eucharist as Covenant Sacrifice," *TS* 21 (1960): 1-44; Johannes Behm, *"diathēkē," TDNT* 2:104-34; Vincent Taylor, *Jesus and His Sacrifice: A Study of the Passion-Sayings in the Gospels* (London: Macmillan, 1937), 39-49, 125-39, 175-79, 203-17.

we can now turn to the most central of Jesus' Mosaic words and deeds for this study: the establishment of a new "covenant" in his "blood" at the Last Supper.

Significantly, in all four accounts of the Last Supper, the images of blood and covenant are present. Compare the following:

> And he took a cup, and when he had given thanks he gave it to them, saying, "Drink of it, all of you; for this is my *blood* of the [new] *covenant,* which is poured out for many for the forgiveness of sins." (Matt 26:27-28)
>
> And he took a cup, and when he had given thanks he gave it to them, and they all drank of it. And he said to them, "This is my *blood* of the [new] *covenant,* which is poured out for many." (Mark 14:23-24)
>
> And likewise the cup after supper, saying, "This cup which is poured out for you is the new *covenant* in my *blood.*" (Luke 22:20)
>
> In the same way also the cup after supper, saying, "This cup is the new *covenant* in my *blood.* Do this, as often as you drink it, in remembrance of me." (1 Cor 11:25)

As I stated in chapter 1, in this study, I will refrain from two tendencies that have characterized twentieth-century study of the eucharistic words of Jesus. First, I will not attempt the (arguably impossible) task of reconstructing a hypothetical original form.[97] Second, I will not try to decide which of two supposed forms of the saying — the so-called "Markan form" and the so-called "Lukan-Pauline" form — is the "more primitive."[98] Rather than attempt to harmonize the details of the Gospels in this way, or set up what are questionable dichotomies, I prefer to let the differences of form and detail between the various accounts stand. My goal here is to focus rather on the basic substance

97. So Tan, *The Zion Traditions and the Aims of Jesus,* 203.

98. For scholars who conclude that the "Markan form" is more primitive, see Gnilka, *Jesus of Nazareth,* 286; Pesch, *Das Abendmahl und Jesu Todesverständnis,* 35-41; Patsch, *Abendmahl und historischer Jesus,* 59-105; Jeremias, *The Eucharistic Words of Jesus,* 138-203; Higgins, *The Lord's Supper in the New Testament,* 24-44. For scholars who conclude that the "Lukan-Pauline form" is more primitive, see Lüdemann, *Jesus after 2000 Years,* 95; Theissen, *The Historical Jesus,* 421-22; Marxsen, *The Lord's Supper as a Christological Problem,* 4-8; Eduard Schweizer, *The Lord's Supper according to the New Testament* (trans. James M. Davis; Facet Books, Biblical Series 18; Philadelphia: Fortress, 1967), 10-17; Behm, *"diathēkē,"* 133. Cf. Tan, *The Zion Traditions and the Aims of Jesus,* 203 n. 30.

(or "gist") of the accounts, interpret these contents in an ancient Jewish context, and then evaluate the arguments for and against the historical plausibility of these contents with regard to Jesus. With that said, as I also mentioned in chapter 1, from a text-critical point of view, I will follow the majority of scholars in utilizing the "long-form" of Luke.[99]

In the case of Jesus' words over the cup, there are obvious differences of detail and form, which make reconstruction of a hypothetical original futile. Nevertheless, once this quest for the original form is abandoned, it is not the differences that stand out so much as the similarities. As Gerd Lüdemann rightly points out:

> [A]ll in all, the difference between the words of institution in Mark and Paul is not all that great.[100]

Indeed, all four accounts of Jesus' words over the cup of the Last Supper agree in claiming that Jesus takes a cup of wine, and speaks words of interpretation over it in which he identifies "my blood" with the establishment of a "covenant." This fourfold testimony is the foundation and starting point for our analysis. Also significant is that in two of the four accounts, Jesus speaks of this blood being "poured out for many" (Mark and Matthew); while in the other two, he explicitly describes the covenant in question as a "new" covenant (Luke and 1 Corinthians).

With these points in mind, several basic questions of interpretation arise. First, what does it mean for Jesus to speak of his own blood as establishing a covenant? Second, what is the meaning of Jesus' blood being "poured out" for "many"? What might such words have meant in an ancient Jewish context? And is the substance of these sayings historically plausible on the lips of Jesus? In order to answer these questions, we will once again attempt to interpret the accounts of the Last Supper in an ancient Jewish context, and then evaluate the arguments for and against historical plausibility.

99. See the most recent and exhaustive work on the subject by Bradly S. Billings, *Do This in Remembrance of Me: The Disputed Words in the Lukan Institution Narrative (Luke 22:19b-20): An Historico-Exegetical, Theological, and Sociological Analysis* (Library of New Testament Studies; London: T. & T. Clark, 2006), as well as François Bovon, *Luke 3* (trans. James Crouch; Hermeneia; Minneapolis: Fortress, 2012), 154-55; see also I. Howard Marshall, "The Last Supper," in *Key Events in the Life of the Historical Jesus* (ed. Darrell L. Bock and Robert L. Webb; WUNT 247; Tübingen: Mohr Siebeck, 2009), 529-41; Joseph A. Fitzmyer, S.J., *The Gospel according to Luke* (AB; New York: Doubleday, 1983, 1985), 2:1387-89.

100. Lüdemann, *Jesus After 2000 Years,* 96.

A Sign of the New Moses

The central interpretive issue of Jesus' words over the cup is what he means by referring his "blood" *(haima)* to the establishment of a "covenant" *(diathēkē)* in the context of the Last Supper (Matt 26:28; Mark 14:24; Luke 22:20; 1 Cor 11:25).[101]

As is widely recognized by commentators, these images hearken back to a key event in the Jewish Torah: Moses' offering of sacrificial blood at Mount Sinai in order to establish the covenant between God and Israel (Exodus 24).[102] As we will see momentarily, this is by no means the only passage from the Old Testament that lies behind the words of interpretation, but it is easily the most explicit,[103] and hence demands our attention first of all:

> And [God] said to Moses, "Come up to the Lord, you and Aaron, Nadab and Abihu, and seventy of the elders of Israel, and worship afar off. Moses alone shall come near to the Lord; but the others shall not come near, and the people shall not come up with him. Moses came and told the people all the words of the Lord and all the ordinances; and all the people answered with one voice, and said, "All the words which the Lord has spoken, we will do." *And Moses wrote all the words of the Lord. And he rose early in the morning, and built an altar at the foot of the mountain, and twelve pillars, according to the twelve tribes of Israel.* And he sent young men of the people of Israel, who offered burnt offerings and sacrificed peace offerings of oxen to the Lord. *And Moses took half of the blood and put it in basins, and half of the blood he threw against the altar.* Then he took *the book of the covenant,* and read it in the hearing of the people; and they said, "All that the Lord has spoken we will do, and we will be obedient." *And Moses took the blood and threw it upon the people, and said, "Behold the blood of the covenant which the Lord has made with you in accordance with all these words."* Then Moses and Aaron, Nadab and Abihu, and seventy of the elders of Israel went up; and they saw the God of Israel; and there was under his feet as it were a pavement of sapphire stone, like the very heaven for clearness. And he did not lay his hand on the chief men of the people of Israel; *they beheld God, and ate and drank.* (Exod 24:1-11)

101. Evans, *Mark,* 386.

102. Perrin, "The Last Supper," 494; Allison, *Constructing Jesus,* 272; Keener, *The Historical Jesus of the Gospels,* 300; Davies and Allison, *Saint Matthew,* 3:465; Marcus, *Mark,* 2:958; Fitzmyer, *The Gospel according to Luke,* 2:1391. See also Joseph A. Fitzmyer, *1 Corinthians: A New Translation with Introduction and Commentary* (AYB 32; New Haven: Yale University Press, 2008), 443.

103. Keener, *The Historical Jesus of the Gospels,* 560 n. 202.

Several aspects of this account present us with significant parallels with the Last Supper.

First, Jesus' identification of the cup with "my blood of the covenant" *(to haima mou tēs diathēkēs)* in two of the four accounts of the words of institution (Matt 26:28; Mark 14:24) presents a precise parallel with Moses' reference to "the blood of the covenant" (Exod 24:8).[104] Significantly, although the allusion is more explicit in Matthew and Mark's accounts than in Luke and Paul's, major commentators have pointed out that Exodus 24:8 appears to lie behind all four accounts of the Last Supper.[105] In particular, the presence of the word "blood" *(haima)* in all four versions of Jesus' words — a word that does not occur in Jeremiah 31 — in the context of a "covenant" sacrifice, establishes a link between all four versions and the covenant ratification ceremony of Sinai.[106]

Second, Jesus' image of his blood being "poured out" *(ekchynnomenon)* in sacrifice (Matt 26:28; Mark 14:24) is similar to the imagery in Exodus, in which the blood of the peace offerings is "thrown against" or "poured out" on the altar (Exod 24:6).[107] Both are images of a sacrificial libation of blood, by which the covenant relationship is established and sealed. Hence, Jesus is describing his blood as being "poured out," just as an ancient priest "poured out" blood of a sacrificial animal (Lev 4:7, 18, 25, 30, 34).[108] As Craig Keener points out, this "sacrificial terminology" is particularly striking, "especially since crucifixion itself technically requires no blood."[109]

Third, just as Jesus celebrates the Last Supper in the presence of the

104. MT *dam hab^erîth;* LXX *haima tēs diathēkēs.*

105. "[E]ven though we do not have 'my blood-of-the-covenant,' as in Mark 14:24, which is a clear allusion to Exod 24:8, yet the identification of the cup of wine with 'the new covenant with my blood' is scarcely any less of an allusion to the covenant sacrifice of Exod 24:3-8 than the Marcan formula, even though it may be overlaid now with an allusion to Jer 31:31, the 'new covenant.' The allusion to the Sinai pact . . . is still clear in the Lucan formula." Fitzmyer, *The Gospel according to Luke,* 2:1391; idem, *1 Corinthians,* 443; Tan, *The Zion Traditions and the Aims of Jesus,* 206-7, 216. For scholars who pit the two against one another, see McKnight, *Jesus and His Death,* 284-89; Beasley-Murray, *Jesus and the Kingdom of God,* 264-65.

106. Tan, *The Zion Traditions and the Aims of Jesus,* 215.

107. MT *waḥ^aṣî hadām;* LXX *haimatos prosecheen.* Barber, "The Historical Jesus and Cultic Restoration Eschatology," 601.

108. Barber, "The Historical Jesus and Cultic Restoration Eschatology," 595 n. 91, citing Collins, *Mark,* 656; Marcus, *Mark,* 2:958; Fitzmyer, *The Gospel according to Luke,* 2:1391, 1402-3; France, *The Gospel of Matthew,* 994.

109. Keener, *The Historical Jesus of the Gospels,* 300, citing Crossan, *The Historical Jesus,* 366, who likens the imagery of blood being "poured out" with a sacrificial libation.

"twelve" disciples, who elsewhere are said to represent the twelve tribes of Israel (Matt 26:20; Mark 14:17; Luke 22:14, 30), so too it is significant that Moses offers the blood of the covenant not with just anyone, but with "the twelve tribes of Israel," who are actually present as well as symbolically represented by "twelve pillars" around the altar (Exod 24:4).

Last, but not least, Jesus speaks of his blood and the covenant in the context of a banquet. Similarly, Moses' offering of the blood of the covenant culminates in a heavenly banquet, in which he and the elders of Israel ascend Mount Sinai into the presence of God, and somehow "eat and drink" (Exod 24:11).[110]

In light of such parallels, we can conclude that Jesus' words over the cup in the accounts of the Last Supper are evocative of the words and deeds of Moses in the Jewish Torah when establishing the covenant at Sinai with the twelve tribes of Israel. In the words of Michael Barber:

> That all four accounts have Jesus linking his *blood* with the motif of a *covenant* while celebrating a *meal* mirrors not only Moses' words concerning the "blood of the covenant" but also the fact that the ceremony in Exodus 24 culminates in a sacred *feast* (cf. Exod 24:8-11). These points of contact are too strong and numerous to be written off as mere coincidence.[111]

The key difference, of course, between the Last Supper and Mount Sinai is that whereas the covenant at Sinai was sealed through the blood of the sacrificial *animals*, the covenant being established at the Last Supper is being inaugurated and sealed through the offering of *Jesus'* own blood.[112] The upshot of these observations for interpreting Jesus' word over the cup is fairly simple, and summed up well by Dale Allison: "Through blood Moses was the mediator of the old covenant. Through blood Jesus is the mediator of the new covenant."[113] In the Last Supper, Jesus is therefore recapitulating the well-known covenant-making actions of Moses, but reconfiguring those actions around his own suffering and death.

110. Davies and Allison, *Saint Matthew*, 3:475.
111. Barber, "The Historical Jesus and Cultic Restoration Eschatology," 601.
112. Tan, *The Zion Traditions and the Aims of Jesus*, 204.
113. Allison, *The New Moses*, 258.

A Sign of the Eschatological Covenant

In addition to this retrospective dimension of the words of institution, there is also a prospective dimension. As the context of the Last Supper makes obvious, Jesus is not simply renewing or reconfirming the covenant established by Moses, he is inaugurating something new, a covenant that will be sealed in his own blood.[114]

Once again, as commentators point out, the idea of a new or eschatological covenant is rooted in various oracles of the Old Testament prophets, which speak on several occasions of a future "everlasting covenant," and, on one famous occasion in Jeremiah, of an explicitly "new covenant."[115] With the Last Supper in mind, consider the following:

> Behold, the days are coming, says the LORD, when I will make *a new covenant with the house of Israel and the house of Judah, not like the covenant which I made with their fathers when I took them by the hand to bring them out of the land of Egypt,* my covenant which they broke, though I was their husband, says the LORD. But this is the covenant which I will make with the house of Israel after those days, says the LORD: I will put my law within them, and I will write it upon their hearts; and I will be their God, and they shall be my people. And no longer shall each man teach his neighbor and each his brother, saying, "Know the LORD," for they shall all know me, from the least to the greatest, says the LORD; *for I will forgive their iniquity, and I will remember their sin no more.* (Jer 31:31-34)

> *I will bring them again into their land which I swore to give to their fathers,* to Abraham and to Isaac and to Jacob, and they will rule over it. . . . *I will make an everlasting covenant with them* to be their God, and they shall be my people, and I will never again remove my people Israel from the land which I have given them. (Bar 2:34-35)

> Yea, thus says the Lord GOD: I will deal with you [Jerusalem] as you have done, who have despised the oath in breaking the covenant, yet I will remember my covenant with you in the days of your youth, and *I will*

114. Perrin, "The Last Supper," 496-97; Barber, "The Historical Jesus and Cultic Restoration Eschatology," 602.

115. E.g., Davies and Allison, *Saint Matthew,* 3:464-65, 473-74; Fitzmyer, *The Gospel according to Luke,* 2:1402.

> *establish with you an everlasting covenant.* Then you will remember your ways, and be ashamed when I take your sisters, both your elder [Samaria] and your younger [Sodom], and give them to you as daughters, but not on account of the covenant with you. *I will establish my covenant with you,* and you shall know that I am the LORD, that you may remember and be confounded, and never open your mouth again because of your shame, *when I forgive you all that you have done,* says the LORD God. (Ezek 16:59-63)

> As for you [daughter Zion] also, *because of the blood of my covenant with you,*
> *I will set your captives free from the waterless pit.*
> *Return to your strongholds, O prisoners of hope;*
> *today I declare I will restore you double.*
> For I have bent *Judah* as my bow; I have made *Ephraim* its arrow. . . .
> On that day the LORD their God will save them; for they are the flock of his people;
> for like the jewels of a crown they shall shine in his land.
> Yea, how good and how fair it shall be!
> Grain shall make the young men flourish, and new wine the maidens. (Zech 9:11-13, 16-17)

Several aspects of these texts contain important links with Jesus' words over the cup.

First, just as Jesus speaks of establishing a "covenant" *(diathēkē)* (Matt 26:28; Mark 14:24; Luke 22:20; 1 Cor 11:25) so too these prophetic oracles all speak of a future "covenant" (MT *b^{e}rîth;* LXX *diathēkē*) which God will establish with his people in the days to come.[116] The clearest parallel between these oracles and the eucharistic words of Jesus is of course that of Jeremiah, who explicitly speaks of a "new covenant," just as Jesus speaks of a "new covenant" *(kainē diathēkē)* in two of the four accounts (Luke 22:20; 1 Cor 11:25). Significantly, even in the accounts that lack the explicit verbal parallel, the very newness of the covenant that Jesus is establishing identifies it implicitly with the eschatological covenant spoken of by the prophets.[117] As Seyoon Kim rightly points out: "Although the word 'new' does not appear before 'cov-

116. Jer 31:31, 33; Bar 2:35; Ezek 16:60, 62; Zech 9:11.

117. Perrin, "The Last Supper," 494; Davies and Allison, *Saint Matthew,* 3:464-65; I. Howard Marshall, *Last Supper and Lord's Supper* (London: Paternoster, 1980), 92.

enant' in Mk 14.24, a covenant established by Jesus' blood can only be a 'new covenant,' different from the Mosaic one. So in Mk 14.24 there is an implicit allusion to Jer 31.31."[118]

Second, though this future covenant is clearly distinct from the covenant made by Moses at Mount Sinai, Jeremiah indisputably associates the "new covenant" with the covenant ratified by Moses at Mount Sinai (Jer 31:31).[119] Some commentators have even suggested that Zechariah may also be alluding to the Mosaic covenant.[120]

Third, it is striking that each of these oracles not only speaks of a future covenant, but links the establishment of this covenant to the restoration of the twelve tribes of Israel. For example, Jeremiah speaks of the new covenant being made with both "Israel" (the ten northern tribes) and "Judah" (the two southern tribes) (Jer 31:31); likewise, Baruch ties the everlasting covenant to the ingathering of the exiles to the promised land (Bar 2:30-34); Ezekiel speaks of the covenant being established with Jerusalem (the south), "Samaria" (the northern kingdom), and even "Sodom" (presumably a reference to the Gentiles (Ezek 16:61; cf. 16:46); finally, Zechariah explicitly links the future covenant to God's plan to "restore" both "Judah" (the southern tribes) and "Ephraim" (the northern tribes) on the day the future "covenant" is established in blood (Zech 9:13). According to the Prophets, the restoration of Israel and the establishment of a new covenant apparently go hand in hand.[121] As Nicholas Perrin notes regarding the allusion to Zechariah:

> [A]n appeal to Zechariah 9:11 ("As for you also, because of the blood of my covenant with you, I will set your prisoners free from the waterless pit") is arguably at play. . . . The Zecharian context serves to cast Jesus' mission in return-from-exile terms and suggest that the cup is somehow instrumental in that restoration.[122]

118. Kim, *The Son of Man as Son of God,* 62.

119. Barber, "The Historical Jesus and Cultic Restoration Eschatology," 601, citing Scott W. Hahn, *Kinship by Covenant* (AYBRL; New Haven: Yale University Press, 2009), 226; A. van der Wahl, "Themes from Exodus in Jeremiah 30-31," in *Studies in the Book of Exodus* (BETL; ed. M. Vervenne; Leuven: Leuven University Press, 1996), 559-67 (esp. 564); John Arthur Thompson, *The Book of Jeremiah* (NICOT; Grand Rapids: Eerdmans, 1980), 580.

120. Allison, *Constructing Jesus,* 272, citing *Targum Zechariah* 9:11: "You also, for whom a covenant was made by blood, I have delivered you from bondage to the Egyptians."

121. Tan, *The Zion Traditions and the Aims of Jesus,* 207; Allison, "Jesus and the Covenant," 61-63.

122. Perrin, "The Last Supper," 494.

We will examine this apparent relationship between the Last Supper and the return from exile in more detail in chapter 6 below. For now, it suffices to highlight the remarkably consistent tendency to link the eschatological covenant with the restoration of the twelve tribes. This restoration context is especially significant when we consider that Jesus is performing the sign of the eschatological covenant in the presence of the "twelve" disciples, who represent the twelve tribes of Israel (Matt 26:20; Mark 14:17; Luke 22:14, 30).

Fourth, it is important to note that in several of the oracles, the establishment of the eschatological covenant is explicitly tied to the forgiveness of Israel's sins. Just as Jesus describes the blood of his covenant in redemptive terms, as being poured "for" *(hyper)* others (Matt 26:28; Mark 14:24; Luke 22:20), so too the prophets speak of the eschatological covenant as atoning for sin. Jeremiah says that when God makes the covenant, he will "forgive" the "iniquity" of Israel and "remember their sin no more" (Jer 31:34); Ezekiel declares that God will "forgive" all that Jerusalem has done (Ezek 16:63); and Zechariah speaks of the blood having the power to "set" the "captives" free from the "waterless pit" (Zech 9:11), a common Old Testament image for the realm of the dead.

These are by no means the only references to a future or eschatological covenant in the prophets, but they are the texts generally cited in discussion of the Last Supper. Although some commentators insist on choosing only *one* of the oracles as the background to the eucharistic words of Jesus — whether Jeremiah 31 or Zechariah 9 — there is no need to be so rigid.[123] For one thing, ancient Jews did not atomize texts as modern readers are sometimes wont to do, but rather tended to read the Bible as a unity. This harmonization of texts was a natural result of their belief in inspiration of the Law and the Prophets. Moreover, the striking number of contextual and intertextual linkages between Jesus' words at the Last Supper and all these biblical prophecies of the future covenant instead suggest that Jesus is taking up the biblical idea of a new covenant and giving it a concrete form in his words and actions at the Last Supper.

Indeed, as we will see momentarily, when the early Jewish use of "covenant" language outside the Bible is surveyed carefully, especially the evidence from the Dead Sea Scrolls, it seems that the difference between the phraseology of an explicitly "new covenant" and (more simply) a renewed covenant or the future "everlasting covenant" spoken of by the prophets is negligible,

123. So Marshall, *Last Supper and Lord's Supper,* 91-92; contrast McKnight, *Jesus and His Death,* 284-89; Beasley-Murray, *Jesus and the Kingdom of God,* 264-65.

if not nonexistent.[124] The phrases can be used interchangeably; hence, the terminological difference between Matthew and Mark's forms of Jesus' saying versus Luke and Paul's forms does not affect the substance of the words: Jesus is establishing the eschatological covenant — which is *per se* new — in his own blood.[125]

A Sign of the Suffering Servant

The final aspect of Jesus' words over the cup that merits attention is their connection with the Old Testament prophecy of the suffering servant (Isaiah 52–53). Although the debate continues over whether Jesus saw himself as the servant — a broader historical question to which we will return below — there are two solid reasons for concluding that in the eucharistic words of interpretation in particular, Jesus describes his own sacrificial death as the suffering and death of the servant of Isaiah.

First and foremost, as is widely recognized by commentators, in two of the four accounts of the Last Supper, there is a fairly explicit allusion to the description of the sacrificial death of the servant in Isaiah 53.[126] When Jesus identifies the wine as his blood which is "poured out" for "many" (Matt 26:28; Mark 14:24), this appears to be an allusion to the suffering servant of Isaiah, who also pours out his life for the many:

> Yet it was the will of the LORD to bruise him; he has put him to grief;
> when he makes himself an offering for sin,
> he shall see his offspring, he shall prolong his days;
> the will of the LORD shall prosper in his hand;
> he shall see the fruit of the travail of his soul and be satisfied;
> by his knowledge shall *the righteous one, my servant,*
> *make many accounted to be righteous;*
> and *he shall bear their iniquities.*
> Therefore I will divide him a portion with the great,
> and he shall divide the spoil with *the many;*

124. Tan, *The Zion Traditions and the Aims of Jesus,* 205, 214-15.

125. Keener, *The Historical Jesus of the Gospels,* 300; Barber, "The Historical Jesus and Cultic Restoration Eschatology," 605.

126. Perrin, "The Last Supper," 494-96; Davies and Allison, *Saint Matthew,* 3:474; Marshall, *Last Supper and Lord's Supper,* 91; Jeremias, *The Eucharistic Words of Jesus,* 226-29.

> because *he poured out his soul to death,*
> and was numbered with the transgressors;
> yet *he bore the sin of many,*
> and made intercession for the transgressors. (Isa 53:10-12)[127]

Despite some protests to the contrary, the parallels between Isaiah's description of the suffering and death of the servant and the eucharistic words of Jesus are solid.[128] Just as the life of the servant is poured out for the "many" (Isa 53:11, 12 [2x]),[129] so too Jesus speaks of his blood being poured out for "many" *(pollōn)* (Matt 26:28; Mark 14:24).[130] As Jeremias points out, the word "many" occurs five times in the account of the suffering servant in Isaiah 52–53; it functions as a kind of technical term for those for whom the servant dies.[131] To be sure, in Isaiah, the servant pours out his "life"[132] whereas Jesus speaks of pouring out his "blood"; but this difference is easily explained by the biblical idea that the "life" is "in the blood" (Lev 17:11): to pour out one, is to pour out the other.[133] Indeed, the connections are even more explicit in Matthew's account: just as the Servant dies for the "sin"[134] of the many (Isa 53:12), so too Jesus pours out his life "for the forgiveness of sins" *(eis aphesin hamartiōn)* (Matt 26:28).[135] Though less explicit, even Luke and Paul's language of Jesus being given "for" *(hyper)* for the disciples (Luke 22:20; 1 Cor 11:24) may be evocative

127. RSV, slightly adapted.

128. The classic case against any such allusion is that of Morna D. Hooker, *Jesus and the Servant* (London: SPCK, 1959), who gives an updated (but unconvincing) defense of her position in "Did the Use of Isaiah 53 to Interpret His Mission Begin with Jesus?" in *Jesus and the Suffering Servant: Isaiah 53 and Christian Origins* (ed. William Farmer and William Bellinger; Harrisburg: Trinity Press International, 1998), 88-103.

129. MT *rabbîm;* LXX *polloi.*

130. Marcus, *Mark,* 2:966-67; Evans, *Mark,* 394; Davies and Allison, *Saint Matthew,* 3:474; Wright, *Jesus and the Victory of God,* 561; Meyer, "The Expiation Motif in the Eucharistic Words," 18-19; France, *Jesus and the Old Testament,* 122; Jeremias, *The Eucharistic Words of Jesus,* 226-27.

131. Jeremias, *New Testament Theology,* 291.

132. MT *nephesh;* LXX *psychē.*

133. William Farmer, "Reflections on Isaiah 53 and Christian Origins," in *Jesus and the Suffering Servant: Isaiah 53 and Christian Origins* (ed. William Farmer and William Bellinger; Harrisburg: Trinity Press International, 1998), 260-80 (here 265).

134. MT *ḥāṭā';* LXX *hamartia.*

135. Perrin, "The Last Supper," 495; Davies and Allison, *Saint Matthew,* 3:474; Léon-Dufour, *Sharing the Eucharistic Bread,* 148, noting that Matt 26:28 uses "for" *(peri),* creating a more exact parallel with the servant who gives himself "for" *(peri)* the sins of others (Isa 53:10 LXX).

of the suffering servant giving his life for others (Isa 53:6, 12).[136] When these various conceptual and verbal parallels are coupled with the general idea of an individual offering his life as a sacrifice for others, it is reasonable to conclude that the background is Isaiah's description of the sacrifice of the suffering servant.[137] However, lest there be any doubt about this connection, another must be taken into account.

Second — and this is important — the otherwise strange idea of Jesus offering his own human blood rather than animal blood in order to establish a covenant can also be explained by reference to the servant in Isaiah. For on at least two occasions, Isaiah explicitly links the offering of the servant *himself* with the establishment of a new covenant:

> Behold *my servant,* whom I uphold,
> my chosen, in whom my soul delights;
> I have put my Spirit upon him, he will bring forth justice to the nations.
> He will not cry or lift up his voice or make it heard in the street;
> a bruised reed he will not break, and a dimly burning wick he will not quench;
> he will faithfully bring forth justice.
> He will not fail or be discouraged till he has established justice in the earth;
> and the coastlands wait for his instruction.
> Thus says God, the LORD, who created the heavens . . .
> "I am the LORD, I have called you in righteousness,
> I have taken you by the hand and kept you;
> *I have given you as a covenant to the people,* a light to the nations,
> to open the eyes that are blind, to bring out the prisoners from the dungeon,

136. Barber, "The Historical Jesus and Cultic Restoration Eschatology," 596 n. 97, citing Peter Stuhlmacher, "Isaiah 53 in the Gospels and Acts," in *The Suffering Servant: Isaiah 53 in Jewish and Christian Sources* (ed. Bernd Janowski and Peter Stuhlmacher; trans. Daniel P. Bailey; Grand Rapids: Eerdmans, 2004), 147-62 (here 152); Meyer, "The Expiation Motif in the Eucharistic Words," 19; Gordon Fee, *1 Corinthians* (NICNT; Grand Rapids: Eerdmans, 1987), 551.

137. Although it is popular to argue that the servant in Isaiah is *not* an individual but merely a representative of all Israel, this is impossible to reconcile with the fact that the text expressly sets up a *contrast* between God's people as a whole, who have "all . . . gone astray" (Isa 53:6), and the servant, who is "numbered with transgressors" but is not himself a transgressor (Isa 53:12).

> from the prison those who sit in the darkness. . . .
> Behold, the former things have come to pass, and *new things* now I
> declare;
> before they spring forth, I tell you of them." (Isa 42:1-7, 9)
>
> And now the LORD says,
> who formed me from the womb *to be his servant,*
> to bring Jacob back to him, and that Israel might be gathered to him,
> for I am honored in the eyes of the LORD, and my God has become my
> strength —
> he says: "It is too light a thing that you should be *my servant*
> to raise up the tribes of Jacob and to restore the preserved of Israel;
> I will give you as a light to the nations,
> that my salvation may reach to the end of the earth."
> Thus says the LORD, the Redeemer of Israel and his Holy One,
> *to one deeply despised, abhorred by the nations, the servant* of rulers:
> "Kings shall see and arise, princes, and they shall prostrate themselves;
> because of the LORD, who is faithful, the Holy One of Israel, who has
> chosen you."
> Thus says the LORD: "In a time of favor I have answered you,
> in a day of salvation I have helped you;
> *I have kept you and given you as a covenant to the people,*
> to establish the land, to apportion the desolate heritages;
> saying to the prisoners, 'Come forth.' . . ." (Isa 49:5-9)

These are truly remarkable parallels with Jesus' words at the Last Supper. Just as Isaiah speaks of the servant himself being "given" in order to establish a "covenant" (MT *bᵉrîth;* LXX *diathēkē*), so too Jesus speaks of his life being poured out to establish a new "covenant" *(diathēkē)* (Matt 26:28; Mark 14:24; Luke 22:20; 1 Cor 11:25). This connection is to my mind decisive: there are no other texts in Jewish Scripture that speak of a *person* being given to establish a *covenant,* yet Isaiah 42 and 49 and the Last Supper accounts do just that.[138] Moreover, in the second oracle cited above, it is clearly the suffering servant that is in view, since he is described as "deeply despised" and "abhorred" by others, just as the servant is later "despised" and rejected (Isa 53:2-3). Finally, in the first oracle from Isaiah, the covenant established by the servant can even legitimately be referred to as a *new* covenant, since its establishment is explicitly

138. Léon-Dufour, *Sharing the Eucharistic Bread,* 152.

set in the context of God doing "new things" (Isa 42:9).[139] Surprisingly, these Isaianic texts are consistently overlooked by commentators on the Last Supper, both by advocates for a link with the suffering servant as well as by those who deny any connection.[140] When the question of Jesus and the servant is taken up, both sets of interpreters seem to overlook the connection between the suffering servant and the establishment of a new covenant.[141] Likewise, many commentators on the Last Supper seem unaware of the connections between the servant and a new covenant in Isaiah.[142]

In light of such considerations, there are good reasons to conclude that all four accounts of Jesus' words over the cup of wine allude to the death of the servant in Isaiah, who is offered for others both as a sacrifice for sins and in order to establish a new covenant.[143] Hence, by means of the words over the cup, Jesus is describing his death as a sacrifice and a sign of the suffering servant.

In sum, when examined against their background in the Law and the Prophets, the words of Jesus over the cup at the Last Supper suggest that he is both hearkening back to the covenant of Moses at Sinai and, as the suffering servant of Isaiah, offering himself as the sacrifice that will establish the new covenant spoken of by the prophets. With this interpretation in place, we can now take up the arguments for and against the historical plausibility of Jesus' words over the cup.

Arguments against Historical Plausibility

When it comes to the identification of the wine of the Last Supper with the blood of the covenant and the death of the servant, there are at least four major arguments against historical plausibility.

139. MT *ḥ*^{a}*dāšôth;* LXX *kaina.*

140. E.g., Jeremias, *The Eucharistic Words of Jesus;* Hooker, "Did the Use of Isaiah 53 to Interpret His Mission Begin with Jesus?," 88-103.

141. For example, there is no discussion of the servant and the covenant in Isa 42:1-9; 49:5-8 in the many essays in William R. Farmer and William H. Bellinger, eds., *Jesus and the Suffering Servant: Isaiah 53 and Christian Origins* (Harrisburg: Trinity Press International, 1998).

142. E.g., Jeremias, *The Eucharistic Words of Jesus,* 225-31.

143. The language of his life being "poured out" is sacrificial language, just as an ancient priest "poured out" blood of the sacrificial animal (Lev 4:7, 18, 25, 30, 34). Barber, "The Historical Jesus and Cultic Restoration Eschatology," 595 n. 91, citing Collins, *Mark,* 656; Marcus, *Mark,* 2:958; Fitzmyer, *The Gospel according to Luke,* 2:1391, 1402-3; France, *The Gospel of Matthew,* 994.

First and foremost, there is the argument from incompatibility with ancient Judaism.[144] In this view, Jesus' identification of the wine with his blood, coupled with his command to the disciples to drink of the cup, is completely irreconcilable with the biblical prohibition against drinking blood in Jewish Scripture (see Gen 9:3-4; Lev 17:10-12; Deut 12:16). As we saw in chapter 1, in light of such evidence, Geza Vermes and Joseph Klausner, both Jewish scholars, conclude:

> [T]he imagery of eating a man's body and especially drinking his blood . . . , even after allowance is made for metaphorical language, strikes a totally foreign note in a Palestinian Jewish cultural setting (cf. John 6.52). With their profoundly rooted blood taboo, Jesus' listeners would have been overcome with nausea at hearing such words.[145]

> [I]t is quite impossible to admit that Jesus would have said to his disciples that they should eat of his body and drink of his blood, "the blood of the new covenant which was shed for many." The drinking of blood, even if it was meant symbolically, could only have aroused horror in the minds of such simple Galilean Jews.[146]

The members of the Jesus Seminar go even further:

> Jews of the first century usually observed the prescriptions in the law — in Leviticus — not to eat or drink blood. The suggestion that those who ate the bread and drank the cup were eating the body of Christ and drinking his blood would have been offensive to Jesus' Judean followers. . . . [T]he symbolism of drinking the blood of a god arose in a pagan rather than a Jewish context.[147]

Clearly, there is widespread agreement among scholars that Jesus' identification of the wine with his blood is one of the strongest cases of incompatibility with Judaism that we possess in all the Gospels.

Second, other scholars argue against the historicity of Jesus' words over

144. Lüdemann, *Jesus after 2000 Years,* 96-97; Theissen and Merz, *The Historical Jesus,* 423; Becker, *Jesus of Nazareth,* 341; Funk and the Jesus Seminar, *The Acts of Jesus,* 139.

145. Geza Vermes, *The Religion of Jesus the Jew* (Minneapolis: Fortress, 1993), 16.

146. Joseph Klausner, *Jesus of Nazareth: His Life, Times, and Teaching* (trans. Herbert Danby; New York: Macmillan, 1925), 329.

147. Funk and the Jesus Seminar, *The Acts of Jesus,* 139.

the cup based on a lack of coherence with other evidence about Jesus. From this point of view, the accounts of the Last Supper cannot be reconciled with the absence of other explicit references to the "covenant" in the teachings of Jesus.[148] Consider the following statements from Jens Schröter, Jürgen Becker, and Scot McKnight:

> Vor allem das Kelchwort bereitet hier Schwierigkeiten, denn die Bundesthematik fehlt ansonsten in der Jesusüberlieferung. Dass Jesus seinen Tod als durch sein vergossenes Blut besiegelten Bundesschluss gedeutet habe, ist deshalb historisch betrachtet kaum wahrscheinlich.[149]

> [T]he covenant concept . . . was not part of the proclamation of Jesus, influenced as the latter was by the preaching of the Baptist (Matt 3:9 par.). Jesus' view of the Kingdom of God nowhere shows the influence of the covenant idea. The Kingdom of God is God's graciousness toward those lost persons who have abandoned the covenant. We will not claim for Jesus himself, therefore, this theological motif of the words of institution.[150]

> We propose that covenant and kingdom are alternative, hermeneutical categories. . . . Inasmuch as Jesus chose kingdom, covenant appears to be left to the side for others to use.[151]

In this view, "kingdom" *(basileia)* and "covenant" *(diathēkē)* are two completely different concepts, and Jesus chose kingdom rather than covenant to express what God was doing through his mission. Moreover, McKnight makes the claim that "in no place in the teachings of Jesus is kingdom coupled with covenant."[152] One scholar even speaks of "covenant avoidance" in the teaching of Jesus.[153] Given such premises, the singular nature of the appearance of covenant in the eucharistic words of Jesus renders it suspect; it must be understood as a creation of the early church.

Third, along similar lines, still other scholars argue against the historicity of the words over the cup based on another argument from a lack of coherence.

148. E.g., McKnight, *Jesus and His Death,* 308; Becker, *Jesus of Nazareth,* 341-42.

149. Schröter, *Das Abendmahl,* 133.

150. Becker, *Jesus of Nazareth,* 341.

151. McKnight, *Jesus and His Death,* 311.

152. McKnight, *Jesus and His Death,* 309.

153. H. Lichtenberger, "'Bund' in Abendmahlüberlieferung," 217; cited in McKnight, *Jesus and His Death,* 304.

From this point of view, the implicitly sacrificial nature of the words over the cup cannot be reconciled with the assumption that Jesus did not view his death as a redemptive sacrifice.[154] Gerd Lüdemann, as usual, puts the point quite bluntly: the words of Jesus at the Last Supper cannot be squared with the fact that "[Jesus] had said nothing about a saving effect of his death."[155] Significantly, this argument is often coupled with the view that Jesus did not identify himself as the suffering servant of Isaiah.[156] In the words of Morna Hooker:

> I suggest, then, that the reason that Jesus did not model himself on the so-called suffering Servant of Isaiah 53 was because it was by no means the obvious passage of scripture to which he would turn. During his ministry, he proclaimed the forgiving love of God, which welcomed repentant sinners back without condition. Particular acts of "atonement" were apparently unnecessary.[157]

From this point of view, the concept of atonement and the identification of Jesus with the suffering Servant in the eucharistic words is "secondary" and hence, unhistorical.[158] Indeed, in his recent book on Jesus, Joseph Ratzinger perceptively identifies "the idea of expiation" that is present in the Last Supper accounts as "the real reason why a good number of modern theologians (not only exegetes) reject the idea that the words of the Last Supper go back to Jesus himself."[159]

A fourth and final argument against historical plausibility is that Jesus' identification of the cup with the blood of the new covenant is too similar to the beliefs of the early church. As is well known to any reader of the New Testament, the idea a new "covenant" is clearly present in the teaching of the post-Easter church (Heb 8:6-13; 9:1-4; 10:16-29; 12:24; 13:20; cf. Gal 4:24). According to this logic, since the concept of a (new) covenant is present in the writings of the early church and absent from the teaching of Jesus elsewhere in the Gospels, then it is necessary to conclude that the identification of Jesus' blood with a new covenant does not go back to him but rather was

154. Schröter, *Das Abendmahl,* 133.

155. Lüdemann, *Jesus After 2000 Years,* 96.

156. Dunn, *Jesus Remembered,* 816-17.

157. Hooker, "Did the Use of Isaiah 53 to Interpret His Mission Begin with Jesus?," 100.

158. E.g., Theissen and Merz, *The Historical Jesus,* 421-23; Gnilka, *Jesus of Nazareth,* 286.

159. Joseph Ratzinger (Pope Benedict XVI), *Jesus of Nazareth, Part Two: Holy Week, From the Entrance into Jerusalem to the Resurrection* (San Francisco: Ignatius, 2011), 119, following Pesch, *Das Abendmahl und Jesu Todesverständnis,* 104.

a creation of the early church in its attempt to make sense of and give value to Jesus' death.[160]

In sum, on the basis of these four major arguments, various scholars of different persuasions have concluded that the words of Jesus over the cup are historically implausible. He did not identify the wine with the blood of a new covenant, and he did not identify his death as the redemptive self-offering of the suffering servant. It was the early church that was responsible for these connections.[161]

On the other hand, there are several positive arguments for the historical plausibility of Jesus' identification of the wine of the Last Supper with the blood of the covenant and the sacrifice of the suffering servant.

Context: Mount Sinai, the Life, and the Atoning Blood of the Covenant

Upon closer inspection, the substance of Jesus' words over the cup is plausible within an ancient Jewish context, in several key ways.

First and foremost, despite the insistence of commentators to the contrary, Jesus' command to drink wine that he identifies as his blood does not actually break any positive command of the Jewish Torah. For the Torah nowhere prohibits the consumption of human blood, much less wine identified as human blood. Rather, it prohibits the consumption of *animal blood.* Examine the evidence again in context, with this distinction in mind:

> [God said to Noah:] The fear of you and the dread of you shall be upon *every beast of the earth,* and upon every bird of the air, upon everything that creeps upon the ground and all the fish of the sea: into your hand they

160. Becker, *Jesus of Nazareth,* 128-29; McKnight, *Jesus and His Death,* 293-321. Cf. Allison, *Constructing Jesus,* 272 n. 211.

161. It is worth noting in passing a common older argument against the authenticity of Jesus' words over the cup. According to this view, because the expression "my blood of the covenant" cannot be successfully retranslated into Aramaic, the words over the cup are called into question. This argument is highly dubious, as it fails to take into account that in the process of translation, formal equivalence need not have been sought. It also reveals a positivistic desire to establish the *ipsissima verba.* As I have said before, we need not search for the original *form* of a saying; the basic *substance* is sufficient, and in all four forms the "blood" of Jesus is linked with the establishment of a covenant. For discussion see McKnight, *Jesus and His Death,* 308 n. 65; Tan, *The Zion Traditions and the Aims of Jesus,* 202; Maurice Casey, "The Original Aramaic Form of Jesus' Interpretation of the Cup," *JTS* 41 (1990): 1-12; Jeremias, *The Eucharistic Words of Jesus,* 193-96.

> are delivered. *Every moving thing that lives shall be food for you,* as I gave you the green plants, I give you everything. Only *you shall not eat flesh with its life, that is, its blood.* (Gen 9:2-4)
>
> If any man among the house of Israel or of the stranger that sojourns among them eats any blood, I will set my face against that person who eats blood, and I will cut him off from among his people. *For the life of the flesh is in the blood; and I have given it for you upon the altar to make atonement for your souls; for it is the blood that makes atonement, by reason of its life.* Therefore I have said to the people of Israel, No person among you shall eat blood, neither shall any stranger who sojourns among you eat blood. (Lev 17:10-12)
>
> *You may slaughter and eat flesh within any of your towns,* as much as you desire . . . as of the gazelle and as of the hart. *Only you shall not eat the blood;* you shall pour it out upon the earth like water. (Deut 12:15-16)

Once again, note carefully: all of these biblical texts are focused on animal sacrifice and animal consumption; none of them has the consumption of human blood even remotely in view. Of course Jesus' command to drink wine identified with his blood is unusual — that should be obvious! However, contrary to popular assumption, *Jesus' instruction to drink the wine he has identified as his blood does not actually represent a positive breach of any law in the Jewish Torah.* In each of these Pentateuchal texts, the command is clearly focused on the cultic consumption of the blood of animals used in sacrifice. Human blood is nowhere in view, much less wine that has been identified as human blood. Because of this, Jesus' command to drink his blood under the appearance of wine is neither prohibited nor condoned by Jewish Scripture: it is simply not in view anywhere in the Law or the Prophets.

Why then does Jesus identify wine, which is meant to be consumed, with his blood, which is meant to be poured out in sacrifice? How is this conceivable within an early Jewish context? At this point in our investigation, we cannot yet answer that question completely. However, for now, I would like to suggest that the seeds of an answer may be contained in the very Jewish context often cited against the historical plausibility of Jesus' words. In the passage from Leviticus above, notice that the reason given for abstaining from animal blood is that "the life is in the blood," and the blood is given by God "to make atonement for your souls" (Lev 17:11). In light of this ancient Israelite view of blood, one can suggest that perhaps the reason God *prohibits* the Israelites from drinking animal blood — because the "life" is in the blood and it is given to make "atonement" — is also the very reason that Jesus *commands* the disciples to drink the wine he identifies as his "blood": *his* "life" is in the blood. Hence, if the twelve disciples are to have a share in the life that will be poured out in his suffering and death, they must consume the wine that is being poured out in sacrifice for sin.[162] At this point, admittedly, there is nothing in the accounts of the Last Supper to confirm this suggestion; we will have to wait for a fuller explanation in chapter 3, when we examine the evidence for his teaching in the synagogue at Capernaum (John 6:53-58). For now, the primary point is that the first argument against the historical plausibility of the words over the cup loses some of its force when we realize that nothing Jesus says actually breaks any of the commandments of Moses in the Torah.

Second, and equally important, the idea that Jesus saw himself as instituting a new or eschatological covenant is completely compatible with his first-century Jewish context. Indeed, references to the eschatological covenant are remarkably abundant in Second Temple Jewish literature. Tom Holmén even goes so far as referring to the covenant as "the basic, fundamental belief" of the Jewish people and the "dominant theme" of Judaism at the time of Jesus.[163] In fact, there are too many examples to give here.[164] For now, let it suffice to note that several passages in the Dead Sea Scrolls make clear that the community saw its members as having entered into "the new covenant" *(haberith hadasah)* (*Damascus Document*[a] [CD[a]] 6:19; 8:21; 19:33-34; 20:12).[165] Likewise, opponents of the community are called "traito[rs of the] new [covenant] si[n]ce they did not believe in the covenant of God . . ." (*1QPesher to Habakkuk* [1QpHab] 2:3). Now, if the authors of the Dead Sea Scrolls could see themselves as establishing

162. In this way, Jesus appears to be fusing the use of blood and wine into one: the former poured out in sacrifice, the latter consumed as a drink offering.

163. Holmén, "Jesus, Judaism, and the Covenant," 4-5. For a full discussion, see idem, *Jesus and Jewish Covenant Thinking.*

164. McKnight, *Jesus and His Death,* 315, lists the following: 1 Macc 1:11-15; 2:19-22; 2:49-70; 4:6-11; 2 Macc 1:2-6; 7:30-38; 8:12-18; Sir 17:12; 24:8-23; 41:19; 44-50; CD[a] 1:4; 2:2; 4:9; 6:11, 18-19; 7:4; 8:18, 20-21; 9:2; 13:14; 19:31, 34; 20:11-13, 17, 25, 29; 1QS 2:26; 5:11, 18; 1QM 13:8; 1QSa 1:5; 1QSb 1:2; 3:24; 1QpHab 2:3; 4Q504 2:9; 1Q34bis 3 ii.5-6; 2 Esd. 2:5, 7; 3:15; 5:29; 7:83; *Jub.* 1:17-18; 2:26-33; 6:12-14; 14:19-20; 15:1-34; 22:15-19; 30:7-12; 33:10-14; 36:8-11; 49:1–50:13. See also David Noel Freedman and David Miano, "People of the New Covenant," in *The Concept of the Covenant in the Second Temple Period* (JSJSup 71; ed. S. E. Porter and J. C. R. De Roo; Leiden: Brill, 2003), 7-26; Dennis E. Smith, "Meals," in *Encyclopedia of the Dead Sea Scrolls* (2 vols.; ed. L. Schiffman and J. C. VanderKam; Oxford: Oxford University Press, 2002), 1:530-32; Holmén, *Jesus and Jewish Covenant Thinking,* 30-59.

165. Tan, *The Zion Traditions and the Aims of Jesus,* 210-15.

the eschatological community of the "new covenant," in a way that was both continuous with the covenant at Sinai and yet new, there is no reason to dispute that Jesus and his disciples could have seen themselves in a similar fashion.[166] As James Dunn states:

> [A]s the Qumran community saw itself as participants in the "new covenant," so Jesus saw the group around him as anticipatory fulfillment of the new covenant (Jer. 31.31-34) which Yahweh was to make with his people. As the twelve somehow represented restored Israel, so they represented Israel under the new covenant.[167]

Indeed, as Dale Allison has shown, Jesus' affirmation of a new covenant even fits in perfectly with his immediate Jewish "predecessor": John the Baptist. According to Allison, one of the most prominent aspects of John the Baptist's preaching was that biological descent from Abraham (and hence membership in his covenant family) was insufficient for eschatological salvation (Matt 3:9; Luke 3:8). By calling into question the permanent validity of the Abrahamic covenant, John thereby paved the way for Jesus himself to speak and act in ways that pointed to the establishment of a new covenant.[168]

Third, Jesus' assertion that his blood — as the blood of the new covenant — has redemptive power is also plausible within the broader context of ancient Jewish beliefs about the blood of the covenant offered by Moses. To be sure, the Torah itself does not make explicit that the blood of Moses' sacrifice at Mount Sinai had the power to atone for sin. Nevertheless, in the Second Temple period, early Jewish interpretations of Exodus 24, in both the Septuagint and Dead Sea Scrolls, identified the covenant sacrifices offered by Moses at Mount Sinai as redemptive, and atoning for sin.[169] Compare the following:

> And he sent the young men of the sons of Israel, and they offered holocausts and they sacrificed *a sacrifice of salvation* to God. And Moses

166. See Tan, *The Zion Traditions and the Aims of Jesus,* 213, 218-19, on continuity between the Sinai Covenant and the new covenant in the Dead Sea Scrolls.

167. Dunn, *Jesus Remembered,* 513.

168. See Allison, "Jesus and the Covenant," 58-61.

169. Barber, "The Historical Jesus and Cultic Restoration Eschatology," 610; Falk, "Moses," in *Encyclopedia of the Dead Sea Scrolls,* 577; Marshall, *Last Supper and Lord's Supper,* 92; Pesch, *Das Abendmahl und Jesu Todesverständnis,* 95-96. In support of this, it is worth noting that in Ezekiel 16:60-63, the future "everlasting" covenant is also connected to atonement for sin. Tan, *The Zion Traditions and the Aims of Jesus,* 217.

> taking half of the blood *poured it* into bowls, and the other half of the blood *he poured out on the altar.* . . . And Moses taking the blood sprinkled it on the people and said, "*Behold, the blood of the covenant,* which the Lord has *covenanted* with you regarding all these words." (Exod 24:5-6, 8 LXX)[170]

> You became angry with them as to destroy them; but you took pity on them in your love for them, and *on account of your covenant — for Moses atoned for their sin* — and so that they would know your great power and your abundant kindness for everlasting generations. (*4QWords of the Luminaries*[a] [4Q504] Frag. 2, col. 2:8-11)

These parallels are extraordinarily significant for how we understand Jesus' actions at the Last Supper regarding the blood of the covenant he is establishing. Not only does the Septuagint explicitly describe the covenant blood as a "sacrifice of salvation" *(thysian sotēriou),* but, even more striking, the Scroll explicitly states that it was on account of the "covenant" *(brth)* that "Moses atoned for their sin" *(kphr mwsh' b'd ht'thm).* Indeed, this early Jewish concept of the atoning blood of the covenant continues and becomes even more explicit in the later Aramaic targums on Exodus.[171] In light of such data, one can posit the following: *If Jesus saw the blood offered by Moses, like other Second Temple Jews, as having atoning power, then it would explain why he uses language evocative of the Sinai covenant sacrifices to describe the atoning power of his own sacrificial blood.* Everything we have seen so far strongly suggests that Jesus not only saw himself as the new Moses; he also saw himself

170. Author's translation.

171. See, e.g., the following Aramaic renditions of the Sinai covenant: "Then Moses took the half of the blood that was in the dashing-basins and dashed (it) against the altar to make atonement for the people; and he said, 'Behold, this is the blood of the covenant which the Lord has made with you in accordance with all these words'" (*Targum Pseudo-Jonathan* on Exod 24:8). "Whereupon Moses took the blood and sprinkled it on the altar to atone for the people, and he said, 'Behold, this is the blood of the covenant which the Lord has established with you in accordance with all these words'" (*Targum Onqelos* on Exod 24:8). For translations, see Bernard Groosfeld, *The Targum Onqelos to Exodus* (ArBib 7; Wilmington: Michael Glazier, 1988), 71-72 (slightly adapted), and translation in Martin McNamara, M.S.C. and Michael Maher, M.S.C., *Targum Neofiti 1: Exodus and Targum Pseudo-Jonathan: Exodus* (ArBib 2; Collegeville: Liturgical Press, 1994), 231. Although from a later period, there are arresting parallels between Moses declaring "*This is (hineh)* the blood of the covenant" (in both Targums) and Jesus' declaration that "This" *(touto)* "is" *(estin)* the cup of his blood (Matt 26:28; Mark 14:24; 1 Cor 11:25).

as both recapitulating the Sinai Covenant and establishing the eschatological covenant in his blood. If this is correct, then it seems plausible that he also saw this sacrifice he was offering at the Last Supper as having the power to atone for sin. This at least is the role that Moses is held to have played by some Second Temple Jews.[172]

Fourth and finally, Jesus' combination of the expectation of a new covenant with the kingdom of God is likewise plausible within his first-century Jewish context. Indeed, even a cursory glance at the evidence shows that it is wrong to pit "kingdom" against "covenant," as do some scholars.[173] To the contrary, as both Jewish Scripture and the Dead Sea Scrolls make abundantly clear, the ideas of kingdom and covenant belong closely together.[174] Consider the following examples, noting the consistently messianic context of the relationship between covenant and kingdom:

> And I will set up over them one shepherd, *my servant David,* and he shall feed them: he shall feed them and be their shepherd. And I, the LORD, will be their God, and *my servant David shall be prince among them;* I, the LORD, have spoken. I will make with them *a covenant of peace. . . .* (Ezek 34:23-25)

> They shall dwell in the land where your fathers dwelt that I gave to my servant Jacob; they and their children and their children's children shall dwell there for ever; and *David my servant shall be their prince for ever. I will make a covenant of peace with them;* it shall be an *everlasting covenant* with them. . . . (Ezek 37:25-27)

> The LORD took away [David's] sins, and exalted his power for ever; *he gave him the covenant of kings and a throne of glory* in Israel. (Sir 47:11; cf. 45:25)

172. Seen in this light, the emphasis on the blood of the covenant in all four accounts of the Last Supper implicitly affirms what is made explicit in Matthew's account: Jesus' blood, the blood of the covenant, is being poured out "for the forgiveness of sins" (Matt 26:28). Cf. Perrin, "The Last Supper," 495; Allison, *The New Moses,* 258-59. McKnight, *Jesus and His Death,* 305, dismisses this as secondary without taking this point into account.

173. Barber, "The Historical Jesus and Cultic Restoration Eschatology," 655-56, following Scott Hahn, *Kinship by Covenant* (AYBRL; New Haven and London: Yale University Press, 2009), 234-37.

174. So Gnilka, *Jesus of Nazareth,* 287, citing G. Q. Quell, *"diathēkē," TDNT* 2:118-24; Moshe Weinfeld, *"b^erîth," TDOT* 2:275-79.

> And he [God] will renew *the covenant* of the [Com]munity for him, *to establish the kingdom* of his people for eve[r, to judge the poor with justice]. (*1QRule of Benedictions* [1Q28b] 5:18)

> The scepter shall [no]t depart from the tribe of Judah. While Israel has the dominion, there [will not] be cut off someone who sits *on the throne of David.* For "the staff" is *the covenant of royalty,* [and the thou]sands of Israel are "the standards." *Blank.* Until *the messiah of righteousness comes,* the branch of David. For to him and to his descendants has been given *the covenant of kingship* of his people for everlasting generations. . . . (*4QCommentary on Genesis A* [4Q252] 5:1-4)

This evidence poses a devastating blow to the argument that Jesus' reference to the covenant at the Last Supper is somehow incompatible with his emphasis on the kingdom of God throughout his public ministry. To the contrary, as Johannes Behm concluded long ago in his famous article on the covenant: "the *kainē diathēkē* [new covenant] is a correlative of the *basileia tou theou* [kingdom of God]."[175] Indeed, McKnight himself admits that "the connection of kingdom and covenant is palpably Jewish."[176] I agree, but would add that these early Jewish texts also make clear that the connection between kingdom and covenant is also palpably messianic. In the Old Testament and the Dead Sea Scrolls, kingdom and covenant tend to be combined precisely in contexts in which the messianic restoration of Israel is in view.

Coherence: The Suffering Servant, the Covenant, and the Kingdom

Jesus' identification of the cup with the blood of a new covenant and the sacrifice of the suffering servant also presents us with a remarkably strong case of coherence, in several ways.

For one thing, the establishment of a new covenant at the Last Supper coheres perfectly with other evidence that Jesus sought to bring about the restoration of the twelve tribes of Israel.[177] As we noted above in our study of the eschatological covenant in the prophets, on more than one occasion, the future covenant is tied to the ingathering of the tribes of Israel in Jewish

175. Behm, "*diathēkē,*" 134; likewise, Jeremias, *The Eucharistic Words of Jesus,* 226.
176. McKnight, *Jesus and His Death,* 309 n. 69.
177. Dunn, *Jesus Remembered,* 513 n. 116.

Scripture (Jer 31; 2 Bar 2; Ezek 16; Zech 9, etc.). In this regard, as Joachim Gnilka points out, Jesus' explicit use of "covenant" language being restricted to the Last Supper is not surprising, since it flows from the singular nature of the situation: it is in the context of the certainty of his imminent death that Jesus reveals to the disciples that he is establishing the eschatological covenant.[178] Or, as Theissen and Merz put it: "Because it is a unique action, it is no wonder that 'covenant' is not a topic elsewhere in the preaching of Jesus. The 'isolation' of this term in the Jesus tradition is no argument against its authenticity."[179]

Second, the identification of the cup with the blood of the new covenant coheres quite well with the Mosaic self-understanding of Jesus evidenced elsewhere in the Gospels. As we have seen over the course of this chapter, a number of scholars have concluded that Jesus saw himself as the long-awaited new Moses, and hence spoke and acted in ways that were deliberately evocative of the words and deeds of Moses.[180] In terms of evidence, his feeding of the multitude in the wilderness with bread, examined above, stands out (Matt 14:13-23; Mark 6:32-45; Luke 9:11-17; John 6:1-13). Now, *if Jesus saw himself as the new Moses, then the idea that he like Moses would establish a covenant between God and his people by means of blood sacrifice is historically quite plausible, perhaps even to be expected.* What else did Moses do for the people of Israel that was more memorable than giving them the Law and establishing the everlasting covenant with YHWH?

Third, Jesus' image of his blood being poured out for many also coheres quite well with other evidence that Jesus saw himself as the suffering Servant of Isaiah.[181] Although this question continues to be the subject of debate, I have argued elsewhere at great length that there are good reasons for concluding that Jesus' declaration that he came "not to be served but to serve and to give his life as a ransom for many *(pollōn)*" (Matt 20:28; Mark 10:45) is also a historically plausible allusion to the sacrifice of the suffering servant, who offers his life as a sacrifice for the "many" (MT *rabbîm;* LXX *polloi*) (Isa

178. Gnilka, *Jesus of Nazareth,* 286.

179. Theissen and Merz, *The Historical Jesus,* 423.

180. McKnight, *Jesus and His Death,* 200; Allison, *The Intertextual Jesus,* 218; Horsley, "The Dead Sea Scrolls and the Historical Jesus," 59; Meyer, "Jesus and the Scriptures," 171; Witherington, *The Christology of Jesus,* 101.

181. See esp. the essays in Bernd Janowski and Peter Stuhlmacher, eds., *The Suffering Servant: Isaiah 53 in Jewish and Christian Sources* (trans. Daniel P. Bailey; Grand Rapids: Eerdmans, 2004). See also Darrell Bock and Michael Glaser, eds., *The Gospel According to Isaiah 53: Encountering the Suffering Servant in Jewish and Christian Theology* (Grand Rapids: Kregel Academic, 2012).

53:11-12).[182] In addition to the connections between the Servant and Jesus in the ransom saying, there is at least one case in which Jesus explicitly describes himself as fulfilling this text from Isaiah:

> And he said to them, "When I sent you out with no purse or bag or sandals, did you lack anything?" They said, "Nothing." He said to them, "But now, let him who has a purse take it, and likewise a bag. And let him who has no sword sell his mantle and buy one. *For I tell you that this Scripture must be fulfilled in me, 'And he was reckoned among transgressors'* [Isa 53:12]; *for what was written about me must have its fulfillment.*" (Luke 22:35-37)

In light of such evidence and for reasons that we do not have the space to go into here, a number of scholars do indeed conclude that Jesus likely saw himself as the Servant of Isaiah.[183] For our purposes, the implications of this proposal are manifold: as we saw at the beginning of this chapter, in the book of Isaiah, the suffering servant is actually modeled on the figure of Moses.[184] This makes sense, since it is the Servant who inaugurates the new exodus in Isaiah.[185] If this conclusion is correct, then it is reasonable to suggest that Jesus

182. Pitre, *Jesus, the Tribulation, and the End of the Exile*, 384-455. Cf. Keener, *The Historical Jesus of the Gospels*, 300; Meyer, "The Expiation Motif in the Eucharistic Words," 33.

183. See McKnight, *Jesus and His Death*, 207-24 (though he demurs on Matt 20:28; Mark 10:45); Pitre, *Jesus, the Tribulation, and the End of the Exile*, 397-98, 404-5, 416-17; Otto Betz, "Jesus and Isaiah 53," in *Jesus and the Suffering Servant: Isaiah 53 and Christian Origins* (ed. William R. Farmer and William H. Bellinger Jr.; Harrisburg: Trinity Press International, 1998), 70-87; Rikki Watts, "Jesus' Death, Isaiah 53, and Mark 10:45: A Crux Revisited," in *Jesus and the Suffering Servant: Isaiah 53 and Christian Origins* (ed. William R. Farmer and William H. Bellinger Jr.; Harrisburg: Trinity Press International, 1998), 125-51; Davies and Allison, *Saint Matthew*, 3:94-100; Wright, *Jesus and the Victory of God*, 579-91. The classic case for Jesus having identified himself with the Suffering Servant of Isaiah remains that of Joachim Jeremias with Walter Zimmerli, *The Servant of God* (London: SCM, 1957, rev. 1965), 99-106. Cf. Dunn, *Jesus Remembered*, 811-12, who rejects Luke 22:35-38 as historically plausible on the basis of literary observations rather than historical argumentation.

184. See above, and R. E. Clements, "Isaiah 53 and the Restoration of Israel," in *Jesus and the Suffering Servant: Isaiah 53 and Christian Origins* (ed. William H. Bellinger Jr. and William R. Farmer; Harrisburg: Trinity Press International, 1998), 47-54; H. P. Hugenberger, "The Servant of the Lord in the 'Servant Songs' of Isaiah: A Second Moses Figure," in *The Lord's Anointed* (ed. P. E. Satterthwaite, R. S. Hess, and G. J. Wenham; Grand Rapids: Baker, 1995), 105-40; Allison, *The New Moses*, 68-71; C. R. North, *The Suffering Servant in Deutero-Isaiah* (2nd ed.; Oxford: Oxford University Press, 1956), 53-55; Jeremias, "*Mōüsēs*," 863-64.

185. Von Rad, *Old Testament Theology*, 2:260-61.

united the figures of Moses and the Servant into one, differing from the book of Isaiah only in that he applied them to himself.

Fourth and finally, Jesus' establishment of a new covenant also is quite consistent with his proclamation of the kingdom of God. Despite what is sometimes claimed by scholars, it is simply not true that Jesus nowhere ever speaks of both "kingdom" and "covenant" together. To the contrary, in the Gospel of Luke, Jesus explicitly connects the ideas of kingdom and covenant in the context of the Last Supper. Compare the following text, which is consistently overlooked by scholars who deny that Jesus could have spoken of the "covenant" because he was focused on the "kingdom":

> You are those who have continued with me in my trials; as my Father *covenanted* a *kingdom* for me, so do I *covenant* for you that you may eat and drink at my table *in my kingdom,* and sit on thrones judging the twelve tribes of Israel. (Luke 22:28-30)[186]

Although English translations frequently obscure the connections with the noun "covenant" *(diathēkē),* in Greek, the links are quite clear.[187] In these verses, Jesus says that just as the Father has "covenanted" *(dietheto)* a "kingdom" *(basileian)* to him, so too do "I covenant" *(diatithemai)* to the disciples so that they might eat and drink "in my kingdom *(basileia)*" (Luke 22:29-30). Strikingly, the context of this language is precisely that which we find in the Old Testament prophets and Dead Sea Scrolls: the messianic restoration of the twelve tribes of Israel. Should there be any doubt about the messianic self-identification implicit here, note that Jesus himself does not take one of the twelve thrones, not because he is beneath the disciples in the kingdom, but because he is above them: i.e., he is the eschatological king of the kingdom. In other words, he is the messiah.[188]

Effects: The New Covenant in Early Christianity

Third and finally, Jesus' identification of the cup of wine with his blood and the connection he draws between his death and the suffering servant also provide

186. RSV, slightly adapted.

187. See Scott Hahn, *Kinship by Covenant,* 227; 1 Chron 19:19; 2 Chron 5:10; Ezek 16:30 LXX.

188. Allison, "Jesus and the Covenant," 66-67.

us with a plausible explanation for the origin of the early church's belief that they were living in the era of the new covenant.

As we saw above, some scholars would use the fact that the idea of a new covenant appears elsewhere in the New Testament as an argument against its origins with Jesus. For one thing, this argument is a non sequitur. It simply does not follow that because the early church believed or emphasized some concept or idea, therefore Jesus did not. The classic example of this is of course Jesus' emphasis on the "kingdom of God," which is found in the New Testament writings outside the Gospels with far more frequency than the idea of a new covenant, over two dozen times.[189] Moreover, when we actually turn to examine the early Christian use of the idea of the "new covenant," we find a prime example of continuity with development, in which the early church is having to adapt the concept to its contemporary circumstances in a manner quite distinct from that of Jesus and the Twelve disciples at the Last Supper. Consider here, for instance, the classic New Testament descriptions of the new covenant found in the epistle to the Hebrews:

> Now the point in what we are saying is this: we have such a high priest, one who is seated at the right hand of the throne of the Majesty in heaven, a minister in the sanctuary and the true tent which is set up not by man but by the Lord. For every high priest is appointed to offer gifts and sacrifices; hence it is necessary for this priest also to have something to offer. Now if he were on earth, he would not be a priest at all, since there are priests who offer gifts according to the law. They serve a copy and shadow of the heavenly sanctuary; for when Moses was about to erect the tent, he was instructed by God, saying, "See that you make everything according to the pattern which was shown you on the mountain." *But as it is, Christ has obtained a ministry which is as much more excellent than the old as the covenant he mediates is better, since it is enacted on better promises.* For if that first covenant had been faultless, there would have been no occasion for a second. For he finds fault with them when he says: "The days will come, says the Lord, when I will establish a new covenant with the house of Israel and with the house of Judah. . . . For I will be merciful toward their iniquities, and I will remember their sins no more." *In speaking of a new covenant he*

189. See Acts 1:3, 8:12; 14:22; 19:8; 20:25, 28:23, 31; Rom 14:17; 1 Cor 4:20; 6:9, 10; 15:24, 50; Gal 5:21; Eph 5:5; Col 1:13; 4:11; 1 Thess 2:12; 2 Thess 1:5; 2 Tim 4:1; 4:18; Heb 12:28; James 2:5; 2 Pet 1:11; Rev 1:6, 9; 5:10; 11:15; 12:10.

> *treats the first as obsolete. And what is becoming obsolete and growing old is ready to vanish away.* (Heb 8:1-8, 12-13)

> For you have not come to what may be touched, a blazing fire, and darkness, and gloom, and a tempest, and the sound of a trumpet, and a voice whose words made the hearers entreat that no further messages be spoken to them. For they could not endure the order that was given, "If even a beast touches the mountain, it shall be stoned." Indeed, so terrifying was the sight that Moses said, "I tremble with fear." But you have come to Mount Zion and to the city of the living God, the heavenly Jerusalem, and to innumerable angels in festal gathering, and to the assembly of the first-born who are enrolled in heaven, and to a judge who is God of all, and to the spirits of just men made perfect, and *to Jesus, the mediator of a new covenant, and to the sprinkled blood that speaks more graciously than the blood of Abel.* (Heb 12:18-24)

Notice the remarkable continuity — but not identity — between these words and those of Jesus. Strikingly, both Jesus at the Last Supper and the epistle to the Hebrews emphasize the coming of a new covenant in connection with the covenant at Mount Sinai and the fulfillment of Jeremiah 31. Moreover, when we compare such texts with Jesus' words over the cup, what stands out is not only the obvious continuity with the central emphasis given to the new covenant by Jesus at the Last Supper but also the equally obvious developments that have taken place by the time of the author of Hebrews. Jesus' words are directed at the fulfillment of the prophecies of Jeremiah and Isaiah in his own person; Hebrews is focused on explaining the implications of this fulfillment for the relationship between the "new covenant" and the "first covenant," especially with reference to its audience's participation in Temple worship (Heb 8:7, 13). Likewise, Jesus' words are tied directly to his own imminent death, whereas Hebrews is using the "new covenant" to explain how it is that Christians might even now enter into the "heavenly Jerusalem" by means of the "sprinkled blood" of Jesus — once again, presumably in the context of early Christian liturgy (Heb 12:18-24). Given everything we have seen so far, the most plausible explanation for the origin of the idea in Hebrews that Christians are living in the era of the new covenant is that Jesus himself declared that he was establishing it by means of his words and deeds at the Last Supper.

In light of all these considerations — compatibility with Judaism, coherence with other words and deeds of Jesus, and continuity with the early church — I consider it reasonable to conclude that Jesus did in fact identify the wine of the Last Supper as his own blood, the blood which, through his death, would be poured out to establish a new covenant.[190] As James Dunn writes:

> Jesus spoke of his anticipated death in terms of a *covenant sacrifice*. . . . The precedent here would be Exod. 24.8: "Moses took the blood and dashed it on the people, and said, 'See the blood of the covenant that the Lord has made with you. . . .'" This meshes well with the earlier possibility . . . that Jesus (somewhat like the Qumran covenanters) saw the group around him as somehow constituting the renewal of God's covenant with Israel, or spoke with a view to the establishment of the new covenant promised in Jer. 31.31-34. Jesus may well have gone willingly to his death because he saw it as the sacrifice which would bring into effect the long-promised covenant. . . . If God was to make a fresh covenant with his people, then presumably a covenant sacrifice was required; Jesus' death would serve as that sacrifice.[191]

I concur with Dunn's presentation, with a few important qualifications. For one thing, if the eucharistic words over the cup are historical — and we have seen that there are very good reasons to believe so — then there is no need to be so circumspect. All the evidence in the Gospels points to the conclusion that Jesus did go willingly to his death precisely because he saw it as the covenant sacrifice that would usher in the eschatological age. Moreover, there is no reason to be vague about how Jesus understood this covenant renewal. Jesus did not see the twelve disciples as "somehow" constituting the renewal of the covenant; if the eucharistic words are historical, then he saw this renewal as taking place precisely through the offering of his body and blood as bread and wine, and through the disciples' participation in that banquet. In other words, he envisioned the eucharistic renewal of the covenant with Israel, embodied in his presence in the persons of the twelve disciples. Lastly, it seems to me that the key to understanding the eucharistic words lies in the fact that Jesus appears to have modeled his actions *both* on the sacrifice of Moses at Mount Sinai *and* the suffering and death of the servant in Isaiah, whose sacrifice inaugurates the new exodus.[192] In short, *Jesus acts like both the new Moses and the Suffering Servant of God, since it is the latter who Isaiah prophesied would inaugurate the new exodus and whose life would be given to establish the eschatological covenant.*

190. So too Tan, *The Zion Traditions and the Aims of Jesus*, 203; Backhaus, "Hat Jesus vom Gottesbund gesprochen?," 347; Behm, "*diathēkē*," 133.

191. Dunn, *Jesus Remembered*, 816, 817-18.

192. Stuhlmacher, "Isaiah 53 in the Gospels and Acts," 153.

The New Bread of the Presence[193]

Before we bring this chapter to a close, it is important to emphasize that it is not only Jesus' words over the cup that suggest a connection with the prophet like Moses. The same thing is true for his words over the bread. Indeed, a case can be made for several striking connections between the Last Supper and the Mosaic institution of the "bread of the presence."

Although these connections are frequently overlooked by commentators on the Last Supper, it is critical to recall — as any Jew familiar with the Torah would have known — that at Mount Sinai, Moses not only offers the sacrificial blood of the covenant with Israel; he also institutes the sacrificial bread of the presence, which is regarded as a memorial of the covenant. Compare the following accounts of Jesus' words over the bread, with their Mosaic background in mind:

> When it was evening, he sat at table with the twelve disciples. . . . Now as they were eating, Jesus took bread, and blessed, and broke it, and gave it to the disciples and said, "Take, eat; this is my body." And he took a cup, and when he had given thanks he gave it to them, saying, "Drink of it, all of you; for this is my blood of the covenant, which is poured out for many for the forgiveness of sins. I tell you I shall not drink of the fruit of the vine until I drink it new with you in my Father's kingdom." (Matt 26:20, 26-29)

> And when it was evening he came with the twelve. . . . And as they were eating, he took bread, and blessed, and broke it, and gave it to them, and said, "Take, this is my body." And he took a cup, and when he had given thanks he gave it to them, and they all drank of it. And he said to them, "This is my blood of the covenant, which is poured out for many. Truly,

193. Barber, "The Historical Jesus and Cultic Restoration Eschatology," 598-602; Brant Pitre, "Jesus, the New Temple, and the New Priesthood," *Letter & Spirit* 4 (2008): 47-83; Mary Douglas, "The Eucharist: Its Continuity with the Bread Sacrifice in Leviticus," *Modern Theology* 15, no. 2 (1999): 209-24; H.-J. Fabry, *"leḥem,"* in *Theological Dictionary of the Old Testament* (15 vols.; ed. G. Johannes Botterweck et al.; Grand Rapids: Eerdmans, 1974-2006), 7:525-27; Roy Gane, "'Bread of the Presence' and Creator-in-Residence," *VT* 42, no. 2 (1992): 179-202; Paul V. M. Flesher, "Bread of the Presence," *ABD* 1:780-81; Menahem Haran, "Shewbread," *Encyclopedia Judaica* (16 vols.; ed. Cecil Roth; Jerusalem: Keter, 1979), 14:1394-95; Jeremias, *The Eucharistic Words of Jesus*, 63-65; Emil G. Hirsch, "Showbread," *The Jewish Encyclopedia* (12 vols.; ed. Isidore Singer; New York: Ktav, 1901), 312-13.

> I say to you, I shall not drink again of the fruit of the vine until that day when I drink it new in the kingdom of God." (Mark 14:17, 22-25)

> And when the hour came, he sat at table, and the apostles with him. . . . And he took bread, and when he had given thanks he broke it and gave it to them, saying, "This is my body which is given for you. Do this in remembrance of me." And likewise the cup after supper, saying, "This cup which is poured out for you is the new covenant in my blood." . . . "You are those who have continued with me in my trials; as my Father covenanted a kingdom to me, so do I covenant to you that you may eat and drink at my table in my kingdom, and sit on thrones judging the twelve tribes of Israel. (Luke 22:14, 19-20, 28-30)

> The Lord Jesus on the night when he was betrayed took bread, and when he had given thanks, he broke it, and said, "This is my body which is for you. Do this in remembrance of me." In the same way also the cup, after supper, saying, "This cup is the new covenant in my blood. Do this, as often as you drink it, in remembrance of me." (1 Cor 11:24-25)

In what follows, I want to explore the significant connections between these words at the Last Supper and the Mosaic bread of the presence. As we will see, when analyzed carefully, (1) Jesus' use of bread and wine, (2) the presence of the twelve disciples, (3) the language of "covenant" *(diathēkē),* and (4) the imagery of "remembrance" *(anamnēsis)* — when situated in the context recapitulating Moses' covenant actions at Sinai — all strongly suggest that Jesus is not only establishing a new covenant; he is also instituting the new bread and wine of his presence.

In order to see these connections clearly, we need to go back to the Jewish Torah and examine the biblical accounts of the bread of the presence in more detail.

Moses and the Bread of the Presence

Significantly, the bread of the presence makes its first appearance in Jewish Scripture in the very section of the Pentateuch that was so pivotal to our examination above: the account of Moses and the Israelites offering the covenant sacrifices at Mount Sinai, sacrifices that climaxed in a heavenly banquet atop the mountain in the very presence of God (Exod 24:1-11). According to the book of Exodus, after the completion of the theophanic banquet, Moses is called by God to come up alone and enter into the glory cloud atop Mount Sinai for forty days and forty nights (Exod 24:12-18). During that time, God gives Moses detailed instructions for building the tabernacle in which he will be worshipped by the Israelites, beginning with three sacred objects that will be kept in the inner sanctum of the Tabernacle: the ark of the covenant, the golden table of the bread of the presence, and the golden lampstand (commonly known as the *menorah*). For our purposes here, it is the golden table that demands our attention:

> [God said to Moses:] "And you shall make *a table* of acacia wood; two cubits shall be its length, a cubit its breadth, and a cubit and a half its height. You shall overlay it with *pure gold,* and make a molding of gold around it. And you shall make around it a frame a handbreadth wide, and a molding of gold around the frame. And you shall make for it four rings of gold, and fasten the rings to the four corners of its four legs. Close to the frame the rings shall lie, as holders for the poles to carry *the table.* You shall make the poles of acacia wood, and overlay them with gold, and *the table* shall be carried by these. And you shall make its plates and dishes for incense, and *its flagons and bowls with which to pour libations;* of pure gold you shall make them. *And you shall set the bread of the Presence on the table before my face always.*" (Exod 25:23-30)[194]

Several aspects of this foundational description are important to highlight.

First, notice that the bread of the presence is not the only item on the golden table. In addition to the "bread of the Presence" *(leḥem pānîm)* which is set before the "face" *(pāneh)* of God (Exod 25:30), there are also "flagons and bowls with which to pour libations" (Exod 25:29). This is a clear reference to sacrificial drink offerings, which consisted of wine (cf. Num 4:7; 15:5-7; 28:7).[195] The reason this is significant for our study of the Last Supper is obvious: according to the book of Exodus, when Moses institutes the perpetual offering of the bread of the presence, it is in fact a dual offering: we can rightly speak of the *bread and wine of the presence.* Unfortunately, it is not clear from this text whether these libations were meant to be poured out by the priests, as some scholars allege.[196] Far more likely is the position of Menahem Haran,

194. RSV, slightly adapted.

195. See Fabry, *"leḥem,"* 527; Menahem Haran, *Temples and Temple-Service in Ancient Israel* (Oxford: Clarendon, 1978), 216-17.

196. For discussion of theories, see Gane, "'The Bread of the Presence,'" 183-85.

who makes a strong case that the text envisages the wine being drunk by the priests, just as the bread is eaten by the priests, in a sacred banquet of bread and wine (cf. Lev 24:5-8).[197]

Second, the central feature of the golden table is obviously the *leḥem happānîm,* commonly rendered in English as the "Bread of the Presence" (RSV).[198] Less obvious is exactly what the expression means. On the one hand, some scholars translate the Hebrew phrase *leḥem happānîm* as "bread of display" or "bread of the offering."[199] From this perspective, the Hebrew expression refers to the bread being placed before God's presence — i.e., in close proximity to the Holy of Holies, where the glory cloud of the divine presence descends above the ark of the covenant.[200] The problem with this explanation is that the expression "[of] the presence" *(happānîm)* is utilized only for the golden table and the bread, and not for other items in the tabernacle such as the lamp or the altar of incense that were in equally close proximity to the Holy of Holies.[201] On the other hand, other interpreters contend that this view tells us what should be done with the cakes, but fails to translate the key expression — *pānîm* — which is the Hebrew word for "presence" or "face."[202] As John Hartley points out: "The Hebrew literally means 'bread of the face' or 'facial bread.'"[203] Roland de Vaux even describes this bread as "the bread of the face (of God)."[204] In support of this interpretation, it is critical to note that this is the way in which *pānîm* is used elsewhere in Exodus, when the text says that

197. Haran, *Temples and Temple-Service in Ancient Israel,* 216-17.

198. Other translations are "bread of the continual offering" (JB) or "showbread" (NAB). The term "showbread" or "shewbread" seems to have come over into English not as a literal translation of the Hebrew but as an Anglicized version of the German *Shaubrod,* which translates the Latin Vulgate's "bread of proposition" *(panes propositionis).* This expression has its roots in those occasions in which the bread is called "the bread of laying out" or "bread of the row" (1 Chron 9:32; 23:29; Neh 10:33; Heb 9:2). See Paul V. M. Flesher, "Bread of the Presence," in *Anchor Bible Dictionary* (6 vols.; ed. David Noel Freedman et al.; New York: Doubleday, 1992), 1:780-81.

199. E.g., Umberto Cassuto, *A Commentary on the Book of Exodus* (trans. Israel Abrahams; Jerusalem: Magnes, 1967), 340; Baruch A. Levine, *Leviticus* (JPS Torah Commentary; Philadelphia: Jewish Publication Society, 1989), 165.

200. Gane, "'The Bread of the Presence,'" 180; Flesher, "Bread of the Presence," 781.

201. Gane, "'The Bread of the Presence,'" 180 n. 6.

202. So H. De Boer, "An Aspect of Sacrifice," in *Studies in the Religion of Israel* (ed. G. W. Anderson et al.; VTSup; Leiden: Brill, 1972), 27-47 (here 32).

203. John F. Hartley, *Leviticus* (Word Biblical Commentary 4; Dallas: Word Books, 1991), 400.

204. Roland de Vaux, *Ancient Israel: Its Life and Institutions* (trans. John McHugh; repr. Grand Rapids: Eerdmans, 1997 [orig. 1961]), 422.

"the LORD used to speak to Moses face to face *(pānîm 'el pānîm)*" (Exod 33:11), or in the famous episode in which Moses asks to see the unveiled glory of God, but God refuses, saying "You shall not see my face *(pānāy)*, for man shall not see me and live" (Exod 33:20, cf. 23).[205] Such parallels strongly suggest that the bread is a visible sign of God's presence. Indeed, research has also shown that in the ancient world, cakes of bread that were offered in temples (and later, in churches), were often stamped with some symbol of the deity (cf. Jer 7:18; 44:19).[206] Hence, taken in its cultic and overall literary context, the most literal translation is "the bread of the face" — i.e., the bread that acts as a visible sign of God's invisible face, his divine presence.[207]

With this in mind, we should stress the context of the instructions regarding the bread of the presence. According to the book of Exodus, Moses' instructions to build the ark, the golden table, and the lampstand are given to him immediately after the banquet in which he and the elders of Israel not only ate and drank, but according to the text saw God:

> Then Moses and Aaron, Nadab and Abihu, and seventy of the elders of Israel went up, and *they saw the God of Israel;* and there was under his feet as it were a pavement of sapphire stone, like the very heaven for clearness. And he did not lay his hand on the chief men of the people of Israel; *they beheld God, and ate and drank.* (Exod 24:9-11)

In light of this overarching context, it seems clear that the bread of the presence/face being described in Exodus 25 is meant to function as a kind of memorial or symbol of the heavenly banquet in which Moses and the elders "beheld" the God of Israel while they "ate and drank" in Exodus 24. Lest there be any doubt about this connection between the heavenly banquet and the earthly tabernacle, we should recall that the text explicitly states at both the opening and the conclusion of the instructions that Moses is to construct the ark, the golden table, and the lampstand according to the heavenly pattern he is shown atop the mountain:

> [God said to Moses:] "And let them make me a sanctuary, that I may dwell in their midst. *According to all that I show you concerning the pattern of*

205. For discussion, see Simian Yofre, "*pānîm*," *Theological Dictionary of the Old Testament* (15 vols.; ed. G. Johannes Botterweck et al.; Grand Rapids: Eerdmans, 1974-2006), 11:589-615.

206. See George Galavaris, *Bread and the Liturgy: The Symbolism of Early Christian and Byzantine Bread Stamps* (Madison: University of Wisconsin Press, 1970), 22.

207. De Boer, "An Aspect of Sacrifice," 34.

> *the tabernacle, and all of its furniture,* so shall you make it. . . . [Proceeds to give instructions on ark, table, and lampstand.] . . . And see that you make them *after the pattern for them, which is being shown you on the mountain.*" (Exod 25:8-9, 40)

When these verses are interpreted in their immediate narrative context, it seems clear that the earthly tabernacle and all its "furniture" — the ark, the table, and the lampstand — are to constitute a visible sign of the invisible heavenly realm of God which is revealed to Moses on the mountain, so that the earthly "bread of the face" *(leḥem happānîm)* likewise functions as a visible sign of the invisible heavenly "face" *(pānîm)* of God.[208]

If this connection is correct, then the link between the bread and the presence and the blood of the covenant is significant: it is *the covenant sacrifice at the foot of the mountain* that enables Moses and the elders to ascend into God's presence and celebrate *the heavenly banquet with him at the summit of the mountain.*[209] In light of such connections, H. De Boer concludes that in the bread of the presence, it is God "himself" who acts, as he did on the mountain, "as the host who presents himself to his believers, giving divine strength, divine life."[210]

The Bread of the Presence and the "Everlasting Covenant"

These initial connections between the bread of the presence and the blood of the covenant are strengthened when we turn to the second most detailed description of the bread of the presence in the Old Testament, located in the book of Leviticus:

208. See Barber, "The Historical Jesus and Cultic Restoration Eschatology," 115-16, for scholarship that argues that the tabernacle was meant to extend the Sinai experience.

209. It is worth noting that this is precisely how the relationship between the blood of the covenant and the heavenly banquet were understood by one ancient Jewish Targum on Exodus, which describes the banquet as follows: "Then Moses and Aaron, Nadab and Abihu, as well as the seventy elders of Israel went up, and they perceived the Glory of the God of Israel and beneath the throne of His Glory was something like the work of a precious stone and in appearance like the sky for purity. Yet the leaders of the Israelites were not injured even though they perceived the Glory of the Lord; *and they rejoiced in their sacrifices which were accepted as though they were eating and drinking*" (*Targum Onqelos* on Exod 24:9-11).

210. De Boer, "An Aspect of Sacrifice," 35.

> The LORD said to Moses. . . . "And you shall take fine flour, and bake *twelve cakes of it;* two tenths of an ephah shall be in each cake. And you shall set them in *two rows, six in a row,* upon the table of pure gold. And you shall put pure frankincense with each row, *that it may go with the bread as a memorial* to be offered by fire to the LORD. Every sabbath day Aaron shall set it in order before the LORD perpetually *on behalf of the people of Israel as an everlasting covenant.* And it shall be for Aaron and his sons, and they shall eat it in a holy place, since it is for him a most holy portion out of the offerings of fire to the LORD, a perpetual due." (Lev 24:5-9)

Again, there are several features of this description that merit highlighting.

First and foremost, the bread of the presence is explicitly described as a sign of the everlasting covenant between God and Israel.[211] This is quite significant. Indeed, as Roy Gane points out, "the 'bread of the presence' is the only offering designated as a *berit ʿolam,* 'an eternal covenant.' . . . Thus, it uniquely symbolizes the relationship itself between YHWH and his people. . . ."[212] One reason this unique terminology is important is that, as we saw above, when the prophets speak of the eschatological covenant, they frequently refer to it as an "everlasting covenant" *(bᵉrîth ʿôlām)* between God and his people, terminology that hearkens back to the liturgical offering of the bread of the presence (Isa 55:3; Ezek 15:59-63; Bar 2:34-35).[213]

Second, there are twelve cakes of bread used in the offering of the bread of the presence, set out in two rows of six. This symbolism is clearly evocative of the twelve tribes of Israel, who entered into the covenant relationship with God at the foot of Mount Sinai by means of sacrifice (cf. Exod 24:8-11). Indeed, not only is the number twelve frequently associated with the tribes of Israel (Exod 24:4; 28:21; Josh 4:2, etc.), but even the division of the twelve into two groups of six finds parallels in other symbols of the twelve tribes, such as the two sets of six stones on the breastplate of the high priest (Exod 28:9-12) and the two sets of six tribes on the mountains (Deut 27:11-13).[214]

Third, the bread of the presence is not just a symbol, it is also a sacrifice. It is important to point this out, since readers sometimes forget that in the Old Testament, there were two types of sacrifice: (1) "bloody" sacrifice, involving the slaughter of bulls, goats, sheep, and turtledoves, and (2) "unbloody" sacri-

211. MT *bᵉrîth ʿôlām;* LXX *diathēkēn aiōnion.*

212. Gane, " 'Bread of the Presence,' " 192.

213. Indeed, even the language of being "set in order" is used for covenant-making. See Barber, "The Historical Jesus and Cultic Restoration Eschatology," 142, citing 2 Sam 23:5.

214. Gane, " 'Bread of the Presence,' " 193.

fice, which often involved grains or bread and wine.[215] This sacrificial identity is indicated above all by the fact that the bread is presented by the priest to God "on behalf of the people of Israel" (Lev 24:8), as well as by the "incense" that is to be kept alongside the bread on the golden table "perpetually" (Lev 24:7). In the Old Testament, such incense always accompanies sacrifices, as a symbol of the offering "ascending" into heaven.[216] Along these lines, some scholars have noted that the books of Malachi and Ezekiel — both interested in matters cultic — explicitly identify the golden table of the bread of the presence as an "altar" (Ezek 41:21-22; Mal 1:7).[217] In other words, the bread and wine of the presence was both a meal (eaten by the priests) and a sacrifice (offered on behalf of the twelve tribes).

Fourth, this incense, which accompanies the offering of the bread of the presence, is described as a sacrificial "remembrance" or "memorial" offering to God.[218] This terminology is used with other unbloody sacrifices of grain (or "cereal offerings") to signify the part of the offering given to God (cf. Lev 2:2, 9, 16; 6:8).[219] Given the connections between the bread of the presence and the events of Mount Sinai, it seems clear that the bread of the presence itself is a "remembrance" of the covenant made by God with the twelve tribes of Israel, one that both recalls and renews the covenant relationship established at Mount Sinai.

Fifth, in support of this connection with the covenant, it is important to stress that the bread of the presence is not depicted as just any kind of sacrifice, but as the premier sacrifice of the sabbath. Indeed, Leviticus is quite clear that the bread of the presence is to be offered "every Sabbath day" by Aaron the high priest and his descendants (Lev 24:8). This link is important to stress, because it reveals an often-overlooked cultic activity that characterizes the biblical sabbath. Not only is the sabbath a day of rest, it is distinctively characterized by the weekly offering of the unbloody sacrifice of the bread and wine of the presence, as a "remembrance" of the "everlasting covenant" between God and the twelve tribes of Israel. To be sure, after the destruction of the Temple in A.D. 70, this connection between the bread, the covenant, and the sabbath sacrifice came to a halt; nevertheless, during the times of a functioning cult, the Pentateuch explicitly envisions the bread of the presence as *the* distinctive

215. See George Buchanan Gray, *Sacrifice in the Old Testament: Its Theory and Practice* (repr.; New York: Ktav, 1971 [orig. 1925]), 298-402.

216. De Vaux, *Ancient Israel*, 430-32.

217. Gane, "'Bread of the Presence,'" 182.

218. MT *'azkārāh;* LXX *anamnēsis.*

219. Gane, "'Bread of the Presence,'" 196.

sacrifice of the most important day of the week, the sabbath. This is probably why, apart from this description of the bread of the presence, the only other time "everlasting covenant" is used with reference to the wilderness period is with reference to the celebration of the sabbath (Exod 31:16).[220]

The connections between these aspects of the bread of the presence and Jesus' actions at the Last Supper constitute a series of striking parallels. Just as the bread of the presence was connected to the twelve tribes of Israel, so Jesus celebrates the Last Supper with the twelve disciples, symbolizing the nucleus of eschatological Israel. And just as the bread of the presence was offered with wine as a sign of the "everlasting covenant," so too Jesus couples his offering of bread with the wine that he ties to the establishment of a new "covenant," spoken of by the prophets. And just as the bread of the presence was an unbloody sacrifice offered as a "remembrance" of the covenant at Sinai, so too Jesus commands the twelve to offer this bread — which he identifies as his body — as a "remembrance" of the sacrifice of his own flesh, which will be given in order to establish the new covenant. In light of such connections, Michael Barber argues:

> [S]ince Jesus uses the term [*anamnēsis*] in connection with bread, wine, and covenant imagery, *anamnēsis* seems to evoke the offering of the bread of the presence, which was also directly linked to the motif of the covenant (cf. Lev 24:8), drink-offerings, and, of course, the term *anamnēsis*. . . . Jesus, in fulfilling hopes for a *new* covenant, also establishes a *new bread of the presence,* a symbol of the eschatological covenant.[221]

When taken together, these various lines of evidence converge and lead to the conclusion that Jesus' words over the bread and wine at the Last Supper are not just evocative of the covenant sacrifices at Mount Sinai, but also of the bread (and wine) of the presence that is instituted by Moses in the Pentateuch as the symbolic and sacrificial memorial of the covenant sacrifices and a kind of earthly participation in the heavenly theophanic banquet.

With this analysis in mind, we can now raise the question of historicity. Are there good reasons to consider historically plausible the conclusion that Jesus, in fulfilling the ancient Jewish hope for a new covenant, acted as a new Moses at the Last Supper and instituted new bread and wine of the presence as a memorial of the new covenant?

220. Gane, "'Bread of the Presence,'" 199.

221. Barber, "The Historical Jesus and Cultic Restoration Eschatology," 598, 634, citing Douglas, "The Eucharist," 209-24.

Arguments against Historical Plausibility

Unfortunately, because Jesus research has almost completely ignored the exploration of any connections between the bread of the Last Supper and the Mosaic bread of the presence, there are a dearth of actual arguments against the historicity of this aspect of Jesus' words and deeds. Indeed, to my knowledge, the connections between the Last Supper and the bread of the presence are ignored by the vast majority of works on the historical Jesus or on the Last Supper.[222] Although one can only guess as to why this is the case, it may reflect the powerful case that Jonathan Klawans has made in showing that there has been a rather marked tendency in modern scholarship on Jesus and Judaism to neglect detailed study of the ancient Jewish cult, in which the bread of the presence figured quite prominently.[223]

Whatever the reason for the neglect of the topic, there are nevertheless at least three possible arguments against historicity that are worth formulating here.

First, one could mount an argument from incompatibility with Jesus' Jewish context. In all of the biblical descriptions of the bread of the presence, the texts are quite clear that it could only be eaten by ordained priests. The Pentateuch explicitly states that the bread is only "for Aaron and his sons" — i.e., the priests (Lev 24:9). But, as is well known, the New Testament is quite explicit that Jesus himself was "descended from Judah" (Heb 7:11), and hence not a Levitical priest.[224] Nor is there any reason to believe that the twelve disciples were all from priestly families, though there may have been exceptions

222. E.g., the bread of the presence and its connections with wine, "remembrance," and the "covenant," receive no discussion in Allison, *Constructing Jesus;* Keener, *The Historical Jesus of the Gospels;* McKnight, *Jesus and His Death;* Dunn, *Jesus Remembered;* Lüdemann, *Jesus After 2000 Years;* Gnilka, *Jesus of Nazareth;* Becker, *Jesus of Nazareth;* Theissen and Merz, *The Historical Jesus;* Wright, *Jesus and the Victory of God;* Beasley-Murray, *Jesus and the Kingdom of God;* Meyer, *The Aims of Jesus;* Bornkamm, *Jesus of Nazareth;* Taylor, *Jesus and His Sacrifice;* Higgins, *The Lord's Supper in the New Testament.* Although Joachim Jeremias discusses the bread of the presence, he only does so in the context of a linguistic argument that *artos* can refer to unleavened bread without qualification; he never draws any connections between the bread, the wine, the covenant, and the eucharistic words of Jesus. Jeremias, *The Eucharistic Words of Jesus,* 62-63.

223. See Jonathan Klawans, *Purity, Sacrifice, and Temple: Symbolism and Supersessionism in the Study of Ancient Judaism* (Oxford: Oxford University Press, 2006), 3-10; Crispin H. T. Fletcher-Louis, "Jesus as the High-Priestly Messiah: Part 1," *JSHJ* 4, no. 2 (2006): 155-75 (here 156-58).

224. See Meier, *A Marginal Jew,* 1:345-94.

to this in the figures of James, John, whose family was apparently familiar with the high priest, and Matthew (if he is identified with Levi).[225] In light of Jesus' identity as a Jewish layman, a case could be made that he could not have deliberately identified the bread and wine of the Last Supper as new bread of the presence, since that bread could only be eaten by Levitical priests.

Second, an argument can also be made based on a lack of coherence with other evidence about Jesus. As we will see below in chapter 5, there are good reasons to conclude that Jesus associated the unleavened bread and the wine of the Last Supper with the Jewish Passover meal. One could argue that we must choose between Passover background or the Mosaic bread of the presence; we cannot have both. From this point of view, either Jesus was instituting a new Passover, or he was instituting the new bread of the presence; it is historically implausible to suggest that he deliberately identified the bread and wine of the Last Supper with both.

Third and finally, one could argue against the historicity of Jesus instituting the new bread of the presence from a lack of continuity with the early church. Significantly, there is no early Christian writing from the first century that we possess — whether in the New Testament or not (e.g., *1 Clement*, the *Didache*) — that ever explicitly identifies the Christian eucharist as the new bread of the presence. From this point of view, the conclusion that Jesus identified the Last Supper with the Mosaic bread and wine of the presence cannot be squared with a lack of visible effects in the early church in this regard. It seems to have left little or no mark on the early church's understanding of the eucharist.

On the other hand, there are several important arguments in favor of the historicity of Jesus' instituting new bread and wine of the presence.

Context: The Bread in the Scrolls, the Therapeutae, and Moses the Priest

For one thing, Jesus' act of instituting new bread and wine of the presence can be situated in his ancient Jewish context, in multiple ways. For the most part, such evidence has not been brought to bear on this question in Jesus research, and so needs to be sketched here in some detail.[226]

First and foremost, Jesus' words and deeds at the Last Supper with reference to the bread and wine are deeply rooted in Jewish Scripture. Although we

225. John 18:15; Matt 9:9; cf. Mark 2:14; Luke 5:27.

226. The exception is Barber, "The Historical Jesus and Cultic Restoration Eschatology," 141-43.

covered these connections above, it may be helpful here to simply chart them out in order to see just how many parallels there are between the Last Supper and the bread and wine of the presence in the Jewish Torah:

Bread of the Presence	**The Last Supper**
1. Twelve Cakes for Twelve Tribes	1. Twelve Disciples for Twelve Tribes
2. Bread and Wine of God's Presence	2. Bread and Wine of Jesus' Presence
3. Sign of "Everlasting Covenant" *(diathēkē)*	3. Sign of New "Covenant" *(diathēkē)*
4. As a "Remembrance" *(anamnēsis)*	4. Do this in "Remembrance" *(anamnēsis)*
5. Offered by High Priest and eaten by Priests (Exodus 24–25, Leviticus 24)	5. Offered by Jesus and eaten by the Twelve (Matthew 26; Mark 14; Luke 22; 1 Corinthians 11)

When such parallels in Jewish Scripture are taken seriously — along with the fact that the bread of the presence was the most holy of all sacrifices, with the possible exception of the Day of Atonement[227] — then it seems that Jesus' actions are so deeply rooted in the Jewish Torah that one could argue that he could not conceivably have associated bread and wine at a sacred meal with a covenant sacrifice and a cultic "remembrance" without intending any connection with the covenant remembrance sacrifice *par excellence:* the bread and wine of the presence.

Second, Jesus' act of identifying the Last Supper with the biblical bread of the presence finds a striking parallel in the Dead Sea Scrolls, in which the future food of the eschatological feast is none other than the bread of the presence, which will be eaten by the priests in the new Temple:[228]

> *They shall arrange the chiefs of the priests behind the High Priest and of his second (in rank), twelve chiefs to serve in perpetuity before God. . . .* And

227. Flesher, "Bread of the Presence," 780.

228. Matthew Black, *The Scrolls and Christian Origins: Studies in the Jewish Background of the New Testament* (New York: Charles Scribner's Sons, 1961), 111.

> the chiefs of their divisions shall each serve in his place. The chiefs of the tribes, and after them the fathers of the congregation, shall take their positions in the gates of the sanctuary in perpetuity. . . . These shall take their positions at the holocausts and the sacrifices, in order to prepare the pleasant incense for God's approval, *to atone for all his congregation and to satisfy themselves in perpetuity before him at the table of glory.* (*1QWar Scroll* [1QM] 2:1-2, 4-6)
>
> *[T]hey [shall] go into the temple [. . .] eight sheahs of finest fl[our . . .] and they shall lift the bread [. . .] first upon [the] al[tar . . . two] rows upon [the] ta[ble . . .] two rows of loa[ves . . . every seventh day before God, a memorial offering . . .] the bread.* And they shall take [the] bread [outside the temple, to the right of] its west side, and it shall be shar[ed . . .]. . . . And] while I was [watching] one of the two loaves was given [to the high] p[riest . . .] with him. And the other was [g]iven to the deputy who was standing close to him [. . .] *Blank* And while I was watching [one of the two breads] was given to a[ll the priests]. . . . (*2QNew Jerusalem ar* [2QNJ ar] frag. 4:1-10, 14-16)[229]

Although the second text is obviously fragmentary, its basic contents can be reconstructed from multiple scrolls that appear to describe the eschatological Jerusalem, both its architecture and its cultic services.[230] For our purposes here, the main point is simple: if the authors of the Dead Sea Scrolls could associate the bread of the presence with the banquet of the age to come, there is no reason to deny that Jesus could have done the same thing at the Last Supper. Indeed, as Matthew Black has argued, these texts suggest that "the sacred meal of bread and/or wine of the Qumran priestly sect was not only an anticipation of the messianic banquet, but also a foretaste of the full Temple rite when that had been fully restored in the New Jerusalem" — a rite that was not just the sacrificial consumption of just any food, but specifically of the bread (and wine) of the presence.[231]

Third, and perhaps even more important, Jesus' act of recapitulating the banquet of Moses on Mount Sinai finds a striking parallel in the first-century

229. Cf. also *11QNew Jerusalem* [11QNJ ar] frag. 20, for the parallel text.

230. See Florentino García Martínez, "New Jerusalem," in *Encyclopedia of the Dead Sea Scrolls* (2 vols.; ed. Lawrence H. Schiffman and James C. VanderKam; Oxford: Oxford University Press, 2000), 606-10.

231. Black, *The Scrolls and Christian Origins,* 111; cf. *1QRule of the Community* 6:2-8; *1QRule of the Congregation*[a] 2:11-22.

Jewish group known as the Therapeutae, who celebrated a sacred meal of bread and wine directly modeled on the bread of the presence in the Tabernacle of Moses.[232] Indeed, according to Philo of Alexandria the Therapeutae directly based their banquet on the actions of Moses and Miriam in the exodus.[233] Although Philo's description of the banquet is somewhat lengthy, because it is so little discussed with reference to the Last Supper, it is well worth quoting in full:

> When everyone has finished his hymn *the young men bring in the tables mentioned a little above on which is set the most holy food of leavened bread seasoned with salt mixed with hyssop, out of reverence for the holy table enshrined in the holy vestibule of the Temple on which lie loaves and salt without condiments, the loaves unleavened and the salt unmixed.* For it was meet that the simplest and purest food should be assigned to the highest caste, namely the priests, as a reward for their ministry, and that the others while aspiring to similar privileges should abstain from seeking the same as they and allow their superiors to retain their precedence. After the supper they hold the sacred vigil which is conducted in the following way. They rise up all together and standing in the middle of the refectory form themselves first into two choirs, one of men and one of women, the leader and chief chosen. . . . Then when each choir has separately done its own part in the feast, having drunk as in the Bacchic rites of the strong wine of God's love, *they mix and both together become a single choir, a copy of the choir set up of old beside the Red Sea in honor of the wonders there wrought.* For at the command of God the sea became a source of salvation to one party and of perdition to the other. . . . This wonderful sight and experience, an act transcending word and thought and hope, so filled with ecstasy both men and women that forming a single choir they sang hymns of thanksgiving to God their Savior, *the men led by the prophet Moses and the women by the prophetess Miriam.* It is on this model above all that the choir of the Therapeutae of either sex . . . create an harmonious content. (Philo, *On the Contemplative Life* 81-83, 85-88)[234]

232. See Patsch, *Abendmahl und historischer Jesus,* 26-28. For a full discussion of the Therapeutae, see Joan Taylor, *Jewish Women Philosophers of First-Century Alexandria: Philo's "Therapeutae" Reconsidered* (Oxford: Oxford University Press, 2004).

233. Barber, "The Historical Jesus and Cultic Restoration Eschatology," 634.

234. Unless otherwise noted, all translations of Philo contained herein are from Philo, *Works* (10 vols. with supp.; trans. and ed. by F. H. Colson, G. H. Whitaker, and R. Marcus; Loeb Classical Library; Cambridge: Harvard University Press, 1929-1953).

This account presents remarkable similarities with Jesus' actions in the Upper Room. In the banquet of the Therapeutae we find a group of Jews, outside the Temple, celebrating a meal of bread and wine that is deliberately modeled on the bread of the presence. Significantly, this banquet hearkens back to the deliverance wrought by God for Israel in the exodus from Egypt. Indeed, even though the crossing of the Red Sea takes place in Exodus 15, and the institution of the bread of the presence takes place in Exodus 24, both Philo and the Therapeutae apparently saw no problem connecting the bread of the presence with earlier events in the exodus. Finally, it is important to emphasize that the male and female leaders of the banquet are deliberately modeling their actions on Moses and Miriam. In other words, the male leader acts like a new Moses, while the female acts like a new Miriam.[235] This is very much like what I am contending that Jesus does at the Last Supper: by identifying the bread and wine of the meal with his own presence and the blood of the covenant, and by speaking of a new act of "remembrance" by which they would be commemorated, Jesus too is acting like a new Moses by instituting a new bread of the presence. The primary difference between Jesus and the Therapeutae — minus the prominent absence of any women at the Last Supper — is that for the Therapeutae, there seems to be a deliberate attempt to distinguish their bread and the true bread of the presence, which is located in the sanctuary.[236] By contrast, all of Jesus' actions suggest that in the Last Supper, he is giving the disciples new bread and wine of the presence, as a perpetual sign of the new and eschatological everlasting covenant.

Fourth — against the argument given above that the Last Supper must be linked with either the Passover or the bread of the presence, but not both — Jesus' apparent fusing of the Passover sacrifice with the covenant sacrifice of Sinai and the bread of the presence is also compatible with ancient Jewish tendencies to synthesize distinct events in the exodus.[237] For one thing, according to the Pentateuch, the bread of the presence was instituted by Moses on Mount Sinai, immediately after the offering of the blood of the covenant (Exodus 24–25). In other words, if Jesus saw himself as the prophet like Moses and saw the Last Supper as recapitulating the actions of Moses at Mount Sinai, then it is but a small step to the idea that the bread and wine that he was offering as a sign of the new

235. It may be also worth noting that in Philo's reference to drinking the "pure wine of the love God" we may have a reference to the fact that the bread of the presence was not only considered a sign of the covenant, but of the "love" of God for his people in making the covenant (cf. Ezekiel 16).

236. Cf. Patsch, *Abendmahl und historischer Jesus*, 28.

237. Barber, "The Historical Jesus and Cultic Restoration Eschatology," 639.

"covenant" was functioning as a new form of the old covenant bread and wine of the presence (Lev 24:1-8). Moreover, if Jesus did in fact draw a connection between the unleavened bread of Passover and the unleavened bread of the presence, he would not have been the only first-century Jew to do so. Significantly, in Philo of Alexandria's lengthy discussion of the feast of Unleavened Bread, he too draws a connection between the *matzoh* and the bread of the presence:

> The bread is unleavened . . . because our forefathers, when under divine guidance they were starting on their migration [in the exodus] were so intensely hurried that they brought the lumps of dough unleavened. . . . Another suggestion made by the interpreters of the holy scriptures is that food, when unleavened is a gift of nature, when leavened is a work of art. . . . Since then, as I have laid down, *the spring-time feast [of Unleavened Bread] is a reminder of the creation of the world, and its earliest inhabitants, children of earth in the first or second generation, must have used the gifts of the universe in their unperverted state* . . . he ordained for use on this occasion the food most fully in accordance with the season. . . . *These statements are especially guaranteed by the setting out of the twelve loaves corresponding in number to the tribes, on the holy table. These are all unleavened,* the clearest possible example of a food free from admixture. . . . (Philo, *Special Laws* 2.158-61)[238]

Note here that for Philo, the primary link between the Passover bread and the bread of the presence is that both were unleavened, which distinguished them from ordinary bread. Although the unleavened character of the bread of the presence is not clear in Scripture, leaven was forbidden to be offered on the altar (Lev 2:11), and ancient Jewish sources unanimously identify it as such (e.g., Josephus, *Antiquities* 3.255; Babylonian Talmud, *Menaḥot* 5a).[239] Note also that Philo seems to suggest that bread without leaven was a kind of primordial or protological food, going back to the time of Adam. For now, the main point is that if Philo could link the Passover and the bread of the presence to one another, there is no reason to doubt that Jesus could have done the same — especially if he too saw the bread of the Last Supper as a foretaste of the kingdom of God, in which the protological conditions of creation would be somehow reestablished.[240]

238. Trans. Colson, LCL (slightly adapted).
239. Hirsch, "Shewbread," 312.
240. See below, chapter 6.

Fifth and finally, although Jesus' act of establishing new bread and wine of the presence at first glance seems to be at odds with the fact that he was not a Levitical priest, it is actually quite compatible with ancient Jewish traditions about Moses in which he is not just identified as a prophet, but as a kind of super-Levitical priest. For example, in Jewish Scripture, Moses performs a whole host of cultic actions that are clearly if not exclusively priestly in character. Above all, there stands the fact that it is Moses who institutes the Aaronic priesthood by ordaining Aaron and his sons (Exod 29:1-9; Lev 8:1-36). In this case, Moses is clearly above even the highest high priest and his sons. Long before their ordination, Moses acts as a priest by offering blood sacrifice (Exod 24:1-11; Lev 8:22-30), interceding for the people (Exod 32:11-14; Num 14:13-25), building the tabernacle (Exod 40:16-33), and entering the sanctuary to speak with God (Exod 33:7-11), all of which are clearly priestly in character.[241] Most explicit of all, Moses is actually referred to as a "priest" *(kōhēn)* in the book of Psalms, arguably one of the best-known books in Jewish Scripture at the time of Jesus:

> Extol the LORD our God; worship at his footstool! Holy is he!
> *Moses and Aaron were among his priests,*
> Samuel also was among those who called on his name.
> They cried to the LORD, and he answered them. (Ps 99:5-6)

In addition to this biblical evidence that Moses was "among his priests" *(bekoh^{a}nāyw)* (Ps 99:6), in Jewish literature in the Second Temple period, Moses' priestly identity becomes even more explicit:

> You [Lord] became angry with them [our fathers] as to destroy them; but you took pity on them in your love for them, and on account of your covenant *(brth)* — for Moses atoned *(kphr)* for their sin — and so that they would know your great power and your abundant kindness for everlasting generations. (*4QWords of the Luminaries*[a] [4Q504] frag. 2, col. 2:8-11)

> Moses will be found to have displayed . . . combined in his single person not only these two faculties — the kingly and the philosophical — but also three others, one of which is concerned with law-giving, the second with the office of a high priest *(archierōsynēn),* and the last with prophecy. . . . For Moses, through God's providence, became king and lawgiver

241. Cf. Num 3:1-10; 18:1-7, in which any non-priest who acts as one shall be "put to death."

> and high priest *(archiereus)* and prophet. . . . [S]uch as he needs the chief priesthood *(tēs prōtēs hierōsynēs),* so that, fortified with perfect rites and perfect knowledge of the service of God, he may ask that he and those whom he rules may receive deliverance from evil *(apotropēn men kakōn)* and participation in good from the gracious One who assents to prayers. (Philo, *Life of Moses* 2.2, 3, 5)[242]

Notice here that in the Dead Sea Scroll, Moses' priestly identity is only implicit, but can be deduced from the fact that he acts as an intercessor on behalf of Israel.[243] By contrast, Philo not only explicitly identifies Moses as a "high priest," he spends pages and pages discussing how Moses exercised "the office of priesthood" (see *Life of Moses* 2.66-186). Moreover, Philo even identifies Moses' reception of instructions from God on "the building of the temple and all its furniture" as "the most important matters which relate to his priesthood" (*Life of Moses* 2.71). It is thus no coincidence that Philo's description of the bread of the presence — which he refers to as the "table on which the bread and salt are laid" (*Life of Moses* 2.104) — takes place in the context of discussing Moses *as a priest.*[244] Perhaps most significant of all, notice that both the Dead Sea Scroll and Philo describe Moses as offering an atoning sacrifice for the people of Israel. In the Old Testament, the act of atoning for sin is a distinctively priestly act (see Lev 4:20, 26, 31, 35).[245] In the Scroll, this act of "atonement" *(kāphar)* is explicitly tied to the "covenant" *(b^erîth)* made by God with Israel, a clear reference to the "blood of the covenant" offered by Moses at Mount Sinai (Exod 24:8).[246]

Coherence: Moses, the Circles of Disciples, and the New Priesthood

The suggestion that Jesus is establishing a new bread and wine sacrifice modeled on the bread of the presence also coheres with other words and deeds of Jesus, in several ways.

242. Trans. F. H. Colson, LCL (slightly adapted).

243. Falk, "Moses," in Collins and Harlow, eds., *The Eerdmans Dictionary of Early Judaism,* 968.

244. For further discussion, see Louis H. Feldman, *Philo's Portrayal of Moses in the Context of Ancient Judaism* (Notre Dame: University of Notre Dame Press, 2007).

245. Cf. de Vaux, *Ancient Israel,* 418-21.

246. For further discussion, see J. Bowley, "Moses in the Dead Sea Scrolls: Living in the Shadow of God's Anointed," in *The Bible at Qumran: Text, Shape, and Interpretation* (ed. P. Flint; Grand Rapids: Eerdmans, 2011), 159-81.

First and foremost, it should be clear by now that idea of Jesus instituting a new sacrificial bread of the presence coheres perfectly with the broad impression given by the Gospels that Jesus spoke and acted on occasion as if he were the long-awaited prophet like Moses (e.g., Matt 14:13-21; Mark 6:30-44; Luke 9:10-17; John 6:1-15; Matt 12:39-42; Luke 11:29-32; Mark 8:12, etc.). Indeed, if the overall thesis of this chapter is correct, and Jesus identified himself as the new Moses, then the fact that he was not a Levitical priest does not mean that he did not see himself as a priestly figure at all. To the contrary, if Jesus saw himself in Mosaic terms, his act of recapitulating the priestly actions of Moses at Mount Sinai with the twelve disciples at the Last Supper with reference to the "bread" of the "covenant" (Matt 26:20, 26-29; Mark 14:17, 22-25; Luke 22:14, 19-20; 1 Cor 11:24-25) would square quite nicely with one another.

Second, this Mosaic picture becomes even clearer when we recognize that the act of instituting new bread and wine of the presence at the Last Supper also coheres perfectly with the often-overlooked evidence that *Jesus seems to have arranged the circles of his disciples according to the priestly hierarchy of Moses and the Israelites at Mount Sinai.* I have argued this at length elsewhere; for now, I simply summarize some main points.[247] Although it is widely recognized that Jesus gathered around himself various followers in different degrees of relation to him, the symbolic significance of these various circles has often gone unnoticed:

1. *Peter, the Chief Disciple:* Directly under Jesus himself stands one disciple: Simon Peter, whom the four Gospels repeatedly depict as both spokesman and chief of the apostles (see Matt 10:2; 16:17-19; Mark 1:36; 3:16; 16:7; Luke 6:14; 9:32; 12:41; 22:31-32; John 1:42; 6:66-69).[248]
2. *The Circle of the Three:* In addition to Peter, the Gospels also depict an intimate circle of three disciples: Peter, James, and John. Among all Jesus' followers, these three figures are the only ones who are explicitly described as being renamed by Jesus, and as being selected to accompany him during significant moments (e.g., Mark 3:16-17; 9:2-8; 14:32-42).
3. *The Circle of the Twelve:* After these three, there stands the wider circle of the twelve: those who are expressly called and commissioned by Jesus to cooperate in the work of the kingdom (e.g., Matt 10:1-2; 19:28; Mark 3:13-15; Luke 9:1; 22:30; John 6:67).

247. Pitre, "Jesus, the New Temple, and the New Priesthood," 78-82.

248. E.g., Meier, *A Marginal Jew,* 3:222.

4. *The Circle of the Seventy:* The fourth and final circle of Jesus' disciples that is delimited by a specific number is the circle of the seventy disciples: a wider group who are chosen and sent out by Jesus on a mission that parallels that of the Twelve (Luke 10:1-20).[249]

Beyond these four circles — the one, the three, the twelve, and the seventy — the wider body of Jesus' disciples is not linked with specific numbers. They consist primarily of other disciples, like the women followers, and the unidentified "crowds," with varying degrees of commitment.[250]

With this numerical organization of Jesus' disciples in mind, compare now the description of the priestly hierarchy of Moses and the elders of Israel, during the covenant-making ceremony of Mount Sinai:

> And [the LORD] said to Moses, "Come up to the LORD, *you and Aaron, Nadab, and Abihu,* and *seventy of the elders of Israel,* and worship afar off. Moses alone shall come near to the LORD; but the others shall not come near, and the people shall not come up with him. . . . And he [Moses] rose early in the morning, and built *an altar* at the foot of the mountain, and *twelve pillars, according to the twelve tribes of Israel.* And he sent young men of the sons of Israel, who offered burnt offerings and sacrificed peace offerings of oxen to the LORD. . . . And Moses took the blood and threw it on the people, and said, "Behold, the blood of the covenant which the LORD has made with you in accordance with all these words." Then Moses and Aaron, Nadab, and Abihu, and seventy of the elders of Israel went up, and they saw the God of Israel; and there was under his feet as it were a pavement of sapphire stone, like the very heaven for clearness. And he did not lay his hand on the chief men of the people of Israel; they beheld God, and ate and drank. (Exod 24:1-11)

249. The number seventy evokes seventy priestly elders of Exod 24:1-11 and Num 11:16-17. The number seventy-two appears to have its origin with the addition of the two elders — Eldad and Medad — who are anointed with the spirit outside the Tabernacle, in the camp (Num 11:26-30). In either case, the number evokes the same body of priestly elders gathered by Moses in the Pentateuch; indeed, one could make a good case that the textual discrepancies in Luke are evidence that the earliest scribes recognized the Old Testament background of Jesus' actions and sought to emend the Gospel manuscripts accordingly. On the question of the textual problem of the "seventy" versus "seventy-two," see Fitzmyer, *The Gospel according to Luke,* 2:845-46; Darrel L. Bock, *Luke* (2 vols.; BECNT; Grand Rapids: Baker, 1994, 1996), 2:1014-16, following Bruce M. Metzger, "Seventy or Seventy-Two Disciples?" *NTS* 5 (1958-59): 299-306.

250. For discussion, see Meier, *A Marginal Jew,* 3:19-124.

To my knowledge, these numerical parallels continue to go undetected by scholarship on Jesus.[251] Yet they are extremely suggestive. Given all of the data we have examined so far regarding the Mosaic identity of Jesus, these parallels strongly suggest that Jesus is deliberately modeling the various circles of his disciples on the priestly hierarchy of Mount Sinai. Peter's priority mirrors that of Aaron, the High Priest.[252] The intimate circle of Peter, James, and John mirrors the threefold circle of Aaron, Nadab, and Abihu (Aaron's high priestly sons).[253] The Twelve disciples parallel the twelve pillars at the foot of the mountain, which appear to have been manned by "young men" "of Israel" — arguably from each of the twelve tribes. And the Seventy disciples provide a direct parallel to the seventy "elders" of Israel. Above all these circles stands Jesus, who — by not counting himself as one of the seventy, the twelve, or even the three — takes upon himself the only role left: that of Moses. In summary fashion:

Moses and Priestly Hierarchy	**Jesus and His Disciples**
Moses	Jesus
The 1: the High Priest, Aaron	The 1: Peter, chief of the Apostles
The 3: Aaron, Nadab, Abihu	The 3: Peter, James, and John
The 12: Twelve Pillars/"Young Men" of the Twelve Tribes	The 12: Twelve Apostles of the Twelve Tribes
The 70: Priestly Elders of Israel	The 70: Appointed and Sent Out

Now, if Jesus did indeed see himself as a new Moses who was establishing a new covenant, then it is eminently plausible that he, like Moses before him, not only offered new blood of the covenant at the Last Supper, but also instituted a new memorial of the covenant: the new bread of the presence.

Third, Jesus' act of instituting new bread and wine of the presence also coheres remarkably well with the sole instance in the Gospels when he speaks explicitly about the bread of the presence with reference to his disciples' act of plucking and eating grain on the Sabbath. Although much could be said about

251. Cf. Meier, *A Marginal Jew,* 3.40-252.

252. See further Michael Barber, "Jesus as the Davidic Temple Builder and Peter's Priestly Role in Matthew 16:16-19," *JBL* 132 (2013): 933-51.

253. It is worth noting that these three are the only ones who accompany Jesus to the top of the mountain in the accounts of the transfiguration (Matt 17:1; Mark 9:2; Luke 9:28).

this episode in the Gospels,[254] for our purposes here, what matters most is the testimony that Jesus draws a parallel between the prerogative of the Jewish priests to eat the bread of the presence in the Temple and the prerogative of his disciples to pluck and eat grain on the Sabbath:

> At that time Jesus went through the grainfields on the Sabbath; his disciples were hungry, and they began to pluck heads of grain and to eat. But when the Pharisees saw it, they said to him, "Look, your disciples are doing what is not lawful to do on the Sabbath." He said to them, *"Have you not read what David did, when he was hungry, and those who were with him: how he entered the house of God and ate the Bread of the Presence, which it was not lawful for him to eat nor for those who were with him, but only for the priests?* Or have you not read in the law how on the Sabbath the priests in the Temple profane the Sabbath, and are guiltless? I tell you, something greater than the Temple is here. And if you had known what this means, "I desire mercy, and not sacrifice" [Hos 6:6], you would not have condemned the guiltless. For the Son of Man is lord of the Sabbath." (Matt 12:1-8)[255]

> One Sabbath he was going through the grainfields; and as they made their way his disciples began to pluck heads of grain. And the Pharisees said to him, "Look, why are they doing what is not lawful on the Sabbath?" And he said to them, *"Have you never read what David did, when he was in need and was hungry, he and those who were with him: how he entered the house of God, when Abiathar was high priest, and at the Bread of the Presence, which it was not lawful for any but the priests to eat, and also gave it to those who were with him?"* And he said to them, "The Sabbath was made for man, not man for the Sabbath; so the Son of Man is lord even of the Sabbath." (Mark 2:23-27)

254. See, e.g., Becker, *Jesus of Nazareth*, 298-99; Joachim Gnilka, *Jesus of Nazareth: Message and History* (trans. Siegfried S. Schatzmann; Peabody: Hendrickson, 1997), 217-18; Wright, *Jesus and the Victory of God*, 393-94; E. P. Sanders, *Jewish Law from Jesus to the Mishnah: Five Studies* (London: SCM; Philadelphia: Trinity Press International, 1990), 12-13, 19-21; Davies and Allison, *Saint Matthew*, 2:304-16, 329-31 (with bibliography); Witherington, *The Christology of Jesus*, 66-71; P. M. Casey, "Culture and Historicity: The Plucking of the Grain (Mark 2.23-8)," *NTS* 34 (1988): 1-23; Jeremias, *New Testament Theology*, 278-79; T. W. Manson, *The Sayings of Jesus* (London: SCM, 1949), 187-88.

255. RSV, slightly altered.

> On a Sabbath, while he was going through the grainfields, his disciples plucked and ate some heads of grain, rubbing them in their hands. But some of the Pharisees said, "Why are you doing what is not lawful to do on the Sabbath?" And Jesus answered, *"Have you not read what David did when he was hungry, he and those who were with him: how he entered the house of God, and took and ate the Bread of the Presence, which it was not lawful for any but the priests to eat, and also gave it to those with him?"* And he said to them, "The Son of Man is lord of the Sabbath." (Luke 6:1-5)

As Crispin Fletcher-Louis has argued, this evidence from the Gospels strongly supports the conclusion that Jesus saw himself as a priestly messiah.[256] I agree, but I would add (as I have argued elsewhere) that in this account, it is significant that Jesus explicitly links the priestly identity of himself and his disciples with the sacrificial bread of the presence (1 Sam 21:6).[257] If this conclusion is correct, and if the substance of this account is historically plausible, then the account of Jesus' exchange with the Pharisees over his disciples' act of plucking grain provides a striking and unexpected convergence with the hypothesis that at the Last Supper, Jesus is both instituting and distributing to his disciples the new bread and wine of the presence. Such a conclusion is the logical outcome of his earlier and more enigmatic statements, in which he seems to arrogate to himself and his disciples priestly prerogatives with specific reference to the Jewish bread of the presence.

Fourth and finally, it is perhaps worth noting that Jesus' act of instituting new bread and wine of the presence at the Last Supper also coheres with a cultic interpretation of his action in the Jerusalem Temple (Matt 21:12-16; Mark 11:15-18; Luke 19:45-48; cf. John 2:14-16).[258] In recent years, a number

256. See Crispin H. T. Fletcher-Louis, "Jesus as the High Priestly Messiah: Part 1," *Journal for the Study of the Historical Jesus* 4, no. 2 (2006): 155-75; "Jesus as the High Priestly Messiah: Part 2," *Journal for the Study of the Historical Jesus* 5, no. 1 (2007): 57-79.

257. See Pitre, "Jesus, the New Temple, and the New Priesthood," 74-82.

258. The most recent and exhaustive treatment of both the primary texts and secondary literature is that of Jostein Ådna, *Jesu Stellung zum Tempel* (WUNT 2.119; Tübingen: J. C. B. Mohr [Paul Siebeck], 2000), see esp. 300-328. See also Michael F. Bird, *Jesus and the Origins of the Gentile Mission* (LNTS 331; Edinburgh: T. & T. Clark, 2007), 155-61; Dunn, *Jesus Remembered,* 636-40; Bryan, *Jesus and Israel's Traditions of Judgement and Restoration,* 206-25; Gerd Lüdemann, *Jesus After 2000 Years: What He Really Said and Did* (London: SCM; Amherst: Prometheus, 2001), 77-78; Bart D. Ehrman, *Jesus: Apocalyptic Prophet of the New Millennium,* 208-9, 211-14; Fredriksen, *Jesus of Nazareth,* 207-12; Theissen and Merz, *The Historical Jesus,* 432-33; Tan, *The Zion Traditions and the Aims of Jesus,* 166-81; Craig A. Evans, "Jesus' Action in the Temple: Cleansing or Portent of Destruction?" in *Jesus in Context: Temple, Purity, and*

of scholars have suggested that Jesus' act of cleansing the Temple should be interpreted as a prophetic sign of the destruction of the old Temple cult and its restoration and replacement by a new Temple.[259] For example, Gerd Theissen and Annette Merz make the case that the Last Supper is the positive cultic counterpart to the cleansing of the Temple:

> The symbolic action against the temple cult was complemented by Jesus' symbolic action at the last supper in founding a cult, though he did not intend to found a cult which would last through time. He simply wanted to replace provisionally the temple cult which had become obsolete: Jesus offers the disciples a replacement for the official cult in which they could either no longer take part, or which would not bring them salvation — until a new temple came. This "substitute" was a simple meal. By a new interpretation, the last supper becomes a substitute for the temple cult — a pledge of the eating and drinking in the kingdom of God which is soon to dawn.[260]

Along similar lines, but with a somewhat different angle, Michael Bird writes:

> [T]he meal Jesus had with his followers was the *sequel* to a demonstration that alleged the redundancy of the temple. As the certainty of death be-

---

Restoration (AGJU 39; Leiden: Brill, 1997), 395-439; Joachim Gnilka, *Jesus of Nazareth: Message and History* (trans. Siegfried S. Schatzmann; Peabody: Hendrickson, 1997), 274-78; Morna D. Hooker, *The Signs of a Prophet: The Prophetic Actions of Jesus* (London: SCM, 1997), 44-48; Bruce D. Chilton, *Pure Kingdom: Jesus' Vision of God* (London: SPCK; Grand Rapids: Eerdmans, 1996), 115-23; Wright, *Jesus and the Victory of God,* 413-28, 430, 490-93, 614, 651; Evans, *Jesus and His Contemporaries: Comparative Studies,* 319-80; Gerd Theissen, "Jesus' Temple Prophecy: Prophecy in the Tension between Town and Country," in *Social Reality and the Early Christians: Theology, Ethics, and the World of the New Testament* (Minneapolis: Fortress, 1992), 94-114; Witherington, *The Christology of Jesus,* 108-16; Jacob Neusner, "Money-Changers in the Temple: The Mishnah's Explanation," *NTS* 35 (1989): 287-90 (here 290); Richard Bauckham, "Jesus' Demonstration in the Temple," in *Law and Religion: Essays on the Place of Law in Israel and Early Christianity* (ed. B. Lindars; Cambridge: Clarke, 1988), 72-89; Sanders, *Jesus and Judaism,* 61-71; Ben F. Meyer, *The Aims of Jesus* (London: SCM, 1977), 197-202; Jeremias, *New Testament Theology,* 145. Jürgen Becker, *Jesus of Nazareth* (trans. James E. Crouch; New York/Berlin: Walter de Gruyter, 1998), 333, 345, is almost entirely alone in insisting that the historical Jesus engaged in no such action.

259. E.g., Bryan, *Jesus and Israel's Traditions of Judgement and Restoration,* 206-25; Fredriksen, *Jesus of Nazareth,* 207-12; Theissen and Merz, *The Historical Jesus,* 432-33; Tan, *The Zion Traditions and the Aims of Jesus,* 166-81; Wright, *Jesus and the Victory of God,* 490-93, 614, 651; Sanders, *Jesus and Judaism,* 61-71.

260. Theissen and Merz *The Historical Jesus,* 434.

> came more inevitable to Jesus, he instituted a meal among his followers that would operate as a symbol of the new exodus that he would achieve in his death by dying like a martyr vicariously for the nation. . . . The meal was symbolic and offered what the temple offered: a symbol of redemption, of covenant, commensality, divine presence and election. In this way a tangible link is forged between the temple episode, the institution of a communal meal, and Jesus' death, in that they all promote the existence of a new temple embodied by Jesus and his community.[261]

From this point of view, the sign in the Temple and the sign in the Upper Room are mutually interpretive: by means of his actions at the Last Supper, Jesus establishes a new sacrificial cult to replace the soon-to-be-destroyed Jerusalem Temple.

Now, if scholars such as Bird, Theissen, and Merz are basically correct and the Last Supper is in fact "the founding" of a counter-temple cult by Jesus, then this would provide a powerful case of coherence with the suggestion that Jesus is instituting new bread of the presence at the Last Supper. In the face of the imminent destruction of the Temple, and with it, the cessation of the bread of the presence as the Mosaic sign of the "everlasting covenant" (Lev 24:1-8), Jesus gathers his twelve disciples and institutes a new sacrificial sign of the new eschatological "covenant" — the bread and wine of the Last Supper.

Effects: The Bread of Jesus' Presence in Early Christianity

Finally, as noted above, the argument from plausibility of effects within the early church is weaker than in other cases we have surveyed so far. The connection between the bread and the wine of the Last Supper and the bread of the presence has left no explicit impact on our earliest extant sources. This must stand as a strike against historical plausibility; in this instance, the case for historicity is not as strong as that regarding the feeding of the five thousand or the conclusion that Jesus instituted a new covenant sacrifice at the Last Supper.

Nevertheless, there are at least two points of contact with the early church that are worth highlighting here.

First, if Jesus implicitly identified the bread and wine of the Last Supper with the bread and wine of the presence in the Tabernacle/Temple, it would provide a plausible explanation for the early Christian language of *personal*

261. Bird, *Jesus and the Origins of the Gentile Mission*, 157-58.

presence when speaking of the bread and wine of the eucharist. Think here, for example, of the words of the apostle Paul:

> I speak as to sensible men; judge for yourselves what I say. The cup of blessing which we bless, is it not a participation *(koinōnia)* in the blood of Christ? The bread which we break, is it not a participation *(koinōnia)* in the body of Christ? (1 Cor 10:15-16)

Because the passing of centuries has made the idea of bread and wine signifying Jesus' body and blood so familiar to many readers of the New Testament, one does not often stop to ask the question: *Where did Paul ever get the idea that bread could effect "communion" with a person?* There is no evidence that such symbolism was ever associated with the bread of the Jewish Passover or other sacrifices in the Jewish Torah. However, the biblical "bread of the presence" — literally, "the bread of the face" *(leḥem happānîm)* (Exod 35:13) — lends itself remarkably easily to being utilized as a sign of personal presence and communion. The key difference, of course, is that in Jewish Scripture, the so-called showbread signified the presence of *God,* whereas the bread of the Last Supper signifies the presence of *Jesus.* On the other hand, that is precisely the kind of development we would expect to take place in the early Christian church, given its intense focus on the person of Jesus, and its claims about his divine identity.

Second, although it is true that there is no explicit identification of the Christian eucharist with the bread of the presence in the extant writings of the first century A.D., we do possess evidence for this identification from the second and early fourth centuries A.D. Such connections are extant both in the writings of Origen of Alexandria and Cyril of Jerusalem:

> The precept is given that, without ceasing, twelve loaves are placed in the sight of the Lord, so that the memory of the twelve tribes is always to be held before him. Through these things, a certain plea or supplication arises for each of the tribes. . . . But if these things are referred to the greatness of the mystery, you will find this "remembrance" to have the effect of a great propitiation. If you return to that bread "which comes down from heaven and gives life to the world" (John 6:33), that bread of the presence "whom God put forward as an expiation by his blood" (Rom 3:25), and if you turn your attention to that remembrance about which the Lord says, "Do this in remembrance of me" (1 Cor 11:25), you will find that this is the only "remembrance" that makes God gracious to men. *Therefore, if you recall*

> *more intently the church's mysteries, you will find the image of the future truth anticipated in these things written in the law.* (Origen, *On Leviticus* 13)
>
> *In the Old Covenant there were the loaves of proposition [the Bread of the Presence], but they, being of the Old Covenant, have come to an end. In the New Covenant there is a heavenly bread and a cup of salvation that sanctify soul and body.* For, as the bread exists for the body, so the Word is in harmony with the soul. *Therefore, do not consider them as bare bread and wine; for, according to the declaration of the Master, they are Body and Blood.* If even the senses suggest this to you [viz., that they are bare bread and wine], let faith reassure you. Do not judge the reality by taste, but, having full assurance from faith, realize that you have been judged worthy of the Body and Blood of Christ. . . . Having learned these things, you have complete certitude that the visible bread is not bread, even if it is such to the taste, but the Body of Christ; and the visible wine is not wine, even if taste thinks it such, but the Blood of Christ. (Cyril of Jerusalem, *Mystagogic Catechesis* 5-6, 9)[262]

Although these texts are far too late to establish any conclusions about the immediate effects of Jesus' words and deeds in the life of the earliest Christian communities, they do nevertheless demonstrate that some ancient Christians eventually recognized connections between the bread and wine of the Last Supper and the bread of the presence. Once again, notice how ancient Christian writers like Origen and Cyril make explicit what is only implicit in the words and deeds of Jesus in the Gospels.

Where then do we stand? In conclusion, the argument from plausibility of effects within the early church is weak. Nevertheless, the Jewish contextual plausibility of Jesus' words over the bread, coupled with the striking and unexpected points of coherence with other words and deeds he is purported to have said and done, make it reasonable, though somewhat less certain, that, at the Last Supper, Jesus, as a new Moses, was not only inaugurating the eschatological covenant spoken of by the prophets; he may also have been instituting the new bread and wine of his own presence. This, at least, would explain why early Jewish Christians like Paul would go on to describe the bread of the eucharist as effecting communion with the person of Jesus himself, just as the Jewish people saw the bread of the presence symbolizing and effecting communion with the person of YHWH at Mount Sinai and in the Tabernacle.

262. Translation in James T. O'Connor, *The Hidden Manna: A Theology of the Eucharist* (2nd ed.; San Francisco: Ignatius, 2010), 28 (emphasis added).

CHAPTER 3

The New Manna

> Manna was not needed in Egypt. Nor would it be needed in the promised land. It is the food of inaugurated eschatology, the food that is needed because the kingdom has already broken in and because it is not yet consummated. The daily provision of manna signals that the Exodus has begun, but also that we are not yet living in the land.
>
> N. T. WRIGHT[1]

In the last chapter, we examined the evidence that during his public ministry and at the Last Supper, Jesus spoke and acted in ways that associated him with the "prophet-like-Moses" of ancient Jewish expectation. In this chapter, I want to build on what we learned by focusing on a second aspect of Jesus' Mosaic self-understanding: the evidence that he also spoke about *the eschatological manna from heaven* that some ancient Jews expected to arrive with the advent of the prophet like Moses, and that Jesus associated this manna with the bread that he would identify as his body at the Last Supper.

In order to do so, we will first have to examine the ancient Jewish beliefs about the manna of the exodus from Egypt and the expectation that it would one day return in a future age of salvation. Then, we will engage in a close analysis of the only two places in the Gospels where Jesus appears to speak about the eschatological manna: (1) the Lord's Prayer, in which Jesus teaches

1. N. T. Wright, "The Lord's Prayer as a Paradigm for Christian Prayer," in *Into God's Presence: Prayer in the New Testament* (ed. Richard N. Longenecker; Grand Rapids: Eerdmans, 2001), 132-54.

the disciples to pray, "Give us this day our *epiousios* bread" (Matt 6:9-13; Luke 11:1-4), and (2) the second half of the so-called "bread of life" discourse at Capernaum, in which Jesus contrasts the food and drink that he identifies with his own "flesh" and "blood" with "the manna in the wilderness" (John 6:48-66).

As I hope to show, when these teachings — the Lord's Prayer and the second part of the Capernaum synagogue discourse — are interpreted in their ancient Jewish context, there are strong reasons for concluding that the *substantia verba Jesu* contained in both of them are historically plausible on the lips of Jesus. If correct, this would prove to be extremely significant, for at least two reasons: (1) the Lord's Prayer is the only prayer Jesus is recorded as ever having taught his disciples and the petition for bread is the very first of the petitions focused on the needs of the disciples; (2) outside of the accounts of the Last Supper themselves, the Capernaum discourse is the most extensive teaching on the consumption of his body and blood attributed to Jesus in the Gospels. And in this discourse, he does not use the imagery of Passover, or the Temple sacrifices, or the messianic banquet. Instead, he draws on the Jewish hope for the eschatological manna. In this regard, I stress, as I did in chapter 1, that despite the obvious differences in the style of the sayings of Jesus in the Gospel of John, scholars still must subject the substance of Jesus' teachings therein to the same evaluation of the evidence in the Synoptic Gospels, before drawing any conclusions about historical plausibility. With that caveat in mind, let us try to set these teachings in context by looking more carefully at the ancient Jewish beliefs about the manna of the first and second exodus.

The Manna in Early Judaism[2]

Before we can turn to the evidence in the Gospels that suggests Jesus may have drawn connections between the manna and his actions at the Last Supper, we must first briefly survey what Jewish Scripture and tradition have to say about both the manna of the exodus and the manna of the eschatological age.

2. William H. C. Propp, *Exodus 1–18* (AB 2; New York: Doubleday, 1998), 582-601; Joel C. Slayton, "Manna," *ABD* 4:511; Cecil Roth, "Manna," in *Encyclopedia Judaica* (16 vols.; Jerusalem: Keter, 1971), 11:884-85; Bruce J. Malina, *The Palestinian Manna Tradition: The Manna Tradition in the Palestinian Targums and Its Relationship to the New Testament Writings* (Leiden: E. J. Brill, 1968); R. Meyer, "Manna," *TDNT* 4:462-66; Louis Ginzberg, *The Legends of the Jews* (7 vols.; repr.; trans. Henrietta Szold; Baltimore and London: Johns Hopkins University Press, 1998), 3:41-50; 6:16-20. See also P. Dumoulin, *Entre la Manne et l'Eucharistie: Étude de Sg 16,15–17,1a* (AnBib; Rome: Pontifical Biblical Institute, 1994).

The Manna in the Old Testament

Although the manna from heaven is mentioned repeatedly in the Old Testament,[3] the foundational account comes from the book of Exodus, which contains the narrative of the origin and nature of the manna in the exodus from Egypt. Immediately following Israel's triumphant crossing of the Red Sea (Exodus 15), the tribes of Jacob begin to complain of hunger and, as a result, God performs one of the most memorable of all his extraordinary acts on their behalf: the giving of the manna (Exodus 16). Over the course of this chapter, we will have occasion to revisit this foundational text several times. For our purposes here, however, I primarily want to stress that in the foundational account from Exodus, the manna of Moses is not ordinary bread but "miraculous food."[4] This is evident in the text in several ways.

First, according to the book of Exodus, the manna is clearly miraculous. For one thing, it is described as "bread from the heavens" *(leḥem min hašāmāyim)* (Exod 16:4). Moreover, its coming is directly tied to the manifestation of the equally miraculous "glory cloud," one of the signs and wonders of the exodus:

> Then the LORD said to Moses, "*Behold, I will rain bread from heaven for you;* and the people shall go out and gather a day's portion every day, that I may prove them, whether they will walk in my law or not. On the sixth day, when they prepare what they bring in, it will be twice as much as they gather daily." So Moses and Aaron said to all the people of Israel, "At evening you shall know that it was the LORD who brought you out of the land Egypt, and in the morning you shall see the glory of the LORD, because he has heard your murmurings against the LORD. For what are we, that you murmur against us?" (Exod 16:4-7)

In light of this emphasis on the heavenly origin of the manna, it is no wonder that later biblical texts would go on to refer to it as the "grain of heaven" *(d^e gan šāmayim)* (Ps 78:24) and the "bread of the mighty ones" *(leḥem 'abîrîm)* (Ps 78:25). In this latter reference, the "mighty ones" is a biblical expression which in context is synonymous with the "angels" (Ps 103:20).[5] In the Greek Septuagint, the supernatural character of the manna becomes even more explicit: it is

3. Exod 16:1-36; Num 11:1-9; 21:5; Deut 8:3, 16; Josh 5:12; Neh 9:20-21; Ps 78:24-25; 105:40; Wis 16:20; 19:21.

4. Meyer, "Manna," 462.

5. Malina, *The Palestinian Manna Tradition*, 35.

the "bread of angels" *(artos angelōn)* (Ps 77:25 LXX), the "food of angels" *(angelōn trophē)* (Wis 16:20), and "heavenly food" *(ambrosias trophēs)* (Wis 19:21).

Second, although the point is often forgotten, the manna is a double miracle. In the morning, God promises to give the Israelites "bread" from heaven, in the form of the manna. But in the evening, God promises to give the people "flesh" *(bāśār)* to eat, in the form of the quail:

> And Moses said, "When the LORD gives you in the evening *flesh to eat* and in the morning *bread to the full,* because the LORD has heard your murmurings which you murmur against him — what are we? Your murmurings are not against us but against the LORD." And Moses said to Aaron, "Say to the whole congregation of the people of Israel, 'Come near before the LORD, for he has heard your murmurings.'" And as Aaron spoke to the whole congregation of the people of Israel, they looked toward the wilderness, and behold, the glory of the LORD appeared in the cloud. And the LORD said to Moses, "I have heard the murmurings of the people of Israel; say to them, *'At twilight you shall eat flesh, and in the morning you shall be filled with bread; then you shall know that I am the LORD your God.'*" (Exod 16:8-12)

Once again, this coupling of the manna miracle with the gift of the quail is reflected elsewhere in Jewish Scripture, as the Psalter says: "They asked, and he brought them quails, and gave them bread from heaven in abundance" (Ps 105:40).

Third, the manna is a daily miracle. It appears each day with the coming of the "dew" (Exod 16:13), and the people are commanded to go out each day and gather the appropriate amount:

> Then the LORD said to Moses, ". . . The people shall go out and gather *a day's portion every day,* that I may prove them, whether they will walk in my law or not. On the sixth *day,* when they prepare what they bring in, it will be twice as much as they gather *daily.*" . . . "This is what the LORD has commanded: 'Gather of it, every man of you, as much as he can eat; you shall take an omer apiece, according to the number of the persons whom each of you has in his tent.'" And the people of Israel did so; they gathered, some more, some less. *But when they measured it with an omer, he that gathered much had nothing left over, and he that gathered little had no lack; each gathered according to what he could eat.* And Moses said to them, "Let no man leave any of it till the morning." But they did not listen

> to Moses; some left part of it till morning, and it bred worms and became foul; and Moses was angry with them. Morning by morning they gathered it, each as much as he could eat; but when the sun grew hot, it melted. (Exod 16:4-5, 16-21)

Note here the extraordinary nature of the manna is manifested in the fact that if the Israelites try to preserve any of it overnight, it always becomes foul and, no matter how much or how little is gathered, it always measures out at an omer's worth. Perhaps most striking of all, in the descent of the manna from heaven, it is described as obeying the laws of sabbath rest:

> On the sixth day they gathered twice as much bread, two omers apiece; and when all the leaders of the congregation came and told Moses, he said to them, "This is what the Lord has commanded: 'Tomorrow is a day of solemn rest, a holy sabbath to the Lord; bake what you will bake and boil what you will boil, and all that is left over lay by to be kept till the morning." So they laid it by till the morning, as Moses had bade them; and it did not become foul, and there were no worms in it. Moses said, "Eat it today, for today is a sabbath to the Lord; *today you will not find it in the field.* Six days you shall gather it, but on the seventh day, which is a sabbath, there will be none." *On the seventh day some of the people went out to gather, and they found none.* And the Lord said to Moses, "How long do you refuse to keep my commandments and my laws? See! The Lord has given you the sabbath, therefore on the sixth day he gives you bread for two days; remain every man of you in his place, let no man go out of his place on the seventh day." So the people rested on the seventh day. (Exod 16:22-30)

Although, as we will see, certain aspects of the manna will come to be associated with natural phenomena in the deserts of the Middle East, the wonders surrounding the gathering of the manna are incontrovertibly being described as miraculous.[6]

Fourth, the manna is an unprecedented miracle. According to the Pentateuch, none of the Israelites have ever seen anything like it.

> In the evenings quail came up and covered the camp; and in the morning dew lay round about the camp. And when the dew had gone up, there was on the face of the wilderness a fine, flake-like thing, fine as hoarfrost on the

6. Malina, *The Palestinian Manna Tradition*, 17.

> ground. When the people of Israel saw it, they said to one another, "What is it?" *For they did not know what it was.* And Moses said to them, *"It is the bread which the* Lord *has given you to eat."* (Exod 16:13-15)

This is implicit in the question asked on the first morning the manna is discovered: " 'What is it?' *(mān hû').* For they did not know what it was" (Exod 16:15).[7] Elsewhere in Jewish Scripture, the unprecedented nature of the manna is stressed when Moses says to the second generation before entering the promised land: "[God] fed you with manna, which you did not know, nor did your fathers know" (Deut 8:3).

Fifth, the manna is a temporary miracle. The Israelites do not discover the manna upon entering the desert, but only after two months of travel (Exod 16:1-2).[8] Moreover, once the manna does appear, the miracle only takes place for the duration of the wilderness wandering: "*And the people of Israel ate the manna forty years,* till they came to a habitable land; they ate the manna till they came to the border of the land of Canaan" (Exod 16:35). Once again, Jewish Scripture elsewhere makes this explicit: as soon as the twelve tribes celebrate the Passover, cross the River Jordan, and enter into the promised land of Canaan, the manna miraculously ceases to fall:

> While the people of Israel were encamped in Gilgal they kept *the passover* on the fourteenth day of the month at evening in the plains of Jericho. *And on the morrow after the passover, on that very day,* they ate of the produce of the land, unleavened cakes and parched grain. *And the manna ceased on the morrow,* when they ate of the produce of the land; and the people of Israel had manna no more, but ate of the fruit of the land of Canaan that year. (Josh 5:10-12)

This connection between the passover and the manna in biblical history is particularly intriguing when we recall that both the Passover bread and the manna were connected with meat that had to be eaten "between the two evenings," and both involved unleavened bread (cf. Exod 12:14-20).[9] Finally, the book of Nehemiah describes the manna as a special provision of God unique to the time of the exodus, coupling it with the miraculous water from the rock of Horeb (Neh 9:20-21).

7. Propp, *Exodus 1–18,* 596.
8. Propp, *Exodus 1–18,* 592.
9. See Propp, *Exodus 1–18,* 600-601.

Sixth, the manna is connected to the cultic sanctuary, the Tabernacle. This is important to stress, given our overall interest in Jesus and the Temple. Although the manna is given first and foremost to sustain the natural life of the Israelites in the desert, God also commands Moses to place some of the manna inside the Israelite sanctuary:

> Now the house of Israel called its name *manna;* it was like coriander seed, *white, and the taste of it was like wafers made with honey.* And Moses said, "This is what the LORD has commanded: 'Let an omer of it be kept throughout your generations, that they may see the bread with which I fed you in the wilderness, when I brought you out of the land of Egypt.'" And Moses said to Aaron, *"Take a jar, and put an omer of manna in it, and place it before the LORD, to be kept throughout your generations."* And the LORD commanded Moses, so Aaron placed it before the testimony, to be kept. (Exod 16:31-34)

Although the reference here to "before the testimony" is somewhat vague, it seems highly likely that the text refers to the manna being stored in the holy place in the tabernacle (cf. Num 17:2-5). Intriguingly, as William Propp points out, the only place where the manna remains incorrupt is in the tabernacle: "Only in the sacred space of the Tabernacle or during the sacred time of the Sabbath can it endure."[10] Along similar lines, Bruce Malina concludes that one of the key aspects of the manna tradition in Jewish Scripture is its connection with a "cultic framework."[11] We will keep this cultic framework in mind as we move into our study of Jesus' words and actions.

In sum, in Jewish Scripture, the manna is an unprecedented daily miracle, unique to the time of the exodus wandering, and directly associated with Moses and the tabernacle. The reason it is necessary for us to emphasize the miraculous nature of the manna in particular is that in modern times it has become remarkably popular, even in scholarly literature, to identify the manna with a purely natural substance of some sort. In the words of William Propp: "Like the Torah's other tales of desert sustenance, the legends of quails and Manna arise from natural phenomena."[12] Commentators differ in their proposals as to what exactly this purely natural substance was: whether the resin

10. Propp, *Exodus 1–18*, 600.

11. Malina, *The Palestinian Manna Tradition*, 39.

12. Propp, *Exodus 1–18*, 599-600, following P. Maiberger, *Das Manna* (Ägypten und Altes Testament 6; Wiesbaden: Harrassowitz, 1983).

secreted by flowering desert plants such as the tamarisk *(Tamarisk gallica)* or flowering ash *(Faxinus ornus)* for several weeks a year, or the excretion of one or more species of desert insects.[13] Such interpretations, however appealing as modern attempts to explain the biblical text, are exegetically impossible to square with the actual claims of Exodus 16, which unequivocally regards the manna as one of the wonders of the exodus from Egypt. As Propp points out: "Admittedly, the statement that the Manna ceased when Israel entered Canaan, taken literally, would preclude identification with ordinary honey-dew (Josh 5:11-12)."[14] As we will see in our study of Jesus and the eschatological manna, the miraculous nature of the manna from an ancient Jewish perspective will prove essential to properly grasping the implications of Jesus' identification of his own flesh and blood with the manna of Jewish eschatology.

The Manna in Early Jewish Literature

When we turn to early Jewish literature outside the Bible, we find many of the same beliefs regarding the manna that were attested in Jewish Scripture, with some noteworthy developments.

First, the manna continues to be regarded as *miraculous*. For example, in the fragmentary accounts of the Hellenistic Jewish writer Artapanus, we find the manna listed as one of the many miraculous "signs" performed by Moses during the exodus: "God rained for them meal like millet, very similar in color to snow" (*Fragments of Artapanus* 3:37).[15] Along similar lines, in the rewriting of Jewish Scripture known as Pseudo-Philo, the manna is identified as one of the three miraculous gifts that God gave to the Israelites during the wilderness wandering:

> And these are the *three things* that God gave to his people on account of the three persons: that is, *the well* of the water of Marah *for Miriam* and *the pillar of cloud for Aaron* and *the manna for Moses*. And when these came to their end, these three things were taken away from them. (*Pseudo-Philo* 20:8)[16]

13. See Slayton, "Manna," 511; Meyer, *"Manna,"* 463.

14. Propp, *Exodus 1–18*, 600.

15. Unless otherwise noted, all translations of the Old Testament Pseudepigrapha contained herein are from Charlesworth, *OTP*, here 2:903.

16. Given Jesus' identification of himself both with the new Moses and the new Manna, this tradition is intriguing insofar as Pseudo-Philo draws a *personal* connection between Mo-

Elsewhere, the same text refers to the manna as the "bread of angels" (*Ps.-Philo* 19:6). Finally, in a somewhat different mode, Philo of Alexandria uses the miraculous nature of the manna as the foundation for his allegorical explanation of its significance. For Philo, both the descent of the manna from heaven and the daily provision of a single measure on most days and a double measure before the sabbath were a sign that God had "wrought wonders" *(ethaumatourgeito)* in the desert; indeed, he admonishes his readers: "And if any one disbelieves these facts, he neither knows God nor has he ever sought to know him" (*Life of Moses* 1.203, 212; cf. *Decalogue* 16). Elsewhere he likewise describes the manna as "heavenly incorruptible food" *(tēn ouranion . . . aphtharton trophēn)* and identifies it with the "word of God" and the food of the soul (*Who Is the Heir of Divine Things?* 79; cf. *Allegorical Interpretation* 3.173-76).

In addition to these brief mentions, the most extensive early Jewish account of the manna comes to us from Josephus. Indeed, although Josephus is sometimes cited as understanding the manna in a purely natural way — i.e., as an ordinary earthly substance — when his comments are cited in full, he clearly stands in the stream of Jewish tradition that regarded the manna of the exodus as a miraculous food:

> Immediately after this first supply of food God sent them down a second. For, *while Moses raised his hands in prayer, a dew descended, and, as this congealed about his hands, Moses, surmising that this too was a nutriment come to them from God, tasted it and was delighted;* and, whereas the multitude in their ignorance took this for snow and attributed the phenomenon to the season of the year, he instructed them that this heaven-descending dew was not as they supposed, but was sent for their salvation *(sōtēria)* and sustenance, and, tasting it, he bade them thus too to convince themselves. They, then, imitating their leader, were delighted with what they ate, for it had the sweet and delicious taste of honey and resembled the spicy herb called *bdellium*, its size being that of a coriander seed; and they fell to collecting it with keenest ardour. Orders, however, were issued to all alike to collect each day but an *assarōn* (that being the name of a measure), since this food would never fail them. . . . Those who nevertheless collected more

ses and the manna, just as he does between Miriam and the well and Aaron and the glory cloud. It seems that in some way the manna represents or is tied to the person of Moses. This would render historical plausibility to the identification of himself with the manna; just as the first Moses was personally identified with the miraculous manna, so too the new Moses, Jesus, radically identifies himself with the new manna that he will give at the Last Supper (cf. Vermes, "He Is the Bread").

> than the prescribed measure reaped therefrom nothing further than their pains, for they found no more than an *assarōn;* while anything left over for the morrow was of no service whatsoever, being polluted by worms and bitterness, *so divine and miraculous was this food.* It is a mainstay to dwellers in these parts against their dearth of other provisions, and to this very day all that region is watered by a rain like to that which then, as a favour to Moses, the Deity sent down for men's sustenance *(diatrophēn).* The Hebrews call this food *manna;* for the word *man* is an interrogative in our language, asking the question "What is this?" So they continued to rejoice in their heaven-sent gift, living on this food for forty years, all the time that they were in the desert. (Josephus, *Antiquities* 3.26-32)

This is an intriguing witness. On the one hand, Josephus appears to link the manna with some kind of rainfall that continues in the region of the wilderness wandering "to this very day" (*Ant.* 3.31), suggesting some kind of natural phenomenon. On the other hand, Josephus attributes the descent of the manna directly to Moses' intercession, describing it as "a nutriment come to them from God." Even more explicitly, he declares that the Israelites were only ever able to gather one measure of manna, and that for but one day, because it was "so divine *(theion)* and miraculous *(paradoxon)*" (*Ant.* 3.30). Unfortunately, Josephus does not tell us how to reconcile these two affirmations. For our purposes here, it is only necessary to point out that despite his reference to a similar contemporary phenomenon in the deserts of Arabia, he still regards the manna of the exodus as a divine wonder.[17]

Moreover, in addition to the identification of the manna as a forty-year miracle (*Pseudo-Philo* 10:7), we also begin to see evidence in early Jewish literature for the belief that the miraculous manna would one day return. For example, we find a hint of such an expectation in one of the Dead Sea Scrolls known as the *Songs of the Sage.* Although the scroll is fragmentary, what we have extant appears to be eschatological in character, since it repeatedly refers to the "periods of wickedness" or the "era of the rule of wickedness" (4Q511 frag. 3:3; 10:3; 35:8-9). In this context, we read the following:

> 8 [*Blank* May] all those of perfect behaviour praise him. *Blank* With the lyre of salvation 9 [may] they [op]en their mouth for God's kindness. *May they search for his manna.* (4Q*Songs of the Sage*[b] [4Q511] frag. 10:9)

17. For discussion, see Louis H. Feldman, *Flavius Josephus: Translation and Commentary: Judean Antiquities 1-4* (ed. Steve Mason; Leiden: Brill, 1999).

As commentators point out, this appears to be one of our earliest references to the idea of eschatological manna that would come in the future, though the fragmentary nature of the document makes it impossible to be sure.[18] Nevertheless, we find a similar but far more explicit description of this expectation in 2 *Baruch*, usually dated to the first century A.D.:

> And it will happen that when all that which should come to pass in these parts is accomplished, *the Messiah* will begin to be revealed. . . . And those who are hungry will enjoy themselves and they will, moreover, see marvels every day. . . . *And it will happen at that time that the treasury of manna will come down again from on high,* and they will eat of it in those years because these are they who will have arrived at the consummation of time. (2 *Baruch* 29:3, 6-8)

As we will see over the course of this chapter, this will prove to be a very significant text for situating Jesus' teachings on the eschatological manna in a Jewish context. For now, we need only point out that there is evidence, however minimal, in both the Scrolls and Pseudepigrapha, of an early Jewish belief that God would bring back the miracle of the manna in the coming age and/or the days of the messiah.[19]

Finally, given our interest elsewhere in the Jewish feast of Passover, it is worth noting that Josephus drew a connection between the manna of the exodus and the unleavened bread of the Passover. In another place in his history, he writes:

18. Craig S. Keener, *The Gospel of John: A Commentary* (2 vols.; Peabody: Hendrickson, 2003), 1:681.

19. Another possible witness to the early Jewish expectation that the messiah would bring back the manna occurs at the very end of the eschatological section in the second Sibylline Oracle: "But you, savior, rescue me, a brazen one, from my scourges, though I have done shameless deeds. I beseech you to give me a little rest from the refrain, *holy giver of manna, king of a great kingdom*" (*Sibylline Oracles* 2:344-47). This seems to be a reference to the coming messiah ("king of a great kingdom") in which the messiah is addressed as "holy giver of manna" *(hagie mannodota).* To the extent that this text reflects certainly early Jewish beliefs about eschatology, it is remarkable that the messiah can be addressed as the holy giver of manna without any further clarification and apart from any direct exodus connections in the context. If this is an early Jewish writing, it would suggest that by the time this oracle was composed, the hope for the return of the manna in the days of the messiah had become a fairly widespread staple of Jewish expectation with which the audience was expected to be familiar. However, in its final form, this oracle is difficult to regard as a purely Jewish (rather than Christian) work, for it seems to explicitly refer to "Christ" coming on the clouds of heaven (*Sib. Or.* 2:241-51). Cf. Keener, *The Gospel of John,* 1:681.

> Quitting the country by the shortest route they arrived on the third day at Beelsephon, a place beside the Red Sea. Being bereft of any sustenance from the barren soil, they kneaded flour, baked it with merely a slight heating, and subsisted on the bread so made; on this they lived for thirty days, for they could make what they had brought from Egypt last no longer, notwithstanding that they rationed the food, limiting the portions to bare needs without eating to satiety. Hence it is that, in memory of that time of scarcity, we keep for eight days a feast called the feast of unleavened bread. (Josephus, *Antiquities* 2.315-17)

What is intriguing about this passage is that it suggests that some Second Temple Jews saw the manna as a replacement for the unleavened bread memorialized during the feast of *Mazzot*.[20] This possible connection will become important as we explore the possibility that Jesus saw the bread of the Last Supper as both the eschatological manna from heaven and the miraculous replacement for the unleavened bread of the Passover.

In sum, the evidence from Jewish Scripture and early Jewish literature outside the Bible reveals a fascinating constellation of beliefs revolving around the wondrous manna of Moses and the exodus.[21] With this essential background in mind, we can now turn to the data in the Gospels.

The Lord's Prayer and the Eschatological Manna[22]

The first piece of evidence that ties Jesus' words and deeds to the Jewish expectation of a new exodus comes from what is arguably the most well-known

20. J. B. Segal, *The Hebrew Passover from the Earliest Times to A.D. 70*, London Oriental Studies 12 (London: Oxford University Press, 1963), 38.

21. As with the ancient Jewish hope for a prophet like Moses, this belief would eventually lead to a veritable explosion of speculation on and writing about the manna in rabbinic literature. See esp. *m. 'Abot* 5:6; *t. Soṭ.* 11:10; *Tg. Ps.-Jon.* on Exod 16:4 and 16:15; *b. Yom.* 75b, 76a; *b. Ḥag.* 12b; *b. Pes.* 54a; *Tg. Pss.* 78:25; *Sifre* on Deut 33:21 (355); *Num. Rab.* 1:2 and 14:20; *Mek.* on Exod 16:13, 16:25; *Gen. Rab.* 82:8; *Ruth Rab.* 5:6; *Eccl. Rab.* 1:9; *Num. Rab.* 11:2. See Keener, *The Gospel of John*, 1:681 and Dodd, *The Interpretation of the Fourth Gospel*, 335.

22. Much of what follows draws directly from Brant Pitre, "The Lord's Prayer and the New Exodus," *Letter & Spirit* 2 (2006): 69-96. For further discussion and bibliography, see Keener, *The Historical Jesus of the Gospels*, 197-98; Dale C. Allison Jr., *The Intertextual Jesus: Scripture in Q* (Harrisburg: Trinity Press International, 2000), 51-53; Dunn, *Jesus Remembered*, 226-28, 409-11, 546-55, 589-91; Dale C. Allison Jr., "Q's New Exodus and the Historical Jesus," in *The Sayings Source Q and the Historical Jesus*, BETL 158, ed. A. Lindemann (Leuven: Leuven

teaching recorded in the Gospels: the Lord's Prayer. This prayer can be found in two slightly different versions in the Gospels of Matthew and Luke, given below, with the disputed Greek word *epiousios* left untranslated:

> Our Father, who art in heaven,
> hallowed be your name.
> Your kingdom come,
> your will be done, on earth as it is in heaven.
> Give us this day our *epiousios* bread;
> and forgive us our debts, as we also have forgiven our debtors.
> And lead us not into temptation
> but deliver us from evil. (Matt 6:9-13)

> Father,
> Hallowed be your name.
> Your kingdom come.
> Give us each day our *epiousios* bread;
> and forgive us our sins, for we ourselves forgive every one who is indebted to us;
> and lead us not into temptation. (Luke 11:2-4)

The contents of the Lord's Prayer are remarkably brief. But what do its petitions actually mean? More specifically, if deemed authentic, what might Jesus

---

University, 2001), 395-428; Gerd Theissen and Annette Merz, *The Historical Jesus: A Comprehensive Guide,* trans. John Bowden (Minneapolis: Fortress, 1998), 261-64; Jürgen Becker, *Jesus of Nazareth,* trans. James E. Crouch (New York and Berlin: Walter de Gruyter, 1998), 265-71; N. T. Wright, *Jesus and the Victory of God* (Minneapolis: Fortress, 1996), 292-94; John P. Meier, *A Marginal Jew: Rethinking the Historical Jesus,* 3 vols. (New York: Doubleday, 1991, 1994, 2001), 2:291-302; W. D. Davies and Dale C. Allison Jr., *A Critical and Exegetical Commentary on the Gospel According to Saint Matthew,* 3 vols. (Edinburgh: T. & T. Clark, 1988, 1991, 1997), 1:590-615; G. R. Beasley-Murray, *Jesus and the Kingdom of God* (Grand Rapids: Eerdmans, 1986), 147-57; Joseph A. Fitzmyer, *The Gospel According to Luke,* 2 vols. (New York: Doubleday, 1983, 1985), 2:896-909; John A. T. Robinson, "The Lord's Prayer," in *Twelve More New Testament Studies* (London: SCM, 1984), 44-64; Joachim Jeremias, *New Testament Theology* (New York: Scribner, 1971), 193-203; and *The Prayers of Jesus* (Naperville, IL: A. R. Allenson, 1967), 82-107; Raymond E. Brown, "The Pater Noster as an Eschatological Prayer," in *New Testament Essays* (New York: Doubleday, 2010 [orig. 1968]), 279-323; Jean Carmignac, *Recherches sur le "Notre Père"* (Paris: Letouzey & Ané, 1969), 200-210; C. B. Houk, "*PEIRASMOS,* The Lord's Prayer, and the Massah Tradition," *SJT* 19 (1966): 216-25; R. F. Cyster, "The Lord's Prayer and the Exodus Tradition," *Theology* 64 (1961): 377-81; Ernst Lohmeyer, *"Our Father": An Introduction to the Lord's Prayer* (trans. John Bowden; New York: Harper & Row, 1965 [orig. 1952]).

himself have meant when he taught it to his disciples? And how would first-century Jews like the disciples have understood its language and imagery in an ancient Jewish context?

Several years ago, N. T. Wright published a brief but thought-provoking article in which he argued that the Lord's Prayer should be understood as a prayer for a "new Exodus."[23] As is widely known, throughout Jewish Scripture, the prophets express the hope that God would once again redeem the people of Israel in much the same way that he had done in the exodus from Egypt. In this new exodus, God would release his people from slavery to sin and death, put an end to their exile from the promised land, and gather them into the promised land, a restored kingdom, and a new Jerusalem.[24] According to Wright, the ancient Jewish hope for a new exodus is the key to unlocking the Jewish meaning of the Lord's Prayer:

> The events of Israel's Exodus from Egypt, the people's wilderness wandering, and their entry into the promised land were of enormous importance in the self-understanding and symbolism of all subsequent generations of Israelites, including Jews of the Second Temple period. . . . When YHWH restored the fortunes of Israel, it would be like a new Exodus — a new and greater liberation from an enslavement greater than that in Egypt. . . . And the Lord's Prayer can best be seen in this light as well — that is, as the prayer of the new wilderness wandering people. . . . This can be seen more particularly as we look at each of the clauses of the Lord's Prayer from a new Exodus perspective.[25]

In my view, Wright has uncovered a fundamental insight into the meaning of the Lord's Prayer in its first-century Jewish context. In this section, building

23. See N. T. Wright, "The Lord's Prayer as a Paradigm for Christian Prayer," in *Into God's Presence: Prayer in the New Testament,* ed. Richard N. Longenecker (Grand Rapids: Eerdmans, 2001), 132-54.

24. For primary texts, see, e.g., Isaiah 40–66; Jeremiah 3, 16, 23, 30–31; Ezekiel 20, 36–37; Hosea 2, 11; Micah 4, 7; Zechariah 9–10; Sirach 36. For secondary literature, see F. Ninow, *Indicators of Typology within the Old Testament: The Exodus Motif* (New York: Peter Lang, 2001); David W. Pao, *Acts and the Isaianic New Exodus,* Wissenschaftliche Untersuchungen zum Neuen Testament 2:130 (Tübingen: Mohr Siebeck, 2000; repr. Grand Rapids: Baker Academic, 2002); Rikki E. Watts, *Isaiah's New Exodus in Mark,* Wissenschaftliche Untersuchungen zum Neuen Testament 2:88 (Tübingen: Mohr Siebeck, 1997; repr. Grand Rapids: Baker Academic, 2000).

25. Cf. Wright, "The Lord's Prayer," 139-40.

on my own previous work,[26] I will attempt to show that his basic suggestion is correct and that the ancient Jewish hope for a new exodus is in fact a very important key to understanding the Lord's Prayer. As I hope to show, when the Lord's Prayer is read against the background of the hope for a new exodus, we discover the very first "we-petition" — the prayer for bread — is not just a general prayer for earthly sustenance, but a very Jewish prayer for the manna of the eschatological exodus.

The Fatherhood of God and the Prophecies of a New Exodus

The first aspect of the Lord's Prayer that evokes both the exodus from Egypt and the new exodus is the opening address to God as "Our Father" *(pater hēmōn)* or "Father" *(pater)* (Matt 6:9; Luke 11:2). Although at first glance, the practice of addressing God as "Father" in prayer may seem unremarkable, when we turn to the Old Testament, it is by no means common. Although on several occasions God is depicted as or compared to a father, he is almost never addressed as "Father" in a prayer — except in a few key instances.[27] When these are examined we find that both the image of God as father and the practice of addressing God as "Father" in prayer are tied with remarkable consistency to the exodus from Egypt and the prophetic hope for a new exodus.

As Wright points out, God's command to Pharaoh to release the Israelites was directly based on his paternal relationship to Israel: "Thus says the LORD: Israel is my first-born son, and I say to you, 'Let my son go that he may worship me'; if you refuse to let him go, behold, I will slay your first-born son" (Exod 4:22-23). Moreover, we find the same link present in the book of Hosea, when God refers to the past Exodus in terms of his paternal relationship to

26. Pitre, "The Lord's Prayer and the New Exodus," 69-96; idem, *Jesus, the Tribulation, and the End of the Exile,* 132-59. I thank the editors of *Letter & Spirit* for permission to reproduce previously published material.

27. Most frequently, Israel is referred to as the sons or children of God, without God explicitly being called "father" (Deut 14:1; Hos 11:1-3; Wis 5:5). In a few cases, God is explicitly called a "father": either with reference to him as creator (Deut 32:6; Mal 2:10), or by way of analogy (Ps 103:13), or as a protector of orphans (Ps 68:5), or with regard to his special relationship with the king of Israel under the Davidic covenant (2 Sam 7:14; Ps 89:26). Apart from the examples we will discuss below, the only cases of God being addressed as "Father" in prayer in the Old Testament come from the books of Sirach and Wisdom, where God is called "Father" on a few occasions (see Wis 14:3; Sir 23:1, 4; 51:10). For a concise discussion of references, see Fitzmyer, *The Gospel according to Luke,* 2:902-3; Davies and Allison, *Saint Matthew,* 1:600-602; Jeremias, *The Prayers of Jesus,* 11-29.

Israel: "When Israel was a child, I loved him, and out of Egypt I called my son" (Hos 11:1). Finally, the first explicit Old Testament use of the Hebrew word "father" *('āb)* for God in the Old Testament comes from the famous "Song of Moses," which is, of course, a recollection of God's past act of deliverance in the exodus from Egypt (Deut 32:9-14). In light of such texts, Wright observes:

> Calling God "Father" not only evokes all kinds of associations of family life and intimacy; more importantly, it speaks to all subsequent generations of God as *the God of the Exodus,* the God who rescues Israel primarily because Israel is God's first-born son. The title Father says as much about Israel, and about the events through which God will liberate Israel, as it does about God.[28]

We can go much further than Wright, however, for this connection between the fatherhood of God and the exodus is not only present in passages that refer to the first exodus. It is even more explicit in prophetic texts concerned with the second exodus.

There are at least two key passages from the Old Testament that utilize the terminology of God as "Father" precisely in the context of describing the eschatological events that will accompany the new exodus. Although these texts are somewhat lengthy, it is important that they be cited here as fully as possible so that the context of their use of "father" terminology is clear. They come to us, not surprisingly, from the books of Isaiah and Jeremiah, both of which are heavily invested in the hope for a future exodus:

> *Then [the LORD] remembered the days of old, of Moses his servant.*
> *Where is he who brought up out of the sea the shepherds of his flock?*
> *Where is he who put in the midst of them his holy Spirit,*
> *who caused his glorious arm to go at the right hand of Moses,*
> *who divided the waters before them to make for himself an everlasting*
> *name, who led them through the depths?* . . .
> So you did lead your people, to make for yourself a glorious name.
> Look down from heaven and see, from your holy and glorious
> habitation.
> Where are your zeal and your might?
> The yearning of your heart and your compassion are withheld from me.
> *For you are our Father,* though Abraham does not know us

28. Wright, "The Lord's Prayer," 140.

> and Israel does not acknowledge us;
> *you, O LORD, are our Father,*
> our Redeemer from of old is your name.
> O LORD, why do you make us err from your ways
> and harden our heart, so that we fear you not?
> Return for the sake of your servants the tribes of your heritage.
> (Isa 63:11-17)

> *In those days, says the LORD, they shall no more say, "The ark of the covenant of the LORD." It shall not come to mind, or be remembered, or missed; it shall not be made again.* At that time Jerusalem shall be called the throne of the LORD, and all the Gentiles shall gather to it, to the presence of the LORD in Jerusalem, and they shall no more follow their own evil heart. *In those days the house of Judah shall join the house of Israel, and together they shall come from the land of the north to the land that I gave your fathers for a heritage.* "I thought how I would set you among my sons, and give you a pleasant land, a heritage most beauteous of all nations. *And I thought you would call me 'My Father,'* and would not turn from following me." (Jer 3:16-19)

Three observations are pertinent here. First, both of these oracles bear strong parallels with the Lord's Prayer. Significantly, Isaiah actually addresses God as "our Father" *('ābînû)* — the same form we find in the longer version of the Lord's Prayer.[29] Similarly, Jeremiah declares that when God gathers Israel and the Gentiles to the restored Jerusalem, they will "call" God "my Father" *('ābî),* likewise paralleling the shorter version of the Lord's Prayer.[30] Second, both of these prophecies address God as father in the context of the hope for a new exodus. This is very clear in Isaiah, in which the prophet calls upon God to look down from heaven and bring the tribes of Israel to the promised land,

29. Isa 63:16; 64:8; cf. Matt 6:9. The Septuagint translation of Isaiah's prayer is identical to the Lord's Prayer; it reads "our Father" *(pater hēmōn)* (Isa 63:16; 64:8 LXX). It is a curious fact of New Testament scholarship that commentators who spend an otherwise enormous amount of time on Jesus' use of "Father" language almost never discuss this passage from Isaiah in which God is actually addressed as "our Father." For example, Isaiah's prayer is listed but not discussed by Dunn, *Jesus Remembered,* 548-49; Darrell L. Bock, *Luke* (2 vols.; Baker Exegetical Commentary on the New Testament; Grand Rapids: Baker, 1996), 2:1051-52; Davies and Allison, *Saint Matthew,* 1:600; Fitzmyer, *The Gospel according to Luke,* 2:902.

30. Luke 11:2. Again, the Septuagint translation is identical to the Lord's Prayer: "And I said: You shall call me Father *(patera)*" (Jer 3:19 LXX).

just as he had done "in the days of old, of Moses his servant" (Isa 63:11, 17).[31] Likewise, Jeremiah tells of future days when people will no longer speak about how God "brought up the people out of the land of Egypt." Instead, they will speak about a new exodus, when God will gather the scattered tribes of Israel "out of all the countries where he had driven them" (Jer 16:14-16; 23:1-8). Finally, and perhaps most significantly, in both Isaiah and Jeremiah, God is *only* addressed as Father in the context of these oracles about the future exodus. This is particularly remarkable when we consider the extraordinary length of these books and the fact that both contain numerous other prayers.[32]

Taken together, these parallels suggest that Jesus' use of "father" language in the Lord's Prayer is not incidental or the result of biblical custom. The occurrences are far too infrequent for that. Rather, the direct address of God as father seems to be drawing on the language of the biblical prophets. Just as God's fatherly love for Israel had compelled him to deliver them from Egypt and bring them home in the first exodus, so too, in the latter days, he will bring his children home to the promised land once more. Seen in the light of this ancient hope, Jesus' address to God as "Father" may signal that he is not merely teaching the disciples about the nature of their relationship with God. More broadly, he is teaching them to pray for the long-awaited new exodus.

The Hallowing of God's Name and the New Exodus in Ezekiel

These connections between the fatherhood of God and the new exodus can be confirmed by turning to the first petition in the Lord's Prayer: "Hallowed

31. On the prominence of the new exodus in Isaiah, see Pao, *Acts and the Isaianic New Exodus,* 51-59, drawing on Dale A. Patrick, "Epiphanic Imagery in Second Isaiah's Portrayal of a New Exodus," *HAR* 8 (1984): 125-41; Carroll Stuhlmueller, *Creative Redemption in Deutero-Isaiah* (Rome: Pontifical Biblical Institute, 1970); Bernhard W. Anderson, "Exodus Typology in Second Isaiah," in *Israel's Prophetic Heritage: Essays in Honor of James Muilenberg,* ed. Bernhard W. Anderson and Walter Harrelson (New York: Harper, 1962), 177-95. See also Gerhard von Rad, who speaks of "the message of the new Exodus" as "one of Deutero-Isaiah's main topics." *Old Testament Theology* (2 vols.; trans. D. M. G. Stalker; New York: Harper & Row, 1965), 2:244-50, 261-62.

32. Apart the passages cited above, there is only one other text in Jeremiah in which God is describes as a "father." Significantly, it is yet another oracle about the ingathering of the exiles in a new exodus. According to Jeremiah, the reason God will one day bring his people home to the promised land is that he is Israel's "father," and Israel is his "first-born son" (Jer 31:7-9). The echoes of God's message to Pharaoh — "Israel is my first-born son. . . . Let my son go" (Exod 4:22-23) — are unmistakable.

be your name" *(hagiasthēto to onoma sou)* (Matt 6:10; Luke 11:2) Although the traditional translation of this line comes across in English as a declarative statement, the Greek is very clearly an imperative request: "May your name be hallowed!"[33] In this case, familiarity may breed a certain lack of awareness for just how peculiar this line of the prayer is. Why should Jesus instruct his disciples to pray that God's name be "hallowed" or "made holy"? Is not the divine name already holy? What might it mean for God to "hallow" his own name?

Here again an answer can be found by recourse to the background of Jesus' words in Jewish Scripture. Although the language of *people* "hallowing" the name of God is found on a couple of occasions in the Old Testament,[34] in the Lord's Prayer, we appear to have a divine passive, with the sense being, "May *God* hallow his name." As many commentators agree, the rather peculiar language of God "hallowing" his "name" is drawn directly from Ezekiel 36, an eschatological prophecy in which the Lord promises to one day sanctify his name.[35] However, while this passage from Ezekiel is widely recognized as a direct parallel to Jesus' words, commentators often ignore the fact that the event that accompanies the hallowing of God's name is nothing other than the journey of the scattered tribes of Israel to the promised land:

> Therefore say to the house of Israel, Thus says the Lord God: It is not for your sake, O house of Israel, that I am about to act, but for the sake of my holy name, which you have profaned among the Gentiles to which you came. *And I will hallow my great name,* which has been profaned among the Gentiles, and which you have profaned among them; and the Gentiles will know that I am the Lord, says the Lord God, *when I vindicate my holiness before their eyes. For I will take you from the Gentiles, and gather you from all the countries, and bring you into your own land. I will sprinkle clean water upon you, and you shall be clean from all your uncleannesses,*

33. Cf. Fitzmyer, *The Gospel according to Luke,* 2:903.

34. See Lev. 22:32; Isa. 29:22-23. In both cases, the subject of the verb is not God but human beings. Among later Jewish literature, see *b. Yeb.* 79a which says that: "It is better that a single jot of the Torah be rooted out of its place so that the Name of heaven be sanctified in public." Translated by Jacob Neusner, *The Babylonian Talmud: A Translation and Commentary* (22 vols.; repr.; Peabody: Hendrickson, 2005). Cf. Dunn, *Jesus Remembered,* 547, who also cites *1 Enoch* 61:12 which, intriguingly, occurs in the midst of a vision of the revelation and enthronement of the Messiah.

35. Meier, *A Marginal Jew,* 2:296-97; Dunn, *Jesus Remembered,* 476-77; Wright, *Jesus and the Victory of God,* 293; Fitzmyer, *The Gospel According to Luke,* 2:898. For a full discussion, see James Swetnam, "Hallowed Be Thy Name," *Bib* 52 (1972): 556-63.

> *and from all your idols I will cleanse you.* A new heart I will give you, and a new spirit I will put within you; and I will take out of your flesh the heart of stone and give you a heart of flesh. And I will put my spirit within you, and cause you to walk in my statutes and be careful to observe my ordinances. You shall dwell in the land which I gave to your fathers; and you shall be my people, and I will be your God. (Ezek 36:22-28)

This is a striking vision of the coming age of salvation. When God's name is hallowed, the people of Israel will be set free from exile among the Gentiles and be gathered "from all the countries" into a restored and renewed promised land, a paradise that will be "like the garden of Eden" (Ezek 36:35). Although in this particular oracle Ezekiel does not use explicit exodus typology, in an earlier parallel oracle, he has already done so. Compare Ezekiel 20, in which the prophet both describes the future return of Israel from the countries in terms of a new exodus, and specifically ties it to the "hallowing" of the Lord God:

> As I live, says the Lord GOD, surely with a mighty hand and an outstretched arm, and with wrath poured out, I will be king over you. I will bring you out from the peoples and gather you out of the countries where you are scattered, with a mighty hand and outstretched arm . . . and I will bring you into the wilderness of the peoples. . . . *As I entered into judgment with your fathers in the wilderness in the land of Egypt, so I will enter into judgment with you,* says the Lord GOD. . . . As a pleasing odor I will accept you, when I bring you out from the peoples, and gather you out of the countries where you have been scattered; and *I will be hallowed among you* in the sight of the nations. And you shall know that I am the LORD, *when I bring you into the land of Israel, the country which I swore to give to your fathers.* (Ezek 20:33-36, 41-42)[36]

In light of such passages, we can conclude that for Ezekiel, the future ingathering of the Israelites to the promised land will recapitulate the journey of the Israelites in the first exodus from Egypt. Once again, this new exodus, and all the events that will accompany it, will take place when God "hallows" his "name" by saving his people.

36. I have slightly altered the RSV's translation of w^{e}*niqdaštî* from "manifest my holiness" to "be hallowed" so that the verbal parallel between Ezekiel 20 and Ezekiel 36 (as well as the Lord's Prayer) is more apparent. Compare the Septuagint, which also reads "I will be hallowed *(hagiasthēsomai)* among you" (Ezek 36:41 LXX).

With this Old Testament background in mind, we can suggest that when Jesus instructs the disciples to pray "Hallowed be your name," he is not giving them a generic prayer for "God's action in human history."[37] Rather, he is giving them a thoroughly biblical prayer, using the language of the prophets, for the new exodus. Indeed, in the case of the second "you-petition," Jesus appears to be drawing directly on the language of Ezekiel's prophecy and instructing his disciples to pray for its fulfillment. If this is correct, then it is worth noting that in the book of Ezekiel, as in Jeremiah, it is elsewhere made clear that the future exodus is expected to coincide with the coming of the messiah and the establishment of the future kingdom (Ezek 37:19-26). It is therefore unsurprising that the next petition deals with the advent of the future kingdom.

The Coming of the Kingdom and the New Exodus in Micah

Perhaps no line from the Lord's Prayer has been more vigorously debated than the petition: "May your kingdom come" *(elthetō hē basileia sou)* (Matt 6:10; Luke 11:2). As many scholars would agree, the hope for the "coming" of God's "kingdom" is arguably the heart not only of the Lord's Prayer, but of Jesus' entire mission and message. But what exactly does Jesus' instruction to pray for the coming of the kingdom mean?

A host of answers have been proposed, far too many to be discussed here.[38] For our purposes here, I simply want to point out that, like other petitions in the Lord's Prayer, the language and imagery of the prayer for the coming of the kingdom appear to be rooted in the prophetic hope for the eschatological journey of the exiles to the promised land in a new exodus.

Despite the curious claim of some scholars that Jesus' combined imagery of the "coming" of the "kingdom" cannot be found in the Old Testament, there is in fact a major prophetic oracle in the book of Micah in which precisely such a combination takes place.[39] Admittedly, this is to my knowledge the only time Jewish Scripture ever speaks about the coming of a kingdom, but this only heightens the importance of Micah's prophecy for interpreting the Lord's Prayer:

37. Cf. Fitzmyer, *The Gospel according to Luke*, 2:899.

38. For discussion, see Meier, *A Marginal Jew*, 2:237-506.

39. *Contra* Meier, *A Marginal Jew*, 2:294; Davies and Allison, *Saint Matthew*, 1:604; Fitzmyer, *The Gospel according to Luke*, 2:904. Cf., however, Dale C. Allison Jr., *Constructing Jesus: Memory, Imagination, and History* (Grand Rapids: Baker Academic, 2010), 37 n. 27.

> It shall come to pass *in the latter days*
> that the mountain of the house of the LORD
> shall be established as the highest of the mountains,
> and shall be raised up above the hills;
> and peoples shall flow to it, and many Gentiles shall come, and say:
> "Let us go up to the mountain of the LORD,
> to the house of the God of Jacob;
> that he may teach us his ways and we may walk in his paths."
> For out of Zion shall go forth the Law,
> and the word of the LORD from Jerusalem. . . .
> *In that day, says the LORD, I will assemble the lame*
> *and gather those who have been driven away,*
> and those whom I have afflicted; and the lame I will make the remnant;
> and those who were cast off, a strong nation;
> *and the LORD will reign over them in Mount Zion*
> from this time forth forever more.
> *And you, O tower of the flock, hill of the daughter of Zion,*
> *to you it shall come, the former dominion shall come,*
> and *the kingdom of the daughter of Jerusalem.* (Mic 4:1-8)

Here we have another striking prophetic parallel to Jesus' prayer for the "coming" *(erchomai)* of the "kingdom" *(basileia)* (Matt 6:10; Luke 11:2). Although this might be easy to overlook in the English translation, the final line of Micah's oracle clearly connects the verb "come"[40] to the noun "kingdom."[41] Given that the immediate context is the proclamation that "the LORD will reign" in Mount Zion, Micah's oracle clearly climaxes with the coming of the kingdom of the LORD — that is, with the coming of the kingdom of God.

The reason this biblical background is significant for us is not only that it uses the same language found in the Lord's Prayer. It is also important because Micah describes the coming of the kingdom to Zion primarily in terms of the eschatological ingathering of the scattered tribes of Israel and the Gentiles. For Micah, the kingdom of the Lord will come when both the Gentile "nations" and the Israelites "who have been driven away" are gathered to Zion (Mic 4:2, 6). Once again, although explicit exodus imagery is not used in the oracle above, Micah elsewhere explicitly describes the return from exile as a new exodus that will surpass the wonders that took place when Israel came out of Egypt:

40. MT *bā'āh;* LXX *eiserchomai.*
41. MT *mamleketh;* LXX *basileia.*

> A day for the building of your walls!
> In that day the boundary shall be far extended.
> *In that day they will come to you,*
> *from Assyria and cities of Egypt,*
> *and from Egypt to the River,*
> *from sea to sea and from mountain to mountain. . . .*
> Shepherd your people with your staff,
> the flock of your inheritance.
> *As in the days when you came out of the land of Egypt*
> *I will show them marvelous things.* (Mic 7:11-15)

It is difficult to overemphasize the importance of these prophetic texts for understanding the Lord's Prayer. Once again, Jesus is drawing on imagery from Jewish Scripture to depict the coming of the kingdom of God. Perhaps even more significant, this imagery reveals that in the biblical prophets, the expectation of the coming of the kingdom of God and the hope for a new exodus overlap.[42] The coming of the kingdom and the journey of the scattered tribes are two ways of speaking about the same eschatological event. The "kingdom" image emphasizes the Davidic shape of the dominion of God: the reign of the messiah, the new Temple, and the establishment of a universal dominion. The exodus imagery emphasizes the Mosaic shape of future salvation, in which God will save his people in the latter days in much the same way he saved them in the Exodus. He will forgive their sins, release them from slavery, and then lead them home to the eschatological promised land. Both the Mosaic and the Davidic dimensions of salvation are important for understanding the age of salvation as depicted by the prophets.

Once this prophetic background is clear, it should be clear that Jesus' prayer for the coming of the kingdom is not a simple invocation of God's presence among them for the present; rather, they are praying for the advent of God's eschatological reign.[43] Indeed, with this biblical background in mind, we can more easily explain Jesus' otherwise awkward language of the "coming" of a "kingdom" — language that continues to puzzle scholars.[44] How can a "kingdom" be said to "come"? The answer is: quite easily, if "the kingdom" in question refers in this context to a people — namely, the scattered children of God. This is especially true if the people in question are in exile, as the tribes

42. Cf. also Isaiah 2, 40; Jeremiah 30–31; Ezekiel 20, 36–37, etc.

43. Keener, *The Historical Jesus of the Gospels,* 198.

44. E.g., Meier, *A Marginal Jew,* 2:298.

of Israel had been for centuries, spread among the Gentile nations.[45] In this light, the coming of God's kingdom for which Jesus instructs his disciples to pray means nothing less than the ingathering of Israel and the Gentiles to the promised land in a new exodus.

The Daily Bread and the Manna from Heaven

If there is any petition in the Lord's Prayer that has long been recognized as connected to the exodus from Egypt, it is the first of the so-called "we" petitions: "Give us this day our *epiousios* bread" (Matt 6:11) or "Give us each day our *epiousios* bread" (Luke 11:3). As we will see, it is certainly the most important line for our investigation of Jesus and the Jewish expectations of a new Moses and a new exodus.

However, while this line may be extremely familiar, its contents raise several important and complicated issues of interpretation. First, exactly what kind of bread is Jesus instructing his disciples to pray for? Is he speaking, as so many take it, about simply earthly bread? If so, how do we square such a mundane interpretation with Jesus' command to his disciples elsewhere, "Do not be anxious about your life, what you shall eat and what you shall drink" (Matt 6:25; Luke 12:22)?[46] Or is he speaking about some other kind of bread? If so, to what does he refer? Far more difficult is the question: What is the meaning of the obscure Greek adjective *epiousios,* commonly translated "daily"? What is the meaning of this word, and what light does its throw on the substance of the petition?[47]

By raising this question, we step directly into what is rightly regarded as "one of the great unresolved puzzles of NT lexicography."[48] It is a sobering fact that by the third century A.D. the expression already had a native Greek speaker and exegetical giant such as Origen perplexed, and the word continues to bewilder interpreters to this day.[49] Although numerous suggestions have been forwarded over the centuries,[50] to my mind, the most significant proposals are four in number:

45. For more on the ingathering of the exiles, see chapter 6 below, and Pitre, *Jesus, the Tribulation, and the End of the Exile,* 31-40.

46. Carmignac, *Recherches sur le "Notre Père,"* 190.

47. See Meier, *A Marginal Jew,* 2:364 n. 48; Fitzmyer, *The Gospel according to Luke,* 2:904-6; W. Foerster, *"epiousios," TDNT,* 2:590-99.

48. Davies and Allison, *Saint Matthew,* 1:607.

49. Origen, *De Oratione* 27:7

50. See John Hennig, "Our Daily Bread," *TS* (1943): 445-54.

1. ***Daily Bread*** "Give us this day our daily bread." In this view, the Greek word *epiousios* is derived from the words "for" *(epi)* and "the being" *(tēn ousan),* with the word "day" *(hēmera)* being implied — i.e., for "the current day" or, more awkwardly, "for the [day] being."

Among ancient authors, a form of this view can be found in John Chrysostom, who interprets the petition as referring to "daily" *(ton ephēmeron)* bread,[51] as well as Jerome's Vulgate translation of Luke 11:3 as "Give us each day our daily *(quotidianum)* bread."[52] Hence, this interpretation has behind it the weight of liturgical usage, as well as being made popular through Martin Luther's German translation of the Bible, as well as the King James Version.[53] Though somewhat less popular these days, it still finds support among modern scholars.[54]

The primary weakness of the "daily" interpretation is twofold. First, it makes the adjective "daily" redundant, since the daily aspect of the bread requested has already been indicated in the prayer, whether in Matthew's version ("this day") or Luke's version ("each day"). Second, if the word "daily" were meant, this could have easily been expressed by a variety of other common Greek adjectives; the word *epiousios* has no clear relationship to the Greek word "day" *(hēmera);* it simply does not mean "daily." Hence, the daily bread view is not really a translation, but rather a loose interpretation in which the wording of the Lord's Prayer is simply altered so that the petition makes sense.

2. ***Natural Bread*** "Give us this day our bread for existence." According to this translation, the Greek word *epiousios* is derived from *epi,* unusually rendered as "for," and "being, substance, essence" *(ousia).*

Among ancient authors, the natural interpretation goes at least as far back as Origen.[55] Among modern scholars, it remains a popular explanation of the petition,[56] who frequently compare it with the request for earthly sustenance in Proverbs: "Feed me with the food that is needful for me" (Prov 30:8).[57]

51. John Chrysostom, *Homilies on the Gospel of Matthew* 19.5.

52. In the Latin Rite, it is also found in the traditional liturgical version of the *Pater Noster.*

53. Jeremias, *The Prayers of Jesus,* 100.

54. E.g., Bornkamm, *Jesus of Nazareth,* 137, 208 n. 50; Matthew Black, *An Aramaic Approach to the Gospels* (2nd ed.; Oxford: Oxford University Press, 1954), 153.

55. "Bread being of service for (our) being." Origen, *De Oratione* 27.7.

56. E.g., Fitzmyer, *The Gospel according to Luke,* 2:900; Foerster, "*epiousios,*" 599.

57. See too Crossan, *The Historical Jesus,* 294, and Robert W. Funk, Roy Hoover, and

Although linguistically a stronger candidate than the daily interpretation, the natural interpretation also suffers from weaknesses. As Albert Schweitzer once forcefully pointed out, it appears to contradict Jesus' injunction to his disciples *not* to be anxious about or focused on material food and material needs, but rather to seek the kingdom.[58] Moreover, Raymond Brown rightly observes that a prayer for mundane earthly bread does not fit the eschatological context of the rest of the Lord's Prayer. This interpretation leaves the petition for bread isolated among the other prayers, which are focused on heavenly realities and eschatological events.[59]

3. ***Supernatural Bread*** "Give us this day our supersubstantial bread." Unlike the previous two solutions, this approach does not view *epiousios* as a form of some other word or words, but translates it as it stands as literally as possible: "on, upon, above" *(epi)* + "being, nature, substance" *(ousia).*

This literal rendering finds its most famous witness in Jerome's translation of the Lord's Prayer in the Vulgate Gospel of Matthew, which reads: "Give us this day our supersubstantial bread."[60] As John A. T. Robinson points out, since there was no such Latin word as "supersubstantial," Jerome's translation of this verse is simply literalistic translation of *epiousios,* which "probably signified something much more like 'supernatural.' "[61]

Among ancient authors, the supernatural interpretation finds remarkably wide support, which strangely often goes unmentioned by modern studies. For example, Cyril of Jerusalem writes in his treatise on the Lord's Prayer: "Common bread is not supersubstantial, but this Holy Bread is supersubstantial."[62] Likewise, Cyprian of Carthage states that the bread Jesus speaks of is "heavenly bread," i.e., the "food of salvation."[63] Above all stands Jerome himself, who explains his rendering as follows: "We can interpret our

---

the Jesus Seminar, *The Five Gospels: The Search for the Authentic Words of Jesus* (New York: Macmillan, 1993), 327.

58. Albert Schweitzer, *The Mysticism of Paul the Apostle* (trans. W. M. Montgomery; London: A. & C. Black, 1931), 239-40.

59. Brown, "The Pater Noster as an Eschatological Prayer," 305.

60. The Latin reads: *Panem nostrum supersubstantialem da nobis hodie.*

61. Robinson, "The Lord's Prayer," 57.

62. Cyril of Jerusalem, *Mystagogic Catechesis* 23.15, in Philip Schaff and Henry Wace, *Nicene and Post-Nicene Fathers: Second Series* (14 vols.; repr.; Peabody: Hendrickson, 1994), 7:155.

63. Cyprian of Carthage, *Treatises* 4.18, cited in Manlio Simonetti, *Matthew* (2 vols.; Ancient Christian Commentary on Scripture; Downers Grove: IVP, 2001, 2002), 135; cf. Roberts and Donaldson, *Ante-Nicene Fathers,* 5:452.

'supersubstantial bread' also as 'the bread which is higher than all substances.'"[64] Likewise, John Cassian, a pupil of John Chrysostom and also a native Greek speaker: "The word 'supersubstantial' expresses . . . a thing above all substances."[65]

The primary weaknesses of the supernatural interpretation are two. First, despite being widely held among ancient Christians, it receives virtually no support among modern exegetes, who either only mention it in passing and or fail to even list it as a viable option, despite the fact that it is easily the most literal translation.[66] Second, it suffers from the fact that, given the limits of our knowledge, it is virtually impossible to translate *epiousios* into an agreed-upon equivalent Aramaic or Hebrew expression.[67] As far as I know, none of the Semitic versions we possess give anything like an equivalent word meaning "supernatural."[68] Given the widespread acceptance of the hypothesis that Jesus spoke Aramaic rather than Greek, this leads scholars to seek a translation that works in both Greek and Aramaic or Hebrew.

4. ***Bread for the Coming Day*** "Give us this day our bread for the coming [day]." According to this translation, *epiousios* is a form of the Greek expression *hē epiousa,* "that which is coming," with the word "day" being implied, not stated. Linguistically, the word would represent a shortened version of the expression "on the following day" *(tē epiousē hēmera),* such as we find elsewhere in the New Testament and early Jewish literature (see Acts 7:26).[69]

Among ancient commentators, this interpretation finds its primary support in a passing comment from Jerome (who by now has taken at least three sides in this debate and clearly seems to have been undecided on the whole matter!):

64. Jerome, *PL* 26:43; cited in Hennig, "Our Daily Bread," 446. See Jerome, Vulgate of Matt 6:11; *Comm. in Ps.* 135:25.

65. John Cassian, *PL* 49:794; cited in Hennig, "Our Daily Bread," 448. Cf. John Cassian, *Conference* 9.21, cited in Just, *Luke,* 187.

66. E.g., Davies and Allison, *Saint Matthew,* 1:608.

67. See the catalogue of competing suggestions in Davies and Allison, *Saint Matthew,* 1:608-9.

68. Fitzmyer, *The Gospel according to Luke,* 2:904-5, lists the Old Syriac as reading "continual *('myn')* bread"; the Peshitta reads "the bread of our need *(desunqanan).*" For what it is worth, it is intriguing that the medieval Hebrew manuscript of the Gospel of Matthew (commonly known as "Shem-Tob's Hebrew Matthew") agrees with the Old Syriac and reads "continual bread" *(lhmnw tamidith).* See George Howard, *Hebrew Gospel of Matthew* (Macon: Mercer University Press, 1995), 24-25.

69. See also Acts 16:11; 20:15; 21:18; 23:11; Josephus, *War* 2.441; *Ant.* 10.170.

> In the Gospel which is called "according to the Hebrews," I have found, instead of "supersubstantial" bread, *maar,* which means "tomorrow's." Thus the sense is: "give us today our tomorrow's, that is, future, bread." (Jerome, *Commentary on Matthew* 6:11)[70]

Remarkably, despite the lost nature of the Gospel according to the Hebrews, modern scholars have been heavily influenced by Jerome's suggestion, such that the future interpretation is now held by a majority of scholars.[71] In his widely influential book on the Lord's Prayer, Joachim Jeremias considered the evidence from Jerome to be the "decisive fact" in favor of the future interpretation.[72]

The primary weakness of this view is its lack of support among ancient Christian interpreters, whose command of Greek was surely as good if not better than that of modern scholars. Indeed, its popularity in modern times seems due to a large extent to the virtual consensus that Jesus did not speak Greek, and that therefore a Semitic original of the Lord's Prayer must be sought, which Jerome provides us.

The Problem of the Bread Petition

What then is one to make of this situation? One has to confess a certain amount of perplexity. How is it possible that what may be among the most well-known verses in the New Testament, both in ancient and modern times, also happens to contain what may be the most obscure word in the Bible?

Given the fact that in this study we are not seeking the *ipsissima verba Jesu* but rather the *substantia verba Jesu,* it seems to me that the best approach is to focus on the overarching context of the bread petition.[73] In the words of W. D. Davies and Dale Allison:

70. St. Jerome, *Commentary on Matthew* (trans. Thomas P. Scheck; Washington, DC: Catholic University of America Press, 2008), 88-89. For an exhaustive survey of the patristic data regarding the Hebrew Gospel(s), see James R. Edwards, *The Hebrew Gospel & the Development of the Synoptic Tradition* (Grand Rapids: Eerdmans, 2009).

71. E.g., Davies and Allison, *Saint Matthew,* 1:609; Jeremias, *The Prayers of Jesus,* 100-101; Brown, "The Pater Noster," 306-7. See BADG, *"epiousios,"* 297; Foerster, *"epiousios,"* 592 nn. 16-17, for extensive older secondary literature.

72. Jeremias, *The Prayers of Jesus,* 100.

73. Cf. Dunn, *Jesus Remembered,* 410.

> In our judgement, the most plausible solution [to the debate over *epiousios*] will have to take into account the implicit allusion to the story of the gathering of the manna in Exodus 16, where God is the source of food, specifically bread (= manna), where several phrases employing *hēmera* ["day"] are found,[74] and where *didōmi* ["give"] is used.[75] Already Tertullian saw the story of the manna as an interpretive key to *epiousios*,[76] and Exod 16:4, which is alluded to elsewhere in the NT[77] runs, "Behold, I will rain bread from heaven for you, and the people shall go out and gather a day's portion every day."[78]

This seems to me to be exactly correct: we should illuminate what is obscure — the meaning of *epiousios* — by means of what is clear: the allusion to the "daily bread" of the manna in the exodus.

When we do this, we discover something remarkable: in both Jewish Scripture and early Jewish literature, there is a consistent emphasis on the daily nature of the manna from heaven. Note that this emphasis on the daily character of the manna is present both in the foundational account of the manna of the exodus as well as one prominent early Jewish witness to the expectation of future manna:

> Then the Lord said to Moses, "Behold, *I will rain bread from heaven for you;* and the people shall go out and gather *a day's portion every day,* that I may test them, whether they will walk in my law or not. On the sixth *day,* when they prepare what they bring in, it will be twice as much as they gather *daily*. . . ." (Exod 16:4-5)

> And it will happen that when all that which should come to pass in these parts is accomplished, *the Messiah will begin to be revealed. . . . And those who are hungry will enjoy themselves and they will, moreover, see marvels every day*. . . . And it will happen at that time that *the treasury of manna will come down again from on high, and they will eat of it* in those years because these are they who will have arrived at the consummation of time. (*2 Baruch* 29:3-8)

74. Exod 16:1, 4, 5, 22, 26, 27, 29, 30.
75. Exod 16:8, 15, 29; cf. Ps 77:24 LXX; John 6:32.
76. Tertullian, *Against Marcion* 4.26.4.
77. John 6:32; 1 Cor 10:3; cf. Rev 2:17.
78. Davies and Allison, *Saint Matthew,* 1:608 (emphasis added; slightly emended).

These are striking parallels to the Lord's Prayer. In the first text, God promises to "give" the "bread" to the people of Israel each "day." Likewise, in the Lord's Prayer, Jesus commands his disciples to pray that God "give" *(didou/dos)* them "bread" *(ton arton)* "today" *(sēmeron)* or "each day" *(to kath' hēmeran)* (Matt 6:11; Luke 11:3).[79] In the second text, the coming of the messiah and his kingdom is not only linked with the return of the manna from heaven, but the emphasis falls on the "daily" nature of the future miracle. Likewise, in the Lord's Prayer, Jesus commands the disciples to pray to God that the bread in question be given each day. Just as the Israelites in the desert had been given manna each day, so too those who live during the days of the messiah should expect to see bread miracles "every day." As C. H. Dodd puts it, Jewish texts like 2 *Baruch* clearly depict the righteous eating the manna during "the period of the temporary messianic kingdom on earth."[80]

In light of such parallels, there are good reasons to conclude that Jesus' emphasis on the daily nature of the bread of the Lord's Prayer is evocative of the manna of the exodus.[81] This conclusion is important for two reasons. First, it strongly suggests that Jesus is not merely instructing the disciples to pray *for* the mundane bread of daily existence. Rather, *he is teaching them to pray for the new manna of the new exodus.* Just as God had provided sustenance for his people during the first exodus, when Israel "ate the bread of angels," so too would God feed the people of his kingdom during the eschatological exodus spoken of by the prophets. Second, and equally significant, it also helps us in drawing a somewhat firmer conclusion about the substance of this petition.

79. Indeed, as Dale Allison points out, in the Septuagint translation of the Old Testament, the word *hēmera* ("day") appears eight times and the word "give" *(didōmi)* three times in the account of the giving of the manna in Exodus 16, emphasizing that the manna is in a unique way the bread given by God to Israel each day: "In the LXX account [of the manna] *hēmera* appears repeatedly (vv. 1, 4, 5, 22, 26, 27, 29, 30), and *didōmi* is used (vv. 8, 15, 29; cf. LXX Ps. 77:24; John 6:32). Further, Luke's redactional "daily" *(to kath' hēmeran)* appears in LXX Exod 16,5." Dale Allison, "Q's New Exodus and the Historical Jesus," 399.

80. C. H. Dodd, *The Interpretation of the Fourth Gospel* (Cambridge: Cambridge University Press, 1953), 335.

81. Allison, *The Intertextual Jesus,* 51-52, lists the following ancient and modern commentators who saw this connection with the manna: Tertullian, Origen, Hugh of St. Victor, Albert the Great, Martin Luther, John Calvin, Cornelius à Lapide, W. Foerster, etc. To this can be added now Pitre, "The Lord's Prayer and the New Exodus," 84-87; Dunn, *Jesus Remembered,* 411; Wright, "The Lord's Prayer," 142-43; Davies and Allison, *Saint Matthew,* 1:608-9; Fitzmyer, *The Gospel according to Luke,* 2:900; Houk, "*PEIRASMOS,* the Lord's Prayer, and the Massah Tradition," 222-23; Brown, "The Pater Noster," 309-10. See the extensive survey by Carmignac, *Recherches sur le "Notre Père,"* 200-210.

Given our current state of knowledge there does not seem to be any definitive way to solve the debate over the meaning of *epiousios*. Nevertheless, when we take into account the connections between this petition and the manna, it is truly remarkable that none of the four major interpretations listed above excludes the allusion to the manna from heaven. Indeed, each one of them coheres quite well with an allusion to the manna:

1. Daily Bread: The manna was daily bread, the people being given "a day's portion every day" (Exod 16:4).
2. Bread for Existence: The manna was also necessary for existence, sustaining the people in the desert by "filling" them (Exod 16:1-3, 8, 12).
3. Supernatural Bread: The manna was clearly miraculous, insofar as it was "bread from heaven" which appeared only six days a week, always in the same measure, and lasted only forty years (Exod 16:4, 13-30).
4. Bread for the Coming Day: The manna was bread for the coming day, since God made good on his promise each week to give the people bread enough "for two days," including the Sabbath rest (Exod 16:5).

In light of these connections, it seems best to conclude that while we remain uncertain as to the exact meaning of the word *epiousios*, we can be much more confident that the petition for bread in the Lord's Prayer is tied to the Jewish eschatological hope for the return of the manna from heaven. Indeed, when the eschatological thrust of the Lord's Prayer as a whole is taken into account, there are strong reasons to conclude that Jesus is teaching his followers to ask God for the manna of the eschatological exodus, the "food of inaugurated eschatology."[82] Significantly, because the exodus was both a day-by-day journey and an event that functions as a prototype of the eschaton, the new exodus interpretation has the added strength of rendering plausible the two poles of exegesis of the Lord's Prayer, which fluctuate between "an eschatological interpretation and one related to everyday life."[83]

The Forgiveness of Debts and the Return to the Land

We now turn to the fourth common petition, in which Jesus instructs the disciples to pray to God for the forgiveness of "debts" (so Matthew) or "sins"

82. Wright, "The Lord's Prayer," 143; cf. Dunn, *Jesus Remembered*, 410-11.
83. Theissen and Merz, *The Historical Jesus*, 262.

(so Luke) based on one's willingness to forgive "debtors" or "those indebted to us" (Matt 6:12; Luke 11:4). Although a prayer for the forgiveness of sins is certainly nothing remarkable, it is curious that Jesus utilizes the language of "debt" *(opheilē)* and "debtor" *(opheiletēs)* (Matt 6:12; Luke 11:4). Whence the economic terminology in an eschatological prayer?

On one level, a linguistic answer to the question is possible. As many scholars have pointed out, in the Old Testament and ancient Judaism, the language and imagery of "debt" was sometimes used as a metaphor for "sin."[84] Although not exactly common, this usage is not unique to the Lord's Prayer. On a deeper level, however, the answer may yet again be rooted in the Old Testament background of the prayer. The choice of "debt" imagery may be meant to evoke the most obvious image of the "forgiveness of debts" from the Old Testament: the year of the Jubilee, when every Israelite would be set free from debt-slavery and allowed to return to one's own land. This year of economic redemption and deliverance, which took place every fifty years, signaled the joy of being forgiven one's debts and being set free from bondage (Lev 25:1-55).[85]

Two aspects of the Jubilee year need to be emphasized as background to Jesus' words. First, the Jubilee did not only mean freedom from debt, as important as that was. It also meant a return to one's land: the Jubilee was to be "a redemption of the land," when every man shall "return to his property" (Lev 25:24, 28). This element of return is sometimes overshadowed by the release from slavery, but it is actually quite significant. For in Leviticus, the practices of the Jubilee year were not merely an act of kindness on the part of Israelites; they were directly rooted in the redemption of Israel from Egypt in *the exodus.* Three times in the course of his instructions regarding the Jubilee year, God emphasizes this connection by declaring: "I am the LORD your God who brought you forth out of the land of Egypt to give you the land of Canaan, and to be your God" (Lev. 25:38, 42, 55). As Wright points out, "The Jubilee provisions . . . look back to the fact that Israel had been enslaved in Egypt and that God had rescued and delivered her. They were part of the Exodus theology."[86] Just as the Lord had set Israel free from slavery in Egypt and returned

84. See Davies and Allison, *Saint Matthew,* 1:611, citing *11QTargumJob* 34:4; Luke 7:41-43; Col 2:13-14; *m. 'Abot* 3:17. See 1 Macc 15:8 for the use of "forgive" with the terminology of "debt." For a history of the idea, see now Gary Anderson, *Sin: A History* (New Haven: Yale University Press, 2010).

85. See also Lev 27:16-25; Num 36:4; Ezek 46:16-18; Isa 49:8-9; 61:1-2; Jer 34:8-22; Neh 5:1-13; *11QMelchizedek* 2:1-9. For a full treatment of the Jubilee in both the Old Testament and Second Temple Judaism, see John S. Bergsma, *The Jubilee from Leviticus to Qumran: A History of Interpretation,* Supplements to Vetus Testamentum (Leiden: E. J. Brill, 2006).

86. Wright, "The Lord's Prayer," 143.

them to their land, the promised land, so too, during the Jubilee year, the people of Israel were to remember their salvation by freeing those enslaved and forgiving those in debt.[87]

Second, the Jubilee was not only something that had happened in the past; it was also a future event that was directly tied to the inauguration of the new Exodus. The basis for this connection is found in the prophet Isaiah, who describes the Servant of the LORD as one who is "anointed" *(māšîaḥ)* to proclaim a great eschatological Jubilee that would precede the restoration of Israel to the promised land:

> *The Spirit of the Lord GOD is upon me,*
> *because the LORD has anointed me*
> *to bring good news to the afflicted;*
> he has sent me to bind up the brokenhearted,
> *to proclaim liberty to the captives,*
> *and the opening of the prison to those who are bound;*
> *to proclaim the year of the Lord's favor. . . .*
> They shall build up the ancient ruins,
> they shall raise up the former devastations;
> they shall repair the ruined cities. . . .
> Therefore *in their land* they shall possess a double portion;
> theirs shall be everlasting joy. (Isa 61:1-2, 4, 7)[88]

While modern Old Testament scholars continue to debate the precise identity of this "anointed" one, there is no doubt that he inaugurates the Jubilee year, "the year of the Lord's favor" (Isa 61:2). This Jubilee is not merely tied to release of various individuals, but to the central hope of Isaiah: the return of the entire people of Israel to the promised land in a new exodus.

In support of this suggestion, it is worth highlighting that the most ancient Jewish interpretation of this passage, found in the Dead Sea Scrolls, not only connects Isaiah 61 with a new exodus, but with the coming of the messiah, who is depicted as a new Melchizedek:

> And as for what he said: "*In [this] year of Jubilee,* [you shall return, each one, to his respective property" (Lev. 25:13), concerning it he said: "Th]is

87. The same principle is at work in the seven-year Sabbatical debt-release. In this case the connection with the Exodus is even more explicit: "At the end of every seven years you shall grant a release. . . . You shall remember that you were a slave in the land of Egypt, and the LORD your God redeemed you; therefore I command you this day" (Deut. 15:1, 15).

88. RSV, slightly altered.

> is [the manner of the release:] every creditor shall release what he lent [to his neighbour. He shall not coerce his neighbour or his brother, for it has been proclaimed] a release for G[od]" (Deut. 15:2). *Its interpretation] for the last days refers to the captives . . . they are the inherita[nce of Melchize]-dek, who will make them return. And liberty will be proclaimed for them, to free them from [the debt of] all their iniquities.* And this [wil]l [happen] in the first week of the Jubilee . . . in which atonement shall be made for all the sons of [light and] for the men [of] the lot of Melchizedek . . . for *it is the time for "the year of favor"* (Isa. 61:2). . . . (*11QMelchizedek* 2:1-9)[89]

In this fascinating text, we find several key eschatological events that help to shed light on the future Jubilee. The "last days" will see the coming of the Messiah, the "anointed one" *(māšîaḥ),* who is depicted as an eschatological Melchizedek, the famous priest-king from the time of Abraham (Gen 14:18; *11QMelch.* 2:18). This messianic priest-king will inaugurate an *eschatological* Jubilee; it will take place in "the last days" in order to set "the captives" free. In addition — and this is important — the "liberty" of this eschatological Jubilee will not be merely economic, but spiritual: it will be proclaimed "to free them from [the debt of] all their iniquities." Hence, the messianic Jubilee is oriented toward "atonement" for sin, and freedom from the power of "Belial," the chief of the evil spirits (*11QMelch.* 2:7, 11-13). This "release" will not only mean the forgiveness of sins, but a return to the promised land. Indeed, it is the Messiah himself who "will make them return" to the land, thereby inaugurating a new Exodus (*11QMelch.* 2:5-6). All of this will take place during "the year of favor," the very Jubilee that Isaiah himself had tied to the coming of one who would be "anointed" by the Spirit of the Lord (Isa 61:2).[90] Indeed, this Scroll also links the Jubilee to the Suffering Servant passage (cf. Isa 53:12).[91]

The upshot of this broader Jewish context of Jubilee imagery is simple:

89. Trans. in Florentino García Martínez and Eibert J. C. Tigchelaar, *The Dead Sea Scrolls Study Edition* (2 vols.; Grand Rapids: Eerdmans, 2000). Brackets represent portions of the text that are damaged or missing.

90. I have also altered the translation of "year of grace" in *11QMelch.* 2:9 to "year of favor" to reflect more clearly that the author is alluding to the "year of favor" in Isa 61:2. Despite the explicit use of "messiah" terminology in this document, it receives little or no treatment in otherwise thorough studies of the Messiah in early Judaism, such as Gerbern S. Oegema, *The Anointed and His People: Messianic Expectations from the Maccabees to Bar Kochba,* Journal for the Study of the Pseudepigrapha Supplement Series 27 (Sheffield: Sheffield Academic, 1998). Compare, however, Timothy H. Lim, "11 QMelch, Luke 4 and the Dying Messiah," *JJS* 43 (1992): 90-92.

91. See Barber, "The Historical Jesus and Cultic Restoration Eschatology," 152-54.

by teaching his disciples to pray for the forgiveness of their "debts," Jesus is not merely instructing them to pray for absolution of one's individual sins — although he is certainly doing that. He is also situating that forgiveness within the broader covenantal context of the eschatological Jubilee and the new exodus. As the Dead Sea Scrolls show, at least some Jews living at the time of Jesus would have understood this eschatological exodus in terms of a spiritual Jubilee — a deliverance from the debt of sin — that would be inaugurated by the messiah himself.[92] In the Lord's Prayer, Jesus is calling on his disciples to live out this messianic redemption by daring to ask God to forgive them their "debts" as they forgive their "debtors."[93]

The Trials and Temptations of the Exodus Journey

The final petition that merits our attention is the plea: "Lead us not into temptation *(peirasmos)*" (Matt 6:13; Luke 11:4). Of all the petitions in this prayer, this one is arguably the most difficult to understand; it has generated a large body of literature, which I have discussed in detail elsewhere.[94] For our purposes here, we need only point out certain connections with the language of the exodus.

On the one hand, if isolated from its context, this petition can be taken as implying that God somehow "leads" human beings into "temptation" *(peirasmos)* to sin, and that humans should ask him not to do so. Both common sense and the New Testament itself make clear that this cannot be the proper interpretation. As the letter of James says, "God cannot be tempted with evil and he himself tempts *(peirazei)* no one" (James 1:13-14). Most commentators agree that temptation to evil is not what Jesus means in the Lord's Prayer.[95]

On the other hand, when this petition is interpreted in light of its Old Testament background, it too seems to display links with exodus language and

92. Cf. David E. Aune, "A Note on Jesus' Messianic Consciousness and 11Q Melchizedek," *EvQ* 45 (1973): 161-65.

93. It is worth noting here that N. T. Wright has argued quite vigorously that throughout the Old Testament, the very notion of "forgiveness of sins" is not only tied to the redemption of the individual Israelite in the eyes of God (see Sir. 28:1-7) but to the *corporate* forgiveness of Israel's sins which led them into exile among the gentile nations (cf. Sir 47:24; 48:15). He argues that, for the Old Testament, "Forgiveness of sins is another way of saying 'return from exile.'" Wright, *Jesus and the Victory of God*, 268 (emphasis eliminated).

94. See Pitre, *Jesus, the Tribulation, and the End of the Exile*, 146-53.

95. Davies and Allison, *Saint Matthew*, 1:613.

imagery.[96] For one thing, the Greek word *peirasmos*, like the Hebrew *nāsāh*, can also mean "trial" or "testing," and its root is frequently used in this connection to describe both the "trials/testings" of the Israelites during the exodus from Egypt and their tendency to put God to "the test" in the face of those trials.[97] The example of the latter usage comes from what the Psalms refer to as "the day of the Testing *(hēmeran tou peirasmou)* in the desert" (Ps 95:8), which took place at the very beginning of the exodus and led to the place being renamed "Testing" — in Hebrew, *Massah*, in Greek, *Peirasmos* (see Exod 17:7 LXX). As for the former, the terminology of "trial" or "testing" is used at least three times in the Pentateuch to refer to the period of plagues and tribulation that preceded the exodus:

> Just remember what the LORD your God did to Pharaoh and to all Egypt, *the great trials that your eyes saw, the signs and wonders,* the mighty hand and the outstretched arm by which the LORD your God brought you out. (Deut 7:18-19)

> Moses summoned all Israel and said to them: You have seen all that the LORD did before your eyes in the land of Egypt, to Pharaoh and to all his servants and to all his land, *the great trials that your eyes saw, the signs, and those great wonders.* (Deut 29:2-3)

> And the LORD will scatter you among the peoples, and you will be left few in number among the nations where the LORD will drive you. . . . But from there you will seek the LORD your God, and you will find him, if you search after him with all your heart and with all your soul. *When you are in tribulation, and all these things come upon you in the latter days, you will return to the LORD your God and obey his voice,* for the LORD your God is a merciful God; he will not fail you or destroy you or forget the covenant with your fathers which he swore to them. For ask now about former ages, long before your own, ever since the day that God created human beings on the earth; ask from one end of heaven to the other: . . . *[H]as any god ever attempted to go and take a nation for himself from the midst of another nation, by trials, by signs and wonders, by war, by a mighty hand and outstretched arm, and by terrifying displays of power, as the LORD your God did for you in Egypt before your very eyes?* (Deut 4:27-34)

96. Wright, "The Lord's Prayer," 145-47; Houk, "*PEIRASMOS*, the Lord's Prayer, and the Massah Tradition," 216-25; Cyster, "The Lord's Prayer and the Exodus Tradition," 377-81.

97. Exod 15:24; 16:4; 17:2, 7; 20:20; Num 14:22; Deut 4:34; 8:2; 13:3; 33:8; Ps 78:41, 56; 95:9.

Taken together, these texts show that the biblical notion of "trials" or "testings"[98] was repeatedly connected with the trials of the exodus — the greatest of which was, of course, the sending of the destroying angel on the night of Passover (Exodus 12–13). Moreover, these trials could also serve as a prototype for a future time of tribulation that was expected to take place "in the latter days" when God would restore Israel in a future exodus by gathering them in from "among the nations" (cf. Deut 30:1-8). In other words, Deuteronomy speaks here of a new exodus, in which God will once again redeem his people through a time of *peirasmos* accompanied by "signs, wonders, and terrifying displays of power": that is, through a period of trial that would inaugurate the age of salvation.

In sum, when the biblical background of the line "Lead us not into temptation" is taken into account, the Lord's Prayer shows itself to be a prayer for God to spare his people in the great *peirasmos* that would accompany the new exodus spoken of by Deuteronomy and the prophets. As I have argued elsewhere, given the eschatological orientation of the Lord's Prayer as a whole, it is likely that the time of "trial" *(peirasmos)* spoken of by Jesus refers to the period of eschatological tribulation that was expected to coincide in ancient Jewish eschatology with the coming of the messianic kingdom of God.[99] In this light, Jesus is teaching the disciples to pray for deliverance, not just from daily trials, but from the eschatological tribulation that was to accompany the advent of the messianic kingdom, just as the Israelites of old were delivered from the trials undergone in Egypt at the inauguration of the first exodus.

Arguments against Historical Plausibility

With all of these observations in mind, we can now take up the question: Keeping in mind the differences in detail between the various versions, should the substance of the Lord's Prayer be regarded — as its common name suggests

98. Hebrew, *massôt;* Greek, *peirasmous.*

99. Pitre, *Jesus, the Tribulation, and the End of the Exile,* 1-130. For similar eschatological interpretations of this petition, see Wright, "The Lord's Prayer," 14; Meier, *A Marginal Jew,* 2:301; Jeremias, *New Testament Theology,* 202; Brown, *New Testament Essays,* 318-19; Lohmeyer, *The Lord's Prayer,* 204-5; Albert Schweitzer, *The Mystery of the Kingdom of God* (trans. Walter Lowrie; London: A. & C. Black, 1925 [orig. 1901]), 143. Indeed, over the course of the last century, this eschatological interpretation of the time of "testing" has become widely accepted and even worked its way into recent English translations of the Bible. "Do not subject us to the final test" (NAB); "Do not bring us to the time of trial" (NRSV); "Do not bring us to the test" (NEB).

— as originating with Jesus himself? Or are there good reasons to believe that it is a creation of the early church?

In contrast to other teachings of Jesus, when it comes to the Lord's Prayer, there is a remarkable amount of scholarly agreement in favor of its historicity, with only a few voices objecting to a positive verdict. Nevertheless, some scholars do object to the historical plausibility of the prayer originating with Jesus, for the following reasons.

First, there is the argument from Jewish contextual implausibility. From this point of view, the idea that Jesus taught a distinctive prayer to his own circle of disciples reflects too much of a "break" with Judaism as a whole. In the words of John Dominic Crossan:

> [T]he establishment of such a prayer seems to represent the point where a group starts to distinguish and even separate itself from the wider religious community, and I do not believe that point was ever reached during the life of Jesus.[100]

Significantly, although Crossan himself admits that the contents of the Lord's Prayer fit quite squarely into a Jewish context,[101] it is the very idea of a unique prayer for Jesus' followers that seems to him at odds with the wider Jewish community.

Second, scholars also argue against the Lord's Prayer based on a lack of coherence with other evidence about Jesus. Consider the views of Crossan and the Jesus Seminar:

> [D]espite the fact that the Lord's Prayer must be a very early summary of themes and emphases from Jesus' own lifetime, I do not think that such a coordinated prayer was ever taught by him to his followers. If there had been a special prayer, specifically and emphatically taught to his followers by Jesus himself, I would expect an even wider attestation for it and also a more uniform version of its contents.[102]

> It is unlikely, in the judgment of the Fellows [of the Seminar], that Jesus taught his disciples the prayer as a whole, even in its reconstructed form.[103]

100. Crossan, *The Historical Jesus,* 294.
101. Crossan, *The Historical Jesus,* 293.
102. Crossan, *The Historical Jesus,* 294.
103. Funk et al., *The Five Gospels,* 327.

Although the reasoning behind these conclusions is admittedly somewhat unclear, their basic logic seems to be that the idea of "a special prayer" or a "whole prayer" being taught by Jesus to his followers is not in keeping with what we know about Jesus from other data. Apparently, the assumption is that other words and deeds of Jesus do not support the conclusion that he deliberately organized his followers into a special group complete with their own special prayer. Moreover, the argument appears to be that if Jesus would have given such a prayer to his followers, he would not have given more than one form of the prayer.

Third and finally, still other scholars argue that the Lord's Prayer is substantially inauthentic because it is identical with the faith and praxis of the early church. According to this point of view, the liturgical character of the Lord's Prayer suggests that it originated in early Jewish-Christian worship services and was only later attributed to Jesus.[104] As the Jesus Seminar concludes: "Someone in the Q community probably assembled the prayer for the first time."[105] The working assumption behind this argument appears to be the idea that Jesus himself did not have as one of his aims the institution of any particular liturgical actions and rites. Hence, the "more liturgical" the evidence, the more likely that it comes from the early church — which was interested in liturgy — than from the historical Jesus, who was not.

Given the questionable force of these arguments against the historical plausibility of the Lord's Prayer, it is perhaps unsurprising that the vast majority of scholars, including those inclined to be skeptical toward the Gospels, affirm the substantial historical plausibility of the Lord's Prayer.[106] The reason is simple: despite the lack of widespread attestation, the Lord's Prayer is historically congruent with ancient Judaism in a number of ways, coheres perfectly with other words and deeds of Jesus, and provides a plausible origin for certain aspects of the faith and praxis of the early church. This is an excellent example of how the three arguments that really matter for historical scholarship are not dissimilarity, multiple attestation, and embarrassment, but contextual plausibility, coherence, and continuity. Let us consider each briefly in turn.

104. Van Tilborg, "A Form-Criticism of the Lord's Prayer," *NovT* 14 (1972): 94-105.

105. Funk et al., *The Five Gospels*, 327.

106. Keener, *The Historical Jesus of the Gospels*, 198; Lüdemann, *Jesus After 2000 Years*, 147; Theissen and Merz, *The Historical Jesus*, 261-64; Becker, *Jesus of Nazareth*, 265-71; Meier, *A Marginal Jew*, 2:294; Sanders, *The Historical Figure of Jesus*, 195; Davies and Allison, *Saint Matthew*, 1:592-93; Beasley-Murray, *Jesus and the Kingdom of God*, 147-57; Fitzmyer, *The Gospel according to Luke*, 2:900; Meyer, *The Aims of Jesus*, 208-9; Jeremias, *New Testament Theology*, 193-203; Bornkamm, *Jesus of Nazareth*, 136-37.

Context: The Baptist's Prayers, Jewish Scripture, and Jewish Daily Prayers

First and foremost, in contrast to the assertions of the scholars cited above, it is not at all implausible that an early Jewish teacher like Jesus taught his disciples prayers. Indeed, according to the Gospel of Luke, it was the fact that John the Baptist taught his disciples to pray that led the disciples to petition Jesus to do the same:

> He was praying in a certain place, and when he ceased, one of his disciples said to him, "Lord, teach us to pray, *as John taught his disciples.*" And he said to them, "When you pray, say: 'Father, hallowed be your name. . . .'" (Luke 11:1-2)

> And they said to him [Jesus], "The disciples of John fast often and *offer prayers,* and so do the disciples of the Pharisees, but yours eat and drink." (Luke 5:33)

Now, if the substance of this memory of John the Baptist teaching his disciples to "offer prayers" or "make prayers" *(deēseis poiountai)* is historically accurate, then the testimony that Jesus taught his disciples to pray in similar manner would fit well into his immediate first-century Jewish context.[107]

Second, as is widely recognized, the contents of the Lord's Prayer also fit remarkably well into an ancient Jewish context.[108] We have already marshaled the most important evidence in this regard, when we showed above how the themes and language of Jesus' prayer are deeply rooted in Jewish Scripture and developed in later Jewish literature and tradition. To briefly recap: the addressing of God as Father is not only attested in the Old Testament, but figures prominently in prophetic prayers for the new exodus (Isa 63:16; 64:8; Jer 3:19).

107. On continuity between John and Jesus, see esp. the excursus on "The Continuity between John the Baptist and Jesus," in Allison, *Constructing Jesus,* 204-20, though he misses the continuity with reference to teaching his disciples to pray. See also Joan E. Taylor, "John the Baptist," in *The Eerdmans Dictionary of Early Judaism* (ed. John J. Collins and Daniel C. Harlow; Grand Rapids: Eerdmans, 2010), 819-21; Robert L. Webb, *John the Baptizer and Prophet: A Sociohistorical Study* (repr.; Eugene: Wipf & Stock, 2006); D. S. Daaph, *The Relationship between John the Baptist and Jesus of Nazareth: A Critical Study* (Lanham: University Press of America, 2005); Meier, *A Marginal Jew,* 2:116-30. Joan Taylor, *The Immerser: John the Baptist within Second Temple Judaism* (Grand Rapids: Eerdmans, 1997), 151-53, takes the continuity in this regard too far when she proposes that John may have composed the Lord's Prayer.

108. Keener, *The Historical Jesus of the Gospels,* 198.

The hallowing of God's name alludes to Ezekiel's prophecy of the restoration of Israel to the land (Ezek 36:23), which is elsewhere described as a new exodus (Ezek 20:33-42). Likewise, the coming of God's kingdom alludes to Micah's prophecy of the journey of the exiles to the promised land (Mic 4:1-12), which is likewise described by the prophet as a recapitulation of God's actions in the exodus (Mic 7:11-15). Above all, the petition for "daily" bread is linguistically rooted in the biblical account of the miracle of the manna from heaven (Exod 16:1-31), and fits into the early Jewish expectation of the future manna of the messiah (2 *Bar.* 29:3-8). The request for forgiveness from "debts" appears to be likewise anchored in the Jewish idea of the year of Jubilee, in which all debts would be forgiven and Israelites would return to their land as they had done during the exodus (Lev. 25:24, 28) and would do in a future jubilee (Isa 61:1-7; *11QMelchizedek* 2:1-9). Finally, the petition for deliverance from "temptation" or "trials" may echo the state of Israel in the wilderness wandering, when they were subjected to many trials and tribulations while on their way to the promised land of Canaan (Deut 4:27-34; 7:19; 29:3).

In addition to this scriptural evidence, it may be worth noting here that there are remarkable parallels between the Lord's Prayer and the Jewish daily prayers preserved in later rabbinic literature.[109] Indeed, these parallels are so striking that even scholars who ordinarily would avoid utilizing later rabbinic literature are inclined to refer to them as significant.[110] Indeed, the similarities with the prayer attributed to Jesus are striking:

> Thou art holy and *thy Name is holy* and the holy praise Thee every day.
> Blessed art thou, Lord, holy God. . . .
> *Forgive us, our Father, for we have sinned;*
> pardon us, our King, for we have transgressed.
> For thou forgivest and pardonest.
> Blessed art thou, Lord, gracious, rich in forgiveness.
> Restore our judges as in former times and our counselors as in the beginning . . .
> and reign over us, thou Lord alone, in grace and mercy. . . .
> Blessed art Thou, Lord, *King,* who lovest justice and judgment.
> (*Shemoneh 'Esreh,* nos. 3, 6, 11)[111]

109. See Vermes, *Jesus and the World of Judaism,* 43; Jakob J. Petuchowski and Michael Brocke, eds., *The Lord's Prayer and Jewish Liturgy* (New York: Seabury, 1978); Jeremias, *The Prayers of Jesus,* 98.

110. E.g., Meier, *A Marginal Jew,* 2:299-300.

111. Trans. in the revised Schürer, *The History of the Jewish People,* 2:456-57.

> Exalted and *hallowed be His great Name*
> in the world which He created according to His will.
> *May He establish His kingdom*
> [and cause His salvation to sprout, and hasten the coming of His messiah]
> *in your lifetime and in your days,*
> and in the lifetime of the whole household of Israel, speedily and at a near time.
> And say: Amen. (*Kaddish* Prayer [Short Version])[112]

What are to we to make of this evidence? It is difficult to know, since the origin and development of these rabbinic prayers is shrouded in obscurity, and a host of complex difficulties attend the question of the dating of the texts in which they are found, the only thing about which is certain is that they are much later than the first century A.D.[113] Because of this, I agree with those scholars who urge caution in the construction of historical hypotheses about the relationship between these later rabbinic texts and the first-century Lord's Prayer.[114] We should certainly not speak about them as background to the Lord's Prayer or of Jesus as drawing upon them. At the very least, however, it seems that, given the striking linguistic and conceptual parallels with the prayer Jesus gives to his Jewish disciples, the later rabbinic parallels offer some support to the conclusion of scholars such as Joseph Fitzmyer: the Lord's Prayer "is a thoroughly Jewish prayer" with a "basically Jewish form and content."[115]

112. Trans. Petuchowski, "Jewish Prayer Texts of the Rabbinic Period," in *The Lord's Prayer and Jewish Liturgy,* 37. The line in brackets is added by some rites in different versions of the Kaddish.

113. For example, although the Eighteen Benedictions are already briefly referred to in the Mishnah (*m. Ber.* 4:3; *Ta'an.* 2:2), we cannot be sure of their exact contents. Likewise, although the Talmud refers to the Kaddish being used as an Aramaic prayer for synagogue worship, we do not know the exact form or contents of the prayer mentioned (*b. Soṭ.* 49a). See Joseph Heinemann, "Amidah," *EncJud* 2:838-45; Cecil Roth, "Kaddish," *EncJud* 10:660-61.

114. Meier, *A Marginal Jew,* 2:363.

115. Fitzmyer, *The Gospel according to Luke,* 2:899, 900. Craig Keener puts it more strongly: "The [Lord's] prayer cannot be an invention of the later gentile church; it closely echoes the Kaddish (as well as the language of other early Jewish prayers)." Keener, *The Historical Jesus of the Gospels,* 198.

Coherence: The Father, the Kingdom, and the New Exodus

In addition to being "thoroughly Jewish" in form and content, the Lord's Prayer also presents a solid case of coherence with other evidence we have about Jesus.

For one thing, the opening address of Jesus' prayer to God as "Father" (Matt 6:9; Luke 11:2) coheres perfectly with other evidence for Jesus' use of the title "Father" for God (Matt 44x, Mark 4x, Luke 15x, John 109x), especially in the context of prayer (Matt 26:39, 42-44; Mark 14:36; Luke 22:42; John 12:28).[116] Similarly, the language of hallowing or sanctifying God's name is attributed to Jesus' prayer to the Father after the coming of the Greeks to see him in Jerusalem: "Father, glorify your name" (John 12:28).[117] It goes without saying that Jesus' prayer for the coming of the "kingdom" fits perfectly with the prominence of "the kingdom of God" in his teaching and preaching as a whole, and is probably one of the primary reasons scholars continue to conclude that the Lord's Prayer goes back to him (e.g., Matt 8:11-12; Luke 13:28-29; Mark 9:1; Matt 12:28; Luke 11:20; 17:20-21; John 3:3, 5).[118] Jesus' concern over forgiveness of sins is manifest in multiple words and deeds attributed to him in the Gospels (Matt 18:23-25; Mark 2:5-12; 11:25; Luke 7:36-50). Indeed, the Isaianic vision of the messianic jubilee and release from debts (Isa 61:1-4) is the very same passage that Jesus himself reads at his inaugural sermon in the synagogue at Nazareth (Luke 4:16-30). By saying that Isaiah's prophecy has been "fulfilled" (Luke 4:21), it seems that Jesus is implicitly identifying himself as the "anointed one" (Isa 61:1) who would inaugurate the eschatological year of release from iniquity.[119] Even the closing reference to deliverance from "temptation" *(peirasmos)* coheres with Jesus' admonitions to his disciples in Gethsemane: "pray that you not come into *peirasmos*" (Matt 26:41; Mark 14:32-42; Luke 22:40).[120]

Most significant for our purposes, if we interpret the daily bread of the Lord's Prayer as a prayer for the new manna of the new exodus, this would produce a striking case of coherence with Jesus' Mosaic sign of feeding the multitude with bread in the desert (Mark 6:30-44; John 6:1-15), as well as other

116. See Keener, *The Historical Jesus of the Gospels,* 271-72; Dunn, *Jesus Remembered,* 548-55; Meier, *A Marginal Jew,* 2:294. See also Marianne Meye Thompson, *The Promise of the Father: Jesus and God in the New Testament* (Louisville: Westminster John Knox, 2000).

117. Meier, *A Marginal Jew,* 2:362 n. 37.

118. Meier, *A Marginal Jew,* 2:298; Schlosser, *Le règne de Dieu,* 1:261.

119. Cf. Wright, *Jesus and the Victory of God,* 268; Aune, "A Note on Jesus' Messianic Consciousness and 11Q Melchizedek," 161-65.

120. On Jesus in Gethsemane, see Pitre, *Jesus, the Tribulation, and the End of the Exile,* 478-504.

texts in which Jesus connects the coming of the kingdom of God with the eschatological banquet (Matt 8:11; Luke 13:28-29; see below, chapter 6). *Indeed, if the Lord's Prayer is in fact a prayer for the new exodus, then the petition for the manna of the kingdom of God stands at the very center of Jesus' and his disciples' hopes for the future.* This point needs to be stressed: the first set of petitions (the so-called "you-petitions") are focused on God, whereas the second set of petitions (the so-called "we petitions") are focused on human needs. Remarkably, in both the longer and shorter forms of the Lord's Prayer, the petition for daily bread is the very first of the we-petitions. This strongly suggests that the gift of the daily manna is being set forth as the most fundamental of human needs. In the context of the eschatological hope for a new exodus, it expresses a deep need and desire for God's miraculous provision for his people during their long and trial-filled journey to their ultimate destination in the promised land, and a similar provision for God's people in the end-times.

Effects: The Lord's Prayer in the Early Church

Third and finally, there is the argument from the plausibility of effects within the early church. If the Lord's Prayer did in fact originate with Jesus himself, it would provide a reasonable explanation for why the early church went on to adopt the prayer as its own, and enjoin it to be said by early Christians.[121]

In this regard, the earliest evidence we have for the recitation of the prayer being joined to its specific attribution to Jesus himself in the early church comes to us from the document known as the *Didache,* which is often dated to the first century A.D. In that document, we find the following:

> But do not let your fasts coincide with those of the hypocrites. They fast on Monday and Thursday, so you must fast on Wednesday and Friday. Nor should you pray like the hypocrites. Instead, pray like this, *just as the Lord commanded in his Gospel:*
>
> "Our Father in heaven,
> hallowed be your name,
> your kingdom come,
> your will be done on earth as it is in heaven.
> Give us today our *epiousios* bread,

121. Cf. Pitre, *Jesus, the Tribulation, and the End of the Exile,* 157; Meier, *A Marginal Jew,* 2:294.

> And forgive us our debt, as we also forgive our debtors;
> and do not lead us into temptation,
> but deliver us from the evil one;
> for yours is the power and the glory forever."
>
> Pray like this three times a day. (*Didache* 8.1-3)[122]

Several aspects of this text are pertinent to the discussion of the plausibility of effects of the Lord's Prayer within the early church. For one thing, it is important to note that the *Didache* expressly attributes the prayer to Jesus himself ("the Lord") as having "commanded" *(ekeleusen)* his followers to pray (*Didache* 8.2). There is no indication that the prayer has any other origin than in the will of Jesus himself, as taught in "his Gospel" — arguably (but not demonstrably) a reference to the Gospel of Matthew.[123]

Moreover — and this is significant — in direct contradiction to those scholars who invoke the "liturgical" character of the Lord's Prayer in the early church as an argument in favor of it having originated in the setting of early Christian worship, the actual testimony of the *Didache* says nothing about the use of the Lord's Prayer in communal worship or the eucharist (despite the assertions of some commentators). Instead, the *Didache* seems to envision the private daily recitation of the prayer by individuals as in early Jewish sources or elsewhere in the New Testament (see Dan 6:9, 11-12; Matt 6:5-6; Acts 10:9), although these ordinarily private prayers could obviously be carried out in a community setting as well (cf. Acts 3:1).[124] In this regard the instructions for how to celebrate the eucharist are given after the command to pray three times a day, at the beginning of a new section, to which the recitation of the Lord's Prayer apparently does not belong: "Now concerning the eucharist, give thanks as follows . . ." (*Didache* 9.1). As Joseph Heinemann once pointed out, a proper form-critical evaluation of the Lord's Prayer reveals that "it displays all of the characteristics of Jewish private prayer" and is "a prayer which every man can recite for himself, rather than one which he must hear recited by the Prayer Leader."[125] Now, for our purposes here, what matters most is that this emphasis

122. Unless otherwise noted, all translations of the Apostolic Fathers contained herein are from Michael W. Holmes, *The Apostolic Fathers: Greek Texts and Translations* (3rd ed.; Grand Rapids: Baker Academic, 2007).

123. See Kurt Niederwimmer and Linda M. Maloney, *The Didache* (Hermeneia; Minneapolis: Fortress, 1998), 134-36.

124. Pitre, *Jesus, the Tribulation, and the End of the Exile,* 155 n. 63.

125. Joseph Heinemann, "The Background of Jesus' Prayer in the Jewish Liturgical Tra-

on the individual would make perfect sense if the prayer originated as a private prayer given by Jesus to his disciples and only later was incorporated into the communal setting of early Christian liturgy.[126]

To sum up: when examined carefully, there are good reasons to conclude that the Lord's Prayer is contextually plausible within a first-century Jewish context, coheres with other evidence about Jesus, and provides a reasonable origin for the individual recitation of the prayer within the early church. In light of such considerations, it seems sound to conclude the substance of the Lord's Prayer is historically plausible on the lips of Jesus of Nazareth. This means that the hope for the new manna was — from the very beginning — one of the central hopes that unified Jesus' disciples in the recitation of the Lord's Prayer. Even before the forgiveness of sins and deliverance from evil, they were to pray for God to give them the eschatological manna of the kingdom each day.

The Teaching in the Synagogue at Capernaum[127]

The next evidence we turn to is without doubt the most controversial and difficult of all of the eucharistic words of Jesus: the teaching in the synagogue at

dition," in *The Lord's Prayer and Jewish Liturgy* (ed. Jakob J. Petuchowski and Michael Brocke; New York: Seabury, 1978), 81-89 (here 88-89).

126. See Gordon J. Bahr, "The Use of the Lord's Prayer in the Primitive Church," in *The Lord's Prayer and Jewish Liturgy* (ed. Jakob J. Petuchowski and Michael Brocke; New York: Seabury, 1978), 149-55.

127. Nicholas Perrin, "Last Supper," *Dictionary of Jesus and the Gospels* (2nd ed.; ed. Joel B. Green, Jeannine K. Brown, and Nicholas Perrin; Downers Grove: IVP Academic, 2013), 497-500; Silke Peterson, *Brot, Licht und Weinstock: Intertextuelle Analysen johanneischer Ich-bin-Worte* (NovTSup 127; Leiden: Brill, 2008); Paul N. Anderson, *The Christology of the Fourth Gospel: Its Unity and Disunity in the Light of John 6* (repr.; Eugene: Wipf & Stock, 2010); Benjamin E. Reynolds, *The Apocalyptic Son of Man in the Gospel of John* (WUNT 2.249; Tübingen: Mohr-Siebeck, 2008), 152-61; Jens Schröter, *Das Abendmahl: Frühchristliche Deutungen und Impulse für die Gegenwart* (SBS 210; Stuttgart: Katholisches Bibelwerk, 2006), 56-60; Craig S. Keener, *The Gospel of John: A Commentary* (2 vols.; Peabody: Hendrickson, 2003), 1:675-99; Craig L. Blomberg, *The Historical Reliability of John's Gospel* (Downers Grove: IVP, 2001), 122-31; Gerd Lüdemann, *Jesus After 2000 Years: What He Really Did and Said* (trans. John Bowden; London: SCM; Amherst: Prometheus, 2001), 468-73; Francis J. Moloney, *The Gospel of John* (SP 4; Collegeville: Liturgical Press, 1998), 217-32; Maurice Casey, *Is John's Gospel True?* (London and New York: Routledge, 1996), 42-50; Robert W. Funk, Roy Hoover, and the Jesus Seminar, *The Five Gospels: The Search for the Authentic Words of Jesus* (New York: Macmillan, 1993), 419-22; Peter Stuhlmacher, *Jesus of Nazareth — Christ of Faith* (trans. Siegfried S. Schatzmann; Peabody: Hendrickson, 1993 [orig. 1988]), 88-102; John A. T. Robinson, *The Priority of John*

Capernaum in John 6:48-66. Unlike the words of institution at the Last Supper, scholars are divided over whether this material even *is* eucharistic. On the one hand, many scholars contend that the language of eating Jesus' flesh and drinking his blood is obviously a reference to the food and drink that he would later give to the disciples at the Last Supper. On the other hand, many other scholars argue that the language of eating Jesus' flesh and drinking his blood is simply a metaphor for believing in him. Still others hold that both meanings are at play. And none of this settles the even more complicated question of whether or not the substance of this account is historically plausible within the setting of Jesus' public ministry in Galilee long before his arrest and execution.

Although much has been written on the sixth chapter of John's Gospel as a whole, for our purposes here, we will be deliberately selective. Given our interests in this book, I will focus our attention in what follows primarily on the teaching of Jesus in the Capernaum synagogue that identifies the new manna from heaven with the "flesh" of Jesus that is to be "eaten" (John 6:48-58), as well as the disciples' decidedly negative response to this "hard teaching" and Jesus' reply (John 6:59-66). For reasons of limited space and scope, I am thus isolating the evidence that is most commonly identified in scholarly literature as "eucharistic," and, therefore, potentially relevant to the interpretation of Jesus' words and deeds at the Last Supper. That evidence consists of the following passage:

(London: SCM, 1985), 302-3; Xavier Léon-Dufour, *Sharing the Eucharistic Bread: The Witness of the New Testament* (trans. Matthew J. O'Connell; New York/Mahwah: Paulist, 1987 [orig. 1982]), 248-77; I. Howard Marshall, *Last Supper and Lord's Supper* (London: Paternoster, 1980), 133-39; C. K. Barrett, *The Gospel according to St. John* (2nd ed.; Philadelphia: Westminster, 1978), 281-308; Rudolf Schnackenburg, *The Gospel according to St. John* (trans. Cecily Hastings et al.; New York: Crossroad, 1990 [orig. 1971]), 53-78; James D. G. Dunn, "John VI — A Eucharistic Discourse?," *NTS* 17 (1970-71): 328-38; Eduard Schweizer, *The Lord's Supper according to the New Testament* (trans. James M. Davis; Philadelphia: Fortress, 1967), 7-9; Raymond E. Brown, *The Gospel according to John* (2 vols.; AB 29-29A; New York: Doubleday, 1966, 1970), 1:281-304; Jeremias, *The Eucharistic Words of Jesus,* 106-7; Rudolf Bultmann, *The Gospel of John* (trans. G. R. Beasley-Murray; Philadelphia: Westminster, 1971 [orig. 1964]), 218-22, 234-37; André Feuillet, *Johannine Studies* (trans. Thomas E. Crane; New York: Alba House, 1965), 53-128; T. Francis Glasson, *Moses in the Fourth Gospel* (SBT 40; London: SCM, 1963); C. H. Dodd, *Historical Tradition in the Fourth Gospel* (Cambridge: Cambridge University Press, 1963), 196-222; Bertil Gärtner, *John 6 and the Jewish Passover* (ConBNT 17; Lund: Gleerup, 1959); C. H. Dodd, *The Interpretation of the Fourth Gospel* (Cambridge: Cambridge University Press, 1953), 333-45; A. J. B. Higgins, *The Lord's Supper in the New Testament* (SBT 6; Chicago: Alec R. Allenson, 1952), 79-84; Vincent Taylor, *Jesus and His Sacrifice: A Study of the Passion-Sayings in the Gospels* (London: Macmillan, 1948), 233-44; David Friedrich Strauss, *The Life of Jesus Critically Examined* (ed. Peter C. Hodgson; London: SCM, 1973), 373-75, 633.

> [Jesus said:] "I am the bread of life. Your fathers ate the manna in the wilderness, and they died. This is the bread that comes down from heaven, that a man may eat of it and not die. I am the living bread which came down from heaven; if any one eats of this bread, he will live for ever; and the bread which I shall give for the life of the world is my flesh."
>
> The Jews then disputed among themselves, saying, "How can this man give us his flesh to eat?" So Jesus said to them, "Amen, amen, I say to you, unless you eat the flesh of the Son of man and drink his blood, you have no life in you; he who eats my flesh and drinks my blood has eternal life, and I will raise him up at the last day. For my flesh is real food, and my blood is real drink. He who eats my flesh and drinks my blood remains in me, and I in him. As the living Father sent me, and I live because of the Father, so he who eats me will live because of me. This is the bread which came down from heaven, not such as the fathers ate and died; he who eats this bread will live forever." This he said in the synagogue, as he taught at Capernaum.
>
> Many of his disciples, when they heard it, said, "This is a hard saying. Who can listen to it?" But Jesus, knowing in himself that his disciples murmured at it, said to them, "Do you take offense at this? Then what if you were to see the Son of man ascending to where he was before? It is the spirit that gives life; the flesh is of no avail; the words that I have spoken to you are spirit and life. But there are some of you that do not believe." For Jesus knew from the first who those were that did not believe, and who it was that should betray him. And he said, "This is why I told you that no one can come to me unless it is granted him by the Father." After this many of his disciples drew back and no longer went about with him. (John 6:48-66)[128]

Before we can analyze these data in detail, it is important to note that in the twentieth century, a number of scholars — most famously, Rudolf Bultmann — theorized that the section of the discourse in which Jesus identifies his flesh with the true manna from heaven and speaks about eating and drinking his blood (John 6:51c-58) should be expunged as a later interpolation of a hypothetical "ecclesiastical editor."[129] From this point of view, the realistic

128. RSV (slightly adapted). In viewing the section dealing with Jesus' blood as food and drink as beginning with John 6:48 (and not 51c), I am following Brown, *The Gospel according to John,* 2:281-304 and Schnackenburg, *The Gospel according to St. John,* 2:53-65.

129. See Bultmann, *The Gospel of John,* 218-20. See also Günther Bornkamm, "Die eucharistische Rede im Johannesevangelium," *ZNW* 47 (1956): 161-69. Brown, *The Gospel ac-*

emphasis on eating and drinking Jesus' blood as food and drink, as well as the eschatological focus on a future resurrection from the dead, is at odds with the fourth evangelist's view that faith in Jesus alone is necessary for salvation. Hence, these teachings of Jesus must reflect a later addition from an unknown redactor. Over the course of the last century, this theory was quite influential, and continues to have a few scholarly advocates.[130]

On the other hand, more recent scholarship has strongly criticized this interpolation theory as unconvincing. From this point of view, John 6:51-58 should be treated as a unity, on the basis of several observations.[131]

For one thing, given the unified nature of the text as it stands, Bultmann and his followers themselves admit that the text employs the "style and language" of Jesus' earlier teachings in the chapter (John 6:35-50), thus giving the appearance of "unity to the whole passage."[132] If the style and vocabulary match that of the entire bread of life discourse so that the text has the "appearance" of unity, then one wonders why an interpolation even has to be postulated. More importantly, the style and language itself argues against the divisions imposed by Bultmann, who breaks the text apart in mid-verse at John 6:51c. Against this textual division, Jesus' statement, "I am the bread of life. Your fathers *ate* the manna in the wilderness, and they died. This is the bread which comes down from heaven, that a man may *eat* of it and not die . . ." (John 6:48-50), clearly signals the beginning of a second section of the discourse, in which the language of "eating" (*esthiō,* six times) or "chewing" (*trōgō,* four times) the flesh of Jesus holds the entire unit together (John 6:48-58). Finally, the response of Jesus' disciples constitutes a reaction both to the "hard saying" about eating Jesus' flesh and drinking his blood and to his teaching on "believing" in him (John 6:60-64).[133] As we will see below, the direct cause of Jesus'

---

cording to John, 1:285-91, agrees that John 6:51c-58 is a later addition, but rejects Bultmann's claim that it is non-Johannine.

130. Lüdemann, *Jesus After 2000 Years,* 469-70; Funk, Hoover, and the Jesus Seminar, *The Five Gospels,* 421.

131. See Perrin, "The Last Supper," 498; Peterson, *Brot, Licht, und Weinstock,* 201-11; Keener, *The Gospel of John,* 1:675; Schnackenburg, *The Gospel according to St. John,* 56-59; Peder Borgen, *Bread from Heaven,* 87-98, 189-92. The foundational critique of Bultmann was made by Eugen Ruckstuhl, *Die literarische Einheit des Johannes-Evangeliums* (Freiburg: Paulus, 1951), 265-71. It is worth noting that Jeremias, *The Eucharistic Words of Jesus,* 107, reversed his earlier opinion that the passage was a later interpolation.

132. Bultmann, *The Gospel of John,* 234, 237. So also Lüdemann, *Jesus After 2000 Years,* 471: "[T]he revisers have evidently made an effort to interlock their addition [in John 6:51c-58] with what has gone before by picking up terms and phrases from [John 6:]49-51b."

133. Reynolds, *The Apocalyptic Son of Man in the Gospel of John,* 159, following J. Web-

losing "many" of his disciples is clearly his shocking statements about eating his flesh and drinking his blood; to excise these makes this singular reaction of the disciples difficult to explain.[134]

For our purposes here, the upshot of these observations is that Bultmann's proposal that John 6:51c-58 should be regarded as a later interpolation disconnected from its immediate context is highly dubious, and should probably be rejected.[135] To the contrary, the evidence as it stands appears to be a unity, in which Jesus identifies himself with the manna from heaven and links this image from Jewish Scripture with the necessity of eating his flesh and drinking his blood. If this is correct, then, there is no reason that we should not treat this evidence as we have every other text examined thus far: first, we will attempt to interpret the teaching of Jesus in the synagogue and the disciples' reaction to it (John 6:48-66); and then we will ask "the historical question of whether the direct eucharistic theme of vss. 51-58 was originally part of Jesus' words to the crowd"[136] — keeping in mind that we are not seeking the *ipsissima verba* but rather asking whether or not the substance of Jesus' teaching in the synagogue and the disciples' reaction are historically plausible. In other words, can the memory that Jesus spoke in such a way — of the idea that consuming his flesh and blood would lead to life and that he linked this promise to the manna — be understood as the result of something Jesus himself actually said? Before we can answer this question, we must, in keeping with our method of proceeding, first interpret the data.

Jesus Identifies His Flesh with the New Manna

The section of Jesus' teachings that demands our attention begins when he not only speaks of himself as "the bread of life," but also contrasts this bread with the "manna" eaten by the Israelites in the desert and identifies it with his "flesh" (John 6:48-51). Three key points should be made about this evidence.

First, Jesus does not identify himself with just any bread. He begins by recalling the manna of the exodus — the miraculous bread from heaven —

ster, *Ingesting Jesus: Eating and Drinking in the Gospel of John* (SBL.ABS 6; Atlanta: SBL, 2003), 78 n. 35.

134. Stuhlmacher, *Jesus of Nazareth,* 94-95.

135. So Keener, *The Gospel of John,* 1:675; Casey, *Is John's Gospel True?,* 46-47; Anderson, *The Christology of the Fourth Gospel,* 32-36, 55; Marshall, *Last Supper and Lord's Supper,* 135; Léon-Dufour, *Sharing the Eucharistic Bread,* 256-61.

136. Brown, *The Gospel according to John,* 1:286 (emphasis altered).

as described in Jewish Scripture. Although we have already had occasion to survey the manna texts and traditions in Jewish Scripture and tradition, it is worth noting here that Jesus' language of "the bread which comes down from heaven" (John 6:50) is directly rooted in Hebrew Scripture and paralleled in ancient Jewish literature:

> Then the LORD said to Moses, "Behold, I shall rain *bread from heaven* for you. . . ." (Exod 16:4)
>
> He rained down upon them manna to eat,
> and gave them *the grain of heaven*. . . . (Ps 78:24)
>
> You did give them *bread from heaven* for their hunger and bring forth water for them from the rock for their thirst. . . . (Neh 9:15)

Although Jesus' reference to the biblical manna is widely recognized by commentators, its significance for interpreting what follows is sometimes underestimated.[137] Above all, it is hard to overemphasize that Jesus' reference to the manna sets the stage for everything that he is going to say about the importance of eating his flesh. Indeed, the entire section of Jesus' discourse normally identified as eucharistic both begins by speaking of the manna eaten by the fathers in the desert (John 6:49) and ends by speaking of the manna eaten by the fathers of the wilderness generation (John 6:58). As we will see, this emphasis is important: *it is the manna that will provide us with the essential key to understanding Jesus' difficult words.*[138] Moreover, as the quotations above demonstrate, the aspect of the manna that receives repeated emphasis, both in Jewish Scripture and the teaching of Jesus here in Capernaum, is that its origin is in heaven.[139] Contrary to naturalistic explanations of the food of the exodus, from the perspective of Jewish Scripture and Jesus in Capernaum, the manna is no ordinary bread — it is miraculous bread from heaven. Finally, when Jesus declares that he is also going to give bread that "comes down from heaven," he is implicitly identifying himself with Moses, who, according to Jewish tradition, was expected to bring back the miracle of the manna. As we saw above in our survey of the manna tradition in ancient Jewish literature,

137. E.g., Barrett, *The Gospel according to St. John*, 293; Brown, *The Gospel according to John*, 1:262-66; Higgins, *The Lord's Supper in the New Testament*, 82; Dodd, *The Interpretation of the Fourth Gospel*, 335.

138. Feuillet, *Johannine Studies*, 57.

139. Anderson, *The Christology of the Fourth Gospel*, 203.

there are a number of texts, beginning in the first century, that reveal the expectation that the future messiah would not only be a new Moses, but that he would bring back the miracle of the manna (2 *Bar.* 29:3-8).[140]

Second, Jesus not only alludes to the manna of the exodus, he also draws a strong contrast between the old bread from heaven and the new bread that he is going to give. He does this by comparing the fate of those who consumed the old manna of the exodus with the fate of those who will eat the new manna: while the wilderness generation died, those who eat the new manna will live forever (John 6:49-50).[141] Here Jesus is again alluding to Jewish Scripture, in this instance to the divine declaration that, because of their murmuring, the congregation of Israel would be sentenced to die in the wilderness:

> And the LORD said to Moses and to Aaron, "How long shall this wicked congregation murmur against me? I have heard the murmurings of the people of Israel, which they murmur against me. Say to them, 'As I live,' says the LORD, 'what you have said in my hearing I will do to you: *your dead bodies shall fall in the wilderness; and of all your number, numbered from twenty years old and upward, who have murmured against me, not one shall come into the land where I swore that I would make you dwell,* except Caleb the son of Jephunneh and Joshua the son of Nun. . . . And your children shall be shepherds in the wilderness forty years, and shall suffer for your faithlessness, until the last of your dead bodies lies in the wilderness. According to the number of days in which you spied out the land, forty days, for every day a year, you shall bear your iniquity, forty years, and you shall know my displeasure.' I, the LORD, have spoken: surely this will I do to all this wicked congregation that are gathered together against me: *in this wilderness they shall come to a full end, and there they shall die.*" (Num 14:26-30, 33-35)

The point of this text from the Torah is that the wilderness generation suffered physical death in the wilderness.[142] For now, the main point is that Jesus is contrasting the physical death — and perhaps the spiritual fate — of the wilderness generation who ate the old manna with the everlasting life of those who eat the new manna from heaven. If anyone eats of this manna, "he will not die" but rather "live forever" (John 6:51), inheriting the life of the world to come. Given the fact that the old manna was regarded as supernatural bread

140. Cf. Schnackenburg, *The Gospel according to St. John,* 2:42.

141. Schnackenburg, *The Gospel according to St. John,* 2:54.

142. Brown, *The Gospel according to John,* 1:284.

from heaven, it is hard to overestimate the striking character of this contrast. As C. H. Dodd points out, even though the manna of the first exodus was of "miraculous origin," Jesus is declaring in no uncertain terms that the manna he will give is greater.[143] Or, to put it another way, he is saying: "Something greater than the manna of Moses is here."

Third and finally, Jesus also explicitly identifies this new manna with his own "flesh," that will be given for the life of the world (John 6:51). It is worth noting here that the manuscript tradition is divided on whether Jesus states that it is his flesh or the bread that is given "for the life of the world."[144] In either case, what matters is that Jesus identifies his flesh with the manna from heaven. In this regard, what matters for us is that even Jesus' mention of his "flesh" in connection with the manna is evocative of Jewish Scripture.[145] Although the point is often overlooked by commentators, in the original biblical account, a double miracle is described: God gives the Israelites both "bread from heaven" and "flesh" from heaven, in the form of the quail.[146] Notice the emphasis on "flesh" *(bāśār)* in the foundational account from the Jewish Torah:

> Then the Lord said to Moses, "Behold, I will rain down bread from heaven for you; and the people shall go out and gather a day's portion every day, that I may test them, whether they will walk in my law or not. On the sixth day, when they prepare what they bring in, it will be twice as much as they gather daily. . . ." And Moses said, *"When the Lord gives you in the evening flesh to eat and in the morning bread to the full. . . ."* And the Lord said to Moses, "I have heard the murmurings of the sons of Israel; say to them, *'At twilight you shall eat flesh, and in the morning you shall be filled with bread;* then you shall know that I am the Lord your God.'" In the evening quails came up and covered the camp; and in the morning dew lay round about the camp. And when the dew had gone up, there was on the face of the wilderness a fine, flake-like thing, fine as hoarfrost on the ground. When the sons of Israel saw it, they said to one another, "What is it?" For they did not know what it was. And Moses said to them, "It is the bread which the Lord has given you to eat." (Exod 16:4-5, 8, 11-15)

143. Dodd, *The Interpretation of the Fourth Gospel,* 336. So too Marshall, *Last Supper and Lord's Supper,* 135.

144. See Brown, *The Gospel according to John,* 1:282, for a discussion of the textual question.

145. Brown, *The Gospel according to John,* 1:282.

146. E.g., Barrett, *The Gospel according to St. John,* 298, seems unaware of the link between "flesh" and the manna in Exodus 16:4-15.

As this passage makes abundantly clear, in the exodus from Egypt, God gives the Israelites both *bread from heaven* and *flesh from heaven* to eat as daily food. Hence, Jesus' identification of the bread with his "flesh" (John 6:51), although undoubtedly mysterious, is not completely unprecedented. Rather, the link between flesh from heaven and bread from heaven is directly rooted in the twofold miracle described in Jewish Scripture.

This biblical background provides a critical key to properly interpreting Jesus' statement that his own flesh shall be given "for the life of the world" (John 6:51). Although some commentators interpret this statement entirely in terms of Jesus' future death, the scriptural evidence in Exodus 16 makes clear that, in context, the primary emphasis seems to be on the flesh that Jesus will give in the form of the eschatological manna from heaven.[147] To be sure, although the gift of Jesus' flesh can never be detached from his sacrificial death, since the immediate context is the giving of the new manna, the imagery of eating flesh and bread points first of all to him giving his flesh as the food of the new exodus.[148]

The Judeans Object to Jesus' Teaching

Should there be any doubt about this, we need only turn to the response of certain members of Jesus' audience, referred to by John as "the Judeans" *(hoi Ioudaioi)* (John 6:52).[149] In their reaction to Jesus' identification of himself with

147. Léon-Dufour, *Sharing the Eucharistic Bread,* 257; Jeremias, *The Eucharistic Words of Jesus,* 198-201; Gärtner, *John 6 and the Jewish Passover,* 23-24.

148. Stuhlmacher, *Jesus of Nazareth,* 96.

149. It goes beyond the boundaries of our investigation to raise the hotly debated question of the identity of "the Jews" *(hoi Ioudaioi)* in the Gospel of John. For our purposes here, it is only important to note that those voicing the objection are Jewish auditors in the synagogue at Capernaum. In my opinion, in this instance, John is using this term in a *geographical* and *genealogical* sense that emphasizes the tension between those of Galilean proximity and descent, and those of Judean proximity and descent, as when he says elsewhere: "After this Jesus went about in Galilee; he would not go about in Judea *(Ioudaia),* because the Judeans *(Ioudaioi)* sought to kill him. Now the Judeans' *(Ioudaiōn)* feast of Tabernacles was at hand" (John 7:1-2). Against this, Brown, *The Gospel according to John,* 1:270, argues that the *Ioudaioi* in John 6 cannot be identified as visitors in Galilee from Judea because they evince personal knowledge of Jesus' family (John 6:42). However, this argument fails to take into account that if the Synoptic Gospels are correct and Joseph is a Judean Davidide by genealogy (Matthew 1; Luke 3), then Jesus would have extended relatives living in Judea who could be visiting Galilee (for whatever reason) and hence referred to as *Ioudaioi* in the geographical and genealogical sense. Indeed, this appears to be the express point of John 4:43-45, which testifies that Jesus

the bread of life, the Judeans focus not on how he will die but rather on how he will give his flesh to be eaten: "The Judeans then disputed among themselves saying, 'How can this man give us his flesh to eat?'" (John 6:52). What exactly is the import of this question?

Above all, the Judeans' objection to Jesus' teaching appears to assume that it is both offensive and absurd. It is offensive insofar as any notion of eating human flesh would have been regarded with disgust by ancient Jews and Greeks alike.[150] The most important evidence for this comes from the Jewish Torah itself, which lists being driven to eat human flesh in time of siege as one of the worst punishments for covenant disobedience:

> *And you shall eat* the offspring of your own body, *the flesh* of your sons and daughters, whom the LORD your God has given you. . . . The man who is the most tender and delicately bred among you will grudge food to his brother, to the wife of his bosom, and to the last of the children who remain with him; so that he will not give to any of them *the flesh* of his children whom he is *eating*. . . . The most tender and delicately bred woman among you, who would not venture to set the sole of her foot upon the ground because she is so delicate and tender, will grudge to the husband of her bosom, to her son and to her daughter, her afterbirth that comes out from between her feet and her children whom she bears, because she will eat them secretly, for want of all things. . . . (Deut 28:53-57)

Other Jewish texts bear witness to a similar revulsion for consuming human flesh (Ezek 5:10-11; Josephus, *War* 6.208-12). To the extent that some in the audience think that Jesus is referring to their eating "the man they see before him,"[151] they are understandably offended.

With that said, however, it is important to note that the emphasis in their

---

leaves Judea and departs to Galilee, because "a prophet has no honor in his own country" — i.e., among the Judeans, who are "his own" (cf. John 1:11). Moreover, just as Galileans like the Beloved Disciple can be both well known by Judeans such as the High Priest and on-site in Judea (John 18:15), so too Judeans can show up in Galilean synagogues for a whole host of reasons, whether sent by Judean authorities (as in Mark 7:1) or because visiting extended family (as in the Galilean Mary's visit to her Judean cousin Elizabeth for three months, during which time Mary presumably attended a Galilean synagogue, Luke 1:39-56), or for some unknown reason. For a thorough discussion of the issue, see Keener, *The Gospel of John,* 1:214-27.

150. Keener, *The Gospel of John,* 1:687; Barrett, *The Gospel according to St. John,* 303; Dodd, *The Interpretation of the Fourth Gospel,* 341.

151. Higgins, *The Lord's Supper in the New Testament,* 82.

question falls on the question of how Jesus can possibly give his flesh to be eaten. In the words of Rudolf Bultmann: "The 'Jews' react by taking offence. . . . In doing so they quite correctly see that a real eating of his flesh is intended, but they regard it as absurd."[152] The reason this point of clarification is important is that it throws light on Jesus' subsequent response. In what follows, Jesus will both heighten the offensive nature of his original identification of his flesh with the true manna from heaven and emphasize how he is going to give them his flesh and blood: under the form of "food" that hearkens back to the manna eaten by the fathers in the desert.

Jesus Responds to the Judeans' Objection

In response to this objection, Jesus proceeds to give what is widely recognized as the most explicit and striking of all his eucharistic words in the Gospels (John 6:53-59). In order to properly interpret what Jesus' response might have meant in a first-century Jewish context, we need to interpret it first and foremost against the backdrop of Jewish Scripture. In this regard, at least five key points should be made.

First, Jesus does not just speak of eating his flesh and blood, but specifically speaks about eating the flesh and drinking the blood of "the Son of Man" (John 6:53). As is widely recognized, in doing so, he is referring to the mysterious "one like a son of man" in the book of Daniel.[153] This biblical background to Jesus' eucharistic words is important for a couple of reasons. For one thing, as I have argued elsewhere, the son of man in Daniel 7 is not only a symbol for the people of God ("the saints of the most high"), but also a messianic figure, a symbol for anointed king.[154] This is quite clear from the fact that the figure of the one like a son of man is set in antithesis to the four great beasts coming from the sea, which are explicitly identified as figures of "four *kings*" (see Dan 7:1-18). Just as the four beasts are explicitly identified as "four kings" of the pagan nations (Dan 7:17), so too the son of man signifies

152. Bultmann, *The Gospel of John,* 2:235; followed by Schnackenburg, *The Gospel according to St. John,* 2:60.

153. See esp. Reynolds, *The Apocalyptic Son of Man in the Gospel of John,* 152-61.

154. Brant Pitre, "Apocalypticism, Apocalyptic Teaching," in *Dictionary of Jesus and the Gospels* (2nd ed.; ed. Joel B. Green, Jeannine K. Brown, and Nicholas Perrin; Downers Grove: IVP Academic, 2013), 24-25; idem, *Jesus, the Tribulation, and the End of the Exile: Restoration Eschatology and the Origin of the Atonement* (WUNT 2.204; Tübingen: Mohr-Siebeck; Grand Rapids: Baker Academic, 2005), 54-55.

the future *king* of Israel — who would later be known as the "messiah" (cf. Dan 9:26). Moreover, the messianic son of man in Daniel 7 is no mere earthly king. Rather, he comes "with the clouds of heaven" and is exalted to the heavenly throne of the "Ancient of Days" (Dan 7:13-14).[155] Thus the son of man in Daniel is a heavenly king. This heavenly identity of the Son of Man is crucial for understanding Jesus' words in the Capernaum synagogue. Above all, Jesus' emphasis on the flesh of the Son of Man emphasizes that he is not speaking about cannibalizing his earthly flesh. Instead, the meal he will give is "not the physical flesh of the earthly Jesus, but the Spirit-filled flesh and blood of the heavenly Son of man."[156] In other words, the heavenly Son of Man will give heavenly, rather than ordinary, food and drink.[157]

Second, in his response to the Judeans' question, Jesus does not retract anything he has said about the necessity of eating his flesh. Rather, he heightens the offense by adding that they must also "drink" his "blood," otherwise, they have no "life" in them (John 6:53-54).[158] As Rudolf Bultmann states: "What was absurd has now become offensive, since the drinking of blood must be regarded as particularly revolting."[159] Once again, the key to understanding Jesus' words can be found in the Jewish Torah. Commentators regularly point out that the prohibition against consuming blood is repeated on several occasions in the Pentateuch (Gen 9:3-4; Lev 17:10-11; Deut 12:16).[160] However, what often goes unnoted is that the prohibition in Leviticus 17 — arguably the *locus classicus* — uses language and imagery similar to Jesus' declaration in the Capernaum synagogue:

> If any man of the house of Israel or of the stranger that sojourns among them *eats any blood,* I will set my face against that person who eats *blood,* and will cut him off from his people. *For the life of the flesh is in the blood;* and I have given it for you upon the altar to make atonement for your souls; *for it is the blood that makes atonement, by reason of its life.*

155. See Michael Bird, *Are You the One Who Is to Come? The Historical Jesus and the Messianic Question* (Grand Rapids: Baker Academic, 2009), 86; cf. 82 n. 22.

156. Schnackenburg, *The Gospel according to St. John,* 2:6.

157. In support of this, it is worth noting that the early Jewish book of Enoch explicitly links the Danielic Son of Man with the celebration of the messianic banquet, in which the righteous dine with the Son of man on the miraculous food and drink of the age of salvation (*1 En.* 62:13-16).

158. Schnackenburg, *The Gospel according to St. John,* 2:61.

159. Bultmann, *The Gospel of John,* 2:235, citing Lev 17:10; Acts 15:20.

160. Keener, *The Gospel of John,* 1:690.

> Therefore I have said to the people of Israel, No person among you shall *eat blood,* neither shall any stranger who sojourns among you *eat blood.* (Lev 17:10-12)

When studied carefully, this text has remarkable potential to throw light on Jesus' difficult teaching about drinking his blood in order to have life. On the one hand, Leviticus raises a seemingly insurmountable difficulty. How can Jesus say that his blood must be drunk when Jewish Scripture explicitly forbids the Israelite people to drink the blood of an animal?[161] On the other hand, when we notice that Jesus declares that those who do not drink his blood have no "life" in them (John 6:53), a possible solution emerges. By linking the drinking of his blood to receiving life, it seems that *the very reason the Mosaic Torah forbids drinking animal blood is the same reason Jesus commands his followers to drink the blood of the Son of Man:* "For the life *(nephesh)* is in the blood . . . and it is the blood that makes atonement, by reason of its life *(nephesh)*" (Lev 17:11). In other words, Jesus' declaration about drinking the blood of the Son of Man seems to presuppose the Torah's teaching that the life of the flesh is in the blood, and that the blood atones for sin. Hence, if Jesus' disciples wish to share in the eschatological life of the resurrection of the dead — in early Jewish and later rabbinic terminology, "eternal life" *(ḥayey 'ôlām)* or "the life of the world to come" *(ḥayey ha'ôlām haba')*[162] — then they have to partake of both his body *and his blood.* In so doing, they will be empowered to receive the eternal life of the messianic Son of man, whose flesh and blood will be given precisely in order to atone for sin — i.e., "for the life of the world" (John 6:51).

Third, when Jesus teaches that his followers will have to both eat his flesh and drink his blood, he is not using this shocking imagery as a mere metaphor for accepting his teaching. Rather, Jesus' language and imagery clearly anticipate the food and drink of the Last Supper, which he will also identify

161. One might point out here that Leviticus speaks specifically against consuming the blood of an *animal,* poured out on "the altar" as a sacrifice for sin. It says nothing against drinking the blood of a man.

162. For "eternal life," see Dan 12:2; 1QS 4:7; 4Q181 frg. 1 col. II 4; *Ps. Sol.* 3:12; *1 En.* 15:4-6; 37:4; 40:9; 58:3; *T. Ash.* 5:2; 6:6; *L.A.B.* 23:13; 4 Macc 5:13; *Jos. Asen.* 8:11; *2 En.* J 42:10; *m. Tam.* 7:4; *y. Ber.* 6a (3:1); *b. Ber.* 21a; *Tg. Ps.-J.* on Lev 18:4; *Tg. Onq.* on Lev 18:5, etc. For "the life of the world to come," see *m. 'Abot.* 4:15; *Mek.* on Exod 20:20; *'Abot R. Nat.* A 2; 19; *'Abot R. Nat.* B 29; 45; *y. Kelim* 32b [9:4]; *b. 'Abod. Zar.* 17a; *Gen. Rab.* 11:10. I owe these citations to Dale C. Allison Jr., *Constructing Jesus: Memory, Imagination, and History* (Grand Rapids: Baker Academic, 2010), 188-89.

as his body and blood.[163] As Rudolf Bultmann writes: "Jesus' reply, cast in solemn terms with 'Amen, Amen, I say to you . . .' and with its marked rhythm, unmistakably refers to the Lord's Supper, since now the drinking of blood is added to the eating of the flesh."[164] This point needs to be stressed, since scholars continue to debate whether Jesus' teaching in John 6:53-58 should be interpreted as referring to the food and drink he would identify with his body and blood at the Last Supper, or whether it should only be interpreted as a metaphor for receiving his teaching.[165] With regard to the latter interpretation, it seems reasonable to expect that those who contend Jesus is using the language of drinking someone's blood as a metaphor for believing in that person should be able to support this conclusion with linguistic evidence. And yet when we examine the parallels with Jesus' words in Jewish Scripture itself, we find something quite different. Although the imagery of eating human flesh and drinking human blood can be used metaphorically in the Old Testament, it is never used as a metaphor for accepting someone's teaching or believing in that person. Consider the following parallels:

> When evildoers assail me, *to eat up my flesh,*
> my adversaries and foes, they shall stumble and fall. (Ps 27:2)

> The LORD of hosts will protect them [the sons of Zion], and *they shall devour* and tread down the slingers; *and they shall drink their blood like wine. . . .* (Zech 9:15)

> So I [Zechariah] said, "I will not be your shepherd. What is to die, let it die; what is to be destroyed, let it be destroyed; and let those that are left *devour the flesh of one another.* (Zech 11:9)

163. E.g., Casey, *Is John's Gospel True?,* 44; Stuhlmacher, *Jesus of Nazareth,* 92; Barrett, *The Gospel according to St. John,* 298-99; Dodd, *The Interpretation of the Fourth Gospel,* 338-39. Brown, *The Gospel according to John,* 1:272.

164. Bultmann, *The Gospel of John,* 235. So also Marshall, *Last Supper and Lord's Supper,* 136: "The inclusion of the blood in the statement of Jesus alongside his flesh is inescapably reminiscent of the Lord's Supper."

165. For the view that eating Jesus' flesh and drinking his blood is a metaphor for believing in him, see Anderson, *The Christology of the Fourth Gospel,* 133; Keener, *The Gospel of John,* 1:690; Blomberg, *The Historical Reliability of John's Gospel,* 126-27; Dunn, "John VI — A Eucharistic Discourse?," 328-38. Anderson's claim that "In using eucharistic terminology in 6:53ff., the evangelist is not emphasizing the importance of the eucharist . . ." reveals the weakness of this position. Keener argues in favor of this view that there is no mention of wine, but this is contradicted by the fact that Jesus explicitly identifies his blood as "drink" *(posis)* (John 6:55).

> As for you, son of man, thus says the Lord God: Speak to the birds of every sort and to all beasts of the field, "Assemble and come, gather from all sides to the sacrificial feast which I am preparing for you, a great sacrificial feast upon the mountains of Israel, and *you shall eat flesh and drink blood. You shall eat the flesh of the mighty, and drink the blood of the princes of the earth* — of rams, of lambs, and of goats, of bulls, all of them fatlings of Bashan. And you shall eat fat till you are filled, and drink blood till you are drunk, at the sacrificial feast which I am preparing for you. And you shall be filled at my table with horses and riders, with mighty men and all kinds of warriors," says the Lord God. (Ezek 39:17-20)

As the last verse of the passage in Ezekiel makes clear, in Jewish Scripture, the metaphorical imagery of "eating" someone's "flesh" and "drinking" someone's "blood" always signifies doing violence to them. *It is never used as a metaphor for "believing" in them.* Remarkably, these biblical parallels with Jesus' words in Capernaum are consistently ignored by scholars who argue that they are a metaphor for accepting his teaching. Significantly, even Craig Keener's massive two-volume commentary on John, which contains over 20,000 ancient Jewish and Greco-Roman parallels, does not even mention the above parallels from Jewish Scripture with Jesus' language of eating his flesh and drinking his blood.[166]

The neglect of these Old Testament parallels with the Capernaum discourse is completely unacceptable. If scholars are going to situate Jesus' teaching in its first-century Jewish context, then the metaphorical use of eating flesh and drinking blood in Jewish Scripture must be taken into account. In the Old Testament, it means to harm or kill someone. There is no linguistic foundation for the assertion that to eat someone's flesh and drink their blood is a metaphor for believing his or her teachings. In the words of Raymond Brown:

> [T]he stress on eating (feeding on) Jesus' flesh and drinking his blood . . . cannot possibly be a metaphor for accepting his revelation. "To eat someone's flesh" appears in the Bible as a metaphor for hostile action. . . . *Thus, if Jesus' words in 6:53 are to have a favorable meaning, they must refer to the Eucharist.* They simply reproduce the words we hear in the Synoptic account of the institution of the Eucharist (Matt xxvi 26-28): "Take, eat; this is my body; . . . drink . . . this is my blood."[167]

166. See Keener, *The Gospel of John,* 1:687-89. They are also ignored in Blomberg, *The Historical Reliability of John's Gospel,* 126-27, and Dodd, *The Interpretation of the Fourth Gospel,* 338-40.

167. Brown, *The Gospel according to John,* 1:284-85 (emphasis altered).

Maurice Casey, as is his custom, is less gentle in his criticism:

> [D]rinking blood is so alien to Judaism that to regard "looking to" and "believing" as metaphors for it is culturally ludicrous.[168]

If Brown and Casey are correct, then, contrary to popular belief, Jesus' declaration about the necessity of eating his flesh and drinking his blood, in an ancient Jewish context, simply cannot function as a metaphor for believing in him. Instead, his use of this imagery represents the beginning of the answer to the Jews' question about how he might give them his flesh to eat.

Fourth, when Jesus speaks about eating his flesh and drinking his blood, he explicitly connects these actions with future eschatology.[169] "He who eats my flesh and drinks my blood has eternal life, and I will raise him up at the last day" (John 6:54). Once again, Jesus' teaching regarding eternal life and resurrection from the dead is drawing directly on Jewish Scripture.[170] In particular, two key biblical texts constitute the background of his words:

> The dead shall *live,* their bodies shall *rise.*
> O dwellers in the dust, awake and sing for joy! (Isa 26:19)

> *And many of those who sleep in the dust of the earth shall awake,* some to *everlasting life* and some to shame and everlasting contempt. And those who are wise shall shine like the brightness of the firmament; and those who turn many to righteousness, like the stars for ever and ever. (Dan 12:2-3)

In these texts from Jewish Scripture, we see the language of "everlasting life" (MT *ḥayey ʿôlām;* LXX *zōēn aiōnion*) and bodily "resurrection" (LXX *anastēsontai*) used interchangeably (Dan 12:2), just as Jesus speaks of both "eternal life" *(zōēn aiōnion)* and "rais[ing] up" *(anastēsō)* the dead (John 6:54). When we take this biblical background into account, Jesus appears to be forging a direct connection between the food and drink that he will give and the ancient Jewish hopes for the resurrection of the dead and the entry of the righteous into everlasting life.

In support of this, it is important to note that Isaiah's description of the

168. Casey, *Is John's Gospel True?*, 50.

169. Keener, *The Gospel of John*, 1:691; Higgins, *The Lord's Supper in the New Testament*, 81.

170. Bultmann, *The Gospel of John*, 236 n. 2 notes the "last day" is a widespread rabbinic conception.

bodily resurrection follows close on the heels of his description of the eschatological banquet in which God will "swallow up death forever" (Isa 25:4-8), suggesting a connection between the two.[171] Moreover, this is exactly how *1 Enoch* interpreted Isaiah's eschatological banquet, linking the feast to the coming of the Son of man and the resurrection of the dead to everlasting life on the final day of judgment:

> And the righteous and the chosen will be saved on *that day;* and the faces of the sinners and the unrighteous they will henceforth not see. And the Lord of Spirits will abide over them, and *with that Son of Man they will eat, and they will lie down and rise up forever and ever.* And the righteous and the chosen will have arisen from the earth, and have ceased to cast down their faces, and have put on the garment of glory. (*1 Enoch* 62:13-15)

In short, when interpreted within the context of Jewish Scripture and early Jewish literature, Jesus' declaration about raising up those who partake of his flesh and blood strongly suggests that the food and drink he will give is a kind of pledge of bodily resurrection to those who receive it.[172] In other words, the messianic Son of man will not only receive an everlasting kingdom, as in Daniel; he will also give everlasting life and bodily resurrection to those who partake of the eschatological banquet. And this eschatological banquet will consist of nothing other than his own flesh and blood.[173]

Fifth and finally, it is this overarching eschatological context — namely, the Jewish hope for the new manna, the coming of the heavenly Son of man, and the future resurrection of the dead — in which we are to understand the realistic language employed by Jesus to describe the fare of this banquet. "For my flesh is *real food* and my blood is *real drink.* He who *chews* my flesh and drinks my blood abides in me, and I in him. As the living Father sent me, and I live because of the Father, so he who *chews me* will live because of me" (John 6:55-57). Despite what some translators suggest, in these verses Jesus does not say that his flesh and blood are "true" *(alēthinos)* food and drink, but "real" *(alēthēs)* food and "real" *(alēthēs)* drink (John 6:55).[174] This gives the teaching

171. Feuillet, *Johannine Studies,* 70.

172. Bultmann, *The Gospel of John,* 236.

173. Feuillet, *Johannine Studies,* 69 n. 33: "Thus the promise of the resurrection is linked to the promise of the Eucharist. In effect, if the glorified Son of Man, whose flesh is vivified by the Spirit of God (VI: 63), is to feed men with His flesh and blood, the salvation which he offers must affect their whole being, body and soul."

174. See Brown, *The Gospel according to John,* 1:283; Feuillet, *Johannine Studies,* 55. Schnack-

a decidedly emphatic realism, something recognized by scholars of widely different viewpoints:

> [I]n vv. 51c-58 "bread" (or "flesh"), "eat," "blood," and "drink" are meant in a real sense: here consumption of the flesh and blood of Jesus is called for. The use of the word "consume" (= "chew") instead of "eat" reinforces the literal understanding.[175]

> [T]he offence is heightened in v. 54 by the substitution of the stronger *trōgein* for *phagein.* It is a matter of real eating and not simply of some sort of spiritual participation. Thus there is every indication that v. 55 should also be taken in this way. It is really so! Jesus' flesh is real food and his blood is real drink![176]

> The necessity of eating the flesh of the Son of Man is driven home uncompromisingly by the transition to the word "munch" *(trōgein)* for "eat" in verses 54, 56-58. It is a real eating that is meant. The Christ at the Eucharist is as real as was his human body.[177]

Although I concur with these sentiments, given our focus on the substance of Jesus' teaching, I do not want to press the issue of vocabulary too far. For our purposes, it is the context and substance that matters most. For when we recall that all of Jesus' statements take place in the context of his allusion to the consumption of the manna in the desert by the wilderness generation, it is reasonable to conclude that he is speaking about real food and drink.[178] Lest there be any doubt about this realism, it is important to recall that Jesus concludes by returning to the image of the manna of the exodus, and contrasting it with the bread that he will give:

---

enburg, *The Gospel according to St. John,* 2:62-63 admits this, but prefers the meaning "reliable." It is worth noting that Greek-speaking Christians interpreted the term as "real" food. See Cyril of Alexandria, *In Joann.* 4.2: "The holy body of Christ, which nourishes us for immortality and eternal life, will indeed be a true food." Cited in Schnackenburg, *The Gospel according to St. John,* 2:454 n. 179. Moreover, many scholars see the shift from the language of "eating" *(phagein)* to "chewing" *(trōgein)* as emphasizing that Jesus is speaking of real food and drink. See Schnackenburg, *The Gospel according to St. John,* 2:62.

175. Lüdemann, *Jesus After 2000 Years,* 470.

176. Bultmann, *The Gospel of John,* 236.

177. Higgins, *The Lord's Supper in the New Testament,* 82.

178. Contra Anderson, *The Christology of the Fourth Gospel,* 208.

> "This is the bread which came down from heaven, *not such as the fathers ate and died; he who eats this bread will live forever.*" This he said in the synagogue, as he taught at Capernaum. (John 6:58-59)[179]

It is hard to overestimate the significance of this final reference to the manna for understanding Jesus' teaching in a Jewish context such as the Capernaum synagogue. By identifying the food and drink he will give not only with the flesh and blood of the Son of man but also with the manna from heaven, Jesus is giving his Jewish audience the most important clue to answering their initial question: "How can this man give us his flesh to eat?" (John 6:52). The answer: he will not give them ordinary food and drink, or ordinary flesh and blood, but miraculous food and drink. He will give them the flesh and blood of the Son of man under the *form* of food and drink. Indeed, not only does Jewish Scripture describe the manna as bread "from heaven," early Jewish literature describes it as miraculous:

> Those who collected more than the prescribed measure [of manna] reaped therefrom nothing further than their pains, for they found no more than an *assarôn* [a measure]; while anything left over for the morrow was of no service whatever, being polluted by worms and bitterness, *so divine and miraculous was this food.* (Josephus, *Antiquities* 3.30)

When the miraculous nature of the manna from a Jewish perspective is taken into account, the question of Jesus' realistic language becomes easier to resolve. In short: *if the old manna of the first exodus was miraculous bread from heaven, then the new manna of the heavenly Son of man must also be miraculous bread from heaven.* Otherwise the old manna of the exodus would be greater than the new manna of the eschaton. And indeed, the food that Jesus will give is no less real than the manna of Moses. But it is no ordinary food; like the manna of old, it will be "miraculous bread" from heaven.[180] Once again, insisting that Jesus is only speaking here of a symbol or metaphor for receiving his teaching fails to do justice to the

179. Intriguingly, a remarkable number of manuscripts make this explicit with the reading: "This is the bread that came down from heaven, not such as the manna *(to manna)* the fathers ate and died, but he who eats this bread will live forever" (John 6:58). See Schnackenburg, *The Gospel according to St. John,* 2:455 n. 185 for the manuscript evidence.

180. Bultmann, *The Gospel of John,* 237: "For this reason he takes up again the concept of the 'bread which comes down from heaven' from v. 51a . . . and he assures his readers by the *houtos estin* that this miraculous bread is indeed the sacrament of the Lord's Supper."

Jewish traditions about the manna and the messiah as well as the Jewish context of his words.

The Disciples Object to Jesus' Teaching

Given the realistic emphasis of Jesus' teaching, it is perhaps unsurprising that John's account describes the disciples' reaction as follows: "Many of his disciples, when they heard it, said, 'This is a hard saying; who can listen to it?'" (John 6:60). Then, after Jesus' response to their question, which we examine below, John also reports: "After this, many of his disciples drew back and no longer went about with him" (John 6:66). Three points should be made here about the meaning of the disciples' distinctively negative reaction.

First, when the disciples describe Jesus' words as a "hard" *(sklēros)* teaching, the language does not mean difficult to understand — though it surely is — but rather "unacceptable" or "offensive."[181] As Craig Keener writes:

> The term connotes harshness and difficulty in following rather than merely difficulty in understanding: not hard to understand, but hard to accept.[182]

In other words, the primary problem is not only that the disciples do not *understand* Jesus' teaching, but also that they do not *accept* it. This distinction will become clear momentarily, when Jesus allows many of his disciples to stop following him without correcting any misunderstanding on their part.

Second, one reason Jesus' teaching about eating his flesh and drinking his blood was so offensive is that, in an ancient Jewish context, the consumption of blood was not only something considered repugnant. Apparently, it was also punishable by scourging, or death.[183] Although the point is often overlooked, according to Jewish Scripture, anyone who consumed blood was not only a law-breaker, but was to be "cut off" from the people:

> Moreover you shall eat no blood whatever, whether of fowl or of animal, in any of your dwellings. Whoever eats any blood, *that person shall be cut off from his people.* (Lev 7:27)

181. Moloney, *The Gospel of John,* 230; Barrett, *The Gospel according to St. John,* 302.

182. Keener, *The Gospel of John,* 1:693, quoting Archibald M. Hunter, *The Gospel according to John* (Cambridge Bible Commentary; Cambridge: Cambridge University Press, 1965), 76.

183. Stuhlmacher, *Jesus of Nazareth,* 95.

In Jewish Scripture, the imagery of being "cut off" is a common expression for being put to death by execution.[184] In light of the gravity of the offense of consuming blood, it is completely understandable that Jesus' demand that his disciples eat his flesh and drink his blood, even if understood only symbolically, would have been particularly "difficult" (and potentially dangerous) teaching for his Jewish disciples. Perhaps that is why the disciples' objection to Jesus' teaching is not only that it is difficult to understand — though it surely was — but rather, that it is difficult to accept.[185] This qualification is important, because it points up the fact that while the disciples seem to recognize the realistic nature of Jesus' language, they find it very hard to swallow.

Third, if the consumption of blood was not only against the Mosaic Law but also punishable by death, this would go a long way toward explaining why "many" of Jesus' disciples react to it by drawing back and no longer following him (John 6:66). What we have here appears to be a permanent abandonment of Jesus by many of his Galilean disciples.[186] Given Jesus' status as a widely known public teacher and prophet, such a public rejection of Jesus by his own disciples is something that would have been a matter of no little seriousness.[187] To be sure, some commentators claim that the "hard teaching" does not refer to Jesus' demand to eat his flesh and drink his blood, since according to their view, Jesus' teaching regarding eating his flesh and drinking his blood was a later interpolation.[188] However, when interpreted against the background of Jewish Scripture and later Jewish tradition, the description of Jesus' words as distinctively difficult and the unprecedented abandonment of Jesus by many of his former disciples make the best sense as a response to his unparalleled

184. E.g., Gen 9:11; 41:36; Ps 37:9; Isa 11:13; 29:20. In later Jewish literature, this punishment of being "cut off" was interpreted to mean either execution for drinking blood, if done intentionally (or "with a high hand" Num 15:31), or scourging (the forty lashes minus one), if done unintentionally. See Herbert Danby, *The Mishnah* (Oxford: Oxford University Press, 1933), 562 n. 16. (Unless otherwise noted, all translations of the Mishnah contained herein are from Danby.) In order to see the gravity of the offense, compare it with some of the other crimes that merit the same punishment: "For thirty-six transgressions is Extirpation ['Cutting-Off'] prescribed in the Law: if a man has a connexion with his mother . . . or with a male or with a beast . . . if a man blasphemes, commits idolatry, offers his seed to Molech, or profanes the Sabbath . . . *or eats the blood*. . . . If in these things he transgressed wantonly he is liable to Extirpation" (Mishnah *Kerithot* 1:1-2; cf. Mishnah *Makkot* 3:1-2).

185. Keener, *The Gospel of John*, 693; Barrett, *The Gospel according to St. John*, 302.

186. Schnackenburg, *The Gospel according to St. John*, 2:75.

187. Keener, *The Gospel of John*, 1:696.

188. Brown, *The Gospel according to St. John*, 1:299-303; Bornkamm, "Die eucharistische Rede," 161-69.

and shocking demand that they eat his flesh and drink his blood in the form of real food and real drink.

Jesus Responds to the Disciples' Objection

With all of this in mind, Jesus' response to the disciples' negative reaction, in which he says in reply: "Do you take offense at this? Then what if you were to see the Son of man ascending to where he was before? It is the spirit that gives life, the flesh is of no avail; the words that I have spoken to you are spirit and life. But there are some of you that do not believe" (John 6:61-64).

As is well known, this response is in some ways both the most difficult and most important part of Jesus' teaching. On the one hand, it is widely regarded as somewhat cryptic, and difficult to interpret.[189] This is particularly so because Jesus' question to the disciples is incomplete; though it has a protasis, it has no apodosis, leaving its implied answer somewhat unclear.[190] On the other hand, Jesus' response is rightly identified as the key to understanding his preceding teaching about eating his flesh and drinking his blood. As C. H. Dodd writes: it is "the clue that the reader must hold fast in attempting to understand the discourse."[191] This is especially true for interpreters who argue that the hard teaching is only a metaphor for believing in him and has nothing to do with an actual act of eating and drinking.[192] Although there is much that could be said about this response, for our purposes here, two key points about how Jesus' words throw light on his teaching in the synagogue should suffice.

First and foremost, Jesus responds to the disciples' objection to eating the flesh and blood of the Son of man by going back once again to what Jewish Scripture has to say about the Son of man. Specifically, he focuses their attention on *the ascension of the Danielic Son of man into heaven.*[193] It is difficult to overemphasize this point: when Jesus speaks about "the Son of man ascending to where he was before" (John 6:62), he is both referring once again to the vision in Daniel 7, and interpreting the movement of the Son of man as an exaltation into heaven:

189. Delbert Burkett, *The Son of the Man in the Gospel of John* (JSNTSup 56; Sheffield: Sheffield Academic Press, 1991), 139.

190. Reynolds, *The Apocalyptic Son of Man in the Gospel of John,* 159; Moloney, *The Gospel of John,* 231.

191. Dodd, *The Interpretation of the Fourth Gospel,* 341.

192. Blomberg, *The Historical Reliability of John's Gospel,* 128; Dunn, "John VI — A Eucharistic Discourse?," 337.

193. Reynolds, *The Apocalyptic Son of Man in the Gospel of John,* 160-61.

> I saw in the night visions, and behold, with the clouds of heaven there came *one like a son of man,* and *he came to the Ancient of Days and was presented before him.* And to him was given dominion and glory and kingdom that all peoples, nations, and languages should serve him; his dominion is an everlasting dominion, which shall not pass away, and his kingdom one that shall not be destroyed. (Dan 7:13-14)

This biblical background to Jesus' response is critically important, for it seeks to aid the understanding of his disciples by drawing their attention to the heavenly identity of Son of man.[194] As Rudolf Schnackenburg writes: "This is why Jesus' reply is deliberately phrased in the form of a question. He wants to make his hearers think further about his identity."[195] Likewise, Raymond Brown points out: Jesus "uses the term Son of man to identify himself with a figure whom both Daniel and Enoch characterize as celestial."[196] In short, by referring to the exaltation of the heavenly Son of Man, Jesus is not attempting to make his teaching more offensive or more difficult. Rather, he is giving the befuddled disciples an essential clue to understanding the riddle of his words.[197] *Jesus' question implies that he is not speaking of eating his earthly flesh in its earthly form* — i.e., cannibalism — *but of eating the heavenly flesh of the exalted Son of Man.* Lest there be any doubt about this, recall the overall context of the identification of his flesh with the new manna. The flesh of the Son of Man, like the manna of old, is both "real food" and yet not of this world: it comes "from heaven" (Exod 16:4).[198]

Second, with this in mind, we can now grasp the meaning of Jesus' (at first glance) puzzling declaration that "the flesh" is of "no avail" (John 6:63). On the one hand, according to some commentators, this declaration means that it is Jesus' own flesh, given as food, that is "of no avail."[199] Consider the following:

194. Barrett, *The Gospel according to St. John,* 301.

195. Schnackenburg, *The Gospel according to St. John,* 2:71; *contra* Bultmann, *The Gospel of John,* 445, and Bornkamm, "Die eucharistische Rede im Johannesevangelium," 166.

196. Brown, *The Gospel according to John,* 1:299.

197. Barrett, *The Gospel according to St. John,* 303.

198. Moreover, just as in some ancient Jewish sources, the manna was believed to be pre-existent, so too, when Jesus speaks of the Son of Man ascending to "where he was before" (John 6:62) he likewise implies "the pre-existence of the Son of Man." See Casey, *Is John's Gospel True?,* 42-43; Barrett, *The Gospel according to St. John,* 304.

199. See Anderson, *The Christology of the Fourth Gospel,* 115-119; Blomberg, *The Historical Reliability of John's Gospel,* 128; Lüdemann, *Jesus After 2000 Years,* 470. This view is typically (though not always) linked to a broader view of John's Gospel, which holds that the Gospel as a whole is "anti-sacramental" or, somewhat more softly, "critically sacramental." For the anti-

> It is the Spirit, through Christ's words, not the Lord's Supper, that gives life.[200]

> It is nothing fleshly which gives life, not even the physical body of Jesus, except as it is given in death.[201]

> The eucharistic flesh avails nothing; life comes through the Spirit and words of Jesus.[202]

At first blush, this is a plausible interpretation — if the terminology of spirit and flesh is detached from its context. On the other hand, when interpreted in context, Jesus' reference to "the flesh" simply cannot mean that his flesh is of no avail.[203] To the contrary, Jesus repeatedly emphasizes that it is precisely his flesh that will be given for the life of the world, and it is precisely his flesh that one must eat in order to receive the eternal life of the resurrection.[204] Reconsider the evidence carefully:

> The bread which I shall give *for the life of the world* is *my flesh.* (6:51)

> How can this man give us *his flesh* to eat? (6:52)

> Unless you eat *the flesh* and blood *of the Son of man* you have no life in you. (6:53)

> He who eats *my flesh* and drinks my blood has eternal life. (6:54)

> *My flesh* is real food and my blood is real drink. (6:55)

---

sacramental view, see Blomberg, *The Historical Reliability of John's Gospel,* 126; Barrett, *The Gospel according to St. John,* 284; Dunn, "John VI — A Eucharistic Discourse?" 328-38; Dalman, *Jesus-Jeshua,* 90. For the critically sacramental view, see Marshall, *Last Supper and Lord's Supper,* 138; Bultmann, *The Gospel of John,* 220. For our purposes here, all such terminology is intrinsically anachronistic; for an incisive critique of the whole discussion, see David E. Aune, "The Phenomenon of Early Christian 'Anti-Sacramentalism,'" in *Studies in the New Testament and Early Christian Literature: Essays in Honor of A. P. Wikgren* (ed. D. E. Aune; Leiden: Brill, 1972), 194-214.

200. Blomberg, *The Historical Reliability of John's Gospel,* 128.

201. Marshall, *Last Supper and Lord's Supper,* 136.

202. James D. G. Dunn, *Baptism in the Holy Spirit* (SBT 2:15; London: SCM, 1970), 184-85, cited in Keener, *The Gospel of John,* 1:690.

203. Higgins, *The Lord's Supper in the New Testament,* 83-84.

204. Schnackenburg, *The Gospel according to St. John,* 2:72.

> He who eats *my flesh* and drinks my blood abides in me. (6:56)

In light of this evidence, the view that Jesus is saying that *his* flesh is "useless" is exegetically indefensible.[205] Jesus' response simply cannot be used to undo everything he has just said about the necessity of eating his flesh and drinking his blood; it must have some other meaning.[206] Of course, one could argue that Jesus' declaration about "the flesh" irreconcilably contradicts his teaching that his disciples eat his "flesh" in the Capernaum synagogue, and must be expunged as a later interpolation.[207] But it seems safer and more plausible to attempt to interpret the words in context.

What then is the meaning of Jesus' reference to "flesh" and "spirit" (John 6:62)? Once again, the answer comes to us from the context provided by Jewish Scripture. It should go without saying that, taken out of context, both "spirit" and "life" can bear a wide range of meanings. However, in this instance, we must resist the remarkably widespread tendency of commentators to detach these terms from Jesus' words about the Son of Man and interpret them in isolation.[208] Instead, when properly situated in the context of the immediately preceding reference to the exaltation of the Danielic Son of Man (John 6:62), Jesus' references to "flesh," "spirit," and "life" (John 6:63) are not isolated abstractions but rather "thoroughly rooted in the Hebrew Scriptures."[209] Indeed, if there is any text in Jewish Scripture where "spirit," "life," and "flesh" converge repeatedly in an unforgettable eschatological context, it is in Ezekiel's vision of the resurrection of the dead in the valley of dry bones:

> The hand of the Lord was upon me [Ezekiel], and he brought me out by *the spirit* of the Lord, and set me down in the midst of the valley, and it was full of bones. And he led me round among them . . . and he said to me, "Son of man, can these bones *live?*" . . . Again he said to me, "Prophesy to these bones, and say to them, 'O dry bones, hear the word of the Lord. Thus says the Lord God to these bones: Behold, I will cause *spirit* to enter you, and you shall *live.* And I will lay sinews upon you, and will cause *flesh*

205. See Moloney, *The Gospel of John,* 231, for an excellent critique.

206. Schnackenburg, *The Gospel according to St. John,* 2:73. Brown, *The Gospel according to John,* 1:300: "If 'flesh' in 63 has nothing to do with the Eucharist, neither then does the emphasis on Spirit have anything to do with a spiritual interpretation of the presence of Jesus in the Eucharist."

207. Bornkamm, "Die eucharistische Rede," 161-69.

208. E.g., Keener, *The Gospel of John,* 1:694-95.

209. Blomberg, *The Historical Reliability of John's Gospel,* 128 (though he does not draw out the implications).

> to come upon you, and cover you with skin, and put *spirit* in you, and you shall *live;* and you shall know that I am the LORD.'" So I prophesied as I was commanded; and as I prophesied, there was a noise, and behold, a rattling, and the bones came together, bone to its bone. And as I looked, there were sinews on them, and *flesh* had come upon them, and skin had covered them; but there was no *spirit* in them. Then he said to me, "Prophesy to *the spirit,* prophesy, son of man, and say to *the spirit,* 'Thus says the Lord GOD: Come from the four winds, O *spirit,* and breathe upon these slain, that they may *live.*'" So I prophesied as he commanded me, and *the spirit* came into them, and they *lived,* and stood upon their feet, an exceedingly great host. Then he said to me, "Son of man, these bones are the whole house of Israel. Behold, they say, 'Our bones are dried up, and our hope is lost, and we are clean cut off.' Therefore prophesy, and say to them, 'Thus says the Lord GOD: Behold, I will open your graves, and raise you from your graves, O my people; and I will bring you home into the land of Israel. And you shall know that I am the LORD, when I open your graves, and raise you from your graves, O my people. And I will put *my spirit within you,* and you shall *live.*' . . . " (Ezek 37:1-14)

The number of parallels between Ezekiel's vision and the response of Jesus to the disciples is striking, and yet they repeatedly go either unmentioned or undiscussed by scholars.[210] Just as Jesus declares that it is the spirit that gives life, so too in Ezekiel it is "the spirit" *(rûaḥ)* that makes the dead "live" *(ḥāyāh)* in the bodily resurrection (Ezek 37:1-6). And just as Jesus describes his words as "spirit" and "life," so too five times Ezekiel speaks of the "spirit" giving the dead the power to "live" (Ezek 37:5, 6, 9, 10, 14). Finally, just as Jesus speaks of "the flesh" alone being unable to give life, so too in Ezekiel, it is the spirit that gives life of the resurrection to the "flesh" *(bāśār)* of the dead bodies in the valley (Ezek 37:6, 8).

The upshot of this Old Testament background to Jesus' words is fairly simple: John 6:63 needs to be interpreted in light of John 6:62 and Jewish Scripture. Contrary to what interpreters who ignore the biblical background assume, when Jesus says that his words are "spirit" and "life," *he is not declaring that they are metaphorical rather than literal.*[211] *Rather, he is saying*

210. E.g., Anderson, *The Christology of the Fourth Gospel,* 209-10; Keener, *The Gospel of John,* 1:694-95; Schnackenburg, *The Gospel according to St. John,* 71-73.

211. E.g., Keener, *The Gospel of John,* 1:694, who, despite his penchant for parallels, completely fails to discuss the striking linguistic convergence between Jesus' response in John 6:63 and Ezekiel 37:1-14. As a result, he sets up a false antithesis between "literal" and the "Spirit"

that his words are heavenly and eschatological. By means of these words, he is pointing his disciples to the eschatological resurrection of the dead and the ascension of the Son of Man into heaven as the essential keys to understanding his teaching about eating his flesh and drinking his blood. It is the spirit that gives life in the resurrection; the flesh not animated by the spirit of God is of no avail, for it remains lifeless, like the "flesh" of the dead bodies of the Israelites in the valley of dry bones. In other words, Jesus' command to eat his flesh is not to be interpreted with reference to his dead body; rather, it must be understood in light of the spirit that will give life to the Son of Man in his resurrection from the dead and exaltation into the heavenly kingdom. As Rudolf Schnackenburg writes: "[I]t is not the flesh and blood of the earthly Jesus, but that of the heavenly Son of man, who, filled with the Spirit, possesses a new mode of existence."[212] I agree, but would qualify this slightly: it is not the flesh and blood of Jesus in its earthly form, but the flesh of the heavenly Son of Man, given in the form of real food and real drink, by the power of the eschatological Spirit, that gives those who partake a share in the life of the world to come and the resurrection of the body. Jesus is trying to lift the eyes of their minds up to "the heavenly, eternal realm, as opposed to the merely natural and passing. . . ."[213]

When this is done, Jesus' teaching about "my flesh" refers to the flesh of the heavenly Son of Man, animated by the spirit in his resurrection and exaltation into the heavenly kingdom (Dan 7:13-14), while his teaching about "the flesh" refers to earthly flesh, unanimated by the eschatological spirit (Ezek 37:1-14). In this way, Jesus' declaration functions as an explanation of the heavenly and eschatological nature of his words. At the same time, it acts as a correction of any earthly or cannibalistic interpretation. As Raymond Brown writes:

> Is its exaltation of the Spirit and deprecation of the flesh a reference to the eucharistic flesh spoken of in 51-58? Zwingli thought so and made 63 the keystone of his argument against the real presence, since it seemed to imply that Jesus wanted his presence in the Eucharist to be interpreted in a spiritual manner. However, such an interpretation of 63 as a deprecation of the importance of the eucharistic flesh is hard to reconcile with the em-

— as if the spirit were metaphorical (cf. John 4:24: "God is spirit" [!]). The real contrast is rather between earthly and heavenly (cf. John 3:12), not literal and metaphorical. So too Reynolds, *The Apocalyptic Son of Man in the Gospel of John,* 157.

212. Schnackenburg, *The Gospel according to St. John,* 2:72.

213. Brown, *The Gospel according to John,* 1:300.

> phasis in 53-56 on the necessity of eating the eucharistic flesh because it is a source of life. . . . *[I]t is not the dead body or flesh of Jesus which will be of benefit in the Eucharist, but his resurrected body full of the Spirit of life.*[214]

Along the same lines, A. J. B. Higgins concludes:

> The contradiction of what has gone before in the statement about the ineffectiveness of the flesh is only apparent, for what imparts their life-giving efficacy to the eucharistic elements is the Spirit released by the ascension. . . . The author's answer, then, to misunderstandings of the sacrament is that the eating and drinking of flesh and blood, while real, is not physical, but spiritual, and corresponds to the physical partaking of the bread and wine.[215]

In short, by means of his declaration about the ascension of the Son of Man and his emphasis on the spirit giving life rather than the flesh, Jesus is directing the understanding of his disciples away from a cannibalistic interpretation and toward one focused on consuming his resurrected and spirit-filled body in the form of food and drink.[216]

Arguments against Historical Plausibility

With all of these exegetical observations in mind, we can now take up the question: Is the substance of John 6:48-66, according to the interpretation given above, historically plausible? Given what we know of ancient Judaism, Jesus, and early Christianity, can we attribute the main points outlined above to the historical Jesus of Nazareth, or should most (if not all) of Jesus' teachings in the Capernaum synagogue be regarded as a creation of the early church?

Even a quick overview of the scholarly literature on this subject shows that most scholarship on Jesus gives either an implicitly or explicitly negative verdict. For example, the vast majority of books on Jesus simply ignore John's account of Jesus' teachings in the Capernaum synagogue, as if they did not

214. Brown, *The Gospel according to John,* 1:299, 303.

215. Higgins, *The Lord's Supper in the New Testament,* 83-84.

216. In the words of Peter Stuhlmacher, with his response, Jesus is declaring that the food and drink he will give is a kind of "sacrament of the resurrection" — a prophetic sign that effects a sharing in Jesus' crucified and resurrected body and blood. Stuhlmacher, *Jesus of Nazareth,* 96.

exist.[217] This is even true of entire monographs devoted to the eucharistic words of Jesus.[218] There is no analysis, no exegesis, and no argument for or against the historical plausibility of Jesus' teaching in the Capernaum synagogue, despite its obvious significance, whatever the exact interpretation. This approach seems to be rooted primarily in the assumption that John's Gospel as a whole — and, in particular, the teachings of Jesus therein — are so obviously unhistorical that there is no need to even examine John's testimony and weigh its historical value.[219] Other scholars do take the time to examine the evidence in John 6, but, curiously, they do so without ever raising the question of whether or not it is historical.[220] This approach suggests either that these scholars believe it to be historical, but do not know of any good arguments for defending it, or believe it unhistorical, but (for whatever reason) do not think their readers can bear that fact. Finally, a third group of scholars both analyze the substance of Jesus' teachings — albeit usually with noticeable brevity — and give reasons for why they deem this material to be unhistorical.[221] From this vantage point, there are a number of arguments against the historical plausibility of Jesus' teaching identifying his own flesh and blood with the true manna from heaven. As usual, they can be divided into three main arguments.

The first major argument against historical plausibility is that Jesus' teachings in John 6:48-66 are not only incompatible with early Judaism, but incomprehensible within an ancient Jewish context. The chief objection in this regard is the frequently repeated assertion that Jesus' pronouncement

217. E.g., Keener, *The Historical Jesus of the Gospels;* Allison, *Constructing Jesus;* Meier, *A Marginal Jew* (4 vols.); Dunn, *Jesus Remembered;* Theissen and Merz, *The Historical Jesus;* Wright, *Jesus and the Victory of God;* Crossan, *The Historical Jesus;* Sanders, *Jesus and Judaism;* Meyer, *The Aims of Jesus;* Vermes, *Jesus the Jew;* Jeremias, *New Testament Theology;* Perrin, *Rediscovering the Teaching of Jesus.*

218. E.g., Pesch, *Das Abendmahl und Jesu Todesverständnis;* Patsch, *Abendmahl und historischer Jesus;* Jeremias, *The Eucharistic Words of Jesus* (only mentions John 6:48-66 in passing; no exegetical or historical *analysis*). Schröter, *Das Abendmahl,* 56-60, is an exception.

219. E.g., Casey, *Jesus of Nazareth;* Dunn, *Jesus Remembered;* Wright, *Jesus and the Victory of God.* However, even scholars who are experts in John's Gospel and consider much of its material to have a claim to substantial historical plausibility ignore Jesus' teachings in the Capernaum synagogue. Two particularly striking examples are Keener, *The Historical Jesus of the Gospels,* and Dodd, *Historical Tradition in the Fourth Gospel,* both of whom completely ignore Jesus' eucharistic teachings in John 6:48-66.

220. E.g., Stuhlmacher, *Jesus of Nazareth,* 88-102; Marshall, *Last Supper and Lord's Supper,* 133-39. The latter never denies the historicity of John 6, but places it in his chapter on "The Lord's Supper in the Early Church," at least implying that it does not originate with Jesus.

221. E.g., Lüdemann, *Jesus After 2000 Years,* 468-73; Casey, *Is John's Gospel True?,* 42-50; Funk et al., *The Five Gospels,* 419-22; Strauss, *The Life of Jesus Critically Examined,* 373-75, 633.

about eating his flesh and drinking his blood would have been impossible to understand before his words and actions at the Last Supper in the Upper Room.[222] This objection goes back at least as far as the work of David Friedrich Strauss, who writes:

> Jesus proceeds to represent his flesh as the bread from heaven, which he will give for the life of the world, and "to eat the flesh of the Son of man, and to drink his blood," he pronounces to be the only means of attaining "eternal life." The similarity of these expressions to the words which the synoptists and Paul attribute to Jesus, at the institution of the Lord's Supper, led the older commentators generally to understand this passage as having reference to the Sacramental supper, ultimately to be appointed by Jesus. The chief objection to this interpretation is, that before the institution of the supper, such an allusion would be totally unintelligible. . . . [Indeed], those allusions, totally unintelligible before the institution of the Supper, cannot have proceeded from Jesus, but only from the Evangelist.[223]

Building on this edifice of Jewish incomprehensibility, Maurice Casey goes one step further. He holds that Jesus' declaration that it is necessary to eat his flesh and drink his blood is not only historically implausible, but decidedly anti-Jewish:

> "Amen, amen, I tell you, unless you eat the flesh of the Son of man and drink his blood, you do not have life in yourselves" (6.53). This is stunningly anti-Jewish. Jewish people drain blood from meat in obedience to biblical injunctions not to eat blood. The requirement that they should drink blood, *even symbolically,* shows that the eucharist has been rewritten to be as offensive as possible to "the Jews."[224]

Although other arguments could be forwarded along these lines, these two suffice to demolish the substantial historical plausibility of Jesus' teaching in the Capernaum synagogue. Clearly, if the identification of his flesh and blood

222. Casey, *Is John's Gospel True?,* 45: "It is also another point at which the Johannine narrative cannot be historically accurate. If one imagines a situation in the ministry of Jesus, the question of 6.52 ['How can this man give us his flesh to eat?'] is never answered for people who were supposed to understand it before the eucharist had ever even been heard of. The twelve were in no better a position than 'the Jews' to do so."

223. Strauss, *The Life of Jesus,* 373-74, 633.

224. Casey, *Is John's Gospel True?,* 44.

as food and drink and his declaration that they must be consumed to receive everlasting life are in fact completely unintelligible before the Last Supper and stunningly anti-Jewish, then it should go without saying that they cannot actually stem from the public ministry of Jesus himself. In this event, the entire account of Jesus' teaching in the synagogue likewise falls to the ground as unhistorical.

The second major argument against historical plausibility is that the teaching of Jesus in Capernaum does not cohere with other evidence we have about what Jesus did and said, how he taught and acted. For one thing, Jesus' identification of himself with the manna from heaven and the "bread of life" (John 6:48-51) is regarded as out of step with his characteristic emphasis on the kingdom of God, rather than himself. Although the Synoptic Gospels provide evidence that Jesus delivered "I am" statements without a predicate (Mark 6:50; 13:6; 14:62 and parallels), only the Gospel of John bears witness to him repeatedly utilizing "I am" statements in order to teach about his identity (John 8:12; 10:7; 10:11; 11:25; 14:6; 15:1).[225] As the Jesus Seminar states: "In virtually every case [of an 'I am'] statement, the reader is being confronted with the language of the evangelist and not the language of Jesus."[226] In addition, Jesus' declaration that eating the flesh and blood of the Son of Man is necessary for being resurrected on the last day is also deemed inconsistent with his other teachings. Consider the words of the Jesus Seminar and Maurice Casey:

> The evangelist appears to contradict the teaching of Jesus in the synoptics: there he advocates unbrokered access to God; all have immediate access to the Father without benefit of priest or religious authority.[227]

> This discourse makes it clear that Jewish people who do not take part in the Christian eucharist will not be saved. That is not a feasible view for Jesus of Nazareth to have taken, not least because he had not instituted the Christian eucharist. More fundamentally, he did not seek to exclude faithful Jews from salvation. His criticisms of his fellow Jews were basically

225. Cf. Blomberg, *The Historical Reliability of John's Gospel*, 124.

226. Funk, *The Five Gospels*, 419.

227. Funk, *The Five Gospels*, 421. So too Lüdemann, *Jesus After 2000 Years*, 469. Ironically, the Jesus Seminar cites as evidence of this "unbrokered access" to God Jesus' denunciation of the scribes for taking away the "key" to the kingdom of heaven (Matt 23:13; Luke 11:52), without noting that the Gospel evidence also testifies that Jesus gave the same "keys of the kingdom" to Peter as chief of the Twelve disciples, using the rabbinic terminology of "binding and loosing" as teaching and juridical authority (Matt 16:19). Funk, *The Five Gospels*, 421.

> aimed at scribes and Pharisees whose attachment to the minutiae of the Law overrode love of God and one's neighbour. Nothing in his teaching is comparable to the exclusion from salvation that we find in the fourth Gospel. We must therefore conclude that the discourse and debate of John 6 belongs to Johannine theology, not to the situation of Jesus' ministry.[228]

Finally, in keeping with the earlier argument that Jesus' statements about eating his flesh and drinking his blood would have been incomprehensible, there is also the argument that Jesus would not have spoken in such a way as to cause himself to lose so many of his own disciples (John 6:60-66). In the words of David Strauss:

> It is indeed said that Jesus wished to sift his disciples, to remove from his society the superficial believers, the earthly-minded, whom he could not trust; but the measure which he here adopted was one calculated to alienate from him even his best and most intelligent followers.[229]

In summary, according to several scholars, even apart from the question of form, the basic content of Jesus' teaching in John 6:48-66 is impossible to reconcile with other historical evidence. From this point of view, the Jesus of history did not teach about himself, much less make obedience to his teachings (or those of any other human being) necessary for salvation. The real Jesus was not "exclusive" in his view of salvation, but inclusive of all. And he would never have deliberately weeded out those of his disciples who were too earthly minded and unwilling to accept his more difficult and radical teachings.

The third major argument against historical plausibility is that Jesus' teaching in Capernaum is simply too similar to the beliefs of the early church to be considered authentic to Jesus. This argument is really the flip-side of the observation noted above that Jesus' words would have been unintelligible in a first-century Jewish context. From this point of view, Jesus' words are only intelligible in an early Christian context, and hence, are reasonably deemed as stemming from the era of the early church, rather than that of Jesus. In this regard, the Jesus Seminar and Raymond Brown appear to agree:

> Many scholars are of the opinion that this section of Jesus' speech was added at a late stage in the gospel's composition. Their judgment is based

228. Casey, *Is John's Gospel True?*, 45-46.
229. Strauss, *The Life of Jesus*, 375.

> on the language found only here in the gospel: note especially vv. 53-58, where the physical acts of "eating" and "drinking" almost certainly refer to the bread and wine of the Christian sacrament.[230]

> Let us now turn to the *historical* question of whether the direct eucharistic theme of vss. 51-58 was originally part of Jesus' words to the crowd. . . . [I]t is enough to raise the question whether, *if* Jesus did speak of the bread of life in the Capernaum synagogue, the doctrine about the Eucharist as reported in 51-58 could have been part of that discourse. . . . [I]s there the slightest evidence that the living bread in 51-58 refers to anything other than the Eucharist? If we answer in the negative, and it seems that we must, then it seems impossible that the words of 51-58 which refer exclusively to the Eucharist could have been understood by the crowd or even by the disciples. . . . The form [of the discourse] in 51-58 represents a more radical rethinking of the discourse in which the eucharistic theme has become primary. It was added to 35-50 at a fairly late stage in the editing of the Fourth Gospel, probably in the final redaction.[231]

It is important to understand the logic of this position. To the extent that Jesus' teachings in John 6:48-66 are about "the Christian sacrament,"[232] "die sakramentale Deutung des Mahles,"[233] or "the doctrine of the Eucharist,"[234] then they are *by definition* necessarily unhistorical. For, during the life of Jesus, a "Eucharistic doctrine" of "the Christian sacrament," strictly understood, did not exist. Even more, if Jesus' command that his followers eat his flesh and drink his blood is about "the superiority of Christianity to Judaism,"[235] then by definition it cannot be authentic to him, since "Christianity" did not as

230. Funk, *The Five Gospels*, 421.

231. Brown, *The Gospel according to John*, 1:286-87. It is intriguing to note here a tension in the scholarly approach to this section. One the one hand, some scholars contend that the discourse is too Johannine to be from Jesus. The discourse is the type of dialogue distinctive of the Gospel according to John, in which Jesus' teaching is misunderstood because it is taken too literally. E.g., Funk, *The Five Gospels*, 421; Strauss, *The Life of Jesus*, 374. On the other hand, other scholars see the contents of the discourse as so at odds with the teachings of John elsewhere that they hypothesize that the section focused on eating and drinking Jesus' flesh and blood (usually isolated as John 6:51b-58) is an interpolation inconsistent with the rest of the Gospel. E.g., Lüdemann, *Jesus After 2000 Years*, 469.

232. Funk, *The Five Gospels*, 421.

233. Schröter, *Das Abendmahl*, 57.

234. Brown, *The Gospel according to John*, 1:286-87.

235. Casey, *Is John's Gospel True?*, 44.

yet exist. Again, if the primary meaning of Jesus' words in the Capernaum synagogue is either "pro-sacramental"[236] or "anti-sacramental" or "critically-sacramental,"[237] they are by definition unhistorical, because such debates over sacramental theology did not (of course) take place during the public ministry of the Jewish prophet from Nazareth. With their characteristic brevity, Gerd Lüdemann and Frank Schleritt state the position clearly:

> The addition by the revisers in vv. 51c-58 presupposes the eucharistic cult after Easter and for that reason alone cannot have preserved any authentic sayings of Jesus.[238]

Intriguingly, the force of this argument against historicity is accepted by scholars who argue in rejoinder that Jesus' teachings in the synagogue are not about the eucharist, but are simply a metaphor for believing in him. These scholars then use this non-eucharistic interpretation as an argument for historical plausibility.[239] In their view, the fact that the discourse is not about the eucharist counts in favor of its historicity, because they have accepted the premise that if it is about the eucharist, then it is by definition unhistorical.

It is in the light of such considerations that many scholars conclude that Jesus' teaching on the flesh and blood of the Son of Man in John 6:48-66 should be deemed substantially (if not entirely) unhistorical, a later creation of the early church. The verdict of Maurice Casey in this regard is representative:

> We must therefore conclude that attempts to defend the historicity of John 6 have not been successful. Nor have the efforts of Protestant scholars to show that the eucharist is not central to it. This discourse does not belong to the Jesus of history. Its *Sitz im Leben* is entirely in the Johannine community, which produced its theology of the eucharist.[240]

236. Schweizer, *The Lord's Supper,* 7, speaks of "unmitigated sacramentalism"; see also Oscar Cullmann, *Early Christian Worship* (trans. A. S. Todd and J. B. Torrance; London: SCM, 1953).

237. Blomberg, *The Historical Reliability of John's Gospel,* 126; Marshall, *Last Supper and Lord's Supper,* 138; Barrett, *The Gospel according to St. John,* 284; Dunn, "John VI — A Eucharistic Discourse?" 328-38; Bultmann, *The Gospel of John,* 220; Dalman, *Jesus-Jeshua,* 90.

238. Lüdemann, *Jesus After 2000 Years,* 473.

239. E.g., Blomberg, *The Historical Reliability of John's Gospel,* 126-27. Casey, *Is John's Gospel True?,* 44-51 gives a helpful survey of scholars (mostly Protestant) who make this argument.

240. Casey, *Is John's Gospel True?,* 51.

With these points in mind, we can now examine the arguments that favor the historical plausibility of Jesus' teaching in the synagogue at Capernaum. Despite the widespread skepticism regarding the historicity of the account, there are in fact several remarkably strong arguments that favor the historicity of this evidence. Indeed, if we focus on the substance of the account (the *substantia verba Jesu*) and remember that we are not looking for the exact words of Jesus (the *ipsissima verba Jesu*), then we find that John's account of Jesus' teaching is historically congruent with ancient Judaism, coheres with other words and deeds of Jesus, and provides a plausible origin for certain aspects of the practice and belief of the early church.

Context: The Manna, the Blood, and the Life of the Son of Man

The first argument for the substantial historicity of Jesus' teaching in the Capernaum synagogue is from its Jewish contextual plausibility. If our analysis above has shown anything, it should have shown that Jesus' teaching about the new manna from heaven is deeply rooted in Jewish Scripture and tradition, and that the reactions of the Judeans and the disciples, given what we know of ancient Jewish beliefs, smack of historical verisimilitude. Indeed, it is remarkable just how many elements in this discourse, including the reactions of the Judeans and his disciples, are either taken straight from the Old Testament or fit quite squarely into an ancient Jewish context. Consider the following points, taken in roughly the same order in which they occur in John's account.

First, Jesus' identification of the food he will give with the true manna "from heaven" (John 6:48-51, 58) is taken directly from the accounts of the manna contained in Jewish Scripture. In particular, his emphasis on the heavenly origin of the manna is explicitly and repeatedly taught in the biblical accounts of the manna (Exodus 16; Psalm 78; Nehemiah 9). Moreover, Jesus' emphasis on the coming of new manna appears to reflect the particular Jewish hope, going back at least as far as the first century A.D., that when the messiah came, he would bring back the miracle of the manna from heaven:[241]

> And it will happen that when all that which should come to pass in these parts is accomplished, the messiah will begin to be revealed. . . . And those who are hungry will enjoy themselves and they will, moreover, see marvels every day. . . . *And it will happen at that time that the treasury of*

241. See survey of the manna above.

> *manna will come down again from on high, and they will eat of it in those years* because these are they who will have arrived at the consummation of time. (2 *Baruch* 29:3, 6-8)

Notice that in both this text and Jesus' Capernaum discourse, the eschatological manna is linked to the advent of the messiah and the resurrection of the dead.[242] Along these lines, Jesus' declaration that he will "give" the new "bread" or new manna that will be greater than the old manna (John 6:51), although clearly demonstrating an implicit claim of remarkable authority — is nevertheless easily situated within the context of the Jewish expectation of a new Moses (cf. Deut 18).[243] It should be clear from the Old Testament background and early Jewish texts like 2 *Baruch* that Jesus' basic declaration that he is going to give the true manna from heaven, a manna greater than that of Moses, is an implicit claim to be the new Moses, as well as a messianic claim that is powerfully congruent with what we know of ancient Jewish beliefs.

Second, contrary to Maurice Casey's claim above, even Jesus' declaration that eating the new manna from heaven is necessary for salvation is also plausible within a Jewish context.[244] In making his argument Casey fails to note that in *Joseph and Aseneth* — an early Jewish account usually dated between the first century B.C. and second century A.D. — we also find the idea that the eating of miraculous food gives heavenly life.[245] Indeed, even Jesus' expression "bread of life" finds a parallel in Second Temple Judaism.[246] In the account of Joseph and Aseneth's courtship, we find several striking parallels with the language and imagery of Jesus:

> And Joseph said: "It is not fitting for a man who worships God, who will bless with his mouth the living God and eat blessed *bread of life (arton zōēs)* and drink a blessed *cup of immortality* and anoint himself with

242. Anderson, *The Christology of the Fourth Gospel,* 205.

243. Cf. Keener, *The Gospel of John,* 1:682; Dodd, *The Interpretation of the Fourth Gospel,* 83; cf. Brown, *The Gospel according to John,* 2:265, though none of these uses this as an argument for historicity.

244. Casey, *Is John's Gospel True?,* 45-46.

245. It should be noted here that some scholars regard *Joseph and Aseneth* as a Christian text. For discussion, see John Collins, "Joseph and Aseneth: Jewish or Christian?" in *JSP* 14, no. 2 (2005): 97-112; Christoph Burchard, "The Importance of Joseph and Aseneth for the Study of the New Testament: A Fresh Look at the Lord's Supper," *NTS* 33 (1987): 102-34.

246. Blomberg, *The Historical Reliability of John's Gospel,* 124; Patsch, *Abendmahl und historischer Jesus,* 26.

> blessed ointment of incorruptibility to kiss a strange woman who will bless with her mouth dead and dumb idols and eat from their table bread of strangulation and drink from their libation a cup of insidiousness and anoint herself with ointment of destruction. (*Joseph and Aseneth* 8:5)

> Lord God of my father Israel,
> the Most High, the Powerful One of Jacob . . .
> bless this virgin and renew her by your spirit,
> and form her anew by your hidden hand,
> and make her alive again by your life,
> *and let her eat your bread of life,*
> *and drink your cup of blessing,*
> and number her among your people
> that you have chosen before all (things) came into being,
> and let her enter your rest which you have prepared for your chosen
> ones,
> and live in your *eternal life* for ever (and) ever.
> (*Joseph and Aseneth* 8:10-11)

Two things stand out as significant from this early Jewish text. For one thing, we find an exact parallel to Jesus' expression, the "bread of life" (John 6:48), which occurs several times over the course of the book (*Jos. Asen.* 8:5, 9; 15:5; 16:16; 19:5; 21:21; cf. 8:11).[247] Although the Jewish author does not explain what this bread refers to, it seems in context to be a reference to a cultic meal of some sort, most likely the unleavened bread of the Jewish Passover. The cultic and initiatory character of the meal can be deduced from the fact that the bread of life is coupled with a reference to the "cup of blessing" in the context of Joseph's prayer for Aseneth's becoming one of the Jewish people. As the Torah makes clear, one had to become an Israelite before being allowed to partake of the Passover meal (Exod 12:43-49).[248] Hence, this suggests that Joseph's reference to the "cup of blessing" may be early Jewish evidence for the expression "cup of blessing" being used as a technical term for the Passover cup of wine (cf. 1 Cor 10:16; *b. Ber.* 51a).[249] Moreover — and this is significant — note well

247. Burchard, "Joseph and Aseneth," 119.

248. For a list of scholarly suggestions, see Burchard, "Joseph and Aseneth," 110-11. It is remarkable that none of the suggestions (Essene meal, Therapeutae meal, everyday Jewish meals) seems aware of the explicit initiatory requirement for the Passover meal in Exod 12:43-49.

249. Cf. Calum Carmichael, "The Passover Haggadah," in *The Historical Jesus in Context*

that much of the language that scholars regularly deem as uniquely "Johannine," and hence, implausible on the lips of Jesus — is present in this early Jewish text. In his prayer, Joseph speaks of "the living God," "life," "darkness," "light," "truth," the "spirit" of God, the "bread of life," and "eternal life" (*Jos. Asen.* 8:10-11). In light of such evidence in Jewish Scripture and ancient Jewish literature, Jesus' basic use of the manna as an image of miraculous bread from heaven — the image that holds all of the evidence in John 6:48-58 together, is congruent with an early Jewish context. In short, Jesus' teaching about the new manna, however elevated, can only be presented as inconceivable in an early Jewish context if one ignores the ancient Jewish parallels to the substance of his teaching.

Third, even Jesus' declaration that unless his followers eat the flesh and "drink the blood of the Son of man," they have no "life" in them (John 6:52-54), is explicable within an early Jewish context. As we noted above, Jesus' words about the necessity of drinking the blood of the Son of Man in order to have "life" presuppose the deeply Jewish belief that "the life" is in the blood:

> If any man of the house of Israel or of the strangers that sojourn among them eats any blood, I will set my face against that person who eats blood, and will cut him off from among his people. *For the life of the flesh is in the blood; and I have given it for you upon the altar to make atonement for your souls; for it is the blood that makes atonement, by reason of the life.* Therefore I have said to the people of Israel, no person among you shall eat blood, neither shall any stranger who sojourns among you eat blood. (Lev 17:10-12)

The point bears repeating: the very reason that Jewish Scripture prohibits the consumption of animal blood — because the life is in the blood — is the reason Jesus requires the disciples to consume the blood of the Son of Man, so that they might be "raised up on the last day" (cf. John 6:54). The Jewish Torah thus provides us both with the reason Jesus' words were so shocking and the eschatological rationale for his command. To be sure, this was clearly not something one would expect to hear at an ordinary synagogue gathering in Galilee! And yet even this portion of Jesus' teaching, when examined carefully, shares the

(ed. Amy-Jill Levine, Dale C. Allison Jr., and John Dominic Crossan; Princeton and Oxford: Princeton University Press, 2006), 343; Gillian Feeley-Harnik, *The Lord's Table: Eucharist and Passover in Early Christianity* (Philadelphia: University of Pennsylvania, 1981), 145; Daube, *The New Testament and Rabbinic Judaism*, 330.

messianic understanding of the "one like a son of man" (Dan 7:13-14) found in our most ancient Jewish interpretations of Daniel 7:13-14; is directly rooted in the description of the bodily resurrection of the dead and their entry into "eternal life" found in Jewish Scripture (Dan 12:1-2); and uses "spirit" and "life" as opposed to "the flesh" in ways that bear multiple connections with Ezekiel's famous vision of the valley of the dry bones and the resurrection of the flesh through the power of the spirit (Ezekiel 37).[250]

Fourth, when Jesus identifies the new manna of Jewish expectations with his own "flesh," the initial objection raised by the Judeans is completely believable (John 6:51-52), and the description of Jesus' words as a "hard teaching" and the abandonment of him by "many" of his disciples (John 6:60-66) are both thoroughly plausible reactions in a first-century Jewish context.[251] Given the potential misunderstanding about his teaching about eating flesh and drinking blood, and the repugnance toward any kind of cannibalism manifested in Jewish Scripture (Deuteronomy 28; Ezekiel 5), the negative response of many of Jesus' disciples is quite believable.[252] Indeed, it is remarkable that Jesus' discourse in Capernaum is so often rejected by scholars as unhistorical because it would have been incomprehensible or difficult to understand.[253] *For that is exactly how John says Jesus' audience reacted.* If John had recorded Jesus delivering such shocking teaching and people reacting to it positively and with complete understanding, one would have strong cause to be suspicious. But this is precisely what does not take place in John's account: instead, both the wider Jewish members of the synagogue and Jesus' own circle of disciples object to his teaching and are apparently repulsed by it. Even when the Twelve accept his teaching, it is clearly not because they understand it (John 6:67-71). If Jesus did in fact teach about the necessity of eating the flesh and blood of the Son of Man, then the responses recorded by John are exactly what one would expect from a Jewish audience and even Jesus' own disciples. Far from counting against the historical verisimilitude of John's account, the difficult nature of Jesus' teaching, coupled with the overwhelmingly negative reaction to it, smacks of historical reality.

Fifth, Jesus' emphasis on the heavenly exaltation of the Son of Man (John 6:61-64) is also plausible in a first-century Jewish context. It consti-

250. Cf. Collins, *Daniel*, 306-7; Vermes, *Jesus the Jew*, 170-72.

251. Blomberg, *The Historical Reliability of John's Gospel*, 128, 130.

252. Schnackenburg, *The Gospel according to St. John*, 2:69, sees the negative response of the disciples in particular as relying on "historical memories" and holds that John is "convinced that in Galilee, there was a falling away, and that people ceased to follow Jesus."

253. Cf. Strauss, *The Life of Jesus*, 373-74.

tutes a clear allusion to Daniel's vision of the exaltation of the Son of Man to the Ancient of Days in Jewish Scripture (Dan 7:13-14). Moreover, his identification of his teachings with "spirit" and "life" as opposed to "the flesh" bears multiple connections with Ezekiel's famous vision of the valley of the dry bones and the resurrection of the flesh through the power of the spirit (Ezek 37). Indeed, even Jesus' fleeting reference to the Son of Man going to "where he was before" (John 6:62) seems to reflect an ancient Jewish belief that the messiah and/or Danielic son of man existed from the very beginning of creation:

> At that hour, *that Son of Man was given a name, in the presence of the Lord of Spirits, the Before-Time; even before the creation of the sun and the moon, before the creation of the stars, he was given a name in the presence of the Lord of Spirits*. . . . For this purpose he became the Chosen One; he was concealed in the presence of (the Lord of Spirits) prior to the creation of the world, and for eternity. (*1 Enoch* 48:2-3, 6)

> And it will happen after these things *when the time of the appearance of the messiah has been fulfilled and he returns with glory, that then all who sleep in hope of him will rise.* And it will happen at that time that those treasuries will be opened in which the number of the souls of the righteous were kept, and they will go out and the multitudes of the souls will appear together, in one assemblage, of one mind. . . . For they know that the time has come of which it is said that it is the end of times. (*2 Baruch* 30:1)

Again, these early Jewish parallels are not meant to suggest that Jesus' teaching in Capernaum would not have been difficult to understand in an ancient Jewish context. It surely was. But such evidence constitutes a strong argument against the widespread idea that his teaching would have been incomprehensible in a Jewish context, and, hence, must be unhistorical. To the contrary, by drawing on Jewish beliefs about the exaltation of the messiah and the resurrection of the dead, beliefs rooted in Scripture and reflected in tradition, Jesus in his response helps his Jewish disciples to see that he is not speaking about the consumption of his earthly flesh in its earthly form, but of the consumption of the heavenly flesh and blood of the resurrected and exalted messiah in the banquet of heaven.

Finally, for what it is worth, even Jesus' language of "eating" the flesh of the "Son of Man" is congruent with a cryptic teaching about *eating the Messiah* that later rabbinic tradition attributed to Rabbi Hillel, the famous first-century older contemporary of Jesus (ca. 110 B.C.–A.D. 10).[254] With the caveat once again in mind that the Talmud comes from a much later period, consider the following text regarding the messianic banquet:

> Rabbi Giddal said in Rab's name: *"Israel is destined to eat in the days of the Messiah."* Rabbi Joseph demurred: "Is this not obvious; who else then shall eat . . . ?" This was said in opposition to Rabbi Hillel, who maintained that *there will be no Messiah for Israel, since they have already eaten him* during the reign of Hezekiah. (Babylonian Talmud, *Sanhedrin* 98b)[255]

While some English translations obscure the point, the teaching attributed to Hillel clearly speaks of "eating" or "consuming" *('ākal)* the "messiah" *(māšîaḥ)*.[256] To be sure, it is by no means clear what Hillel means by saying this. Perhaps he is referring to the famous Passover feast that was celebrated during the reign of Hezekiah (see 2 Chron 30:1-26).[257] In order to attempt to explain this passage, David Daube once connected it with the later Jewish tradition of eating a piece of bread during Passover known as the *aphikomen*, which symbolized the Messiah.[258] (I for one find the early medieval Jewish evidence utilized by Daube far too late to put any confidence in his proposal about the *aphikomen* at the Last Supper.) However we explain this rabbinic tradition, for our purposes, the upshot of these data is this: Jesus' language of "eating" the flesh of the Son of Man, though obviously shocking, is not entirely unparalleled in ancient Jewish literature. Indeed, one can put the point more strongly: to my knowledge, *the only individual that ancient rabbinic tradition ever speaks about "eating" is the messiah, and this tradition is attributed to Rabbi*

254. See James H. Charlesworth and Loren L. Johns, eds., *Hillel and Jesus: Comparisons of Two Major Religious Leaders* (Minneapolis: Fortress, 1997). Remarkably, this saying attributed to Hillel, despite its obvious parallels with the New Testament, goes undiscussed.

255. Unless otherwise noted, all translations of the Babylonian Talmud contained herein are from Isidore Epstein, ed., *The Babylonian Talmud, Soncino Edition* (35 vols.; London: Soncino, 1933-35).

256. Cf. Jacob Neusner, *The Babylonian Talmud: A Translation and Commentary* (22 vols.; Peabody: Hendrickson, 2005), 16:527.

257. On the significance of Hezekiah's Passover for Jesus, see Brant Pitre, "Jesus, the Messianic Wedding Banquet, and the Restoration of Israel," *Letter & Spirit* 8 (2013): 35-54.

258. See David Daube, *He That Cometh* (St. Paul's Lecture 5; London: London Diocesan Council for Christian-Jewish Understanding, 1966), 9-10; idem, *Wine in the Bible* (St. Paul's Lecture 13; London: London Diocesan Council for Christian-Jewish Understanding, 1974), 12-20. For a defense of Daube, see Calum B. Carmichael, "David Daube on the Eucharist and the Passover Seder," *JSNT* 42 (1991): 45-67.

Hillel, the first-century contemporary of Jesus.[259] At the very least, a rabbinic tradition such as this suggests that it was not impossible for Jesus, in an ancient Jewish context, to have spoken to his disciples about eating the flesh of the Son of Man.[260] To the contrary, although Jesus' teaching about eating the flesh and drinking the blood of the Son of Man is certainly an arresting formula, it is an arresting teaching that can be plausibly situated within his early Jewish context and finds at least one remarkable parallel with a later rabbinic tradition ascribed to the first century.

Of course, even in light of these parallels in Jewish Scripture and tradition, one cannot contend that Jesus' command that his disciples eat his flesh and drink his blood is identical to anything we find in Jewish sources, rabbinic or other. However, these elements of congruence strengthen the case that Jesus' teaching is explicable within an ancient Jewish context.

Coherence: Teaching in Synagogues, the Son of Man, and the Last Supper

The second major argument for historical plausibility is from coherence with other words and deeds of Jesus. If we once again remind ourselves that we are not looking for the *ipsissima verba Jesu,* but rather the *substantia verba Jesu,* then the Capernaum synagogue teaching is remarkably coherent with other words and deeds of Jesus in several ways that are consistently overlooked.

First, Jesus' teaching on the new manna fits remarkably well with the evidence for his teaching in Jewish synagogues in general and the Capernaum synagogue in particular.[261] John's claim that Jesus spoke about the new manna while "in the synagogue, as he taught at Capernaum" (John 6:59) is thus in accord with other data in which Jesus teaches in the Capernaum synagogue (Luke 4:31; 7:4) and other local Jewish synagogues throughout Galilee (Matt 4:23; 9:35; 12:8-9; 13:54; Mark 1:21, 39; 6:2; Luke 4:15-16, 33, 44; 6:6; 13:10; John 18:20).[262] One reason

259. For a similar tradition, see also Babylonian Talmud, *Sanhedrin* 99a.

260. Blomberg, *The Historical Reliability of John's Gospel,* 126.

261. See Allison, *Constructing Jesus,* 307; Graham H. Twelftree, "Jesus and the Synagogue," *Handbook for the Study of the Historical Jesus* (4 vols.; ed. Tom Holmén and Stanley E. Porter; Leiden: Brill, 2011), 4:3105-34; James D. G. Dunn, "Did Jesus Attend the Synagogue?," in *Jesus and Archaeology* (ed. James H. Charlesworth; Grand Rapids: Eerdmans, 2006), 206-22.

262. Keener, *The Gospel of John,* 1:692, citing archaeological evidence confirming the presence of the synagogue at Capernaum in Jesus' day. Cf. Brown, *The Gospel according to John,* 1:284. As Josephus says, the synagogue was used for the study of Scripture (*Ag. Ap.* 2.175; Philo, *Hypoth.* 7.12-13), which accords well with Jesus' use of the exodus traditions.

this synagogue context is significant is that it provides a reasonable explanation for the dialogical and homiletical shape of Jesus' teaching on eating the flesh and drinking the blood of the Son of Man. As Dale Allison rightly points out:

> The authors [of the canonical Gospels] . . . have it that, on several occasions, Jesus taught in a synagogue, which implies that he composed short homilies. There are also the various editorial commentaries that envisage him addressing the crowds in the open; and surely readers are left with the impression that people did not come together only to be accosted by a cryptic sentence or two, followed by Jesus' immediate departure. Must we not rather think that he was a little less enigmatic than that and so went on for at least a little while? As John A. T. Robinson once put it, "It is hardly to be supposed that Jesus went round peppering his audience with pellets of disconnected apophthegms."[263]

Allison goes on to conclude that "[i]f Jesus was more than an aphorist, then maybe we should expect to have more than just aphorisms, more than just isolated fragments of his speech."[264] In other words, we should expect Jesus' synagogal teaching to be somewhat more lengthy and dialogical than his aphorisms and parables, as indeed it is in this case. The reason this observation matters to us is that I suspect that one of the primary reasons many Jesus scholars do not even examine the potential historical plausibility of the data in question is because of the assumption that the substance of the "bread of life discourse" is too long to go back to Jesus, unlike the shorter parables and aphorisms in the Synoptics. When we keep in mind that we are not looking for the *ipsissima verba* but the substance or "gist" of Jesus' teaching in the Capernaum synagogue, this assumption is unwarranted, since in the case of

263. Allison, *Constructing Jesus,* 307-8, citing Robinson, *The Priority of John,* 304. Significantly, the broader context of Robinson's words quoted by Allison above regards Jesus' discourse in the Capernaum synagogue: "This 'earthing' of the discourses in real time, and space . . . has led to the question whether some of them at least may not reflect actual, and datable, occasions within the ministry of Jesus, in a way again that it would be impossible to derive from the Synoptic material. Even, or especially, such a highly theological and 'Johannine' discourse as that of ch. 6 on the bread of life turns out to reflect synagogue preaching patterns. . . . Clearly, not least in strong eucharistic overtones, it reflects the teaching of the church, but I see no reason why the homiletic structure, which . . . fits precisely the *Sitz im Leben* of teaching 'in the synagogue' (6.59), should not represent how Jesus himself spoke in these circumstances." Robinson, *The Priority of John,* 302-3, following Borgen, *Bread from Heaven.*

264. Allison, *Constructing Jesus,* 308.

Jesus' exchange regarding the manna and eating the flesh of the Son of Man, it only takes about two minutes or so to slowly read John 6:48-55 aloud in Greek. (Even by contemporary standards, a few minutes of material is hardly a long "homily" or lengthy "discourse"!) Rather, when the basic content of Jesus' teaching regarding the new manna from heaven is carefully interpreted in context, the basic content coheres well with what we can surmise about his method and manner of teaching in the Jewish synagogue.

Second, the enigmatic nature of Jesus' teaching in Capernaum coheres with other evidence we have that he regularly employed riddle-like speech and difficult sayings.[265] It should go without saying that we have substantial evidence that he spoke in "parables" or "riddles" *(mešālîm)* (Matt 13:34; Mark 4:33-34; John 16:25). But it also needs to be said that even many of Jesus' teachings that do not fit the exact parameters of what modern scholars normally designate as "parables" are often extremely enigmatic, such that their meaning continues to be debated even to this day.[266] Ancient teachers, Jesus included, could use more obscure teachings to separate the "wheat" and "chaff" among truly dedicated disciples and those whose faith would fail.[267] The most obvious example of this is of course the words of institution at the Last Supper, in which Jesus mysteriously identifies the bread and wine of the Passover meal with his own body and blood (Matt 26:26-28; Mark 14:24; Luke 22:19-20; 1 Cor 11:23-24). Also important is the account of Jesus warning the disciples to "beware of the leaven of the Pharisees," in which they respond by thinking him to be upbraiding them for having brought no bread along on their journey (Matt 16:5-12; Mark 8:13-21). In this evidence, as in the Capernaum synagogue, Jesus delivers a teaching about bread that is easily misunderstood if taken too literalistically.[268] This element of coherence is important to emphasize given David Friedrich Strauss's statement discussed above, that Jesus' identification of the new manna with his own flesh must be unhistorical simply because the disciples would not have understood it.[269] Such an objection completely fails

265. See Keener, *The Gospel of John*, 1:692; Klyne R. Snodgrass, *Stories with Intent: A Comprehensive Guide to the Parables of Jesus* (Grand Rapids: Eerdmans, 2008); Tom Thatcher, *Jesus the Riddler: The Power of Ambiguity in the Gospels* (Westminster: John Knox, 2006).

266. See Pitre, *Jesus, the Tribulation, and the End of the Exile*, 131-218; Daniel Fanous, *Taught by God: Making Sense of the Difficult Sayings of Jesus* (Rollinsford, NH: Orthodox Research Institute, 2010).

267. Keener, *The Gospel of John*, 1:687 n. 233; cf. Keener, *The Gospel of Matthew*, 378-79, citing Diogenes Laertius 3.63; 8.1.15.

268. Keener, *The Gospel of John*, 1:688.

269. Strauss, *The Life of Jesus Critically Examined*, 375.

to reckon with the apparent delight Jesus (and sometimes his Jewish audience) takes in propounding *m^e^šālîm* whose meanings are not immediately obvious, such as in the riddle about the Messiah and David's son (Matt 22:41-46; Mark 12:35-37; Luke 20:41-44).[270] In short, Jesus' identification of the bread from heaven with his own flesh, and his command to eat his flesh and drink his blood are by no means his only teachings that are quite difficult to understand.

Third, Jesus' teaching on the new manna coheres with other evidence for a Mosaic self-understanding on his part.[271] When Jesus declares that he will be the one to give the new manna from heaven (John 6:49-51), he is implicitly identifying himself with the prophet like Moses of Jewish Scripture (Deuteronomy 18), if not the Mosaic messiah of early Jewish messianism (e.g., Josephus, *Ant.* 20.97-98, 169-70; *4QTestimonia* [4Q175] 1-8). This Mosaic self-understanding coheres quite well with other evidence that Jesus frequently acted and spoke like Moses, such as when he feeds the multitude in the desert with bread (Matt 14:13-21; Mark 6:30-44; Luke 9:10-17; John 6:1-15), teaches his disciples to pray for the eschatological manna of the kingdom (Matt 6:11; Luke 11:3), and repeatedly describes his contemporaries as "this [evil] generation," in the manner of Moses himself (Matt 12:39-42; Luke 11:29-32; Mark 8:12). Perhaps most striking of all, even Jesus' climactic declaration that they will see the Son of Man "ascending" to heaven coheres with ancient Jewish traditions about Moses, who was believed by some Jews to have ascended into heaven at the end of his life:[272]

> Afterwards the time came *when he [Moses] had to make his pilgrimage from earth to heaven, and leave this mortal life for immortality, summoned thither by the Father.* . . . For when he was already being exalted and stood at the very barrier, *ready at the signal to direct his upward flight to heaven,* the divine spirit fell upon him and he prophesied with discernment while still alive the story of his own death. . . . Such, as recorded in the Holy Scriptures, was the life and such the end of Moses, king, lawgiver, high priest, prophet. (Philo, *Life of Moses* 2.288, 291-92)[273]

270. See Keener, *The Gospel of Matthew,* 371-75, 381-84.

271. See Allison, *Constructing Jesus,* 270-73 and chapter 2 above.

272. Schapdick, "Moses," 610-11. For later references to the ascension of Moses into heaven, see also *Sifre* on Deut 34:5 (357); *Deut. Rab.* 34:5. The tradition may also be assumed in the New Testament passages regarding the appearance of Moses at the Transfiguration (Matt 17:1-9; Mark 9:2-10; Luke 9:28-36) and the dispute between Michael the archangel and Satan over the body of Moses (Jude 9).

273. Trans. F. H. Colson, LCL (slightly adapted).

> When he [Moses] arrived on the mountain called Abaris . . . he dismissed the elders. And, while he bade farewell to Eleazar and Joshua and was yet communing with them, *a cloud of a sudden descended upon him and he disappeared in a ravine.* But he has written of himself in the sacred books that he died, *for fear lest they should venture to say that by reason of his surpassing virtue he had gone back to God.* (Josephus, *Jewish Antiquities* 4.325-26)

In the light of such early Jewish evidence, there is nothing implausible whatsoever about Jesus' declaration in the Capernaum synagogue that he will give bread from heaven that will be greater than the manna given by Moses in the exodus. Indeed, such a connection is particularly plausible if the manna of the exodus was associated with the Jewish Passover, the feast during which Jesus apparently will go on to perform the sign of the Last Supper (Josh 5:10-12).

Fourth, in the Capernaum discourse, Jesus implicitly identifies himself as the heavenly "Son of Man" from the book of Daniel (John 6:53, 62). It should go without saying that this self-identification coheres with the abundant evidence elsewhere that Jesus frequently spoke of the eschatological Son of Man (e.g., Mark 8:38; Luke 12:8-9; Matt 24:30-31; Mark 13:26-27; Luke 21:27; Matt 24:44; Luke 12:40; Matt 24:27; Luke 17:24; Matt 10:23; 13:41; 16:27; John 5:25-29).[274] It is also congruent with the evidence in which Jesus implicitly identifies himself as the messianic Son of Man (e.g., Matt 9:6; Mark 2:10; Luke 5:24; Matt 20:28; Mark 10:45; Matt 26:24; Mark 14:21; Luke 22:22; John 9:35-37).[275] In particular, in Jesus' response to the disciples' objection, he speaks of the ascension of the Son of Man into heaven (John 6:62), apparently with reference to Daniel's vision of the "son of man" being exalted into the heavenly kingdom (Dan 7:13-14). This emphasis on the disciples seeing the ascension of the Son of Man, though with different language, dovetails perfectly with Jesus' declaration before Caiaphas and the Sanhedrin that they would see the Son of Man ascending to the heavenly throne of God in his kingdom (Matt 26:64; Mark 14:62; Luke 22:69). It also fits with other evidence in which Jesus or the disciples assume his eventual enthronement as Son of Man and the exaltation of his disciples along with him (Matt 20:20-28; Mark 10:35-45; Matt

274. Blomberg, *The Historical Reliability of John's Gospel,* 123; on the Son of man, see Allison, *Constructing Jesus,* 293-303; Keener, *The Historical Jesus of the Gospels,* 200-202; John J. Collins, "The Son of Man in Ancient Judaism," in *Handbook for the Study of the Historical Jesus* (4 vols.; ed. Tom Holmén and Stanley E. Porter; Leiden: Brill, 2011), 2:1545-68.

275. See Bird, *Are You the One Who Is to Come?,* 78-104.

19:28; Luke 22:30; Matt 25:31).[276] In short, the evidence suggests that the Jesus of history is one who identified himself as the eschatological Son of Man who would be enthroned in heaven, and this is exactly the Jesus we meet in the Capernaum discourse.

Fifth, Jesus' teaching regarding the new manna (John 6:48-58) and his response to the disciples' objection (John 6:61-64) cohere remarkably well with the eschatological teaching of Jesus evidenced elsewhere in the Gospels. For example, in his Capernaum discourse, the emphasis falls on the promise of receiving "eternal life" through partaking of the new manna and, as result, being resurrected on the last day (John 6:54-55). It should go without saying that such an emphasis on the resurrection of the dead is exactly what we find in a plethora of other teachings of Jesus (e.g., Matt 5:29-30; 18:6-9; Mark 9:42-48; Luke 17:1-2; Matt 22:23-33; Mark 12:18-27; Luke 20:27-38; Matt 11:21-23; Luke 10:13-14; Matt 12:39-42; Luke 11:29-32; John 5:25-29).[277] With regard to Jesus' emphasis on "eternal life," it is critical to note that the expression "life" or "eternal life" *(zōē aiōnios)* is simply another way of referring to the "kingdom of God" *(basileia tou theou)*. This can be seen in a number of teachings of Jesus, in which "eternal life" and the "kingdom of God" are used interchangeably and treated as equivalent (e.g., Matt 18:7-9; Mark 9:43-47; Matt 19:16-30; Mark 10:17-25; Luke 18:18-30; John 3:3-15).[278] In addition, Jesus not only affirms the common Jewish belief in the reality of eternal life and the resurrection of the body. Rather, he repeatedly identifies himself as the mediator of eschatological life (John 6:48, 51, 54, 56, 57). This emphasis coheres well with other similar teachings in which he makes the life of the eschaton hinge on one's response to him, such as his striking declaration that salvation is contingent on whether someone acknowledges him before others (Matt 10:33; Mark 8:38; Luke 12:8-9) and his promise that anyone who has left family and possessions in order to follow him will receive "eternal life" in "the age to come" (Matt 19:29; Mark 10:29-30; Luke 18:28-30). In light of such parallels, the argument the Capernaum teaching is unhistorical because the historical Jesus taught an unmediated and non-eschatological salvation can only be maintained by ignoring a substantial amount of evidence to the contrary.[279] When the evidence for Jesus'

276. See Pitre, *Jesus, the Tribulation, and the End of the Exile*, 264-92.

277. See Allison, *Jesus of Nazareth*, 136-48.

278. See Klaus Haacker, "What Must I Do to Inherit Eternal Life? Implicit Christology in Jesus' Sayings about Life and the Kingdom," in *Jesus Research: An International Perspective* (ed. James H. Charlesworth and Petr Pokorný; Grand Rapids: Eerdmans, 2009), 140-53; Allison, *Constructing Jesus*, 186-89.

279. Contra Funk, *The Five Gospels*, 421.

eschatological outlook is properly taken into account, it seems clear that Jesus' teaching on the new manna is coherent with similar eschatological statements contained elsewhere in the Gospels.

Sixth — and this is important — Jesus' identification of the new manna with his "flesh" that would be given for "the life of the world" implies that he knows he will die and that he views his future death as redemptive (John 6:51, 53-54). Now, as we saw in chapter 1, during the twentieth century it became very popular to maintain that Jesus neither foresaw his demise nor interpreted it as salvific, but rather met with an unexpected collapse at the end of his life.[280] If this were the case, then Jesus' teaching in the Capernaum synagogue about giving his life for the salvation of others would *de facto* be anachronistically unhistorical. However, as several recent studies have shown, a strong case can be mounted that Jesus did in fact anticipate being executed (as John the Baptist was before him) and that he saw his death as instrumental in ushering in the age of salvation (in contrast to the death of the Baptist).[281] For example, there is evidence in which Jesus anticipates death for himself and his followers (Mark 9:9-13) and declares that any disciple of his must "take up his cross" — a well-known instrument of Roman execution — and follow him, presumably to death (Matt 10:38; 16:24; Mark 8:34; Luke 9:23; Luke 14:27). Then of course there are the numerous texts in which he declares that he, as Son of Man, will suffer like John the Baptist before him (Matt 17:1-13; Mark 9:11-13; Luke 9:28-36) and eventually die (Mark 8:31 pars.; 9:31 pars.; 10:33-34 pars.; Luke 17:25; John 3:14; 12:23-26). Above all, there is the evidence in which Jesus identifies his own passion and death with that of the suffering servant in Isaiah (Luke 22:35-38; citing Isaiah 53) and describes his death, like that of the Isaianic servant, as a "ransom for many" (Matt 20:28; Mark 10:45).[282] While the differences in vocabulary and detail in these various texts are obvious, Jesus' teaching in the Capernaum synagogue about his future death coheres well with other evidence in which Jesus anticipates his death and describes it as redemptive. Indeed,

280. Famously, Rudolf Bultmann, "The Primitive Christian Kerygma and the Historical Jesus," in *The Historical Jesus and the Kerygmatic Christ: Essays on the New Quest for the Historical Jesus* (ed. Carl E. Braaten and Roy A. Harrisville; Nashville: Abingdon, 1964), 22-23. See also S. K. Williams, *Jesus' Death as a Saving Event: The Background and Origin of a Concept* (HDR 2; Missoula: Scholars Press, 1975); Bart Ehrman, *Jesus: Apocalyptic Prophet of the New Millennium* (New York: Oxford University Press, 1999), 209-10.

281. See esp. Scot McKnight, *Jesus and His Death: Historiography, the Historical Jesus, and Atonement Theory* (Waco: Baylor University Press, 2005); Pitre, *Jesus, the Tribulation, and the End of the Exile,* passim; Wright, *Jesus and the Victory of God,* 563-611.

282. See Pitre, *Jesus, the Tribulation, and the End of the Exile,* 384-454.

even Jesus' description of his flesh being offered for the life of "the world" — i.e., all peoples — coheres with the suffering Servant's offering of his life for the "many" or "multitude" gathered from both Israel and the Gentile nations (Isa 53:12).[283] In sum, despite frequent claims to the contrary, Jesus' teaching in the Capernaum synagogue regarding his death as instrumental for eschatological salvation cannot be deemed historically implausible based on an argument from a lack of coherence.

Seventh, Jesus' declaration that his followers must eat his flesh and drink his blood in order to have eternal life (John 6:53-57) — arguably the heart of the discourse in the synagogue — presents a striking case of coherence with his words and actions at the Last Supper (Matt 26:26-28; Mark 14:22-25; Luke 22:19-20; 1 Cor 11:23-25). Just as Jesus speaks about eating his "flesh" in the Capernaum discourse (John 6:51, 53, 54, 56), so too in all of the extant accounts of the Last Supper, he instructs the disciples to eat the bread, which he identifies as his "body" (Matt 26:26; Mark 14:22; Luke 22:19; 1 Cor 11:24).[284] And just as Jesus speaks about consuming his "blood" and identifies it as real "drink" in Capernaum (John 6:53-56), so too in the accounts of the Last Supper, he identifies the wine with his "blood" and commands them to "drink" of it (Matt 26:27-28; Mark 14:24; Luke 22:20; 1 Cor 11:25).[285] Along similar lines, in the Capernaum discourse, Jesus connects the consumption of his flesh and blood with the reception of "eternal life" and the promise of bodily resurrection (John 6:53-55). Likewise, in all of the accounts of the Last Supper, Jesus speaks of his body and/or blood being offered as a sacrifice for others (Matt 26:28; Mark 14:24; Luke 22:19-20; 1 Cor 11:24), with the implication that it is a redemptive sacrifice.[286] Indeed, in at least one account of the Last Supper, Jesus links the act of eating and drinking with him at the Last Supper with entry into the "kingdom" of God (Luke 22:29-30), which, as we just saw above, is a synonym for eternal life or the life of the world to come. Even Jesus' language of "abiding" in and with the disciples as a result of eating his flesh and drinking his blood (John 6:56) may find a conceptual parallel in the evidence that Jesus saw

283. Pitre, *Jesus, the Tribulation, and the End of the Exile,* 416-17; Jeremias, *The Eucharistic Words of Jesus,* 227-29. So too Schnackenburg, *The Gospel according to St. John,* 2:56, though he does not use this point of coherence to argue for historicity.

284. *Contra* Schröter, *Das Abendmahl,* 60, who claims that in the Synoptic and Pauline accounts Jesus does not identify the elements themselves with his body and blood, only the act of breaking and the symbol of the covenant.

285. The express command to drink is only present in Matthew and 1 Corinthians; in Mark and Luke, the drinking of the cup is implied but not expressly stated by Jesus.

286. See above, chapter 3; Taylor, *Jesus and His Sacrifice,* 125.

himself as establishing a "covenant" at the Last Supper with his disciples — i.e., an intimate sacred bond of communion with the disciples — through their reception of his body and blood (Matt 26:28; Mark 14:24; Luke 22:20; 1 Cor 11:25).[287] Finally, if we should interpret John as testifying that Jesus spoke of eating his flesh in blood in the synagogue at Capernaum when the Passover feast "was at hand" (cf. John 6:4), then this too coheres with his performance of the prophetic sign of the Last Supper during the feast of Passover.[288] In light of so many parallels in substance, it is not surprising that scholars have described Jesus' dialogue in the synagogue as "an expanded transcription of the 'words of institution' "[289] or as "the Johannine form of the words of institution."[290] The fact that in the Capernaum synagogue Jesus speaks of his "flesh" *(sarx),* whereas at the Last Supper he speaks of his "body" *(sōma),* does not weaken the coherence, since the basic meaning is the same.[291] Given these multiple points of correspondence, it is truly remarkable that so many scholars continue to deny the historical plausibility of the eucharistic elements in Jesus' teaching in the synagogue at Capernaum.[292]

287. Brown, *The Gospel according to John,* 1:293: "Just as the Eucharist itself echoes the theme of the covenant ('blood of the covenant' — Mark xiv 24), so also the mutual indwelling of God (and Jesus) and the Christian may be a reflection of the covenant theme. . . . At Qumran (1QS i 16ff.) the communion of the sectarian with God was looked on as a mark of the new covenant."

288. Marshall, *Last Supper and Lord's Supper,* 134 (though he does not use this to argue for historicity).

289. Dodd, *The Interpretation of the Fourth Gospel,* 338.

290. Brown, *The Gospel according to John,* 1:285.

291. Schnackenburg, *The Gospel according to St. John,* 2:55; Brown, *The Gospel according to John,* 1:285.

292. In fact, contrary to the normal canons of historical argumentation, coherence with the words of institution at the Last Supper is often used as an argument *against* the historicity of the Capernaum teaching. According to this point of view, the substantial correspondence between Jesus' teaching on the manna and his words at the Last Supper is explained by proposing that the words of institution have been "transposed" back into Jesus' public ministry and erroneously set during the days of his Galilean preaching in the synagogue. See, e.g., Brown, *The Gospel according to John,* 1:287. The problems with this theory are several. For one thing, the entire hypothesis that John has "moved" the words of institution seems to be founded on the questionable assumption that Jesus did not expect to suffer and die and could not possibly have anticipated the sign he was going to perform at the Last Supper. See Strauss, *The Life of Jesus Critically Examined,* 633. Against this, as we have already pointed out above, stands the evidence in all four Gospels that Jesus did anticipate his death and viewed it as having redemptive significance. If this is correct, then the evidence that Jesus spoke and acted in ways that pointed forward to future actions that would bring his ministry to its climax is coherent with what we know of him from elsewhere. Blomberg, *The Historical Reliability of John's Gospel,*

In sum, when Jesus' teaching in the Capernaum synagogue is interpreted in context, it provides what is perhaps the strongest argument from coherence with other teachings of Jesus that we possess. For it is a case involving the Gospel of John (John 6:48-66), the Synoptic Gospels (Matt 26:26-28; Mark 14:24-25; Luke 22:18-22), and even the letters of Paul (1 Cor 11:23-25). Following ordinary arguments for historical plausibility, this striking case of coherence should lead us to the conclusion that just as Jesus began preparing his disciples for his death during his public ministry, so too, in the synagogue at Capernaum, Jesus used the language of Jewish Scripture and the expectation

---

129. Moreover, the transposition theory has absolutely no textual or manuscript evidence to support it. Contrast this with the account of the woman caught in adultery (John 7:53–8:11), for which we have actual manuscript evidence of transposition into different places in manuscripts of both John and Luke. In addition, the theory that the words of Jesus regarding the manna have been "moved" from the Last Supper directly contradicts the explicit testimony that Jesus said these things "in the synagogue, as he taught at Capernaum" (John 6:59). Jesus' teaching on the new manna is no "floating logion" from the Gospel of Mark, unanchored by time or space, and stitched to what precedes and what follows with only the word "immediately" *(euthys).* Rather, it is concretely anchored in a time and place far antecedent to Jesus' actions at the Last Supper. See Dodd, *Historical Tradition in the Fourth Gospel,* 315-17. Above all, the identification of the manna teaching as anachronistic completely glosses over the differences between Jesus' discourse in Capernaum and the actual accounts of the Last Supper. Although, as I have argued above, the episodes are coherent with one another in terms of Jesus' mode of teaching, eschatology, self-understanding, they are not identical. Rather, the two are inextricably tied to two different times and places in the life of Jesus of Nazareth. Despite the fact that scholars consistently refer to Jesus' teachings in Capernaum as "the Johannine form of the words of institution" (Brown, *The Gospel according to John,* 1:285), it is precisely the idea of the *institution* of a ritual that is missing. Once again, overinterpretation leads to an incorrect judgment in the question of historical plausibility. It would of course be completely implausible for Jesus to institute the eucharist in the Capernaum synagogue long before his passion and death. But that is exactly what does not take place in John's account. Instead, Jesus uses the imagery of the eschatological manna and the exaltation of the Son to speak about his future death and how he will fulfill the role of the new Moses who was expected to give the new manna. Such teaching would have served as an excellent preparation — if not a complete explanation — to prepare his disciples in advance for some of his most puzzling words and deeds by means of preliminary instructions. In this regard, it is perhaps worth noting, that not one of the extant accounts of the Last Supper registers any surprise, disbelief, or consternation on the part of the Twelve disciples when Jesus identifies the bread and wine with his body and blood. This stands in stark contrast to John's account of the Capernaum discourse, in which many of his disciples abandon him (John 6:60-66). The fact that neither his passion predictions nor his manna teachings were completely understood in no way counts against their historical plausibility. To the contrary, the express testimony of the Gospels that the Judean audience and even Jesus' own disciples had difficulty with these teachings and ultimately failed to understand is extremely plausible and exactly how we would expect them to react to such difficult words.

of Jewish eschatology regarding the return of the manna from heaven to prepare his disciples for the mysterious prophetic sign that he would eventually perform at the Last Supper.

Effects: The Manna of the Messiah in Early Christianity

The third and final argument for the historical plausibility of Jesus' teaching on the true manna of his flesh and blood is from continuity with the beliefs and practices of the early church. As we saw in chapter 1, if evidence about what Jesus did or said has the power to explain why the early church acted in certain ways or believed certain things, then — if it has already been established as congruent with an ancient Jewish context and coherent with other words of Jesus — it is reasonable to conclude that the evidence originated with Jesus himself. When it comes to Jesus' teachings in the Capernaum synagogue, there are several aspects that provide a plausible origin for the faith and praxis of the early church.

First and foremost, Jesus' identification of his flesh and blood with the eschatological manna of Jewish expectation stands in strong continuity with the apostle Paul's typological interpretation of the manna of the exodus with the early Christian eucharist celebrated at Corinth. Although the passage is lengthy, I will cite it in full, so that we might compare it with Jesus' Capernaum discourse:

> I want you to know, brethren, that *our fathers were all under the cloud, and all passed through the sea, and all were baptized into Moses in the cloud and in the sea, and all ate the same spiritual food and all drank the same spiritual drink.* For they drank from the spiritual rock which followed them, and the rock was Christ. Nevertheless with most of them God was not pleased; for they were overthrown in the wilderness. Now these things are warnings for us, not to desire evil as they did. Do not be idolaters as some of them were; as it is written, "the people sat down to eat and drink and rose up to dance." We must not indulge in immorality as some of them did, and twenty-three thousand fell in a single day. We must not put the Lord to the test, as some of them did and were destroyed by serpents; nor grumble, as some of them did and were destroyed by the Destroyer. Now these things happened to them as a warning, but they were written down for our instruction, upon whom the end of the ages has come. Therefore let anyone who thinks that he stands take heed lest

> he fall. No temptation has overtaken you that is not common to man. God is faithful, and he will not let you be tempted beyond your strength, but with the temptation will also provide the way of escape, that you may be able to endure it. Therefore my beloved, shun the worship of idols. *I speak as to sensible men; judge for yourselves what I say. The cup of blessing which we bless, is it not a participation in the blood of Christ? The bread which we break, is it not a participation in the body of Christ?* Because there is one bread, we who are many are one body, for we all partake of the one bread. (1 Cor 10:1-17)

It is important to note in this regard that Paul uses the manna "in a way similar to but not identical with" Jesus' teaching in the synagogue at Capernaum.[293] On the one hand, they are remarkably alike. Just as Jesus identifies his own flesh and blood with the true manna from heaven (John 6:48-51, 58), so too Paul begins his discussion of the eucharist at Corinth with the typological analogy of the "spiritual food" *(pneumatikon brōma)* of the manna (1 Cor 10:3). Likewise, just as Jesus emphasizes the death of the wilderness generation (John 6:49, 58), so Paul uses the demise of the wilderness generation as a warning against presumption. Just because the Corinthians receive the new spiritual food of the body and blood of Christ, they should not presume that they then have the license to indulge in immorality and idolatry without suffering any consequences. Eschatological salvation is not assured by eucharistic "participation" *(koinōnia)* any more than the wilderness generation's entry into the promised land was assured by their consumption of the manna.[294] On the other hand, there are also significant differences between the Capernaum discourse and Paul's teaching on the manna.[295] Gone are Jesus' distinctively Jewish references to the Son of Man, eternal life, the living Father, the use of Ezekiel's imagery of the spirit and life in the context of the resurrection of the body. Significantly, any apparent difficulties regarding the use of body/flesh and blood imagery are also missing in Paul; unlike Jesus, he assumes that the Corinthians should know what he means (being "sensible") when he uses the explicitly Christian language of "the blood of Christ" and "the body of Christ" (1 Cor 10:16). From the perspective of the plausibility of effects, this is precisely the kind of development that we would expect in a case of continuity between Jesus and the early church. In sum, Jesus' identification of the manna provides

293. Higgins, *The Lord's Supper in the New Testament*, 82.
294. Marshall, *Last Supper and Lord's Supper*, 119.
295. Cf. Brown, *The Gospel according to John*, 1:274.

a plausible historical starting point for Paul's identification of the manna with the Christian eucharist.[296] In this regard, Dale Allison reasons rightly: "There is also 1 Cor 10:1-5, where the Eucharist is likened to the supernatural food that Israel ate in the wilderness. From a very early time, then, Christian tradition consistently linked the Last Supper to exodus themes. *Maybe it did this in part because Jesus himself had already done so.*"[297]

Second, Jesus' emphasis in the Capernaum synagogue on the power of his flesh and blood to communicate eternal life and a share in the bodily resurrection (John 6:53-55) also presents an important case of continuity with the early church. As recognized by many scholars, Jesus' teaching in the synagogue at Capernaum stands in continuity with the thought of Ignatius of Antioch.[298] In his letter to the Ephesians, usually dated to the early second century, Ignatius has this to say about the relationship between the eucharist and eschatology:

> All of you, individually and collectively, gather together in grace, by name, in one faith and one Jesus Christ, who physically was a descendant of David, who is Son of Man and Son of God, in order that you may obey the bishop and the council of presbyters with an undisturbed mind, breaking one bread, which is the medicine of immortality, the antidote we take in order not to die but to live forever in Jesus Christ. (*To the Ephesians* 20.2)[299]

Once again, note that this is a case of plausible continuity between what Jesus has to say and the words of Ignatius. Indeed, the Capernaum synagogue discourse differs from Ignatius precisely where the former is most Jewish in formulation.[300] In Jesus' teachings, the salvation promised is described in a thoroughly Jewish fashion: his followers are to eat the flesh and blood of the Danielic Son of Man (cf. Dan 7:14), and in doing so, they will receive a share in the Jewish hope for "eternal life" and the bodily resurrection of the dead (cf.

296. This is particularly true when we recall that there is no explicit connection drawn between the bread of the Last Supper and the manna from heaven. In all of our accounts of the Last Supper, the Passover lamb, not the exodus manna, dominates.

297. Allison, *Constructing Jesus,* 272 (emphasis added). Cf. Schnackenburg, *The Gospel according to St. John,* 2:60.

298. E.g., Lüdemann, *Jesus After 2000 Years,* 470; Bultmann, *The Gospel of John,* 219.

299. Trans. Michael W. Holmes, *The Apostolic Fathers: Greek Texts and English Translations* (3rd ed.; Grand Rapids: Baker Academic, 2007).

300. Cf. Schnackenburg, *The Gospel according to St. John,* 2:61-62.

Dan 12:1-2). By the time we get to Ignatius, the basic connection is still present between the consumption of the bread and the reception of everlasting life, but now delivered in the idiom of Greek-speaking, predominantly Gentile Christianity. Jesus' very Jewish connection between the manna and "eternal life" *(zōē aiōnios)* has been transformed into a link between the eucharist and "immortality" *(athanasias),* so that one might not die but "live for all time" *(zēn . . . dia pantos).*[301] Gone is the explicit reference to the resurrection of the body on the last day. Everything in Ignatius' letter speaks of an explicitly Christian context: the affirmation of "faith" in "Jesus Christ," the concern over obedience to the bishop and presbyters, and the language of the "breaking" of the "bread" (cf. Acts 2:42). *Hence, what begins as a very Jewish way of describing the life-giving power of the true manna from heaven in the Capernaum synagogue becomes in Ignatius' letter a very Christian way of saying much the same thing:* the bread that is broken has the power to give everlasting life. We have here a textbook case of the teaching of Jesus in Capernaum being translated from an early Jewish key into the language of a more developed Gentile Christianity. In light of such continuity and development, it is reasonable to conclude that Jesus' teachings on the new manna provide a plausible point of origin for Ignatius' description of the Christian eucharist as having the power to communicate everlasting life.

Third and finally, but by no means least significantly, the realistic language and imagery of Jesus' words in Capernaum also stand in strong continuity with the realistic emphases of early Christian descriptions of the eucharist.[302] It would also explain why the earliest Christian texts we possess

301. Regarding Ignatius' statements in *Eph.* 20.2, Schnackenburg, *The Gospel according to St. John,* 2:62, notes: "John never uses the word *athanasia,* which is generally connected with the idea of the immortality of the soul, and thereby shows himself to be more dependent on Semitic attitudes, which are characterized by a view of man as a totality, and in which the fulfillment of life came only with bodily resurrection."

302. For an analysis of the eucharistic texts in Ignatius and Justin, see Schröter, *Das Abendmahl,* 73-90; Paul Bradshaw, *Eucharistic Origins* (Oxford: Oxford University Press, 2004), 87-90; James T. O'Connor, *The Hidden Manna: A Theology of the Eucharist* (2nd ed.; San Francisco: Ignatius, 2005), 1-22. For what it is worth, if Jesus did in fact emphasize the realistic nature of eating his flesh and drinking his blood, it would provide a ready explanation for why early Christians in the second century A.D. would go on to be accused of cannibalism (see *Athenagoras* 3; *Theophilus* 3.4, 15; Origen, *Contra Celsus* 6.27). See Keener, *The Gospel of John,* 1:688 n. 240. Indeed, we can ask the question of whether the early church would have created teaching of Jesus about eating his flesh and drinking his blood, teachings that in any context — not just Jewish — would be easily misunderstood and potentially lead to exactly these kinds of dangerous accusations.

— Ignatius of Antioch and Justin Martyr — interpret Jesus' language and imagery with reference to the eucharist:[303]

> Now note well those who hold heretical opinions about the grace of Jesus Christ that came to us; note how contrary they are to the mind of God. . . . They abstain from eucharist and prayer because they refuse to acknowledge that the eucharist is the flesh of our savior Jesus Christ, which suffered for our sins and which the Father by his goodness raised up. (Ignatius, *To the Smyrnaeans* 6.2)

> And this food is called among us the eucharist, of which no one is allowed to partake but the man who believes that the things which we teach are true, and who has been washed with the washing that is for the remission of sins, and unto regeneration, and who is living as Christ has enjoined. For not as common bread and common drink do we receive these; but in like manner as Jesus Christ our Savior, having been made flesh by the Word of God, had both flesh and blood for our salvation, so likewise we have been taught that the food which is blessed by the prayer of His word, and from which our blood and flesh by transmutation are nourished, is the flesh and blood of that Jesus who was made flesh. (Justin Martyr, *1 Apology* 66)[304]

Once again, we have a strong case of continuity with Jesus' discourse in Capernaum.[305] Just as he identifies the manna that he will give with his own "flesh" and "blood" (John 6:51, 53-55), so too Ignatius emphatically identifies the "eucharist" as the "flesh" *(sarx)* of Jesus. Likewise, Justin declares in no uncertain terms that the eucharist is "not" treated as "common food" *(koinon arton)* or "common drink" *(koinon poma)* but "is the flesh and blood of Jesus *(sacra kai haima . . . einai).*"[306] It is worth noting that this realism is so significant for Ignatius that he uses it as a dividing line to separate the heretics who refuse

303. Keener, *The Gospel of John,* 1:689 (arguing, however, that Ignatius and Justin misinterpret Jesus' teaching).

304. Trans. Alexander Roberts and James Donaldson, *The Ante-Nicene Fathers* (10 vols.; repr.; Peabody: Hendrickson, 1994), 1:185.

305. Cf. Schnackenburg, *The Gospel according to St. John,* 2:452 n. 154, 455 n. 192, citing A. J. Bellinzoni, *The Sayings of Jesus in the Writings of Justin Martyr* (Leiden: Brill, 1967), who makes a case for Justin's dependence on John's Gospel in this regard.

306. Bradshaw, *Eucharistic Origins,* 87, 89, noting the connection with the evidence in John's Gospel.

to accept the idea that the eucharist really is the flesh of Jesus from orthodox Christians, in a manner continuous with Jesus' own allowance of many of his disciples to separate from him because of their unwillingness to accept the shocking realism of his teaching. For our purposes here, the main point is that yet again we have a strong case of continuity, but not identity, with the teachings of Jesus. Indeed, these two texts are particularly important in pointing up what is *not* present in Jesus' discourse in Capernaum: namely, any explicit reference to "the eucharist" *(eucharistia)*.[307] Note this well: whereas Jesus speaks about "bread from heaven" or "the manna" or "real food" — all perfectly plausible within a Jewish context — it is not until we get to Ignatius and Justin Martyr that we see any explicit reference to the Christian "eucharist" *per se.*

In closing, one reason these differences are important to highlight is that commentators who reject the historicity of the Capernaum discourse consistently overlook them and transform Jesus' teaching on the new manna into an anachronistically Christian discourse on "the Eucharist." By means of this vocabulary change, they thereby introduce content and conceptual development into Jesus' teaching that is not actually present. Consider, for example, the words of Raymond Brown:

> Let us now turn to the historical question of whether the direct eucharistic theme of vss. 51-58 was originally part of Jesus' words to the crowd. . . . [I]t is enough to raise the question whether, if Jesus did speak of the bread of life in the Capernaum synagogue, the doctrine about the Eucharist as reported in 51-58 could have been part of that discourse. . . . Is there the slightest evidence that the living bread in 51-58 refers to anything other than the Eucharist? If we answer in the negative, and it seems that we must, then it seems impossible that the words of 51-58 which refer exclusively to the Eucharist could have been understood by the crowd or even by the disciples. They are really out of place anywhere during the ministry except at the Last Supper.[308]

This is a textbook example of how judgments about historicity are ultimately based on prior judgments about interpretation. Note well that it is Brown who employs the language of "the Eucharist," not Jesus in the Capernaum discourse. "The Eucharist" — to use Brown's language — is never mentioned in the bread of life discourse; it must be read into the text by Brown himself. If

307. As in Justin, *1 Apol.* 66.1.

308. Brown, *The Gospel according to John,* 1:286-87.

such anachronistic language were present, Brown would be correct; it would be unintelligible at the level of history. But as have seen in our exegesis above, Jesus does not speak about "the Eucharist." Rather, Jesus speaks about *the manna* from heaven — "the bread of life," "the manna in the wilderness," "the bread that comes down from heaven," and "the living bread," "the bread which I shall give" (John 6:48-51) — all of which are, as I have demonstrated above, completely plausible and quite intelligible in a first-century Jewish context.[309] In other words, while it is certainly true that Jesus' Jewish audience had never heard of "the Eucharist," it is equally certain that they had heard of the manna. And it is the manna from heaven that constitutes the substance of Jesus' Capernaum teaching — not "the Eucharist."

Hence, even the very emphasis on the bread from heaven and the true manna reveals a powerful case of causal continuity with early Christian belief. Jesus' teachings in the Capernaum synagogue are consistent with but not the same as early Christian identification of the "body of Christ" and "blood of Christ" as "spiritual food" and "spiritual drink" (Paul), early Christian emphasis on the eucharist as an efficacious communicator of "immortality" (Ignatius), or the realistic identification of the eucharist with the "flesh" of Jesus (Justin, Ignatius). When we add to this that they are also plausible and explicable (albeit shocking) within a Jewish context, and coherent with a broad spectrum of other evidence about Jesus in the Gospels, then one can reasonably conclude that the substance of the Capernaum teaching (the *substantia verba Jesu*) in John 6:48-66 is in fact historically plausible as deriving from Jesus during his public ministry in Galilee.

309. Contra Léon-Dufour, *Sharing the Eucharistic Bread,* 258.

CHAPTER 4

The Date of the Last Supper

> [I]s the last supper *Pesaḥ?* . . . If Jesus saw in *Pesaḥ* a prefigurement of his own death, we would know that Jesus saw his death as analogous to the victim of the *Pesaḥ*. If the last supper is not *Pesaḥ,* however, then an interpretation of his death would have to be altered.
>
> SCOT MCKNIGHT[1]

As anyone familiar with Jesus research knows, one of the perennial questions in historical reconstructions of his life and death revolves around the date of the Last Supper. This complex issue can be formulated in terms of a single question: *Was the Last Supper a Jewish Passover meal?* Unfortunately, to ask this question is to enter into what is easily the most disputed chronological issue in New Testament studies. It is certainly the most complex and difficult topic we will address in this book.

For the sake of clarity, then, our treatment will consist of several basic components. First, we will briefly examine the textual evidence for an apparent contradiction between the Synoptic Gospels and the Gospel of John on the date of the Last Supper. Second, we will then survey several major solutions to the question that have been proposed by modern scholars, analyzing their strengths and their weaknesses. Third, in somewhat more detail, I will propose a fourth solution to the problem supported by fresh evidence and arguments from ancient Jewish language and liturgy, evidence that has been remarkably

1. Scot McKnight, *Jesus and His Death: Historiography, the Historical Jesus, and Atonement Theory* (Waco: Baylor University Press, 2005), 259.

neglected in recent studies of the topic by Jesus scholarship. As I will attempt to show, when the chronological evidence in the Gospels, especially the Gospel of John, is properly interpreted in its early Jewish context, there are very solid reasons to conclude that Jesus' Last Supper was indeed a Jewish Passover meal and that the chronological contradiction between the Synoptic Gospels and John is based on a misinterpretation of the Johannine data. This misinterpretation stems from a lack of familiarity with ancient Jewish Passover terminology, chronology, and sacrifices.

Before we begin, however, there is one preliminary point that needs to be emphasized. On the one hand, as we will see in a moment, the debate over the date of the Last Supper obviously centers on the apparent contradiction between the Synoptic Gospels and the Gospel of John regarding whether or not the Last Supper was a Jewish Passover meal. On the other hand, as a closer examination of Johannine scholarship reveals, there is a second major issue: the problem of the chronology of John's Gospel itself. Although the fact is not widely recognized in Jesus research, a number of major twentieth-century scholars admit that at least some of the evidence in John's Gospel appears to reflect "traces of the Synoptic chronology" by depicting the Last Supper as a Passover meal and the death of Jesus as occurring after the sacrifice of the Passover lambs. Consider the following:

> Julius Wellhausen: "Jesus and his disciples are here still at table, and in fact *at the passover meal, i.e. at the Lord's supper of the synoptics;* in contradiction to 13:1; 18:28; 19:14 — it is idle to shut one's eyes to this contradiction."[2]

> Rudolf Bultmann: "The expression ['lying close to the breast of Jesus'] is certainly an indication that the meal which is spoken of in [John 13] vv. 21-30, in contrast to [John 13] vv. 2-20, *is the Passover meal;* for on this occasion reclining at table was obligatory."[3]

> Rudolf Bultmann: "Certainly it is surprising that no mention is made of the Passover [in John 19:31]. . . . *That may well be due to the fact that this story is derived from a tradition according to which Jesus was crucified on the 15th Nizan* [sic], *as in the Synoptics.*"[4]

2. Julius Wellhausen, *Das Evangelium Johannis* (Berlin: Georg Reimer, 1908), 60 (emphasis added); translation in Jeremias, *The Eucharistic Words of Jesus,* 82 n. 3.

3. Rudolf Bultmann, *The Gospel of John: A Commentary* (trans. G. R. Beasley-Murray; Philadelphia: Westminster, 1971), 480 n. 3 (emphasis added).

4. Bultmann, *The Gospel of John,* 676 n. 6.

> Joachim Jeremias: "There are other *traces of the synoptic chronology in the fourth gospel,* especially in the account of Jesus' last supper (John 13.2ff.). . . . *Some of the remarks made by John presuppose that this was a passover meal.*"[5]

> Raymond Brown: "That there are Passover characteristics in the meal, *even in John,* is *undeniable.*"[6]

> C. K. Barrett: "The supposed command [of Jesus] to give to the poor would be particularly appropriate on Passover night. . . . In going into the darkness Judas went to his own place. So far as the remark is historical it suggests that *the event took place on Passover night (in agreement with the Markan tradition).*"[7]

> Craig S. Keener: "Although Jewish people in Palestine usually sat on chairs when available, they had adopted the Hellenistic custom of reclining for banquets, including *the Passover,* a setting that the Fourth Gospel and its first audience might assume from the Gospel tradition despite the Fourth Gospel's symbolic shift of the Passover to one day later. It probably implies that *John has, after all, revised an earlier Passover tradition.*"[8]

This is a striking series of assertions. Virtually every introduction to or discussion of the infamous "date of the Last Supper" debate construes the question as a simple choice between the Synoptics (which view it as a Passover meal) and the Gospel of John (which views it as some other kind of meal).[9] But according to some of the most influential Johannine scholars, we are not just dealing with an apparent contradiction between John and the Synoptics, but also with chronological confusion *within the Fourth Gospel itself.* From this point of view, John's Gospel occasionally contradicts itself in depicting the Last Supper as a Passover meal, and thus contains

5. Joachim Jeremias, *The Eucharistic Words of Jesus* (trans. Norman Perrin; London: SCM, 1966), 81 (emphasis added).

6. Raymond E. Brown, *The Gospel according to John* (2 vols.; Anchor Bible 29-29A; New York: Doubleday, 1966, 1970), 2:556 (emphasis added).

7. C. K. Barrett, *The Gospel according to St. John* (2nd ed.; Philadelphia: Westminster, 1978), 448, 449 (emphasis added).

8. Craig S. Keener, *The Gospel of John* (2 vols.; Peabody: Hendrickson, 2003), 2:900-901.

9. E.g., Jens Schröter, *Das Abendmahl: Frühchristliche Deutungen und Impulse für die Gegenwart* (SBS 210; Stuttgart: Katholisches Bibelwerk, 2006), 44.

certain "trace[s] of the earlier synoptic tradition in which the supper was a Paschal meal."[10]

As we will see later, I find the suggestion that the Gospel of John contains two different chronologies ultimately unconvincing and will instead suggest another path, based on reexamination of the key passages in John in their first-century Jewish context. For now, however, the fact that these supposed traces of "the Synoptic chronology" in John are almost universally ignored by Jesus research on the date of the Last Supper provides us justification for a fresh investigation of the whole issue. As we will see, the date of the Last Supper is as much an issue of how one interprets the Fourth Gospel as it is a historical problem of whether the Last Supper was a Passover meal.

The Apparent Contradiction

The classic problem of the date of the Last Supper can be summed up in a relatively brief antithesis: On the one hand, according to the Synoptic Gospels of Matthew, Mark, and Luke, the Last Supper appears to have taken place *the evening after* the Passover lambs were sacrificed in the Jerusalem Temple (15 Nisan). On the other hand, according to the Gospel of John, the Last Supper appears to have taken place *the evening before* the Passover lambs were sacrificed in the Temple (14 Nisan).

This apparent chronological contradiction is of no little significance. Rather, it has a direct bearing on both the calendar date and historical character of the Last Supper.[11] If Jesus celebrated his final meal the evening after the Passover lambs were sacrificed in the Temple, then *the Last Supper was clearly a Jewish Passover meal,* and everything Jesus did and said at that meal needs to be interpreted in that context. However, if Jesus celebrated his final meal the evening before the Passover lambs were sacrificed in the Temple, then *the Last Supper was not a Passover banquet,* but some other kind of meal. Which is it? Before turning to scholarly answers to the question, it is important to take a moment to closely examine the actual data in question, so that we can properly evaluate the various solutions that have been proposed.[12]

10. Barrett, *The Gospel According to St. John,* 447.

11. McKnight, *Jesus and His Death,* 244.

12. The literature on this subject is unbelievably vast; we will engage much of it over the course of this chapter. For overviews of the question in recent Jesus research, see esp. Harold W. Hoehner, "The Chronology of Jesus," in *The Handbook for the Study of the Historical Jesus* (ed. Tom Holmén and Stanley E. Porter; 4 vols.; Leiden: Brill, 2011), 3:2315-59; McKnight, *Jesus and*

The Testimony of the Synoptic Gospels

On the one hand, the Gospels of Matthew, Mark, and Luke unequivocally and repeatedly identify the Last Supper as a Jewish Passover meal, eaten after the Passover lambs were sacrificed in the Temple (15 Nisan). Consider the following:

> Now on the first day of Unleavened Bread the disciples came to Jesus, saying, "Where will you have us *prepare for you to eat the Passover?*" He said, "Go into the city to such a one, and say to him, 'The Teacher says, My time is at hand; *I will keep the Passover* at your house with my disciples.'" And the disciples did as Jesus had directed them, and *they prepared the Passover.* When it was evening, he sat at table with the twelve disciples. . . . (Matt 26:17-20)

> And on the first day of Unleavened Bread, *when they sacrificed the Passover lamb,* his disciples said to him, "Where will you have us go and *prepare for you to eat the Passover?*" And he sent two of his disciples, and said to them, "Go into the city, and a man carrying a jar of water will meet you; follow him, and wherever he enters, say to the householder, 'The Teacher says, Where is my guest room, *where I am to eat the Passover* with my disciples?' And he will show you a large upper room furnished and ready; there prepare for us." And the disciples set out and went to the city, and found it as he had told them; and *they prepared the Passover.* And when it was evening he came with the Twelve. And as they were at table eating . . . (Mark 14:12-17)

> Then came the day of Unleavened Bread, *on which the Passover lamb had to be sacrificed.* So Jesus sent Peter and John, saying, "Go and *prepare the Passover for us, that we may eat it.*" They said to him, "Where will you have us prepare it?" He said to them, "Behold, when you have entered

---

His Death, 259-73; John P. Meier, *A Marginal Jew* (4 vols.; AYBRL; New Haven: Yale University Press, 1991, 1994, 2001, 2009), 1:386-401; Raymond E. Brown, *The Death of the Messiah: From Gethsemane to the Grave* (2 vols.; ABRL; New York: Doubleday, 1994), 2:1350-78 (with bibliography); Joseph A. Fitzmyer, *The Gospel according to Luke* (2 vols.; AB 28A-B; New York: Doubleday, 1983-1985), 2:1378-85; I. Howard Marshall, *Last Supper and Lord's Supper* (London: Paternoster, 1980), 57-75; Harold W. Hoehner, *Chronological Aspects of the Life of Christ* (Grand Rapids: Zondervan, 1977). Even though his bibliography is dated, Joachim Jeremias, *The Eucharistic Words of Jesus* (trans. Norman Perrin; London: SCM, 1966), 15-88, provides a clear and extensive overview of the primary data and various scholarly solutions. Also helpful is Jack Finegan, *Handbook of Biblical Chronology* (Princeton: Princeton University Press, 1964), 285-98.

> the city, a man carrying a jar of water will meet you; follow him into the house which he enters, and tell the householder, 'The Teacher says to you, Where is the guest room *where I am to eat the Passover* with my disciples?' And he will show you a large upper room furnished; there make ready." And they went, and found it as he had told them; and *they prepared the Passover.* And when the hour came, he sat at table, and the apostles with him. And he said to them, "*I have earnestly desired to eat this Passover with you* before I suffer; for I tell you that I shall not eat it until it is fulfilled in the kingdom of God." And he took a cup, and when he had given thanks, he said, "Take this . . ." (Luke 22:7-17)

Taken together, the Synoptic Gospels identify the Last Supper as a Jewish "Passover" meal *(pascha)* some twelve times (Matt 26:17, 18, 19; Mark 14:12 [2x], 14, 16; Luke 22:7, 8, 11, 13, 15). Nine times they refer to the disciples going into Jerusalem to "prepare" *(hetoimazō)* the Passover meal on the afternoon before the Last Supper (Matt 26:17, 19; Mark 14:12, 15, 16; Luke 22:8, 9, 12, 13). Six times they speak of Jesus and the disciples "eating" *(phagō)* the Passover meal (Matt 26:17; Mark 14:12, 14; Luke 22:8, 11, 15). Indeed, in Luke's account, Jesus specifically refers to the Last Supper as a "Passover" *(pascha)* during the meal itself (Luke 22:15).[13] Most significantly for our purposes, both Mark and Luke explicitly state that the Last Supper took place the evening after the Passover lambs were "sacrificed" *(thyō)* before being eaten (Mark 14:12; Luke 22:7). This reference to the sacrifice of the lambs is one of the clearest chronological indicators that the Synoptic Gospels date the Last Supper to the same evening as the ordinary Jewish Passover meal.[14]

By ancient Jewish reckoning, then, all of this evidence places the Last Supper on the evening after the slaughter of the lambs in the Temple during the afternoon. As most scholars agree, if anything in the Gospels is clear, it is that "the Synoptics portray the Last Supper on Thursday evening as a Passover meal."[15]

The Testimony of the Gospel of John

When we turn from the Synoptics to the Gospel of John, we find something quite different. For one thing, as is widely known, John's Gospel does not

13. Brown, *The Death of the Messiah,* 2:1358.
14. Jeremias, *The Eucharistic Words of Jesus,* 17.
15. Meier, *A Marginal Jew,* 1:389.

contain any narrative of the so-called "words of institution," in which Jesus identifies the bread and wine of the Last Supper with his own body and blood. Moreover, although it speaks of Jesus' last "supper" *(deipnon)* with his disciples (John 13:2), John's Gospel never unambiguously identifies this supper as a Passover taking place after the sacrifice of the lambs. Above all, John contains three key texts that — at least at first glance — appear to date the Last Supper before the lambs were sacrificed in the Jewish Temple. Although the Greek terminology used by John will become very important to our discussion, for now, I offer a standard English translation of the texts:

> Now *before the feast of the Passover,* when Jesus knew that his hour had come to depart out of this world to the Father, having loved his own who were in the world, he loved them to the end. And during supper, when the devil had already put it into the heart of Judas Iscariot, Simon's son, to betray him . . . (John 13:1-2)

> Then they led Jesus from the house of Caiaphas to the praetorium. It was early. They themselves did not enter the praetorium, so that they might not be defiled, but might *eat the Passover.* (John 18:28)

> When Pilate heard these words, he brought Jesus out and sat down on the judgment seat at a place called The Pavement, and in Hebrew, Gabbatha. Now *it was the day of Preparation of the Passover;* it was about the sixth hour [noon]. (John 19:13-14)

Taken at face value, the first text states that Jesus' Last Supper — the meal at which Judas betrayed him — took place "before the feast of Passover." If the expression "the feast of the Passover" *(tēs heortēs tou pascha)* (John 13:1) refers to the sacrifice of the initial Passover lambs on 14 Nisan, then the Last Supper seems to have taken place twenty-four hours before 14 Nisan, before the Passover lambs were killed and eaten. As Rudolf Bultmann comments: "The day immediately before the Passover feast is intended, that is to say, the 13th Nisan."[16]

The second text is even more concrete. When Jesus' Jewish accusers brought him to Pontius Pilate early Friday morning, they refused to enter Pilate's praetorium lest they be defiled and therefore unable to "eat the Passover." If the Greek expression "eat the Passover" *(phagōsin to pascha)* (John

16. Bultmann, *The Gospel of John,* 464-65.

18:28) refers to the consumption of the Passover lambs that were sacrificed in the Temple, then, again, John seems to be claiming that the Last Supper took place twenty-four hours ahead of the ordinary Jewish Passover meal that would be eaten by Jesus' accusers the Friday night after he was handed over to Pilate. John Meier puts the point forcefully: "The phrase used here, *phagein to pascha* ('to eat the Passover'), is the very one used by the Synoptics to describe what was to be done at the Last Supper (Mark 14:12; Matt 26:17; Luke 22:8, 15). Clearly, according to John's chronology, the Passover meal had not yet been celebrated."[17]

Finally, in the third passage, John tells us that Jesus was handed over by Pilate to be crucified on the morning of "the day of Preparation of the Passover." If the Greek expression "preparation of the Passover" *(paraskeuē tou pascha)* (John 19:14) refers to a day of preparation *for* the eating of the Passover lambs that had been sacrificed in the Temple on Friday night, then the Last Supper obviously could not have coincided with the eating of the initial Passover lambs. On this reading, the Jewish Passover meal was prepared for on Friday morning and eaten on Friday night *after* Jesus was crucified — not on the Thursday night before he was crucified. In short, "in John's reckoning," the Last Supper "was not a Passover meal."[18]

In brief, these are the primary texts in the Gospels that have generated the debate over whether the Last Supper was in fact a Jewish Passover meal. Although we will examine other evidence for and against the Last Supper being a Passover below, the texts given above constitute the primary data in question, and any solution stands or falls primarily on how one deals with the evidence they present.

Four Solutions to the Problem

With these data in mind, we can now turn to the hypotheses that have been proposed by scholars for dealing with the historical problem of the date of the Last Supper. Among the various solutions, four approaches stand out as the dominant hypotheses:

1. *The Essene Hypothesis:* Both John and the Synoptics are right; the differences are a result of different Jewish liturgical calendars in use in the

17. Meier, *A Marginal Jew,* 1:389.
18. Meier, *A Marginal Jew,* 1:389-90.

first century. The chronological contradiction is only apparent and can be resolved.

2. *The Johannine Hypothesis:* John is right and the Synoptics are wrong; the Last Supper was not a (ordinary) Jewish Passover meal. The contradictory evidence is irreconcilable.
3. *The Synoptic Hypothesis:* The Synoptics are right and John is wrong; the Last Supper was a Jewish Passover meal. The contradictory evidence is irreconcilable.
4. *The Passover Hypothesis:* Both John and the Synoptics are right; the apparent contradiction is based on a misinterpretation of Jewish Passover terminology in John's Gospel. The contradictory evidence has been misinterpreted by scholars who do not give adequate attention to the cult, chronology, and terminology of the Jewish Passover.

Although these are not of course the only solutions to the date of the Last Supper, they are by far the most influential in recent Jesus research.[19] And while scholars who embrace these solutions differ about various details, as a general rule, most fall into one of these four categories.[20] As we will see, the fourth solution — the Passover hypothesis — has been almost totally ignored in a number of recent studies as if it did not exist.[21] Nevertheless, the Passover

19. Recently, the Cambridge scientist Colin J. Humphreys proposed that Jesus celebrated the Last Supper on a Wednesday night, following an ancient solar calendar that had its origins in Egypt. See Colin J. Humphreys, *The Mystery of the Last Supper: Reconstructing the Final Days of Jesus* (Cambridge: Cambridge University Press, 2011). Although Humphreys's proposal is brilliant in many ways, it is beset by serious weaknesses that, in my mind, render it untenable (see below). Another hypothesis that is worth noting is the theory that the Galileans (represented by the Synoptic Gospels) reckoned the day from sunrise to sunrise, as opposed to the Judeans (represented by the Gospel of John and the temple), who reckoned the day from sunset to sunset. According to this view, the Galileans would sacrifice their lambs a day early because they calculated the day differently. The main problem with this view is a total lack of evidence that the Galileans followed a sunrise-to-sunrise day while Judeans followed sunset to sunset. (*M. Pes.* 4:5, cited in this regard, does not actually provide evidence for different reckonings of the day.) In support of this view, see esp. Hoehner, "The Chronology of Jesus," 2348-49. See also David Instone-Brewer, *Feasts and Sabbaths: Passover and Atonement* (TRENT 2A; Grand Rapids: Eerdmans, 2011), 128-35; idem, "Jesus' Last Supper: the Synoptics and John," *ExpTim* 112 (2001): 122-23. Instone-Brewer attempts to revive Strack-Billerbeck's theory that the Passover sacrifice could be brought on two different days (cf. *t. Pes.* 4:8). Unfortunately, this solution still suffers from the lack of evidence that the temple priests would have actually sacrificed Passover lambs on 13 Nisan.

20. Schröter, *Das Abendmahl,* 44-45, simply leaves the chronological question "open."

21. E.g., McKnight, *Jesus and His Death,* 259-73; Meier, *A Marginal Jew,* 1:386-401; Gerd

hypothesis, when strengthened by ancient Jewish evidence that has not yet been properly taken into account, has merits that have not yet been adequately appreciated.

With this introductory matter in mind, we can now turn to our analysis of each of these proposals. As we review each one of them, I want to stress that in what follows, I am seeking to be both as brief and as fair as possible. An entire monograph could easily be composed on this very complex subject, with many pages dedicated to each of these scholarly proposals. However, for the sake of space, I will not evaluate every possible argument associated with each theory. Rather, my purpose here is simply to isolate and summarize what I consider the primary strengths and weaknesses of each theory. In this regard, I beg the reader not to skip the analysis of each hypothesis. In what follows, the analysis of all four solutions — the Essene, Johannine, Synoptic, and Passover hypotheses — is not merely for the sake of overview, but is essential to my overarching argument. As I hope to show, it is necessary to evaluate the arguments for and against each one in order to build up a complete picture of the problem so that we can see more clearly which solution makes the best sense of the most evidence. This is especially true of the Johannine hypothesis, which — though currently the most popular solution — has rarely been subjected to critical scrutiny.

The Essene Hypothesis

The first solution we will examine is the Essene hypothesis, which was first forwarded in the brilliant and creative work of Annie Jaubert in her book *The Date of the Last Supper.*[22]

According to this solution, at the time of Jesus, the authors of the Dead Sea Scrolls of Qumran, who were Essenes, disagreed with the Temple authorities in Jerusalem about the calendar date of the annual Jewish feasts, including the Passover. On the one hand, the Essenes followed a *solar* calendar, in which the sacrifice and consumption of the Passover lambs always fell on a Tuesday night. On the other hand, the Temple priests followed a *lunar* calendar, in which the Passover meal was celebrated each year on different days of the

---

Theissen and Annette Merz, *The Historical Jesus: A Comprehensive Guide* (trans. John Bowden; Minneapolis: Fortress, 1998), 423-27; Brown, *The Death of the Messiah,* 2:1350-78.

22. Annie Jaubert, *The Date of the Last Supper* (trans. I. Rafferty; Staten Island: Alba House, 1965 [orig. 1957]).

week, as calculated by the authorities on the basis of observing the moon. From this perspective, the chronological discrepancy in the Gospels is best explained by the hypothesis that in his final week, Jesus kept the Passover on Tuesday night, at the same time as the Essenes. Hence, on the one hand, when the Synoptics say that the Last Supper was a Passover meal, they reflect the Essene solar calendar. On the other hand, when John says that Jesus was condemned before the priests at the Passover, he reflects the lunar calendar of the Temple officials.

In other words, when the Synoptics claim that the Last Supper was a Passover meal, they are correct, reflecting the Jewish festal calendar of the Essenes. Likewise, when the Fourth Gospel says that Jesus was arrested before the Passover meal was eaten, it too is correct, reflecting the liturgical calendar of the Temple authorities. The apparent contradiction in the Gospels is the result of the fact that the Synoptic Gospels are utilizing a different Jewish liturgical calendar than the Gospel of John. In the year that Jesus was crucified, the Essenes (along with Jesus and his disciples) and the Temple authorities ate the Passover on different days of the week.

Since its initial publication, the Essene hypothesis has drawn a remarkable amount of attention. On the one hand, since Jaubert originally forwarded the theory in the late 1950s, it has had a number of scholarly advocates, especially among Catholic exegetes and archaeologists.[23] Perhaps the most visible support for a form of the Essene hypothesis took place in 2007, when Pope Benedict XVI mentioned the Essene calendar in his Holy Thursday homily and described the idea that Jesus celebrated the Last Supper early as "a highly plausible hypothesis" — although it seems that the Pope speaks of the meal taking place only twenty-four hours before the Passover rather than several days.[24] Other supporters of the hypothesis are scholars familiar with the Dead Sea Scrolls and the calendrical debates that punctuated the landscape of Sec-

23. See esp. E. Nodet, "On Jesus' Last Supper," *Bib* 91 (2010): 348-69; Bargil Pixner, *Paths of the Messiah: Jesus and Jewish Christianity in Light of Archaeological Discoveries* (San Francisco: Ignatius Press, 2010), 242-44; idem, "Mount Zion, Jesus, and Archaeology," in *Jesus and Archaeology* (ed. James H. Charlesworth; Grand Rapids: Eerdmans, 2006), 309-22; Eugen Ruckstuhl, *Chronology of the Last Days of Jesus: A Critical Study* (trans. Victor J. Drapela; New York: Desclée, 1965); Patrick W. Skehan, "The Date of the Last Supper," *CBQ* 20 (1958): 192-99. For a positive view of the connections between the Last Supper and the Essenes, see David Flusser, "The Last Supper and the Essenes," in *Judaism and the Origins of Christianity* (Jerusalem: Magnes, 1988), 202-6.

24. See Pope Benedict XVI, "Homily for the Mass of the Lord's Supper," Basilica of St. John Lateran, Holy Thursday, 5 April 2007 (available at www.vatican.va).

ond Temple Judaism.[25] In recent years, the work of Jaubert was honored with a collection of essays, and her solution has received a book-length defense in the learned work of Stéphane Saulnier.[26]

On the other hand, the Essene hypothesis has also been repeatedly criticized since its initial publication.[27] This criticism is especially strong in the work of scholars who are suspicious of any attempt to reconcile the apparent chronological discrepancy regarding the date of the Last Supper.[28] After some fifty years, it continues to be a staple of discussion, with many scholars feeling the need to interact with it directly when taking up the question of the date of the Last Supper.[29] This is undoubtedly due to the fact that the Essene hypothesis is rooted in the study of Second Temple Judaism and has several noteworthy arguments in its favor.

1. *Evidence for Solar and Lunar Calendars in Early Judaism*

First and foremost, by far the strongest argument for the Essene hypothesis is the solid and incontrovertible ancient Jewish evidence for competing liturgical calendars in the Second Temple period.[30] As is widely recognized, during the time of the Second Temple, there appears to have been a divide among various Jewish groups over whether the annual feasts such as Passover, Pentecost, and Tabernacles should be celebrated according to (1) a 354-day lunar calendar or (2) a 364-day solar calendar.[31]

25. E.g., James VanderKam and Peter Flint, *The Meaning of the Dead Sea Scrolls* (San Francisco: HarperCollins, 2002), 256-60. For early positive responses by experts in the Scrolls and Hebrew literature, see H. Braun, *Qumran und das Neue Testament* (Tübingen: Mohr, 1966), 2:43-45; G. R. Driver, *The Judean Scrolls* (Oxford: Oxford University Press, 1965), 330-35.

26. Stéphane Saulnier, *Calendrical Variations in Second Temple Judaism: New Perspectives on the 'Date of the Last Supper' Debate* (JSJSup 159; Leiden: Brill, 2012). B. Lourié, M. Petit, and A. Orlov, *L'Église des deux Alliances: Mémorial Annie Jaubert (1912-1980)* (OJC 1; Piscataway: Gorgias, 2008).

27. Jeremias, *The Eucharistic Words of Jesus*, 21-26; Marshall, *Last Supper and Lord's Supper*, 71-75.

28. See Meier, *A Marginal Jew*, 1:391-95; Brown, *The Death of the Messiah*, 2:1366-69; Fitzmyer, *The Gospel according to Luke*, 2:1378-85.

29. E.g., Humphreys, *The Mystery of the Last Supper*, 94-109.

30. Saulnier, *Calendrical Variations in Second Temple Judaism*, 44-45.

31. For discussion, see Saulnier, *Calendrical Variations in Second Temple Judaism*, 115-37; Sacha Stern, *Calendar and Community: A History of the Jewish Calendar, 2nd Century* BCE *to 10th Century* CE (Oxford: Oxford University Press, 2001), 1-52; James C. VanderKam, *Calendars in the Dead Sea Scrolls: Measuring Time* (London: Routledge, 1998).

Such a divide would have had a direct effect on when the various annual feasts were celebrated. In particular, according to the lunar calendar (as with the Jewish calendar in use to this day), the dates of annual feasts such as Passover, Pentecost, and Tabernacles would change with the shifting cycles of the moon. By contrast, for those Jews inclined to follow the solar calendar, the annual feasts would, in theory, always take place on the same day of the week.[32] In her study, Jaubert marshals a number of texts that bear witness to this regular solar festal calendar from early Jewish Pseudepigrapha (*Jub.* 6:32-38) as well as the Dead Sea Scrolls (*Damascus Document*[a] [CD[a]] 3:13-15; 6:18-19; 16:1-5; *1QRule of the Community* [1QS] 1:15-16; 10:5-7).[33] For our purposes here, however, perhaps the clearest and most explicit evidence comes to us from one of the Dead Sea Scrolls that is specifically focused on the solar calendar and hence spells out exactly on which days of the week the Jewish feasts would fall according to this calendar:

> The festivals of the first year: *On the third day from Sabbath (Tuesday)* of the course of the sons of Maaziah *is the Passover.* On the first day (Sunday) of the course [of] Jeda[iah] is the Waving of the [Omer]. On the fifth day (Thursday) of the course of Seorim is the [Second] Passover. On the first day (Sunday) of the course of Jeshua is the Feast of Weeks. On the fourth day (Wednesday) of the course of Maaziah is the Day of Remembrance. [On the] sixth day (Friday) of the course of Jehoiarib is the Day of Atonement, [in the] seventh [month]. [On the] fourth day (Wednesday) of the course of Jedaiah is the Feast of Booths. (*4QCalendrical Document A* [4Q320] frag. 4, col. 3:1-9)[34]

For our purposes here, the most significant feature of this evidence is that according to the ancient Jewish solar calendar, the annual spring feast of the Passover always falls three days after the Sabbath. Given the Jewish custom of beginning the liturgical day at sunset, this would mean that the Passover meal would be eaten on a Tuesday evening.[35] In the light of such evidence, advocates of the Essene hypothesis consider it plausible that Jesus chose to

32. Jaubert, *The Date of the Last Supper,* 97.

33. See Jaubert, *The Date of the Last Supper,* 15-30.

34. Translation by Michael Wise, Martin Abegg Jr., and Edward Cook, *The Dead Sea Scrolls: A New Translation* (San Francisco: HarperCollins, 1996), cited in VanderKam and Flint, *The Meaning of the Dead Sea Scrolls,* 259.

35. Saulnier, *Calendrical Variations in Second Temple Judaism,* 118; Jaubert, *The Date of the Last Supper,* 27-28.

follow the solar calendar reflected in the Dead Sea Scrolls rather than the lunar calendar used by the priests in the Temple. As a result, when he celebrated his final Passover meal with his disciples, he did so on the Tuesday night before he died, while other Jews ate the Passover on Friday night.[36]

2. *Patristic Evidence for a Tuesday Last Supper*

The second major argument in favor of the Essene hypothesis is that it not only has ancient Jewish calendrical evidence in its favor; there are also several pieces of patristic evidence that Jesus ate the Last Supper on the Tuesday night — not Thursday, as is commonly thought — before he was crucified.[37]

The most important witness in this regard is the *Didascalia Apostolorum*, usually dated by scholars to the third-fourth century A.D.[38] In its account of the Last Supper (told in the first person plural by the apostles themselves), we find the following chronology of Jesus' last days:

> While he was still with us before his passion, when we were eating the Pasch with him, he said to us: Today, on this very night, one of you will betray me. And each one of us said to him: Will it be I, Lord? He answered and said to us: It is he who dips his hand in the plate with me. And Judas Iscariot, who was one of us, rose up to betray him. . . . Judas came with the scribes and with the priests of the people and he delivered up our Lord Jesus. This took place on Wednesday. *After eating the Pasch, on Tuesday evening, we went to the Mt. of Olives and, in the night, they took our Lord Jesus. The following day, which is Wednesday, he was kept in the house of the high priest, Caiaphas;* the same day the leaders of the people met and discussed his case. The following day, Thursday, they brought him to the governor, Pilate, and he was kept with Pilate through the night following Thursday. On the morning of Friday they made many accusations concerning him before Pilate, but they could prove nothing against him, and they brought false witnesses against him, and they called upon Pilate to put him to death. They crucified him that same Friday, and he suffered on Friday for six hours. (*Didascalia Apostolorum* 14.1-9)[39]

36. Saulnier, *Calendrical Variations in Second Temple Judaism*, 38-39.

37. Saulnier, *Calendrical Variations in Second Temple Judaism*, 33-38; Pixner, *Paths of the Messiah*, 250-52; Jaubert, *The Date of the Last Supper*, 69-80.

38. Saulnier, *Calendrical Variations in Second Temple Judaism*, 33.

39. Cited in Jaubert, *The Date of the Last Supper*, 71-72 (emphasis altered).

In addition to the *Didascalia,* Jaubert also cites two fourth-century church fathers: Epiphanius, who followed the *Didascalia* in dating the arrest of Jesus to Wednesday (see Epiphanius, *De Fide* 22; cf. *Panarion* 51.2); and Victorinus, bishop of Pettau, who writes that "the man Jesus Christ . . . was arrested by evil-doers on the fourth day [= Wednesday]," and enjoined his audience to fast in remembrance of this event (*De Fabrica Mundi* 3).

Taken together, these three pieces of early Christian evidence, whatever their exact literary relationship with one another, provide substantial patristic support for the idea that Jesus did not actually celebrate the Last Supper on Thursday night, as generally assumed, but on the Tuesday evening of his final week.[40]

3. *The Three-Day Passion Allows More Time for Events*

The third major argument in support of the Essene hypothesis is not from direct evidence, but from general considerations of historical plausibility. According to this argument, the hypothesis that Jesus ate the Passover meal on Tuesday night — and hence, there was a three-day passion chronology — allows much more time for all of the various events described in the Gospel accounts of the passion to take place.[41]

Indeed, according to the Gospels, the time between the time of Jesus' betrayal and arrest and his crucifixion is punctuated by a remarkable number of events:

1. Nocturnal meeting with Annas (John 18:12-24);
2. Meeting with Caiaphas and the Sanhedrin (Matt 26:57-66; Mark 14:53-64; Luke 22:54);
3. Meeting with the "chief priests and elders of the people in the morning" (Matt 27:1-2; cf. Mark 15:1; Luke 22:66-71);
4. Meeting with Pontius Pilate, also in the morning (Matt 27:11-14; Mark 15:1-5; Luke 23:1-5; John 18:28-40);

40. Saulnier, *Calendrical Variations in Second Temple Judaism,* 33-38. Jaubert also cites in her favor Tertullian's statement that the traditional Wednesday and Friday fasts were meant to commemorate "the taking away of the Spouse" (*On Fasting, against the Psychics* 2, 14). Jaubert, *The Date of the Last Supper,* 88. But this evidence is of less weight, and may even support the counterargument that the Wednesday arrest tradition derived from the practice of fasting, and not vice versa.

41. Saulnier, *Calendrical Variations in Second Temple Judaism,* 40-41.

5. Meeting with Herod (Luke 23:6-12);
6. Exchange with the crowds over release of Barabbas (Matt 27:15-26; Mark 15:6-16; Luke 23:13-25);
7. Jesus is scourged, mocked, and crucified (Matt 27:26-50; Mark 15:15-37; Luke 23:25-46; John 19:16-30).

As Jaubert puts it: "The space of time is very short and it is extremely difficult to imagine how so many events were compressed into so few hours."[42] This argument from the historical implausibility of the Gospel records has won the Essene calendar hypothesis many of its supporters.[43]

4. Archaeology and the "Gate of the Essenes" in Jerusalem

A fourth and final observation in favor of this hypothesis is based on ostensible links between the traditional site of the Upper Room in Jerusalem and archaeological excavations involving what some have contended is the "gate of the Essenes" mentioned by Josephus (*War* 5.145).

In a series of studies, both Bargil Pixner and Rainer Riesner have sought to strengthen Jaubert's hypothesis by arguing that a strong case can be made that the site where the Last Supper took place can be located within the ancient Essene quarter in Jerusalem.[44] In the late 1970s, Pixner undertook excavations in Jerusalem near the traditional site of the Upper Room on Mount Zion; he summarizes the findings of his excavations (along with those of others in the area) as follows:[45]

42. Jaubert, *The Date of the Last Supper,* 107.

43. Cf. Saulnier, *Calendrical Variations in Second Temple Judaism,* 40-41, 53-54, citing Ruckstuhl, *Chronology of the Last Days of Jesus,* 35-55; C. S. Mann, "The Chronology of the Passion and the Qumran Calendar," *CQR* 160 (1959): 446-56 (here 451).

44. See Bargil Pixner, *Paths of the Messiah,* 192-220; idem, "Mount Zion, Jesus, and Archaeology," in *Jesus and Archaeology* (ed. James H. Charlesworth; Grand Rapids: Eerdmans, 2006), 309-22; Rainer Riesner, "Jesus, the Primitive Community, and the Essene Quarter of Jerusalem," in *Jesus and the Dead Sea Scrolls* (ed. James H. Charlesworth; New York: Doubleday, 1992), 198-234; Bargil Pixner, D. Chen, and S. Margalit, "Mount Zion: The 'Gate of the Essenes' Reexcavated," *ZDPV* 105 (1989): 85-95 and plates 6-16; Rainer Riesner, "Josephus' 'Gate of the Essenes' in Modern Discussion," *ZDPV* 105 (1989): 105-9; Bargil Pixner, "The History of the 'Essene Gate' Area," *ZDPV* 105 (1989): 96-104; idem, "An Essene Quarter on Mount Zion?," in *Studia Hierosolymitana in onore del P. Belarmino Bagatti,* vol. 1: *Studi archeologici* (SBF.CMa 22; Jerusalem: Franciscan, 1976), 245-86.

45. See Pixner, *Paths of the Messiah,* 198-215.

1. A town wall on the southwest side of the hill, suggesting Mount Zion was included within the wall of the city.
2. A gate added to the Hasmonean town during the Herodian period (37 B.C.–A.D. 70), one of the capitals of which shows traces of having been burnt;
3. Evidence of paths leading southeast out from the remains of the gate;
4. Two ritual baths *(mikvaoth)* some forty meters northwest of the remains of the gate, dated to the Roman period (63 B.C.–A.D. 70).[46]

On the basis of this archaeological evidence, combined with Josephus' mention of a "gate of the Essenes" (*War* 5.145), Pixner and Riesner argue that there was an "Essene quarter" in Jerusalem and that it was located within the city walls on Mount Zion. When this conclusion is coupled with the fact that the traditional site of the Last Supper is also on Mount Zion, Pixner comes to the following conclusion:

> The thesis that the Jerusalem meal took place on Mount Zion supports [the theory that the date of the Last Supper was connected with the Essene calendar] because the proximity of the Essene settlement to the traditional Last Supper room strengthens the assumption that Jesus actually celebrated his last Passover meal according to the calendar of the Essenes.[47]

In other words, if Jesus celebrated the Last Supper in the Essene quarter of Jerusalem, then it is plausible to suggest that he likewise followed the solar calendar of the Essenes and hence consumed the Passover meal on the Tuesday before he was crucified rather than Thursday.

On the one hand, one can easily see why the Essene hypothesis has been a remarkably popular and enduring approach to the date of the Last Supper. Despite the fact that the theory is close to fifty years old, scholars writing on the subject, whether they accept it or not, demonstrate the force of its arguments by consistently engaging it. On the other hand, the theory suffers from several serious weaknesses. What follows are what I consider to be the most significant.

46. On these ritual baths, which were not discovered by Pixner, see R. Reich, "*Mishnah Sheqalim* 8:3 and the Archaeological Evidence" [in Modern Hebrew], in A. Oppenheimer, U. Rappaport, and M. Stern, *Jerusalem in the Second Temple Period: Abraham Schalit Memorial Volume* (Jerusalem: Magnes, 1980), 225-56.

47. Pixner, *Paths of the Messiah*, 251.

1. *The Essene Hypothesis Contradicts the Synoptic Testimony*

The first and most important argument against the Essene hypothesis is that it explicitly contradicts the Synoptic testimony that Jesus ate the Last Supper the evening after the Passover lambs were sacrificed by the Jewish people. In this regard, two of the three Synoptic accounts are explicit:

> Then Judas Iscariot, who was one of the twelve, went to the chief priests in order to betray him to them. And when they heard it they were glad, and promised to give him money. And he sought an opportunity to betray him. And on the first day of Unleavened Bread, *when they sacrificed the Passover lamb,* his disciples said to him, "Where will you have us go and prepare for you to eat the Passover?" (Mark 14:10-12)

> Then came the day of Unleavened Bread, *on which the Passover lamb had to be sacrificed.* So Jesus sent Peter and John, saying, "Go and prepare the Passover for us, that we may eat it." (Luke 22:7-8)

In both of these texts, Mark and Luke unequivocally identify the Last Supper as taking place the evening after the Passover lambs were being "sacrificed" *(ethyon)* (Mark 14:12; Luke 22:7). The reason this is significant is that, according to the Jewish Torah, the only lawful place for a Passover lamb to be sacrificed was in the chosen sanctuary — i.e., the later Jerusalem Temple (Deut 12:1-14; 16:2-6).[48]

Therefore, when interpreted against the backdrop of Jewish Scripture, the Synoptic claims that Jesus celebrated the Last Supper after the cultic sacrifice of the lambs in the Temple is extremely problematic for the Essene hypothesis. The reason: the Essene hypothesis rests entirely on the assumption that it is the Synoptic Gospels that reflect the Essene calendar (what Jaubert calls "the old Pasch"), while John's Gospel reflects the Jerusalem Temple calendar (what Jaubert calls "the official Pasch").[49] Yet here we see two of the three Synoptic Gospels themselves explicitly tying the date of the Last Supper to the time when the lambs were sacrificed in the Temple. The upshot of this is simple but significant: *the very Gospels that supposedly bear witness to the*

48. E.g., Evans, *Mark 8:27–16:20,* 373; Fitzmyer, *The Gospel according to Luke,* 2:1382, points out that the sacrifice of the Passover lamb in the first century was to be carried out "in the court of the priests" — i.e., in the temple.

49. Jaubert, *The Date of the Last Supper,* 97.

Essene calendar — that is, the Synoptic Gospels — are the same texts that actually link the Last Supper to the sacrifices in the Temple, and by extension, to the ordinary Temple calendar.

Because of this conflict between the Essene hypothesis and the testimony of the Synoptics regarding the sacrifice of the lambs, Jaubert and others have been forced to jettison the evidence in Mark 14:12-16 and Luke 22:7-8 as "later interpolations":

> The explanatory phrase, "when they sacrificed the Pasch" [Mark 14:12], which does not appear in the text of Matthew, seems to be a secondary gloss. . . . It is also possible that the glossator, who was so concerned to stress that it was the eve of the Pasch, no longer knew which Pasch was in question.[50]

> The passage introducing the synoptical accounts of the Last Supper (Mark 14:12-16, and par.) can be clearly recognized as a later addition to the narratives. . . . Apparently, it is not genuine.[51]

Unfortunately, neither Jaubert nor Eugen Ruckstuhl gives any evidence for Mark and Luke's testimony regarding the sacrifice of the lambs on Thursday afternoon as being later textual "glosses." Their rejection of these data seems to be entirely "gratuitous."[52]

Indeed, the reason the Essene theory is forced to jettison the evidence regarding the time of the Passover sacrifices is that, in the final analysis, it cannot make sense of the Synoptic testimony. As Joachim Gnilka rightly points out:

> [I]f one attempted to assume that Jesus wanted to celebrate the Passover Tuesday, it would not have been possible for him to secure a lamb that had been slaughtered in the Temple in keeping with the regulations. Yet this must be absolutely presupposed for this festival. The assertion that the Essenes had permission to slaughter lambs in the temple on their date is pure invention.[53]

50. Jaubert, *The Date of the Last Supper,* 97-98.

51. Ruckstuhl, *Chronology of the Last Days of Jesus,* 19.

52. Meier, *A Marginal Jew,* 1:393.

53. Joachim Gnilka, *Jesus of Nazareth: Message and History* (trans. Sigfried S. Schatzmann; Peabody: Hendrickson, 1997), 280. In a footnote, Gnilka rightly rejects the appeal sometimes made to Josephus, *Ant.* 18.18-19, which says nothing of the Essenes having a place in the temple accorded exclusively to them (280 n. 32).

In sum, the conflict between the Essene hypothesis and the testimony of the Synoptics regarding the sacrifice of the lambs in the Temple before the celebration of the Last Supper is a major weakness. For it not only puts the Essene theory at odds with the chronology of Mark and Luke, but also strongly suggests that the Synoptics are working with the liturgical calendar of the Jewish Temple, not with a distinctly solar calendar.

2. *Jesus Seems to Have Followed the Ordinary Temple Calendar*

The second major argument against the Essene hypothesis is that the Gospels contain no clear evidence that Jesus ever followed a different liturgical calendar than that of the Jerusalem Temple, much less that he followed the solar calendar of the Essenes.[54]

Ever since the Dead Sea Scrolls were discovered, scholars have expended enormous energy trying to show some direct connection between Jesus and the sect of the Essenes.[55] Despite such attempts, there remains no clear evidence in the Gospels that Jesus had any direct connection with the Essenes.[56] Indeed, when we carefully examine the Gospel accounts of Jesus' participation in various Jewish feasts, there is quite simply no evidence that Jesus ever followed the solar calendar of the Essenes, as opposed to the lunar calendar used in the Jerusalem Temple. We find evidence of this lunar calendar as normative, for example, in the book of Sirach:

> [The Lord] made the moon also, to serve in its season, to mark the times and to be an everlasting sign. *From the moon comes the sign for feast days,* a light that wanes when it has reached the full. The month is named for the moon, increasingly marvelous in its phases, an instrument of the hosts on high shining forth in the firmament of heaven. (Sir 43:6-7)

54. Ratzinger, *Jesus of Nazareth,* 111; Meier, *A Marginal Jew,* 1:392; Brown, *The Death of the Messiah,* 2:1368; Fitzmyer, *The Gospel according to Luke,* 2:1381. This was pointed out long ago by J. T. Milik, *Ten Years of Discovery in the Wilderness of Judea* (London: SCM, 1959), 112-13.

55. E.g., Pixner, *Paths of the Messiah,* 157-252; Rainer Riesner, "Das Jerusalemer Essenerquartier und die Urgemeinde," in *Aufstieg und Niedergang der Römischen Welt* 26.2 (ed. H. Temporini and W. Haase; Berlin: De Gruyter, 1995), 1175-1222.

56. See Meier, *A Marginal Jew,* 3:488-613 for the most exhaustive treatment of Jesus and the Essenes to date.

In keeping with this non-polemical description of the moon as regulating the festal cycle,[57] whenever the Gospels do depict Jesus participating in the various annual feasts, he always does so in the Temple at the same time as the majority of Jews. For example, in the Gospel of John, Jesus clearly keeps the feast of Tabernacles at the same time everyone else "goes up" to the feast (see John 7:1-10, 37).[58] In light of this and other evidence, John Meier writes:

> Jaubert . . . sweeps away the whole of the Johannine tradition with a wave of the hand, but with no detailed discussion. One can see why. If, early on in the Fourth Gospel, Jesus' observance of Jewish feasts in the Jerusalem temple *at the same time that other Jews observe them* is allowed to stand as basically historical, there is no good reason to think that his observance of his last Passover in Jerusalem would diverge from his set custom.[59]

Meier's critique is on target, but I would strengthen it by adding that it is not just the Gospel of John, but the Synoptic accounts of the Last Supper that imply that Jesus followed the sacrificial rites of the Jerusalem Temple. As we just mentioned above, it is the Synoptics — which are supposed to reflect the Essene calendar — which explicitly describe Jesus and his disciples celebrating the Last Supper the evening after the lambs were "sacrificed" (Mark 14:10-12; Luke 22:7-8), something which had to take place in the Jerusalem Temple (Deut 12:12-16).

Hypothetically speaking, if one or more of the Gospels bore witness to Jesus following a different festal calendar, then the Essene hypothesis would have a high degree of probability. But if all four Gospels themselves suggest instead that Jesus celebrated the annual feasts along with the majority of common Jews, then the Essene hypothesis once again labors under the burden of failing to square with the textual data. As a result, what is perhaps the strongest argument for Jaubert's hypothesis — the external Jewish evidence for a distinctively solar calendar in use among the Essenes — is seriously weakened in the face of what the Gospels actually tell us about Jesus' relationship to the Jewish authorities and the Jerusalem Temple.[60] Indeed, in the most recent defense

57. Saulnier, *Calendrical Variations in Second Temple Judaism*, 195.

58. See Craig S. Keener, *The Gospel of John* (2 vols.; Peabody: Hendrickson, 2003).

59. Meier, *A Marginal Jew*, 1:393.

60. It is worth noting here that Matthew's Gospel in particular raises problems for the suggestion that Jesus and the disciples followed the Essene calendar. According to Matthew, Jesus commands the disciples to be obedient to the teachings of the Pharisees — not the Essenes: "Then Jesus said to the crowds and to his disciples, 'The scribes and Pharisees sit on Moses' seat; so practice and observe whatever they tell you, but not what they do; for they

of the Essene theory, Stéphane Saulnier is forced to admit that "there appears to be no evidence that Jesus followed the old 'solar' calendar for Passover or any other festivals" and that "there are no (explicit) references to an Essene Passover in the Gospels."[61]

3. *No Evidence for a Three-Day Passion in the Gospels*

A third argument against the theory has to do with the suggested chronology of Jesus' last week. According to the Essene hypothesis, Jesus was arrested Tuesday night and spent all of Wednesday and Thursday in prison before being executed sometime Friday morning. This would lead to the conclusion that the "passion" of Jesus took place over a period of some three days.

The problem with a three-day passion is that it too contradicts the explicit chronological testimony of both the Synoptics and John that Jesus was crucified the morning after his betrayal and arrest.[62] The framework of a single evening is made quite clear by the chronological indicators given in the accounts of Peter's betrayal on the morning of Jesus' crucifixion:

> Jesus said to [Peter], "Amen, I say to you, *this very night,* before the cock crows twice, you will deny me three times." (Mark 14:30)

> And as Peter was below in the courtyard . . . immediately the cock crowed a second time. And Peter remembered how Jesus had said to him, "Before the cock crows twice, you will deny me three times." And he broke down and wept. *And as soon as it was morning,* the chief priests, with the elders and scribes, and the whole Sanhedrin held a consultation; and they bound Jesus and led him away and delivered him to Pilate. (Mark 14:66, 72; 15:1)

> Jesus answered [Peter], "Will you lay down your life for me? Amen, amen, I say to you, *the cock will not crow,* till you have denied me three times." (John 13:38)

---

preach, but do not practice'" (Matt 23:1-3). Given the evidence suggesting that it was the Pharisees who followed the lunar calendar (e.g., *t. Sanh.* 2:2-9; *b. Sanh.* 11b), one is hard pressed to convincingly argue that the very Gospel in which Jesus commands his disciples to follow the Pharisees in "whatever" they teach is the same Gospel in which he and his disciples observe the Essene calendar for the celebration of the Last Supper.

61. Saulnier, *Calendrical Variations in Second Temple Judaism,* 60, 61.

62. See Raymond E. Brown, *New Testament Essays* (New York: Image, 1968), 212-14.

> One of the servants of the high priest, a kinsman of the man whose ear Peter had cut off, asked, "Did I not see you in the garden with him?" Peter again denied it; and *at once the cock crowed. Then they led Jesus from the house of Caiaphas to the praetorium. It was early.* They themselves did not enter the praetorium, so that they might not be defiled, but might eat the Passover. (John 18:26-28)

Taken together, this evidence from the passion narratives manifests an explicit chronology of a single evening elapsing between the night of Jesus' betrayal and arrest and the morning he was handed over to Pilate and crucified. Notice in this regard that we are dealing here with the Passion narratives, in which the evangelists' interest in a more precise chronology becomes very pronounced. This stands in contrast to the somewhat vaguer chronology associated with the public ministry of Jesus. In this regard, the Essene hypothesis rests on the contrary assumption that when it comes to the Passion, the evangelists are uninterested in matters "chronological."[63] To the contrary, it is precisely when we turn to the passion and death of Jesus that all four evangelists become very interested in the chronological sequence of events.[64]

In short, the chronological evidence for a single evening makes it impossible to gratuitously insert some three days between the night of Jesus' betrayal and the morning of his crucifixion. Indeed, in the face of the Gospel evidence, Jaubert herself admits that *"The Gospels do not appear to have kept any memory of the three days of the passion."*[65] I agree, but would put it more strongly: not only is there no evidence for a three-day passion, but such a chronology contradicts the apparent one-day chronology of the Synoptics and John. John Meier puts it well when he points out that the Essene hypothesis necessitates that we conclude that "the Synoptics and John are *both wrong* when they *agree* that the Last Supper and Jesus' arrest took place on Thursday evening."[66] Once again, in order to make the Essene hypothesis work, time signals such as the ones quoted above either have to be ignored or eliminated as evidence.[67]

63. Jaubert, *The Date of the Last Supper*, 114.

64. See Brown, *The Death of the Messiah*, 1350-78 (with bibliography), on the passion chronology.

65. Jaubert, *The Date of the Last Supper*, 103 (emphasis added). Jaubert earlier on claims that the three day chronology was "lost" by the early church (89).

66. Meier, *A Marginal Jew*, 1:394 (emphasis original).

67. Jaubert, *The Date of the Last Supper*, 103-17.

4. *The Patristic Evidence Contradicts the Solar Calendar Theory*

A fourth argument against the Essene hypothesis is that the patristic evidence cited in support of the theory actually claims that Jesus celebrated the Last Supper according to the *lunar calendar* of the Jewish people.

In this regard, the *Didascalia Apostolorum,* which is the primary patristic evidence used to support the Essene hypothesis, explicitly enjoins its audience to follow the lunar calendar of the Jewish priests in the Temple and the Hebrew people:

> *Reckoning by the moon — we calculate as do the Hebrew faithful — on the tenth day, a Monday, the priests and the ancients of the people assembled and came into the fore-court of Caiaphas, the high priest.* . . . Because of the crowds of all the (Jewish) people, from every town and every village, who were coming up to the Temple to celebrate the Pasch at Jerusalem, *the priests and the ancients took counsel, ordained and established that they would celebrate the feast immediately so that they might arrest him without disturbance.* The inhabitants of Jerusalem took part in the paschal sacrifice and the meal and the people from outside the city had not yet arrived; because they changed the days. . . . Thus they celebrated the Passover three days before its time; on the eleventh day of the moon, Tuesday. (*Didascalia Apostolorum* 17.2, 6-7)[68]

This evidence poses two key problems for the Essene theory. First, it hardly constitutes a patristic witness to Jesus' following the solar calendar of the Essenes. Indeed, not only does the *Didascalia* say nothing about a solar calendar, but on more than one occasion enjoins its audience to follow the lunar calendar with regard to Passover.[69] Second, the *Didascalia*'s claim that the Jewish priests moved the Passover up three days for the sole purpose of arresting Jesus before the Jews from outside Jerusalem could get there does not seem to be historically plausible.

In short, Jaubert uses the patristic evidence for Jesus' Tuesday supper very selectively, accepting the pieces that fit her hypothesis (like the Tuesday date of the Last Supper), but rejecting the elements that do not (like the explicit

68. Quoted in Jaubert, *The Date of the Last Supper,* 73-74.

69. See also *Didascalia Apostolorum* 20.10: "Observe the fourteenth day of the Pasch, wherever it falls, for the month and the day do not fall at the same time every year, but at different times. Hence, when this (Jewish) people celebrates the Pasch, you are to fast."

references to the lunar calendar and the claim that the Temple priests moved the date of Passover). In light of these difficulties Jaubert is again forced to admit that in *Didascalia*'s chronology the issue is "lacking any homogeneity."[70] Given this fact, it seems precarious to choose the questionable chronological and cultic claims of the *Didascalia* over the multiply attested one-day chronology of the Synoptics and John.

5. *An Etiology for the Christian Custom of Wednesday Fasting*

How then do we explain the existence of these patristic references to a Tuesday Last Supper? Since Jaubert first proposed the Essene hypothesis, scholars have pointed out that the patristic evidence for a Wednesday arrest can also be explained as an early Christian attempt to link the Christian practice of fasting on Wednesday and Friday with the days of Jesus' Passion (Friday) and arrest (Wednesday).[71]

In order to see this, it is important to recall that in the first century A.D., the *Didache* explains the Christian practice of fasting on Wednesday and Friday as a reaction to the traditional Pharisaic days of fasting:

> But do not let your fasts coincide with those of the hypocrites. *They fast on Monday and Thursday, so you must fast on Wednesday and Friday.* (*Didache* 8.1-3)[72]

By the time of the patristic evidence cited in Jaubert — evidence usually dated to the fourth century or later — this practice of fasting on Wednesday and Friday is being rooted by a few sources in the events of Jesus' passion week. Strikingly, in all three of the patristic sources cited by Jaubert in support of the Essene hypothesis, the chronology of Jesus' passion is explicitly tied to the Christian custom of fasting on Wednesdays and Fridays:

> [Jesus speaking in an apparition to his disciples:] "You will *fast* for them (for the Jews) *on Wednesday, for it is on Wednesday that they began to lose their souls and that they apprehended me.* The night which follows Tuesday belongs to Wednesday as it is written: "It was evening and morning, one

70. Jaubert, *The Date of the Last Supper,* 74.
71. Jeremias, *The Eucharistic Words of Jesus,* 25.
72. Trans. Holmes, *The Apostolic Fathers,* 355-57.

> day"; thus the evening belongs to the following day. Tuesday evening, I ate my Pasch with you, and during the night, they took me. . . . *And on Friday fast for them,* because on that day they crucified me. (*Didascalia Apostolorum* 14.18-21)[73]

> Wednesday and Friday are *days of fasting* up to the ninth hour because, *as Wednesday began, the Lord was arrested* and on Friday he was crucified. (Epiphanius, *De Fide* 22)[74]

> The man Jesus Christ, the author of all these things just mentioned, was arrested by evil-doers on the fourth day [= Wednesday]. *We make the fourth day a day of fast by* reason of his imprisonment. (Victorinus of Pettau, *De Fabrica Mundi* 3)[75]

In light of such evidence, and given the other historical difficulties with the Essene hypothesis enumerated thus far, it is reasonable to conclude that the patristic tradition of a Tuesday Last Supper is not a historically reliable memory of Jesus' use of a solar calendar, but rather a mistaken patristic etiology for the custom of the Christian Wednesday fast.[76] Indeed, in support of the conclusion that the Wednesday fast preceded the Tuesday-supper explanation, it is worth noting that the fourth-century writer Peter of Alexandria also attempted to explain the Wednesday fast with reference to the events of Jesus' passion, but linked it with the plotting of the Jewish authorities against Jesus, not with his imprisonment (*Ep. Can.* 15).[77]

6. No Evidence for an "Essene Quarter" in Jerusalem

Although at first glance the argument from the archaeological evidence that Jesus celebrated the Last Supper in the Essene quarter seems to marshal concrete data in its favor, on further analysis, this claim is also problematic.

The most devastating point against this otherwise plausible suggestion is the fact that we do not actually possess any explicit textual evidence for an Essene quarter in Jerusalem. Indeed, when the primary data from Josephus

73. Cited in Jaubert, *The Date of the Last Supper,* 72.
74. Cited in Jaubert, *The Date of the Last Supper,* 77.
75. Cited in Jaubert, *The Date of the Last Supper,* 79.
76. Cf. Meier, *A Marginal Jew,* 1:423 n. 77.
77. Cf. Saulnier, *Calendrical Variations in Second Temple Judaism,* 37.

are examined carefully, he does not actually say anything about an "Essene quarter" in Jerusalem; he only mentions a "gate" used by the Essenes.[78] In his description of the western wall of the city, Josephus writes:

> On the west side it is extended from the same starting point along a piece of land called Bethso until the Gate of the Essenes *(epi tēn Essēnōn pylēn),* then bent to the south and then ran its course on the other side of the Pool of Siloam. (Josephus, *War* 5.145)[79]

This evidence from Josephus is extremely significant for evaluating the arguments from archaeology. As Riesner himself admits, the existence of an Essene quarter in Jerusalem is a modern scholarly assumption, going back to the work of J. B. Lightfoot and M. J. Lagrange.[80] No ancient author actually mentions such a quarter. This modern theory is a deduction based on Josephus' mention of the gate: "the 'Gate of the Essenes' implies the existence of an Essene quarter in Jerusalem."[81]

The existence of such a quarter is, of course, possible; but it is equally plausible that the "gate of the Essenes" described the gate leading *out* of the city toward an Essene settlement (just as the modern-day Damascus gate bears this name because it is the gate leading north toward Damascus). Because of this, even Rainer Riesner, who has published extensively on this subject, can only speak of "the *possible* Essene quarter on Zion."[82]

Now, if the very existence of the Essene quarter is only a possibility, then the likelihood of being able to demonstrate that the Last Supper took place within this section of Jerusalem is significantly diminished. The problems with this theory become even more pronounced if we remain uncertain about exactly where the Last Supper itself took place. Although at first glance the Essene hypothesis appears to have archaeology in its favor, the textual and archaeological data are far too meager to conclude that Jesus probably

78. See Rainer Riesner, "Josephus 'Gate of the Essenes' in Modern Discussion," *ZDPV* 105 (1989): 105-9.

79. Cited in Riesner, "Jesus, the Primitive Community, and the Essene Quarter," 208 (emphasis added).

80. Riesner, "Jesus, the Primitive Community, and the Essene Quarter," 208, following M. J. Lagrange, *Le Judaïsme avant Jésus-Christ* (Paris: Gabalda, 1931), 316-19, and J. B. Lightfoot, *Saint Paul's Epistles to the Colossians and Philemon* (London: Macmillan, 1879), 94 n. 2.

81. Riesner, "Jesus, the Primitive Community, and the Essene Quarter," 208.

82. Riesner, "Jesus, the Primitive Community, and the Essene Quarter," 209, following Pixner, "An Essene Quarter on Mount Zion," 245-85.

celebrated the Last Supper in an Essene quarter for which we have no explicit evidence. Indeed, even if the archaeological data for the existence and location of the Essene quarter were more solid, the hypothesis would still run aground of the express testimony of the Synoptic Gospels that Jesus celebrated the Last Supper not with any special group or according to any special calendar, but at the time the lambs were being "sacrificed" (Mark 14:12; Luke 22:7) in the Jerusalem Temple, which was controlled by the Sadducees and Pharisees, and not the Essenes (cf. Josephus, *Antiquities* 18.5).

7. The Problem of Intercalation and the Timing of the Solar Passover

Seventh and finally, one of the most serious weaknesses of the Essene hypothesis regards our ignorance of ancient Jewish methods of intercalation, by which the 365-day solar calendar and the 354-day lunar calendar would be kept in line with one another. In modern times, the two are kept in harmony by means of quadrennial "leap years"; when it comes to the ancient Jewish solar calendar — and this is crucial — *we have no idea what method of intercalation, if any, was followed.* There is simply no evidence.[83]

The reason the question of intercalation is important is simple. The hypothesis that Jesus celebrated the Last Supper on a Tuesday night rather than a Thursday night following the solar calendar of the Essenes is based entirely on the assumption that the solar Passover would have taken place *before* the lunar Passover and *during the same week.* But this is precisely what we do not know, because we have no evidence as to how the Essene calendar was intercalated. Indeed, after a book-length study of ancient Jewish calendars in defense of the Essene hypothesis, Stéphane Saulnier is still forced to admit:

> The main difficulty with the 364DY tradition [= solar calendar] was to assert whether it was aligned with the lunisolar calendar the year that Jesus died, so much that its Passover celebration fell on the Tuesday of passion week. . . . [T]his particular issue still remains to be considered further. . . .[84]

83. Cf. Saulnier, *Calendrical Variations in Second Temple Judaism,* 212 n. 26 and 246: "The question of intercalation of the 364-day calendar remains an unresolved issue for want of a 'smoking gun.' . . . If it is becoming increasingly difficult to doubt the practicability of the 364-day year, scholars are still at a loss to explain how the calendar was kept in line with the seasons."

84. Saulnier, *Calendrical Variations in Second Temple Judaism,* 244.

In other words, although Saulnier does an excellent job of showing that the evidence suggests that some method of intercalation was used to keep the solar calendar in line with the seasons, he admits the evidence does not allow us to know how the Essenes kept their solar calendar in line with the seasons.[85] But this information is essential to the Essene solution to the date of the Last Supper, since for the theory to work, the solar Passover had to have taken place before the lunar Passover and during the same week. But that is precisely what we are unable to show.

In fact, in his recent study, Colin J. Humphreys goes even further and argues that ordinarily, the solar Passover of the Essenes falls after the lunar Passover, sometimes by two weeks.[86] He bases this argument on the description of the solar calendar in *1 Enoch* — of which multiple copies were found at Qumran — in which the month of Passover ("the first month") according to the solar calendar is clearly designated as beginning *after* the spring equinox — i.e., the time in the spring when the days and nights are of equal (Latin *aequus*) length:

> It [the sun] rises in *the first month* in the large gate, namely it rises in the fourth of those six gates which are towards the east . . . and on those days *the day grows daily longer and the night grows nightly shorter*. . . . (*1 Enoch* 72:6-9)[87]

In light of this evidence, Humphreys argues as follows:

> In the first century AD (and today), the [lunar] Jewish calendar was intercalated so that *Passover* [Nisan 14] must fall after the spring equinox. However, the Qumran community followed 1 Enoch, which stated that *Nisan 1* must fall after the spring equinox. Since Passover (in the middle of Nisan) necessarily falls after Nisan 1, it follows that Passover in the Qumran calendar, if it was intercalated, *always* fell after Passover in the [lunar] Jewish calendar. . . .[88]

This is a fascinating observation, especially if one recalls that, even to this day, it is ordinarily the case that the modern-day Jewish Passover (following

85. Saulnier, *Calendrical Variations in Second Temple Judaism*, 244.
86. Humphreys, *The Mystery of the Last Supper*, 106.
87. Cited in Humphreys, *The Mystery of the Last Supper*, 105, 106.
88. Humphreys, *The Mystery of the Last Supper*, 107.

a lunar calendar) ordinarily occurs before the celebration of Catholic Easter (following a luni-solar calendar based on the spring equinox). If Humphreys is correct — and there is strong reason for caution here, given our ignorance of ancient Jewish methods of intercalation — and the solar Passover ordinarily would have taken place *after* the lunar Passover, then the effect for the Essene solution to the date of the Last Supper is fairly devastating. As he puts it:

> We conclude then that Jesus could not have used the Qumran calendar to celebrate his last supper as a Passover meal since, whether it was intercalated or not, Passover in the Qumran calendar did not fall in the same week as Passover in the official Jewish calendar.[89]

If this is correct, then the postulate of a Tuesday last supper does not aid in solving the contradiction between John and the Synoptics, because at the time of Jesus' execution, the Essenes would not yet have celebrated their Passover until after he was already dead.

In sum, there are several remarkable strengths to the Essene hypothesis. Chief among these is the indisputable evidence that ancient Jews disputed over whether feast days should be celebrated according to a lunar or solar liturgical calendar, and that the authors of the *Jubilees* and some Dead Sea Scrolls favored the latter. Because of this fact, this hypothesis has rightly been considered a serious historical possibility for explaining the apparent contradiction between the Gospels. Nevertheless, upon closer examination of the data, its weaknesses appear to outweigh its strengths. It is difficult to reconcile with the Synoptic testimony that Jesus ate the Last Supper the same evening the lambs were being sacrificed by other Jews. It is based on a few questionable patristic chronologies of Jesus' last days, and even contradicts them with regard to the use of the solar calendar. It is forced to insert a three-day imprisonment into the one-day chronology found in the Synoptics and John. There is no actual evidence, literary or archaeological, for the existence of an "Essene quarter" in southwest Jerusalem, and, as such, it cannot really make the case that Jesus celebrated the Last Supper in this (hypothetical) quarter, following the calendar of the Essenes. Finally, we do not even know if the solar Passover was celebrated the same week as the lunar Passover, and there is some reason to believe that it may ordinarily have come after, thus making Jesus' celebration of the Essene Passover during his last week unlikely, if not impossible.

89. Humphreys, *The Mystery of the Last Supper,* 109.

The Johannine Hypothesis

The second major solution to the problem of the date of the Last Supper is what I will call the Johannine hypothesis. According to this theory, the Synoptic and Johannine chronologies of Jesus' last days are irreconcilably contradictory, and it is John, not the Synoptics, who is more historically accurate. The Last Supper took place on the evening before the Passover lambs were slaughtered in the Temple (14 Nisan), and the ordinary Jewish Passover meal was celebrated on the Friday evening after Jesus was crucified (15 Nisan). Hence, whatever kind of meal the Last Supper was, it was not an ordinary Jewish Passover meal.

In this regard, it is important to stress that in contemporary scholarship, the Johannine hypothesis usually takes two fundamentally different forms.

1. *The Non-Paschal Meal:* The first form of the Johannine hypothesis argues that the Last Supper was not a Passover meal at all, but some other kind of meal, ranging anywhere from an "ordinary meal" with his disciples to "a farewell meal," to a "special farewell meal." According to this point of view, "Jesus gave a heightened significance to . . . their last meal together," but that is all.[90] A key argument for this version of the theory is that the Last Supper in John's Gospel is not described as a Passover meal. Instead, it is the Synoptic Gospels who have retroactively transformed the Last Supper into a Passover meal for "theological" reasons. The Synoptic depiction of the Last Supper as a Passover meal is "a theologoumenon, i.e. . . . a dramatization of the preGospel proclamation of Jesus as the paschal lamb."[91] Along these lines, the Synoptics are historically in error when they repeatedly refer to the Last Supper as a "Passover" and say that Jesus celebrated it at the same times as other Jews. This form of the Johannine hypothesis is currently the most widely held solution to the date of the Last Supper.[92]

90. Dunn, *Jesus Remembered*, 772-73.

91. Brown, *The Death of the Messiah*, 2:1370.

92. See, e.g., D. Moody Smith, "Jesus Tradition in the Gospel of John," in *Handbook of the Study of the Historical Jesus* (ed. Tom Holmén and Stanley E. Porter; 4 vols.; Leiden: Brill, 2011), 3:1997-2039 (here 2022-24); Mark A. Matson, "The Historical Plausibility of John's Passion Dating," in *John, Jesus, and History*, vol. 2: *Aspects of Historicity in the Fourth Gospel* (ed. Paul N. Anderson, Felix Just, S.J., and Tom Thatcher; Atlanta: Society of Biblical Literature, 2009), 291-312; James D. G. Dunn, *Jesus Remembered* (Christianity in the Making, vol. 1; Grand Rapids: Eerdmans, 2003), 772-73; Paula Fredriksen, *Jesus of Nazareth, King of the Jews* (New York: Vintage Books, 1999), 223; Jürgen Becker, *Jesus of Nazareth* (trans. James Crouch; New

2. *The Anticipatory Passover Meal:* The second form of the Johannine hypothesis argues that the Last Supper was some kind of Passover meal, but that Jesus held this meal twenty-four hours in advance of the ordinary Jewish Passover meal on Friday night. In this view, the Synoptics are not incorrect in referring to the Last Supper as a "Passover," because Jesus celebrated the meal according to the norms of an actual Passover meal, and because the Passover feast was only twenty-four hours away. Indeed, from this point of view, the Last Supper is a kind of "*quasi*-Passover meal" celebrated by Jesus "a day ahead of the real thing," given the imminence of his death.[93] This second form of the Johannine hypothesis also has a strong contemporary following: I myself once held this view, and it has recently found a prominent supporter in Joseph Ratzinger (Pope Benedict XVI), who adopts it, albeit with certain "reservations," in his recent book on the last days of Jesus.[94]

In order to see why the Johannine hypothesis (in both forms) has been so widely accepted, we need first to review the strength of the major arguments in its favor.[95] Then we will subject these arguments to critical scrutiny, something that has not been done very frequently in the scholarly literature.

York/Berlin: Walter de Gruyter, 1998), 340-41; Gerd Theissen and Annette Merz, *The Historical Jesus: An Introduction* (trans. John Bowden; Minneapolis: Fortress, 1998), 426-27; Brown, *The Death of the Messiah,* 2:1370; Meier, *A Marginal Jew,* 1:399; Anthony J. Saldarini, *Jesus and Passover* (New York: Paulist, 1984), 51-79; Brown, *The Gospel according to John,* 2:555-58; Günther Bornkamm, *Jesus of Nazareth* (trans. Irene McLuskey, Fraser McLuskey, and James Robinson; London: Hodder & Stoughton, 1960), 160-62; Solomon Zeitlin, "The Last Supper as an Ordinary Meal in the Fourth Gospel," *JQR* 42 (1951-52): 251-60; idem, "The Date of the Crucifixion according to the Fourth Gospel," *JBL* 51 (1932): 263-71; Rudolf Bultmann, *The History of the Synoptic Tradition* (trans. J. H. Marsh; rev. ed.; Oxford: Basil Blackwell, 1972 [orig. 1931]).

93. N. T. Wright, *Jesus and the Victory of God* (Minneapolis: Fortress, 1996), 556-59.

94. See, e.g., Joel Marcus, "Passover and Last Supper Revisited," *NTS* 59 (2013): 303-24; Joseph Ratzinger (Pope Benedict XVI), *Jesus of Nazareth: Holy Week* (San Francisco: Ignatius Press, 2011), 2:113; McKnight, *Jesus and His Death,* 272-73; Brant Pitre, *Jesus, the Tribulation, and the End of the Exile: Restoration Eschatology and the Origin of the Atonement* (WUNT 2.204; Tübingen: Mohr-Siebeck; Grand Rapids: Baker Academic, 2005), 441-42; Wright, *Jesus and the Victory of God,* 556-59; Craig Evans, *Mark 8:27–16:20* (WBC 34b; Nashville: Thomas Nelson, 2001), 371-72; Markus Bockmuehl, *This Jesus: Martyr, Lord, Messiah* (Edinburgh: T. & T. Clark, 1994), 92-95; Vincent Taylor, *The Gospel according to St. Mark* (2nd ed.; London: Macmillan, 1966), 664-67.

95. Other minor arguments could be adduced, but these are the ones that I think lead most people to accept this position as the most compelling solution. For responses to some of the minor arguments, see Jeremias, *The Eucharistic Words of Jesus,* 62-84.

1. No Mention of a Lamb at the Last Supper

The first major argument for the Johannine hypothesis is that none of the four Gospels ever mentions a Passover lamb at the Last Supper.[96] According to this point of view, although the Last Supper is described as a "Passover" *(pascha)* meal by the Synoptics (Mark 14:12-16; Luke 22:7-8), there is never any explicit reference to a "lamb" *(arnion)*. In the words of Raymond Brown:

> [I]t is peculiar to place the whole burden of solving the Gospel discrepancies on the availability of a slain lamb, when no Gospel ever mentions that a lamb was part of the meal.[97]

Along similar lines, James Dunn claims:

> There is no allusion to the normal elements in the Passover meal, the last supper tradition itself does not speak of it as a Passover. . . .[98]

For many scholars, this apparent absence of the Passover lamb, even in the Synoptic Gospels, is the "most decisive" argument in favor of the Johannine hypothesis.[99] The reason the Gospels do not explicitly mention the lamb in their accounts of the actual supper is that the Passover lambs would not be sacrificed until the next day. The Gospel silence in this case is a remnant of a historically reliable tradition about the non-paschal character of the meal.

In support of this position, advocates of the Johannine hypothesis often point to the fact that in Mark's account of the passion, the Jewish leaders expressly state that they do not want to arrest Jesus during the Passover feast:

> It was now two days before the Passover and the feast of Unleavened Bread. And the chief priests and the scribes were seeking how to arrest him by stealth, and kill him; for they said, "*Not during the feast,* lest there be a tumult of the people." (Mark 14:1-2)

On the basis of this evidence, it is commonly claimed that Mark's Gospel itself bears witness to the fact that Jesus was not arrested "during the feast"

96. Schröter, *Das Abendmahl,* 44.
97. Brown, *The Death of the Messiah,* 2:1364.
98. Dunn, *Jesus Remembered,* 772.
99. McKnight, *Jesus and His Death,* 270.

but rather killed before the Passover.[100] From this point of view, the accounts of Jesus sending the disciples into Jerusalem to "prepare the Passover" (Mark 14:12-16) the afternoon before the Last Supper were added later, since they contradict the "primitive" Markan passion chronology in which the meal was not a Passover at all. In the words of John Meier:

> The intriguing fact is that, if Mark's Passion Narrative is shorn of two passages that probably come from either a secondary level of the tradition or from Mark's own redactional activity [i.e., Mark 14:1a and 14:12-16], the remaining Passion Narrative contains no clear indication that the Last Supper was a Passover meal or that Jesus died on Passover day.[101]

Put another way, if we simply remove the evidence for "the Passover" taking place after two days (Mark 14:1a) and the evidence that Jesus sent his disciples into Jerusalem to "prepare the Passover" (Mark 14:12-16), then there is no longer any evidence that the Last Supper was a Passover meal. Once again, in the words of Meier:

> Once the Synoptic Passion Narratives are deprived of their late or redactional references to Passover, we realize that the Last Supper in the underlying Synoptic tradition is no more a Passover meal than is the Last Supper in John's Gospel.[102]

In sum, according to the Johannine hypothesis, the Synoptic Gospels have only partially transformed the Last Supper into a Passover meal. First, they all fail to add the Passover lamb to their accounts of the words of institution, revealing evidence of a "primitive form" in which the Last Supper was an ordinary meal. Second, they also fail to remove the evidence that the Jewish leaders did not kill Jesus "during the feast" (Mark 14:2), thereby establishing internal contradictions that also point away from the "original" form of the Last Supper having been a Jewish Passover meal.

100. E.g., Meier, *A Marginal Jew*, 1:396-97; Gerd Theissen, *The Gospels in Context: Social and Political History of the Synoptic Tradition* (Minneapolis: Fortress, 1991), 166-67.

101. Meier, *A Marginal Jew*, 1:396.

102. Meier, *A Marginal Jew*, 1:398.

2. *Jesus Was Hanged "On the Eve of Passover"*

The second major argument in favor of the Johannine hypothesis is based on external evidence from the Babylonian Talmud that Jesus was crucified before the Passover lambs were sacrificed in the Temple.

Given the widespread scholarly skepticism towards the use of later rabbinic evidence in Jesus research, this common appeal to the Talmud as evidence for the historical date of the Last Supper is remarkable. Almost without fail, scholarly advocates of the Johannine hypothesis (in both of its forms) cite the rabbinic evidence that "Jesus (of Nazareth)" was "hanged on the eve of Passover" (Babylonian Talmud, *Sanhedrin* 43a).[103] This evidence from the Babylonian Talmud is seen as Jewish support for "the Johannine chronology" of Jesus' death before the Passover lambs were eaten.[104] N. T. Wright's treatment of this rabbinic data in this regard is representative:

> The synoptic evangelists . . . date [the Last Supper]: they have Jesus and the disciples speak of "eating the Passover": they have the disciples "preparing the Passover-meal." John, however, indicates that the meal took place *before* the feast; he does not, however, describe the meal, or any symbolic actions concerned with the bread or the wine, but only the footwashing. This fits with the Talmudic evidence, which as we saw had Jesus being executed "on the eve of the Passover."[105]

Likewise Mark Matson:

> If this baraita [rabbinic tradition] has any claim to deriving from an early period in the Jewish memory of Jesus — and I think its claim is strong — it clearly suggests that Jesus was crucified (or hung) on the day *before* the Passover, or Nisan 14, in agreement with John's Gospel.[106]

According to the logic of this argument, there is no reason to see any theological motivation on the part of the Talmudic rabbis to change the date of Jesus' death (in contrast to the Synoptic Gospels). Hence, preference should be given to the Talmudic chronology and hence to the conclusion that the Last Supper

103. E.g., Moody Smith, "Jesus Tradition in the Gospel of John," 2023; Matson, "The Historical Plausibility of John's Passion Dating," 299-300; Meier, *A Marginal Jew*, 1:96-97.

104. Brown, *The Death of the Messiah*, 2:1360.

105. Wright, *Jesus and the Victory of God*, 555, citing *b. Sanh.* 43a.

106. Matson, "The Historical Plausibility of John's Passion Dating," 300.

was not a Passover meal. For many scholars, this rabbinic text alone places the crucifixion of Jesus "without a doubt on the eve of Passover," before the slaughter and eating of the Passover lambs, thereby contradicting the claims of the Synoptic Gospels.[107]

In addition to this rabbinic evidence, it is worth noting here that there is also testimony from the second-third century A.D. *Gospel of Peter* cited in support of the Johannine hypothesis. According to this text, we read the following:

> And he [Pilate] turned him over to the people on the day before the Unleavened Bread, their feast. (*Gospel of Peter* 2.5)[108]

For the Johannine hypothesis, the phrase "the day before the Unleavened Bread, their feast" *(pro mias tōn azymōn tēs heortēs autōn)* means that Pilate delivered Jesus over to be crucified on 14 Nisan.[109] In light of these two pieces of external data from the Talmud and one of the patristic-era apocryphal gospels, some scholars conclude that the Last Supper was not a Passover meal.[110]

3. *Unlawful Activities on a Feast Day (15 Nisan)*

A third major argument used in support of the Johannine hypothesis is that many of the activities described in the Gospels as happening on the Friday of Jesus' execution could not possibly have taken place on the first day of Passover (15 Nisan), since that day was a solemn day of festal rest.

The primary evidence for this point comes from the Pentateuch itself. In the description of the annual feasts given in the book of Leviticus, we find a clear injunction to rest on both the first and last days of the Passover week:

> In the first month, on the fourteenth day of the month between the two evenings is the LORD's Passover. And on the fifteenth day of the same month is the feast of unleavened bread to the LORD; seven days you shall eat unleavened bread. *On the first day* you shall have a holy convocation; *you shall do no laborious work.* (Lev 23:5-7)

107. Josef Blinzler, *The Trial of Jesus* (trans. Isabel McHugh and Florence McHugh; Westminster: Newman, 1959), 76.

108. Wilhelm Schneemelcher, ed., *New Testament Apocrypha* (2 vols.; trans. R. McL. Wilson; Louisville: Westminster John Knox, 1991, 1992), 1:223.

109. Matson, "The Historical Plausibility of John's Passion Dating," 300.

110. So Dunn, *Jesus Remembered,* 772 n. 41.

The "first day" mentioned here refers to the first day of the week of unleavened bread (= 15 Nisan), which would by the first century simply be referred to as "the feast of Passover" (see discussion below). Leviticus clearly describes this as a solemn day of festal rest, upon which no laborious work is to be done.

But when we turn to the Gospel accounts of the Friday of Jesus' crucifixion, we find several key activities taking place. The most commonly cited examples are the following:

1. Purchase of a linen cloth for Jesus' shroud by Joseph of Arimathea (Mark 15:46).
2. Preparation of spices and ointments by the women followers of Jesus (Luke 23:55-56).
3. Removal from the cross and burial of Jesus' body (Matt 27:59-60; Mark 15:46; Luke 23:53-54).
4. Simon of Cyrene's coming in "from the field" (Mark 15:21; Luke 23:26).

For many advocates of the Johannine hypothesis, the argument from the amount of activity described as taking place on 15 Nisan by the Synoptics is "the most persuasive argument" against the Synoptic testimony that the Last Supper was a Passover meal.[111] As Raymond Brown argues: "The main reason for doubting this chronology is the amount of activity that the Synoptics describe as taking place on what should have been a solemn festal day."[112]

From this point of view, given the difficulties in reconciling the Synoptic testimony with the biblical prohibition of "laborious work" on 15 Nisan, it makes more sense to accept John's chronology, which has all of this activity taking place on 14 Nisan — that is, on "an ordinary day, not a holyday."[113]

4. Improbability of a Trial and Execution on Passover (15 Nisan)

The fourth major argument in support of the Johannine hypothesis is that the Jewish Sanhedrin could not have held a formal trial of Jesus and handed him over for execution on the solemn feast of Passover.

Although no such prohibition is mentioned in Jewish Scripture, advocates of the Johannine hypothesis once again appeal to rabbinic evidence

111. Brown, *The Death of the Messiah,* 2:1360. So too Meier, *A Marginal Jew,* 1:396.
112. Brown, *The Death of the Messiah,* 2:1358.
113. Brown, *The Gospel according to John,* 2:556.

from the Mishnah, which states that "none may sit in judgment" on "a Festival-day" (Mishnah, *Betzah* 5:2; cf. Tosefta *Betzah* 4:4).[114] In light of this rabbinic prohibition against having a trial on a feast day, scholars conclude that the Sanhedrin could not have tried Jesus and handed him over to be executed the night after the Passover lambs were eaten, since that day was indeed the inaugural feast day of Passover week (15 Nisan).[115] In his response to Joachim Jeremias's defense of Jesus' having been executed on the feast of Passover (which we will examine below), John Meier sums up the position eloquently:

> Despite Jeremias' deft command of the material, he cannot really establish the likelihood that, at the time of Jesus, the supreme Jewish authorities in Jerusalem would arrest a person suspected of capital crime, immediately convene a meeting of the Sanhedrin to hear the case (a case involving the death penalty), hold a formal trial of witnesses, reach a decision that the criminal deserved to die, and hand over the criminal to the Gentile authorities with a request for execution the same day — all within the night and early day hours of Passover Day, the fifteenth of Nisan! Yet this is what the Synoptic passion chronology and presentation of the Jewish "process" basically demand. In contrast, John's dating of Jesus' arrest at the beginning of the fourteenth of Nisan and his presentation of a more informal "hearing" before some Jewish officials during the night hours — while not without its own problems — does not labor under the same immense weight of historical improbability.[116]

Indeed, Amy-Jill Levine likens the practical implausibility of assembling the Jewish Sanhedrin on the same night the Passover lambs were eaten to assembling the Supreme Court on Christmas Eve![117] If this modern analogy holds, then obviously, this fourth argument for the Johannine hypothesis is perhaps the one that has had the most persuasive power in leading to the conclusion

114. It should be noted here that in this regard, scholars often cite Philo of Alexandria's statement that Jews may not "bring accusations or conduct suits of law," or "do any other of the things which are usually permitted at times which are not days of festival" (*Migration* 91). In context, however, Philo is speaking exclusively about the Sabbath; it is not exactly clear what he means when he draws the analogy with "days of festival."

115. So McKnight, *Jesus and His Death*, 269.

116. Meier, *A Marginal Jew*, 1:396; cf. also 425 n. 90.

117. Amy-Jill Levine, *The Misunderstood Jew: The Church and the Scandal of the Jewish Jesus* (San Francisco: HarperCollins, 2006), 208.

that Synoptic chronology of Jesus' arrest and execution during Passover is historically implausible, if not impossible, in a first-century Jewish context. In the words of Joseph Ratzinger (Pope Benedict XVI): "Despite all academic arguments, it seems questionable whether the trial before Pilate and crucifixion would have been permissible and possible on such an important Jewish feast day."[118]

5. *The Argument from Modern Astronomical Calculations*

The fifth and final argument for the Johannine hypothesis — and one which is particularly convincing to modern-day readers — is that contemporary astronomical calculations seem to lend scientific support to the theory that the Last Supper was not a Passover meal.

According to this position, modern-day astronomical calculations lead to the conclusion that in the most probable years of Jesus' death — A.D. 30 or 33 — it was the 14 Nisan that fell on a Friday, not 15 Nisan (as in the Synoptics).[119] Although the calculations have been made by a number of different astronomers over the years, there is fairly widespread agreement, at least since the mid-twentieth century, that, according to astronomical calculations regarding the phases of the moon, 14 Nisan would have fallen on a Friday in two of the most likely years for Jesus' crucifixion. Consider, for example, the recent calculations of the Oxford astrophysicist Graeme Waddington and Cambridge Professor of Materials Science and Metallurgy Colin Humphreys, outlined in the table on page 290, which are fairly representative.[120] It is beyond the scope of this work (not to mention my expertise) to go into the details of these calculations, much less to critique them. Presuming for the sake of argument that they are correct, and if we assume other standard chronological conclusions about the timing of Jesus' public ministry, then one can clearly see that the only

118. Ratzinger, *Jesus of Nazareth*, 2:107.

119. For discussion of the use of astronomy in this regard, see esp. Humphreys, *The Mystery of the Last Supper*, 14-25, 39-79; Hoehner, "The Chronology of Jesus," 2315-59; Meier, *A Marginal Jew*, 401-2; Brown, *The Death of the Messiah*, 1:547-56; Colin J. Humphreys and W. G. Waddington, "Astronomy and the Date of the Crucifixion," in *Chronos, Kairos, Christos: Nativity and Chronological Studies Presented to Jack Finegan* (ed. Jerry Vardaman and Edwin Yamauchi; Winona Lake: Eisenbrauns, 1989), 165-81; idem, "Dating the Crucifixion," *Nature* 306 (1983): 743-46; Jack Finegan, *Handbook of Biblical Chronology* (Princeton: Princeton University Press, 1964), 298-301; Jeremias, *The Eucharistic Words of Jesus*, 38-40.

120. Humphreys, *The Mystery of the Last Supper*, 62.

Jewish Day	Gospel Interpretation	Date (Julian Calendar)
Nisan 14	John correct.	Friday, April 11, A.D. 27 Friday, April 7, A.D. 30 Friday, April 3, A.D. 33
Nisan 15	Synoptics correct.	Friday, April 11, A.D. 27 Friday, March 26, A.D. 34 Friday, April 23, A.D. 34

years in which 15 Nisan falls on a Friday (as in the Synoptic Gospels) are A.D. 27 and A.D. 34, which would be widely regarded by specialists in the chronology of Jesus' life as too early and too late to be the year he was crucified. In the words of John Meier: "For all practical purposes, then, we are left with a choice between A.D. 30 and 33."[121] Thus, assuming the accuracy of these calculations, one is left with the conclusion that it is only the Johannine hypothesis — i.e., the theory that the Last Supper was not a Passover meal — that finds support from contemporary astronomy. For the modern mind, such scientific support, however supplementary, lends the Johannine hypothesis the appearance of being particularly airtight.

For these and other reasons, the Johannine hypothesis, in either form, is without a doubt the most popular solution to the problem of the Date of the Last Supper. It commands the assent of many commentators, historians, and theologians who write on the subject today. However, despite this substantial list of supporting arguments and advocates, when critically analyzed, the Johannine hypothesis actually suffers from some serious weaknesses. Because it is currently the most popular solution, I will take a few moments to outline these weaknesses in detail, most of which have not been sufficiently discussed in literature on the historical Jesus. Indeed, while there are numerous extensive critiques of the various other proposals, very few critical evaluations of the merits of the Johannine hypothesis have been written.

1. *The Last Supper Accounts Do Mention a Passover Lamb*

First and foremost, as C. K. Barrett demonstrated a long time ago, and as even a cursory reading of the Gospels in Greek makes clear, the widespread claim

121. Meier, *A Marginal Jew,* 1:402.

that the Synoptics do not mention a Passover lamb in their accounts of the Last Supper is simply wrong.[122]

Now, it is true that the Synoptic Gospels do not use the word "lamb" *(arnion)* with reference to the Last Supper. However, this is completely unsurprising, since in Jewish literature *arnion* was not the customary way of referring to the Passover lamb. Rather, in the Bible and early Judaism, the customary way of referring to the Passover lamb was simply to call it the "Passover," both in Hebrew *(pesaḥ)* and Greek *(pascha)* (e.g., Exod 12:1-14).[123]

Moreover — and this is critical — on at least two occasions, the Synoptics *do* refer to the Passover lamb in the context of the Last Supper. Consider the following evidence again, in which I leave the Greek word *pascha* untranslated, so that its connection with the Passover lamb is clear:

> And on the first day of Unleavened Bread, *when they sacrificed the pascha,* his disciples said to him, "Where will you have us go and prepare for you *to eat the pascha?*" (Mark 14:12)

> Then came the day of Unleavened Bread, *on which the pascha had to be sacrificed.* So Jesus sent Peter and John, saying, "Go and prepare the *pascha* for us, that we may eat it. . . ." And when the hour came, he sat at table, and the apostles with him. And he said to them, "I have earnestly desired *to eat this pascha* with you before I suffer. . . ." (Luke 22:7-8, 14-15)

According to advocates of the Johannine hypothesis, in both of these cases, although the first use of the Greek word *pascha* unequivocally refers to the Passover lambs that were "sacrificed" in the Temple (Mark 14:12; Luke 22:7), in the very next verses (and every time thereafter), the word *pascha* does not refer to a lamb, but rather somehow is meant to signify a "lambless Passover."[124]

Such exegesis is contextually indefensible. The most natural reading of the Greek text is that the first use of *pascha,* which explicitly refers to the sacrificial Passover lamb, establishes the basic sphere of meaning for those that immediately follow. Unlike many modern English translations (RSV, NAB), the Greek text does not use different terms to refer to the lambs that were sacrificed and the meal that was eaten: both of them are referred to (rightly)

122. C. K. Barrett, "Luke XXII.15: To Eat the Passover," *JTS* 9 (1958): 305-7. See also Jeremias, *The Eucharistic Words of Jesus,* 18-19.

123. Joachim Jeremias, "*pascha,*" *TDNT* 5:896-904.

124. Cf. McKnight, *Jesus and His Death,* 270, 272.

as *pascha*. After the initial reference to the sacrificial lambs (Mark 14:12; Luke 22:7), if the Synoptics had wanted to then go on to use the word *pascha* to refer to a lambless Passover meal, they would have had to make that explicit — if such a usage was even possible in first-century Judaism. Hence, when Jesus says during the Last Supper that he has "earnestly desired to eat this *pascha*" with the disciples (Luke 22:15), the burden of proof is on anyone who claims that this means "Passover-without-a-lamb." Again, the linguistic evidence is unequivocal: Jesus is sending his disciples into the city to prepare for eating the ordinary Passover meal, including the sacrificial lamb sacrificed that afternoon.[125] Any claim to the contrary only shows that the popular hypothesis that the Last Supper was not a Passover meal (or that Jesus celebrated it twenty-four hours in advance) appears to have become so deeply ingrained that the theory of a lambless Last Supper is overshadowing what the Gospel texts explicitly state.[126] In short, common though the argument may be, the suggestion that the Synoptic accounts do not mention a Passover lamb is verifiably false and should be discarded as such.

2. *The Talmud Is Not Referring to Jesus of Nazareth*

A second major problem with the Johannine hypothesis is that the ancient evidence from the Talmud that Jesus was crucified "on the eve of Passover" is historically worthless, since the rabbinic tradition in question is probably not even about Jesus of Nazareth.[127]

At first glance, the rabbinic data that Jesus was crucified "on the eve of Passover" — which is consistently cited by scholars in favor of the Johannine hypothesis — appears to give us an external Jewish witness to Jesus' crucifixion before the Passover lambs were eaten.[128] Nevertheless, as Johann Maier has shown, if one actually goes back and examines the text in its context, there are extremely strong reasons to doubt that it has anything to do with Jesus of Nazareth.[129] Consider the entire passage:

125. Jeremias, *The Eucharistic Words of Jesus*, 19.

126. E.g., Dunn, *Jesus Remembered*, 772.

127. Gnilka, *Jesus of Nazareth*, 281 n. 34.

128. E.g., Wright, *Jesus and the Victory of God*, 555; Meier, *A Marginal Jew*, 1:96-97; Brown, *The Death of the Messiah*, 2:1360.

129. See Johann Maier, *Jesus von Nazareth in der talmudischen Überlieferung* (Erträge der Forschung 82; Darmstadt: Wissenschaftliche Buchgesellschaft, 1978), 263-75. For an earlier critique, see Jeremias, *The Eucharistic Words of Jesus*, 19. In light of such discrepancies, the

> *On the eve of the Passover Yeshu was hanged. For forty days before the execution took place, a herald went forth and cried,* "He is going forth *to be stoned* because he has *practiced sorcery* and enticed Israel to apostasy. Anyone who can say anything in his favor, let him come forward and plead on his behalf." But since nothing was brought forward in his favor he was hanged on the eve of the Passover! — 'Ulla retorted: Do you suppose that he was one for whom a defense could be made? Was he not a *Mesith* [enticer], concerning whom Scripture says, "Neither shall you spare, neither shall you conceal him" [Deut 13:9]. With Yeshu however it was different, for *he was connected with the government.* Our Rabbis taught: *Yeshu had five disciples, Matthai, Nakai, Nezer, Buni, and Todah.* (Babylonian Talmud, *Sanhedrin* 43a)[130]

Using this evidence to establish the date of the Last Supper is riddled with problems. For one thing, while the first line of this text is frequently cited in part, the full text is almost never actually quoted by advocates of the Johannine hypothesis.[131] Whatever the reason for such an omission, when examined carefully, it is not the similarities but the differences between this rabbinic evidence and the Gospel claims that stand out.

In the Talmud, Yeshu's execution was preceded by "forty days" of public heralding for witnesses on his behalf. In the Gospels, Jesus' arrest and execution appears to have taken place in less than twenty-four hours. Even more striking, in the Talmud, Yeshu was "stoned" and then "hanged" after having died — a common practice in antiquity.[132] In the Gospels, Jesus is scourged and then crucified while still alive.[133] In fact, the surrounding context of the discussion in the Talmud is actually the Mishnah text about rules for execution by stoning, not crucifixion! In the Talmud, Yeshu is executed for "practicing sorcery." In the Gospels, Jesus is charged with "blasphemy" and put to death by crucifixion at the hands of the Romans (Matt 26:65-66; Mark 14:64-65; cf.

---

recent study of Peter Schäfer, *Jesus in the Talmud* (Princeton and Oxford: Princeton University Press, 2007), 63-74, wisely insists that he is focused on "the (possible) *talmudic reading* of the Gospels, not with the historical reality" (here 168-69).

130. Trans. Soncino Talmud (archaic English slightly adapted).

131. E.g., Wright, *Jesus and the Victory of God,* 555; Meier, *A Marginal Jew,* 1:96-97; Brown, *The Death of the Messiah,* 2:1360. Joseph Klausner, *Jesus of Nazareth: His Life, Times, and Teaching* (trans. Herbert Danby; New York: Macmillan, 1925), 27-30 is an exception.

132. See David W. Chapman, *Ancient Jewish and Christian Perceptions of Crucifixion* (WUNT 2.244; Tübingen: Mohr Siebeck, 2008; Grand Rapids: Baker Academic, 2010), 1-33.

133. Schäfer, *Jesus in the Talmud,* 71.

Luke 22:71).[134] In the Talmud, Yeshu was "connected with the government." In the Gospels, Jesus is a "carpenter" from a small village in Galilee (Mark 6:3), who does not appear to have any personal ties with Pontius Pilate or the Herodian family.[135] To be sure, while it is true that the Gospels claim that Jesus is a Davidide (Matt 1:1-17; Luke 3:23-38), it should go without saying that the Davidic royal family was decidedly not in power in the first century A.D. In the Talmud, Yeshu had "five disciples," all of whom were executed, at least one for murder (Nakai). In the Gospels Jesus has twelve disciples, only one of whose names even comes to close to matching the name of Yeshu's followers (Matthew) (Matt 10:1-4; Mark 3:16-19; Luke 6:14-16). Indeed, the logical gymnastics one must employ to make these names fit Jesus' disciples are in themselves an argument against identifying the Yeshu of the Talmud with Jesus of Nazareth.[136] Finally, but by no means least significantly, as Gustaf Dalman pointed out a century ago, when compared with other rabbinic evidence, the Talmud actually appears to be describing the execution of some other Jewish man named "Yeshu," who was known for his idolatry during the time of King Jannai (104-78 B.C.); this Yeshu thus may have lived over a century before Jesus himself was even born.[137]

In short, even a cursory reading of this frequently used passage from the Babylonian Talmud reveals that it provides no credible external evidence for when Jesus of Nazareth was crucified, much less whether the Last Supper was a Passover meal. The fact that major scholars continue to quote pieces of this text out of context as support for the Johannine hypothesis represents a serious failure in historical method and a prime example of how later rabbinic literature should *not* be used in Jesus research.[138] More importantly, it also constitutes a major weakness of the Johannine hypothesis. Given the close

134. Maier, *Jesus von Nazareth,* 227.

135. The attempt of Schäfer, *Jesus in the Talmud,* 72-73, to salvage the idea that "Jesus was close to the government" by interpreting John 19:12 as a reference to Pilate as Jesus' "protector" shows just how much of a stretch it is to apply this to Jesus of Nazareth.

136. See Klausner, *Jesus of Nazareth,* 27-30.

137. So Gustaf Dalman, *Jesus-Jeshua: Studies in the Gospels* (trans. P. P. Levertoff; New York: Macmillan, 1929), 89. He cites *b. Sanh.* 107b (uncensored version), which speaks of a man named Yeshu/Jesus who was the disciple of Rabbi Joshua, a contemporary of King Jannai (104-78 B.C.), and who was known for idolatrous action (which may explain the reference to his execution in *b. Sanh.* 43a). See also *b. Soṭ.* 47a.

138. Meier, *A Marginal Jew,* 1:96-97, attempts to separate the "correct information" about chronology from the more "confused" elements, but his interpretation of the text as an "apologetic" reaction to the canonical Gospels' depiction of a "twenty-four-hour period" trial and arrest is ultimately unconvincing.

attention that has been paid to ancient Jewish sources in recent years, the fact that such a dubious Talmudic text continues to be cited to reject the testimony of the Synoptic Gospels is almost breathtaking. It too should be discarded by serious scholars as historical support for the Johannine solution to the date of the Last Supper.[139]

3. The Activities in the Synoptics Were Permitted on Feast Days

Third, the argument that the activities described by the Gospels as having taken place on a feast day (15 Nisan) were unlawful is based more on modern scholarly imagination than ancient Jewish evidence. Indeed, when subjected to critical analysis, this *prima facie* reasonable objection fails on several important counts.

For one thing, proponents of this argument frequently fail to take into account the distinction in Jewish Scripture between the *absolute* prohibition of work on a Sabbath and the *lesser* prohibition of work on a feast day. Although the Torah forbids a person to engage in "any work" whatsoever on the Sabbath (Exod 20:10), it only prohibits "occupational work" or "laborious work" on a feast day.[140] This is particularly clear in the book of Leviticus when it contrasts Sabbath and Passover/Unleavened Bread:

> Six days shall work be done; but on the seventh day is a Sabbath of solemn rest; a holy convocation; *you shall do no work (kol mela'kah);* it is a Sabbath

139. To be fair, it remains true that the extracanonical *Gospel of Peter* does state that Pilate delivered Jesus over to be crucified "on the day before the unleavened bread, their feast" (*Gos. Pet.* 2.5), presumably a reference to 14 Nisan. But as we saw above, similar evidence can be marshaled from the patristic era that Jesus did eat the Lamb at the Last Supper and that he was crucified on 15 Nisan *(Chronicon Paschale).* The conflicting patristic evidence seriously undermines the weight of any extracanonical references. At the very least, it seems problematic (if not inconsistent) for scholars to lean too heavily on a single reference in the apocryphal *Gospel of Peter,* not usually treated by Jesus researchers as a bastion of historically reliable information.

140. For the importance of this distinction, see esp. Jacob Milgrom, *Leviticus: A New Translation with Introduction and Commentary* (3 vols.; AB 3, 3A, 3B; New York: Doubleday, 1991, 2000, 2001), 1977-78. So too Victor Hamilton, *Handbook on the Pentateuch* (Grand Rapids: Baker Academic, 2005), 194: "In contrast to the days of public sacrifices when laborious or heavy work *(mele'ket 'abodah)* is forbidden (Num. 28:18, 25, 26; 29:1), only on the Sabbath and Yom Kippur/Day of Atonement is no work at all to be done *(kol mela'ka).* See Num. 29:7 and Lev. 23:3, 28." George Buchanan Gray, *Sacrifice in the Old Testament: Its Theory and Practice* (New York: Ktav, 1971 [orig. 1925]), 386.

> to the LORD in all your dwellings. . . . On the fifteenth day of the same month is the feast of unleavened bread. On the first day you shall have a holy convocation; *you shall do no laborious work (mele'keth 'abodah).* (Lev 23:3, 6-7; see Num 28:18)

Significantly, Jewish Scripture nowhere makes clear exactly what the difference is between "no work" whatsoever and "no laborious work" or "servile work." What is clear, however, is that "[o]ne can only speak of a feast day possessing the character of a Sabbath to a limited extent."[141] Moreover, the Pentateuchal distinction between no work whatsoever (Sabbath) and no laborious work (feast day) continues into the Second Temple period, where it is present in the Dead Sea Scrolls' most detailed description of the Passover feast:

> The fifteenth day of this month there will be a ho[ly] assembly. In it you shall do no laborious work *(ml'kth 'bwdah).* It is the feast of unleavened breads, during seven days, for YHWH. . . . The seventh day [there will be a solemn assembly] for [YH]WH. On it you shall do no laborious work *(ml'kth 'bwdah).* (*11QTemple*[a] [11Q19] 17:10-11, 15)

Eventually, this Pentateuchal and early Jewish distinction between different kinds of prohibited labor ultimately leads to a situation where even into the rabbinic period, there is a longstanding debate among observant Jews about exactly what kind of activities were permitted on a feast day as opposed to a Sabbath. In this regard, E. P. Sanders makes an extremely significant point in his study of Second Temple Judaism:

> [T]he debate on which there are more surviving Pharisaic opinions than any other concerns what work could be done "on a festival day."[142]

Indeed, an entire tractate of the Mishnah is devoted to cataloguing the many different opinions among the rabbinic sages themselves about this question (see tractate *Betzah*). Even in this regard, we have no certainty that the later regulations described by the rabbis were actually in force in the first century A.D. and, if they were, which groups followed them.[143] In light of this situation,

141. Jeremias, *The Eucharistic Words of Jesus*, 75.

142. E. P. Sanders, *Judaism: Practice and Belief* 63 BCE–66 CE (London: SCM; Philadelphia: Trinity Press International, 1992), 425.

143. Blinzler, *The Trial of Jesus*, 149-63.

at the very least, historians should be cautious in their claims regarding what kind of work was forbidden on a feast day.

Moreover, scholars who claim that the Gospels' description of the activities taking place on the Passover is historically incredible invariably make this case without citing any explicit early Jewish evidence that what the Synoptic Gospels describe could not have taken place on the feast day of Passover. (The primary exception is the question of Jesus' trial, which I will deal with below.) Arguments given for this view tend not to be based on objective evidence but on what the scholar is personally able to envision. This point of view was given a classic expression when Eduard Schweizer wrote in his influential essay on the Lord's Supper:

> The execution of Jesus on Passover day is *not impossible,* although it is *hard to imagine.*[144]

Many advocates of the Johannine hypothesis have followed Schweizer's lead in his argument, claiming that the Gospel chronology of Jesus' being executed on the feast of Passover (15 Nisan) is "hard to imagine";[145] it "seems highly implausible";[146] it labors under "the immense weight of historical improbability."[147] On the other hand, it is claimed that the execution of Jesus on the day the lambs were sacrificed (14 Nisan) is "much more credible"[148] and "seems more plausible."[149] Even John Meier, who is well known for his exhaustive study of Second Temple texts, does not cite any early Jewish evidence to support his claim that "the whole chain of events" described by the Gospels could not have taken place on Passover day. Rather he simply states: "I think that John presents the more historically probable scenario."[150] In each of these scholars, the Johannine hypothesis does not rest upon primary source evidence but on the subjective evaluation ("I think") of what the scholar is able to imagine. To be sure, there is nothing inherently wrong with subjective reasoning — each scholar can only view the evidence from his or her respective vantage point. Nevertheless, it should give one pause to recognize that with regard to the activities accomplished on a feast day, supporters of the Johannine hypothesis

144. Schweizer, *The Lord's Supper according to the New Testament,* 31 (emphasis added).
145. Fredriksen, *Jesus of Nazareth,* 223.
146. Brown, *The Death of the Messiah,* 2:1358.
147. Meier, *A Marginal Jew,* 1:396.
148. Fredriksen, *Jesus of Nazareth,* 223.
149. Brown, *The Gospel according to John,* 2:556.
150. Meier, *A Marginal Jew,* 1:425 n. 90.

consistently fail to accompany their skepticism with any concrete evidence against the claims in the Gospels.

Perhaps most significant of all, while advocates of the Johannine hypothesis appeal to rabbinic evidence for the importance of the rest associated with a feast day (*m. Betz.* 5:2, cited above), at the same time, they consistently either ignore or dismiss other rabbinic evidence that certain activities described by the Gospels were in fact permitted on Sabbath days, and, *a fortiori,* on feast days.[151] For example, the Gospels describe Joseph of Arimathea purchasing a shroud for Jesus' burial on the feast day (Mark 15:46). Although the Mishnah requires that such a purchase wait until the very end of the day, it permits the acquisition of a coffin or shroud on the Sabbath:

> They may await nightfall at the Sabbath limit to see to the business of [the reception of] a bride or of [the burial of] a corpse, *to fetch its coffin and wrappings.* (Mishnah, *Shabbat* 23:4)[152]

In a similar vein, the Gospels describe the women preparing ointments for Jesus' burial on the day of Passover (Luke 23:55-56). According to the Mishnah, such preparations are also permitted for the dead, even on the Sabbath:

> [On the Sabbath] *they may make ready all that is needful for the dead,* to anoint it and wash it, provided they do not move any member of it. (Mishnah, *Shabbat* 23:5)

Note this well: if preparations for the dead could be made during the solemn rest of a Sabbath, then *a fortiori* they would have been permissible on a feast day. The same point holds true for the removal of Jesus' body from the cross and his subsequent entombment (Matt 27:59-60; Mark 15:46; Luke 23:53-54). This is easily explained, even on a feast day, as obedience to the biblical command that anyone "hang[ed] on a tree" must be buried "the same day" (Deut 21:23).

151. See Jeremias, *The Eucharistic Words of Jesus,* 74-79; Dalman, *Jesus-Jeshua,* 93-106, for a complete list.

152. It is also possible, too, that under necessity Joseph simply left some kind of surety with the seller of the shroud, with the intention of squaring away after the feast day. The Mishnah allows for this possibility as well, and explicitly connects it with Passover. "So, too, in Jerusalem on the eve of Passover when it falls on a Sabbath, a man may leave his cloak and take his Passover-lamb and make his reckoning with the seller after the close of the Festival-day" (Mishnah, *Shabbat* 23:1).

Finally, even the description of Simon of Cyrene coming in "from the field" (Mark 15:21; Luke 23:26) on the morning of Jesus' crucifixion can be plausibly explained. In this instance, it is true that rabbinic literature prohibits work in the fields, either on a Sabbath or feast day, since such work would obviously fall under the category of "laborious work."[153] However, as Adela Yarbro Collins notes: "the statement in [Mark] 15:21 that Simon was coming *ap' agrou* could be translated 'from the country' as well as 'from the fields.' In the former case, work is not necessarily implied."[154] In support of this point, compare a similar use of the word "field" *(agros)* in the longer ending of Mark:

> After this [Jesus] appeared in another form to two of them, as they were journeying to the field/to the country *(eis agron)*. (Mark 16:12)

If this is, as is commonly thought, an abbreviated summary of the story of Jesus' appearance to the two disciples on the road out of Jerusalem to Emmaus (Luke 24:13-35), then the phrase "to the field" does not mean that the two disciples were headed out of Jerusalem to a hard day of agricultural labor. Rather, it only indicates that they were going from the city to the country. Taken in this way, the Gospel reference to Simon of Cyrene coming in *ap' agrou* means that he was coming in "from outside the city."[155] This interpretation is especially plausible when we consider the time of Simon's arrival in Jerusalem. As Gustaf Dalman once quipped:

> In the Gospel narrative, it was not in the evening but in the morning before nine o'clock that Simon came (cf. Mk. xv. 25), a time when no one goes home from work in the field.[156]

More recently, Joachim Gnilka makes the same point:

> Certain difficulties that one encounters in opting for the synoptic dating are easily removed, namely, that Simon of Cyrene comes in from the country (Mark 15:21). . . . Simon does not come from work in the country at this time of day.[157]

153. See *Jub.* 1:8; *b. 'Erub.* 38b; Dalman, *Jesus-Jeshua,* 100-101.
154. Adela Yarbro Collins, *Mark* (Hermeneia; Minneapolis: Fortress, 2007), 624.
155. Jeremias, *The Eucharistic Words of Jesus,* 77.
156. Dalman, *Jesus-Jeshua,* 100-101.
157. Gnilka, *Jesus of Nazareth,* 281 n. 34.

The point is well taken: I for one am inclined to doubt that Simon was coming in from a hard day's work in the field at nine o'clock in the morning. The more likely explanation of the Gospel description is that Simon, like other Jews, is coming in from outside the city, perhaps on his way to the Temple for morning prayer at the third hour (Acts 3:1) or perhaps coming in to the Temple to offer the festal sacrifice that was customary during the feast of Unleavened Bread, especially on 15 Nisan.[158]

In short, when examined carefully, the activities described by the Gospels as happening on the day of Jesus' execution, often described as implausible (or even impossible), can in fact be accounted for when the distinction between Sabbath rest and rest on a feast day is taken into account. Though a major proponent of the Johannine hypothesis, Raymond Brown is forced to admit:

> One can find indications in Jewish tradition allowing *every one of these actions* [described in the Synoptics] on a feast.[159]

If Brown and Sanders are correct, and there was more rabbinic debate about work and rest on a feast day than any other area, and rabbinic tradition contains permissions for every one of the actions described by the Synoptics, then the argument from the historical implausibility of the activities described by the Gospel narratives is far from the "most compelling" argument for the Johannine hypothesis. Indeed, on closer inspection, it looks as if it is almost a figment of modern imagination. Indeed, perhaps this is why at least three of the four evangelists, who actually lived in the first-century A.D., saw no problem whatsoever in describing these various activities as taking place on 15 Nisan, the beginning of the feast of Unleavened Bread.

4. Rabbinic Tradition Requires False Prophets to Be Executed during Festivals

Fourth, there is the argument that Jesus could not have been tried and executed on a feast day because the Mishnah forbids "sitting in judgment" during a festival (*Betzah* 5:2). Of all the ostensibly impossible activities described by the Gospels as occurring on the feast of Passover, it is the trial and execution of Jesus during Passover that is widely considered the decisive argument against

158. Jeremias, *The Eucharistic Words of Jesus,* 77.

159. Brown, *The Death of the Messiah,* 2:1358 (emphasis added).

the Last Supper having been a Passover meal. Yet, like some of the other arguments we have analyzed in favor of the Johannine hypothesis, scholars who make this claim consistently take rabbinic evidence that favors their position out of context and ignore rabbinic evidence against the theory.

Consider for example the evidence from the Mishnah that is consistently cited to show that it would have been impossible for the Sanhedrin to try Jesus on a feast day (*m. Betz.* 5:2). As with the earlier passage from the Talmud, this teaching is usually quoted in brief (if at all) and then treated as a first-century rule that would have bound the members of the Jerusalem Sanhedrin, whether or not they were Pharisees, Sadducees, or of some other Jewish persuasion. However, when we actually go back to the Mishnah itself and read the text in its context, we find that *the rabbinic teaching against sitting in judgment on a feast day has nothing to do with the great Sanhedrin in Jerusalem, much less with a public case of capital punishment.* Rather, the surrounding context clearly suggests that the rabbis are giving an opinion on the ordinary kind of judicial activities such as betrothals and levirate marriage rituals that would be carried out by local judges but which, on feast days, should be avoided:

> Any act that is culpable on a Sabbath, whether by virtue of the rules concerning Sabbath rest *(shebuth)* or concerning acts of choice *(reshuth)* or concerning pious duties *(mitzvah),* is culpable also on a Festival-day *(yom tob).* And these [acts are culpable] by virtue of the rules concerning Sabbath rest *(shebuth):* none may climb a tree or ride a beast or swim on water or clap the hands or slap the thighs or stamp with the feet. And these [acts are culpable] by virtue of the rules concerning acts of choice *(reshuth): none may sit in judgment* or conclude a betrothal or perform *halitzah*[160] or contract levirate marriage. And these [acts are culpable] by virtue of the rules concerning pious duties *(mitzvah):* none may dedicate aught or make a vow of Valuation or devote aught or set apart Heave-offering or Tithes. All these things have they prescribed [as culpable] on a Festival-day: still more so [are they culpable] on the Sabbath. A Festival-day differs from the Sabbath in naught save in the preparing of needful food. (Mishnah, *Betzah* 5:2)

Note here that the immediate context of the prohibition against sitting in judgment is clearly a technical rabbinic discussion of what kinds of activities

160. "The ceremony prescribed (Deut. 25.7ff) when a man refuses to contract levirate marriage, i.e. to marry his deceased, childless brother's widow (Deut. 25.5-6)." Danby, *The Mishnah,* 187 n. 4.

the "Sages . . . have forbidden on the Sabbath."[161] This alone should make us extremely cautious about assuming that these particular opinions of the sages were in force in Jerusalem in the first-century A.D., as do advocates of the Johannine hypothesis. Moreover, in this passage from the Mishnah, there are three different kinds of prohibited actions:

1. Acts of Sabbath rest *(shebuth),*
2. Acts of choice *(reshuth),* and
3. Simple pious duties *(mitzvah).*[162]

Strikingly, the prohibition against sitting in judgment — which the Johannine hypothesis treats as if it is a universal law — is specifically ascribed to the second category, "acts of choice." These are apparently of even a lesser weight than the prohibitions against clapping one's hands, slapping the thighs, and dancing! Clearly, such a text has everything to do with the opinions of the rabbis and very little to do with what the great Sanhedrin in Jerusalem could or could not do during a feast with regard to a case of capital punishment. As with the death of Yeshu on "the eve of the Sabbath," we seem once again to have before us a situation in which New Testament scholars are citing rabbinic evidence against the first-century testimony of the Gospels without closely examining what the rabbinic text is actually about. It is stunning that such sloppy recourse to the rabbis continues to figure even in prominent scholarship favoring the Johannine hypothesis. One wonders if scholars are even going back and reading the Mishnaic text before arguing that the Synoptics depict something historically impossible.

However, when we turn to what the rabbis do say about the Sanhedrin and cases of capital punishment, we find something quite significant for our study of the date of the Last Supper. In the tractate on the Sanhedrin, rabbinic literature actually requires certain kinds of criminals to be executed *during the feasts* of Passover, Pentecost, and/or Tabernacles, so that Jewish pilgrims would be able to see them die.[163] Consider the following teaching from the Tosefta, regarding crimes such as false prophecy, apostasy, and perjury:

161. Philip Blackman, *Mishnayoth* (6 vols.; New York: Judaica, 1963), 2:372 n. 3.

162. Philip Blackman defines *shebuth* as a technical rabbinic term for "rest" meaning "abstention from secular work or pursuit" because it is "out of keeping with the importance, dignity, and observance of the holyday." Blackman, *Mishnayoth,* 2:517.

163. Jeremias, *The Eucharistic Words of Jesus,* 78-79; Dalman, *Jesus-Jeshua,* 98-100.

> A rebellious and incorrigible son, a defiant elder, one who leads people astray to worship idols, one who leads a town to apostasy, *a false prophet,* and perjured witnesses — they do not kill them immediately. *But they bring them up to the court in Jerusalem and keep them until the festival,* and *then they put them to death on the festival,* as it is said, "And all the peoples shall hear and fear, and no more do presumptuously" (Deut 17:13). The words of Rabbi ʿAquiba. (Tosefta, *Sanhedrin* 11:7)[164]

Strikingly, this evidence from the Tosefta is consistently either ignored or dismissed by scholars who claim that it was "illegal" or impossible for the Sanhedrin to have Jesus executed on the feast of Passover.[165] Nevertheless, the tradition is clearly describing the Second Temple period, since it envisions a time when pilgrims would still go up to the Temple in Jerusalem to sacrifice at the major festivals — something which was no longer possible after the destruction of Jerusalem in A.D. 70. Indeed, this is not the only evidence we have for the idea that certain criminals should be executed during festivals (*m. Sanh.* 11:4-5; *b. Sanh.* 89a; *Sifre* on Deut 17:3 [105a]). Last, but certainly not least, the idea that certain criminals should be executed during festivals is not mere rabbinic opinion, but is directly based on Jewish Scripture, taken from the teaching in Deuteronomy regarding the trial and execution of serious criminals by the priestly leaders in cases of grave "evil" (see Deut 17:2-13).

Now, I want to stress here that I am not claiming that the first-century Sanhedrin necessarily followed this teaching recorded in the Tosefta. What I am suggesting, however, is that *the very existence of an ancient Jewish tradition that required a "false prophet" to be kept "until the festival" for public execution before the people demolishes the widespread assertion that it would have been unthinkable for the Sanhedrin to have Jesus executed during Passover.* At least some early rabbis not only thought it possible; they also thought the Mosaic teaching on capital punishment in Deuteronomy 17 required it. Once again, perhaps this is why the Synoptic Gospels writers — who are very familiar with first-century Judaism — do not hesitate to claim that the Sanhedrin tried Jesus and handed him over to be executed on the 15th of Nisan, the first day of Passover week.[166] Indeed, in light of this evidence, advocates of the Johannine

164. Unless otherwise noted, all translations of the Tosefta contained herein are from Jacob Neusner, *The Tosefta* (2 vols.; Peabody, MA: Hendrickson, 2002).

165. E.g., Levine, *The Misunderstood Jew,* 208; McKnight, *Jesus and His Death,* 269.

166. As Dalman, *Jesus-Jeshua,* 98-99, points out, the members of the Sanhedrin do not say that they want to avoid arresting Jesus during the feast because it would be against the law, but because they were afraid of the crowds (Matt 26:5; Mark 14:2; Luke 22:2).

hypothesis find themselves unable to refute the fact that "it was not impossible for a criminal to be executed on a feast day."[167] If this is true, then the now-popular argument that it would have been "unthinkable" for Jesus to be executed on a feast day should no longer be used as an argument against the Last Supper being a Jewish Passover meal.

5. *Rabbinic Tradition Also Prohibits Trials on the* Eve *of a Feast Day*

Fifth, it is ironic that while advocates of the Johannine hypothesis frequently use the rabbinic tradition against "sitting in judgment" on a feast day against the Synoptic chronology (e.g., 15 Nisan) (*m. Betz.* 5:2) — even though it has nothing to do with capital cases of the Sanhedrin in Jerusalem — they often fail to point out that the same rabbinic tradition actually does prohibit trials on the *eve* of a feast day: i.e., the day on which, according to Johannine theory, Jesus was tried and put to death.

Indeed, when we turn to the Mishnah tractate on the Sanhedrin, what we find regarding trials on the eve of a feast day poses a direct challenge to the Johannine hypothesis:

> In non-capital cases the verdict, whether of acquittal or of conviction, may be reached the same day; in capital cases a verdict of acquittal may be reached on the same day, but a verdict of conviction not until the following day. Therefore *trials may not be held* on the eve of a Sabbath *or on the eve of a Festival-day.* (Mishnah *Sanhedrin* 4:1)[168]

This evidence poses a significant problem for scholars who want to cite the rabbinic literature against the Synoptic chronology but still hold on to the claim that Jesus was tried by the Sanhedrin on the evening before the lambs were sacrificed (14 Nisan). To be sure, some scholars attempt to minimize the impact of this evidence by pointing out that John's Gospel does not narrate a "formal trial" anyway.[169] Nevertheless, they are still left with the problematic description of Jesus having some kind of formal meeting with the high priests Annas and/or Caiaphas before being officially handed over by Jewish leaders to

167. Meier, *A Marginal Jew,* 1:396.

168. Cf. *b. Sanh.* 35a for similar data.

169. E.g., Matson, "The Historical Plausibility of John's Passion Dating," 309-10; Meier, *A Marginal Jew,* 1:425.

Pilate to be executed on the eve of a feast (John 18:13-14, 19-24, 28). Moreover, according to the Johannine hypothesis, all this interaction with the Jewish priests is supposed to take place on the morning when these same priests would be immersed in preparations for the largest sacrificial celebration in the Temple of the entire liturgical year: the sacrifice of thousands of Passover lambs in a single afternoon (see chapter 5 for further details). Indeed, in this regard, one cannot help but wonder if the Synoptic testimony is actually more believable, since the arrest, hearings, and execution of Jesus would have taken place after the Jewish high priests and leaders were finished engaging in the labor intensive sacrifices of 14 Nisan in the Temple.

In any case, the upshot is that the invocation of rabbinic rules regarding the Sanhedrin is a double-edged sword for the Johannine hypothesis: its claim that Jesus was tried and sentenced to death on the eve of the feast of Passover (14 Nisan) is in fact just as problematic as the claim that he was tried and executed on the feast day itself (15 Nisan). As Raymond Brown admits:

> It may be false to suppose that the 14th of Nisan, the day when the lambs were being sacrificed in the temple area, was not a festal day. Even if it was looked on purely as the "preparation day for the Passover" (John 19:14), according to later Jewish law . . . *some of the activities would be forbidden on the eve of a feast day as well, e.g., a Jewish trial for a capital offense.* We are not certain, however, how much of this highly protective attitude toward legalities was in effect in the 1st cent[ury].[170]

I agree with Brown that we should not assume that the later rabbinic rules regarding the Sanhedrin were in place in the first century. However, this is precisely the assumption that is used to argue against the Synoptic depiction of Jesus being put to death on 15 Nisan. Indeed, as we saw above, the argument that the trial and execution of Jesus on 15 Nisan would have been "unlawful" is considered the "most decisive" argument against the Synoptic testimony.

Obviously, there is a need for a more critical and consistent treatment of rabbinic evidence about when capital cases could take place by advocates of the Johannine hypothesis. Either all four Gospel accounts of Jesus' passion and death are unhistorical because they go against later rabbinic rules, or these rabbinic rules were not being followed by the great Sanhedrin in the first century. In this regard, it seems to me that we have at least four witnesses — the four Gospels — that constitute first-century evidence that hearings and an

170. Brown, *The Death of the Messiah,* 2:1361 (emphasis added).

execution could take place on the eve of a feast day or on the feast day itself (i.e., 14 or 15 Nisan). In this case, in other words, we have grounds from the Gospels themselves to conclude that the Mishnah is describing rabbinic teachings that do not appear to have been in force among the Jerusalem Sanhedrin in the first century A.D.[171]

Once again, perhaps this is why the Synoptic Gospels show no awareness of the supposedly impossible conflict between the actions of the people on the night of 15 Nisan and Jewish law and custom. Perhaps it is not the Gospels that are ignorant of first-century Jewish custom, but we who are in error in assuming there was a conflict. As one scholar puts it: "The Synoptic narratives are in conflict with Jewish custom, though without displaying the least consciousness of the fact."[172]

6. No Evidence for a "Lambless" Passover Meal in the Second Temple Period

A sixth major argument against the Johannine hypothesis applies only to the second form of the theory, according to which the Last Supper was a "quasi-Passover meal" that took place twenty-four hours in advance of the ordinary Jewish Passover.[173] N. T. Wright sums up this view well when he writes:

> [W]e have no reason to suppose, granted all that we have seen of Jesus' agenda and normal way of operating, that he would have felt bound to celebrate the [Passover] festival on the officially appointed day. . . . [T]here is no reason to suppose that Jesus might not have celebrated what we might call a *quasi*-Passover meal a day ahead of the real thing. This, of course, would have meant doing without a lamb (since the priests would not be killing them for Passover until the following day); that would be no bar to treating the meal as a proper Passover. . . . Granted that Jesus had, throughout his work, reorganized the symbolic world of his contemporaries around his own life and mission, it certainly does not strain credulity to think that he might organize *a special quasi-Passover meal* a day early.[174]

171. See Blinzler, *The Trial of Jesus,* 149-57.

172. Gray, *Sacrifice in the Old Testament,* 390.

173. Ratzinger, *Jesus of Nazareth,* 113-15; McKnight, *Jesus and His Death,* 272-73; Pitre, *Jesus, the Tribulation, and the End of the Exile,* 441-42; Wright, *Jesus and the Victory of God,* 556-59; Evans, *Mark 8:27–16:20,* 371-72.

174. Wright, *Jesus and the Victory of God,* 556 (emphasis added).

Although at first glance this seems like a very reasonable argument — I myself once held this view — when it is held up to the realities of Jewish law and Temple liturgy, there are several serious problems with this version of the Johannine hypothesis.

Above all, the celebration of Passover on the appointed day of 14 Nisan was not just a "scribal rule" from which Jesus could demur if he saw fit.[175] Rather, it was the divinely revealed law of God, given to Israel through the hand of the prophet Moses. Seven times the Mosaic Torah explicitly commands that the Passover lamb be sacrificed on 14 Nisan (Exod 12:6, 18; Lev 23:5; Num 9:3, 5, 11; 28:16), with no allowance made for a "private" act of keeping the feast in advance.[176] Indeed, the book of Numbers clearly states that the Passover must be kept on 14 Nisan, the appointed day:

> And the LORD spoke to Moses in the wilderness of Sinai. . . . "Let the sons of Israel *keep the Passover at its appointed time.* On the fourteenth day of the month, in the evening, you shall keep it *at its appointed time;* according to all its statutes and ordinances you shall keep it." (Num 9:1-3)

Nor can appeal here be made to the biblical concession that Israelites in a state of ritual impurity may keep the Passover one month later, on the 14th of Iyar (Num 9:9-13).[177] According to the Johannine hypothesis, Jesus celebrates the Passover a day in advance, not a month behind. Moreover, the only allowance for such a shift in date is a case of ritual impurity. Most importantly, even in the case of the later date, Jewish Scripture still requires the sacrifice and consumption of a lamb: "they shall eat it with the unleavened bread and bitter herbs" and not "break a bone of it" (Num 9:11-12).

Moreover, advocates of the twenty-four-hour-in-advance Passover are forced to theorize that Jesus celebrated the "Passover" meal without a lamb. The problem with this proposal is that there is absolutely no basis for asserting

175. So R. T. France, *The Gospel of Matthew* (NICNT; Grand Rapids: Eerdmans, 2007), 985, following Wright, *Jesus and the Victory of God,* 556.

176. Contra France, *The Gospel of Matthew,* 985 n. 18, who uses the analogy of having a birthday or Christmas party one night in advance. This is not only anachronistic, but reflects a deep misunderstanding of the solemn nature of liturgical events. By their very nature, the annual feasts of ancient Judaism were communal events, not "private" occasions that people could keep whenever they wished. A more accurate contemporary analogy would be the celebration of Easter vigil Mass on Friday night rather than Saturday, which would be, in a Catholic context, unthinkable.

177. As does Wright, *Jesus and the Victory of God,* 556.

that in the Second Temple period "a lambless meal can be Pesaḥ."[178] And to be sure, proponents of this theory can cite no ancient evidence to support this claim. More recently, in his full-length study of the ancient Jewish Passover, Baruch Bokser concedes:

> Despite the probability that some Jews who lacked access to a paschal sacrifice felt the need to do something on Passover eve, none of the pre-rabbinic accounts of the celebration mentions a meal without a sacrifice.[179]

Even less plausible is the idea that the Temple priests in Jerusalem would have permitted Jesus' disciples to sacrifice their Passover lamb twenty-four hours ahead of schedule. As Joachim Jeremias rightly observes: "There is no evidence that passover lambs were ever slaughtered on two consecutive days in the Temple, and it seems most unlikely that such a thing ever could have happened."[180]

In short, the second form of the Johannine hypothesis that postulates a lambless "Passover" meal twenty-four hours before the actual feast day is contradicted by the Mosaic Torah, the historical practice of ancient Judaism, and the Synoptic Gospels. The only reason scholars propose such a notion is based on the attempt to reconcile the apparent discrepancy between the Synoptic and Johannine chronologies. Despite its initial appeal, on closer inspection, the idea of an anticipatory, lambless "Passover" meal should be deemed historically implausible if not impossible in a first-century Jewish context.

7. Modern Astronomy Cannot Determine Ancient Jewish Calendar Dates

The seventh and final argument against the Johannine hypothesis regards the use of astronomical calculations to support the conclusion that Jesus died on Friday, 14 Nisan in A.D. 30 or 33. At first glance, this procedure seems extremely reasonable, providing a contemporary scientific corroboration for this scholarly solution to the date of the Last Supper. However, as experts in ancient calendars agree, and as Roger Beckwith has recently argued in detail, contemporary astronomical calculations cannot be used to solve the problem of the date of the Last Supper, for two main reasons.[181]

178. So McKnight, *Jesus and His Death*, 272.

179. Baruch M. Bokser, *The Origins of the Seder* (Berkeley: University of California Press, 1984), 53, 54.

180. Jeremias, *The Eucharistic Words of Jesus*, 23-24.

181. See esp. Roger T. Beckwith, "The Date of the Crucifixion: The Misuse of Calendars

First and foremost, as far as we can tell, *the ancient Jewish lunar festal calendar was based on human observation, not astronomical calculation.* As Beckwith notes: "Jewish months, years, and festivals were fixed not by calculation in advance but by continuous observation. The beginning of each month was announced when the new moon was sighted in Palestine."[182] The most ancient and detailed description of this process that we possess can be found in the Mishnah tractate on the New Year, which describes how the new moons of each liturgical month were established "while the Temple still stood" — i.e., in the first century A.D.:

> *Because of six New Moons do messengers go forth* [to proclaim the time of their appearing]: *because of Nisan, to determine the time of Passover,* because of Ab, to determine the time of the Fast, because of Elul, to determine the New Year; because of Tishri, to determine aright the set feasts; because of Chislev, to determine the time of [the feast of] the Dedication; and because of Adar, to determine the time of Purim. *And while the Temple still stood they went forth also because of Iyyar, to determine the time of the Lesser Passover.* Because of two New Moons may the Sabbath be profaned: [the New Moon] of Nisan and [the New Moon] of Tishri, *for on them messengers used to go forth to Syria, and by them the set feasts were determined.* And while the Temple still stood the Sabbath might also be profaned because of any of the New Moons, to determine aright the time of the offerings. *Whether [the New Moon] was manifestly visible or not,* they may profane the Sabbath because of it. Rabbi Jose says: If it was manifestly visible they may not profane the Sabbath because of it. . . . If it was a far journey enduring a night and a day they may profane the Sabbath and go forth to bear witness about the New Moon, for it is written, "These are the set feasts of the Lord, even holy convocations which ye shall proclaim in their appointed seasons" (Lev 23:4). (Mishnah, *Rosh Hashanah* 1:1-5, 9)

Several aspects of this evidence are worth highlighting. First, notice that the determination of the time of the Passover feast (as with all the other feasts) is completely based on whether or not the new moon is "manifestly visible or

---

and Astronomy to Determine the Chronology of the Passion," in *Calendar and Chronology, Jewish and Christian: Biblical, Intertestamental, and Patristic Studies* (Leiden: Brill, 2001), 276-96.

182. Beckwith, "The Misuse of Calendars," 187.

not." Second, as a reading of the entire tractate makes even clearer, notice also that the determination of the time of the Passover was based on the official proclamation of the "messengers" who would be sent throughout the land, not on any astronomical calculations. Third, notice also that the Mishnah is consciously distinguishing between the present and the time while "the Temple still stood." It thereby roots this practice of establishing feast days by lunar observation in the first century.

The reason all of this is important is simple: if, while the Temple still stood, the official dates of the monthly festivals — starting with the Passover — were determined by observation of the new moon and not by calculation, *then this means that there was always at least a forty-eight-hour margin of error involved in the determination of the beginning of the month.* For the moon could on any given day be obscured by atmospheric conditions for at least twenty-four hours before becoming visible.[183] As John Meier, himself a proponent of the Johannine hypothesis, rightly admits:

> [S]ome exegetes call upon the insights of astronomy to calculate in which years — within the range of A.D. 29-34 — the fourteenth of Nisan fell on a Friday. At first glance, the use of science to solve this problem of biblical chronology looks very promising; but there is more than one obstacle to a clear scientific solution. (1) In the official lunar calendar, the new month (e.g., Nisan) was declared on the evening of the twenty-ninth day of the old month *if* two trustworthy eyewitnesses could attest to the calendar commission in Jerusalem that they had seen the new light of the new moon after sunset. The declaration therefore depended not on whether the new light actually existed, but on whether human beings had seen it. Clouds, rain, dust, and other atmospheric disturbances of which we cannot now be sure could have delayed the sighting of the new light. This difficulty was mitigated somewhat by the rule that months could be neither shorter than twenty-nine days nor longer than thirty. *Hence the delay was only one day at most.*[184]

183. Even Humphreys, *The Mystery of the Last Supper,* 50, who is very confident about his astronomical calculations, has to admit beneath his chart of possible dates: "Nisan 14 AD 27 and AD 32 could have been on the following day if the new moon was not detected owing to poor atmospheric transparency." This is one of the main problems with the solution given by Humphreys, *The Mystery of the Last Supper.* He gives far too much weight to his astronomical calculations and too little to reconciling his theory with the actual accounts of Jesus' passion in the Gospels.

184. Meier, *A Marginal Jew,* 1:401-2 (emphasis added).

Notice here the variable of "one day at most" in any and all calculations. It should go without saying that one cannot solve the twenty-four-hour discrepancy in the date of the Last Supper by using astronomical calculations that have precisely this margin of error! This fact alone renders all arguments from astronomical calculation completely useless. We simply cannot ever know whether the modern-day calculations of the calendar days match the first-century Jewish observations of the liturgical calendars at the time of Jesus.

Second, and even more devastating, any use of astronomical calculation must be based on some system of intercalation, which harmonizes the disjunction between the 365-day solar calendar and the 354-day lunar cycle (as does our modern "leap year"). And yet, we have no idea whether and when first-century Jews intercalated their solar and lunar calendars in any given year.[185] Moreover, what evidence we do possess suggests that the *system of intercalation was based on changing seasonal and agricultural conditions,* which could be different in any given year, and about which astronomical calculations can tell us nothing.[186] Compare the following evidence, noting in particular the first quotation, which is ascribed to the first-century Rabbi Gamaliel:

> [Rabbi Gamaliel said:] May your peace be great for ever! We beg to inform you that the turtledoves are still tender and the lambs too thin and that the first-ripe grain has not yet appeared. It seems advisable to me and my colleagues to add thirty days to this year. (Tosefta, *Sanhedrin* 2:5-6)

> A year may be intercalated on three grounds: on account of the premature state of the corn-crops; or that of the fruit-trees; or the lateness of the *tekuphah* [= new season]. On the basis of any two of these they may intercalate, but no one only." (Tosefta, *Sanhedrin* 2:2; cf. *b. Sanh.* 11b)[187]

> He used to say: "In that the turtledoves are still tender and the spring-lambs too thin, it is advisable in my opinion to add thirty days to this year." (Babylonian Talmud, *Sanhedrin* 11a-b)[188]

Once again, if this evidence is in any way reflective of how the lunar calendar in the Second Temple period was regulated, then the upshot is that we have no way

185. See esp. Saulnier, *Calendrical Variations in Second Temple Judaism,* 244-45.
186. Beckwith, "The Misuse of Calendars," 189-98.
187. Cited in Beckwith, "The Misuse of Calendars," 192.
188. Cited in Beckwith, "The Misuse of Calendars," 190, 191.

of telling whether our astronomical calculations match the observational intercalation methods used by first-century Jews. Hence, the problem of intercalation introduces a margin of error of not just one or two days, but an entire month!

In short, due to the nature of the ancient Jewish calendar, we have absolutely no way to access exactly where the intercalation cycle was at the time of Jesus in the year that he died. Therefore, we also have no way of correlating contemporary calculations with the reality of the first-century Passover celebration. In the words of John Meier:

> To adjust the lunar calendar to the actual solar year, every now and then a leap year would have to be added to the Jewish calendar. There was probably no regular cycle of leap years in the early 1st century A.D.; they were added whenever the authorities decided from concrete observation (especially of agriculture) that they were needed. We cannot be sure whether a leap year fell between A.D. 29 and 32. *All calculations must therefore remain tentative.*[189]

I would put this more strongly: all astronomical calculations, because they can be off anywhere between a day (because of divergence between observation and calculation) and a month (because of divergence between modern and ancient Jewish methods of intercalation/leap-years), are of *no value whatsoever* in solving the problem of the date of the Last Supper. Indeed, as Roger Beckwith points out, following the calculations of Graeme Waddington and Colin Humphreys, when the above variables are taken into account, one can in fact calculate two years in which 14 Nisan would have fallen on a Thursday, as in the Synoptic testimony:

Jewish Day	Gospel Interpretation	Date (Julian Calendar)
Nisan 14	Synoptics correct	Thursday March 5 A.D. 30 (Delay of New Moon because of low visibility)
		Friday, March 6 A.D. 33 (Early Passover, due to variation in climate and intercalation)

189. Meier, *A Marginal Jew,* 1:402, citing Blinzler's "sobering warning" against depending too much on astronomical calculations.

I am, of course, not suggesting that such calculations make the case for the Last Supper having been a Passover meal. Instead, I am using them to show that *we just do not know* exactly where the first-century Jewish calendar was in terms of intercalation and atmospheric conditions in the year Jesus died. In fact, we are not even certain what year that was.[190] For better or for worse, the question of when the Last Supper took place and whether or not it coincided with the Jewish Passover meal must be settled on the basis of the textual evidence in the Gospels. Modern-day astronomy simply cannot help us; we have no way of correlating it with the observational and agriculturally based liturgical calendar of the first-century Jewish Temple authorities. We must go instead to the first-century sources themselves. Indeed, scholars should not continue to ignore the complex and variable nature of the ancient Jewish lunar calendar and at the same time uncritically call upon astronomy to support the Johannine hypothesis as a solution to the date of the Last Supper.

In sum, despite the widespread popularity of the Johannine hypothesis in recent years, when it is actually subjected to scrutiny, both forms of the theory suffer from a host of grave weaknesses, above all its uncritical and selective use of rabbinic literature. It begins by erring in its demonstrably false claim that the Synoptic Gospels do not describe a Passover lamb at the Last Supper. It appeals to rabbinic evidence that is probably not even about Jesus of Nazareth to support its theory that he was executed before the ordinary Jewish Passover. It rejects the chronology of the Synoptic Gospels on the basis of unsubstantiated claims while ignoring rabbinic traditions that contradict it, especially the traditions requiring that executions of false prophets should take place on feast days such as Passover and prohibiting trials on the days before feast days. In its second form, it suggests the implausible (if not impossible) scenario that Jesus held a private, lambless Passover meal twenty-four hours in advance, in direct disobedience to Mosaic Law and ancient Jewish practice. Finally, it misuses astronomy to support its conclusions without taking into account the observation-based nature of the first-century Jewish lunar calendar and our complete ignorance of the method of intercalation utilized in the year Jesus died. For these reasons, which are grave, the Johannine hypothesis does not deserve the widespread approval it currently holds, and, barring some stronger defense of its positions, should be abandoned as the dominant solution to the date of the Last Supper.

190. See the stunning array of proposals for the year of Jesus' death — ranging from A.D. 21 to 36! — in Hoehner, "The Chronology of Jesus," 2351-52, with full bibliography.

The Synoptic Hypothesis

The third solution we will examine may be referred to as the Synoptic hypothesis. Like the Johannine hypothesis, this solution describes the chronologies of John and the Synoptics as irreconcilable. Unlike the Johannine hypothesis, this solution argues that it is the Synoptic accounts that are chronologically accurate, while John's Gospel is not. In other words, the Last Supper took place on *the evening after* the Passover lambs had been sacrificed in the Temple (14 Nisan); and Jesus was crucified the morning after the Passover lambs had been eaten (15 Nisan). According to this hypothesis, then, the Last Supper was a Jewish Passover meal.

A central pillar of the Synoptic hypothesis is the argument that in the Fourth Gospel, the date of Jesus' death has been altered for theological reasons. In the words of E. P. Sanders, if forced to choose, we must conclude "that it was John who changed the day of the execution."[191] In particular, this theory posits that John's Gospel moves the Last Supper twenty-four hours ahead of the Passover in order to have Jesus be condemned at the same time that the Passover lambs were being sacrificed in the Temple. The words of Gerhard Lohfink and C. K. Barrett are representative:

> While the tradition of the first three evangelists clearly speaks of a Paschal meal in the night before the fifteenth of Nisan, the Fourth Gospel stresses that the day of Jesus' crucifixion was the fourteenth of Nisan, so that Jesus died at exactly the hour in which the Paschal lambs were being slaughtered in the Temple. But precisely that would be Johannine theology: Jesus is thus depicted as the true Paschal lamb.[192]

> [John's chronology] may not be good history; but it does seem to be Johannine theology. . . . The Johannine date of last supper and crucifixion seems to be due to John's determination to make clear that Jesus was the true Paschal Lamb of God.[193]

191. E. P. Sanders, *The Historical Figure of Jesus* (London: Penguin, 1993), 285-86.

192. Gerhard Lohfink, *Jesus of Nazareth: What He Wanted, Who He Was* (trans. Linda M. Maloney; Collegeville: Liturgical Press, 2012), 252.

193. C. K. Barrett, *The Gospel according to St. John* (2nd ed.; Philadelphia: Westminster, 1978), 48-51. Barnabas Lindars, *John* (Sheffield: Sheffield Academic Press, 1990), 446, makes the same point when he states that the death of Jesus (supposedly) during the sacrifice of the lambs is "purely a Johannine invention, dictated by his theological interests." Cited in McKnight, *Jesus and His Death,* 265.

From this point of view, the chronological contradiction between John and the Synoptics is ultimately the result of a theological adaptation carried out to show that Jesus is the true Passover "lamb of God who takes away the sin of the world" (John 1:29).

In recent years, the Synoptic hypothesis has had fewer advocates than the Johannine hypothesis. Nevertheless, it continues to find support among prominent scholars in Jesus research, especially those known for their expertise in ancient Judaism, such as Martin Hengel, Craig Keener, and E. P. Sanders.[194] It was given its classic form in Joachim Jeremias's work *The Eucharistic Words of Jesus.*[195] One reason it continues to find support among scholars of ancient Judaism is that the hypothesis has several important arguments in its favor.

1. *The Synoptics Explicitly Refer to a Passover Meal with a Lamb*

The first and most important argument in favor of the Synoptic hypothesis is the abundant evidence in all three Synoptic Gospels that the Last Supper was in fact a Jewish Passover meal.

As we saw in the opening section of this chapter, the Gospels of Matthew, Mark, and Luke *explicitly* and *repeatedly* identify Jesus' Last Supper as a Jewish Passover meal some twelve times (Matt 26:17, 18, 19; Mark 14:12 [2x], 14, 16; Luke 22:7, 8, 11, 13, 15). Moreover, in contrast to the chronological data in the Gospel of John (which we will survey below), the Synoptic data are unambiguous, especially since they not only refer to the Last Supper as a "Passover" *(pascha),* but explicitly state that Jesus and the disciples ate the supper on the evening after the Passover lambs were sacrificed: "on the first day of Unleavened Bread, when they sacrificed the Passover lamb *(pascha)*" (Mark 14:12; Luke 22:15). In light

194. E.g., Lohfink, *Jesus of Nazareth,* 252-56; Maurice Casey, *Jesus of Nazareth* (London: T. & T. Clark, 2010), 429-37; Craig S. Keener, *The Historical Jesus of the Gospels* (Grand Rapids: Eerdmans, 2009), 372-74; Martin Hengel and Anna Maria Schwemer, *Jesus und das Judentum* (Tübingen: Mohr Siebeck, 2007), 582-86; Marcus J. Borg and John Dominic Crossan, *The Last Week: The Day-by-Day Account of Jesus's Final Week in Jerusalem* (San Francisco: HarperCollins, 2006), 110; Joachim Gnilka, *Jesus of Nazareth* (trans. Siegfried S. Schatzmann; Peabody: Hendrickson, 1997), 279-87; Sanders, *The Historical Figure of Jesus,* 285-86; Marshall, *Last Supper and Lord's Supper,* 58-62; Rudolf Pesch, *Das Abendmahl und Jesu Todesverständnis* (QD 80; Freiburg, Basel, Vienna: Herder, 1978); A. J. B. Higgins, *The Lord's Supper in the New Testament* (SBT 6; Chicago: Alec R. Allenson, 1957), 13-23; Gustaf Dalman, *Jesus-Jeshua: Studies in the Gospels* (trans. Paul P. Levertoff; London: SPCK, 1929), 86-93.

195. Joachim Jeremias, *The Eucharistic Words of Jesus* (trans. Norman Perrin; New York: Charles Scribner's, 1966), 1-61.

of such explicit cultic and chronological data, one can easily see why scholars consider the testimony of the Synoptics sufficient to conclude that Jesus' Last Supper coincided with the celebration of the Jewish Passover.[196]

In addition to this explicit evidence, the Synoptic hypothesis also makes its case on the basis of implicit evidence that the Last Supper was a Passover meal. In his famous study, Joachim Jeremias listed some fourteen parallels between aspects of the Last Supper and ancient Jewish descriptions of the Passover meal.[197] Not all of these parallels are of equal value, and scholars have rightly raised objections to some of the more tenuous ones. Nevertheless, no complete refutation of Jeremias's cumulative argument has ever been forthcoming.[198] Many of his arguments continue to be utilized by experts in Second Temple Judaism such as Martin Hengel and Anna Maria Schwemer in support of the conclusion that the Last Supper was a Passover meal.[199] Of the fourteen arguments listed by Jeremias, in my opinion, the three given below are particularly strong.

2. *The Last Supper Is Eaten at Night in Jerusalem, not Bethany*

Second, Jesus and the Twelve disciples eat the Last Supper at night in "the city" of Jerusalem — not in the town of Bethany where they were staying (Matt 26:18; Mark 14:13; Luke 22:10). This combination of time and proximity is an extremely significant argument in favor of the Last Supper having been a Passover meal.[200]

196. E.g., Lohfink, *Jesus of Nazareth,* 252.

197. See Jeremias, *The Eucharistic Words of Jesus,* 41-62.

198. E.g., Schröter, *Das Abendmahl,* 44, simply asserts that Jeremias's proposal is difficult to reconcile with the Synoptic texts, without drawing on a single piece of ancient Jewish evidence to refute his cumulative argument. Likewise, Xavier Léon-Dufour, *Sharing the Eucharistic Bread: The Witness of the New Testament* (trans. Matthew J. O'Connell; New York/Mahwah: Paulist, 1982), 306-8, devotes an appendix to the attempt to refute Jeremias point by point. The result is telling: Léon-Dufour simply dismisses several of Jeremias's strongest arguments without counterevidence, and ends by admitting: "In my opinion, the only datum that tips the balance in favor of a Passover meal is the fact that the Synoptics seem to say that the Supper was in fact a Passover meal" [!]. That is quite a significant datum; when added to fourteen other arguments, perhaps it does more than "tip the balance." See Ben F. Meyer, "The Expiation Motif in the Eucharistic Words: A Key to the History of Jesus?," *Greg* 69 (1988): 461-87 (esp. 467-68).

199. Hengel and Schwemer, *Jesus und das Judentum,* 583-84.

200. Hengel and Schwemer, *Jesus und das Judentum,* 583; Gnilka, *Jesus of Nazareth,* 279; Jeremias, *The Eucharistic Words of Jesus,* 42-43.

According to the Synoptic Gospels, during his last week in Jerusalem, Jesus and the disciples "lodge" in Bethany (Matt 21:17). Indeed, it is from Bethany, located on the Mount of Olives, that Jesus sends the disciples to acquire a colt for his triumphal entry (Mark 11:1-2; Luke 19:29). According to the Gospel of Mark, each evening, when "it was late," Jesus would go "out to Bethany with the Twelve," and then come back "from Bethany" in the morning in order to go into Jerusalem (Mark 11:12). Clearly then, when it comes to the Last Supper, the celebration of the evening meal in the city is unusual and demands an explanation.[201]

The most obvious reason for Jesus' geographical movement from Bethany to Jerusalem — especially considering the potentially grave danger he is in from certain of the authorities — is that the Last Supper was a Passover meal. In accordance with Jewish custom, it would have to be eaten at night in the city of Jerusalem. This connection between the Passover and the central sanctuary is, of course, based directly on the commands of the Pentateuch:

> You may not offer the Passover sacrifice within any of your towns which the LORD your God gives you; but *at the place which the LORD your God will choose, to make his name dwell in it, there you shall offer the Passover sacrifice, in the evening* at the going down of the sun, at the time you came out of Egypt. And you shall boil it and eat in the place which the LORD your God will choose; and in the morning you shall turn and go to your tents. (Deut 16:5-7)

When we turn to how this biblical command was interpreted by Second Temple and early rabbinic Jewish literature, we find all of the evidence speaking with one voice that the Passover meal has to be eaten at night within the city of Jerusalem:

> [And it is not fitting to sacrifice it [the Passover] during any time of light except during the time of the border of the evening. *And they shall eat it during the time of evening until a third of the night.* (*Jubilees* 49:12)

> [And on the four]teenth day of the first month, [at twilight], they [will celebrate] [the Passover of YHWH] and they will perform sacrifice; prior to the evening offering they will sacrifice [it. Every male of] twenty years and older shall celebrate it. *And they shall consume it [at night] in the*

201. Higgins, *The Lord's Supper in the New Testament,* 21.

> *courtyards of [the] sanctuary, and every one shall rise early and will go to [his] tent.* (*11QTemple*[a] [11Q19] 17:6-9)

> When the first group went out they remained within the Temple Mount. . . . *After nightfall* they went out and roasted their Passover-offerings. (Mishnah, *Pesaḥim* 5:10; cf. 10:1)

When the requirement from the Jewish Torah that the Passover must be eaten in the chosen sanctuary is combined with the early Jewish evidence that this meant consuming the Passover lamb in the city of Jerusalem, we have a clear explanation for the account of the Last Supper in the Synoptics. Jesus' act of eating the Last Supper at night in the city of Jerusalem — especially given how crowded the city would have been just before the Passover festival — coheres perfectly with ancient Jewish descriptions of how the Passover lamb was eaten while the Temple still stood. It gives important support to the conclusion that the Last Supper was not an ordinary meal, but a first-century Jewish Passover.

3. *Jesus Interprets the Bread and Wine of the Last Supper*

A third major argument for the Synoptic hypothesis is that Jesus explains the meaning of the elements of the meal by identifying them as his own "body" and "blood" (Matt 26:26-28; Mark 14:22-24; Luke 22:19-20; 1 Cor 11:23-25). This act of interpreting the elements is completely out of keeping with an ordinary evening meal, but easily explained if the Last Supper was a Passover meal.[202]

Indeed, one of the key elements of the Passover, in both Jewish Scripture and tradition, is that the symbolism of the ritual be explained by an act of interpretation. For example, the Jewish Torah already associates an act of explanation with the consumption of the Passover meal:[203]

> You shall observe this rite [the Passover] as an ordinance for you and your sons for ever. And when you come to the land which the LORD will give you, as he has promised, you shall keep this service. *And when your children say to you, "What do you mean by this service?" you shall say, "It*

202. Hengel and Schwemer, *Jesus und das Judentum*, 583.

203. Lohfink, *Jesus of Nazareth*, 374 n. 13, rightly points out that this act of interpretation is already present in Jewish Scripture, contra Günter Stemberger, "Pesachhaggada und Abendmahlsberichte des Neuen Testaments," in idem, *Studien zum rabbinischen Judentum* (SBAB 10; Stuttgart: Katholisches Bibelwerk, 1990), 360-61.

> *is the sacrifice of the LORD's Passover,* for he passed over the houses of the sons of Israel in Egypt. . . ." (Exod 12:24-27)
>
> You shall offer the passover sacrifice to the LORD your God, from the flock or the herd, at the place which the LORD will choose, to make his name dwell there. You shall eat no leavened bread with it; seven days you shall eat it with unleavened bread, *the bread of affliction* — for you came out of the land of Egypt in hurried flight. . . . (Deut 16:2-3)

In light of such passages in the Pentateuch itself, the claim of some scholars that there is no "pre-Jesus" evidence for the interpretation of the Passover elements is baffling.[204] To the contrary, patterns of liturgical explanation are already present in the Torah. Although we cannot be sure what form and content the answers to these questions took in biblical times, the link between the Passover and ritual explanation is ancient and explicit, and the book of Deuteronomy provides one of the first interpretations of the Passover bread as the "bread of affliction" *(leḥem ʿoniy)* (Deut 16:3).

These biblical texts alone would suffice to establish the paschal context of Jesus' act of interpreting the bread and wine. However, it is also worth noting here that in both Second Temple literature and the Mishnah the connection between the Passover meal and the interpretation of the bread and other elements of the meal becomes even more pronounced.[205]

> *Unleavened bread is (a sign) of great haste and speed,* while the bitter herbs (are a sign) of the life of bitterness and struggle which they endure as slaves. That is that which is said. (Philo, *Questions and Answers on Exodus* 1.15)
>
> Rabban Gamaliel used to say: Whosoever has not said [the verses concerning] these three things at Passover has not fulfilled his obligation. And

204. McKnight, *Jesus and His Death,* 268.

205. See esp. Joel Marcus, "Passover and Last Supper Revisited," *NTS* 59 (2013): 303-24, against certain recent scholars who have tried to argue that a fixed order of service and ritual retelling of the exodus events were only post–A.D. 70 developments. See, e.g., Clemens Leonhard, *The Jewish Pesach and the Origins of the Christian Easter: Open Questions in Current Research* (Studia Judaica 35; Berlin and New York: De Gruyter, 2006), 1-118; Jonathan Klawans, "Was Jesus' Last Supper a Seder?," *BRev* 17 (2001): 24-33; Joseph Tabory, "Towards a History of the Passover Meal," *Passover and Easter: Origin and History to Modern Times* (ed. Paul F. Bradshaw and L. A. Hoffman; Notre Dame: University of Notre Dame, 1999), 63; Bokser, *The Origins of the Seder,* 14-28.

> these are they: Passover, unleavened bread, and bitter herbs: "Passover" — because God passed over the houses of our fathers in Egypt; *"unleavened bread" — because our fathers were redeemed from Egypt;* "bitter herbs" — because the Egyptians embittered the lives of our fathers in Egypt. (Mishnah, *Pesaḥim* 10:5)

Several things are worth noting about this evidence. For one thing, Philo's witness makes quite clear that the unleavened bread of the Passover was already being interpreted as a symbolic element in the first century A.D. Moreover, although the Mishnah was not written down until the late second century (ca. A.D. 200), this particular tradition of interpreting the elements is attributed to Rabbi Gamaliel I, who would have been a contemporary of Jesus himself.[206] As Maurice Casey points out, if this attribution is in any way reliable, then the Mishnah provides important support for the conclusion that the act of interpreting the elements of the meal was already in place at the time of Jesus, although the Gamaliel tradition appears to imply that the details in this regard were not yet uniform.[207] Finally, it is worth noting that the explanation of the "unleavened bread" *(matzah)* in the Mishnah contains a specifically redemptive significance, in a manner strikingly akin to Jesus' identification of the bread with his "body" that would be given in sacrifice (Matt 26:26; Mark 14:22; Luke 22:19; 1 Cor 11:24).[208]

Once again, Jesus' act of interpreting the bread and wine as his own body and blood and attributing to them redemptive significance is extremely difficult to explain in the context of an ordinary meal, however solemn. When his actions are situated in the context of a Jewish Passover meal, however, they find a plausible historical explanation. In light of ancient Jewish Passover customs, Jesus' acts of interpreting the bread and wine and explaining their redemptive significance make eminent sense if he was building on (and transforming) the ritual interpretations that were part of the ancient Jewish Passover meal.

Indeed, I know of no counterargument that provides a more plausible explanation for why Jesus interpreted the bread and wine of the Last Supper. To be sure, some scholars have claimed that "words of interpretation could be proffered at any meal one chose to interpret"; but they give no actual ev-

206. For the identification with Gamaliel I, see Jeremias, *The Eucharistic Words of Jesus,* 56; David Daube, *The New Testament and Rabbinic Judaism* (repr.; Peabody: Hendrickson, n.d. [orig. 1956]), 187.

207. Casey, *Jesus of Nazareth,* 433.

208. Lohfink, *Jesus of Nazareth,* 253. See chapter 5 for more detailed discussion.

idence to support this claim.[209] In light of this situation, Joachim Jeremias influentially concluded that Jesus' act of interpreting the bread and wine at the Last Supper was of "absolutely decisive significance" and "the convincing argument" for identifying the Last Supper as a Passover meal.[210]

4. Jesus and the Disciples Sing the Passover "Hymn"

Fourth and finally, but by no means least significantly, the Last Supper ends with the singing of a hymn. According to both Matthew and Mark, when Jesus and his disciples "had sung a hymn *(hymnos)*, they went out to the Mount of Olives" (Matt 26:30; Mark 14:26). Like the interpretation of the elements of the meal, the singing of a hymn was not part of an ordinary Jewish meal, but was a key component in the celebration of the Passover.[211]

Indeed, according to both Second Temple Jewish literature and the Mishnah, the ancient Passover meal is described as having involved the singing of hymns, which are in one case specifically associated with the psalms of David. This evidence goes back to the first century A.D.:

> And *David*, son of Jesse, was wise. . . . *And he wrote psalms:* three thousand six hundred; and songs to be sung before the altar over the perpetual offering of every day, for all the days of the year; three hundred and sixty-four; and for the sabbath offerings: fifty-two songs . . . *and for all the days of the festivals*, and for the Day of Atonement: thirty songs. (*11QPsalms*[a] [11Q5] 27:2, 4-8)

> On this day [the Passover] every dwelling-house is invested with the outward semblance and dignity of a temple. The victim is then slaughtered and dressed for the festal meal which befits the occasion. The guests assembled for the banquet have been cleansed by purificatory lustrations, and are there not as in other festive gatherings, to indulge the belly with wine and viands, but to fulfill with *prayers and hymns* the custom handed down by their fathers. (Philo, *Special Laws* 2.148)

209. McKnight, *Jesus and His Death*, 268. See also Léon-Dufour, *Sharing the Eucharistic Bread*, 308, who can only say that Jeremias's point is "a questionable hypothesis," without offering any counterexplanation.

210. Jeremias, *The Eucharistic Words of Jesus*, 55 (emphasis added).

211. Hengel and Schwemer, *Jesus und das Judentum*, 583.

> After they have mixed for him [the host] the third cup he says the Benediction over his meal. [Over] a fourth [cup] *he completes the Hallel and says after it the Benediction over song.* (Mishnah, *Pesaḥim* 10:7; cf. *T. Pes.* 10:7)

To be sure, the Scroll does not explicitly identify which "psalms" *(thlym)* of David were sung during Passover, nor does Philo tell us what these Passover "prayers and hymns" *(euchōn te kai hymnōn)* exactly were. In the Mishnah, however, the "Hallel" refers to the singing of certain psalms from the portion of the Psalter sung during Passover (Psalms 113–118). In light of such parallels, scholars have argued that the Synoptic Gospels are "undoubtedly" depicting Jesus and the disciples as singing the second set of Hallel psalms (Psalms 115–118) at the conclusion of the Last Supper.[212] Indeed, in a remarkable case of correspondence, even the word sometimes used to describe the second part of the Hallel in rabbinic literature is the loan-word *hiymnon,* taken from the Greek word *hymnos* ("hymn") — exactly the same Greek word found in the Synoptics (Matt 26:30; Mark 14:26).[213]

To be sure, from time to time, critics of the Synoptic hypothesis have claimed that any ordinary Jewish meal could end with the singing of hymns — although such arguments are infrequent because the evidence cannot support it.[214] As Jeremias rightly objected long ago: "[T]he '*hallel* at the conclusion of an ordinary meal,' mentioned in several modern studies of our subject, is a product of fantasy."[215] By contrast, Jesus' actions at the Last Supper are easily explained by and fit perfectly well with the most ancient evidence we possess regarding the liturgy of the Second Temple Jewish Passover meal. Therefore, all things being equal, the most plausible explanation for the incidental but striking convergence between the Synoptic testimony and ancient Jewish descriptions of the Passover is that the Last Supper itself was in fact a Jewish Passover meal.

212. Keener, *The Historical Jesus of the Gospels,* 299-301; Casey, *Jesus of Nazareth,* 435; Jeremias, *The Eucharistic Words of Jesus,* 55. Keener cautions that the exact sequence of psalms was not likely standardized in Jesus' day, since later rabbis were still debating the point (*t. Pes.* 10:8; *b. Pes.* 118a). Keener, *The Historical Jesus of the Gospels,* 561 n. 219.

213. Higgins, *The Lord's Supper in the New Testament,* 21.

214. Léon-Dufour, *Sharing the Eucharistic Bread,* 308, appeals to the songs sung during the banquet of the celibate ascetic Therapeutae sect. However, this only strengthens the case against the Last Supper being an ordinary meal, since their banquets were hardly ordinary and were in fact connected with the remembrance of the exodus. (See chapter 3 above for discussion of the meal of the Therapeutae and the bread of the presence.)

215. Jeremias, *The Eucharistic Words of Jesus,* 55.

Second-Century Evidence for the Last Supper as a Passover Meal

As we saw above, one of the reasons both the Essene and Johannine hypotheses have appealed to many is the patristic evidence cited in support of a Tuesday-night arrest of Jesus (*Didascalia Apostolorum*, Epiphanius, Victorinus of Pettau), and, in the case of the latter, the evidence for Jesus' being crucified on the eve of Passover (Babylonian Talmud, *Gospel of Peter*). Given the fact that scholars consistently appeal to such evidence from the patristic period to support the contention that the Last Supper did *not* take place at the same time as the ordinary Jewish Passover, it is worth noting here the often-overlooked point that the earliest patristic evidence we possess supports the position that the Last Supper was a Jewish Passover meal.

In this regard, the most significant patristic witnesses date from the mid to late second century A.D., in the writings of Justin Martyr and Irenaeus of Lyons:

> The Passover, indeed, was Christ, who was later sacrificed, as Isaiah foretold when he said: "He was led as a sheep to the slaughter" (Isa 53:7). It is also written that *on the day of the Passover you seized him,* and that *during the Passover you crucified him.* (Justin Martyr, *Dialogue with Trypho* 111.3)[216]

> "He came to Bethany six days before the Passover" (John 12:1), and going up from Bethany to Jerusalem, *He there ate the Passover, and suffered on the following day.* (Irenaeus, *Against Heresies* 2.22.3)[217]

It is remarkable that these texts are not more frequently brought into the discussion of the date of the Last Supper, given that Justin Martyr clearly interprets the evidence in the Gospels ("It is written") as affirming that Jesus was arrested on "the day of Passover" (i.e., evening following 14 Nisan) and crucified "during Passover" (i.e., at the start of the Passover week, the morning

216. Trans. in Raniero Cantalamessa, *Easter in the Early Church: An Anthology of Jewish and Early Christian Texts* (trans. James M. Quigley S.J. and Joseph T. Lienhard S.J.; Collegeville: Liturgical Press, 1993), 41.

217. Translation from Roberts and Donaldson, *Ante-Nicene Fathers,* 1:391 (slightly adapted). Jaubert, *The Date of the Last Supper,* 85, is to be commended for citing this text. However, her dismissal of it as "nothing more than an interpretation of the Gospel" is puzzling. All of the patristic texts she cites are interpretations of the Gospel chronology in one way or another; the only difference between Irenaeus and the texts she cites in favor of her chronology is that his witness is centuries earlier.

of 15 Nisan). Likewise, Irenaeus, in the context of having just referred to the Jewish Passover, affirms without hesitation that at the Last Supper Jesus "ate the Passover" (evening following 14 Nisan) and was executed "on the following day" (15 Nisan). The evidence from Irenaeus in this regard is particularly striking, given his familiarity with the Gospel of John. In contrast to advocates of the Johannine hypothesis, Irenaeus does not manifest any awareness of a chronological tension between the Gospel of John and his assertion that Jesus was executed after eating the Passover meal. To the contrary, the text cited above explicitly quotes the Gospel of John's chronological reference to the Jewish Passover celebrated during Jesus' last days (John 12:1).

In sum, the Synoptic hypothesis has in its favor the explicit testimony of Matthew, Mark, and Luke that the Last Supper was a Jewish Passover meal, as well as the implicit evidence from parallels between the Last Supper and ancient Jewish descriptions of the Passover. Jesus' unusual act of eating a meal with the Twelve at night in the city of Jerusalem; his act of interpreting and explaining the elements of the meal; and the singing of a hymn at its conclusion, among other things, produce converging lines of evidence to support the conclusion that the Last Supper was indeed a Jewish Passover meal. Taken together, this explicit and implicit evidence make the Synoptic hypothesis a formidable solution to the question of the date of the Last Supper. Perhaps that is why the arguments for the Synoptic hypothesis, though frequently dismissed, are not actually refuted on the basis of any ancient Jewish evidence.[218]

With that said, despite the strength of the Synoptic hypothesis's positive arguments, the theory does suffer from one major flaw when it comes to its interpretation of the death of Jesus in the Gospel of John. (Other weaknesses will only become fully apparent when we turn below to the fourth solution, the Passover hypothesis.) As we saw above, one of the pillars of the Synoptic hypothesis is its rejection of the Gospel of John as evidence for the date of Jesus' death — a rejection based on the claim that the Fourth Gospel alters the timing of the death of

218. For example, in his case against the Synoptic hypothesis, John Meier does not actually respond to Jeremias's positive arguments for the paschal character of the Last Supper. Rather, he argues that Jeremias is proposing a "false dichotomy' between a Passover meal and an ordinary everyday meal. Instead, Meier proposes instead that Jesus arranged "a solemn farewell meal," which was "accompanied by all the formalities (reclining at table, drinking wine, singing hymns, etc.) that Jeremias uses to prove the Passover nature of the supper." See Meier, *A Marginal Jew,* 398-99. In contrast to Jeremias, however, Meier does not give any Second Temple Jewish evidence for the category of a "solemn farewell meal" that would need to be eaten in the city of Jerusalem, include the interpretation of the elements, and conclude with the singing of hymns. McKnight, *Jesus and His Death,* 269, also does not offer any actual evidence.

Jesus. In closing, then, we need to take a few moments to outline what I consider the most significant weakness of this solution to the date of the Last Supper.

1. The Gospel of John Does Not Correlate the Crucifixion with the (Supposed) Sacrifice of the Passover Lambs at "Noon"

The major weakness of the Synoptic hypothesis can be formulated as follows: contrary to what is widely claimed, John's Gospel does *not* call attention to the fact that Jesus was crucified "the very hour" the Passover lambs were being sacrificed in the Temple — i.e., noon (John 19:14). For, as ancient Jewish evidence makes clear, the Passover lambs were not sacrificed at noon, but later, sometime between the ninth hour (3 p.m.) and eleventh hour (5 p.m.). And of these hours John makes absolutely no mention; nor does he in any way attempt to link the timing of Jesus' death with them. Because this erroneous interpretation is so widely assumed, we need to take a few moments to address it in detail.

The key text upon which proponents of the Synoptic hypothesis base their claim that John has Jesus crucified at the same hour as the Passover lambs is from the fact of Jesus' being sentenced to death by Pilate at the judgment seat:

> Upon this Pilate sought to release him, but the Jews cried out, "If you release this man, you are not Caesar's friend; every one who makes himself a king sets himself against Caesar." When Pilate heard these words, he brought Jesus out and sat down on the judgment seat at a place called the Pavement, in Hebrew Gabbatha. Now it was the preparation of Passover; *it was about the sixth hour* [= noon]. He said to the Jews, "Here is your King!" They cried out, "Away with him, away with him, crucify him!" Pilate said to them, "Shall I crucify your King?" The chief priests answered, "We have no king but Caesar." Then he handed him over to them to be crucified. (John 19:12-16)[219]

On the basis of this text, commentators repeatedly claim that John is calling attention to the fact that Jesus' crucifixion coincided with the sacrifice of the Passover lambs in the Temple. Significantly, this claim is made by support-

219. There are two issues involved in the interpretation of this text. The first is the meaning of the phrase "preparation of the Passover" *(paraskeuē tou pascha)* (John 19:14). We will deal with this in the next section. For now, let us simply focus on the second, which is John's reference to Jesus' being crucified at "the sixth hour," i.e., noon (John 19:14).

ers of both the Synoptic hypothesis and the Johannine hypothesis. Perhaps its most famous proponent is Raymond Brown, whose extremely influential commentary claims:

> If the fourth evangelist does not identify the day itself as Passover, he still has Jesus condemned to death at noon on Passover Eve (xix 14), *the very hour at which the priests began to slaughter the paschal lambs in the temple area.*[220]

Notice here that Brown does not cite any ancient Jewish evidence in support of his claim that the Passover lambs were sacrificed at noon.[221] Nor do the many other scholars who argue that John altered the chronology of Jesus' crucifixion in order to have his condemnation by Pilate coincide with the sacrifice of the Passover lambs at noon. Indeed, this assertion has become something of an unquestioned exegetical conclusion; it is repeated over and over again as if it needed no evidence to support it.[222]

From this point of view, the Gospel of John's emphasis on the chronological coinciding of Jesus' crucifixion with the noontide sacrifice of the Passover lambs is intended to reveal Jesus as the true Passover "lamb of God" who takes away the sins of the world (John 1:29). In his recent book against the historical reliability of John's Gospel, Maurice Casey, a supporter of the Synoptic hypothesis, argues:

> We must infer that the Johannine phrase [in 19:14] means about midday on Friday, 14 Nisan. Jesus is sentenced to die, and is crucified on Golgotha, so that the whole process coincides approximately with the slaughter of the Passover victims in the Temple.[223]

Along similar lines, Craig Keener argues that in altering the chronology of Jesus' crucifixion, "John has simply provided a theological interpretation of

220. Brown, *The Gospel according to John,* 2:556 (emphasis added).

221. Cf. Brown, *The Gospel according to John,* 2:883. Unfortunately, in his later work, Brown does mention all the counterevidence from Jubilees, Philo, Josephus, and the Mishnah, but he relegates it to a footnote and continues to insist that "Jesus the Lamb of God was sentenced to death at the very hour when lambs for the Jewish Passover began to be killed." Brown, *The Death of the Messiah,* 1:847 n. 47.

222. E.g., Matson, "The Historical Plausibility of John's Passion Dating," 293; Dunn, *Jesus Remembered,* 772, although he admits in a footnote that "the time of day when the slaughtering began is not clear."

223. Maurice Casey, *Is John's Gospel True?* (London and New York: Routledge, 1996), 24.

Jesus' death, as many commentators . . . have argued."[224] Joachim Jeremias sums up the view of proponents of the Synoptic hypothesis well when he writes that in John's Gospel, the "typology" of Jesus the new Passover lamb "came to be understood as chronology."[225]

Despite the widespread influence of this interpretation, it faces a major problem of historical plausibility. For according to all of the ancient Jewish evidence we possess, *the sacrifice of the Passover lambs did not take place at noon, but from around 3 p.m. to 5 p.m. — hours that are never even mentioned in the Gospel of John.* Consider the following pieces of evidence, from both the Second Temple period and rabbinic literature:

> The children of Israel . . . come and observe Passover on its appointed day on the fourteenth of the first month between the evenings from the third (part) of the day [ca. 2 p.m.] until the third (part) of the night [ca. 6 p.m.] because the two parts of the day are given for light and one third for evening. This is what the Lord commanded you so that you might observe it between the evenings. And it is not fitting to sacrifice it during any time of light except during the time of the border of evening. And they shall eat it during the time of evening until a third of the night. (*Jubilees* 49:10-11)

> [On the four]teenth day of the first month, [at twilight], they [will celebrate] [the Passover of YHWH] and they will perform sacrifice; prior to the evening offering they will sacrifice [it . . .]. (*11QTemple*[a] [11Q19] 17:6-7)

> Why is the Passover sacrificed *at evening?* Perhaps because good things were about to befall at night (and because) it was not custom to offer a sacrifice in darkness, and for those who were about to experience good things at night *it was not (proper) to prepare it before the ninth hour* [= 3 p.m.]. (Philo, *Questions and Answers on Exodus* 1.11)

> After the New Moon comes the fourth feast, called the Crossing Feast, which the Hebrews in their native tongue call Passover *(Pascha)*. In this festival many myriads of victims from midday until evening *(apo mesēmbrias achri hesperas)* are offered by the whole people, old and young alike, raised for that particular day to the dignity of the priesthood. (Philo, *Special Laws* 2.145)[226]

224. Keener, *The Historical Jesus of the Gospels*, 374.
225. Jeremias, *The Eucharistic Words of Jesus*, 83.
226. Trans. LCL, slightly adapted.

> Accordingly, on the occasion of the feast called Passover, at which they sacrifice from the ninth [= 3 p.m.] to the eleventh hour [= 5 p.m.] *(hen thyousin men apo enatēs hōras mechris hendekatēs)* and a little fraternity, as it were, gathers around each sacrifice, of not fewer than ten persons. (Josephus, *War* 6.423-24)

> The Daily Whole-offering [the Tamid][227] was slaughtered at a half after the eighth hour [2:30 p.m.] and offered up at a half after the ninth hour [3:30 p.m.]; [but] on the eve of Passover it was slaughtered at a half after the seventh hour [1:30 p.m.] and offered up at a half after the eighth hour [2:30 p.m.], whether it was a weekday or the Sabbath. If the eve of Passover fell on the eve of a Sabbath, it [the Daily Whole-offering] was slaughtered at a half after the sixth hour [12:30 p.m.] and offered up at a half after the seventh hour [1:30 p.m.]. And, after this, the Passover-offering [was slaughtered]. (Mishnah, *Pesaḥim* 5:1)

Given the ready access that scholars have to these ancient Jewish texts, it is baffling how John's reference to "the sixth hour" (John 19:14) ever came to be identified as "the very hour at which the priests began to slaughter the paschal lambs in the temple area."[228] Although it is possible that scholars have misinterpreted Philo's general reference to the Passover lambs being sacrificed at "midday" *(mesēmbrias)* (Philo, *Special Laws* 2.145), he elsewhere clarifies this vague reference and corroborates Josephus' evidence that it was not lawful to sacrifice the Passover Lamb until "the ninth hour" — i.e., 3 p.m. (*Questions on Exodus* 1.11). However, this still does not explain why scholars continue to ignore the evidence from *Jubilees,* Josephus, and the Mishnah. According to Josephus — whose testimony should be considered particularly weighty, given that he served as a priest in the Second Temple — the Passover sacrifices ordinarily did not begin until 3 p.m. According to the Mishnah, even when this time was pushed up in the years that Passover fell on the eve of a Sabbath (as in Jesus' final week), at the very earliest, the Passover lambs would be sacrificed sometime around 2 p.m., because it could not be offered until the daily Whole-offering of the Tamid was complete.[229] Somewhat less valuable

227. See Num 28:1-18.

228. Brown, *The Gospel according to John,* 2:556; idem, *The Death of the Messiah,* 1:847 n. 47.

229. It is worth noting here that none of this evidence is annulled by Mishnah *Pesaḥim* 5:3, which says that a lamb slaughtered before noon is invalid. This is simply a legal text making explicit that any animal slaughtered before the sun began to decline after noon would not meet

is the description from the Temple Scroll, since it describes an idealized cult; yet even that document does not place the sacrifice of the Passover lambs anywhere near noon, but "before the evening sacrifice" *(lphny minḥth h'rb)*.

In short, when taken together, the one thing that none of the ancient Jewish sources say is that the Passover lambs were sacrificed at the sixth hour — i.e., noon. This is a powerful argument against the claim that the Gospel of John has altered the chronology of Jesus' passion in order to highlight the fact that he was crucified at the same hour that the lambs were being sacrificed in the Temple. As Josef Blinzler concedes in his study of the trial of Jesus:

> Others assume that John made out Jesus to be condemned in the sixth hour solely because he wanted to achieve a certain symbolism: Jesus was to die at the same hour at which the paschal lambs were being slaughtered in the Temple.[230] But one can reasonably doubt the correctness of this conjecture. . . . If John had really wished to express this symbolism in 19:14, then it would have been more sensible for him to have given the time, not in the report of the condemnation but in the report of the *crucifixion* (19:18-23).[231]

Along the same lines, Rudolf Schnackenburg points out in his commentary on the Fourth Gospel:

> It is usually said that [John] wanted to present Jesus as the true Passover lamb who died on the cross at the same time that the Passover lambs were slaughtered in the Temple. *Even this idea, however, lacks a firm foundation in the gospel. The evangelist does not in fact say this* — it is simply a conclusion drawn from his chronology and his interest in the event of the passover.[232]

---

the biblical standards of being sacrificed "between the evenings" (Exod 12:6). It is not describing a custom of sacrificing the lambs beginning at noon, since the Mishnah itself explicitly states that "the Passover offering [was slaughtered] after" the daily whole offering, which was sacrificed at 2:30 p.m. generally, and 1:30 p.m. if the eve of Passover coincided with the eve of a Sabbath (*m. Pes.* 5:1, cited above). See Jacob Neusner, *The Mishnah: A New Translation* (New Haven: Yale University Press, 1988), 236-37.

230. Here Blinzler cites Bultmann, *Das Evangelium des Johannes,* 514 n. 5.

231. Blinzler, *The Trial of Jesus,* 267.

232. Schnackenburg, *The Gospel according to St. John,* 3:36 (emphasis added). See also Dalman, *Jesus-Jeshua,* 92.

Schnackenburg's observation is very telling here. Contrary to advocates of the Synoptic hypothesis claim, John's Gospel does not actually say anything about Jesus' dying at the same time that the Passover lambs were being sacrificed in the Temple. Indeed, it is the Synoptic Gospels, and not John, who tell us that Jesus died at the ninth hour (3 p.m.) (Matt 27:46; Mark 15:34; Luke 23:44-46). The idea that Jesus died at the same hour that the Passover lambs were being slaughtered can only be achieved by harmonizing the chronological indicators present in John, which mentions 12 noon, and the Synoptics, which mention 3 p.m.[233] It does not occur on the level of redaction in any Gospel.

In sum, when the data from the Gospels and ancient Jewish descriptions of the Passover are properly taken into account, it seems clear that the explanation given by advocates of the Synoptic hypothesis for why John both altered the date of the crucifixion and emphasized Jesus' crucifixion at noon does not hold up to historical scrutiny. To put it bluntly: the popular theory that John has altered the chronology of Jesus' death in order to have Jesus' condemnation in John 19:14 coincide with the noon sacrifice of the Passover lambs founders on the fact that *there does not appear to have ever been a noon sacrifice of the Passover lambs.* This is a serious flaw. Indeed, the Synoptic hypothesis's misinterpretation of Johannine chronology is in fact symptomatic of a larger problem of chronological misinterpretation of John's Gospel, a problem that plagues both the Synoptic hypothesis's rejection of John and the Johannine hypothesis's rejection of the Synoptic chronology.

What then are we to do with the Synoptic hypothesis? I propose that we take the four major arguments in favor of the Synoptic hypothesis seriously; I for one consider all of the arguments for the Last Supper having been a Passover meal to be convincing. The fact that they remain unrefuted by counterevidence is telling. However, I will not follow the Synoptic hypothesis in its dismissal of the chronology of John's Gospel. Rather, I will attempt to explain the data in the Gospel of John by reexamining them in light of ancient Jewish language, literature, and liturgy. As we will see in the next section, when the strengths of the Synoptic hypothesis regarding the Passover character of the Last Supper are combined with a careful linguistic and historical analysis of the chronological data in John's Gospel, a viable solution to the problem of the date of the Last Supper does in fact present itself in the form of a fourth hypothesis.

233. Cf. Keener, *The Gospel of John,* 2:1131, who also admits this.

The Passover Hypothesis

Now that we have surveyed three of the most influential hypotheses regarding the date of the Last Supper and reviewed their weaknesses, we can turn to the fourth major proposal that demands our attention. I will call this the Passover hypothesis.

According to this solution, the apparent contradiction between John and the Synoptics regarding the date of the Last Supper is the result of the misinterpretation of ancient Jewish Passover terminology and chronology in the Gospel of John. Specifically, interpreters who see a contradiction between John and the Synoptics assume that on the three occasions when John uses the word "Passover" *(pascha)* he is referring to the Passover lamb sacrificed on 14 Nisan. However, these interpreters consistently fail to take into account that in Jewish Scripture, Second Temple Jewish literature, and rabbinic literature, the word "Passover" had at least four different meanings:

1. The Passover *lamb,* sacrificed on 14 Nisan;
2. The Passover *meal,* during which the initial lamb was eaten (15 Nisan);
3. The Passover *peace offering,* sacrificed and eaten during the seven-day feast of Unleavened Bread (15-21 Nisan);
4. The Passover *week,* consisting of seven days of sacrifice/celebration (15-21 Nisan).

I will give examples of each of these uses momentarily. For now, I simply want to stress that in any ancient Jewish text dealing with "Passover," the meaning of the word must always be determined by the context. One cannot simply assume that when one comes across the word "Passover," it is referring to the lamb sacrificed on 14 Nisan. In this regard, a modern liturgical analogy may be helpful: even in our own day, the liturgical use of the word "Easter" can have several meanings: (1) the Easter Vigil on Saturday evening; (2) the Easter Sunday solemnity on Sunday morning; (3) any day of the octave of Easter week; or (4) the forty-nine-day Easter season as a whole. Indeed, this liturgical ambiguity is inherited from the church's Jewish roots, since the Latin word for "Easter" is of course *Pascha.* Hence, the only way to establish the modern meaning of the word "Easter" is to examine its context; so too with the ancient word "Passover."

With this in mind, when the Gospel of John's account of Jesus' death is interpreted in its ancient Jewish context — in which all four meanings of the word "Passover" were still in use — there are very sound reasons to conclude that there is no real contradiction between the Synoptic and Johannine chronologies. To be specific, in the three key uses of the word "Passover" *(pascha)* that scholars use to establish his chronology (John 13:1; 18:28; 19:14), the Fourth Gospel is using definitions #2, 3, and 4 above, not definition #1 (the initial Passover lamb):

"Before the feast of Passover" (John 13:1)	=	just before the Passover *meal* on 15 Nisan (definition #2)
"To eat the Passover" (John 18:28)	=	the Passover *peace offering,* eaten on 15 Nisan (definition #3)
"The preparation of Passover" (John 19:14)	=	the Friday of Passover *week,* which lasts from 15 Nisan to 21 Nisan (definition #4)

In order to establish this conclusion, of course, we will have to examine the evidence in the Gospel of John below. As we will see, when this is done, a strong case can be made that *in both John and the Synoptics, the Last Supper is being depicted as a Jewish Passover meal, eaten the evening after the lambs were sacrificed (15 Nisan).* Hence, in both John and the Synoptics, Jesus was crucified on the first day of the weeklong feast of Passover/Unleavened Bread (15-21 Nisan). If these points are correct, then the contradiction between John and the Synoptics on the date of the Last Supper is more apparent than real, and the result of a misconstrual of the linguistic and historical realities of the Passover festival in the Second Temple period.

With this in mind, I should stress that in what follows, I will not simply be rehearsing previous scholarly arguments that would support certain aspects of the Passover hypothesis.[234] Instead, I will be presenting fresh evidence and arguments based on a firsthand study of the primary sources regarding the ancient Jewish Passover as well as key texts in the Gospel of John. Indeed, as I hope to show, it is highly ironic that the Passover hypothesis should be ignored at the very same time that contemporary Jesus research is unanimously

234. Previous forms of this solution often tend to be cursory and, as a result, somewhat unconvincing. See, e.g., Roger T. Beckwith, *Calendar and Chronology, Jewish and Christian: Biblical, Intertestamental and Patristic Studies* (Leiden: Brill, 2001), 276-96; Barry D. Smith, "The Chronology of the Last Supper," *WTJ* 53 (1991): 29-45; Cullen I. K. Story, "The Bearing of Old Testament Terminology on the Johannine Chronology of the Final Passover of Jesus," *NovT* 31 (1989): 316-24; C. C. Torrey, "In the Fourth Gospel the Last Supper Was a Passover Meal," *JQR* 42 (1951-52): 237-50; P. J. Heawood, "The Time of the Last Supper," *JQR* 42 (1951): 37-44; C. C. Torrey, "The Date of the Crucifixion according to the Fourth Gospel," *JBL* 50 (1931): 227-41.

insisting on the importance of situating him in his Jewish context.[235] As we will see, more than any other solution to the date of the Last Supper, the Passover hypothesis takes seriously the complexity of ancient Jewish language and liturgy at the time of Jesus as well as the Gospel of John's assumption that its readers are familiar with the realities of the first-century Jerusalem Temple.

1. *The Word "Passover" Had Four Meanings in Early Judaism*

The first major argument for the Passover hypothesis is that in ancient Jewish literature, both biblical and nonbiblical, the word "Passover" — in both Hebrew *(pesaḥ)* and Greek *(pascha)* — can have at least four different meanings.[236] In any given case, the precise definition of the word must be determined by the context. Specifically, the word "Passover" can be used with reference to:

1. The Passover Lamb — sacrificed in the afternoon, on 14 Nisan.[237]
2. The Passover Meal — eaten in the evening, on 15 Nisan.[238]
3. The Passover Peace Offering — offered and eaten during 15-21 Nisan;[239]
4. The Passover Week — 15-21 Nisan, the seven-day feast.[240]

235. E.g., this solution is not even mentioned by Dunn, *Jesus Remembered;* Brown, *The Death of the Messiah;* Meier, *A Marginal Jew;* Wright, *Jesus and the Victory of God,* etc. McKnight, *Jesus and His Death,* 264-65, mentions this solution in passing in a footnote. However, he manifests an unfamiliarity with it when he lumps it in with the Synoptic hypothesis.

236. See F. W. Danker, *A Greek-English Lexicon of the New Testament and Other Early Christian Literature* (3rd ed.; Chicago and London: University of Chicago Press, 2000), 784-85 (hereafter BDAG); J. Lust, E. Eynikel, and K. Hauspie, *A Greek-English Lexicon of the Septuagint* (2 vols.; Stuttgart: Deutsche Bibelgesellschaft, 1992), 361; Joachim Jeremias, *"pascha," TDNT* 5:896-904; Theodor Zahn, *Introduction to the New Testament* (trans. J. M. Trout et al.; 3 vols.; London: T. & T. Clark, 1909), 3:296-97; Francis Brown, S. R. Driver, and Charles A. Briggs, *The Brown-Driver-Briggs Hebrew and English Lexicon* (repr. Peabody: Hendrickson, 1996 [orig. 1906]), 820.

237. See Exod 12:21; Deut 16:6; 2 Chron 30:15, 17; *Jub.* 49:1; Matt 26:17; Mark 14:12-14; Luke 22:7, 11, 15; 1 Cor 5:7.

238. See Exod 12:48; Deut 16:1; *Jub.* 49:1-2; Philo, *De Sept.* 18.19; Josephus, *Ant.* 2.313; 3.248; 17.213; *War* 6.9; Matt 26:18; Mark 14:1; Heb 11:28.

239. Deut 16:1-3; 2 Chron 35:7-9; and (as I will argue below) John 18:28. It is significant that these two occurrences in Jewish Scripture go unmentioned by lexicons that do not mention the Passover peace offering as a fourth definition. E.g., BDAG, 784-85; Lust et al., *A Greek-English Lexicon of the Septuagint,* 2:361.

240. Josephus, *War* 2.10; 6.243; *Ant.* 14.21; 17.213; 18.29; Luke 22:1; John 2:23; 18:39. Zahn, *Introduction to the New Testament,* 3:297, holds that "there is clearly no intention of distinguish-

Several points are worth noting about this list. First, as the footnotes reveal, the multiple meanings of the word "Passover" are present in Jewish Scripture, Second Temple literature, and rabbinic tradition. Hence, the inherent ambiguity of the term spans a great deal of time, and is not limited to extrabiblical literature. Second, the ambiguity of the word "Passover" is true of Hebrew, Aramaic, and Greek. Hence, the multiple meanings of Passover are not peculiar to any one particular language. Both these points are important for seeing just how easily the Gospels might use the word "Passover" in a way that could lead to confusion among interpreters. However, in order to make clear the existence of these multiple meanings, we shall take a few moments to look closely at examples of each definition, before we turn to how the terms are used in the Gospel of John.

1. ***The Passover Lamb*** The first definition of the word "Passover" refers to the initial sacrificial Passover lamb that would be killed on the afternoon of 14 Nisan.[241] This usage is often easy to identify because it is frequently accompanied by the language of killing or sacrificing the Passover:

> Select lambs for yourselves according to your families, and *kill the Passover.* (Exod 12:21)
>
> And they *killed the Passover* on the fourteenth day of the second month. (2 Chron 30:15)
>
> Remember the commandment which the Lord commanded you concerning *Passover,* that you observe it in its time, *on the fourteenth of the first month, so that you might sacrifice it* before it becomes evening. . . . (*Jubilees* 49:1)
>
> And on the first day of Unleavened Bread, when *they sacrificed the Passover,* his disciples said to him. . . . (Mark 14:12)
>
> Then came the day of unleavened bread, on which *the Passover* had to be *sacrificed.* (Luke 22:7)

In these texts and others, the context makes clear that the word "Passover" (Hebrew *pesaḥ;* Greek *pascha*) is being used to refer to the Passover lamb, and

---

ing the Passover proper from the feast of Azyma [= Unleavened Bread]" in John 2:13; 6:4; 11:55; 12:1; 13:1; Luke 2:41, and includes these as examples as well.

241. BDAG, 784, lists this as the first definition of *pascha.*

it alone. In order to reflect this, many English translations such as the RSV will add the word "lamb" (reading "kill the Passover lamb") in order to make the precise meaning of the term explicit.

2. ***The Passover Meal*** The second definition of the word "Passover" refers to the Passover meal in which the sacrificial lamb was eaten.[242] This definition is really only a slight variation of the first. However, in an ancient Jewish context, it needs to be distinguished from the first definition since the initial Passover lamb was not actually eaten until the next calendar day, after sunset (15 Nisan). Once again, this meaning can be established by the context whenever reference is made to the meal in which the initial lamb would be eaten on the night of 15 Nisan:

> And when a stranger shall sojourn with you and would *keep the Passover* of the LORD, let all his males be circumcised, then he may come near and keep it. . . . *But no uncircumcised person shall eat of it.* (Exod 12:48)

> Remember the commandment which the LORD commanded you concerning *Passover,* that you observe its time, on the fourteenth of the first month, so that you might sacrifice it before it becomes evening and *so that you might eat it during the night on the evening of the fifteenth* from the time of sunset. (*Jubilees* 49:1-2)

> At this time there came round *the feast,* during which it is the ancestral custom of the Jews to serve unleavened bread. It is *called Passover,* being a commemoration of their departure from Egypt. (Josephus, *Antiquities* 17.213)

> [Jesus] said to [the disciples], ". . . Tell the householder, 'The Teacher says to you, Where is the guest room, where I am *to eat the Passover* with my disciples?' And he will show you a large upper room furnished; there make ready." (Luke 22:11-12)

As one would expect, given the connection between the sacrifice and the meal, some texts appear to refer to both.[243] For our purposes, however, there is an

242. BDAG, 784, lists this as the third definition of *pascha.*

243. Zahn, *Introduction to the New Testament,* 3:296, points out that when "Passover" is used with the verb "prepare" *(hetoimazein),* either meaning can be at work. E.g., Matt 26:19; Mark 14:16; Luke 22:8, 13.

important difference in time: when the word "Passover" is used to refer to the lamb apart from the meal, it is describing 14 Nisan; when it is used to refer to the meal with the lamb, it is referring to 15 Nisan.

3. ***The Passover Peace Offering*** The third definition of the word "Passover" refers to the sacrificial peace offering eaten during the weeklong feast of Unleavened Bread (15-21 Nisan).[244] This third definition of Passover is the one with which many readers, even some scholars, are unfamiliar.[245] In order to recognize this usage, it must be stressed that, according to the Jewish Torah, the initial Passover lamb was not the only sacrifice to be offered and eaten during the weeklong festival (15-21 Nisan). Another sacrificial lamb, in the category of a "peace offering," was to be offered and eaten over the course of the seven-day festival.[246] Consider, for example, the description of the weeklong feast of Unleavened Bread in the biblical book of Chronicles:

> And the sons of Israel that were present at Jerusalem kept the feast of unleavened bread seven days with great gladness. . . . So *the people ate the feast for seven days, sacrificing peace offerings* and giving thanks to the LORD the God of their fathers. (2 Chron 30:21-22)[247]

Notice here that, in contrast to the one-day contemporary Jewish Passover Seder familiar to many modern-day readers and scholars, the biblical celebration of Passover was tied to seven days of sacrifices and feasting in the sanctuary. It was, for lack of a better term, a kind of "Passover octave."

With this liturgical context of eight days of sacrificial feasting in mind,

244. See Num 28:17-25; 2 Chron 30:22; *Jub.* 49:22. On these Passover week sacrifices in early Jewish and rabbinic literature, see Smith, *Jesus' Last Passover Meal,* 20-21, citing Josephus, *Ant.* 3.224, 228; 8.271; *m. Pes.* 6:3; *t. Pesaḥ* 5:3; *Mek.* 12:5-8; *Sifre* on Deut 16:2 (129).

245. It is overlooked in BDAG, 784-85; Lust et al., *A Greek-English Lexicon of the Septuagint,* 2:361. Jeremias, *"pascha,"* 899, notes the evidence for this definition in 2 Chron 30:22, only then to dismiss it. Cf. Brown-Driver-Briggs, *Hebrew and English Lexicon,* 820, subsumes the usage in Deut 16:2 and 2 Chron 30:22 (cited below) under the first definition of the "sacrifice of passover, involving a communion-meal, hence a species of peace offering." The identification of these "Passovers" as peace offerings is of course, correct, but fails to note the calendrical distinction between when the initial Passover would be sacrificed (14 Nisan) and when the Passover peace offering would be killed and eaten (15-21 Nisan).

246. See Gary Anderson, "Sacrifice and Sacrificial Offerings (OT)," *ABD,* 5:878, who rightly notes that the peace offering is "the basic form of sacrifice brought on feast days (1 Sam 1:3-4; Deut 12:11-12)."

247. RSV (slightly adapted).

the key point is this: in Jewish Scripture, the peace offerings of the weeklong festival of Unleavened Bread are also referred to as "Passovers." It is extremely significant that this third definition can be found in the Hebrew Bible itself, in both the Law and the Prophets:

> Observe the month of Abib, and keep the Passover to the LORD your God; for in the month of Abib the LORD your God brought you out of Egypt by night. And *you shall sacrifice the Passover (pesaḥ) to the LORD your God, from the flock or the herd,* at the place which the LORD will choose, to make his name dwell there. *You shall eat no leavened bread with it; seven days you shall eat it with the unleavened bread,* the bread of affliction. . . . (Deut 16:1-3)

> Then Josiah contributed to the lay people, as *Passovers (pesaḥim)* for all that were present, *lambs and kids* from the flock to the number of thirty thousand, *and three thousand bulls.* . . . Hilkiah, Zechariah, and Jehiel, the chief officers of the house of God, gave to the priests *for Passovers* two thousand six hundred lambs and kids and three hundred bulls. Conaniah also . . . gave to the Levites *for Passovers (pesaḥim)* five thousand lambs and kids and five hundred bulls. (2 Chron 35:7-9)

In the passage from Deuteronomy, we find the word "Passover" *(pesaḥ)* used to refer both to the sheep or goat offerings from the flock and the cattle offerings from the herd (Deut 16:1-2). However, the initial Passover lamb could not be a bull, but had to be a sheep or goat (Exod 12:5). Therefore, in these verses, the word "Passover" is also being used to refer to the peace offerings that would be sacrificed and eaten over the course of the weeklong feast, which could be cattle (cf. Num 28:17-25). Indeed, that is why the very next verse states: "Seven days you shall eat it with unleavened bread" (Deut 16:3). In this sentence, the antecedent for the Hebrew word "it" is "Passover," so that it means: "Seven days you shall eat *the Passover* with unleavened bread." Again, this cannot refer to eating the initial lamb over the course of seven days, but rather to the peace offerings of the festal week.[248] In the passage from Chronicles, we find even more explicit evidence: Josiah and Hilkiah give thousands of bulls as "Passovers"

248. See Anderson, "Sacrifices and Sacrificial Offerings (OT)," 878, on the sacrificial meal that was an essential component of the peace offering. Regarding the interpretation of this text among the rabbis, see Bernard Grossfeld, *The Targum Onqelos to Deuteronomy* (Aramaic Bible 9; Wilmington: Michael Glazier, 1988), 53 n. 2.

(pesaḥim) for the people to eat (2 Chron 35:7, 8, 9). These "Passovers" cannot refer to the initial Passover lambs, since, once again, a bull could not be offered for that sacrifice. Rather, in this text, the word "Passover" refers to the peace offerings of the seven-day feast. In sum, a close reading of the Hebrew Bible reveals clear biblical precedent for using the word "Passover" to refer to these sacrifices. In short: *there is clear evidence from the Old Testament itself that the word "Passover" was used to refer to the peace offerings that would be sacrificed and eaten during the weeklong feast of Unleavened Bread (15-21 Nisan).*[249]

4. ***The Passover Week*** The fourth and final definition of the word "Passover" refers to the weeklong festival of Unleavened Bread. This definition, unlike the previous three, is not explicitly found in Jewish Scripture, which consistently designates the seven-day feast of 15-21 Nisan as "the feast of Unleavened Bread" *(ḥāg hamaṣṣôth)* (Lev 23:6-8; Num 28:17-25; Ezek 45:21).[250] However, by the first century A.D., this distinction had all but disappeared, and the term "Passover" also came to be used to refer to the seven-day feast as well.[251] Awareness of this linguistic shift is important for interpreting the Gospels in their Second Temple context. Consider, for example, the following:

> Now the feast of *Unleavened Bread* drew near, *which is called the Passover.* (Luke 22:1)

> As this action took place at the time of observing the feast of *Unleavened Bread, which we call Passover,* the Jews of best repute left the country and fled to Egypt. (Josephus, *Antiquities* 14.21)[252]

> When *the feast of Unleavened Bread, which we call Passover,* was going on, the priests were accustomed to throw open the gates of the temple after midnight. (Josephus, *Antiquities* 18.29)

> Wherein does the Passover of Egypt differ from the Passover of the generations [that followed after]? At the Passover of Egypt the lamb was got on the 10th [of Nisan] . . . and it was eaten in haste and during one night,

249. *Contra* Jeremias, *"pascha,"* 899, who rejects this usage in explaining Deut 16:1-2; 2 Chron 35:7-9, much less the early Jewish evidence outside the Bible.

250. Cf. BDB, 820, 595.

251. Jeremias, *"pascha,"* 897, lists as examples Josephus, *Ant.* 14.21; 17.213; 18.29; 20.106; *War* 2.10; *m. Pes.* 9:5; *m. Ḥag.* 1:3.

252. Some manuscripts of Josephus read *phaska,* which also means "Passover."

> whereas *the Passover of the generations* [that followed after] *continued throughout seven days.* (Mishnah, *Pesaḥim* 9:5)

Of these texts, the first is the most significant for our purposes, since it shows that even the Gospel of Luke was aware that in first-century Jewish parlance, "the feast of Unleavened Bread" *(hē heortē tōn azymōn)* was commonly "called Passover" *(legomenē pascha).* Luke's assertion is confirmed by Josephus, who says on more than one occasion that Jews in his own day refer to the weeklong feast of Unleavened Bread as "Passover" *(pascha).* By the time of the Mishnah, this fourth definition has become common, and the word "Passover" *(pesaḥ)* is used to refer to the whole Passover week, the seven-day feast (15-21 Nisan).

In light of the textual evidence cited above, scholarly studies of Passover in ancient Judaism and the New Testament agree on the following significant conclusion:

> Whereas the Old Testament distinguishes between the Passover, which was celebrated on the night of 14th-15th Nisan, and the feast of unleavened bread, held from the 15th to the 21st Nisan, in later Judaism the two were popularly combined and "passover" was generally used for both. This is the predominant usage in the New Testament.[253]

> [T]he NT treats Passover as part of the festival of Unleavened Bread . . . or even uses the latter term to refer to the former festival.[254]

It is impossible to overemphasize the importance of this linguistic point: the New Testament documents reflect the Second Temple Jewish custom of referring to the seven-day feast of unleavened bread simply as "Passover." Although readers familiar with the Old Testament may tend to separate Passover and Unleavened Bread, this was not so in Judaism at the time of Jesus. Indeed, the Gospel of Luke itself provides us with evidence for multiple uses of the word "Passover" in a single text:

"Then came the day of Unleavened Bread, on which the Passover had to be sacrificed." (Luke 22:7)	=	Passover *lamb,* sacrificed on 14 Nisan (definition #1)

253. Jeremias, *"pascha,"* 898.

254. Baruch M. Bokser, "Unleavened Bread and Passover, Feasts of," *Anchor Bible Dictionary* (6 vols.; ed. David Noel Freedman et al.; New York: Doubleday, 1992), 755-65 (here 763).

"Where is the guest room, where I am to eat the Passover with my disciples?" (Luke 22:11; cf. 22:15)	=	Passover *meal,* eaten on 15 Nisan (definition #2)
"The feast of Unleavened Bread drew new, which is called the Passover." (Luke 22:1)	=	Passover *week,* which lasts from 15 Nisan to 21 Nisan (definition #4)

As we will see, if the Gospel of Luke — written by a Gentile author probably for Gentile readers — could use multiple meanings of "Passover" *(pascha)* in the same Gospel, then there is no reason to doubt that the Gospel of John could do the same, especially given the latter's deep familiarity with the Jewish Temple and its feasts (see discussion below). Indeed, it seems clear that in the first century A.D., one could speak of all of the realities associated with the festival — the sacrificial lamb, the meal, the sacrifices, and the seven-day festival — as "Passover" without further qualification. These linguistic data will provide important support for the conclusion that the Gospel of John's multivalent use of the word "Passover" not only coheres with the Synoptic Gospels, but also is congruent with the extant Jewish festal terminology from the first century.

In sum, there is indisputable evidence for four definitions of the word "Passover": (1) the Passover lamb; (2) the Passover meal; (3) the Passover peace offering; and (4) Passover week. With this evidence in mind, we can now turn back to the Gospel of John's account of Jesus' death and try to situate it properly in the context of ancient Jewish Passover terminology. As we will see, unlike the Essene, Johannine, and Synoptic hypotheses, the Passover hypothesis takes all four meanings into account and in doing so is able to make sense of the Gospel data.

2. *"Before the Feast of Passover" = Before the Passover Lamb Was Eaten*

The second major argument in favor of the Passover hypothesis is far less well known, but equally significant. In short: contrary to what many assume, the phrase "before the feast of Passover" (John 13:1) does not mean before the Passover lamb was *sacrificed* (14 Nisan). To the contrary, in an ancient Jewish context, the phrase "before the feast of Passover" means before the Passover lamb was *eaten* (15 Nisan). Hence, the Gospel of John begins its account of the Last Supper on the same afternoon as the Synoptics: *the afternoon of 14 Nisan,* "just before the feast of Passover," the night when the lambs would be eaten.

In order to see this clearly, we must reexamine the beginning of the Gospel of John's account of the Last Supper, and interpret it carefully in light of ancient Jewish Passover language:

> Now *before the feast of Passover,* when Jesus knew that his hour had come to depart out of this world to the Father, having loved his own who were in the world, he loved them to the end. And during supper, when the devil had already put it into the heart of Judas Iscariot, Simon's son, to betray him. . . . (John 13:1-2)

Almost without fail, when modern commentators come to this passage, they assume that John's expression "the feast of Passover" refers to the day the lambs were sacrificed (14 Nisan).[255] From this point of view, then, John's opening time reference would be to the afternoon of the day before the lambs were sacrificed (13 Nisan). The recent statements of Mark Matson are representative:

> The Fourth Evangelist then explicitly marks out the chronological progression of the final days so that there is little question that the final meal was not Passover but was celebrated *the day before Passover, that is, on Nisan 13.* John's account begins in 13:1 by introducing the meal as taking place "before the Passover" *(pro de tēs heortēs tou pascha).*[256]

Along similar lines, Ernst Haenchen writes:

> The temporal notice, "before the feast of the Passover" [refers to] *the thirteenth of Nisan* and not the fourteenth, as in the synoptic tradition.[257]

According to this interpretation, John 13:1 refers to the afternoon of 13 Nisan (John 13:1), twenty-four hours before the lambs were sacrificed, and the remainder of John's account takes place during the "night" of 14 Nisan (John 13:30) — twenty-four hours before the lambs were eaten.[258] In the words of

255. E.g., Smith, "Jesus Tradition in the Gospel of John," 2022: "John seems to go out of his way to emphasize that Jesus died before Passover eve, not on the first day of the feast." Meier, *A Marginal Jew,* 1:427 n. 100: "John pointedly places the meal just before Passover (13:1)"; Bultmann, *The Gospel of John,* 465.

256. Matson, "The Historical Plausibility of John's Passion Dating," 292.

257. Ernst Haenchen, *John* (2 vols.; trans. E. Haenchen; Hermeneia; Philadelphia: Fortress, 1984), 105.

258. Westcott, *The Gospel according to St. John,* 2:145.

Raymond Brown: "The evening of this meal and the next day, on which Jesus will die, constitute Passover Eve."[259]

As widespread as this interpretation is, it is quite wrong, and reveals modern scholarly confusion about the first-century Jewish Passover and festal terminology. In an ancient Jewish context, "the feast" *(heortē)* of Passover always refers to 15 Nisan, the day on which the lambs were eaten. Therefore, "before the feast of Passover" means 14 Nisan, not 13 Nisan. It is difficult to overstress this point, as it is essential to a correct interpretation of the chronology of Jesus' death in the Gospel of John. Consider, for example, the following evidence:

> On the fourteenth day of the first month is the LORD's Passover. And *on the fifteenth day of the month is a feast* [= 15 Nisan]; seven days shall unleavened bread be eaten. (Num 28:16-17)

> Remember the commandment which the LORD commanded you concerning Passover, that you observe it in its time, on the fourteenth of the first month, so that you might sacrifice it before it becomes evening and so that you might eat it during the night on the *evening of the fifteenth from the time of sunset* [= 15 Nisan]. *For on this night there was the beginning of the feast. . . .* (*Jubilees* 49:1-2)

> Rabbi Judah says: They may search out [the leaven] on the night of the 14th or on the morning of the 14th or at the very time for its removal. But the Sages say: If a man has not searched on the night of the 14th let him search on the 14th; if he has not searched on *the 14th* let him search *during the Feast* [= 15 Nisan]; if he has not searched *during the Feast* let him search *after the Feast.* (Mishnah, *Pesaḥim* 1:3)

As these data demonstrate, in early Jewish parlance, the terminology of "the feast" of Passover is used for 15 Nisan, the night the Passover meal was eaten.[260] Indeed, it is a remarkable fact that in Jewish Scripture the word "feast" (MT *ḥāg;* LXX *heortē*) is never used for 14 Nisan, the day of "the LORD's Passover"; it is always used for 15 Nisan and the seven subsequent days.[261] (This makes

259. Brown, *The Gospel according to John,* 2:550.

260. As demonstrated above, the "feast" could of course also refer to the seven days beginning with 15 Nisan — i.e., 15-21 Nisan. But the effect is the same for our question.

261. See Exod 12:14-15 ("feast" is tied to the "seven days"); Exod 23:15; 34:18 ("the feast" is the seven days of Unleavened Bread); Exod 34:25 ("feast" refers to the meal eaten on the night

sense, of course, since a feast involves eating, and the consumption of the lamb does not take place on the 14th, but on the 15th.) The same thing is true in the Second Temple evidence. For example, *Jubilees* speaks of the sacrifice of the Passover lambs on the fourteenth. But it is the night of the 15th — when the Passover meal is eaten — that is designated "the beginning of the feast." Finally, and quite significantly, the Mishnah, like other rabbinic literature, repeatedly refers to 14 Nisan, the day on which the lambs were sacrificed, simply as "the fourteenth" *('arbā'āh 'āśār)*. Contrary to what Raymond Brown said above, it is 14 Nisan — not 13 Nisan! — that is called "the Eve of Passover" *('ereb pesaḥim)*.[262] Why? Because 15 Nisan, the night the lambs were eaten, is when "the Feast" *(hamô'ēd)* actually begins.[263] This distinction should be obvious to anyone familiar with ancient Jewish Passover customs, since 14 Nisan, the day on which the lambs were sacrificed, was apparently a day of fasting, not feasting (Mishnah, *Pesaḥim* 10:1).

The upshot of these data is simple: when John says "before the feast of Passover," he cannot mean 13 Nisan, before the lambs were sacrificed, as so many modern scholars suggest. All of the linguistic parallels suggest that the Gospel of John is referring to the afternoon of 14 Nisan, just "before the feast of Passover" — i.e., before the night on which the lambs would be eaten.

In support of this conclusion, it is also worth noting that John does not say "one day" or "twenty-four hours" before the feast of Passover, as so many commentators suggest; he only says "before" *(pro de)* the feast (John 13:1). The idea of an entire day is something that must be read into the text.[264] In order

of 15 Nisan); Lev 23:6 (the "feast" is on "the fifteenth day of the month" — not the fourteenth); Deut 16:16 (the "feast" is of "Unleavened Bread"); 2 Chron 8:13 ("the feast" is of "Unleavened Bread"); 2 Chron 35:17; Ezra 6:22 (the "feast" of Unleavened Bread lasts "seven days"); Ezek 45:21, 23 (although "the Passover" happens on "the fourteenth day of the month," the "feast" lasts "seven days," during which "unleavened bread" is eaten). It is remarkable that this fact is not more frequently acknowledged. Cf. Raymond Brown, *The Death of the Messiah,* 2:1356 n. 9, who acknowledges that "There is a debate whether 'feast' means Passover, Unleavened Bread, or both," but then goes on to assert without citing any evidence whatsoever that "in the 1st cent. AD the usage was changing, so that 'feast' was being used more frequently (and soon exclusively) for Passover rather than for Unleavened Bread." In Mishnah, the exact *opposite* is the case; the 14th is just "the fourteenth," the 15th or 15th-21st is "the Feast."

262. See *m. Shabb.* 23:1; *m. Pes.*4:5.

263. See David Instone-Brewer, *Feasts and Sabbaths: Passover and Atonement* (TRENT 2A; Grand Rapids: Eerdmans, 2011), 115-16.

264. Barrett, *The Gospel according to St. John,* 437, admits this, when he says of John 13:1: "That John *means* in fact *the day* before the Passover is shown by 18.28, 19.14, 31, 42." In other words, taken by itself, John 13:1 does not clearly state "the day before Passover," but "just before the Passover feast." A similar admission can be found in Bultmann, *The Gospel of John,* 465.

to see this point clearly, it is helpful to compare the chronology of John 13:1 to a parallel reference at the beginning of the previous chapter:

> *Six days before the Passover,* Jesus came to Bethany, where Lazarus was, whom Jesus had raised from the dead. There they made him a supper. . . . (John 12:1-2)

> *Before the feast of Passover,* when Jesus knew that his hour had come to depart out of this world to the Father, having loved his own who were in the world, he loved them to the end. And during supper. . . . (John 13:1-2)

This parallel is quite revealing. It shows that when John wants to speak of whole days before Passover, he explicitly says "six days before the Passover" *(pro hex hēmerōn tou pascha)* (John 12:1). But there is no reference to an entire "day" *(hēmera)* before the feast of Passover in John 13:1; there he simply says "before the feast of the Passover" *(pro de tēs heortēs tou pascha).* To my mind, this difference places the burden of proof on the interpreter who wants to claim that John is setting the Last Supper twenty-four hours before the Passover meal. Significantly, this point is admitted by advocates of the Johannine hypothesis, who state:

> In themselves, the words *pro de tēs heortēs tou pascha* ["before the feast of Passover"] need only designate the proximity of the Passover feast.[265]

> It was just before the Passover feast.[266]

> John pointedly places the meal just before Passover (13:1).[267]

If Bultmann, Brown, and Meier are correct in their interpretations and translation of the meaning of "before" in John 13:1, and we recognize that "the feast of Passover" refers to the day on which the lambs were eaten (15 Nisan), then it seems fairly clear that the chronological reference in John 13:1 means: "Just before 15 Nisan."

In sum, while modern commentators on John may think of 14 Nisan as "the feast of Passover," ancient Jews apparently did not.[268] The feast of Passover

265. Bultmann, *The Gospel of John,* 465 n. 1.

266. Brown, *The Gospel according to John,* 2:548.

267. Meier, *A Marginal Jew,* 1:427 n. 100.

268. Contra Bernard, *St. John,* 454, who holds that "what is now to be narrated takes place on the eve of the Passover, i.e., on the evening of Nisan 13." But 13 Nisan is never called

did not begin until the lambs were being eaten, and that meant 15 Nisan. Hence, the correct interpretation of "before the feast of the Passover" (John 13:1) is "just before 15 Nisan." It is hard to overemphasize the importance of this point, since the misconstrual of John's opening verse in his description of Jesus' Last Supper is one of the primary factors that leads scholars to misinterpret the rest of the Fourth Gospel's chronology.[269] A correct interpretation would place John's opening chronological indicator on the late afternoon before the meal would be eaten that night — *the very same afternoon identified in the Synoptic Gospels before they give their descriptions of the Last Supper* (cf. Mark 14:12; Luke 22:7).

3. *The Last Supper in John Is a Passover Meal*

The third major argument for the Passover hypothesis is that the Last Supper in the Gospel of John, when interpreted in its ancient Jewish context, contains several striking indications that it is not an ordinary meal, but rather a Jewish Passover meal.

This conclusion would, of course, follow logically from a correct interpretation of John 13:1.[270] However, it can also be established by analyzing the

---

"the eve of the Passover" *('ereb pesaḥ);* that is reserved for 14 Nisan. See, e.g., *m. Pes.* 4:5, where morning-afternoon of 14 Nisan is called "the eve of Passover"; the night following 13 Nisan is simply called "the night." If that is true, then the late afternoon of 13 Nisan could never merit being called "the eve of Passover."

269. It is also one of the primary weaknesses of certain presentations of the Passover hypothesis, which recognize the polyvalence of the word "Passover" in early Judaism, but fail to clearly explain the chronological indicator in John 13:1. See, e.g., Andreas J. Köstenberger, "Was the Last Supper a Passover Meal?," in *The Lord's Supper: Remembering and Proclaiming Christ Until He Comes* (ed. T. R. Schreiner and M. R. Crawford; NACSBT 10; Nashville B. & H. Academic, 2011), 1-25; "John," in *Commentary on the New Testament Use of the Old Testament* (ed. G. K. Beale and D. A. Carson; Grand Rapids: Baker Academic, 2007), 500; Craig L. Blomberg, *The Historical Reliability of the Gospels* (2nd ed.; Downers Grove: IVP, 2007), 221-25; *The Historical Reliability of John's Gospel: Issues & Commentary* (Downers Grove: IVP, 2001), 187, 193-94, 238-39, 246-47; Darrell L. Bock, *Jesus according to Scripture* (Grand Rapids: Baker Academic, 2002), 357-66, 495-97, 617-18; idem, *Luke* (2 vols.; BECNT; Grand Rapids: Baker, 1994), 2:1951-60; Barry D. Smith, "The Chronology of the Last Supper," *WTJ* 53 (1991): 29-45; idem, *Jesus' Last Passover Meal* (Lewiston: Edwin Mellen, 1993); D. A. Carson, *The Gospel according to John* (Grand Rapids: Eerdmans, 1991), 457-58, 460, 473-76, 587-90, 603-4; William L. Lane, *The Gospel According to Mark* (NICNT; Grand Rapids: Eerdmans, 1974), 496-98; Norval Geldenhuys, *Commentary on the Gospel of Luke* (NICNT; Grand Rapids: Eerdmans, 1951), 649-70.

270. Blomberg, *The Historical Reliability of John's Gospel,* 193-94.

details of John's description of the Last Supper. After the account of Jesus' act of washing the disciples' feet (John 13:3-20), the Gospel of John says the following about the Last Supper:

> When Jesus had thus spoken, he was troubled in spirit, and testified, "Amen, amen, I say to you, one of you will betray me." The disciples looked at one another, uncertain of whom he spoke. *One of his disciples, whom Jesus loved, was lying close to the breast of Jesus;* so Simon Peter beckoned him and said, "Tell us who it is of whom he speaks." So *lying thus, close to the breast of Jesus,* he said to him, "Lord, who is it?" Jesus answered, *"It is he to whom I shall give this morsel when I have dipped it." So when he dipped the morsel,* he gave it to Judas, the son of Simon Iscariot. Then after the morsel, Satan entered into him. Jesus said to him, "What you are going to do, do quickly." Now no one at the table knew why he said this to him. *Some thought that, because Judas had the money box, Jesus was telling him, "Buy what we need for the feast"; or that he should give something to the poor.* So, after receiving the morsel, he immediately went out, and it was night. (John 13:21-30)

As advocates of both the Johannine and Synoptic hypotheses admit, several aspects of this account suggest that John, like the Synoptics, is describing the Last Supper as a Jewish Passover meal:

1. The reclining posture of Jesus and the disciples (John 13:23-25);
2. The dipping of the morsel by Jesus (John 13:26-27);
3. The custom of giving something to the poor during a festal meal (John 13:29);
4. The last-minute purchase of something for the feast (John 13:29-30);

We will take a few moments to examine each of these in more detail.

First, as Rudolf Bultmann points out, Jesus and the disciples are "lying" down or reclining at table (John 13:23, 25). This posture coheres perfectly with ancient Jewish tradition that required everyone to "recline" while eating the Passover meal:[271]

271. So Bultmann, *The Gospel of John,* 480 n. 3; Barrett, *The Gospel According to St. John,* 446. Cf. Dalman, *Jesus-Jeshua,* 115: "Jesus had at table John 'at His breast' (John xiii.25; xxi.20), or 'in His bosom' (John xiii.23). A disciple of the Rabbis thus described the Passover meal of his teacher: 'We lay on one another's knees.' As it was always the custom to lean upon the left arm, in order to keep the right arm free for the food, one had the neighbor at the right, in

> Even the poorest in Israel must not eat unless he *reclines* at table, and they must not give him less than four cups of wine to drink. (Mishnah, *Pesaḥim* 10:1)[272]

> Even the poorest in Israel should not eat [the Passover] until he *reclines* at his table. (Tosefta, *Pesaḥim* 10:1)[273]

Although these rabbinic parallels are certainly later than the Gospels, they provide a plausible explanation for John's description of the disciples' posture at the Last Supper, which coheres with and is perhaps even meant to emphasize that the meal took place on the night the Passover was eaten.

Moreover, as C. K. Barrett points out, Jesus' act of dipping of the "morsel" and handing it to Judas "refers most naturally to the dipping of bitter herbs of the Passover meal in the *haroseth* sauce," which took place before the Passover meal proper began.[274] Again, a similar action is described in the rabbinic tractates on Passover:

> [When] they bring him [the food], he dips the lettuce [in vinegar] before he comes to the breaking of the bread. They brought him unleavened bread, lettuce and *haroset* and two dishes. . . . (Mishnah, *Pesaḥim* 10:3)[275]

> Rabbi Judah says: "Even if one has eaten only one small savory, even if he has dipped only one piece of lettuce, they still toss unleavened bread to the children, so that they won't fall asleep." (Tosefta, *Pesaḥim* 10:9)

---

front of the breast, and lay behind his back. Therefore, if John was in this position, he was at second place of honour after the Master. . . ."

272. Author's translation.

273. See Jeremias, *The Eucharistic Words of Jesus,* 49 n. 2, who also cites the Jerusalem Talmud: "Rabbi Levi has said: 'because slaves eat standing, here (at the passover meal) people should recline to eat, to signify that they have passed from slavery to freedom'" (*y. Pes.* 10:37b; cf. *b. Pesaḥim* 108a).

274. Barrett, *The Gospel According to St. John,* 447. Strikingly, he goes on to say that John contradicts himself: "John represents the supper as taking place before the Passover, and therefore cannot have been thinking of the bitter herbs and *haroseth,* but his use of *baptein* and *psōmion* . . . may be regarded as a trace of the earlier synoptic tradition in which the supper was a Paschal meal (cf. v. 23). In the Passover *Haggadah* the Passover supper is distinguished from all other meals in several ways including 'on all other nights we do not dip . . . even once, but on this night twice.'"

275. Trans. Jacob Neusner, *The Mishnah: A New Translation* (New Haven and London: Yale University Press, 1988), 249.

In addition, as Raymond Brown concedes, the disciples' interpretations of Judas' actions — as going to buy something "for the feast" or to give something "to the poor" — together suggest that John 13:21-30 depicts the Last Supper being eaten on Passover night.[276] For in ancient Jewish tradition, it appears to have been customary to provide for the poor on the evenings of feast days.[277] Consider, for example, a striking parallel from the book of Tobit regarding a similar action during the feast of Pentecost:

> When I [Tobit] arrived home and my wife Anna and my son Tobias were restored to me, at the feast of Pentecost, which is the sacred festival of the seven weeks, a good dinner was prepared for me and I sat down to eat. *Upon seeing the abundance of food I said to my son, "Go and bring whatever poor man of our brethren you may find* among the exiles of Nineveh, who is mindful of the Lord, *and he shall eat together with me.* I will wait for you until you come back." *So Tobias went out to look for some poor person* of our people. (Tobit 2:1-3)

This text is remarkable insofar as it not only suggests that the poor would be provided for on the feast of Pentecost, but that the festal meal could be interrupted just before it began in order to carry out this pious duty. That is exactly what appears to be happening with the disciples' reaction to Judas' departure in John. Along similar lines, the Mishnah alludes to a similar concern for the poor being exercised during the feast of Passover:

> Even the poorest in Israel must not eat [the Passover] until he sits down to table, and they must not give them less than four cups of wine to drink, even if it is from the [Pauper's] Dish. (Mishnah, *Pesaḥim* 10:1)

Taken together, this evidence sheds much light on the disciples' otherwise puzzling reaction to Judas' departure from the Last Supper. For it provides a precise parallel with John's account of the Last Supper: the table is set, the participants have reclined at table. However, before the festal meal proper is eaten, Judas gets up from table and leaves, and some disciples interpret him

276. Brown, *The Gospel according to John,* 2:576; cf. Jeremias, *The Eucharistic Words of Jesus,* 53-54. It should be noted here that in making this point I find no basis for Jeremias's suggestion that Josephus' reference to the opening of the city gates on Passover night (*Ant.* 18.29) has anything to do with the custom of giving to the poor.

277. Keener, *The Gospel of John,* 2:920.

as departing "in order to give something to the poor" (John 13:29).[278] Lastly, these parallels explain why the other disciples apparently think that Judas is dashing out to make a last-minute purchase "for the feast" (John 13:29). As even advocates of the Johannine hypothesis admit, the disciples' interpretation of Judas' actions makes no sense according to the common assumption that the Passover meal was still twenty-four hours away. As Raymond Brown notes:

> Why would Judas be sent out to make the purchases on Thursday *night* when all Friday remained for shopping?[279]

The only reason for Judas to go out shortly before "night" (John 13:30) to buy something "for the feast" was that "the feast" — i.e., the Passover meal — was about to begin. The disciples thus appear to imagine Judas going out to the nearby street (perhaps containing festal vendors about to close up shop) just before nightfall to make a final purchase for the Passover feast.[280]

In short, despite the assumption of many that the Last Supper in John's Gospel is not a Passover meal, a close examination of his text in the light of Jewish parallels points in precisely the opposite direction. In this regard, it is essential to note that this conclusion is not simply drawn by advocates of the Passover hypothesis. To the contrary, as I pointed out at the beginning of the chapter, a remarkable number of major scholars admit that the Last Supper in John 13 is in fact being described as a Passover meal. In light of what we have seen so far, consider again the following observations with reference to the text in question:

> Julius Wellhausen: "Jesus and his disciples are here still at table, and in fact at the passover meal, i.e. at the Lord's supper of the synoptics; in

278. In terms of the ancient debate over whether Judas partook of the first eucharist, this evidence suggests that Judas leaves the Last Supper before the consumption of the lamb takes place. In support of this suggestion, note that it is only after Judas leaves the table that "night" falls (John 13:30). Hence, in the preceding verses John appears to be describing what is happening on Thursday dusk, shortly "before the feast of Passover" (John 13:1), as Jesus and the disciples reclined at a table prepared for eating the main festal meal that night.

279. Brown, *The Gospel according to John,* 2:576; see also Smith, "The Chronology of the Last Supper," 32; Jeremias, *The Eucharistic Words of Jesus,* 53.

280. At the risk of being anachronistic, I expect some readers have had the experience of arriving at a party at which one of the hosts has dashed off for some last-minute purchase before the evening banquet, even if the table is set and the opening appetizers have already begun.

contradiction to 13:1; 18:28; 19:14 — it is idle to shut one's eyes to this contradiction."[281]

Rudolf Bultmann: "The expression ['lying close to the breast of Jesus'] is certainly an indication that the meal which is spoken of in vv. 21-30, in contrast to vv. 2-20, is the Passover meal; for on this occasion reclining at table was obligatory."[282]

Joachim Jeremias: "There are other traces of the synoptic chronology in the fourth gospel, especially in the account of Jesus' last supper (John 13.2ff.). . . . Some of the remarks made by John presuppose that this was a passover meal."[283]

Raymond Brown: "That there are Passover characteristics in the meal, even in John, is undeniable."[284]

C. K. Barrett: "The supposed command [of Jesus] to give to the poor would be particularly appropriate on Passover night. . . . In going into the darkness Judas went to his own place. So far as the remark is historical it suggests that the event took place on Passover night (in agreement with the Markan tradition)."[285]

Craig S. Keener: "Although Jewish people in Palestine usually sat on chairs when available, they had adopted the Hellenistic custom of reclining for banquets, including the Passover, a setting that the Fourth Gospel and its first audience might assume from the Gospel tradition despite the Fourth Gospel's symbolic shift of the Passover to one day later. It probably implies that John has, after all, revised an earlier Passover tradition."[286]

281. Julius Wellhausen, *Das Evangelium Johannis* (Berlin: Georg Reimer, 1908), 60; translation in Jeremias, *The Eucharistic Words of Jesus,* 82 n. 3.

282. Bultmann, *The Gospel of John,* 480 n. 3.

283. Jeremias, *The Eucharistic Words of Jesus,* 81.

284. Brown, *The Gospel according to John,* 2:556, citing P. Benoit, "The Holy Eucharist," *Scripture* 8 (1956): 97-108.

285. Barrett, *The Gospel according to St. John,* 448, 449. In discussing the departure of Judas to give something to the poor, Barrett is forced to conclude that "the historical setting" of the Last Supper changes in these verses from twenty-four hours in advance of Passover to Passover night itself (448).

286. Keener, *The Gospel of John,* 2:900-901. Elsewhere Keener admits that Judas' going to give to the poor "is not incompatible with Passover" (2:920).

Given the widespread assumption that John's Gospel goes out of its way to stress that the Last Supper was not a Passover meal, this is a weighty catena of scholarly assertions to the contrary. Indeed, it shows that some of the most influential and exhaustive modern commentaries on John consistently recognize that the Last Supper in John resembles a Passover meal. This admission is particularly significant when we consider that none of the scholars listed above is an advocate of the Passover hypothesis. To the contrary, all of them either support the Johannine or Synoptic hypothesis. In short: *a number of major scholars agree that at least some of the data in John's Gospel actually support the conclusion that the Last Supper was a Passover meal.*

Once again, this conclusion leads these scholars to conclude that the Gospel of John is in conflict with its own account of the Last Supper. On the one hand, all of these commentators think that the Fourth Gospel dates Jesus' crucifixion on the day the lambs were sacrificed. On the other hand, all of them also admit that the Last Supper in John is a Passover meal, despite his apparent chronology. As a result, they are forced to conclude that John's Gospel contradicts itself on the date and character of the Last Supper. As Wellhausen puts it, "it is idle to shut one's eyes to this contradiction."[287] Likewise, Jeremias contends that there are "traces of the synoptic chronology in the fourth gospel."[288] In order to explain the problem, Rudolf Schnackenburg posits that the passages that identify the meal as a Passover are later "interpolations."[289] Such appeals to competing chronologies within the same Gospel and hypothetical interpolations are both unconvincing and unnecessary. Given the multiple meanings of the word "Passover" in Jewish Scripture and extrabiblical literature, a much more plausible solution is that modern commentators have simply misinterpreted John's Passover terminology.

Indeed, the very admission of these scholars that John depicts the Last Supper as a Passover meal constitutes one of the most powerful arguments for the Passover hypothesis. If the major Johannine commentators of the twentieth century are correct and the Fourth Gospel depicts the Last Supper as a Passover meal, then it follows that *all four Gospels agree that the Last Supper was a Passover meal.* Hence, in order to maintain the position that the Last Supper was not a Passover meal, one has to reject the testimony of all the Gospels, not just three. From the vantage point of historical methodology, it seems more reasonable to accept their testimony, and to continue to interpret

287. Wellhausen, *Das Evangelium Johannis,* 60.

288. Jeremias, *The Eucharistic Words of Jesus,* 81.

289. Schnackenburg, *The Gospel according to St. John,* 3:36.

the subsequent chronological references in the Gospel of John within this chronological and festal context.

4. *"To Eat the Passover" = the Passover Peace Offering*

The fourth major argument for the Passover hypothesis is that the description of the Jewish leaders refusing to enter the praetorium on the Friday of Jesus' execution so that they might "eat the Passover" (John 18:28) refers to the consumption of the Passover peace offering (15 Nisan), not to the consumption of the initial Passover lamb (14 Nisan). In an ancient Jewish context, both the initial lamb and the peace offerings eaten during Passover week could be referred to as "Passovers" *(pesaḥim),* and a state of ritual purity was necessary for the consumption of both. Moreover, since John has already identified the Last Supper as the initial Jewish Passover meal (John 13:1-20), it follows that the only consistent and contextually plausible meaning for the word "Passover" *(pascha)* is the sacrificial lamb eaten during the seven-day festival (John 18:28).

In order to see this, we must carefully reexamine the account of Jesus being brought to Pilate's praetorium early Friday morning:

> Then they led Jesus from the house of Caiaphas to the praetorium. It was early. They themselves did not enter the praetorium, so that they might not be defiled, but might *eat the Passover.* (John 18:28)

For many commentators, this verse is the decisive argument in favor of the conclusion that Jesus was crucified before the Jewish Passover lambs were eaten (Friday night), and that the Synoptic description of the Last Supper as a Jewish Passover meal is thus incorrect.[290] However, according to the Passover hypothesis, in John 18:28, the Greek word *pascha* does not refer to the Passover lamb or to the "feast of Passover" at which the lamb was eaten (cf. John 13:1) but to the Passover peace offering, which would be eaten over the course of the seven-day festival.[291]

In support of this position, several points need to be made.

290. Meier, *A Marginal Jew,* 1:389; Zeitlin, "The Last Supper as an Ordinary Meal in the Fourth Gospel," 256.

291. Blomberg, *The Historical Reliability of John's Gospel,* 237-38; Smith, "The Chronology of the Last Supper," 39-41; Torrey, "In the Fourth Gospel the Last Supper Was the Paschal Meal," 242-44; Zahn, *Introduction to the New Testament,* 3:297-98.

For one thing, *John has already identified the Last Supper as a Passover meal* (John 13:1, 21-30). This observation is critically important. If John has already indicated the Last Supper was a Passover meal, then it follows that when the word "Passover" occurs in John 18:28, if read in context, the first two definitions of "Passover" — the Passover lamb and the Passover meal — are excluded. This leaves only the Passover week and its peace offerings as candidates. As Craig Blomberg states:

> When we read 18:28 in its narrative sequence, after the account of chapters 13-17, we would naturally assume that by "eating the Passover" John is referring to upcoming meals in the week-long feast of the Unleavened Bread.[292]

This crucial point is often overlooked, even by advocates of the Passover hypothesis.[293] If John has already identified the Last Supper as a Passover meal taking place on the night of 15 Nisan, then the word "Passover" in John 18:28 must refer to something other than the Passover lamb. *Hence, it is only by taking John 18:28 out of context that it can be made to refer to the initial Passover lamb.* Again, this point is admitted by commentators on John when they claim that the reference to "eat[ing] the Passover" in 18:28 "contradicts" John's earlier description of the Last Supper as a Passover.[294]

Moreover, as we saw above, in the Old Testament itself, the word "Passover" (Hebrew *pesaḥ;* Greek *pascha*) can be used to refer to the Passover peace offerings. The Pentateuch commands the Israelites to eat the "Passover" *(pesaḥ)* for "seven days . . . with unleavened bread" (Deut 16:1-3), clearly referring to the Passover week peace offerings. The book of Chronicles speaks of Josiah giving lambs, kids, and "bulls" as "Passovers *(pesaḥim)* for all that were present" during the weeklong festival (2 Chron 35:7-9). Now, if this biblical evidence were all we had, it would to establish the linguistic plausibility of the Fourth Gospel using the word "Passover" in the same way: to refer to the Passover peace offerings.

For what it is worth, in later rabbinic literature, we also find several cases in which the word "Passover" *(pesaḥ)* is explicitly defined as referring to the Passover peace offerings.[295] Compare the following texts:

292. Blomberg, *The Historical Reliability of John's Gospel,* 238.

293. E.g., Smith, "The Chronology of the Last Supper."

294. E.g., Jeremias, *The Eucharistic Words of Jesus,* 82.

295. See Smith, "The Chronology of the Last Supper," 35-39; Lightfoot, *A Commentary on the New Testament from the Talmud and Hebraica,* 3:420-23.

> Wherein does the Passover of Egypt differ from the Passover of the generations? At the Passover of Egypt *it was acquired on the tenth* [of Nisan] . . . *and it was eaten* in haste and during *one night;* whereas *the Passover of the generations,* according to custom, *throughout seven days.* (Mishnah, *Pesaḥim* 9:5)[296]

> Can the Passover be offered on any of the festivals? The Passover has a fixed date: if it is brought then, well and good, but if not, it is rejected. Rabbi Hisda replied. The Passover is mentioned incidentally. Rabbi Shesheth said: *"Passover" here means the peace offerings of Passover.* (Babylonian Talmud, *Rosh Hashanah* 5a)[297]

> Rabbi Shesheth said: "*What does the 'Passover' mean? The peace-offerings of Passover.*" If so, is it identical with peace-offerings? — He teaches about peace-offerings which are brought on account of Passover, and he teaches about peace-offerings which are brought independently. (Babylonian Talmud, *Zebaḥim* 99b)

> [I]t is written: "And you shall sacrifice the Passover unto the Lord your God, of the flock and of the herd" [Deut 16:2]; yet surely the Passover is only from lambs or goats? But "flock" here refers to the Passover, [while] *"herd" refers to the festival offering,* as the Divine Law says: "And *you shall sacrifice the Passover.*" (Babylonian Talmud, *Pesaḥim* 70b)

Remarkably, this linguistic evidence is consistently ignored or dismissed by critics of the Passover hypothesis. Yet it provides important lexical support for the contextual interpretation of the Gospel of John's Passover terminology. For example, the Mishnah draws a direct contrast between "the Passover of Egypt" *(pesaḥ mitzraim),* which was "eaten" *('ākal)* in "one night," and "the Passover of generations" *(pesaḥ dōrōth),* which is "throughout seven days." In other words, the word "Passover" not only refers to the initial lamb sacrificed on 14 Nisan and eaten on 15 Nisan, but also to the other offerings sacrificed and eaten during the entire Passover week.[298] Moreover, the other texts cited

296. Author's translation; I have rendered the text literally, so that the absence of the verb in the final clause is clear. Most English translations add a verb such as "continued" (Danby) or "applies" (Neusner) that is not present in the Hebrew. See Zahn, *Introduction to the New Testament,* 3:297, who notes: "Since no new verb takes the place of 'eating' the Passover in the original celebration, this same verb is to be supplied in the second instance also."

297. Soncino translation slightly adapted.

298. Smith, "The Chronology of the Last Supper," 37.

above explicitly state that the word "Passover" *(pesaḥ)* can be used to refer both to the Passover lamb and to "the peace offerings of Passover" *(shelamiy pesaḥ).* This is exactly what I am arguing takes place in John 18:28: the expression "to eat the Passover" refers to the Passover peace offering. Notice also how the rabbinic traditions interpret Deuteronomy 16:1-3 precisely as I argued above: when the Pentateuch speaks about "eating" the "Passover" for "seven days with unleavened bread," it is referring to the peace offerings of Passover week. As one modern scholar notes, the sacrifice from the flock refers to the lamb, while the sacrifice from the herd refers to the peace offering, but "both are called by the same name" — the name of "Passover."[299]

Finally, there is the reason the Jews do not wish to enter Pilate's praetorium: "so that they might not be defiled, but might eat the Passover" (John 18:28). Critics of the Passover hypothesis sometimes argue that it was not necessary to eat the Passover peace offering in a state of ritual purity, and that therefore John must be referring to the initial Passover lamb.[300] But this is demonstrably false; according to the Jewish Torah, the Passover peace offering was like all other peace offerings — it had to be eaten in a state of ritual purity:

> All who are clean may eat flesh, but the person who eats of the flesh of the sacrifice of the LORD's peace offerings while an uncleanness is on him, that person shall be cut off from his people. (Lev 7:19-20)[301]

Clearly, the act of eating any peace offering — much less the festal peace offerings of Passover week — in a state of ritual defilement, was a serious breach of Mosaic Law. This appears to be the driving force behind the Jews' unwillingness to enter Pilate's praetorium.[302] It is also a weighty argument against the

299. See the note by H. Freedman in the *Hebrew-English Soncino Talmud,* Tractate *Pesaḥim* 70b, n. 4. Cf. Marcus Jastrow, *Dictionary of the Targumim, Talmud Babli, Yerushalmi and Midrashic Literature* (2 vols.; New York: Judaica Press, 1971), 1:423.

300. Cf. Matson, "The Historical Plausibility of John's Passion Dating," 293-94; Zeitlin, "The Last Supper as an Ordinary Meal in the Fourth Gospel," 256.

301. Cf. Deut 16:1-3 (on eating the peace offering with unleavened bread).

302. It is not clear exactly what kind of ritual defilement is actually envisioned here. Most commentators suggest that John's account appears to reflect the ancient Jewish belief that all Gentile homes were ritually impure, probably because of the Gentile custom of disposing of their aborted children by throwing their bodies down the drains beneath their homes. For example, *11QTemple* [11Q19] 48:11-12 reads: "And you shall not do as the gentiles do: they bury their dead in every place, they even bury them in the middle of their houses." Likewise, *m. 'Ohal.* 18:7: "The dwelling-places of gentiles are unclean." Regarding this rabbinic tradition,

popular argument by supporters of the Johannine hypothesis that Barabbas was released in order that he might partake of the Passover.[303] This otherwise ingenious suggestion fails to take the first-century Jewish context into account, in which Barabbas, having been in a Gentile prison, would have been in a state of ritual defilement and would have missed all the preliminary cleansings necessary for offering and eating the Passover (see Num 9:11-12; Josephus, *War* 1.229; John 11:55; Acts 21:24-27). By contrast, the Passover hypothesis coheres perfectly with the linguistic complexity and liturgical realities of ancient Jewish practice and belief.

In sum, when John's account of the Jews refusing to enter Pilate's praetorium so that they might "eat the Passover" in John 18:28 is interpreted both in its literary context as following the Passover meal described in John 13:1-20 and in the historical context of ancient Jewish Passover terminology, the expression does not appear to refer to consuming the initial Passover lamb, but rather to consumption of the Passover peace offering. In light of such evidence, the widespread assertion that "[t]he *chagiga* [= Passover peace offering] was never called Passover"[304] is erroneous. There are, in fact, solid linguistic and historical reasons for interpreting John 18:28 as a reference to the consumption of the Passover peace offering, which is referred to by the word "Passover" in both the Old Testament and ancient Jewish literature.

---

the footnote in Danby, *The Mishnah*, 675 n. 10 reads: "Because they throw abortions down their drains." Cf. Acts 10:28; 11:3; Keener, *The Gospel of John*, 2:1099; S. Safrai and Menahem Stern, eds., with David Flusser and W. C. van Unnik, *The Jewish People in the First Century: Historical Geography, Political History, Social, Cultural, and Religious Life and Institutions* (2 vols.; CRINT 1; Assen: Van Gorcum, 1974-76), 829; Jaubert, *The Date of the Last Supper*, 112; Brown, *The Gospel according to John*, 845-46, gives a number of other parallels regarding Jewish views of Gentile impurity, including the Temple Scroll, which expresses disdain for the Gentile practice of burying "the dead everywhere, even in their houses." Cf. Josephus, *Ant.* 18.93-94, on Jews going to get priestly vestments from the Romans seven days before the festival. This is intriguing, since the ritual defilement of touching a graveyard or entering into a home where someone has died is "seven days" (Num 19:14-16), the exact length of the Passover week festival. As such, in John 18:28, the Jews may be concerned about being excluded from the entire seven-day festival.

303. E.g., Meier, *A Marginal Jew*, 1:400, who regards the "obvious premise" of the release of Barabbas as being given "precisely so that the Jew, upon release, could take part in the Passover meal." None of the Gospels suggests this, nor is it as obvious as Meier purports. A far more plausible explanation of the amnesty is the perennial political principle of *quid pro quo:* in exchange for the peaceful celebration of the Passover in the city, the people are allowed the release of one political prisoner.

304. Zeitlin, "The Last Supper as an Ordinary Meal in the Fourth Gospel," 256.

5. *The "Preparation of Passover" = the Friday of Passover Week*

The fifth major argument for the Passover hypothesis is that the phrase "preparation of the Passover" *(paraskeuē tou pascha)* (John 19:14) does not refer to "the Preparation Day for the Passover" — that is, 14 Nisan. Instead, it refers to "the Friday *(paraskeuē)* of Passover week." In other words, it utilizes the fourth definition of the word "Passover" given above, in which *pascha* refers to the entire weeklong festival.

In order to see this, we need to go back and examine carefully the Gospel of John's account of Jesus being brought before Pilate:

> [Pilate] brought Jesus out and sat down on the judgment seat at a place called the Pavement, and in Hebrew, Gabbatha. Now it was *Preparation of the Passover;* it was about the sixth hour. (John 19:13-14)

For many exegetes, John's statement that Jesus was crucified on "Preparation of the Passover" *(paraskeuē tou pascha)* suggests that Jesus was crucified *before* the Jewish Passover lambs were eaten. From this perspective, the phraseology refers to "day of Preparation for the Passover"[305] — meaning that Jesus was crucified on 14 Nisan at the very same time the Jewish pilgrims were preparing to eat the initial Passover lamb later that evening.[306]

Of the three key chronological indicators in John's Gospel, this is the one that is easiest to clarify, by means of a few simple observations.

First, many English Bibles exacerbate the confusion caused by this verse by failing to translate the text in John literally. For example, in various translations, we read "It was preparation day for Passover" (NAB); "Now it was the day of Preparation of the Passover" (RSV); "Now it was the day of preparation for the Passover" (NRSV). Unfortunately, none of these are what the Gospel of John actually says. The Greek text simply reads: "Now it was preparation of the Passover" *(ēn de paraskeuē tou pascha).* Notice that there is no reference to any supposed "day" of preparation; this must be added in the translation. Notice also that "Passover" is in the genitive case: it is the preparation "*of* the Passover," not "*for* the Passover."[307] In other words, in order to give the appearance of dating Jesus' crucifixion to the time before the consumption of

305. Haenchen, *John,* 2:178.

306. Schnackenburg, *The Gospel according to St. John,* 3:264; Brown, *The Gospel according to John,* 2:882; Barrett, *The Gospel According to St. John,* 545; Zeitlin, "The Last Supper as an Ordinary Meal in the Fourth Gospel," 251-55.

307. Zahn, *Introduction to the New Testament,* 3:295-96.

the Passover lambs, the English translations must add elements that simply are not present in the original Greek text.

Second, in the first-century A.D., the Greek word "preparation" *(paraskeuē)* is simply the Jewish name for "Friday," because that was the day of the week on which one would "prepare" *(paraskeuazō)* for the Sabbath, which began at sundown Friday evening.[308] Consider the following examples:

> And when evening had come, since it was *Preparation, that is, the day before the Sabbath,* Joseph of Arimathea . . . took courage and went to Pilate, and asked for the body of Jesus. (Mark 15:42-43)

> Then [Joseph] took [Jesus' body] down, and wrapped it in a linen shroud, and laid him in a rock-hewn tomb, where no one had ever yet been laid. It was *the day of Preparation,* and *the Sabbath was beginning.* (Luke 23:54)

> [The Jews] need not give bond (to appear in court) on *the Sabbath* or on *the Preparation* for it, after the ninth hour. (Josephus, *Antiquities* 16.163)

Here we see clearly that the "Preparation" *(paraskeuē)* or "day of Preparation" *(hēmera paraskeuēs)* is simply the common Jewish way of referring to the day before the Sabbath — that is, Friday. In fact, every other time the word occurs in the New Testament apart from the debated text, John 19:14, it is simply used to refer to Friday in this way.[309]

Third, and even more telling, in the Gospel of John itself, the only two other occurrences of "Preparation" are likewise used to refer to Friday, i.e., the day before the Sabbath:

> Since it was *Preparation,* in order to prevent the bodies from remaining on the cross *on the Sabbath* (for that Sabbath was a great day), the Jews asked Pilate that their legs might be broken, and that they might be taken away. (John 19:31)

308. BDAG 771; cf. Blomberg, *The Historical Reliability of John's Gospel,* 246-47; Smith, "Chronology of the Last Supper," 42-43; Story, "The Bearing of Old Testament Terminology on the Johannine Chronology," 318; Torrey, "In the Fourth Gospel the Last Supper Was the Paschal Meal," 239-42. See also E. A. Abbot, *Johannine Grammar* (London: A. & C. Black, 1906), 92, who holds that John 19:14 is "more probably" a possessive genitive, and hence should be translated as the "Friday of passover (week)."

309. Blomberg, *The Historical Reliability of John's Gospel,* 247. For similar early Christian usage, see Matt 27:62; *Did.* 8.1; *Mart. Poly.* 7.1.

> They took the body of Jesus, and bound it in linen cloths with the spices. . . . So because of *the Preparation of the Jews,* as the tomb was close at hand, they laid Jesus there. (John 19:40, 42)

In both these Johannine texts, the word "Preparation" *(paraskeuē),* especially "the Preparation of the Jews" *(tēn paraskeuēn tōn Ioudaiōn)* is simply a reference to the Jewish Friday.[310] For example, despite his being an advocate of the Johannine hypothesis, Rudolf Schnackenburg admits that John 19:14 "does not leave any room for doubt that the day of preparation for the sabbath (that is Friday) is intended — the normal Jewish usage."[311]

When these linguistic parallels from external and internal evidence are taken into account, and when we recall that John has already identified the Last Supper as a Passover meal, then the most accurate translation of his description of when Jesus was condemned by Pilate is as follows:

> Now it was *Friday of Passover-week (paraskeuē tou pascha);* it was about the sixth hour. (John 19:14)

Indeed, some English translations and one prominent Greek lexicon accurately reflect this point:

> And it was Friday in Passover. (NEB, John 19:14)

> It was the day of Preparation of Passover Week. (NIV, John 19:14)

> "The Friday of Passover week" (BDAG, regarding John 19:14)[312]

Hence, upon closer analysis, yet another apparent contradiction between John and the Synoptics regarding the chronology of Jesus' death vanishes. For in both John and the Synoptics, Jesus is indeed crucified on the Friday of Passover week, the Jewish preparation day for the Sabbath.[313] As conceded by Rudolf Bultmann: "If *pascha* can signify the entire seven days feast . . . *paraskeue tou pascha* could mean 'the Friday of Passover week.'"[314]

310. Blomberg, *The Historical Reliability of John's Gospel,* 254; Story, "The Bearing of Old Testament Terminology on the Johannine Chronology," 318 n. 3.

311. Schnackenburg, *The Gospel according to St. John,* 3:288.

312. Cf. BDAG 771.

313. Segal, *The Hebrew Passover,* 36 n. 4; Torrey, "The Date of the Crucifixion according to the Fourth Gospel," 235.

314. Bultmann, *The Gospel of John,* 664 n. 5.

Once again, it is fascinating to note that this evidence has led certain scholars to propose that there are internal chronological contradictions — so-called "traces" of the Synoptic chronology — in the Gospel of John. Consider the comments of Rudolf Bultmann regarding the account of the reason for Jesus' body being taken down:

> Since the sabbath is mentioned at the same time, *paraskeuē* [in John 19.31] seems to be understood as "Friday." Certainly it is surprising that no mention is made of the Passover. . . . That may well be due to the fact that this story is derived from a tradition according to which Jesus was crucified on the 15th Nizan [sic], as in the Synoptics.[315]

One cannot help but wonder: Is it plausible, as Bultmann here suggests, that John contradicts his own chronology in the space of a few verses? Or is it more likely that scholars have misinterpreted the Jewish Passover terminology utilized earlier in John's Gospel? To my mind, Bultmann's exegesis of John 19:31 is right on target: "preparation" does mean "Friday." However, the reason for this is not that this piece of John's account is derived from a hypothetical tradition according to which Jesus was crucified on the 15th Nisan, as in the Synoptics. *Rather, the Gospel of John contains evidence for the crucifixion of Jesus on the 15th of Nisan because that is the day he was crucified.* Contrary to what is assumed by so many, it is the Gospel of John itself that dates the crucifixion to 15 Nisan, "the Friday of Passover week."

6. The "Great Sabbath" = 16 Nisan, the Feast of the Sheaf Offering

A sixth important argument for the Passover hypothesis is that the description of the Saturday after Jesus' death as a "great day" (John 19:31) is best explained if that Sabbath coincided with the feast of the sheaf of first-fruits (16 Nisan). This feast is one of the seven major "appointed times" described in the liturgical calendar in the Jewish Torah: Passover, Unleavened Bread, First Fruits, Weeks, Trumpets, the Day of Atonement, and Tabernacles (Lev 23:1-44).

This important chronological indicator takes place in the Gospel of John's explanation for why the bodies of Jesus and the other crucified men were removed by the Romans from the crosses:

315. Bultmann, *The Gospel of John,* 676 n. 6.

> Since it was Friday *(paraskeuē)*, in order to prevent the bodies from remaining on the cross on the Sabbath — *for that Sabbath was a great day* — the Jews asked Pilate that their legs might be broken, and that they might be taken away. (John 19:31)[316]

What is the meaning of this chronological aside? Why does the Gospel of John go out of its way to emphasize that the Sabbath after Jesus' death was "a great day"? What is the meaning of this enigmatic expression?

Remarkably, some commentators pass over this description of the Sabbath without even attempting to explain what it means.[317] Others argue that the "great Sabbath" refers to the feast of Passover (15 Nisan), presupposing the chronology of the Johannine hypothesis, according to which the feast of Passover was eaten Friday night after sunset and continued throughout the day on Saturday.[318] According to this view, the reason the Gospel refers to the Sabbath after Jesus' death as a "great day" is that "The 15th of Nisan, the first day of Passover, was a holy day (LXX of Exod xii 16), and the fact that in this particular year it fell on a Sabbath would make it even more solemn."[319] Or, to put it another way, because in the Jewish Torah the feast of Passover (15 Nisan) is a day of rest from "laborious work" (Lev 23:7), if it fell on the same day as the weekly Sabbath it would constitute a kind of "double sabbath."[320] There are a couple of serious problems with this interpretation.

For one thing, as advocates of this view admit, "we have no early Jewish attestation of the word 'solemn' ['great'] being used to designate a Sabbath that is also a feast day."[321] So the theory is conjectural. Even more significant, while it is possible that the Gospel of John could refer to the Sabbath as "great" because it coincided with the feast of Passover (15 Nisan), if this were his meaning, it would be very strange for him to not simply say so explicitly. As Roger Beckwith rightly points out:

> The statement of John 19:31, "the day of that Sabbath was a high day," is curiously vague if it refers to Nisan 15 and not Nisan 16. John has already stated seven times that they have to come up to Jerusalem for the Passover (John 11:55 [twice]; 12:1; 13:1; 18:28, 39; 19:14). It would surely have been

316. RSV, slightly adapted.
317. E.g., Moloney, *The Gospel of John;* Haenchen, *John.*
318. E.g., Brown, *The Gospel according to John,* 2:934.
319. Brown, *The Gospel according to John,* 2:934.
320. E.g., Westcott, *The Gospel according to St. John,* 2:278.
321. Brown, *The Gospel according to John,* 2:934.

> more natural, therefore, to say "the day of that sabbath was the Passover" or "the day when they ate the Passover," had he thought of it as such. If, however, it was Nisan 16, the day of the offering of the Sheaf (Lev 23:9-14), his expression is a very natural one.[322]

Beckwith makes an extremely important point: if John wanted to emphasize that the bodies needed to be removed from the crosses because that Sabbath was Passover, he simply could have said: "that Sabbath was the feast of Passover." But he doesn't say that, because it wasn't Passover; it was a different festal Sabbath — the day of the sheaf offering, which took place during Passover week. Indeed, on further reflection, it is almost absurd to suggest that John would avoid identifying the Sabbath after Jesus' death as the Passover, given his emphasis on and interest in the Passover feast thus far. By contrast, John's identification of the Sabbath as "the great day" makes perfect sense if the Saturday after Jesus' death was the festal offering of the first "sheaf" *('ōmer)* of barley in the Temple (16 Nisan). This feast is one of the seven major "appointed times" described in the Pentateuch (Leviticus 23). However, unlike the Passover, the feast of the sheaf offering never developed a single name by which it could be easily identified, and it does not seem to play any clear role in the theological emphases of John's Gospel.[323] Hence, John simply refers to the Sabbath as a festal day, because he wants to explain why it was necessary to get the bodies off the crosses before sundown.

However, because many readers are unfamiliar with the sacrificial offering of the sheaf of barley, it is important to cite descriptions of what would be taking place in the Temple on this feast day from Jewish Scripture, the Second Temple period, and early rabbinic literature:

> The LORD said to Moses: "Say to the people of Israel, When you come into the land which I give you and reap its harvest, *you shall bring the sheaf of the first fruits of your harvest to the priest; and he shall wave the sheaf before the LORD,* that you may find acceptance. On the morrow after the sabbath the priest shall wave it. And on the day when you wave the sheaf, you shall offer a male lamb a year old without blemish as a burnt offering

322. Beckwith, "The Misuse of Calendars and Astronomy," 203.

323. In support of this suggestion, notice how earlier in John's Gospel, he is equally vague about the exact identity of "the feast of the Jews" mentioned before the healing of the man born blind (John 5:1). Because the exact feast day has no immediate theological significance that John wishes to draw out, he simply relates it in order to explain why Jesus is in Jerusalem.

to the LORD. . . . And you shall eat neither bread nor grain parched or fresh until this same day, until you have brought the offering of your God; it is a statute forever throughout your generations in all your dwellings." (Lev 23:9-14)[324]

But within the feast [of Passover] there is also another feast following directly after the first day. *This is called the "Sheaf" (dragma), a name given to it from the ceremony which consists in bringing to the altar a sheaf as a first-fruit (aparchē),* both of the land which has been given to the nation to dwell in and of the whole earth. . . . (Philo, *Special Laws* 2.162)[325]

The prescribed rite for the Sheaf is that it should be brought from nearby. If [the crop] near Jerusalem was not yet ripe, it could be brought from any place. . . . How was it made ready? *The messengers of the court used to go out on the eve of the Festival day and tie the barley in bunches while it was yet unreaped to make it the easier to reap; and the towns near by all assembled there together that it might be reaped with much pomp.* When it grew dark he called out, "Is the sun set?" and they answered, "Yea!" . . . "Is this a sickle?" and they answered "Yea!" . . . "Is this a basket?" and they answered, "Yea!" . . . On the Sabbath he called out, "On this Sabbath?" and they answered, "Yea!" . . . "Shall I reap?" and they answered, "Reap!" . . . He used to call out three times for every matter, and they answered "Yea!" "Yea!" "Yea!" Wherefore was all this? Because of the Boethuseans who used to say: The Sheaf may not be reaped at the close of a Festival-day. *They reaped it, put it into baskets, and brought it to the Temple Court.* They used to parch it with fire to fulfill the ordinance that it should be "parched with fire" (Lev 2:14). . . . They spread it out in the Temple Court so that the wind blew over it. . . . After the Sheaf had been offered they used to go out and

324. As is widely known, the ambiguity of the phrase "the morrow after the Sabbath" in Lev 23:15 generated a debate within Second Temple Judaism about whether the feast of the Sheaf-offering should take place on 16 Nisan, the day after the festival "sabbath" of 15 Nisan (so the Pharisees and rabbis); on the first weekly Sabbath during Passover week (so the Sadducees/Boethusians); or on the first weekly Sabbath after Passover week (so the book of *Jubilees* and the Dead Sea Scrolls). For our purposes here, it is worth noting that in the first century A.D., Philo describes the celebration of the sheaf offering as taking place on 16 Nisan, in accordance with the later rabbinic traditions. Saulnier, *Calendrical Variations in Second Temple Judaism,* 75, 150. Regarding the controversy, see Mishnah, *Ḥag.* 2:4; *Men.* 10:3; Danby, *The Mishnah,* 506 n. 1, 213 n. 12.

325. Trans. Colson, LCL.

> find the market of Jerusalem full of meal and parched corn, though this was not with the consent of the Sages. . . . (Mishnah, *Menaḥot* 10:1-5)[326]

With this trajectory of Jewish texts in mind, John's identification of the Sabbath after Jesus' death as a "great day" (John 19:31) makes sense. Unlike an ordinary Sabbath, where everyone would remain in their homes observing the day of rest, on the feast of first fruits (16 Nisan), the Jewish pilgrims residing in Jerusalem would have been going up to the Temple in Jerusalem for the offering of the sheaf of first fruits — a celebration, as the Mishnah says, carried out "with great pomp." On such a day, the pilgrim crowds would have easily seen that the bodies of Jesus and the two thieves had been left on the crosses overnight, in direct contradiction to Jewish Scripture and tradition, which held that failing to bury the body of a hanged man would bring defilement on the whole land (Deut 21:23; Josephus, *War* 4.317).[327] In this context, it would make good sense for the Jewish leaders to urge Pilate to get the bodies down from the crosses, lest a riot break out among the crowds in response to the direct violation of Mosaic law.

Should there be any doubt about this interpretation, it is important to note that once again major advocates of the Johannine hypothesis admit that the reference to the "great Sabbath" (John 19:31) seems to refer to 16 Nisan, and thus to support the Synoptic chronology. Consider the remarks of Rudolf Bultmann, Raymond Brown, Rudolf Schnackenburg, and John Meier — none of whom accept the Passover hypothesis:

> Rudolf Bultmann: Since the sabbath is mentioned at the same time, *paraskeue* [in John 19.31] seems to be understood as "Friday." Certainly it is surprising that no mention is made of the Passover. . . . That may well be due to the fact that this story is derived from a tradition according to which Jesus was crucified on the 15th Nizan [sic], as in the Synoptics.[328]

> Raymond Brown: Bultmann, p. 524[5], thinks that this verse reflects a tradition where Jesus died on the 15th of Nisan (the Synoptic position . . .) so that the next day, a Sabbath, would have been the 16th of Nisan, a particularly solemn day, for in the Pharisaic tradition it was the day for offering sheaves (cf. Lev xxiii 6-14). We can make no decision about a

326. Trans. Danby (slightly adapted, translating *'ōmer* as "sheaf").

327. Blomberg, *The Historical Reliability of John's Gospel*, 254.

328. Bultmann, *The Gospel of John*, 676 n. 6.

> single verse. . . . Perhaps the phraseology of the clause is dependent on Mark xv 42.[329]
>
> Rudolf Schnackenburg: It is surprising that the source accentuates the Sabbath . . . whether one may conclude from the information that the synoptic chronology (according to which, the day of the passover feast was already on the Friday) still breaks through here, is to be doubted. If the following remark comes from the evangelist, then he intended to underline the coincidence of the day of the passover feast and the Sabbath.[330]
>
> John Meier: The adjective "great" could also be applied to the Sabbath that fell during Passover week, since, in Pharisaic tradition, it was the day for the offering of the sheaves.[331]

If these exegetes are correct about the identification of the great Sabbath with the feast of the sheaf offering, then we find ourselves with yet another so-called "trace of the Synoptic chronology" in the Gospel of John. And yet, all of their attempts to explain this away — that John contradicts his own chronology (now more than once), that this stray verse has been influenced by Mark 15:42, that a "single verse" cannot be determinative — seem to be special pleading. Significantly, these admissions show that the Johannine hypothesis not only has trouble explaining the Synoptic descriptions of the Last Supper as a Passover; it also has trouble explaining the data in the Gospel of John! Why not simply consider the Passover hypothesis, which is able to make sense of the data in both the Synoptics and John together, without continually jettisoning pieces that do not fit?

Before closing, it is worth noting an important difference between the argument as I have just presented it here and previous research. In the past, some advocates of the Passover hypothesis have argued that the Saturday after Jesus' death would have been a "great Sabbath" because it was "the Sabbath of Passover week, which was thus doubly sacred."[332] Although this is possible,

329. Brown, *The Gospel according to John,* 2:933.

330. Schnackenburg, *The Gospel according to St. John,* 3:288. Schnackenburg goes on to posit that the chronological designation is an interpolation: "The designation 'high,' not supported in rabbinic sources, was also used by him for the last day of the feast of Tabernacles, remarkable for its special rites . . . so it can easily be supposed that he added these few words" (3:288).

331. Meier, *A Marginal Jew,* 1:422.

332. Blomberg, *The Historical Reliability of John's Gospel,* 254.

it is not what I am claiming. I am arguing that the Sabbath after Jesus' death is called "great" because it is the day on which the first fruits were offered in the Temple, not simply because it fell "during Passover week." In support of this specific liturgical interpretation, consider the other use of the adjective "great" *(megalē)* in the Gospel of John with regard to a particular day of Jewish festivities in the Temple:

> On the last day of the festival [of Tabernacles], *the great day,* Jesus stood up and proclaimed, "If any one thirst, let him come to me and let him who believes in me drink. As the scripture says, 'Out of his heart shall flow rivers of living water.'" (John 7:37-38)

As Raymond Brown points out in his commentary, this reference to "the great day" *(hēmera tē megalē)* is a reference to the seventh day of the feast of Tabernacles.[333] For that day there took place the climax of the seven-day "water-libation" ceremony, which has its roots in the book of Zechariah's description of "living waters" flowing out of Jerusalem during the Feast of Tabernacles (Zech 14:8, 16-19) and which is described in the Mishnah tractate on the feast of Tabernacles (see Mishnah, *Sukkah* 4:9–5:1).[334] If this interpretation is correct, then the first mention of a "great day" (John 7:37) can help us to solidify the mention of a "great Sabbath" (John 19:31). Just as the Gospel of John uses the "great day" to refer to the solemn festal offering of the water in the Temple during the weeklong festival of Tabernacles, so too he uses the expression "the great day" to refer to the solemn festal offering of the first sheaf of grain in the Temple on the Saturday after Jesus was executed.[335] In other words, a close reading of the Gospel in the light of external evidence from Jewish liturgy and internal evidence from the Gospel itself provides converging lines of support for the Passover hypothesis.

In sum, when the chronological evidence in the Gospel of John is interpreted in its linguistic, literary, and historical contexts, there are good reasons for concluding that the date of the Last Supper in the Gospel of John and the Synoptics is basically the same: the account of Jesus' final meal begins on the

333. Brown, *The Gospel according to John,* 1:326.

334. Brian D. Johnson, "The Jewish Feasts and Questions of Historicity in John 5–12," in *John, Jesus, and History,* vol. 2: *Aspects of Historicity in the Fourth Gospel* (ed. Paul N. Anderson, Felix Just, S.J., and Tom Thatcher; Atlanta: Society of Biblical Literature, 2009), 117-29 (here 122-23), following Jeffrey L. Rubenstein, *The History of Sukkot in the Second Temple and Rabbinic Periods* (Atlanta: Scholars Press, 1995).

335. This is missed by Blomberg, *The Historical Reliability of John's Gospel,* 136.

afternoon of 14 Nisan, continues through the night of 15 Nisan, on which Jesus and his disciples celebrate a Passover meal together, and then concludes with the crucifixion of Jesus on 15 Nisan, the first day of the weeklong feast of Passover celebrated by the Jews in the city of Jerusalem, and the day before a Sabbath which, in that year, coincided with the feast of the sheaf offering in the Temple (Nisan 16).

The Passover Hypothesis, the Gospel of John, and the Jewish Feasts

With all of this in mind, before we bring this chapter to a close, it is important to raise and respond to one final objection that continues to be levied against the Passover hypothesis. As I noted at the beginning of this chapter, in most recent Jesus research, the solution to the date of the Last Supper which I have referred to as the Passover hypothesis is simply ignored, not refuted. As a result, arguments against it are often lacking; when they are given, they tend to take the form of positive arguments for the Johannine hypothesis. (Once these are considered established, the case is usually considered closed.) However, when scholars do actually engage the Passover hypothesis itself, the major objection levied against it is that the Gospel of John's Gentile audience would never have understood the various meanings of the word "Passover," and, therefore, the author of the Gospel of John did not intend them.

This argument finds its most influential expression, as is so often the case, in the work of Joachim Jeremias. In the space of a couple of sentences, Jeremias both admits the basic argument of the Passover hypothesis but rejects the possibility that the audience of the Gospel could have understood the word "Passover" in this way:

> It is true that the paschal sacrifices *(ḥagigah)* which were eaten during the seven days of the feast (Nisan 15-21) sometimes are called *pesaḥ* in accordance with Deut 16.2 and II Chron 35.7, so that John 18.28 could be referred to 15 Nisan. . . . But it is extremely questionable whether the Gentile Christians for whom John wrote would be able to understand such a linguistic subtlety.[336]

Along similar lines, at the very beginning of his recent treatment on the date of the Last Supper, Stéphane Saulnier concedes to the linguistic evidence in favor

336. Jeremias, *The Eucharistic Words of Jesus,* 21.

of the Passover hypothesis but dismisses it by quoting Jeremias's argument that the audience of John's Gospel would not have understood it:

> Billerbeck has shown that the sacrifices of this feast were occasionally called *pesach,* in line with Deut 16:2 and 2 Chr 35:7. However, "it is extremely questionable whether the Gentile Christians for whom the fourth evangelist wrote would be able to understand such linguistic subtlety." Rather, their understanding is likely to have been literal, with the inference that the Passover lamb was eaten on the evening following Jesus' death.[337]

For critics of the Passover hypothesis, this appears to be a decisive blow against this solution. Indeed, both Jeremias and Saulnier apparently feel they need say nothing further; once this argument regarding the Gentile audience of the Gospel of John is made, the Passover hypothesis is never mentioned again.

In response to this objection, I would make here at least four points.[338]

First, when Jeremias was writing some sixty years ago, the Gospel of John was widely regarded as the "Hellenistic" Gospel — as opposed to the Synoptics. However, as numerous studies of the parallels between the Dead Sea Scrolls and John's Gospel in particular have shown, this outdated view of John's Gospel as Hellenistic rather than Jewish has been all but obliterated.[339] In the words of Craig Keener:

> The trend of recent scholarship has been away from a non-Jewish Hellenistic milieu and toward a Jewish matrix for early Christianity. . . . In few places in the study of the New Testament has this shift in perspective proved as dramatic as in the case of the Fourth Gospel, the Jewishness of which has come to be increasingly recognized in recent decades.[340]

337. Saulnier, *Calendrical Variations in Second Temple Judaism,* 4.

338. Incidentally, as I noted above, scholarly advocates of the Johannine hypothesis easily accept the idea (even though it is erroneous) that John's Gentile readers would have been able to catch his allusion to "the very hour" when the Passover lambs were being sacrificed (cf. John 19:14). If scholars accept the idea that John's readers would know about the hour the lambs were sacrificed in the temple — which is not in the Bible — then why is it so hard to believe they would have been familiar with the multiple meanings of Passover — which are in the Bible?

339. E.g., Mary L. Coloe and Tom Thatcher, eds., *John, Qumran, and the Dead Sea Scrolls: Sixty Years of Discovery and Debate* (Atlanta: Society of Biblical Literature, 2011); Elizabeth W. Mburu, *Qumran and the Origins of Johannine Language and Symbolism* (JCT 8; London: T. & T. Clark, 2008); James H. Charlesworth, ed., *John and Qumran* (London: Geoffrey Chapman, 1972).

340. Keener, *The Gospel of John,* 1:171.

Indeed, there has been an explosion of research affirming the deeply Jewish character of the Fourth Gospel, and it shows no sign of abating.[341] For our purposes here, the basic point is that Jeremias's criticism of the Passover hypothesis is based on an erroneous assumption about the "Hellenistic" character of John's Gospel.

Second, and even more important, although scholars continue to debate the exact identity of the audience of the Gospel of John, one thing is indisputable: *If there is anything that John clearly assumes on the part of his readers, it is an intimate familiarity with the Jerusalem Temple and the Jewish feasts.* It is widely recognized, and has been for some time, that John assumes firsthand knowledge of Jerusalem and the holy land on the part of his readers. He repeatedly mentions, without explanation, places such as the "pool" called "Bethzatha" which is "by the Sheep-Gate" (John 5:2) or "the portico of Solomon" which is "in the Temple" (John 10:23), as if his readers were familiar with the topography of Jerusalem before its destruction.[342] Moreover, as several recent studies have shown, the basic framework of John's Gospel revolves entirely around the ancient Jewish feasts and the Jerusalem Temple.[343] Consider, by way of example, the following references to Jewish feasts:

1. Passover (John 2:13, 23)
2. Passover (John 4:45)
3. Unnamed "Feast" (John 5:1)
4. Sabbath (John 5:9, 10, 16, 18)
5. Passover (John 6:4)
6. Tabernacles (John 7:2)
7. Sabbath (John 7:22, 23)
8. "Last and great day" of the Feast of Tabernacles (John 7:37)

341. See Keener, *The Gospel of John,* 1:171-232, for an extensive discussion with bibliography.

342. See Blomberg, *The Historical Reliability of John's Gospel,* 56-62.

343. See, e.g., Brian D. Johnson, "The Jewish Feasts and Questions of Historicity in John 5–12," in Anderson, Just, and Thatcher, eds., *John, Jesus, and History,* vol. 2: *Aspects of Historicity in the Fourth Gospel,* 117-29; Michael A. Daise, *Feasts in John: Jewish Festivals and Jesus' "Hour" in the Gospel of John* (WUNT 2.229; Tübingen: Mohr Siebeck, 2007); Keener, *The Gospel of John;* Gale A. Yee, *Jewish Feasts and the Gospel of John* (Wilmington: Michael Glazier, 1989). For an earlier study along these lines, see also Aileen Guilding, *The Fourth Gospel and Jewish Worship: A Study in the Relation of St. John's Gospel to the Ancient Jewish Lectionary System* (Oxford: Clarendon, 1960). Although Guilding's overall "Jewish lectionary" hypothesis suffers from serious methodological weaknesses, her basic point about the festal framework of John's Gospel remains a significant contribution.

9. Sabbath (John 9:14, 16)
10. Dedication (Hannukah) (John 10:22)
11. Passover (John 11:55; 12:1)
12. Passover (John 13:1)
13. Passover (John 18:28, 39, 19:14, 31)
14. Sabbath (John 19:31)[344]

What matters most for our purposes here is that the Gospel of John does not simply mention these Jewish feasts in passing. Instead, it assumes that his audience is familiar both with the chronology of these feasts as well as their symbolic meaning, often highlighting them when there is a significant thematic connection between the Jewish feasts and the words and deeds of Jesus.[345] For example, the reference to "the Passover" in the account of the feeding of the five thousand (John 6:4) assumes that his readers will pick up on the connection between the feast of Passover and the miracle of the manna in Jewish Scripture (see Exodus 12–13; Joshua 5). Likewise, the reference to the feast of Tabernacles (John 7:2, 37) assumes that readers will pick up on connections between Jesus' statements about rivers of "living water" and the expectation that rivers would flow from the Temple in Jerusalem during the eschatological feast of Tabernacles (Zechariah 14), not to mention the water libation and light rituals that the rabbis tell us took place in the first century (*m. Sukk.* 4:9; *t. Sukk.* 3:11-12). Indeed, John assumes so much familiarity with these feasts on the part of his readers that on one occasion, he describes a "feast" (John 5:1) the identity of which even modern scholars and experts in Judaism continue to debate.[346] These examples could be multiplied. For now, the basic point is that far from being implausible, the Passover hypothesis is quite consistent with the Fourth Gospel's tendency to assume firsthand familiarity on the part of (at least some of) his readers with the Jerusalem Temple and the Jewish festal calendar.[347]

344. Reproduced from Johnson, "The Jewish Feasts and Questions of Historicity in John 5–12," 117.

345. Compare the parallels between Jesus' statements about "rivers of living water" (John 7:37-39) and "the light of the world" (John 8:12), which appear to be delivered during the feast of Tabernacles, and the water and light rituals of that very festival. See *m. Sukk.* 4:9; *t. Sukk.* 3:11-12; Yee, *Jewish Feasts and the Gospel of John,* 80-82; Guilding, *The Fourth Gospel and Jewish Worship,* 92-112.

346. See, e.g., John 5:1-47 for the unnamed "feast," as well as Daise's argument that most readers have misidentified the Passover in John 6 as referring to the first Passover (Nisan 14) when in fact it refers to the second Passover (14 Iyar), which Jews would be obligated to celebrate one month later if they were ritually defiled for some reason. Daise, *Feasts in John,* 140-52.

347. See John A. T. Robinson, "The Destination and Purpose of St John's Gospel," *NTS*

Third, even *if* John's Gospel was written primarily for Gentile Christians, this does not mean that they would not have been familiar with the various meanings of the word "Passover." Indeed, we know for certain that at least one first-century Gentile Christian — the author of Luke and Acts — was well aware of the fact that the Greek word "Passover" *(pascha)* could be used to refer to the seven-day festival of Unleavened Bread. Again, recall Luke's description of the preparation for the Last Supper:

> Now the feast of Unleavened Bread *(heortē tōn azymōn)* drew near, which is called Passover *(hē legomenē pascha).* (Luke 22:1)

Now, if a Gentile Christian author like Luke could be familiar with the fact that the word "Passover" was used to refer to the weeklong festival of Unleavened Bread, then it is by no means clear why the implied readers of the Gospel of John could not have had access to the same knowledge. This is especially so when we recall, as we saw above, that the multiple meanings of the word "Passover" are found in Jewish Scripture itself (Deut 16:1-3; 2 Chron 35:7-9). Moreover, even if John's readers misinterpreted the word "Passover" (as I have argued modern scholars do), it should go without saying that this in no way changes the meaning intended by the author. Indeed, it would be far from the only time something in the Fourth Gospel was misunderstood by its readers.

Fourth and finally, as we have already seen, by the time John's Gospel was written, the terminology of "the Feast of Unleavened Bread" was already beginning to be eclipsed by the word "Passover" (Greek *pascha;* Hebrew *pesaḥ*). Once again, Raymond Brown concedes the point:

> By the 1st cent. AD . . . *the names were becoming interchangeable.* By the next century "Passover" had become the name of the whole feast, so that "the feast of the Unleavened Bread" never appears in Tannaitic literature.[348]

If this is true, then it makes perfect sense to suggest that the Gospel of John is using Jewish Passover terminology in much the same way as other Jewish writings in the first century. Just as Jewish Scripture uses the word "Passover" to refer to the seven-day feast and its peace offerings, so too the Gospel of

6 (1960): 117-31, for the theory that the Fourth Gospel was written primarily for Jews in the Diaspora.

348. Brown, *The Death of the Messiah,* 2:1352 (emphasis added), following Solomon Zeitlin, "The Time of the Passover Meal," *JQR* 42 (1951-52): 45-50. Given that both Brown and Zeitlin ultimately reject the Passover hypothesis, this is yet another argument in its favor.

John uses "Passover" to refer to the initial Passover meal and the Passover peace offering. In other words, the Passover hypothesis has in its favor that in John's first-century context, the use of such language is not only plausible, but to be expected, and will later emerge as the dominant terminology of early rabbinic literature.[349]

To sum up what we have seen so far: (1) In the Old Testament and ancient Jewish literature, the word "Passover" (Hebrew *pesaḥ;* Greek *pascha*) can have multiple meanings. It can refer to the Passover lamb, the initial Passover meal, the entire Passover week, or the Passover peace offerings. In any given case, the meaning must be determined by the context. (2) As is widely admitted by commentators on John's Gospel — and not just by advocates of the Passover hypothesis — there are strong reasons to believe that, contrary to popular opinion, the Last Supper in the Gospel of John is in fact described as a Passover meal. John's reference to "before the feast of Passover" (John 13:1) does not mean "just before 14 Nisan," but "just before 15 Nisan" — the night the Passover lambs were eaten. Moreover, his description of the Last Supper — with participants reclining, the dipping of the morsel in the dish, and Judas' departure to give something to the poor — collectively indicate that he is describing the feast of Passover just mentioned. (3) Once this is established, the subsequent reference to the Jews refusing on Friday morning to enter the praetorium so that they might "eat the Passover" (John 18:28), when interpreted in context, must refer to the consumption of the Passover peace offerings, which were eaten on 15-21 Nisan and had to be consumed in a state of ritual purity. In confirmation of this, both the Old Testament and rabbinic literature contain several cases in which the "peace offerings of Passover" *(shelmaiy pesaḥ)* are referred to simply by the word "Passover" *(pesaḥ).* John thus appears to reflect the common Jewish Passover terminology. (4) Along the same lines, when subjected to close linguistic comparison with ancient Jewish idioms, John's reference to Jesus' being condemned by Pilate on "the preparation of Passover" (John 19:14) does not refer to "the preparation day for Passover," but rather to "the Friday of Passover week." John, like the other Synoptics, is

349. Incidentally one could also argue that if the Synoptic Gospels are in circulation when the Gospel of John is written, and if John assumes that his readers are familiar with them — both ideas widely, though not universally accepted — then it seems difficult to believe that he would deliberately alter the chronology without being more explicit about it. I realize that this implausibility rests on a whole host of other assumptions about early Christian literature and history. Nevertheless, I think it worth pointing out that it seems more plausible to suggest that John has not altered the Synoptic chronology, but that readers unfamiliar with the language and liturgy of the Second Temple period have misinterpreted him as doing so.

simply emphasizing the fact that Jesus was crucified on "Preparation, that is, the day before the Sabbath" (cf. Mark 15:42). (5) The entire Passover hypothesis is not only consistent with the inherent ambiguity of common ancient Jewish Passover terminology, but with John's own distinctive interest in the Jewish feasts, as well as the assumption that runs throughout his Gospel that his readers are familiar with the liturgical calendar and cultic realities of Second Temple Judaism.

In short, of the four major hypotheses regarding the apparent chronological contradiction between the Synoptic Gospels and the Gospel of John, I submit that the Passover hypothesis — when it is combined with the strengths of the Synoptic hypothesis — is the most plausible solution to the question of whether the Last Supper was a Passover meal. A close analysis of these four positions reveals that while each has its various strengths, the first three hypotheses suffer from weaknesses that seriously cripple their overall historical plausibility. In particular, the Johannine hypothesis, though it currently reigns supreme, is plagued by a number of serious problems that continue to go unaddressed by many of its advocates. Most damaging of all, in order for the Johannine solution to work, it must not only reject the explicit testimony of the Synoptics, it must also jettison the "traces of the Synoptic chronology" in the Gospel of John. Although I obviously do not wish to be dogmatic about a matter that is so clearly fraught with complexities and difficulties, it nevertheless seems to me that the Passover hypothesis, by contrast, provides a historical solution to the date of the Last Supper which has in its favor the fact that it draws on the triple testimony of the Synoptic Gospels, a close reading of the language and imagery in the Gospel of John, as well as an abundance of ancient parallels from both the Old Testament and ancient Judaism. Like the Essene hypothesis, the Passover hypothesis takes seriously Jewish liturgical realities of the Second Temple period; like the Johannine hypothesis, it pays close attention to the historical testimony of the Gospel of John; and like the Synoptic hypothesis, it reckons with the weight of the triply attested chronology. But unlike these other hypotheses, the Passover hypothesis does all this without jettisoning the Gospel data that fail to fit its theory. In other words, the Passover hypothesis makes the best sense of the most evidence. For this reason, and for all those detailed above, this study will proceed on the conclusion that Jesus' Last Supper was in fact a Jewish Passover meal.

CHAPTER 5

The New Passover

> Passover looked back to the exodus, and on to the coming of the kingdom. Jesus intended this meal [the Last Supper] to symbolize the new exodus, the arrival of the kingdom through his own fate. The meal, focused on Jesus' actions, with the bread and the cup, told the Passover story, and Jesus' own story, and wove these two into one.
>
> N. T. WRIGHT[1]

Now that we have made a case for regarding the Last Supper as a Passover meal, we can ask: If Jesus' final meal was in fact a Passover meal, what significance does it have for our understanding of the Last Supper? What light does the Passover shed on the meaning of his words and actions in the Upper Room? In a first-century Jewish context, how are Jesus' actions at the Last Supper similar to an ordinary Jewish Passover, and how are they different? What are the implications of these similarities and differences?

In this chapter, we will try to answer these questions in three stages. First, we will briefly survey the shape of the Passover in the Old Testament and early Jewish literature. The primary goal of this survey is to familiarize the reader with the main features of the Jewish Passover so that these features or the absence thereof can be seen with greater clarity when we turn to the Last Supper itself. Second, we will study the important account of Jesus sending the disciples to prepare the Passover in the Upper Room on the afternoon before

1. N. T. Wright, *Jesus and the Victory of God* (*Christian Origins and the Question of God*, vol. 1; Minneapolis: Fortress, 1996), 559.

he celebrated the Last Supper (Matt 26:17-19; Mark 14:12-16; Luke 22:7-13). This is intended both to solidify earlier conclusions about the date of the Last Supper, and to root Jesus' actions at the Last Supper more firmly in their Passover context. Third, we will then return to Jesus' identification of the Passover bread as his "body" and the Passover wine as his "blood," and his command to the disciples to repeat his actions in "remembrance" of him (Matt 26:26-28; Mark 14:22-24; Luke 22:14-20; 1 Cor 11:23-25).

As we have already seen, the Passover context of the Last Supper does not exhaust the meaning of Jesus' words and deeds at his final meal. Nevertheless, given the emphasis in all four Gospels on the Passover meal as the overarching and dominant context of the Last Supper (see chapter 4), I am suggesting that the fact that Jesus chooses the Passover as the occasion upon which to perform his final prophetic sign is significant. After all, he conceivably could have performed the Last Supper during some other Jewish feast, such as the Day of Atonement, or Tabernacles, or during no feast at all. Given the fact that Jesus chose the Passover, it is important to ascertain what significance this has for how we understand his words and deeds in context.

As I hope to show, the Last Supper represents (1) the institution of a New Passover meal, wherein believers eat the eschatological Passover lamb; participation in this meal involves participation (2) in his death and (3) in the redemptive power of the new exodus that will be set in motion by his death. In other words, Jesus' last Passover meal was a prophetic sign in which he identified himself as the eschatological Passover lamb, the redemptive sacrifice that would inaugurate the new exodus. In this way, Jesus reconfigured the ordinary Jewish Passover meal — originally centered on the historical sacrifice of the Passover lamb and the deliverance of the Israelites from Egypt — around the eschatological offering of his own body and blood. By identifying himself as the new Passover lamb, he sought both to signify and set in motion the exodus spoken of by the prophets, which would take place through his suffering and death.

The Passover in Early Judaism[2]

In order to understand Jesus' actions at his final Passover meal in their ancient Jewish context, it is important first to study the shape of the Passover in

2. For helpful overviews of the key primary sources, see Daniel K. Falk, "Festivals and Holy Days," in *The Eerdmans Dictionary of Early Judaism* (ed. John J. Collins and Dan-

the Old Testament and early Jewish literature. Because I will draw on many of the texts covered in this survey in our study of the Gospel accounts below, this overview will function more as a summary of key points than a detailed analysis.

The Passover in Jewish Scripture

In the Old Testament, there are a number of texts that describe the shape of the Passover ritual.[3] From an ancient Jewish perspective,[4] the most important description is found in the Pentateuch's account of the night of Israel's exodus from Egypt (Exodus 12–13). It is here that we first find a detailed account of the ritual actions that constitute the basic shape of the Passover sacrifice and meal:

> The Lord said to Moses and Aaron in the land of Egypt: "This month shall be for you the beginning of months; it shall be the first month of the year for you. Tell all the congregation of Israel that on the tenth day of this month *they shall take every man a lamb according to their fathers' houses,* a lamb for a household; and if the household is too small for a

---

iel C. Harlow; Grand Rapids: Eerdmans, 2010), 636-45; McKnight, *Jesus and His Death* 243-58; James C. VanderKam, "Passover," in *Encyclopedia of the Dead Sea Scrolls* (2 vols.; ed. Lawrence H. Schiffman and James C. VanderKam; Oxford: Oxford University Press, 2000), 2:637-38; Roland de Vaux, *Ancient Israel: Its Life and Institutions* (repr.; Grand Rapids: Eerdmans, 1997), 484-92; Barry D. Smith, *Jesus' Last Passover Meal* (Lewiston: Edwin Mellen, 1993), 1-57; Baruch M. Bokser, "Unleavened Bread and Passover, Feasts of," *Anchor Bible Dictionary* (6 vols.; ed. David Noel Freedman et al.; New York: Doubleday, 1992), 755-65; E. P. Sanders, *Judaism: Practice and Belief* 63 BCE–66 CE (London: SCM; Philadelphia: Trinity Press International, 1992), 132-38; Baruch M. Bokser, *The Origins of the Seder* (Berkeley: University of California Press, 1984); Abram Kanof, "Passover," in *Encyclopedia Judaica* (16 vols.; ed. Cecil Roth; Jerusalem: Keter, 1972), 13:163-73; Roger Le Déaut, C.S.Sp., *La Nuit Paschale: Essai sur la signification de la Pâque juive à partír du Targum d'Exode XII 42* (Rome: Institut Biblique Pontifical, 1963); George Buchanan Gray, *Sacrifice in the Old Testament: Its Theory and Practice* (New York: Ktav, 1971 [orig. 1925]), 337-97; H. H. Rowley, *Worship in Ancient Israel: Its Forms and Meaning* (London: SPCK, 1967), 47-50, 117-18; J. B. Segal, *The Hebrew Passover from the Earliest Times to A.D. 70* (London Oriental Studies 12; London: Oxford University Press, 1963), 1-41, 230-69.

3. Exod 12:1-28, 43-49; Lev 23:5; Num 28:16; Deut 16:1-8; Josh 5:10-11; 2 Chron 30:1-27; 35:1-19.

4. Throughout this overview, we will forego any interaction with modern scholarly theories about the hypothetical sources behind the Pentateuch and other Jewish Scriptures, as these are not relevant for a study of ancient Jewish thought.

> lamb, then a man and his neighbor next to his house shall take according to the number of persons; according to what each can eat you shall make your count for the lamb. Your lamb shall be without blemish, a male a year old; you shall take it from the sheep or from the goats; and you shall keep it until the fourteenth day of this month, when *the whole assembly of the congregation of Israel shall kill their lambs in the evening.* Then they shall take some of the blood, and put it on the doorposts and the lintels of the houses in which they eat them. *They shall eat the flesh that night, roasted; with unleavened bread and bitter herbs they shall eat it.* Do not eat any of it raw or boiled with water, but roasted, its head with its legs and its inner parts. And you shall let none of it remain until the morning, anything that remains until the morning you shall burn. In this manner you shall eat it: your loins girded, your sandals on your feet, and your staff in your hand; and you shall eat it in haste. *It is the* L*ORD's Passover.* For I will pass through the land of Egypt that night, and I will strike all the first-born in the land of Egypt, both man and beast. . . . *The blood shall be a sign for you, upon the houses where you are; and when I see the blood, I will pass over you, and no plague shall fall upon you to destroy you, when I strike the land of Egypt.* This day shall be for you *a memorial day,* and you shall keep it as a feast to the LORD; throughout your generations you shall observe it as an ordinance for ever. (Exod 12:1-14)

Several aspects of this foundational text are worthy of our attention.

First, it is important to point out that the original "Passover" *(pesaḥ)* is described as a domestic sacrifice of all twelve tribes of Israel. In the biblical narrative, the exodus from Egypt takes place before the establishment of the exclusively Levitical priesthood (cf. Exod 32:25-29); hence, at this point in Israel's history, all twelve tribes have not yet lost their "priestly faculties" and thus can act as priests, by both sacrificing the lamb and by pouring the blood into a "basin" and anointing the home with it. Second, note the prominence assigned to eating the flesh of the Passover lamb. While a single verse is devoted to the slaughter of the lamb, a whole series of prescriptions revolve around its consumption. This emphasis is significant, for it suggests that the original Passover is a "sacrificial meal,"[5] and therefore that the Passover is not completed by the death of the lamb, but by eating its flesh. Third, note also the implicit redemptive power of the blood of the Passover lamb. Its sacrificial blood, when spread upon the doorposts and lintel, is an efficacious "sign": by means of the blood,

5. Bokser, "Unleavened Bread and Passover," 737.

the Israelites are protected from the plague of death.[6] In the Old Testament, such "signs" are often reminders and renewals of covenant, such as the "sign" of the rainbow (Gen 9:12), circumcision (Gen 17:11), and the Sabbath (Exod 31:13, 17).[7] Again, as we will see later on, a rather heated debate has taken place regarding whether the Passover sacrifice was viewed as having expiatory power or not; for now, we need only note that, at least in the Passover of the exodus, the blood of the lamb clearly has some kind of redemptive or apotropaic power.[8] Fourth and finally, from its inception, the original Passover is instituted to be repeated: it is to be a "memorial day" or "remembrance" *(zikkārôn)* throughout all generations (Exod 12:14). In particular, Passover is to be celebrated annually, along with the seven-day "feast of unleavened bread" (Exod 12:17). Indeed, the book of Exodus even bears witness to a ritualized questioning of the father by the son that would accompany the celebration of this annual memorial in order to explain its significance (Exod 12:21-23, 26-27; 13:6-8).

In addition to this foundational text, other biblical passages bear witness to features associated with the Passover. Although the importance of the description in Exodus can tend to overshadow these other biblical descriptions, they too are important for highlighting the multiple associations that the feast of Passover would have had for an ancient Jew familiar with the Scriptures. For the sake of space, I will simply enumerate them as follows:

1. ***The Passover and the Seven-Day Feast of Unleavened Bread*** As we saw in chapter 4, the Passover is not an isolated event, but is closely tied to the weeklong festival of Unleavened Bread, whose beginning coincides with the eating of the initial Passover lamb (Exod 12:14-27; Lev 23:4-8; Num 28:16-25; Deut 16:1-8; Ezra 6:19-22).[9] One reason this connection is significant is that it permanently links the command to "eat the flesh" of the Passover lamb with the consumption of a meal of "unleavened bread and bitter herbs" (Exod 12:8; Num 9:11). Eating the flesh of the lamb and the "unleavened bread" *(maṣṣôth)* go together (Exod 12:8). Moreover, in the Pentateuch itself, the *maṣṣāh* is identified as having symbolic significance:

> Seven days you shall eat it [the Passover] with unleavened bread, *the bread of affliction* — for you came out of the land of Egypt in hurried flight —

6. See Victor Hamilton, *Exodus: An Exegetical Commentary* (Grand Rapids: Baker Academic, 2011), 184-85 on the Hebrew *pāsaḥ* as "protect" (Exod 12:13).

7. Propp, *Exodus 1–18*, 400.

8. Bokser, "Unleavened Bread and Passover," 757.

9. Bokser, "Unleavened Bread and Passover," 757.

> that all the days of your life you may remember the day when you came out of the land of Egypt. (Deut 16:3)

Here we see the unleavened bread functioning both as a symbol for the "affliction" *(ʿānî)* suffered by Israel in their exodus from Egypt, and as a memorial of the day on which they were delivered from Egypt. Hence, the *maṣṣāh* is inextricably bound up with the Passover itself.

2. ***The Passover and the Entry into the Promised Land*** The Passover is not only connected to the departure from Egypt, but to the eventual entrance of the wilderness generation into the promised land, as well as the return to the land by the Judeans after the Babylonian exile. According to the books of Joshua and Ezra, one of the ways in which the Israelites celebrated the entry into the land (in the case of the exodus) or the return to the land (in the case of the exiles) was by keeping the Passover:

> While the sons of Israel were encamped at Gilgal they *kept the Passover on the fourteenth day of the month at evening* in the plains of Jericho. And on the next day after the Passover, on that very day, they ate of the produce of the land, unleavened cakes and parched grain. And the manna ceased on the next day, when they ate of the produce of the land; and the sons of Israel had manna no more, but ate of the fruit of the land of Canaan that year. (Josh 5:10-12)

> On the fourteenth day of the first month *the returned exiles kept the passover.* For the priests and the Levites had purified themselves together; all of them were clean. So *they killed the passover lamb for all the returned exiles,* for their fellow priests, and for themselves; *it was eaten by the people of Israel who had returned from exile, and also by every one who had joined them and separated himself from the pollutions of the peoples of the land to worship the* Lord, *the God of Israel.* And they kept the feast of unleavened bread seven days with joy; for the Lord had made them joyful, and had turned the heart of the king of Assyria to them, so that he aided them in the work of the house of God, the God of Israel. (Ezra 6:19-22)

Although these descriptions of the Passover are easy to overlook because they are located outside the Pentateuch proper, they are important because they suggest that the Passover feast constitutes a kind of "ritual frame" for the entire exodus, as well as specific connections with the return to the land.[10] This connection between Passover, entry into the promised land, and return from exile already present in the Hebrew Scriptures may explain some of the eschatological significance that would later link the celebration of the Passover with the ingathering of the exiles and the restoration of Israel.

3. ***The Passover as a Temple Sacrifice*** Although "the Passover of Egypt" is clearly a domestic sacrifice, offered in the homes of the Israelites, other Scriptures explicitly transform it into a sacrifice that could only be offered in the Jerusalem Temple. According to the Pentateuch:

> You may not offer the Passover sacrifice within any of your towns which the LORD your God gives you; but at the place which the LORD your God will choose, to make his name dwell in it, there you shall offer the Passover sacrifice, in the evening at the going down of the sun, at the time you came out of the land of Egypt. And you shall boil it and eat it at the place which the LORD your God will choose, and in the morning you shall turn and go to your tents. (Deut 16:5-7)

As we will see, it is critical to stress this explicit link in the Mosaic Torah between a central sanctuary and every Passover after the initial exodus, especially if we want to understand exactly how the Passover was celebrated at the time of Jesus. Jesus lived while the Temple still stood: hence, the Passover sacrifice was still tied by the Torah to the sacrificial offering of the lamb in the Temple and the eating of the lamb in Jerusalem. As far as our evidence suggests, it is only after the destruction of Jerusalem and its Temple in A.D. 70, when the command in Deuteronomy 16 could no longer be fulfilled, that rabbinic Judaism was forced to transform the Passover from a Temple sacrifice into a non-sacrificial banquet, one that could be celebrated anywhere by relatively anyone. In the words of E. P. Sanders:

> Jews could celebrate Passover only in Jerusalem and only when they were pure. The removal of corpse impurity required a mixture of water and ashes that ran out fairly soon after the temple was destroyed. After the fall of the temple, therefore, those who interpreted these passages [Deut 16:1-8; Num 9:10-12] in their obvious sense no longer celebrated Passover,

10. Frank H. Gorman, "Passover, Feast of," in *Eerdmans Dictionary of the Bible* (ed. David Noel Freedman; Grand Rapids: Eerdmans, 2000), 1013-14.

> but only Unleavened Bread. In the course of history, however, the term "Passover" prevailed, with the result that the modern Jewish calendar Passover begins on the 15th Nisan.[11]

This is a significant observation: Sanders is basically saying that the Temple was so central to the biblical idea of Passover that when the Temple was destroyed, the Passover feast was not simply transformed, but, in a certain sense, actually ceased. The *meal* continued, but the *sacrifice* of the lamb and the pouring out of the blood by the priests in the sanctuary — both of which are central and required by the Pentateuch — could no longer be accomplished. The reason is of course that the Pentateuch specifies the central sanctuary (later identified as the Jerusalem Temple) as "the sole legitimate seat of worship" and thus the sole legitimate place of the Passover offering.[12] Indeed, it is this cultic dimension of the Passover as an exclusively Temple sacrifice that transforms it into a pilgrimage festival in the Old Testament, in which Israelites living outside of Jerusalem are required to travel to the city in order to offer the Passover sacrifice and celebrate the accompanying feast of Unleavened Bread (cf. Exod 23:14-17).

4. ***The Passover as a Priestly Sacrifice*** Once the Passover sacrifice is transferred to the Temple, it is by definition also established as a sacrifice that can only be offered by ordained priests. The reason is simple: although a layman could slit the throat of the lamb, the sacrificial libation of the lamb's blood could only be performed by the Levitical priests in the Temple.[13] This stands in stark contrast to the original exodus, which was a domestic sacrifice, in which the father of each household from every tribe acted as priest over his family:

> When the service had been prepared for, the priests stood in their place, and the Levites in their divisions according to the king's command. *And they killed the Passover lamb, and the priests sprinkled the blood which they received from them while the Levites flayed the victims.* . . . And they roasted the Passover lamb with fire according to the ordinance; and they boiled the holy offerings in pots, in caldrons, and in pans, and carried them quickly to all the lay people. (2 Chron 35:10-11, 13)

11. Sanders, *Judaism,* 133.
12. Moore, *Judaism,* 40.
13. Segal, *The Hebrew Passover,* 15.

Along the same lines, the book of Ezra states that the "priests and Levites" sacrifice the Passover lambs on behalf of the sons of Israel (Ezra 6:19-20). Again, this constitutes a fundamental difference between the Passover in the Old Testament and Second Temple period and the later rabbinic Passover meal as it will be celebrated after the destruction of the Temple. The biblical texts not only inextricably tie the Passover sacrifice to the Jewish Temple; they restrict the performance of the blood ritual to the Jewish priesthood.[14]

5. ***The Passover as a Royal Feast of the Davidic King*** In at least three key biblical texts, the Passover feast is not only connected with the exodus from Egypt, but with the Davidic king and the restoration of the twelve tribes of Israel. This Davidic aspect is frequently overlooked, but very important for situating Jesus' actions in their Jewish context.[15]

For example, a central section of the selective history given to us in the book of Chronicles emphasizes the fact that, at the time of King Hezekiah, the Passover celebration is led by the "royal decree" of the Davidic king.[16] Moreover, the Passover is clearly described as the mechanism by which the Davidic kingdom will be redeemed from sin and the twelve tribes restored from exile:

> *Hezekiah sent to all Israel and Judah,* and wrote letters also to Ephraim and Manasseh, *that they should come to the house of the LORD at Jerusalem, to keep the Passover.* . . . So couriers went throughout all Israel and Judah with letters from the king and from his princes, as the king had commanded, saying, "O people of Israel, return to the LORD, the God of Abraham, Isaac, and Israel, that he may turn again to the remnant of you who have escaped from the hand of the kings of Assyria. . . . Yield yourselves to the LORD, and *come to his sanctuary,* which he has sanctified forever, *and serve the LORD your God, that his fierce anger may turn away from you. For if you return to the LORD, your brethren and your children will find compassion with their captors, and will return to this land.*" (2 Chron 30:1, 6, 8-9)

Notice Hezekiah's concern that the Passover include all twelve tribes of Israel — the two southern tribes of Judah and the ten northern tribes of Israel — which have been divided since the death of King Solomon (ca. 922 B.C.). This

14. McKnight, *Jesus and His Death*, 248.

15. See Scott W. Hahn, *The Kingdom of God as Liturgical Empire: A Theological Commentary on 1-2 Chronicles* (Grand Rapids: Baker Academic, 2012), 181.

16. Segal, *The Hebrew Passover*, 18.

is the meaning of the effort Hezekiah makes to invite the "remnant" of the scattered tribes of "Ephraim, Manasseh, and Zebulun" to come and keep the Passover celebration. In this way, the Passover sacrifice of the Davidic king has both restoration and redemptive power: by keeping the Passover, the "fierce anger of God" will be turned away from Israel, and the scattered exiles will "return to this land."[17]

Along similar lines, King Josiah's famous cultic reforms climax in a Passover feast initiated by the Davidic king himself:

> So all the service of the LORD was prepared that day, *to keep the Passover* and to offer burnt offerings on the altar of the LORD, *according to the command of King Josiah.* And the sons of Israel who were present kept the Passover at that time, and the feast of unleavened bread seven days. *No Passover like it had been kept in Israel since the days of Samuel the prophet; none of the kings of Israel had kept such a Passover as was kept by Josiah,* and the priests and the Levites, *and all Judah and Israel who were present,* and the inhabitants of Jerusalem. (2 Chron 35:16-18)

Once again, Passover and the Davidic king are closely linked: it is "the kings of Israel" who were supposed to "keep" the Passover but failed, in contrast to King Josiah, who restores right worship through a royal edict.[18] Likewise, the connection between Passover and the restoration of the twelve tribes reappears. Indeed, the reason Josiah's Passover is so memorable is that "all Judah and Israel" — i.e., representatives of all twelve tribes — are present. Clearly the Chronicler has an interest in showing that one thing that makes a Davidic king great is the extent to which he is able to unify the twelve tribes of Israel through the celebration of the Passover.

Finally, Passover and the Davidic monarch are connected in Ezekiel's prophetic description of the future Temple. Ezekiel emphasizes that it is the "duty" of the eschatological "prince" *(nāśîʾ)* — i.e., the future Davidic king — to keep the appointed feasts of the house of Israel.[19] Special prominence is given

17. So Bokser, *The Origins of the Seder,* 18.

18. Segal, *The Hebrew Passover,* 6.

19. On the "prince" as an eschatological Davidic king in Ezekiel, see Ezek 34:23-24: "I will set over them one shepherd to tend them, my servant David; he shall feed them and be their shepherd. I, the LORD, will be their God, and my servant David shall be prince *(nāśîʾ)* among them." On the use of this term in Ezekiel, see P. M. Joyce, "King and Messiah in Ezekiel," in *King and Messiah in Israel and the Ancient Near East* (ed. J. Day; JSOTSup 270; Sheffield: Sheffield Academic Press, 1998), 323-27.

to the fact that the eschatological king will take the lead role in the feast of Passover and Unleavened Bread:

> In the first month, on the fourteenth day of the month, you shall celebrate *the feast of the Passover,* and for seven days unleavened bread shall be eaten. *On that day the prince shall provide for himself and all the people of the land a young bull for a sin offering.* And on the seven days of the festival he shall provide as a burnt offering to the LORD seven young bulls and seven rams without blemish, on each of the seven days; and a he-goat daily for a sin-offering. (Ezek 45:21-23)

Once again, it is the Davidic king who takes the "central role" in the celebration of the eschatological Passover.[20] Notice also that Passover seems to be being "merged with ideas of atonement,"[21] when Ezekiel states that it will be the future king's responsibility to provide both the peace offerings of Passover week and a "sin-offering" for all the people (cf. Ezek 45:17). Strikingly then, in Ezekiel's vision of the eschatological Temple, it is the eschatological Davidic king — later known as the Messiah — who offers an atoning sacrifice for the sins of the people during the eschatological Passover.

As we can see from this brief survey, the Old Testament provides a rich and variegated description of the shape of the Passover feast. In addition to the foundational description in Exodus, we find a feast connected with Israel's entry into the promised land, an essentially cultic and Temple-centered feast, and a feast that is linked to redemptive sacrifice and the restoration of the Davidic kingdom and the tribes of Israel.

The Passover in Early Jewish Literature

When we turn to descriptions of the Passover in early Jewish literature outside the Bible, we find, as one would expect, a number of themes consistent with what we've already seen in the Jewish Scriptures.[22] In addition to these elements, however, there are several distinctive features of the Passover in the literature of the Second Temple period that will help us focus on certain associations that may have been circulating at the time of Jesus.

20. Segal, *The Hebrew Passover,* 7; McKnight, *Jesus and His Death,* 248.

21. McKnight, *Jesus and His Death,* 248.

22. For summaries, see Segal, *The Hebrew Passover,* 31-32; McKnight, *Jesus and His Death,* 252-53.

1. ***The Passover as a Feast of Wine and Hymns of Praise*** In the Hebrew Scriptures' descriptions of Passover, mentions of a joyful atmosphere are fairly infrequent, and there is only a little evidence that wine or special hymns ever accompanied the Passover sacrifice (cf. 2 Chron 35:11-15). By contrast, the drinking of wine and the singing of hymns, both of which characterize the joyfulness of the feast, take on a certain prominence in Greek writings such as the Wisdom of Solomon and extrabiblical Second Temple descriptions of Passover. For example, in its description of the Passover, Wisdom speaks of the fact that the Israelites "were already singing the praises of their fathers" (Wisd 18:9). Along similar lines, *Jubilees* states that the "beginning of the feast" of Passover means "the beginning of joy" (*Jub.* 49:2). Indeed, it even goes on to claim that at the very first Passover in Egypt, the Israelites "remained eating the flesh of the Passover and drinking wine and praising and blessing and glorifying the LORD the God of their fathers" (*Jub.* 49:6). As scholars note, in this text, written centuries before Jesus' day, we find the first mention of wine as a constitutive part of the Passover meal.[23] Perhaps most interesting of all, the Dead Sea Scrolls provide evidence that certain psalms were sung during the annual festivals, including the Passover:

> And David, son of Jesse, was wise. . . . And he wrote psalms: three thousand six hundred; and songs to be sung before the altar over the perpetual offering of every day, for all the days of the year; three hundred and sixty-four; and for the sabbath offerings: fifty-two songs . . . *and for all the days of the festivals,* and for the Day of Atonement: thirty songs. (*11QPsalms*[a] [11Q5] 27:2, 4-8)

In short, by the time we get to the first century, both the drinking of wine and the singing of hymns and psalms are firmly anchored in the Passover celebration. Indeed, Philo not only speaks of the "joy" with which Passover is celebrated by the Jewish people, but explicitly states that the Passover sacrifice would be accompanied by the drinking of "wine" and the singing of "songs of praise" to God (*Special Laws* 2.146-48).

2. ***The Passover as a Jerusalem Temple Feast*** Although the biblical accounts presuppose that pilgrims (especially men) would travel to Jerusalem to celebrate Passover, the accounts of Hezekiah and Josiah's Passovers as unique events clearly indicate that for much of Israel's history, many people did not

23. Segal, *The Hebrew Passover,* 22; Bokser, *The Origins of the Seder,* 19.

follow the Law and come to Jerusalem to keep the feast. In stark contrast to this, descriptions of Passover from Philo and Josephus in the Second Temple period describe it as an extremely popular pilgrimage festival, which led to Jerusalem being virtually overrun with Jewish pilgrims from both inside and outside the promised land:

> *Countless multitudes from countless cities come, some over land, others over sea, from east and west and north and south at every feast.* They take the temple for their port as a general haven and safe refuge from the bustle and great turmoil of life . . . to enjoy a brief breathing-space in scenes of genial cheerfulness. Thus filled with comfortable hopes they devote the leisure, as is their bounden duty, to holiness and the honouring of God. Friendships are formed between those who hitherto knew not each other, and the sacrifices and libations are the occasion of reciprocity of feeling and constitute the surest pledge that all are of one mind. (Philo, *Special Laws* 1.69-70)[24]

In similar fashion, Josephus tells us that, during the first century A.D., at every Passover, "a vast multitude" would be collected "out of remote places" to gather in Jerusalem and keep the feast (*War* 6.428). Because of this, Josephus also claims that more sacrifices were offered at Passover-tide than at any other annual feast (*Antiquities* 17.213).[25] In other words, during the Second Temple period, Passover seems to have become the most popular pilgrimage festival, to which multitudes of Jews would come, from both the promised land and the Diaspora.[26] One reason the ingathering of so many Jews is significant is that it may have provided a concrete liturgical connection between the cele-

24. LCL translation, cited in Bokser, *The Origins of the Seder,* 82.

25. Cf. Bokser, *The Origins of the Seder,* 117 n. 23.

26. It is worth noting at this point the currently popular idea that Jews outside Jerusalem during the Second Temple period would celebrate Passover in the Diaspora without sacrifice. For example, Baruch Bokser, "Was the Last Supper a Passover Seder?," 28, claims that Jews outside Jerusalem gathered to celebrate a "special meal" that resembled the Passover, but was missing the sacrificial lamb. Significantly, however, he can cite no textual evidence in support of this claim. Indeed, Bokser himself admits elsewhere: "Before 70 C.E., did such meals take place *without* the paschal lamb? *No firm evidence* exists that confirms this." And again: "Despite the probability that some Jews who lacked access to a paschal sacrifice felt the need to do something on Passover eve, *none* of the prerabbinic accounts of the celebration mentions a meal without a sacrifice." Bokser, *The Origins of the Seder,* 53, 54 (emphasis added). For similar speculation without evidence, see Marcus, *Mark,* 2:945; Wright, *Jesus and the Victory of God,* 556; Sanders, *Judaism,* 133-34.

bration of Passover and the restoration of the people of Israel from exile. Every year, in a partial way, it was the Passover pilgrim feast in particular that gave Second Temple Jews a taste of what the future ingathering of the exiles might indeed be like.

3. ***The Passover as a Night-Time Feast*** In addition to the requirement that the Passover be sacrificed in the Jerusalem Temple, the Dead Sea Scrolls also depict the meal as taking place at night (restored texts are placed in brackets):

> [And on the four]teenth day of the first month, [at twilight], they [will celebrate] [the Passover of YHWH] and they will perform sacrifice; prior to the evening offering they will sacrifice [it. Every male of] twenty years and older shall celebrate it. And *they shall consume it [at night], in the courtyards of [the] sanctuary, and every one shall rise early and go to [his] tent.* (*11QTemple* [11Q19] 17:6-9)

Although it is not clear how the author of this Scroll envisioned the relationship between this Temple, the present-day Jerusalem cult, and the Temple to come at the end of time (cf. *11QTemple* 29:8-10), it nevertheless jibes with what we have seen elsewhere about the nocturnal timing of the consumption of the Passover lamb in Jerusalem.

4. ***The Passover as a Redemptive Sacrifice*** Although there is no evidence that Second Temple Jews saw contemporary celebrations of the Passover memorial as redemptive or atoning, there is some evidence that they saw the original Passover of the exodus as a redemptive sacrifice.[27] Again, *Jubilees* emphasizes the original Passover's apotropaic effect when stating that the Israelites were "saved" from the "powers of Mastema" — the destroying angel — because of "the blood" of the Passover lambs (*Jub.* 49:3).[28] Along similar lines, Josephus tells us that the blood of the Passover lambs in Egypt "purified" *(hagnizō)* the homes of the Israelites, which at least one scholar sees as implying the "removal of guilt" through the blood of the lamb (*Antiquities* 2.312).[29] This connection may aid us as we attempt to understand how Jesus might have viewed the inaugural Passover of the eschatological exodus.

27. McKnight, *Jesus and His Death,* 248; Bokser, *The Origins of the Seder,* 18; Segal, *The Hebrew Passover,* 23.

28. Bokser, *The Origins of the Seder,* 20.

29. Smith, *Jesus' Last Passover Meal,* 46. Later rabbinic literature intriguingly compares the doorposts and lintels of the Israelite homes in Egypt to "altars" (*Mek.* 12:7).

5. ***The Passover, Future Eschatology, and the Messiah*** Perhaps this is why the first hints of an eschatological dimension to the Passover emerge during the Second Temple period. Although the evidence is fairly meager, there are two passages worth noting. First, Josephus mentions in passing that at the three pilgrimage feasts in Jerusalem, the Jewish people would "intercede for future mercies" (*Antiquities* 4.203-4). This suggests that in the first century A.D., all three feasts — Passover, Pentecost, and Tabernacles — not only looked back to Israel's history of salvation, but forward to future redemption. Second, and far more significant, is the Greek translation of Jeremiah's prophecies of the restoration of Israel from the same period. According to the Septuagint, Jeremiah's famous oracles of the coming of the Messiah, the restoration of Israel, and the forging of a new covenant will not only take place in the general future, but "during the feast of Passover" *(en heortē phasek)* (Jer 38:7-9 LXX = Jer 31:7-9 MT). In this extremely important witness, we see clearly that the Greek version of Jeremiah places the eschatological restoration of Israel and the establishment of the new covenant during Passover.[30]

Unfortunately, it is impossible to tell whether this connection between Passover and the messianic restoration was present in the Hebrew original used by the Septuagint — it is absent in the current Masoretic Text and the Hebrew copies of Jeremiah among the Dead Sea Scrolls.[31] Nevertheless, there is no doubt that the Septuagint was widely read by Jews in the Second Temple period. This widespread influence may be one factor in the ubiquity of the later rabbinic expectation that the coming of the Messiah and the eschatological redemption of Israel would take place during the feast of Passover. It may also lie behind the custom, described by Josephus, of opening the gates at midnight on Passover night: "When the Festival of Unleavened Bread, which we call Passover, was going on, the priests were accustomed to throw open the gates of the temple after midnight" (*Antiquities* 18.29). One of the most exhaustive studies of the Passover ever written suggests that this Second Temple ritual was tied to the expectancy of the coming of the messiah at midnight.[32] Whatever we make of this suggestion, the Septuagint provides us with solid evidence that a link between the celebration of Passover and the messianic restoration of Israel was already circulating some two centuries or more before the public ministry of Jesus.

30. Smith, *Jesus' Last Passover Meal,* 49; Pitre, *Jesus, the Tribulation, and the End of the Exile,* 448.

31. Cf. Martin Abegg Jr., Peter Flint, and Eugene Ulrich, *The Dead Sea Scrolls Bible* (San Francisco: HarperOne, 1999), 399-400.

32. Le Déaut, *La Nuit Paschale,* 288-89, suggests that the explanation for this custom, otherwise difficult to explain, may be "l'idée d'une apparition du Messie dans cette nuit pascale."

In short, in early Jewish literature, the feast of Passover not only preserves the various elements found in the Bible, but also emphasizes Passover as a pilgrim feast of joy which, in some circles at least, was seen as a foretaste of the future age of restoration.[33] Although much more could be said, this brief survey should provide the reader with enough information to lay the groundwork for our study of Jesus' final Passover meal. As we will see, several of the themes we have unearthed — the connection with the exodus, the sacrificial nature of the Passover lamb, the drinking of wine, the connections with the messianic restoration of Israel, the hymns of praise, etc. — are also present in the accounts of his words and actions.

The Temple Context of the Last Supper[34]

Now that we have traced out the shape of the Jewish Passover meal in the Bible and ancient Jewish literature, we can turn to the accounts of Jesus' final Passover preserved in the Gospels themselves.

Before doing so, it is worth highlighting that at this point in the investigation, some scholars leap immediately into an examination of the so-called

33. Many of these same constellations of ideas are present in later rabbinic literature: the Passover as a Temple sacrifice (*m. Pes.* 5:5-10; *t. Pes.* 4:10-15); an atoning sacrifice (*m. Pes.* 10:6; *Exod. Rab.* 15:12; 17:3; 19:5); a multi-stage liturgical meal (*m. Pes.* 10; *t. Pes.* 10); associated with the coming of the Messiah (*Targ. Neof.* on Exod 12:42; *Mek.* on Exod 12:42; *Exod. Rab.* 15:1; cf. Jerome, *Commentary on Matthew* 4 on 25:6). On the rabbinic Passover, see esp. Bokser, *The Origins of the Seder,* passim; Le Déaut, *La Nuit Paschale,* 279-91.

34. I. H. Marshall, "The Last Supper," in *Key Events in the Life of the Historical Jesus* (ed. Darrell L. Bock and Robert L. Webb; WUNT 247; Tübingen: Mohr Siebeck, 2009), 485-504; McKnight, *Jesus and His Death,* 266-70; R. Routledge, "Passover and Last Supper," *TynBul* 53 (2002): 203-21; Jonathan Klawans, "Was Jesus' Last Supper a Seder?" *BibRev* 17 (2001): 24-33, 47; Evans, *Mark,* 367-79; Davies and Allison, *Saint Matthew,* 3:456-60; Sanders, *The Historical Figure of Jesus,* 250-51; Rudolf Pesch, "The Gospel in Jerusalem: Mark 14:12-26 as the Oldest Tradition of the Early Church," in *The Gospel and the Gospels* (ed. Peter Stuhlmacher; Grand Rapids: Eerdmans, 1991), 106-48; Smith, *Jesus' Last Passover Meal,* 148-49; Fitzmyer, *The Gospel according to Luke,* 2:1376-84; Rudolf Pesch, *Das Abendmahl und Jesu Todesverständnis* (QD 80; Freiburg: Herder, 1978), 69-90; R. H. Hiers, *The Historical Jesus and the Kingdom of God: Present and Future in the Message and Ministry of Jesus* (UFHM 38; Gainesville: University of Florida, 1973), 96-101; Hermann Patsch, *Abendmahl und historischer Jesus* (Calwer Theologische Monographien 1; Stuttgart: Calwer, 1972), 62-63; Jeremias, *The Eucharistic Words of Jesus,* 92-93; Bultmann, *History of the Synoptic Tradition,* 263-64; Gustaf Dalman, *Jesus-Jeshua: Studies in the Gospels* (trans. P. P. Levertoff; New York: Macmillan, 1929), 86-184.

"words of institution."[35] Many works, even those specifically focused on the Last Supper, do not bother to spend any time on the Gospel accounts of the preparation for the Last Supper (Matt 26:17-19; Mark 14:12-16; Luke 22:7-13). But to skip this material is a serious mistake. For one thing, it creates a false impression that originally, "the words of institution were contextless."[36] This is simply not true. According to all three Synoptic Gospels, the immediate context of the words of institution is explicitly sacrificial (or cultic) and implicitly tied to the Jerusalem Temple.

Indeed, in stark contrast to Jesus scholarship's tendency to ignore these data, the Gospels themselves spend as much space recounting the preparations for the Passover/Last Supper in Jerusalem as they do recounting the words of institution at the Last Supper. Given our interest in not just the words of Jesus but the context in which they may have been spoken, this material demands our attention:

> Now on the first day of Unleavened Bread the disciples came to Jesus, saying, "Where will you have us prepare for you to eat the Passover?" He said, "Go into the city to such a one, and say to him, 'The Teacher says, My time is at hand; I will keep the Passover at your house with my disciples.'" And the disciples did as Jesus had directed them, and they prepared the Passover. (Matt 26:17-19)

> And on the first day of Unleavened Bread, when they sacrificed the Passover, his disciples said to him, "Where will you have us go and prepare for you to eat the Passover?" And he sent two of his disciples, and said to them, "Go into the city, and a man carrying a jar of water will meet you; follow him, and wherever he enters, say to the householder, 'The Teacher says, Where is my guest room, where I am to eat the Passover with my disciples?' And he will show you a large upper room furnished and ready; there prepare for us." And the disciples set out and went to the city, and found it as he had told them; and they prepared the Passover. (Mark 14:12-16)

> Then came the day of Unleavened Bread, on which the Passover had to be sacrificed. So he sent Peter and John, saying, "Go and prepare the Passover for us, that we may eat it." They said to him, "Where will you have us prepare it?" He said to them, "Behold, when you have entered the city, a man

35. E.g., McKnight, *Jesus and His Death,* chapters 13 and 14.

36. Smith, *Jesus' Last Passover Meal,* 85.

> carrying a jar of water will meet you; follow him into the house which he enters, and tell the householder, 'The Teacher says to you, Where is the guest room, where I am to eat the Passover with my disciples?' And he will show you a large upper room furnished; there make ready." And they went, and found it as he had told them; and they prepared the Passover. (Luke 22:7-13)

Several important questions are raised by these accounts. First, both Mark and Luke identify the afternoon of the Last Supper as the time when the Passover lamb was being sacrificed. What would the Passover sacrifice have been like during the first century A.D.? What exactly would it have entailed? Second, what is the nature of the rendezvous that Jesus has arranged in the Upper Room? Why not just enter Jerusalem as a group and find a place to celebrate the Passover meal, like every other pilgrim? Third, what exactly is Jesus commanding the disciples to do when he sends them into Jerusalem to "prepare" the Passover? Exactly what preparations are envisioned? Fourth and finally, as always, are the accounts of the disciples preparing the Passover historically plausible in a first-century context? What are the arguments for and against historicity?

The Requirement for the Passover Sacrifice to Be in Jerusalem

We will take up the question of the rendezvous first, since it can be answered rather briefly. It seems evident from all three Gospels that arrangements have been made for a private Passover to be held at an anonymous host's home in the city of Jerusalem. In light of these arrangements, Jesus sends the disciples (who are identified in Luke as Peter and John) into the city on the afternoon that the Passover lambs were "sacrificed" *(ethyon)* (Mark 14:12; Luke 22:7). Their instructions: to meet "a man carrying a jar of water" who would lead them to the home where Jesus and the Twelve would keep the feast. Several aspects of this somewhat mysterious episode call for clarification.

First, despite frequent remarks to the contrary, there is no clear evidence in the Gospels that this rendezvous necessarily represents a case of prophetic or supernatural foreknowledge on Jesus' part.[37] Such an interpretation fails

37. *Contra* A. Y. Collins, *Mark*, 646; Gerd Lüdemann, *Jesus after 2000 Years: What He Really Said and Did* (London: SCM; Amherst: Prometheus, 2001), 96; Bultmann, *History of the Synoptic Tradition*, 264.

to reckon with the fact that the man carrying the jar of water and the anonymous owner of the upper room also appear to know in advance that Jesus and his disciples will be coming to celebrate the Passover in their home. As Mark says very clearly, it is *he* who approaches *them:* "a man carrying a jar of water will meet you *(apantēsei hymin)*" (Mark 14:13).[38] Thus, barring prophetic foreknowledge on the part of these unknown men, it seems best to conclude that what is in view is a meeting that has been prepared in advance by Jesus, in some unknown manner.

Why does Jesus celebrate Passover in this somewhat secretive fashion? The most plausible suggestion is that Jesus is taking the necessary precautions because he is aware that he has already been marked out by the Jerusalem authorities for arrest. This is the impression given by the Synoptic Gospels, in which the description of the rendezvous comes immediately after the conferral of the chief priests with Judas as to how he might betray Jesus to them (Matt 26:3-5; Mark 14:1-2; Luke 22:1-6).[39] As Craig Evans states: "Jesus . . . has made arrangements — evidently unknown to the disciples whom he has sent — for observing the Passover in a private room. The clandestine rendezvous with the man carrying the jar of water may have had to do with precautions that Jesus felt were necessary. He knew he was a wanted man."[40] This is an especially plausible interpretation given the importance of the Last Supper taking place that night: Jesus has one final prophetic sign to perform, and he cannot have Judas handing him over to the authorities before the Last Supper is complete.

Second, the rather common assertion that the disciples are able to recognize a man carrying a jar of water because only women did this (men used water-skins) should probably be abandoned.[41] For one thing, this interpretation, which has gained remarkably widespread currency in contemporary commentaries, is entirely based on modern-day observations. There is no ancient evidence, Jewish or otherwise, to support it.[42] Moreover, there is evidence

38. So Marcus, *Mark,* 2:945; Keener, *A Commentary on the Gospel of Matthew,* 624; France, *The Gospel of Mark,* 564; Fitzmyer, *The Gospel according to Luke,* 2:1383.

39. Cf. John A. T. Robinson, *The Priority of John* (London: SCM, 1985), 223-29, who convincingly argues on the basis of John 11:45-53 that a formal meeting of the Sanhedrin has already taken place in which they "passed a resolution" *(ebouleusanto)* (John 11:53) that "Jesus should be put to death and at which he is publicly declared a wanted man." As John goes on to say: "Now the chief priests and the Pharisees had given orders that if any one knew where he was, he should let them know, so that they might arrest him" (John 11:57).

40. Evans, *Mark,* 373.

41. Marcus, *Mark,* 2:945; Davies and Allison, *Saint Matthew,* 3:457 n. 15.

42. Marcus, *Mark,* 2:945, traces the suggestion back to the great Dominican M.-J. La-

in the Old Testament that men, especially servants, did carry water, even if it is not clear whether it was in jars or water-skins (Deut 29:10-11; Josh 9:21-27).[43] Furthermore, the suggestion lacks practical plausibility: in a city brimming with thousands of pilgrims, how are the disciples of Jesus supposed to happen upon the one man carrying a jar of water? Once again, it seems more likely that Jesus has arranged in advance a meeting between the disciples and one of the servants of the owner of the Upper Room.

Third and finally, and most important of all, the very reason Jesus and his disciples would even need to secure the hospitality of the unknown host stems from the fact that the sacrificial feast of the Passover, according to Jewish Scripture and other Second Temple literature, had to take place in Jerusalem.[44] The Pentateuch is unequivocal on the restriction of all sacrifice to the central sanctuary, and other Second Temple literature bears witness to the continued practice of the Temple as the exclusive locale of the Passover sacrifice:

> You shall seek the place which the LORD your God will choose out of all your tribes to put his name and make his habitation there; thither shall you go, and thither shall you bring your burnt offerings and your sacrifices . . . and there you shall eat before the LORD your God, and you shall rejoice, you and your household. . . . *Take heed that you do not offer your burnt offerings at every place that you see; but at the place which the LORD will choose in one of your tribes,* there you shall offer your burnt offerings, and there you shall do all I am commanding you. (Deut 12:5-6, 13-14)

> In the days when a house is built in the name of the LORD in the land of their inheritance, *they shall go there and they shall sacrifice the Passover* at evening when the sun is setting on the third (part) of the day. And they shall offer up its blood on the threshold of the altar. And its fat they shall place on the fire which is above the altar. And they shall eat its flesh cooked in fire within the court of the house which is sanctified in the name of the LORD. *And they shall not be able to observe the Passover in their cities or in any district except before the tabernacle of the LORD or before his house in*

---

grange, *The Gospel of Saint Mark,* 373, who bases his interpretation entirely on his personal observations of "modern custom" at the turn of the twentieth century.

43. Marcus, *Mark,* 2:945. Cf. Keener, *A Commentary on the Gospel of Matthew,* 624, citing *T. Job* 21:2-3; *Gen. Rab.* 53:13; 93:6. Neither of these texts makes any distinction between men using skins and women using jars.

44. Smith, *Jesus' Last Passover Meal,* 14-15; Fitzmyer, *The Gospel according to Luke,* 2:1377.

> *which his name dwells.* And let them not stray from after the LORD. (*Jub.* 49:19-21)[45]

As we will see in a moment, *Jubilees*' vision of all Israel eating the Passover within the very Temple courts itself is idealized, and, by the first century A.D., was certainly impossible, given the thousands of pilgrims descending upon the city for the festival. Nevertheless, the biblical requirement that the Passover sacrifice only be offered in one place — the city of Jerusalem — was in force at the time of Jesus. Indeed, it is quite clearly the primary reason that Jesus sends the disciples into Jerusalem to prepare the Passover, rather than simply remaining in Bethany and celebrating Passover there. As adult Jewish men, they were obligated to perform this sacrificial ritual in the Temple.[46]

The practical effect of this biblical requirement for the Passover to be sacrificed in Jerusalem is that Jerusalem would be filled to the brim with pilgrims from every corner of the known world, coming to keep the feast as the Torah required (see Josephus, *War* 2.10; *Ant.* 17.213-14; 20.106). Indeed, in the first century, the feast of Passover was not just *a* pilgrim feast; it was *the* most popular of all three pilgrimage festivals. According to Josephus, many pilgrims apparently brought their own tents to Passover and stayed outside Jerusalem, while the city locals would offer rooms and beds in exchange for the hides of the animals offered in sacrifice during Passover (*Antiquities* 17.217).[47] In light of such a situation, it is easy to see why Jesus arranges for a private room in which to celebrate the Passover meal, as well as why he and the disciples, like many other pilgrims, do not stay the night in the city, but retire to the garden of Gethsemane, outside the city walls (Matt 26:36-46; Mark 14:32-42; Luke 22:39-46; John 18:1-11).

The Thousands of Passover Lambs Sacrificed in the Temple

With this basic context in mind, we can now explain what exactly the Gospels mean when they state that on the afternoon when the lambs were being

45. Notably, the later rabbis, even though they were no longer able to keep the Passover sacrifice in the Temple, concur with the biblical and Second Temple evidence regarding the restriction of the sacrifice to Jerusalem: "At the Passover observed in Egypt each and every one slaughters [his Passover-offering] in his own house. But the Passover observed in the coming generations [sees] all Israel slaughtering [the Passover-offering] in one location [the Temple]." (Tosefta, *Pesaḥim* 8:16)

46. Dalman, *Jesus-Jeshua,* 111.

47. Cf. Sanders, *Judaism,* 129.

"sacrificed" *(ethyon)* (Mark 14:12; Luke 22:7), the disciples went into Jerusalem and "prepared the Passover" *(hētoimasan to pascha)* (Matt 26:19; Mark 14:16; Luke 22:13). What was the sacrifice and preparation of the Passover like in the first century? What does Jesus' instruction to the disciples to prepare the meal entail?

The first point that needs to be emphasized is that both actions — the sacrifice of the Passover lamb in the Temple and the preparation of the meal in the upper room — are presupposed by the evangelists.[48] Indeed, two of the three accounts of the preparation explicitly mention the sacrifice of the Passover lambs and connect that sacrifice to the disciples' preparations for the Last Supper. If we leave the Greek word for "passover" untranslated, this is particularly clear:

> And on the first day of Unleavened Bread, *when they sacrificed* the *pascha,* his disciples said to him, "Where will you have us go and *prepare* for you to eat the *pascha*"? (Mark 14:12)

> Then came the day of Unleavened Bread, on which the *pascha* had *to be sacrificed.* So Jesus sent Peter and John, saying, "Go and *prepare* the *pascha* for us, *that we may eat it.*" They said to him, "Where will you have us *prepare* it?" (Luke 22:7-9)

There is a widespread tendency in English translations to render the first occurrence of *pascha* as "Passover *lamb*" and the second just as "the Passover," leaving the impression of preparations simply for the Passover meal (so RSV). In the Greek texts, however, the connection is much stronger; in context, it is clearly the same *pascha* — i.e., the Passover lamb — that is being both sacrificed and prepared for consumption.[49]

48. So Marshall, "The Last Supper," 495-96; Marcus, *The Gospel of Mark,* 2:944; Evans, *Mark,* 373.

49. In support of this, it is worth noting that the evidence in the Gospel of Mark in particular reveals that the preparation the disciples engage in must refer primarily to the preparation of the lamb (with the other elements of the meal being implied), since the room itself is described as already having been prepared: "And he will show you a large upper room furnished and prepared *(hetoimon);* there prepare *(hetoimasate)* for us" (Mark 14:15). As Joel Marcus points out: "If the room is already prepared *(hetoimon),* why do the disciples need to prepare there *(hetoimasate)?* . . . Perhaps the room is already prepared but the meal is not" (Marcus, *Mark,* 2:946). Again, English translations usually obscure this by translating the first reference as "ready" and the second as "prepare" (so RSV). But, again, there is no such difference in Greek, and it seems that a particular interpretation of the Last

The reason this is important is that it highlights the cultic and sacrificial context of the Last Supper as a Jewish Passover meal. Modern readers can be easily tempted to imagine the Passover described by the Gospels as a modern-day "Seder," which is a non-sacrificial, non–Temple centered, non-priestly meal, that can be celebrated and eaten anywhere. As a result, there is no blood involved. *The Passover in the Second Temple period, however, was strikingly different: it took place in the Temple, was offered by priests, and involved not only the preparation of the bread and wine of the meal, but the cultic slaughter of thousands and thousands of lambs.* Significantly, it is precisely this bloody and sacrificial aspect of the pilgrim festivals that receives emphasis in descriptions from the Second Temple period. For example, in the Greek document known as the *Letter of Aristeas* (usually dated ca. second-first century B.C.), we find this description of the festal sacrifices in the Temple:

> Now the House faces the east with its back towards the west. And the whole floor is paved with stone and has slopes to the appropriate places, to allow for the flushing of water which occurs so as to clean the blood from the sacrifices. For many tens of thousands of beasts are brought for sacrifice on the days of the festivals. (*Letter of Aristeas* 88)[50]

Even more significant for understanding the Gospels is the firsthand description of Josephus, who claims to have been a priest in the Second Temple before its destruction in A.D. 70. He not only describes the sacrifices of the festivals in general, but the quantity of lambs slaughtered on the Passover in particular:

> Accordingly, on the occasion of the feast called Passover, at which they sacrifice from the ninth to the eleventh hour, and a little fraternity, as it were, gathers around each sacrifice, of not fewer than ten persons (feasting alone being not permitted), while the companies often include as many as twenty, *the victims were counted and amounted to two hundred and fifty-five thousand six hundred;* allowing an average of ten diners to each victim,

Supper seems to be guiding these translation choices. The two words refer to two different acts of preparation: one focused on the room, which is taken care of by the owner, the other focused on the Passover lamb and the meal, which is carried out by the disciples. Hence, this description appears to include both the acquisition and sacrifice of the Passover lamb in the Temple and the preparation of the Passover lamb for the meal that would be celebrated in the Upper Room itself.

50. Trans. C. T. R. Hayward, *The Jewish Temple: A Non-Biblical Sourcebook* (London: Routledge, 1996), 28.

> we obtain a total of two million seven hundred thousand [pilgrims], all pure and holy. (Josephus, *War* 6.423-24)[51]

A total of 250,000 lambs for 2,000,000 pilgrims is a stunning figure.[52] Even if the number is exaggerated, as most scholars think,[53] the testimony of Josephus is critical for reconstructing what a first-century Passover in the Temple was actually like, and how it differed from the later rabbinic seder. To the modern reader, who has probably never witnessed the sacrifice of a single lamb, much less the slaughter of tens of thousands, the immensity of such crowds being gathered for such a bloody act of worship is difficult to imagine. For our purposes here, whatever the exact count, the primary point is that the Last Supper is set at a time when the Temple and the city of Jerusalem were filled to capacity. In the first century A.D., the 14th of Nisan was a day of blood and sacrifice, the blood of the Passover lambs.[54]

In sum, when the Gospel accounts of Jesus sending the disciples to prepare the Passover are read closely and compared with ancient evidence, they depict Jesus as sending the disciples (explicitly identified by Luke as Peter and

51. Trans. LCL, cited in Bokser, *The Origins of the Seder,* 24-25.

52. Elsewhere Josephus estimates the number of Passover pilgrims in the first century at "no fewer in number than three million" (*War* 2.280).

53. See Sanders, *Judaism,* 126-28.

54. Second Temple sources do not tell us exactly how so many lambs were sacrificed in the space of one afternoon. However, early rabbinic literature claims that while the Temple still stood, the sacrifice took place in an assembly-line style, with the throats of the lambs being slit by the laymen, while the priests' task was restricted to pouring out the blood on the altar. See Mishnah, *Pesaḥim* 5:5-7: "The Passover was slaughtered in three groups, for it is written, 'And the whole assembly of the congregation of Israel shall slaughter it' [Exod 12:6] — 'assembly,' 'congregation,' and 'Israel.' When the first group entered in and the Temple Court was filled, the gates of the Temple Court were closed. [On the shofar] a sustained, a quavering, and again a sustained blast were blown. The priests stood in rows and in their hands were basins of silver and basins of gold. In one row all the basins were of silver and in another row all the basins were of gold. . . . An Israelite slaughtered his offering and the priest caught the blood. The priest passed the basin to his fellow, and he to his fellow, each receiving a full basin and giving back an empty one. The priest nearest to the Altar tossed the blood in one action against the base [of the Altar]. When the first group went out the second group came in; and when the second group went out the third group came in. As the rite was performed with the first group so was it performed with the second and the third. [In the meantime the Levites] sang the Hallel. If they finished it, they sang it anew. . . ." Translation by Herbert Danby, *The Mishnah* (Oxford: Oxford University Press, 1933), slightly adapted. This "assembly-line" approach will strike a note of familiarity to any Catholic who has attended one of the papal Masses at a "World Youth Day," where over a million people are documented as having been present and received communion at a single liturgy.

John) into the city of Jerusalem on the afternoon when the Passover lambs were being sacrificed in the Temple. They also depict Jesus as having already established an encounter between the disciples and a young man who would show them where the Passover meal would be celebrated. Given the fact that Jesus both commands the disciples to "prepare" the Passover and states that the Upper Room itself was already "made ready," the logical implication of the texts is that the disciples go into the city to acquire a lamb, sacrifice it in the Temple, and prepare it and the rest of the cultic meal according to Jewish custom in the first century. With this basic picture in mind, we can now take up the question of whether the Gospel accounts of Jesus and the disciples' preparation for the Last Supper are historically plausible.

Arguments against Historical Plausibility

When it comes to the question of historical plausibility, the evidence that Jesus sent the disciples to prepare the Jewish Passover on the afternoon before the Last Supper (Matt 26:17-19; Mark 14:12-16; Luke 22:7-13) is somewhat difficult to assess, insofar as most major works on Jesus simply ignore it.[55]

When on occasion this evidence is rejected as unhistorical, at least two major arguments are utilized against it.[56]

First, there is the argument from the impossibility of miracles and prophecy. Once again, this is, properly speaking, a philosophical rather than

55. E.g., Keener, *The Historical Jesus of the Gospels;* Wright, *Jesus and the Victory of God;* Sanders, *Jesus and Judaism;* Becker, *Jesus of Nazareth;* Meyer, *The Aims of Jesus;* Jeremias, *New Testament Theology;* Bornkamm, *Jesus of Nazareth.*

56. One argument against historical plausibility barely merits mention, but I will briefly address it here because it continues to appear in the literature. According to some scholars, Jesus' act of sending the disciples to meet the young man (Matt 26:18; Mark 14:13-15; Luke 22:10-13) demonstrates a prophetic foreknowledge that is literarily derived from the Old Testament account of the prophet Samuel sending Saul to retrieve his father's lost donkeys, and knowing in advance that Saul will "meet two men by Rachel's tomb in the territory of Benjamin at Zelzah," who will tell him that "the asses" he seeks "are found" (see 1 Sam 10:1-4). For some scholars, the fact that in this account Samuel foretells that Saul will meet a man leads to the conclusion that the accounts of Jesus sending his disciples into Jerusalem were "suggested by the anointing of Saul and its aftermath of signs" (Funk and the Jesus Seminar, *The Acts of Jesus,* 138). It should go without saying that the parallel between the story of Samuel sending Saul to find his donkeys and Jesus sending the disciples into Jerusalem to meet someone and prepare the Passover does not justify any such historical conclusion. Indeed, even a cursory comparison of the accounts reveals that the differences far outweigh the similarities, perhaps the most prominent being that there are no donkeys.

a historical argument. Nevertheless, according to this proposal, in the accounts of the preparation for Passover, Jesus displays prophetic foreknowledge of the young man whom the disciples will meet in the city and Judas' imminent betrayal, the latter of which prompts him to hold the Last Supper in an unknown place (Matt 26:18; Mark 14:13-15; Luke 22:10-13). From this point of view, the discovery of the room is "miraculous."[57] For scholars who adopt this view, since prophetic foreknowledge of any sort is *a priori* impossible, the accounts are not historically plausible and therefore did not happen.[58] This philosophical objection is often couched as a literary argument, by scholars who claim on the basis of the supposed miracle that the "genre" of these sending accounts in the Gospels is that of a "legend" or "fairy-tale motif," and thus, by definition, unhistorical.[59]

Second, and probably more important, is the argument from incoherence or incompatibility with other evidence about Jesus. From this point of view, the accounts of Jesus sending his disciples to prepare the Passover meal are not historically plausible because they directly contradict the Johannine hypothesis regarding the date of the Last Supper, which places the meal twenty-four hours before the Passover lambs were sacrificed and eaten (see chapter 4 for discussion).[60] For scholars who have already concluded on other grounds that the Last Supper was not a Jewish Passover meal and that the chronology of the Synoptic accounts is erroneous, the logical implication is that the accounts of the preparation for Passover are also unhistorical. In the words of John Meier:

> The intriguing fact is that, if Mark's Passion Narrative is shorn of two passages that probably come from either a secondary level of the tradition or from Mark's own redactional activity [Mark 14:1a, 12-16 and parr.], the remaining Passion narrative contains no clear indication that the Last Supper was a Passover meal or that Jesus died on Passover day.[61]

In other words, Jesus could not have sent the disciples to slaughter the Passover lamb in the Jerusalem Temple and prepare the Passover banquet if the Last Supper was not in fact a Passover meal. The force of this argument, if the

57. Schröter, *Das Abendmahl,* 44.

58. Lüdemann, *Jesus after 2000 Years,* 96.

59. A. Y. Collins, *Mark,* 646; Léon-Dufour, *Sharing the Eucharistic Bread,* 193; Bultmann, *History of the Synoptic Tradition,* 263-64; Dibelius, *From Tradition to Gospel,* 189.

60. E.g., Schröter, *Das Abendmahl,* 44; Meier, *A Marginal Jew,* 1:393; Ruckstuhl, *Chronology of the Last Days of Jesus,* 19; Jaubert, *The Date of the Last Supper,* 97-98.

61. Meier, *A Marginal Jew,* 1:396.

premise were correct, would be weighty. Indeed, it is probably the reason that many major works on Jesus simply ignore the accounts of the preparation for the Passover in their treatments of the Last Supper. From this point of view, there is no reason to even examine this material, because conclusions about the date of the Last Supper have already settled the matter. However, as we argued extensively above, the premise of this argument is erroneous, and there are good reasons to conclude that the Last Supper was in fact a Passover meal (see chapter 4).

Arguments for Historical Plausibility

On the other hand, there are also several positive arguments levied by scholars in favor of the historical plausibility of Jesus' sending the disciples into Jerusalem to prepare the Passover on the afternoon of the Last Supper.[62]

First, it should go without saying that Jesus' act of sending the disciples to prepare the Passover is eminently plausible with what we know about his first-century Jewish context. For one thing, in contrast to post-70 A.D. customs, the evangelists presuppose that the Passover had to be celebrated in the Temple at Jerusalem (cf. Deut 16:5-7; Josephus, *War* 6.428). Moreover, the Gospel accounts explicitly tie the celebration of the Passover to the "sacrifice" of the lambs (Mark 14:12; Luke 22:7). This emphasis on cultic sacrifice in the Jerusalem Temple coheres with the reality of the Passover celebration before the destruction of the Temple in Jerusalem, as we saw above (Deut 12:4-14; *Jub.* 49:19-21). This requirement to offer and eat the Passover lamb in the city of Jerusalem also provides a contextually plausible rationale for why Jesus does not celebrate the Passover in Bethany but rather sends the disciples into the city.[63] In short, there is absolutely nothing in the accounts that contradicts or

62. For scholars favoring historicity, see Marshall, "The Last Supper," 489-97; Sanders, *The Historical Figure of Jesus,* 250-52; Marshall, *Last Supper and Lord's Supper,* 76-77; Pesch, *Das Abendmahl,* 69-90; idem, *Das Markusevangelium,* 2:340-45; Lagrange, *The Gospel according to Saint Mark,* 371-75.

63. Davies and Allison, *Saint Matthew,* 3:458. For what it is worth, the Gospel accounts are even congruent with early rabbinic traditions which claim that while the Second Temple still stood, it was permissible for a representative of a group to buy a Passover lamb and slaughter it in the Temple on behalf of the group (Mishnah, *Pesaḥim* 8:2-3). This is, of course, exactly what we see Jesus doing in the Gospels, when he sends a couple of his disciples (in Luke's account, Peter and John) on ahead to prepare the Passover on behalf of himself and the rest of the Twelve (Matt 26:17-19; Mark 14:12-16; Luke 22:7-13). So Dalman, *Jesus-Jeshua,* 111.

is incompatible with what we know about the Judaism of Jesus' day, and much to commend it.

Second, and equally important, Jesus' act of sending the disciples to prepare the Passover also coheres with other evidence about him, in two ways. For one thing, it depicts a Jesus who participates regularly in the Jewish Temple cult, just as we find elsewhere: Jesus is purportedly raised by a family that went up "every year" to Jerusalem "for the feast of Passover" in the Temple (Luke 2:41); he instructs those he heals to follow purity regulations and show themselves "to the priest" (Matt 8:2-4; Mark 1:40-45; Luke 5:12-16); he even speaks to his disciples of bringing their sacrifices to "the altar" (Matt 5:23-26). In particular, the Gospel of John emphasizes that Jesus celebrates the Jewish festivals at the same time as the rest of the Jewish people, with crowds debating whether he will "go up" to the pilgrimage feast of Tabernacles, despite apparent danger to himself (John 7:1-10, 37).[64] Moreover, if, as I argued in chapter 4, the Last Supper was in fact a Jewish Passover meal, then the evidence for Jesus sending the disciples to prepare the Passover also coheres with the date of the Last Supper itself, and the second argument against its historicity falls to the ground.[65] Of course, my conclusions regarding the date above were, in part, based on the evidence in question (Matt 26:17-19; Mark 14:12-16; Luke 22:7-13), so this point only gains force from the other evidence upon which that conclusion was based (see chapter 4). Finally, it may be worth noting here that Luke's testimony that Jesus sent "Peter and John" to prepare the meal (Luke 22:8) also coheres with the fact they are specially chosen from among the twelve on other occasions, such as Jesus' prayer in the garden of Gethsemane (Matt 26:36-46; Mark 14:32-42; Luke 22:40-46).[66] In short: if the Last Supper was in fact a Jewish Passover meal, then it would have been historically necessary for someone to prepare that meal.

Third and finally, there is no discernible argument from plausibility of effects in the early church. I for one can see no effects of this event, other than the tendency of the early church to associate the Last Supper with the Passover (1 Cor 5:7-8; more on that below). With that said, it should be noted here that the argument against this passage from the impossibility of prophetic foreknowledge on Jesus' part is not only philosophically debatable,

64. Meier, *A Marginal Jew,* 1:393. For a full study that recognizes Jesus' participation in the Temple cult while outlining his complex relationship with it, see esp. Nicholas Perrin, *Jesus the Temple* (Grand Rapids: Baker Academic, 2010).

65. Marshall, "The Last Supper," 497.

66. In favor of the historical plausibility of Jesus' prayer in Gethsemane, see Pitre, *Jesus, the Tribulation, and the End of the Exile,* 478-504.

but exegetically weak. There is quite simply nothing in the text of the Gospels that asserts the miraculous character of Jesus' establishing a rendezvous with the anonymous young man. To the contrary, given the massive number of pilgrims in the city during Passover, not to mention the potentially dangerous nature of Jesus' situation with reference to both Judas and the authorities, it is highly plausible that he would have taken steps to arrange in advance the celebration of the Last Supper in an unknown location. As Joel Marcus writes:

> This whole chain of events could be interpreted in a non-supernatural manner, as reflecting prearrangement between Jesus and the owner of the room. Jesus was a wanted man, and it may have been necessary for him to communicate clandestinely with an accomplice in Jerusalem in order to make a Passover seder there possible.[67]

This would certainly explain why Jesus can reveal the location of the room to Peter and John (via the prearrangement with the young man), while simultaneously keeping the rest of the twelve (notably Judas) in the dark. In other words, the argument from the impossibility of Jesus' prophetic foreknowledge, in contrast to the anonymous man with the jar, does not hold water.

In light of such considerations, and especially in light of the analysis of the date of the Last Supper given in the last chapter, it seems that there are good reasons to conclude that the accounts of Jesus' sending the disciples into Jerusalem on the afternoon of the Last Supper to sacrifice and prepare the Passover are historically plausible, even if the case is not supported by any discernible effects in the early church. In the words of E. P. Sanders:

> I think that it is highly likely . . . that one of the disciples took a lamb to be slaughtered in the Temple. The readers of the gospels knew that animals were sacrificed at festivals. . . . This was part and parcel of ancient life: Jews, Greeks, Syrians, Romans and the other inhabitants of the Roman empire all participated in such rites. Only the details were different. Thus failure to say that Jesus and his followers did what everyone else did is probably not significant. Had they not observed the laws and traditions, that would have been remarkable, but observance would cause no comment.[68]

67. So Marcus, *Mark,* 2:948. See also Marshall, "The Last Supper," 490-92; idem, *Last Supper and Lord's Supper,* 77; cf. Fitzmyer, *The Gospel according to Luke,* 2:1377.

68. Sanders, *The Historical Figure of Jesus,* 251.

With this said, in order to see the significance of this sacrificial context more clearly, we will have to turn to the words and deeds of Jesus at the supper itself in order to examine them against the backdrop of the Passover meal itself.

The Body and Blood of the Lamb[69]

Now that we have established the Passover as the chronological and cultic context of the Last Supper, we can turn directly to the so-called "words of institution," in which Jesus identifies the bread of the Passover meal with his body and the wine with his blood and commands the disciples to repeat his actions in memory of him. Although we examined Jesus' words and deeds at the Last Supper in chapter 2 with reference to the blood of the covenant and the bread of the presence, it is important here to supplement that discussion with specific attention to the context of the Passover. In the multiple accounts

69. The literature on the words of institution is vast. For a sampling, see Nicholas Perrin, "Last Supper," *Dictionary of Jesus and the Gospels* (2nd ed.; ed. Joel B. Green, Jeannine K. Brown, and Nicholas Perrin; Downers Grove: IVP Academic, 2013), 492-501; Marshall, "The Last Supper," 560-88 (with bibliography); Lohfink, *Jesus of Nazareth,* 252-56; Keener, *The Historical Jesus of the Gospels,* 296-301; Hengel and Schwemer, *Jesus und das Judentum,* 582-86; Marcus, *Mark,* 2:956-68; Jonathan Klawans, *Purity, Sacrifice, and Temple: Symbolism and Supersessionism in the Study of Ancient Judaism* (Oxford: Oxford University Press, 2006), 214-22; James D. G. Dunn, *Jesus Remembered* (Grand Rapids: Eerdmans, 2003), 229-31, 512-13, 771-73, 795-96; Barry D. Smith, "Last Supper, Words of Institution," in *Encyclopedia of the Historical Jesus* (ed. Craig A. Evans; London: Routledge, 2008), 365-68; McKnight, *Jesus and His Death,* 259-92; Dennis E. Smith, *From Symposium to Eucharist: The Banquet in the Early Christian World* (Minneapolis: Fortress, 2003), 219-78; Jonathan Klawans, "Interpreting the Last Supper: Sacrifice, Spiritualization, and Anti-Sacrifice," *NTS* 48, no. 1 (2002): 1-17; Davies and Allison, *Saint Matthew,* 3:464-81 (with bibliography); C. Ham, "The Last Supper in Matthew," *BBR* 10 (2000): 53-69; Wright, *Jesus and the Victory of God,* 554-63; Ben F. Meyer, "The Expiation Motif in the Eucharistic Words: A Key to the History of Jesus?," *Gregorianum* 69 (1988): 461-87; Léon-Dufour, *Sharing the Eucharistic Bread,* 102-79; G. R. Beasley-Murray, *Jesus and the Kingdom of God* (Grand Rapids: Eerdmans, 1985), 258-73; Fitzmyer, *The Gospel according to Luke,* 2:1385-1406 (with bibliography); I. Howard Marshall, *Last Supper and Lord's Supper* (London: Paternoster, 1980), 76-106; Willi Marxsen, *The Beginnings of Christology: Together with the Lord's Supper* (Philadelphia: Fortress, 1979), 87-122; Pesch, *Das Abendmahl und Jesu Todesverständnis,* 90-101; Patsch, *Abendmahl und historischer Jesus,* passim; Gordon J. Bahr, "The Seder of the Passover and the Eucharistic Words," *NovT* 12 (1970): 181-202; Eduard Schweizer, *The Lord's Supper according to the New Testament* (FBBS 18; Philadelphia: Fortress, 1967); Günther Bornkamm, *Jesus of Nazareth* (trans. Irene McLuskey, Fraser McLuskey, and James M. Robinson; repr.; Minneapolis: Fortress, 1995 [orig. 1960]), 160-62; Jeremias, *The Eucharistic Words of Jesus,* passim.

of the words of institution that we possess, several features, when interpreted in their ancient Jewish context, suggest that Jesus is not only speaking of the sacrifice of a new covenant; he is also instituting a new Passover:

> Now as they were eating, Jesus took bread, and blessed, and broke it, and gave it to the disciples and said, "Take, eat; this is my *body.*" And he took a cup, and when he had given thanks he gave it to them, saying, "Drink of it, all of you; for this is my *blood* of the covenant, which is poured out for many for the forgiveness of sins." (Matt 26:26-28)
>
> And as they were eating, he took bread, and blessed, and broke it, and gave it to them, and said, "Take; this is my *body.*" And he took a cup, and when he had given thanks he gave it to them, and they all drank of it. And he said to them, "This is my *blood* of the covenant, which is poured out for many." (Mark 14:22-24)
>
> And when the hour came, he sat at table, and the apostles with him. And he said to them, "I have earnestly desired to eat this Passover with you before I suffer; for I tell you that I shall not eat it until it is fulfilled in the kingdom of God." And he took a cup, and when he had given thanks he said, "Take this, and divide it among yourselves; for I tell you that from now on I shall not drink of the fruit of the vine until the kingdom of God comes." And he took bread, and when he had given thanks he broke it and gave it to them, saying, "This is my *body* which is given for you. Do this in remembrance of me." And likewise the cup after supper, saying, "This cup which is poured out for you is the new covenant in my *blood.*" (Luke 22:14-20)[70]

70. In some ancient manuscripts of Luke's Gospel, vv. 19b-20 are omitted. An enormous body of text-critical discussion has grown up around this issue, debating whether the so-called "longer version" (including vv. 19b-20) or "shorter version" (omitting vv. 19b-20) is original. In my opinion, the manuscript evidence for the longer version is simply too abundant to maintain the minority position, which has only a single Greek manuscript in its favor. For these and other reasons, I will adopt the longer version herein, referring the reader to the discussion in Marshall, "The Last Supper," 529-41; Bradly S. Billings, *Do This in Remembrance of Me: The Disputed Words in the Lukan Institution Narrative (Luke 22:19b-20): An Historico-Exegetical, Theological, and Sociological Analysis* (Library of Biblical Studies; London: T. & T. Clark, 2006). Fitzmyer, *The Gospel according to Luke,* 2:1387-89, sums up well two of the main arguments favoring the longer version as original: (1) the "overwhelming number" of Greek manuscripts supporting the longer version; (2) "the principle of *lectio difficilior,*" by which

> For I received from the Lord what I also delivered to you, that the Lord Jesus on the night when he was betrayed took bread, and when he had given thanks, he broke it, and said, "This is my *body* which is for you. Do this in remembrance of me." In the same way also the cup, after supper, saying, "This cup is the new covenant in my *blood*. Do this, as often as you drink it, in remembrance of me." (1 Cor 11:23-25)

With the Passover context in mind, at least three key questions arise about this particular evidence: First, why does Jesus identify the Passover bread with his own "body" (Matt 26:26; Mark 14:22; Luke 22:19; 1 Cor 11:24)? Why does Jesus identify the Passover wine with his "blood" (Matt 26:28; Mark 14:24; Luke 22:20; cf. 1 Cor 11:25)? Third and finally, what is the meaning of the command for his disciples to "Do this in remembrance of me" (Luke 22:19; 1 Cor 11:24-25)? Although this final directive is only present in two of the accounts (Luke and Paul), it is still necessary that we interpret its meaning and evaluate its historical plausibility. In order to answer these questions, we will have to situate the accounts of the words of institution in their ancient Jewish context. Once this is done, we will then take up the highly contested question of their historical plausibility.

The Body of the Eschatological Passover Lamb

The first aspect of Jesus' actions that demands our attention is his identification of the unleavened bread with his own body and his command for the disciples to eat it. In all four accounts, Jesus says over the bread: "This is my body" *(touto estin to sōma mou)* (Matt 26:26; Mark 14:22; Luke 22:19; 1 Cor 11:24).[71] In both Luke and Paul's accounts, he adds that his body is given "for you" *(hyper hymōn)* (Luke 22:19; 1 Cor 11:24). And in the other two accounts, Jesus commands the disciples to "take, eat" *(labete phagete)* or just "take" *(labete)* (Matt 26:26; Mark 14:22). What can Jesus mean by identifying the bread as his body? Why does he speak of it being given or offered for the disciples? And, above all, what are the implications of his command that they receive it by consuming it? Does the Passover context of the Last Supper provide any clues to what such an action might have meant in a first-century Jewish context?

Luke's account of multiple cups provides a ready explanation for why a baffled scribe would shorten the longer version.

71. There are slight variations in word order, which do not affect the substance.

First and foremost, Jesus not only blesses the bread and distributes it; he interprets its meaning.[72] As we saw above, this act of interpreting the paschal bread is something rooted in the Pentateuch. With Jesus' words in mind, consider again the following texts:

> Remember this day, in which you came out of Egypt, out of the house of bondage, for by strength of hand the LORD brought you out from this place, no leavened bread shall be eaten. . . . Seven days you shall eat unleavened bread, and on the seventh day there shall be a feast to the LORD. *Unleavened bread shall be eaten for seven days; no leavened bread shall be seen with you,* and no leaven shall be seen with you in all your territory. *And you shall tell your son on that day, "It is because of what the LORD did for me when I came out of Egypt."* And it shall be to you as a *sign* on your hand and as a *memorial* between your eyes, that the law of the LORD may be in your mouth; for with a strong hand the LORD has brought you out of Egypt. (Exod 13:3, 6-9)

> You shall offer the passover sacrifice to the LORD your God, from the flock or the herd, at the place which the LORD will choose, to make his name dwell there. You shall eat no leavened bread with it; *seven days you shall eat it with unleavened bread, the bread of affliction — for you came out of the land of Egypt in hurried flight. . . .* (Deut 16:2-3)

Notice here that in the passage from Exodus, the Pentateuch clearly links the consumption of the "unleavened bread" *(maṣṣôth)* not only with the deliverance from slavery in Egypt, but also with some kind of festal explanation of the unleavened nature of the bread to the son by the father: "It" — i.e., the unleavened bread — "is because of what the LORD did for me when I came out of Egypt." Even more, the feast of unleavened bread is meant to call to mind the deliverance wrought: it is both a "sign" and a "memorial" of what God has done. Deuteronomy develops this further, and interprets the unleavened bread with the suffering of the people of Israel: it is "the bread of affliction" *(leḥem 'oniy),* referring apparently to the afflictions faced by the people when they came out in hurried flight — i.e., at the Passover. Even if we had no evidence for similar interpretations from later Jewish texts (which we do; see below), these two passages from the Torah would provide sufficient background to

72. See Keener, *The Historical Jesus of the Gospels,* 299; Marcus, *Mark,* 2:956-57; Marshall, *Last Supper and Lord's Supper,* 84.

explain Jesus' otherwise bizarre act of interpreting the unleavened bread of the Passover meal. To the extent that the bread of the Last Supper is exodus bread, it demands an explanation.[73]

Second, Jesus not only interprets the bread, he identifies it as his body, which in two of the accounts he speaks of as being given for the disciples. Unlike the act of interpretation, this represents of course a striking divergence from anything found in Jewish Scripture.[74] As we just saw, in the Torah, the meaning of the unleavened bread is always explained with reference to the redemption of Israel from slavery, the haste with which they departed, and/or the sufferings they endured in the exodus. Presumably, given the Passover context, one would expect Jesus to say something similar over the bread. Yet he departs entirely from the precedents in the Torah and instead identifies the bread as his "body." As far as I can tell, the most plausible explanation for this lies in the fact that Jewish Scripture not only links the unleavened bread with the redemption from Egypt, but with the flesh of the Passover lamb.

> The whole assembly of the congregation of Israel shall kill their lambs in the evening. . . . *They shall eat the flesh* that night, roasted; *with unleavened bread* and bitter herbs *they shall eat it.* Do not eat any of it raw or boiled with water, but roasted, its head with its legs and its inner parts. (Exod 12:6, 8-9)

73. As Joel Marcus, "Passover and Last Supper Revisited," *NTS* 59 (2013): 303-24 has demonstrated, despite the contentions of some that the act of interpreting the unleavened bread does not go back to the Second Temple period, he shows that it is already assumed in an often-overlooked passage in Philo, in which the Alexandrian interprets the elements of Passover with reference to the exodus: "*Unleavened bread is (a sign) of great haste and speed,* while the bitter herbs (are a sign) of the life of bitterness and struggle which they endure as slaves. That is that which is said" (Philo, *Questions and Answers on Exodus* 1.15). Such an act is also described in the Mishnah's description of the Passover ritual, in a passage that is attributed to Rabbi Gamaliel, who Marcus holds to be Gamaliel I, a first-century rabbi mentioned in the New Testament (idem 319 n. 62). According to the Mishnah: "Rabban Gamaliel used to say: Whosoever has not said these three things at Passover has not fulfilled his obligation. And these are they: Passover, unleavened bread, and bitter herbs: 'Passover' — because God passed over the houses of our fathers in Egypt; 'unleavened bread' — because our fathers were redeemed from Egypt; 'bitter herbs' — because the Egyptians embittered the lives of our fathers in Egypt" (Mishnah, *Pesaḥim* 10:5). Among others Marcus is responding to Jonathan Klawans, "Was Jesus' Last Supper a Seder?" *BRev* 17 (2001): 24-33; C. Leonhard, "Das alttestamentlich und das jüdische Pesachfest," in *Die Osterfeier in der alten Kirche* (ed. H. auf der Maur, R. Messner, W. G. Schöpf; LO 2; Münster: Lit, 2003), 22.

74. Theissen and Merz, *The Historical Jesus,* 425.

Notice here that the "flesh of the lamb" is specially associated with the bread: it is to be eaten "with unleavened bread *(maṣṣôth)* and bitter herbs." Notice also that it is the whole body of the lamb that is to be consumed; it is roasted whole, with all its parts, and not dismembered or diced. The reason this is significant for our purposes is that the earliest accounts of the Passover in rabbinic literature consistently utilize the language of the "body" of the lamb when speaking of the Passover sacrifices that were offered and eaten during the time of the Second Temple:

> When [food] is brought before him he eats it seasoned with lettuce, until he is come to the breaking of the bread; they bring before him unleavened bread and lettuce and the haroseth. . . . *And in the Holy Temple they used to bring before him the body of the Passover offering.* (Mishnah, *Pesaḥim* 10:3)[75]

> Unleavened bread, lettuce, and haroset — even though there is no haroset, there must be unleavened bread. Rabbi Eleazar son of Rabbi Sadoq says, "It is a religious duty." *And in the Temple they bring before him the body of the Passover offering.* (Tosefta, *Pesaḥim* 10:9)[76]

Significantly, both the Mishnah and Tosefta explicitly speak of "the body of the Passover lamb" *(guphow shel pasah)* with reference to the main course consumed during the Jewish Passover meal. This establishes a direct verbal link with the part of the meal being described in the accounts of the Last Supper. Moreover, both the Mishnah and Tosefta also explicitly tie this language of the "body" *(guph)* to the Passover as it was served at the Passover meal while the Temple still stood.[77] In other words, they use this language with reference to the Second Temple period, and hence to Jesus' own day. Finally, this language of the "body" of the lamb continues to be prominent in later Jewish descriptions of the Passover. Although it is obviously a much later text, it is nonetheless striking to note that the Babylonian Talmud tractate on Passover uses the word "body" *(guph)* eight times to refer to the Passover lamb (*b. Pesaḥim* 36d). It seems unreasonable to chalk this striking correspondence with the Gospels

75. Trans. Danby (slightly adapted). Cf. Bokser, *The Origins of the Seder,* 30, who translates the same phrase as "The carcass of the Passover offering."

76. Trans. Neusner (slightly adapted).

77. As Bokser points out, some manuscripts of the Mishnah lack the word "used to" *(hayu).* Bokser, *The Origins of the Seder,* 119. Even without this word, however, the sense remains the same.

up to coincidence.[78] Rather, these rabbinic descriptions of the Passover in the Second Temple strongly suggest that Jesus, by explicitly identifying the bread as his body, is also implicitly identifying himself with the sacrificial body of the Passover lamb.[79] In the words of Scot McKnight: "Jesus saw the bread as a replacement for the lamb."[80]

Third, in two of the four accounts of the Last Supper, Jesus speaks of his body as being given for the disciples. In Luke's account he says, "This is my body which is given for you" *(to hyper hymōn didomenon);* in Paul, more simply, "This is my body which is for you" *(to hyper hymōn)* (Luke 22:19; 1 Cor 11:24). The basic implication of these words is rather straightforward: Jesus expects to die, but he does not see his impending death as ineffective or fruitless; rather, his body is being offered on behalf of the disciples. Once again, although this is certainly a shocking statement, it can be explained in a Passover context: Jesus seems to be drawing yet another parallel between the fate of the Passover lamb(s) and his own suffering and death. In the Torah, the Passover lamb does not die for nothing, but so that the people of Israel might be delivered from slavery to Pharaoh and from death:

> You shall eat it in haste. It is the LORD's Passover. For I will pass through the land of Egypt that night, and I will smite all the firstborn in the land of Egypt, both man and beast. . . . The blood shall be a sign for you, upon the houses where you are; and when I see the blood, *I will pass over you, and no plague shall fall upon you to destroy you,* when I smite the land of Egypt. (Exod 12:11-13)

As we saw above, this redemptive meaning of the Passover sacrifice is already present in Jewish Scripture and becomes amplified in later Jewish tradition. Just as the Passover lamb was sacrificed on behalf of and in order to protect the first-born sons of the twelve tribes of Israel, so too Jesus offers his body as a sacrifice on behalf of the twelve disciples.

Fourth and finally, Jesus also commands the disciples to take the bread in order that they might eat it. To be sure, the explicit command to "take, eat" *(labete phagete)* or just "take" *(labete)* is only present in two of the four accounts (Matt 26:26; Mark 14:22). However, there is no good reason to deny that

78. According to Gustaf Dalman, the Aramaic word for "body" is used nine times in one rabbinic commentary on Numbers to refer to the Passover lamb (*Sifre* on Numbers 69 [18a]). See Dalman, *Jesus-Jeshua,* 143.

79. Smith, *Jesus' Last Passover Meal,* 154.

80. McKnight, *Jesus and His Death,* 281.

the other two accounts imply that the bread will be eaten by the disciples (Luke 22:19; 1 Cor 11:24). Given everything we've seen so far, this final command can be readily explained. If Jesus' words over the bread identify his body with the body of the Passover lamb, then the logical implication is twofold: (1) first, like the Passover lamb, he will suffer a sacrificial death; (2) second, also like the Passover lamb, his body will be ritually eaten in a meal. In support of this suggestion, recall the emphasis that Jewish Scripture places on the necessity of eating the flesh of the sacrificial lamb:

> *They shall eat the flesh* that night, roasted; with unleavened bread and bitter herbs *they shall eat it.* Do not eat any of it raw or boiled with water, but roasted, its head with its legs and its inner parts. And you shall let none of it remain until the morning, anything that remains until the morning you shall burn. *In this manner you shall eat it:* your loins girded, your sandals on your feet, and your staff in your hand; and *you shall eat it* in haste. It is the LORD's Passover. (Exod 12:8-11)

> In the second month on the fourteenth day in the evening *they shall keep it; they shall eat it* with unleavened bread and bitter herbs. *They shall leave none of it until the morning,* nor break a bone of it. . . . But the man who is clean and is not on a journey, yet refrains from keeping the passover, *that person shall be cut off from his people,* because he did not offer the LORD's offering at its appointed time; that man shall bear his sin. (Num 9:11-13)

The upshot of these passages from the Torah is simple: to *keep* the Passover is to *eat* the Passover (with unleavened bread); anyone who fails to do this sins gravely, and is cut off from Israel. This emphasis on the consumption of the lamb shows clearly that *the sacrifice of the Passover was not completed by the death of the lamb, but by eating its flesh.* Hence, if Jesus is identifying himself as the new Passover lamb, then it follows that he will not only die a sacrificial death; he will also be consumed (in some manner) by those who would benefit from his death. For this reason, he invites the disciples to take and eat the bread of his Passover.

In short, the Gospel accounts of Jesus' actions over the unleavened bread can be explained when we pay close attention to the accounts of Passover in Jewish Scripture. On the basis of such background, scholars of very different perspectives agree that it is first and foremost the Passover that provides the context for the meaning of the words of interpretation:

> Er deutet die Mazza auf sich selbst. Die Mazza erhält in der Deutung Jesus also eine neue Bedeutung — und sie deutet Jesus selbst![81]

> *Jesus reinterprets elements of the Passover meal in terms of himself.* His words over the bread and "the cup after the meal" are to be understood as a reinterpretation of the declaration of the *paterfamilias* over the bread taken with the meal proper, "This is the 'bread of affliction' (Deut 16:3), which our fathers had to eat as they came out of Egypt. . . ." Instead of identifying the unleavened *mazzot* as "the bread of affliction," Jesus identifies the bread with his "body," i.e., with himself.[82]

> Finally, Jesus does not merely speak of bread and wine as symbols of his body and blood. Rather, he has all of the Twelve (including Judas!) actually partake of the food and drink — they all *participate* in the bread-as-body and blood-as-wine. It is, as it were, a final attempt to bring all of them with him through execution to resurrection, through death to new life.[83]

> The disciples' partaking the bread signals their own participation in the redemption of the new exodus, just as any first-century A.D. Jew would have signified participation in the first exodus by eating the Passover lamb.[84]

In light of such connections, one can argue that Jesus' act of interpreting the bread of the Last Supper is a kind of prophetic sign of his own personal fate, by means of which he is declaring: "I am the eschatological Passover lamb whose death initiates the time of salvation."[85] Moreover, given the context of a Passover meal, Jesus' prophetic sign also has an added dimension of meaning: "I am the eschatological Passover lamb, *whose body must be eaten*."

The Blood of the Eschatological Passover Lamb

The next significant aspect of Jesus' actions is his identification of the paschal wine with his own "blood" and his command for the disciples to drink it. This

81. Pesch, *Das Abendmahl und Jesu Todesverständnis*, 91.

82. Fitzmyer, *The Gospel according to Luke*, 2:1390-91 (emphasis added).

83. Marcus J. Borg and John Dominic Crossan, *The Last Week: The Day-by-Day Account of Jesus's Final Week in Jerusalem* (San Francisco: HarperCollins, 2006), 120 (emphasis added).

84. Perrin, "The Last Supper," 493.

85. Cf. Jeremias, *The Eucharistic Words of Jesus*, 224.

feature is likewise present in various forms in all four accounts of the Last Supper, although differences of form and content are greater than with his words over the bread. In two accounts, Jesus identifies the wine as "my blood of the covenant" *(to haima mou tēs diathēkēs)* (Matt 26:28; Mark 14:24). In the other two accounts, he identifies the cup as "the new covenant in my blood" *(hē kainē diathēkē en tō haimati mou)* (Luke 22:20; cf. 1 Cor 11:25).[86] In three of the four accounts, this blood is specifically said to be is "poured out" *(ekchynnomenon)* for others (Matt 26:28; Mark 14:24; Luke 22:20). Significantly, all four accounts explicitly link the "blood" of Jesus with the establishment of a "covenant" *(diathēkē)* (Matt 26:28; Mark 14:24; Luke 22:20; 1 Cor 11:25). Granted these differences in detail, what is the significance of Jesus' basic action over the cup of wine? What can he mean by identifying it as his blood and tying it to the establishment of a covenant?[87] Once this identification is made, how then can he possibly command the disciples to drink it? Does the Passover context of the Last Supper provide any clues as to how such an action might be interpreted in an ancient Jewish context? In order to answer these questions, three basic observations are in order.

First, Jesus identifies the wine with his blood.[88] In two of the accounts,

86. 1 Cor 11:25 reads a bit differently: *hē kainē diathēkē . . . en tō emō haimati.*

87. Unlike the words over the bread, here we find a clear syntactical difference between Matthew's and Mark's accounts of Jesus' words ("This is my blood of the covenant") and Luke and Paul's ("This cup . . . is the new covenant in my blood"). Faced with this difference, and with the fact that the words of institution were (presumably) only uttered once, many scholars feel compelled to choose one or the other form as more original. I feel no such compunction, since, as I said earlier, I do not think that, when faced with divergences in the Gospel accounts, we have the tools to determine an original form. However, we are on much firmer ground when we focus on the substance of the words. In this regard, they are remarkably coherent. In all four accounts, Jesus does two key things: (1) First, he identifies the Passover wine with his own "blood." (It should go without saying that, given the analogy drawn by Jesus, "cup" in Luke 22:20 and 1 Cor 11:25 is obviously a metonym for the wine it contains.) (2) Second, he links his blood to the establishment of a "covenant." Even though the adjective "new" is only found in Luke and Paul, there is no reason to hesitate in describing this as a new covenant in all four accounts, since, even in Matthew and Mark, the newness of the covenant is implicit by the fact that, unlike all previous covenants, it is made in Jesus' blood. Presumably, this is one reason later scribes added the word "new" to certain manuscripts of Matthew and Mark; they were only making explicit what was implicit in the text, as well as (perhaps) harmonizing the eucharistic words with the Lukan and Pauline accounts. For a speculative attempt at a tradition history, see Pesch, *Das Abendmahl und Jesu Todesverständnis,* 21-53. For an approach emphasizing the substance of the agreements over differences in detail, see Keener, *The Historical Jesus of the Gospels,* 559 n. 200; Wright, *Jesus and the Victory of God,* 560-62.

88. Theissen and Merz, *Jesus of Nazareth,* 425.

Jesus says that the wine "is my blood" *(estin to haima mou)* (Matt 26:28; Mark 14:24) and in two, he identifies the wine as the covenant "in my blood" *(en tō haimati mou/en tō emō haimati)* (Luke 22:20; 1 Cor 11:25), but in all four instances, it is his blood that is signified. What can this mean? Thankfully, in this case, the symbolism is rather straightforward. In Jewish Scripture, wine — presumably the red variety — is regularly used as a metaphor for blood. For example, a number of texts in Jewish Scripture use the expression "blood of the grape":[89]

> Binding his foal to the vine, and his ass's colt to the choice vine, he washes his garments in *wine,* and his vesture in *the blood of grapes.* (Gen 49:11)

> With the finest of the wheat, and of *the blood of the grape* you drank *wine.* (Deut 32:14)

> Finishing the service of the altars, and arranging the offering to the most High, the Almighty, he [the high priest] reached out his hand to *the cup* and *poured a libation of the blood of the grape; he poured it out at the foot of the altar,* a pleasing odor to the Most High, the King of all. (Sir 50:14-15)

In light of such parallels, the meaning of Jesus' sign is fairly clear. As the bread signifies his body that will be offered in sacrifice and eaten in this new Passover, so the wine signifies his blood that will be offered in sacrifice and, likewise, drunk in this new Passover.[90]

Second, Jesus also says that this blood will be "poured out" *(to ekchynnomenon)* on behalf of others, whether "for many for the forgiveness of sins" (Matt 26:28), or just "for many" (Mark 14:24), or "for you" (Luke 22:20). Following the identification of the wine with his blood, Jesus' language should strike us as somewhat odd. Isn't wine meant to be drunk, not poured out? Although, as we saw in chapter 2, there are echoes here of the suffering Servant who pours out his life for others (Isa 53:10-12), given the cultic and sacrificial context of the Last Supper, the Passover provides us another explanation.[91] *For while the cups of Passover wine were never poured out, the blood of the Passover lamb was poured out* — on the altar of sacrifice, in the Temple. Consider the following texts:

89. Davies and Allison, *Saint Matthew,* 3:473.
90. Cf. Pesch, *Das Abendmahl und Jesus Todesverständnis,* 94.
91. Jeremias, *The Eucharistic Words of Jesus,* 226.

> The holy things which are due from you, and your votive offerings, you shall take, and you shall go to the place which the LORD will choose, and offer your burnt offerings, the flesh and the blood, on the altar of the LORD your God; *the blood of your sacrifices shall be poured out on the altar of the LORD your God*, but the flesh you may eat. (Deut 12:26-27)

> *And they killed the passover lamb* on the fourteenth day of the second month. And the priests and the Levites were put to shame, so that they sanctified themselves, and brought burnt offerings into the house of the LORD. They took their accustomed posts according to the law of Moses the man of God; *the priests sprinkled the blood* which they received from the hand of the Levites. (2 Chron 30:15-16)

> When the service had been prepared for, the priests stood in their place, and the Levites in their divisions according to the king's command. *And they killed the passover lamb, and the priests sprinkled the blood* which they received from them while the Levites flayed the victims. (2 Chron 35:10-11)

Clearly, the pouring out (or "sprinkling") of the blood on the altar in the Temple sanctuary was an important component of blood sacrifice in general, and the Passover sacrifice in particular.[92] Given the Passover context of the Last Supper, it seems reasonable to conclude that when Jesus speaks of his blood being "poured out," he is not merely talking about the fact that he will die, or even the manner of his death. Even more he is identifying his death as a cultic act, indeed, as a Passover sacrifice.[93]

Once again, then, he is not only performing a prophetic sign of his own imminent death; he is also saying to his disciples, "I am the eschatological Passover lamb, whose blood will be poured out as a sacrifice for others."

92. In later rabbinic literature, the pouring out of the Passover lambs' blood is described as being carried out by the priests in the assembly line (Mishnah, *Pesaḥim* 5:6), and, given the large number of lambs, the Tosefta even claims that there was so much poured out during Passover that the priests stood in blood up to their ankles: "How do they mop up the [Temple] courtyard? They stop it up and slosh a stream of water through it until it is as clean as milk. Rabbi Judah says: 'A cup was filled with the mingled blood [which had been spilled]. One tossed it with a single act of tossing on the altar.' . . . He said to them, 'If so, then why do they stop up the courtyard, so that the Priests slipped around in blood up to their ankles?' They said to him, 'It is a good thing for the priests to walk in blood up to their ankles'" (Tosefta, *Pesaḥim* 4:12). Cf. Dalman, *Jesus-Jeshua*, 123, citing *y. Pes.* 32c.

93. Keener, *The Historical Jesus of the Gospels*, 300; Crossan, *The Historical Jesus*, 366; Davies and Allison, *Saint Matthew*, 3:474.

Third, in all four accounts of the Last Supper, Jesus links his "blood" *(haima)* to the establishment of a "covenant" *(diathēkē)* (Matt 26:28; Mark 14:24; Luke 22:20; 1 Cor 11:25). What are we to make of this? On the one hand, in chapter 2, I argued that the primary background of Jesus' words was Moses offering the blood of the covenant at Mount Sinai to seal the sacred family bond between YHWH and the twelve tribes of Israel (see Exod 24:8). Moreover, as numerous scholars have pointed out, the Pentateuch does not ever describe the Passover sacrifice itself as establishing or sealing a "covenant" (see Exodus 12–13). On the other hand, within the narrative of the Pentateuch itself, the Passover sacrifice in Egypt at the beginning of the exodus and the covenant sacrifice at Mount Sinai which was the goal of the exodus can hardly be disassociated from one another.[94] In other words, *the Passover is ordered to the covenant at Mount Sinai. For it is the Passover sacrifice that sets the exodus in motion,* and ultimately makes it possible for the twelve tribes to fulfill the goal of offering the covenant sacrifice on Mount Sinai. Contrary to what Scot McKnight suggests, "covenant and *Pesaḥ*" are *not* "countries and ideas apart."[95]

The reason this causal connection between the Passover, the exodus, and the blood of the covenant matters for us is that when we turn to the book of Zechariah, the blood of the covenant is directly tied to the coming of the messiah and the inauguration of a new exodus, in which the people of Israel will once again be set free, though this time, not from slavery in Egypt, but from "the Pit":

> Rejoice greatly, O daughter of Zion! Shout aloud, O daughter of Jerusalem! *Lo your king comes to you; triumphant and victorious is he, humble and riding on an ass, on a colt the foal of an ass.* I will cut off the chariot from

94. Indeed, a close reading of the Pentateuch reveals that, on more than one occasion, the release from Egypt (which is effected by the Passover plague) is repeatedly tied to the sacrificial "worship" *(ʿᵃbōdāh)* which Israel will offer to Moses in the covenant sacrifice on Mount Sinai. Consider the following: "Moses said, 'Who am I that I should go to Pharaoh, and bring the sons of Israel out of Egypt?' He said, 'But I will be with you; and this shall be the sign for you, that I have sent you; when you have brought forth the people of Egypt, you shall worship God on this mountain'" (Exod 3:11-12). "And you [Moses] shall say to Pharaoh, 'Thus says the LORD, Israel is my first-born son, and I say to you, "Let my son go that he may worship me"; if you refuse to let him go, behold, I will slay your first-born son [i.e., in the Passover]'" (Exod 4:22-23). "Then they [Moses and Aaron] said, 'The God of the Hebrews has met with us; let us go, we pray, a three days' journey into the wilderness, and sacrifice to the LORD our God, lest he fall upon us with pestilence or with the sword'" (Exod 5:3).

95. McKnight, *Jesus and His Death,* 308.

> Ephraim and the war horse from Jerusalem; and the battle bow shall be cut off, and he shall command peace to the nations; his dominion shall be from sea to sea, and from the River to the ends of the earth. As for you also, *because of the blood of my covenant with you, I will set your captives free from the waterless pit.* Return to your stronghold, O prisoners of hope; today I declare that I will restore to you double. . . . On that day, the LORD their God will save them, for they are the flock of his people, for like jewels of a crown they shall shine on his land. Yea, how good and how fair it shall be! *Grain shall make the young men flourish, and new wine the maidens.* (Zech 9:9-12, 16-17)

Significantly, this oracle constitutes the sole instance in all of Jewish Scripture in which the expression "blood of the covenant" (MT *dam b^{e}rîth;* LXX *haimati diathēkēs*) is used apart from the account of Moses and the twelve tribes at Mount Sinai (Exod 24:8). Moreover, in its immediate context, the blood of the covenant is tied to the triumphal entry of the future "king" — the messiah — into the city of Jerusalem. Finally, and most significant of all, the blood of the covenant is described as inaugurating a new exodus, in which the captives of Israel will be "set free," not from slavery to Pharaoh, but from the "waterless Pit" — an image used elsewhere to describe Sheol, the realm of the dead (cf. Ps 28:1; 30:3; 143:7; Isa 38:18; Ezek 31:16; 32:24-30). In other words, this exodus is not just new, it is eschatological. Last, but not least, like the exodus from Egypt, the new exodus culminates in a banquet of "grain" and "new wine."[96]

In short, if Jesus is not only alluding to Mount Sinai, but to biblical prophecies of the new exodus, then his apparent fusion of Passover and covenant imagery makes perfect sense. By the blood of his covenant — the new covenant — he is setting in motion the eschatological exodus spoken of by the prophets.[97] This exodus, like the exodus from Egypt, revolves around both the Passover sacrifice (which sets it in motion) and the blood of the covenant (which seals the relationship between God and the twelve tribes). In other words, *there is no need to choose between "Passover" or "covenant," for the exodus unites them both.* Jesus is performing a sign of the new Passover and the new covenant, the constitutive elements of a new exodus.

96. McKnight, *Jesus and His Death,* 291, shows that Zechariah 9:11 is interpreted as the blood of the Passover lamb in *Targum Zechariah* 9:11, which reads: "You also, for whom a covenant was made by blood, I have delivered you from bondage to the Egyptians."

97. Perrin, "The Last Supper," 497.

A New Memorial of a New Passover Sacrifice

Should there be any doubt about this, the final aspect of Jesus' words over the bread and wine that establish a connection between his actions and the Jewish Passover is the command to the disciples to "do this" *(touto poieite)* — i.e., repeat his actions — "in remembrance of me" *(eis tēn emēn anamnēsin)* (Luke 22:19; 1 Cor 11:24-25). In Paul's account, Jesus speaks the command over both the bread and the cup. In Luke's account, this command to repeat his actions is only spoken over the bread, though it may be implied in the fact that immediately after stating the command "Do this in remembrance of me" with regard to the bread, Luke states that Jesus did "likewise" *(hōsautōs)* with the cup after supper (Luke 22:20). In any case, the command itself is attested in both the Gospel and in Paul, and therefore needs to be interpreted.[98] When situated in an ancient Jewish context, what is the meaning of the command?

First, although the point is sometimes overlooked, Jesus' instruction to the disciples to "Do this" *(touto poieite)* (Luke 22:19; 1 Cor 11:24-25), when situated in a Jewish context, is remarkably evocative of a cultic action or the repetition of a rite.[99] Compare the following texts in which the command to "Do this" is used to describe the repetition of some kind of cultic rite:

98. It is very important to note here Jesus' command to the disciples to "do this" in "remembrance" of him is likewise multiply attested, in both Luke and Paul (Luke 22:19; 1 Cor 11:24-25). Scholars usually consider the rare case of an attestation of a saying of Jesus in both the Gospels and Paul to be a significant factor in favor of historicity. (Jesus' teaching against divorce is the premier example.) Yet, when it comes to the words of institution, a curious inconsistency arises. Scholars will frequently begin speaking about "the Lukan-Pauline tradition," as if there were but *one* text, rather than *two* testimonies. See, e.g., McKnight, *Jesus and His Death,* 305, and Theissen and Merz, *The Historical Jesus,* 415-20, who speak of the "Pauline type." This fusion of the Lukan and Pauline testimonies into one is historically unwarranted and methodologically inconsistent: in no other instance does scholarship treat the Gospel of Luke as if it is literarily dependent on 1 Corinthians. Indeed, as Joseph Fitzmyer points out, such a literary relationship between the Gospel of Luke and Paul's letter may even be deemed "impossible." See Fitzmyer, *The Gospel according to Luke,* 2:1386. Nevertheless, because some scholars treat Paul and Luke as if they were but one text, they are often reluctant to conclude that Jesus' command to repeat his actions is historically plausible. See, e.g., McKnight, *Jesus and His Death,* 334. Jesus' command to "Do this in remembrance of me" is multiply, not singly, attested; the tendency to completely ignore this fact when it comes to the first-century sources should be banished from Jesus scholarship.

99. Barber, "The Historical Jesus and Cultic Restoration Eschatology," 673-74; Léon-Dufour, *Sharing the Eucharistic Bread,* 109; Jeremias, *The Eucharistic Words of Jesus,* 249-50; cf. Hans Lietzmann, *Mass and Lord's Supper: A Study in the History of the Liturgy* (trans. D. H. G. Reeves; Leiden: Brill, 1953-79), 182.

> "You shall take the ram of ordination, and boil its flesh in a holy place; and Aaron and his sons shall eat the flesh of the ram and the bread that is in the basket, at the door of the tent of meeting. They shall eat those things with which atonement was made, to ordain and consecrate them. . . . *You shall do this* (MT *ʿāśîtāh . . . kākāh;* LXX *poiēseis . . . houtōs*) to Aaron and his sons according to all that I have commanded you; through seven days you shall ordain them. . . ." (Exod 29:31-33, 35)[100]

> "And when you prepare a bull for a burnt offering, or for a sacrifice, to fulfil a vow, or for peace offerings to the LORD, then one shall offer with the bull a cereal offering of three tenths of an ephah of fine flour, mixed with half a hin of oil, and you shall offer for the drink offering half a hin of wine, as an offering by fire, a pleasing odor to the LORD. *Thus they shall do* (MT *kākāh yēʿāśeh;* LXX *houtōs poiēseis*) for each bull or ram, or for each of the male lambs or the kids . . . a perpetual statute throughout your generations. . . ." (Num 15:8-11, 15)[101]

> "All those who enter the covenant shall respond and shall say after them, 'Amen, Amen.' They shall *do this (kkh yʿsw)* year after year, all the days of Belial's dominion." (*1QRule of the Community* [1QS] 2:19)[102]

> "Afterwar[ds,] the Messiah of Israel [shall stre]tch out his hands towards the bread. [And afterwards, they shall ble]ss all the congregation of the community, each [one according to] his dignity. *And in accordance with this precept he shall do (chwq hzh yʿs) at each me[al,* when] at least ten me[n are gat]hered." (*1QRule of the Congregation* [1QSa] 2:20-22)[103]

When examined carefully, these texts are not just illuminating linguistic parallels; in some ways, it is their context that is even more striking: the priestly ordination ritual, in which the "flesh" and "bread" of the ordination sacrifice, which are said to have atoning power, are eaten by Aaron and his sons; the

100. Trans. RSV, slightly adapted.

101. See Num 15:1-16 for multiple occurrences.

102. Trans. G. Martínez and E. J. Tigchelaar, *The Dead Sea Scrolls Study Edition,* slightly adapted.

103. Intriguingly, the requirement in the Dead Sea Scroll that at least ten men be present may even suggest that the messianic banquet is being identified as a Passover meal, since in the first century "no less than ten men" was the exact minimum required for the celebration of the Passover (Josephus, *War* 6.423).

sacrifice of the peace offering with "flour" and "wine"; the eschatological "covenant" assembly envisioned in the Scrolls; and the banquet of the messiah. In every instance, the context is a cultic rite, which is meant to be ritually reenacted over time, and which, in the last case, is an anticipation of the messianic banquet (see below, chapter 6). This strongly suggests that the same cultic and ritual meaning is present in Jesus' command to "do this" at the Last Supper.

Second, in support of this suggestion, in both Jewish Scripture and Second Temple Jewish literature, the ritualized reenactment of the Passover sacrifice that set the exodus in motion is consistently associated with the remembrance of the original saving event.[104] With Jesus' command to the disciples to repeat his actions "in remembrance" *(anamnēsin)* of him (Luke 22:19; 1 Cor 11:24-25), compare the following:

> This day [Passover] shall be for you *a memorial* (MT *zikkārôn;* LXX *mnēmosynon*), and you shall keep it as a feast to the LORD; throughout your generations you shall observe it as an ordinance for ever. (Exod 12:14)

> And you command the children of Israel to observe the Passover in their days every year, once per year, on its appointed day. And it will come as an acceptable *memorial* from before the LORD. And the plague will not come to kill or to smite during that year when they have observed the Passover in its (appointed) time in all (respects) according to his command. (*Jub.* 49:15)

> The festival [Passover] is a remembrance *(hypomnēma)* and thank-offering for that great migration from Egypt. . . . This practice which on that occasion was the result of a spontaneous and instinctive emotion, was sanctioned by the law once in every year as a memorial *(hypomnēsin)* of thanksgiving for their deliverance. (Philo, *Special Laws* 2.146)[105]

> Hence it is that, in *memory (mnēmēn)* of that time of scarcity, we keep for eight days a feast called the feast of unleavened bread. (Josephus, *Antiquities* 2.317)

104. Perrin, "The Last Supper," 497; Keener, *The Historical Jesus of the Gospels,* 296; Marcus, *Mark,* 2:965; Wright, *Jesus and the Victory of God,* 562; Léon-Dufour, *Sharing the Eucharistic Bread,* 110; Fitzmyer, *The Gospel according to Saint Luke,* 2:1390. For references to the concept of "memorial" in Judaism, see Gabrielle Boccachini, *Middle Judaism: Jewish Thought 300 B.C.E. to 200 C.E.* (Minneapolis: Fortress, 1991), 231-39.

105. Trans. Colson, LCL (slightly adapted).

Although various forms of the root word "remember" in Hebrew and Greek appear in these texts, the basic meaning is the same. All of them clearly conceive of the Passover as a ritualized act of remembering God's saving action on behalf of Israel in the exodus from Egypt.[106] In the words of Craig Keener: "Mention of 'memory' in a Passover context involved not mere recollection but more of a participatory commemoration."[107]

In sum, when Jesus' command for the disciples to repeat his actions is situated in an early Jewish context and coupled with the language of remembrance in the course of a Passover meal, then the logical implication of his words and deeds is rather straightforward: *he is deliberately instituting a new Passover ritual that he expects the apostles to reenact after his death.*[108] In the words of Joseph Fitzmyer:

> Just as the Passover meal was for Palestinian Jews a yearly *anamnēsis,* so too Jesus now gives a directive to repeat such a meal with bread and wine as a mode of re-presenting to themselves their experience of him, especially at this Last Supper. . . . Thus Jesus gives himself, his "body" and his "blood," as a new mode of celebrating Israel's feast of deliverance. His own body and blood will replace the Passover lamb as the sign of the way God's kingdom will be realized from now on, even though its fullness will not be achieved until the eschaton.[109]

If Fitzmyer's interpretation is correct, then we can legitimately speak of Jesus' words over the bread and wine — his identification of them with his body and blood, and his command to repeat his action in remembrance of him — as words of institution. In these words of interpretation and command, Jesus is establishing a new cultic act, a new Passover sacrifice and meal. While this new rite Jesus is performing clearly has numerous points of continuity with the old Passover sacrifice and meal, he is also radically reconfiguring it around his own impending sacrificial death and thereby filling it with new meaning. By means of his Passover, the disciples will both recall and make present the

106. Cf. Marcus, *Mark,* 2:965, citing Exod 12:14; 13:3, 9; Deut 16:3; *Jub.* 49:7; Josephus, *Antiquities* 2:317; and Ottfried Hofius, "The Lord's Supper and the Lord's Supper Tradition: Reflections on 1 Corinthians 11:23b-25," in *One Loaf, One Cup: Ecumenical Studies of 1 Cor 11 and Other Eucharistic Texts* (ed. Ben F. Meyer; New Gospel Studies 6; Macon: Mercer University Press, 1993), 75-115 (here 104 n. 164).

107. Keener, *The Historical Jesus of the Gospels,* 296.

108. Léon-Dufour, *Sharing the Eucharistic Bread,* 109-16.

109. Fitzmyer, *The Gospel according to Luke,* 2:1391-92.

saving effects of Jesus' sacrificial death, above all through the cultic repetition of his actions over the Passover bread and wine.

Arguments against Historical Plausibility

With all of this in mind, the question now before us is: Are these words of institution historically plausible on the lips of Jesus? Or are they a later development, a creation of the early church? Or is the evidence too slim for us to decide?

A remarkable amount of ink has been spilled over the historicity of the words of institution.[110] For the sake of space and clarity, however, I will focus our attention on the most compelling arguments for and against historicity, following the methodology outlined in chapter 1. In this regard, there are at least three major arguments against the historicity of the words of institution as I have interpreted them herein.

First and foremost, there is the argument from the implausibility of the words of Jesus in an ancient Jewish context.[111] According to this view, Jesus' identification of the bread and wine with his body and blood, coupled with his command to the disciples to eat and drink them, is simply too discontinuous with the Jewish prohibition against the consumption of blood to be historical:

> The supper thus described is not historical. . . . Jews were strictly forbidden to consume blood.[112]

> Any suggestion of drinking blood would have been intolerable for Jewish ears.[113]

> Jews of the first century usually observed the prescriptions in the law — in Leviticus — not to eat or drink blood. The suggestion that those who ate the bread and drank the cup were eating the body of Christ and drinking his blood would have been offensive to Jesus' Judean followers. . . . [T]he

110. For helpful overviews of arguments, see Marshall, "The Last Supper," 504-30; McKnight, *Jesus and His Death,* 275-92, 304-12; Theissen and Merz, *The Historical Jesus,* 414-27; Léon-Dufour, *Sharing the Eucharistic Bread,* 157-79; Pesch, *Das Abendmahl und Jesus Todesverständnis,* 21-53; Patsch, *Abendmahl und historischer Jesus,* 59-105; Jeremias, *The Eucharistic Words of Jesus,* 189-96.

111. For examples, see Klawans, "Interpreting the Last Supper," 5 n. 14.

112. Lüdemann, *Jesus after 2000 Years,* 96-97.

113. Becker, *Jesus of Nazareth,* 341.

> symbolism of drinking the blood of a god arose in a pagan rather than a Jewish context.[114]

> [T]he imagery of eating a man's body and especially drinking his blood . . . , even after allowance is made for metaphorical language, strikes a totally foreign note in a Palestinian Jewish cultural setting (cf. John 6.52). With their profoundly rooted blood taboo, Jesus' listeners would have been overcome with nausea at hearing such words.[115]

> To try to derive [the eucharist of the early church] from the passover ritual or any other Jewish rite is ludicrous. Strange as some rituals of Judaism may be, they do not include eating people.[116]

> [I]t is quite impossible to admit that Jesus would have said to his disciples that they should eat of his body and drink of his blood, "the blood of the new covenant which was shed for many." The drinking of blood, even if it was meant symbolically, could only have aroused horror in the minds of such simple Galilean Jews.[117]

As should be eminently clear from these statements, for a number of scholars, the eucharistic words of interpretation and institution fail to pass historical muster, quite simply because Jesus was a first-century Jew. As such, he could never have commanded his disciples to eat his body and drink his blood, even if he only meant it symbolically.

A second argument against the historicity of the words of institution is from their apparent incompatibility with other sayings and deeds of Jesus. This objection takes two principal forms: (1) the argument from Jesus' imminent eschatology; and (2) the argument from the non-messianic self-understanding of Jesus.[118] With regard to the first, the argument is actually not often explicitly articulated. Instead, it functions more as an assumption that undergirds a tendency to ignore the words of institution by scholars who affirm that Jesus

114. Funk and the Jesus Seminar, *The Acts of Jesus*, 139.

115. Geza Vermes, *The Religion of Jesus the Jew* (Minneapolis: Fortress, 1993), 16.

116. Morton Smith, *Jesus the Magician* (San Francisco: Harper & Row, 1978), 123. Cited by McKnight, *Jesus and His Death*, 282-83.

117. Joseph Klausner, *Jesus of Nazareth: His Life, Times, and Teaching* (trans. Herbert Danby; New York: Macmillan, 1925), 329.

118. Becker, *Jesus of Nazareth*, 341-42; Funk, Hoover, and the Jesus Seminar, *The Five Gospels*, 118, 388, 260. Cf. Smith, *Jesus' Last Passover Meal*, 165 n. 49 for further bibliography.

expected the end of time to happen immediately.[119] From this point of view, Jesus expected the final coming of the kingdom to happen immediately. Hence, he did not intend to institute a cult "with the deliberate intention of providing a basis for a new tradition"; rather, he "expected the imminent transformation of the world and the end of all traditions."[120] With regard to the second argument, Jesus cannot have spoken the words of institution, because they presuppose that he saw his death as having redemptive significance for others:

> Some would argue that Jesus had a premonition that he would die soon. But the Last Supper tradition does more than simply predict his death. Rather, it provides a highly developed and ritualized interpretation of his death. To place the seeds of Christological interpretation in the thought and words of Jesus himself does not make good historical sense, though it is comforting theologically. Historical probability would suggest that such interpretations of Jesus' death developed in the years following his death, not before.[121]

> If it is certain that according to the accounts of Paul and Mark (the same is probably true of the accounts of Matthew and Luke) Jesus celebrated the first Lord's Supper with his disciples, at which he distributed to them his body and blood and at which they ate his body and drank his blood symbolically, really, or in whatever way, then it is equally certain that the institution of the supper thus described is not historical. . . . [For Jesus] had said nothing about a saving effect of his death or even his resurrection.[122]

> [The expression "for many"] is reminiscent of Isa 53:12, but Jesus cannot have spoken that way. . . . [T]he idea of an individual's vicarious death on behalf of an entire group can be documented with any certainty only for Hellenistic Judaism. When we examine Jesus' message elsewhere, we find nowhere the suggestion that God's gracious acceptance of the lost was dependent in any way on the sacrifice of Jesus' own life.[123]

119. E.g., Dale Allison, *Constructing Jesus;* idem, *Jesus of Nazareth;* Bart Ehrman, *Jesus of Nazareth;* E. P. Sanders, *Jesus and Judaism;* Albert Schweitzer, *The Quest of the Historical Jesus* — none of which deal with the words of institution.

120. Theissen and Merz, *The Historical Jesus,* 436.

121. Dennis E. Smith, *From Symposium to Eucharist: The Banquet in the Early Christian World* (Minneapolis: Fortress, 2003), 226.

122. Lüdemann, *Jesus after 2000 Years,* 96.

123. Becker, *Jesus of Nazareth,* 341-42.

In other words, Jesus either did not anticipate his own death and/or did not see his death as having any redemptive power; therefore the words of institution, which do both of these things, are historically inadmissible.

Third, there is the argument from a lack of plausible effects in the early church. This argument also takes two forms: one holding that (1) the early Christian eucharist is too different from the Jewish Passover to have originated with a paschal Last Supper; and the other holding that (2) the early Christian eucharist is too liturgical to have originated from the non-liturgical meal of Jesus and the disciples. With regard to the former argument, Gerd Theissen and Annette Merz write:

> An intrinsic probability tells against the identification of the last supper as a Passover meal. The Passover is celebrated annually. Had Jesus celebrated his farewell meal as a Passover meal, it would have led to the origin of an emphatically annual meal. But all Christians celebrated the Lord's Supper, which they derived from that last supper, every week. . . . And there are other difficulties: the Passover is celebrated in the family (with women and children), but Jesus (according to Mark) is alone with his twelve disciples. The women who followed him to Jerusalem are not present.[124]

In support of this argument, scholars frequently cite the testimony of early Christian writings such as the *Didache* and Justin Martyr, which make it abundantly clear that the Christian eucharist, in contrast to the Jewish Passover, was being celebrated on "each day of the Lord" (*Didache* 14.1) or "on the day we call the day of the sun," i.e., Sunday (Justin Martyr, *1 Apology* 1:65).

The second form of this argument for implausibility of effects in the early church is by far the most common objection to the historicity of the eucharistic words.[125] According to this view, the accounts of the Last Supper are simply too "cultic" or "liturgical" to have been derived from the non-cultic meal of Jesus and the twelve:

> Of course it is open to anyone to assume a last meal of Jesus with his twelve disciples. . . . However, such a meal has no genetic relationship to the Lord's Supper which was understood in cultic terms.[126]

124. Theissen and Merz, *The Historical Jesus*, 426.

125. Smith, *Jesus' Last Passover Meal*, 165. See, e.g., Funk, Hoover, and the Jesus Seminar, *The Five Gospels*, 118, 388.

126. Lüdemann, *Jesus after 2000 Years*, 96-97.

> All of the texts that deal with the Last Supper of Jesus reflect the liturgical concerns of the meal celebrations of the various churches. No text reports the historical event. The purpose of each text, rather, is to justify why the church celebrates the Lord's Supper as it does.[127]

From this perspective, one begins with the assumption that it is historically impossible that Jesus could have founded a cult or ever commanded his disciples to engage in liturgical actions. Therefore, any trace of liturgical or cultic elements in the Last Supper accounts must be regarded as an unhistorical "cult etiology" and ascribed instead to the creative activity of the early church.[128] This applies in a preeminent way to Jesus' application of sacrificial language of "body" and "blood" to the bread and wine of the Last Supper, and even more so to his command for the disciples to repeat his liturgical actions in the command: "Do this in remembrance of me." The premise of the argument is that cult and liturgy originate in the early church, not with the historical Jesus.[129]

Finally, it is worth noting here that a number of scholars, while accepting the historicity of the words of institution, reject the historical plausibility of the Passover interpretation I have forwarded above. From this point of view, Jesus did not identify the bread and wine as the body and blood of the new Passover lamb, and he did not institute a new Passover memorial, because historically, the Last Supper was not a Passover meal.[130] I trust that I have adequately dealt with the question of date of the Last Supper above (see chapter 4). Nevertheless, there is an aspect of this proposal that would affirm the historicity of the Last Supper but deny the Passover character of the words of institution, and needs to be addressed. For example, John Meier, who holds this perspective, writes:

> Once the Synoptic Passion Narratives are deprived of their late or redactional references to Passover, we realize that the Last Supper in the underlying Synoptic tradition is no more a Passover meal than is the Last Supper in John's gospel. . . . *Jesus instead arranged a solemn farewell meal with his inner disciples just before Passover.* . . . There is another possible scenario. . . . The supper, though not a Passover meal and not celebrated as a

127. Becker, *Jesus of Nazareth*, 340.

128. Becker, *Jesus of Nazareth*, 340; Bultmann, *History of the Synoptic Tradition*, 265.

129. For a book-length exposition of this perspective, see Dennis E. Smith, *From Symposium to Eucharist: The Banquet in the Early Christian World* (Minneapolis: Fortress, 2003).

130. E.g., Theissen and Merz, *The Historical Jesus*, 426.

> substitute Passover meal, was nevertheless anything but an ordinary meal. With Jesus bidding farewell to his closest disciples as he prepared himself for the possibility of an imminent and violent death, the tone of the meal would naturally be both solemn and religious, accompanied by all the formality (reclining at table, drinking wine, singing hymns, etc.) that Jeremias uses to prove the Passover nature of the supper. Moreover, if we should allow the basic historicity of the eucharistic narrative (Mark 14:22-25 parr.) we would have to admit that Jesus did and said some astounding things at the Last Supper, things that cannot be explained simply by positing the context of some Jewish ritual meal, Passover or otherwise.[131]

I hope that it is clear by now that the Passover (and exodus) characteristics of the Last Supper are not limited to the supposedly late "redactional references to Passover" (here Meier means the account of Jesus sending the disciples to Jerusalem in Mark 14:12-16 and par.). Instead, as we have just demonstrated, the cultic language and Passover features are deeply imbedded in the words of institution themselves, when they are properly situated in the context of Jewish Scripture and the Jerusalem Temple sacrifices. In light of this, in order to come to the conclusion that the Last Supper was simply a solemn farewell meal, one must not only eliminate all the explicit data describing the Last Supper as a Passover meal, but ignore the cultic and paschal language of the words of institution themselves. This position can only be held by claiming — against a remarkable swath of biblical and early Jewish evidence — that the paschal features of the words of institution we have outlined in detail above "remain vague."[132] As a result, this attempt to salvage historicity as a farewell meal without reference to the Passover is ultimately unconvincing.

In light of such arguments, a significant number of modern scholars have concluded that the eucharistic words of institution cannot and do not originate with Jesus himself; they are historically implausible and should not be part of any historical portrait of Jesus' life and teaching. Or, at the very least, some accept the words of institution as historical, but reject any connection between them and the Jewish Passover.

131. Meier, *A Marginal Jew,* 1:398-99 (the entire context is instructive).

132. E.g., Schröter, *Das Abendmahl,* 44, who claims: "Die Schilderung der Umstände des Pesachmahles is also wenig konkret, die Bezüge zum letzten Mahl Jesu bleiben vage."

Context: The Passover Meal, the Thanksgiving Sacrifice, the Blood Taboo, and Jewish Martyrdom

On the other side of the ledger, there are several important arguments in favor of the historicity of the words of institution, interpreted against the backdrop of the Jewish Passover meal. Indeed, despite the *prima facie* difficulty of Jesus commanding his disciples to eat and drink bread and wine he has identified as his body and blood, several considerations argue in favor of the Jewish contextual plausibility of the words of institution.

First, despite the obvious differences with an ordinary Jewish Passover meal, Jesus' words and deeds at the Last Supper cohere remarkably well in multiple ways with what we know about ancient Jewish Passover meals.[133] Although we've already gone through this in the exegesis above, it may be helpful to summarize it here in the form of a chart adapted from the recent work of Craig Keener (see p. 428). Notice here that the parallels are not contingent on rabbinic texts and traditions; they are all present either in Jewish Scripture or Second Temple sources. As such, they serve to point up how well the overall picture of Jesus' Last Supper fits with what we know of the Passover in the Second Temple period: his blessings of the bread and wine are parallel to similar Jewish blessings during the Passover meal; his identification of the bread with his body and the wine with his blood parallels the centrality of the body and blood of the Passover lamb in the celebration of the paschal feast; even his command to the disciples to repeat his actions in "remembrance" of an original saving event parallels biblical and early Jewish conceptions of the Passover feast as a memorial or remembrance of the original deliverance of the exodus from Egypt.

Second, along these lines, it is significant that even Jesus' act of giving thanks or blessing the bread and wine of the Last Supper fits quite perfectly into a first-century Jewish Passover context. As more than one scholar has shown,[134] by the first century A.D., the Passover was not regarded as just any kind of sacrifice, but as a sacrifice of thanksgiving for deliverance:

> The [Passover] festival is a reminder *(hypomnēma)* and thank-offering *(charistērion)* for that great migration from Egypt which was made by

133. For standard charts of parallels, see McKnight, *Jesus and His Death,* 256; Marshall, *Last Supper and Lord's Supper,* Table 1 (appendix).

134. See Jutta Leonhardt, *Jewish Worship in Philo of Alexandria* (TSAJ 84; Tübingen: Mohr-Siebeck, 2001), 29-31; Jean Laporte, *Eucharistia in Philo* (Lewiston: Edwin Mellen, 1984).

Paul's Report	Mark's Report	Early Jewish Setting
At night (1 Cor 11:23)	At night (Mark 14:30)	Passover meal at night (Exod 12:8; Deut 16:4-8; Josephus, *Ant.* 18.29)
Jesu took bread, gave thanks and broke it (1 Cor 11:23-24)	Jesus took bread, gave thanks, and broke it (Mark 14:22)	Passover is a sacrifice of "thanksgiving" *(eucharistias)* for deliverance (Philo, *Spec. Laws* 2.146)
Jesus interpreted the bread (1 Cor 11:24-25)	Jesus interpreted the bread (Mark 14:22)	The bread interpreted symbolically at Passover (Exod 12:26-27; 13:7-10; Deut 16:2-3; Philo, *Questions on Exod.* 1.15)
Jesus identified the cup as a (new) covenant in his blood (1 Cor 11:25)	Jesus identified the cup as his blood of the (new) covenant, poured out for "the many" (Mark 14:24)	The blood of a covenant evokes the first covenant with Israel (Exod 24:8), and the exodus (Zech 9:10-11) Passover lamb's blood is poured out on the altar (2 Chron 30:15-16; 35:10-11; cf. Deut 12:26-27)
His followers would eat and drink in memory of him (1 Cor 11:24-25)	Missing in Mark; but in Luke Jesus' followers would eat in memory of him (Luke 22:19, most MSS)	Passover is an annual memorial of the first redemption of Israel (Exod 12:14; 13:3; Deut 16:2-3; *Jub.* 49:15; Philo, *Spec. Laws* 2.146)
The meal looked forward to his future coming (1 Cor 11:26)	The meal prefigured the future kingdom banquet (Mark 14:25)	Jewish expectation of eschatological Passover and new exodus (Ezek 45:21-23; LXX Jer 38:7-9; cf. Josephus, *Ant.* 4.203-4)
	They sang a hymn (Matt 26:30; Mark 14:26)	Hymns accompany Passover (2 Chron 35:11-15; Wisd 18:9; *Jub.* 49:6; Philo, *Spec. Laws* 2.146-48)

> more than two millions of men and women in obedience to the oracles vouchsafed to them. . . . This practice which on that occasion was the result of a spontaneous and instinctive emotion, was sanctioned by the law once in every year to remind them of their duty of thanksgiving *(eucharistias).* (Philo, *Special Laws* 2.46)[135]

Here we find a striking convergence between Philo's description of Passover and the accounts of Jesus' last supper: just as Philo connects the Jewish Passover with a "reminder" *(hypomnēma)* of God's deliverance and "thanksgiving" *(eucharistias)* for it, so too in the accounts of Jesus' words and deeds, he both "gives thanks" *(eucharistēsas)* over the elements of the meal (Matt 26:27; Mark 14:23; Luke 22:17, 19; 1 Cor 11:24) and speaks of them as a "remembrance" *(anamnēsin)* of the deliverance about to be wrought through his death (Luke 22:19; 1 Cor 11:24, 25). Although for some commentators, the word *eucharisteō* (present in all four accounts) is a clear sign of later Christian editing, the historical fact of the matter is that before it was ever linked with the eucharist of the early church, it was already closely associated with the Jewish Passover feast. Hence, even Jesus' act of giving thanks is contextually plausible in a first-century Jewish Passover context.

Third — and this is important — although Jesus' identification of the bread and wine with his body and blood, along with his command for the disciples to consume them, is arresting, he does not in fact abrogate any Jewish Scripture or tradition. Indeed, although the Jewish Torah does forbid drinking animal blood (Gen 9:3-4; Lev 17:10-12; Deut 12:16), it never explicitly forbids the consumption of human blood, and it certainly never prohibits drinking human blood under the appearance of wine. And Jesus is commanding the disciples to eat his body and drink his blood under the form of bread and wine. As contemporary Jewish scholar Jonathan Klawans points out:

> It is indeed nearly impossible to conceive of a plausible Jewish teacher of the first century C.E. who advocates the eating of human flesh, or the drinking of blood of any species. Yet, as has been often pointed out, neither human flesh nor blood of any species was consumed by Jesus, his followers, members of the early church, or even, for that matter, by Catholics after the fourth Lateran Council in 1215. Even when performed by Christians with a firm belief in the doctrine of transubstantiation, no

135. Trans. Colson, LCL (slightly adapted).

> violation of *Jewish* purity codes is taking place in any enactment of eucharistic traditions.[136]

Klawans's point bears repeating: contrary to the common scholarly assertion, in the words of institution, Jesus does not explicitly contradict any prohibition of the Law and the Prophets. Thus, the argument that Jesus could not have said this without breaking the Jewish Law does not hold. Indeed, according to the New Testament, within apostolic circles, the Jewish prohibition of the drinking of animal blood was never lifted.[137] To the contrary, the Jerusalem council, at which Peter, James, and Paul were all present, commanded both Jewish and Gentile Christians to "abstain . . . from blood" (Acts 15:20, 29). Evidently, the early church did not see any conflict between the biblical blood taboo and participation in the eucharist (cf. 1 Cor 10:16; 11:23-25). If Jewish Christians such as Peter and James saw no conflict between the two, then it is reasonable to conclude that Jesus' actions were not historically impossible within a first-century Jewish context.[138]

136. Klawans, *Purity, Sacrifice, and the Temple,* 216. He is following W. D. Davies, *Paul and Rabbinic Judaism: Some Rabbinic Elements in Pauline Theology* (London: SPCK, 1968), 245-56.

137. McKnight, *Jesus and His Death,* 282.

138. It may also be worth noting here that the contention that the words of institution arose among Gentile Christians fails to take into account how potentially difficult Jesus' identification of the wine with his blood would have been for *Gentiles.* As several scholars have pointed out, there is no solid evidence that the consumption of blood — much less human blood — was a part of ancient Gentile worship experience. See Johannes Behm, *"haima," TDNT* 1:172-77 (here 174). To the contrary, as Craig Keener has shown, there is evidence that the idea of eating and drinking human flesh and blood "would have revolted . . . even most Greeks and Romans." See Keener, *The Historical Jesus of the Gospels,* 560. As an example, Keener cites a story from Herodotus of how some Scythians plotted to get back at Cyaxeres king of the Medes by taking a man, chopping him in pieces, and serving "his flesh" to Cyaxeres under the pretense that it was animal flesh, only for him to later learn the horrifying truth that he had consumed human flesh and blood (Herodotus, *Histories,* 1.74, 129). Along similar lines, another story tells of Astyages, king of the Medes, performing a similar act of treachery when he slew the son of his rival, Harpagos, and had his "flesh" cooked and served to Harpagos at a banquet while everyone else ate lamb's flesh (Herodotus, *Histories,* 1.119). Both of these stories, written for a Greek audience, operate on the assumption that the consumption of human flesh was so horrifying that it would be a great victory to trick an enemy into engaging in such consumption. Such Gentile revulsion toward consumption of human flesh and blood is of course the only logical explanation for why the early church later suffered criticism and distrust from pagan outsiders who accused them of engaging in cannibalism during their eucharistic assemblies. See Keener, *The Historical Jesus of the Gospels,* 560 n. 208 (citing Athenagoras, *Plea* 3; Tertullian, *Apology,* 4.11; 7.1). Such evidence undermines scholars who would argue that the Gentile church created the idea of drinking Jesus' blood under the form of wine. Indeed, it is

Fourth, the idea that Jesus' suffering and death would have redemptive power also fits quite squarely into a Second Temple Jewish context. As numerous scholars have shown,[139] the concepts of martyrdom and blood atonement for sin are present in the early Jewish descriptions of the Maccabean martyrs:

> [The young Jewish man to King Antiochus:] "Our brothers after enduring a brief suffering have drunk of everflowing life under God's *covenant;* but you, by the judgment of God, will receive just punishment for your arrogance. I, like my brothers, give up body and life for the laws of our fathers, appealing to God to show mercy soon to our nation and by afflictions and plagues to make you confess that he alone is God, and *through me and my brothers to bring to an end the wrath of the Almighty which has justly fallen on our whole nation.*" (2 Macc. 7:36-38)

> The tyrant himself and all his council marveled at their [the Jewish martyrs'] endurance, *because of which they now stand before the divine throne and live through blessed eternity.* For Moses says, "All who are consecrated are under your hands." These, then, who have been consecrated for the sake of God, are honored, not only with this honor, but also by the fact that *because of them our enemies did not rule over our nation, the tyrant was punished, and the homeland purified* — they having become, as it were, *a ransom for the sin of our nation.* And *through the blood of those devout ones and their death as an expiation,* divine Providence preserved Israel that previously had been afflicted. (4 Macc. 17:17-22)

Notice the striking connections between the understanding of the blood of martyrs manifested in these texts and in the Last Supper accounts: redemptive suffering delivers from bondage, atones for sin, is tied to the covenant between God and Israel, and leads to the exaltation of the suffering righteous to the heavenly throne of God. In light of such parallels, Craig Keener rightly concludes that "Jesus' salvific understanding of his death was intelligible in the tradition precisely because it was not isolated, but belonged to a wider framework of understanding about atoning blood sacrifice, suffering, and martyrs' sacrificial death."[140]

---

remarkable to note that the blood identification is least explicit in 1 Corinthians and the Gospel of Luke — the two accounts usually regarded as written for Gentiles.

139. See Keener, *The Historical Jesus of the Gospels,* 301; McKnight, *Jesus and His Death,* 168-69; Witherington, *The Christology of Jesus,* 252. For further discussion, see Pitre, *Jesus, the Tribulation, and the End of the Exile,* 384-454.

140. Keener, *The Historical Jesus of the Gospels,* 301.

Coherence: Prophetic Signs, the Suffering Servant, the Interim Period, and the Temple Action

In addition to being explicable within a first-century Jewish context, Jesus' words over the bread and wine also cohere with other important data about him, in at least three ways.

First and foremost, Jesus' words over the cup and the bread cohere with the evidence that suggests that he sought to bring about the eschatological restoration of Israel in a new exodus. For one thing, he gathers around himself the Twelve disciples, who both symbolize the twelve tribes of Israel and embody in themselves the nucleus of a new Israel, centered on Jesus (Matt 19:28; Mark 3:14; Luke 22:28-30). As we saw in chapter 2, he acts like a new Moses when he brings a multitude out into the desert and feeds them with bread (Matt 14:13-23; Mark 6:32-45; Luke 9:11-17; John 6:1-15; cf. Exodus 16), leading some to declare him "the prophet" like Moses (John 6:1-15). As we saw in chapter 3, he also promises to give the true bread from heaven, that is, the new manna of the Messiah (John 6:48-59). The reason such evidence matters is simple: *if Jesus is going to inaugurate the new exodus, then it is fitting for there to be a new Passover.* In the words of N. T. Wright,

> Passover looked back to the exodus, and on to the coming of the kingdom. Jesus intended this meal [the Last Supper] to symbolize the new exodus, the arrival of the kingdom through his own fate. The meal, focused on Jesus' actions, with the bread and the cup, told the Passover story, and Jesus' own story, and wove these two into one.[141]

Wright's insight here is key, especially if we recognize that Jesus is not simply celebrating one more Jewish Passover; he is enacting a prophetic sign of the new exodus, which is intended to effect what it signifies.[142] As John Meier has emphasized, the symbolic actions of the biblical prophets — Isaiah's going naked to signify the coming exile (Isa 20:1-6), Jeremiah smashing a wineflask to signify the judgment of Jerusalem (Jer 13:12-14), and Ezekiel constructing

141. Wright, *Jesus and the Victory of God,* 559.

142. See Pitre, *Jesus, the Tribulation, and the End of the Exile,* 444. See also Morna D. Hooker, *The Signs of a Prophet* (Harrisburg: Trinity Press International, 1997), 48-54, 80-95; David E. Aune, *Prophecy in Early Christianity and the Ancient Mediterranean World* (Grand Rapids: Eerdmans, 1983), 161-63; N. A. Beck, "The Last Supper as an Efficacious Symbolic Act," *JBL* 89 (1970): 192-98. On signs in general see also Scot McKnight, "Jesus and Prophetic Actions," *BBR* 10 (2000): 197-232.

a model of Jerusalem under siege (Ezek 4:1-8), just to name a few — are not just symbolic but efficacious:

> [I]n the minds of the prophets and their followers, these symbolic gestures did not simply point forward to the future events they prophesied; the symbolic gestures unleashed the future events, setting them inexorably in motion.[143]

The same holds true for the sign of the new Passover and new exodus that Jesus is performing with the twelve disciples. Once again, in the words of Wright: "Jesus' actions with the bread and the cup . . . must be seen in the same way as the symbolic actions of certain prophets in the Hebrew Scriptures. . . . The actions carry prophetic power, effecting the events (mostly acts of judgment) which are then to occur."[144] In other words, the Last Supper not only symbolizes the restoration of Israel through a new passover, new covenant, and new exodus, it actually sets these events in motion. It thus not only coheres with the other data in the Gospels in which Jesus seems bent on the restoration of Israel in a new exodus; it brings these other words and actions to their climax.

Second, Jesus' words over the bread and wine of the Last Supper also cohere with the evidence that Jesus saw himself as the Suffering Servant of Isaiah and his death as redemptive (Matt 20:28; Mark 10:45; cf. Luke 22:35-38).[145] In the words of Craig Keener:

> Like Jesus at the Last Supper, the saying in Mark 10:45 probably alludes to the suffering servant of Isaiah, particularly in Jesus not only serving but offering his "soul" or "life" (Isa 53:12) as a ransom or redemption price (cf. Isa 53:10-11) on behalf of the "many" (Isa 53:11-12; cf. Rom 5:15).[146]

143. Meier, *A Marginal Jew,* 3:153.

144. Wright, *Jesus and the Victory of God,* 558.

145. See Pitre, *Jesus, the Tribulation, and the End of the Exile,* 384-455, for extensive arguments regarding the historical plausibility of Jesus describing his death as a ransom. See also McKnight, *Jesus and His Death,* 207-24; Graham Stanton, *The Gospels and Jesus* (Oxford: Oxford University Press, 2002), 278; Otto Betz, "Jesus and Isaiah 53," in *Jesus and the Suffering Servant: Isaiah 53 and Christian Origins* (ed. William R. Farmer and William H. Bellinger Jr.; Harrisburg: Trinity Press International, 1998), 70-87; Wright, *Jesus and the Victory of God,* 579-91.

146. Keener, *The Historical Jesus of the Gospels,* 301.

I agree, but would strengthen the point by adding that Jesus' image a "ransom for many" is drawing on numerous biblical texts describing a new exodus, in which the twelve tribes of Israel will be "ransomed" from exile among the nations.[147] In both the ransom saying and the words of interpretation, Jesus links his own fate with the inauguration of a new exodus: in the one, with the ransom that the prophets link to the new exodus (Matt 20:28; Mark 10:45), in the other, with the death of the Passover lamb that set the first exodus in motion (Matt 26:27-28; Mark 14:24; Luke 22:17; 1 Cor 11:25).[148] Indeed, although there is no clear reference to the Passover in Isaiah's description of the Passover, it is nevertheless remarkable that the suffering and death of the Servant is compared to that of a sacrificial lamb:

> All we like sheep have gone astray; we have turned every one to his own way; and the LORD has laid on him the iniquity of us all. He was oppressed, and he was afflicted, yet he opened not his mouth; *like a lamb that is led to the slaughter,* and *like a sheep that before its shearers is dumb,* so he opened not his mouth. (Isa 53:6-7)

In short, Jesus' description of his own death as a redemptive sacrifice in the context of the prophetic hope for a new exodus fits well with other sentiments about the meaning and power of his death in the Gospels.

Third, in direct contrast to the objection given above, Jesus' identification of his own blood as establishing a "covenant" (Matt 26:28; Mark 14:24; Luke 22:20; 1 Cor 11:25) and his command for his disciples to repeat his actions in "remembrance" of him (Luke 22:19-20; 1 Cor 11:23-25) coheres quite well with other evidence that he expected an interim period of unknown length between his own death and the passing away of heaven and earth.[149] For example, Jesus' appointment of twelve disciples (Matt 10:1-11; Mark 6:7-13; Luke 9:1-5) suggests the intention to establish the nucleus of a community that would perpetuate his teachings in his absence.[150] The parables of the kingdom, such as those of the mustard seed (Matt 13:31; Mark 4:30-32; Luke 13:18-19), the leaven (Matt 13:33; Luke 13:20-21), the seed growing secretly (Mark 4:26-29), and the weeds

147. See Pitre, *Jesus, the Tribulation, and the End of the Exile,* 404-13.

148. Similarly, Wright, *Jesus and the Victory of God,* 557-59.

149. See Brant Pitre, "Apocalypticism and Apocalyptic Teaching," in *Dictionary of Jesus and the Gospels* (2nd ed.; ed. Joel B. Green, Jeannine K. Brown, and Nicholas Perrin; Downers Grove: IVP Academic, 2013), 23-33; T. F. Glasson, *Jesus and the End of the World* (Edinburgh: St. Andrew Press, 1980).

150. Keener, *The Historical Jesus of the Gospels,* 199-200.

and the wheat (Matt 13:24-30, 36-43) all depict the coming of the kingdom as taking place in stages and over an extended period of time.[151] This is to say nothing of the parables of the apparent delay of the Son of Man, such as the householder and the thief (Matt 24:43-44; Luke 12:39-40), the wicked servant and the delay of the master (Matt 24:45-51; Luke 12:41-48), the talents (Matt 25:14-30; Luke 19:11-27), and the ten virgins (Matt 25:1-13). Particularly intriguing are the parables of the banquet, which presuppose missionary activity among Israel and the nations and an interim of some sort between Jesus' public ministry and the final realization of the kingdom (Matt 22:1-14; Luke 14:15-24). Finally, in my earlier work, I also argued at great length for the authenticity of Jesus' discourse on the mount of Olives, in which he explicitly speaks of a roughly forty-year period of eschatological tribulation that would take place after he was gone, during which the disciples would both suffer and continue proclaiming the kingdom among Israelites and Gentiles in his absence (Matt 24:1-31; Mark 13:1-27; Luke 21:5-28).[152] In light of such data, T. Francis Glasson writes of the Last Supper:

> Even a "short interval" does not appear to do justice to the conception of a new covenant and a period in which it would operate. . . . The words "my blood of the covenant" (Mark 14:24) and "This cup is the new covenant in my blood" (1 Corinthians 11:25) look back, as the commentators remind us, to Exodus 24. . . . Jesus knew that the covenant at Sinai had been instituted many centuries before. Is it conceivable that he envisaged only a "short interval" before the Last Judgment and a supernatural new world? . . . When Jesus in the upper room referred to this [the covenant], surely he cannot at the same time have thought that a catastrophic kingdom was imminent, bringing history to an end, and touching off the resurrection of the dead, the last judgment, a new heaven and earth. This just does not make sense. Judas had departed, and Jesus knew that in all probability he had not many hours to live. Was the new covenant to operate for merely a few hours, or a few days, or a "short interval"?[153]

If this is correct, then not only is there no conflict between the eucharistic words of institution and Jesus' eschatological outlook, but the two fit quite well

151. Pitre, "Apocalypticism and Apocalyptic Teaching,'" 28. Regarding questions of authenticity, see especially Klyne R. Snodgrass, *Stories with Intent: A Comprehensive Guide to the Parables of Jesus* (Grand Rapids: Eerdmans, 2008), loc. cit.

152. See Pitre, *Jesus, the Tribulation, and the End of the Exile*, 219-379.

153. Glasson, *Jesus and the End of the World*, 67-68.

with one another. Both look beyond Jesus' death to a time when the disciples will be acting in his absence. Indeed, the fact that Jesus will be *absent* when the disciples repeat his actions "in memory" of him reveals something very significant about his eschatology: it shows that he expects there to be some kind of *interim period* in which the new covenant will already be inaugurated but the messianic kingdom will not yet be fully consummated.

Fourth and finally, Jesus' reconfiguration of the Passover sacrifice and meal around his own suffering and death coheres remarkably well with the implications of his prophetic sign in the Temple (Matt 21:12-16; Mark 11:15-18; Luke 19:45-48; cf. John 2:13-16).[154] Obviously, we do not have the space here to engage the vast and complex literature that has been generated in recent years on Jesus' action in the Temple.[155] For now, let us simply highlight the fact that a number of scholars have called attention to the complementary character of the Last Supper and the action in the Temple. Compare the conclusion of Gerd Theissen and Annette Merz:

> The symbolic action against the temple cult was complemented by Jesus' symbolic action at the last supper in founding a cult, though he did not intend to found a cult that would last through time. He simply wanted to replace provisionally the temple cult which had become obsolete: Jesus

154. Perrin, "The Last Supper," 494.

155. See esp. Nicholas Perrin, *Jesus the Temple* (Grand Rapids: Baker Academic, 2010), 80-109. See also Klyne R. Snodgrass, "The Temple Incident," in *Key Events in the Life of the Historical Jesus* (ed. Darrell L. Bock and Robert L. Webb; WUNT 247; Tübingen: Mohr Siebeck, 2009), 429-80; Dunn, *Jesus Remembered,* 636-40; Bryan, *Jesus and Israel's Traditions of Judgement and Restoration,* 206-25; Lüdemann, *Jesus after 2000 Years,* 77-78; Jostein Ådna, *Jesu Stellung zum Tempel* (WUNT 2.119; Tübingen: J. C. B. Mohr [Paul Siebeck], 2000); Bart D. Ehrman, *Jesus: Apocalyptic Prophet of the New Millennium,* 208-9, 211-14; Fredriksen, *Jesus of Nazareth,* 207-12; Theissen and Merz, *The Historical Jesus,* 432-33; Tan, *The Zion Traditions and the Aims of Jesus,* 166-81; Craig A. Evans, "Jesus' Action in the Temple: Cleansing or Portent of Destruction?" in *Jesus in Context: Temple, Purity, and Restoration* (AGJU 39; Leiden: Brill, 1997), 395-439; Joachim Gnilka, *Jesus of Nazareth: Message and History* (trans. Siegfried S. Schatzmann; Peabody: Hendrickson, 1997), 274-78; Morna D. Hooker, *The Signs of a Prophet: The Prophetic Actions of Jesus* (London: SCM, 1997), 44-48; Wright, *Jesus and the Victory of God,* 413-28, 430, 490-93, 614, 651; Evans, *Jesus and His Contemporaries: Comparative Studies,* 319-80; Witherington, *The Christology of Jesus,* 108-16; Jacob Neusner, "Money-Changers in the Temple: The Mishnah's Explanation," *NTS* 35 (1989): 287-90 (here 290); Richard Bauckham, "Jesus' Demonstration in the Temple," in *Law and Religion: Essays on the Place of Law in Israel and Early Christianity* (ed. B. Lindars; Cambridge: Clarke, 1988), 72-89; Sanders, *Jesus and Judaism,* 61-71; Ben F. Meyer, *The Aims of Jesus* (London: SCM, 1977), 197-202; Jeremias, *New Testament Theology,* 145.

> offers the disciples a replacement for the official cult in which they could either no longer take part, or which would not bring them salvation — until a new temple came. . . . Anyone who follows the Synoptics in dating the "last supper" to Passover night can bring out the "substitute function" of the last supper even more strongly.[156]

In the next chapter we will query whether Jesus expects this new cultic act to "last through time"; for now, I simply want to emphasize that Theissen and Merz have put their finger on an important connection between the cultic nature of the words of institution and the implications of Jesus' action for the Jerusalem Temple cult. If Jesus' Temple action signifies the destruction of the old cult, as in the prophecy of the "den of robbers" cited by Jesus (Jer 7:11),[157] then it would make sense for him to institute a new sacrificial cult, with its own rite, reconfigured around the efficacious sacrifice of himself. And to the extent that the Jerusalem Temple was the place where the Mosaic covenant between God and Israel was renewed and sustained, yet Jesus spoke about instituting an eschatological "covenant" in *his blood,* then it makes sense that he would anticipate the end of the cult of animal sacrifices.[158] And if Jesus' Temple action also signifies the coming of the eschatological Temple spoken of by Isaiah (the "house of prayer for all peoples" [Isa 56:7]),[159] then it makes sense for him to establish a new Passover sacrifice and meal, since the Passover was one of if not the most popular, influential, and prominent Temple events in the life of a first-century Jew.

In sum, the words of institution, interpreted as a new Passover, cohere with the often shocking and cultically charged prophetic signs of Jesus, the evidence that Jesus saw himself as the eschatological fulfillment of figures and events from Jewish Scripture, the evidence that Jesus saw his imminent death as the Suffering Servant as having sacrificial and redemptive power, and the evidence that he expected his disciples to carry on his mission after his death.

156. Theissen and Merz, *The Historical Jesus,* 434. The final line of the text above is from n. 28, which follows the reference to the new temple directly.

157. See Perrin, *Jesus the Temple,* 87-88.

158. Note the contrast here with the Maccabean martyrs: although the literature speaks of their blood as atoning, it does not speak of it as establishing the new covenant spoken of by the prophets.

159. See Perrin, *Jesus the Temple,* 84-86.

Effects: Christ as Passover Lamb in Early Christianity

Finally, if Jesus is indeed instituting a new Passover at the Last Supper, then this would provide a plausible historical explanation for why the apostle Paul, less than twenty years after Jesus' crucifixion (ca. A.D. 54-55), can identify Jesus as the true Passover lamb that has been sacrificed.[160] In his first letter to the Corinthians, Paul writes:

> Your boasting is not good. Do you not know that a little leaven leavens the whole lump? Cleanse out the old leaven that you may be a new lump, as you really are unleavened. *For Christ, our passover lamb, has been sacrificed.* (1 Cor 5:6-7)

There is much that could be said about this dense and significant little text, but for our purposes here, two points are worth highlighting.[161]

First, notice that Paul does not speak of Christ as "fulfilling" the Jewish Passover but as being the "Passover lamb" *(to pascha)* who has been "sacrificed" *(etythē).* As John Meier points out, this is historically quite significant:

> [Paul] apparently can presuppose that his Gentile converts understand the metaphor without any explanation. This implies that as early as the mid-fifties of the 1st century the idea of Christ's death as a Passover sacrifice was common Christian tradition.[162]

I agree, but would add to this that it is not only Jesus' death that is described as a Passover sacrifice, but Jesus' *person* who is identified as the Passover *lamb (pascha).* Although this may seem commonplace to anyone familiar with the history of Christianity, it is, upon further reflection, a very strange thing to say about a person. How do we explain such an identification so early on in the history of the church? Given everything we have seen so far in this chapter, the most plausible explanation for why Paul refers to Christ as "our passover lamb" *(to pascha hēmōn)* is that Jesus identified himself as the Passover lamb at the Last Supper, when he spoke of the bread as his body, his blood being

160. See Marshall, "The Last Supper," 559; Jeremias, *The Eucharistic Words of Jesus,* 222-23. So too, Schröter, *Das Abendmahl,* 45, though he is non-committal on the exact date of the Last Supper.

161. See Gordon D. Fee, *The First Epistle to the Corinthians* (NICNT; Grand Rapids: Eerdmans, 1987), 216-18, for a concise overview.

162. Meier, *A Marginal Jew,* 1:429 n. 108.

poured out like the Passover lambs in the Temple, and his meal as something to be done in remembrance of his death.

Second, in this vein, it is remarkable the extent to which advocates of the Johannine hypothesis — i.e., that the Last Supper was not a Passover meal (see chapter 4) — will go in insisting that Paul is only talking about the death of Jesus and not referring to the Last Supper or the Lord's Supper. For example, Scot McKnight and John Meier write:

> The Pauline tradition of the Eucharist shows no signs of a connection to *Pesaḥ,* even though Paul understands Jesus as the *Pesaḥ* victim (1 Cor 5:7).[163]

> [T]he immediate context in 1 Corinthians 5 has nothing to do with the eucharist or the Last Supper, and so the natural reference of "our Passover lamb has been sacrificed — namely, Christ" is to the physical death of Christ on the cross.[164]

Although it is certainly the case that Paul does not explicitly refer to the Lord's Supper in 1 Corinthians 5, I submit that these scholars are overstating their case in the attempt to bolster the Johannine hypothesis. Their interpretation ignores the context of Paul's argument, in which the identification of Christ as the Passover lamb is certainly not to tell us information about the date of the crucifixion or the physical death of Christ on the cross.

Instead, Paul's purpose is to exhort the Corinthian Christians to "keep the feast" in a worthy fashion by cleansing out the "leaven" of evil that is currently plaguing their assembly, because of the presence of the infamous man "living with his father's wife" (1 Cor 5:1). Look again at the passage, in its full context:

> *When you are assembled, and my spirit is present,* with the power of our Lord Jesus, you are to deliver this man [who is guilty of *porneia*] over to Satan for the destruction of the flesh, that his spirit may be saved in the day of the Lord Jesus. Your boasting is not good. Do you not know that a little leaven leavens the whole lump? Cleanse out the old leaven that you may be a new lump, as *you really are unleavened bread. For Christ, our paschal lamb, has been sacrificed. Let us, therefore, keep the feast, not*

163. McKnight, *Jesus and His Death,* 272.
164. Meier, *A Marginal Jew,* 1:429.

> *with the old leaven, the leaven of malice and evil, but with the unleavened bread of sincerity and truth.* I wrote to you in my letter not to associate with immoral men; not at all meaning the immoral of this world, or the greedy and robbers, or idolaters, since then you would need to go out of the world. But rather I wrote to you not to associate with any one who bears the name of brother if he is guilty of immorality or greed, or is an idolater, reviler, drunkard, or robber — *not even to eat with such a one.* (1 Cor 5:4-11)

As the context makes abundantly clear, Paul's identification of Christ as the Passover lamb is part of a larger description of the Christian assembly as the true feast of Unleavened Bread, during which the Corinthians "keep the feast" with the "unleavened bread" of sincerity and truth. Far from being an abstract metaphor for the moral life,[165] this is a liturgical description of what should take place when the Corinthians assemble to eat with one another, presumably to eat the Lord's Supper.[166] That, of course, is why the exhortation climaxes with Paul commanding the Corinthians "not even to eat with *(synesthiein)* such a one." Given the fact that Paul refers to the context of the "assembl[ing]" *(synagō)* (1 Cor 5:4), uses the explicit Passover language of "to keep the feast" *(heortazō)* with "unleavened bread" *(azymos)* (1 Cor 5:7, 8), and does so in order to stop the Corinthians from "eating with" *(synesthiō)* the brother who is committing sexual immorality (1 Cor 5:11), it strains credulity to insist that Paul's language of keeping the feast has "nothing to do with the eucharist." To the contrary, when Paul does explicitly speak of the Lord's Supper later in the epistle, we find the similar language of "assembling *(synerxomenōn)*" for "the Lord's Supper" (1 Cor 11:18), and repeating warnings that anyone who "eats" *(esthiō)* the bread of the Lord's Supper in an unworthy manner will eat judgment upon themselves (cf. 1 Cor 11:26, 27, 28, 29, 33, 34). All this to say quite simply that, contrary to what some scholars claim, Paul is not just identifying Christ as the Passover lamb, he is also describing the Lord's Supper in terms taken directly from the Jewish feast of Passover and Unleavened Bread.[167] Just

165. Cf. Raymond F. Collins, *First Corinthians* (SP 7; Collegeville: Liturgical Press, 1999), 214-15.

166. Cf. Anthony Thiselton, *The First Epistle to the Corinthians: A Commentary on the Greek Text* (NIGTC; Grand Rapids: Eerdmans, 2000), 406, who recognizes that the Christian "feast" is continuous, but does not draw any connection with the regular celebration of the "breaking of the bread" (cf. Acts 2:42).

167. See Jeremias, *The Eucharistic Words of Jesus*, 223; Rupert Feneberg, *Christliche Passafeier und Abendmahl. Eine biblisch-hermeneutische Untersuchung der neutestamentlichen*

as the Jewish people were to cleanse out the "leaven" before keeping Passover and Unleavened Bread, so now are the Corinthians to cleanse out the old "leaven" *(zymē)* of sin and evil in order to keep the new feast of Christ the new Passover lamb (1 Cor 5:8).

In light of such considerations, the argument that the Last Supper was not a Passover meal because the early Christians celebrated the eucharist weekly (cf. Acts 20:7; 1 Cor 16:2) or even daily (Acts 2:42) loses its force. For Paul provides with solid, early evidence that within two decades of Jesus' death, the eucharist is being associated with the Jewish Passover meal, however often it is being celebrated. The differences between this eucharist and the Jewish Passover can be easily explained by the fact that it is a *new* Passover, centered on the death of Jesus, not a mere replication of the Jewish Passover, as our study of the words of institution has made clear. Moreover, as it has been the burden of chapters 2-3 to demonstrate, the Passover does not exhaust the meaning of the Last Supper or, for that matter, the Christian eucharist. As we have already seen above, the Last Supper was also associated with the new manna (which was eaten daily! see Exodus 16), the new covenant, and, as we will see in the next chapter, with the coming of the kingdom of God.[168]

Einsetzungsbericht (Munich: Kösel, 1971); Georg Walther, *Jesus, das Passalamm des Neuen Bundes: Der zentralgedanke des Herrenmahles* (Gütersloh: Bertelsmann, 1950).

168. It may be worth noting here that, while it is true that the Christian eucharist seems to have been celebrated every week, rather than just annually, it does not follow that this is an argument against Jesus identifying himself as the new Passover lamb at the last. To make such an argument is to completely ignore the abundant patristic evidence that the most important (and controversial) eucharistic celebration during the first centuries of the church was the annual Spring feast of the "Pascha" (later known in English as "Easter"). Indeed, the importance of the annual *Pascha* was so widespread that by the second century the debate over its exact character and date rocked early Christianity in both East and West with the most volatile debate of its day and almost led to schism in the famous "Quartodeciman Controversy." See, e.g., Eusebius, *Ecclesiastical History* 5.23-25; Hippolytus of Rome, *Refutation of All the Heresies* 8, 18.1-2. Although there is of course no evidence for the celebration of a special annual Christian eucharist in the New Testament documents, I raise the issue here because those scholars who would argue that the weekly celebration of the eucharist somehow undermines the paschal character of the Last Supper completely fail to reckon with the fact that the early church, across a wide swath of geographical territory, *did* accord special significance to the celebration of the eucharist that annually coincided with the Jewish Passover. Once again, in both East and West, this annual feast was known as "Passover" *(pascha).* Such an early and widespread celebration of a supremely significant annual eucharist known as "Passover" (Easter) coheres quite well with the hypothesis that Jesus himself celebrated the first eucharist, the Last Supper, at the time of the Jewish Passover. For an excellent overview of the primary texts, see Raniero Cantalamessa, *Easter in the Early Church: An Anthology of Jewish and Early*

Now, I am well aware that it is precisely the cultic or liturgical character of the early Christian eucharist that is often used as an argument against the historicity of the words of institution. From this point of view, the words of institution (in their paschal form) are simply too continuous with the cultic practice of the early church for them not to be suspected of having been created by the early church. But this argument is a logical non sequitur, and historically unsatisfying, because it leaves unanswered the question of why early Christians used such cultic and paschal language in the first place to describe a meal which, in its original form, was non-liturgical, non-cultic, and non-sacrificial. By contrast, if we posit that the paschal features of the Christian eucharist (like the presence of bread and wine) originated with the words and actions of Jesus himself at his final Passover meal, then we find a plausible historical explanation. The reason the early eucharist can be associated with sacrificial and cultic language without detriment to the sacrifice of Jesus on the cross is that its origin lay with Jesus himself, who associated both his last meal and his death with the sacrificial body and blood of the Passover lamb in the Temple. Moreover, if we grant this, then we find in 1 Corinthians 5 precisely the combination of continuity and development between Jesus and early Christianity that we have witnessed elsewhere: Paul makes explicit what is only implicit in the words and deeds of Jesus at the Last Supper. Jesus does not say "I am the new Passover lamb"; he says "This is my body and this is my blood" during a Passover meal. Paul, however, draws out the implication, and makes the meaning of the sign clear: Jesus the prophet is now "Christ our Passover" (1 Cor 5:7).

Taken together, when interpreted in light of ancient Jewish Passover beliefs and parallels, it is reasonable to conclude that Jesus is not only celebrating the annual Jewish Passover meal. Rather, he appears to be reconfiguring the sacrifice and consumption of the Passover lamb around his own passion and death as well as instituting a new Passover memorial thereby. The primary implication of this reconfiguration and institution is that Jesus is identifying himself as the eschatological Passover lamb and his actions at the Last Supper as the foundation for a new Passover meal. In other words: Jesus is the new Passover lamb who will be sacrificed for the redemption of the new Israel in a

---

Christian Texts (Collegeville: Liturgical Press, 1993). For a recent study of the subject, see esp. Wolfgang Huber, *Passa und Ostern: Untersuchungen zur Osterfeier der alten Kirche* (BZNW 35; Berlin: Walter de Gruyter, 2011); Clemens Leonhard, *The Jewish Pesach and the Origins of the Christian Easter: Open Questions in Current Research* (Studia Judaica 35; Berlin and New York: De Gruyter, 2006).

new exodus; as such, he commands his disciples to eat his flesh — under the form of unleavened bread — as part of a new Passover meal.

In short, a close examination of the words of institution reveals that Jesus not only saw his own imminent death as a redemptive sacrifice, but that by means of the words of institution, he revealed himself as the eschatological Passover lamb of the eschatological exodus. Moreover, by means of his command to repeat his actions, he deliberately instituted a new Passover sacrifice, and thus, a new cultic act. All of this taken together shows that Jesus' eschatological scenario, though clearly centered on his own passion and death, looked beyond those events to an interim period in which the disciples would continue to celebrate the new Passover ritual. Moreover, if the words of institution were in fact a kind of prophetic sign, then we may have discovered the historical origins of the early church's realistic interpretation of the words of institution. As any ancient Jew would have known, prophetic signs were not merely symbolic; they were also efficacious: i.e., they effected what they signified. When the identification of Jesus with the Passover lamb is combined with the identification of the Last Supper as a prophetic sign of the new Passover, then we have good reason to believe that early Jewish Christians would have recognized the realistic logic of this new Passover. If Jesus is the new Passover lamb, and the eucharist is the new Passover meal, then the bread and wine must in some way really be his body and blood. As any first-century Jew would have known: in order for the Passover to be properly kept, *one has to eat the flesh of the lamb.* This connection between Passover and prophetic sign provides a plausible historical explanation for the early Christian designation of Jesus as the Passover lamb and the early Christian realism with regard to the eucharist. In the words of Saint Paul: "Christ our Passover has been sacrificed; therefore let us keep the feast!" (1 Cor 5:7-8).

CHAPTER 6

The Eucharistic Kingdom of God

> Above all, in the Sacrament of the Eucharist the Church recapitulates the historic crisis in which Christ came, lived, died, and rose again, and finds in it the "efficacious sign" of eternal life in the Kingdom of God. In its origin and in its governing ideas it may be described as a sacrament of realized eschatology.
>
> C. H. DODD[1]

As recent scholarship has demonstrated, although Judaism was characterized by a diversity of eschatological expectations, arguably the most widespread hope was for the ingathering of the twelve tribes of Israel. In his magisterial study of Second Temple Judaism, E. P. Sanders concludes that "the general hope for the restoration of the people of Israel," including the lost ten tribes, is "the most ubiquitous hope of all."[2] In his earlier work, Sanders even went so far as to claim that "[i]n general terms it may be said that 'Jewish eschatology' and 'the restoration of Israel' are almost synonymous."[3]

If Sanders is correct — and I think he is — then it is significant for our purposes that in the last fifty years or so, a number of scholars have made a

1. C. H. Dodd, *The Parables of the Kingdom* (rev. ed.; London: Nisbet; New York: Scribner's, 1961), 164.

2. E. P. Sanders, *Judaism: Practice and Belief: 63 BCE–66 CE* (London: SCM; Valley Forge: Trinity Press International, 1992), 294.

3. E. P. Sanders, *Jesus and Judaism* (Philadelphia: Fortress, 1985), 97; so too T. F. Glasson, "What Is Apocalyptic?," *NTS* 27 (1980): 98-105 (esp. 100)

strong case that Jesus' proclamation of *the kingdom of God* should be understood within the broader context of this ancient Jewish hope for *the restoration of Israel.* This case is based, first of all, on the abundant evidence in the Gospels for Jesus having called and gathered "the Twelve" disciples. Consider the following statements of major works on Jesus:

> There is no complete kingdom of God without a complete Israel. It is within this overarching hope for the regathering in the end time of *all* Israel, all twelve tribes, that Jesus' choice of an inner circle of twelve disciples must be understood.[4]

> Most of the twelve tribes had disappeared into the mists centuries before Jesus, and he could not possibly have thought of himself as ministering to them. So if his appointment of a group of twelve was intended to put people in mind of all Israel, what was the point? It is hard to avoid thinking that Jesus shared the expectation, so widely attested, of the eschatological restoration of the twelve lost, or rather hidden, tribes.[5]

> The very existence of the twelve speaks, of course, of the reconstitution of Israel; Israel had not had twelve visible tribes since the Assyrian invasion of 734 BC, and for Jesus to give twelve followers a place of prominence, let alone to make comments about them sitting on thrones judging the twelve tribes, indicates pretty clearly that he was thinking in terms of the eschatological restoration of Israel.[6]

> The number twelve was symbolic; hence "the twelve" were themselves a "sign." Generically, the reference was to the people of God, in its fullness twelve tribes. But inasmuch as the loss of the Northern Kingdom (722 BC) had left only two and a half tribes, twelve is the eschatological herald. . . . By his appointment, then, Jesus made the twelve a sign of the future, i.e., of the imminent restoration of Israel.[7]

4. John P. Meier, *A Marginal Jew* (3 vols.; ABRL; New York: Doubleday, 1991, 1994, 2001), 3:153.

5. Dale C. Allison Jr., *Jesus of Nazareth: Millenarian Prophet* (Minneapolis: Fortress, 1998), 101.

6. N. T. Wright, *Jesus and the Victory of God* (*Christian Origins and the Question of God,* vol. 2; Minneapolis: Fortress, 1996), 300.

7. Ben F. Meyer, *The Aims of Jesus* (London: SCM, 1977), 154.

This list could easily be extended.[8] For our purposes here, the basic point is that the idea that Jesus shared the ancient Jewish hope for the ingathering of the twelve tribes has become part and parcel of recent historical Jesus scholarship.

However, while the idea of Israel's restoration has become a commonplace, there are still several important unanswered questions associated with how Jesus connected the restoration of Israel with the coming of the kingdom of God. In 1985, E. P. Sanders admitted that "we have not yet achieved precision and nuance in understanding just how Jesus thought of restoration and what it would involve."[9] This problem can be reformulated as a series of questions: Did Jesus expect a literal, geographical return of the lost tribes to the earthly land of Israel?[10] To this day, this is how some see the fulfillment of the biblical prophecies of the return of the scattered Israelites to Jerusalem. Or, by contrast, did Jesus expect a purely spiritual or moral restoration of God's people, for which he used the biblical images of ingathering as metaphors?[11] Or did he envision a miraculous ingathering of the exiles, something more than a merely earthly "return to the land"?[12] If so, where exactly did he think the lost tribes would go? And how exactly did he think they would get there? And when did he think the ingathering would

8. E.g., Chris Tilling, "Tribes of Israel," in *The Routledge Encyclopedia of the Historical Jesus* (ed. Craig A. Evans; London: Routledge, 2008), 662-63; James M. Scott, "Exile and Restoration," in *Dictionary of Jesus and the Gospels* (2nd ed.; ed. Joel B. Green, Jeannine K. Brown, and Nicholas Perrin; Downers Grove: IVP Academic, 2013), 251-58; Craig S. Keener, *The Historical Jesus of the Gospels* (Grand Rapids: Eerdmans, 2009), 246-47; Michael F. Bird, *Jesus and the Origins of the Gentile Mission* (LNTS 331; Edinburgh: T. & T. Clark, 2007), 26-45; James D. G. Dunn, *Jesus Remembered* (*Christianity in the Making*, vol. 1; Grand Rapids: Eerdmans, 2003), 507-11; R. P. Meye, *Jesus and the Twelve* (Grand Rapids: Eerdmans, 1968); Joachim Jeremias, *New Testament Theology*, vol. 1: *The Proclamation of Jesus* (trans. John Bowden; New York: SCM; London: Charles Scribner's Sons, 1971), 234; idem, *Jesus' Promise to the Nations* (trans. S. H. Hooke; London: SCM, 1958), 20-21.

9. Sanders, *Jesus and Judaism*, 119.

10. E.g., Dale C. Allison Jr., *Constructing Jesus: Memory, Imagination, and History* (Grand Rapids: Baker Academic, 2010), 51, cf. 67-76; George Wesley Buchanan, *Jesus: The King and His Kingdom* (Macon: Mercer University Press, 1984), 34-35, 114.

11. This appears to be the position of N. T. Wright, *Jesus and the Victory of God*, who has on several occasions stressed that when he uses the phrase "end of the exile," he means it as a "metaphor." See especially N. T. Wright, "In Grateful Dialogue," in *Jesus and the Restoration of Israel: A Critical Assessment of N. T. Wright's* Jesus and the Victory of God (ed. Carey C. Newman; Downers Grove: IVP, 1999), 244-77 (esp. 258-61).

12. E.g., Paula Fredriksen, *Jesus of Nazareth, King of the Jews* (New York: Random House, 1999), 98.

take place? Would the twelve tribes only be restored at the end of history, as some scholars suggest? Or was there some means by which this hope might be realized before the end?

In an earlier book, I argued that Jesus saw himself as inaugurating the ingathering of the exiles, and that he saw his own death as playing the pivotal role in this event.[13] What I did not do, however, was spell out how Jesus thought the restoration of Israel would take place, to where he thought the scattered people of God would be gathered, and how this ingathering was related to the Last Supper. In this chapter, I want to offer a fuller description of Jesus' vision of the future by making two basic points.

First, Jesus closely ties the ingathering of the twelve tribes of Israel to the banquet in the kingdom of God. He does this above all when he speaks of many coming "from east and west" to dine with Abraham, Isaac, and Jacob "in the kingdom" (Matt 8:11-12; Luke 13:28-29). When this saying is interpreted in light of early Jewish traditions about the messianic banquet, it seems clear that, for Jesus, the primary destination of the ingathering is not the earthly promised land or the earthly city of Jerusalem, but the banquet in the heavenly kingdom. Moreover, as we will see, Jesus' teaching also implies that he expects both Israelites and Gentiles to be gathered from "east and west" to the banquet. The coming of the kingdom of God thus entails the restoration of Israel and the ingathering of the nations, precisely by means of their participation in the feast "for all peoples" (cf. Isa 25:6-9).

Second, at the Last Supper, Jesus describes his own post-mortem destination as the banquet of the heavenly kingdom of God. This happens when Jesus vows not to drink of "the fruit of the vine" until he does so "in the kingdom" of God (Matt 26:29; Mark 14:25; Luke 22:14-18). This vow implies that Jesus' eschatological Passover that begins in the city of Jerusalem will not end in Jerusalem. Instead, it will be completed by his exaltation into the heavenly banquet of the kingdom of God. In other words, for Jesus, the hope for the future cannot be summarized with the words "next year in Jerusalem," but "next time at the heavenly banquet." Moreover, by sharing the wine of the Last Supper with the disciples, Jesus gives them a "foretaste" of the heavenly kingdom into which he himself will be exalted. In this way, the Last Supper functions as an efficacious prophetic sign, not just of Jesus' death, but also of eternal life in the kingdom of God. In order to see clearly these connections

13. Brant Pitre, *Jesus, the Tribulation, and the End of the Exile: Restoration Eschatology and the Origin of the Atonement* (WUNT 2.204; Tübingen: Mohr Siebeck; Grand Rapids: Baker Academic, 2005).

between the Last Supper, the restoration of Israel, and the kingdom of God, we will have to begin by looking carefully at how the messianic banquet was understood in the Old Testament and ancient Judaism.

The Messianic Banquet in Early Judaism[14]

In his famous study of Jewish apocalyptic, D. S. Russell states that the notion of an "eschatological banquet" is "a familiar one" in ancient Judaism.[15] And as Dennis Smith writes in his article on the messianic banquet, "the messianic banquet theme is especially prominent in the gospel tradition."[16] Nevertheless, in the study of Jesus, Jewish descriptions of the messianic banquet are often only mentioned in passing and not studied in detail.[17]

Therefore, in order to situate Jesus' teachings as much as possible in their ancient Jewish context, we need to look more closely at the shape of the messianic banquet in ancient Jewish literature. This survey is by no means exhaustive. Rather, the purpose is to select key texts and examine them in enough detail to throw some light on the wider context of Jesus' teaching with specific reference to the Last Supper.

14. On the entire subject of the banquet, see especially Philip J. Long, *Jesus the Bridegroom: The Origin of the Eschatological Feast as a Wedding Banquet in the Synoptic Gospels* (Eugene: Pickwick, 2013), 1-9, 43-67. See also Peter-Ben Smit, *Fellowship and Food in the Kingdom: Eschatological Meals and Scenes of Utopian Abundance in the New Testament* (WUNT 2:234; Tübingen: Mohr-Siebeck, 2008), 21-34; Dennis E. Smith, *From Symposium to Eucharist: The Banquet in the Early Christian World* (Minneapolis: Fortress, 2003), 133-72; idem, "Messianic Banquet," *Anchor Bible Dictionary* 4:787-91; J. Priest, "A Note on the Messianic Banquet," in *The Messiah: Developments in Earliest Judaism and Christianity* (ed. James H. Charlesworth; Minneapolis: Fortress, 1992), 222-38; Lawrence H. Schiffman, "The Messianic Banquet," in *The Eschatological Community of the Dead Sea Scrolls* (SBLMS 38; Atlanta: Scholars Press, 1989), 53-67; Frank Moore Cross, *The Ancient Library of Qumran* (3rd ed.; Minneapolis: Fortress, 1995), 168-70; Emil Schürer, *The History of the Jewish People in the Age of Jesus Christ (175 B.C.–A.D. 135)* (rev. and ed. Geza Vermes et al.; 3 vols.; Edinburgh: T. & T. Clark, 1973, 1979, 1986, 1987), 2:534 n. 73; Johannes Behm, *"deipnon," TDNT* 2:34-35; George Foot Moore, *Judaism in the First Centuries of the Christian Era: The Age of the Tannaim* (3 vols.; Cambridge, MA: Harvard University Press, 1927), 2:363-65.

15. D. S. Russell, *The Method and Message of Jewish Apocalyptic* (Philadelphia: Westminster, 1964), 322, cited in Priest, "A Note on the Messianic Banquet," 222.

16. Smith, "Messianic Banquet," 789.

17. Long, *Jesus the Bridegroom,* 43-67 is a notable exception.

The Messianic Banquet in the Old Testament

Multiple passages in the Jewish Scriptures use the image of a banquet or feast to describe the joy of the coming age of salvation.[18] However, by far the most explicit description of an eschatological banquet in the Old Testament is in the book of Isaiah.[19] In the midst of a series of descriptions of the coming day of the Lord (Isaiah 24–27), the prophet speaks of a future banquet for Israel and the nations:

> *On this mountain the* Lord *of hosts will make for all peoples a feast of fat things, a feast of wine on the lees, of fat things full of marrow, of wine on the lees well refined.* And he will destroy on this mountain the covering that is cast over all peoples, the veil that is spread over *all nations. He will swallow up death for ever,* and the Lord God will wipe away tears from all faces, and *the reproach of his people he will take away* from all the earth, for the Lord has spoken. It will be said on that day, "Lo, this is our God; we have waited for him, that he might save us." (Isa 25:6-9)

Because this passage is the foundational witness to the eschatological feast, several aspects of its description are worth highlighting.

First, the coming feast is no ordinary banquet; it is an eschatological event.[20] This eschatological dimension is evident from the fact that the banquet culminates in the overthrow of suffering and death: God will "swallow up death for ever" and wipe away "tears" from "all faces." Indeed, just a few verses after describing the banquet, Isaiah goes on to speak about the resurrection of the "bodies" of the "dead" (Isa 26:19). As Joseph Klausner suggests, the overall context of the banquet is Isaiah's vision of "the cessation of death and the resurrection of the dead in the Age to Come."[21] Second, the banquet is a feast of redemption; it will be tied to the forgiveness of sins. At the time of the banquet, God will take away "the reproach of his people" and give them salvation (Isa 25:8-9). Third, the coming feast will be a cultic or sacrificial banquet. This is the meaning of the strange imagery of "fat things" and "wine on the lees." This is technical terminology for sacrificial offerings of the Temple cult, as when Deuteronomy speaks of "the fat of their sacrifices"

18. Priest, "A Note on the Messianic Banquet," 234-37.

19. Smit, *Fellowship and Food in the Kingdom*, 22, considers it "the only certain" example.

20. See Long, *Jesus the Bridegroom*, 43-45.

21. Joseph Klausner, *The Messianic Idea in Israel: From Its Beginning to the Completion of the Mishnah* (trans. W. F. Stinespring; London: George Allen & Unwin, 1956), 180.

and "the wine of their drink offering" (Deut 32:37-38; cf. Lev 3:3; 4:8-9).[22] This cultic dimension is important to stress, since Isaiah explicitly states that the banquet will take place on "the mountain of the LORD," which in context refers to "Mount Zion . . . in Jerusalem" (Isa 24:23).[23] Fourth, in Isaiah, the eschatological banquet will be an international banquet, which will include both the restored tribes of Israel and the Gentile nations.[24] The feast will be "for all peoples" and will result in the "veil" that is cast over all the "nations" or "Gentiles" *(goyim)* being lifted. This is a startlingly universal vision of salvation, nestled right in the heart of one of the most widely read prophets of the Old Testament.

Fifth and finally, given our focus in chapter 2 on Moses and Mount Sinai, it is significant that several scholars have suggested that the banquet in Isaiah 25 alludes to and is modeled on the heavenly banquet of Moses and the elders atop Mount Sinai (cf. Isa 24:23).[25] In his commentary on Isaiah, Otto Kaiser writes:

> Just as Yahweh once revealed himself on Sinai before the elders of his people in the whole fullness of his light when the covenant was made (cf. Ex. 24.3ff., 9f.), he will once again show himself to the elders of Israel in order, needless to say, to ratify the covenant for all time.[26]

If this suggestion is correct, it has enormous implications for how Jesus and other Jews may have understood the eschatological banquet described in Isaiah 25. For, as we saw in chapter 2, the banquet of Moses and the elders atop Mount Sinai is not just any kind of banquet. Rather, it is a covenantal banquet, insofar as it follows the sacrificial offering of the blood of the covenant and

22. John N. Oswalt, *The Book of Isaiah Chapters 1–39* (NICOT; Grand Rapids: Eerdmans, 1986), 463-64.

23. Davies and Allison, *Saint Matthew,* 2:566.

24. Long, *Jesus the Bridegroom,* 58-61.

25. See Long, *Jesus the Bridegroom,* 52-55; James Todd Hibbard, *Intertextuality in Isaiah 24–27: The Reuse and Evocation of Earlier Texts and Traditions* (FAT 2/16; Tübingen: Mohr-Siebeck, 2006), 79; Theissen and Merz, *The Historical Jesus,* 426, following Peter Stuhlmacher, *Biblische Theologie des Neuen Testaments* (2 vols.; Göttingen: Vandenhoeck und Ruprecht, 1992), 1:130; Priest, "A Note on the Messianic Banquet," 235. So too Ben-Smith, *Fellowship and Food in the Kingdom,* citing Catherine Lynn Nakamura, "Monarch, Mountain, and Meal: The Eschatological Banquet of Isaiah 24:21-23; 25:6-10a" (Ph.D. Dissertation, Princeton Theological Seminary, 1992), 12-19.

26. Otto Kaiser, *Isaiah 13–39: A Commentary* (OTL; Philadelphia: Westminster, 1974), 195.

the sealing of the sacred bond between the twelve tribes of Israel and God.[27] Second, it can be quite fittingly referred to as an ecclesial banquet, insofar as it represents the communion of the "assembly" (Hb *qāhāl;* Gk *ekklēsia*) of Israel and God. Finally — and this is important — the banquet atop Sinai is described as a heavenly banquet, insofar as it takes place in a kind of luminal realm where heaven and earth meet in a theophany: Moses and the elders "beheld God, and ate and drank" (Exod 24:11). If Isaiah is indeed alluding to Exodus 24 in his description of the eschatological feast, then one can safely assume that some (or all) of these aspects carry over into Isaiah's vision of the future. Indeed, this is the *locus classicus* of any discussion of the eschatological feast in Jewish Scripture and tradition.

In addition to this text, several other occurrences of banquet imagery in Jewish Scripture also seem to point forward to a future feast.[28] Admittedly, the evidence is slim, as well as less clear than in Isaiah 25. Nevertheless, at least four texts in particular may reflect the hope for a coming feast in the age of salvation:

> *Ho, every one who thirsts, come to the waters; and he who has no money, come, buy and eat!* Come, buy wine and milk without money and without price. Why do you spend your money for that which is not bread, and your labor for that which does not satisfy? *Hearken diligently to me, and eat what is good, and delight yourselves in fatness.* Incline your ear, and come to me, hear that your soul may live; and *I will make with you an everlasting covenant, my steadfast sure love for David.* (Isa 55:1-3)

> The LORD has sworn by his right hand and by his mighty arm: "I will not again give your grain to be food for your enemies, and foreigners shall not drink your wine for which you have labored; *but those who garner it shall eat it and praise the LORD, and those who gather it shall drink it in the courts of my sanctuary.*" (Isa 62:8-9)

> Therefore thus says the Lord GOD: "*Behold, my servants shall eat, but you shall be hungry; behold, my servants shall drink, but you shall be thirsty;* behold, my servants shall rejoice, but you shall be put to shame. . . . For behold, *I create new heavens and a new earth;* and the former things shall not be remembered or come into mind. But be glad and rejoice forever

27. See Long, *Jesus the Bridegroom*, 50-51.
28. Priest, "A Note on the Messianic Banquet," 234-37; Behm, "*deipnon*," 35.

> in that which I create; for behold, I create Jerusalem a rejoicing, and her people a joy. (Isa 65:13, 17-18)
>
> *As for you also, because of the blood of my covenant with you, I will set your captives free from the waterless pit.* Return to your stronghold, O prisoners of hope; today I declare I will restore you double. . . . On that day the LORD their God will save them for they are the flock of his people; for like the jewels of a crown they shall shine on his land. Yea how good and how fair it shall be! *Grain shall make the young men flourish and new wine the maidens.* (Zech 9:11-12, 16-17)

If Isaiah 55 and Zechariah 9 are depicting a future banquet in the age of salvation, then they are noteworthy insofar as both texts link the banquet imagery with the renewal of the covenant between God and Israel. This is especially true of the latter, which attributes the release to the "blood of the covenant" (Zech 9:11), a direct allusion to the "blood of the covenant" that established the bond between the twelve tribes and YHWH at Mount Sinai (Exod 24:8).[29] Moreover — and this too is significant — both Isaiah and Zechariah appear to connect the future feasting with the miraculous restoration of Israel. Indeed, Isaiah not only speaks of eating bread and drinking wine in the eschatological temple "sanctuary" (Isa 62:9), it even speaks of feasting in "a new heaven and a new earth" (Isa 65:17). Likewise, Zechariah arguably speaks of the return of the captives, not from Babylon, but from the realm of the dead: the "waterless pit" (Zech 9:11; cf. Ps 28:1; 30:3; 143:7; Isa 38:18; Ezek 31:16; 32:24-30). In this regard, it is perhaps significant that this oracle from Isaiah will go on to become one of the primary Scripture texts cited in rabbinic literature as a basis for the expectation of the eschatological banquet of the Messiah.[30]

The Messianic Banquet in Early Jewish Literature

When we turn to early Jewish literature outside the Old Testament like the Dead Sea Scrolls and the ancient Jewish Pseudepigrapha, the expectation of an eschatological banquet that is sometimes explicitly messianic becomes far more pronounced.

29. Carol L. Meyers and Eric M. Meyers, *Zechariah 9–14* (AB 25C; New York: Doubleday, 1993), 139.

30. See *b. Shab.* 153a; *Eccl. Rab.* 9:8; *Exod. Rab.* 25:7 on Exod 16:4.

By far the most explicit witness is found in the Dead Sea Scroll known as the *Rule of the Congregation* (1QSa). This document presents itself as a "rule" for righteous Israelites living "in the final days" (1QSa 1:1), a kind of eschatological charter. It closes with a striking depiction of a great banquet at which the messiah will be present:

> At [a ses]sion of the men of renown, [those summoned to] the gathering of the community council, *when [God] begets the Messiah* with them: [the] chief [priest] of all the congregation of Israel shall enter, and all [his] br[others, the sons] of Aaron, the priests [summoned] to the assembly, the men of renown, and they shall sit be[fore him, each one] according to his dignity. *After, [the Mess]iah of Israel shall [enter] and before him shall sit the heads of the th[ousands of Israel, each] one according to his dignity, according to [his] po[sition] in their camps and according to their marches.* . . . And [when] they gather [at the tab]le of community [or to drink the n]ew wine, and the table of the community is prepared [and the] new wine [is mixed] for drinking, [no-one should stretch out] his hand to the first-fruit of the bread and of [the new wine] before the priest, for [he is the one who bl]esses the first-fruit of the bread and of the new win[e and stretches out] his hand towards the bread before them. *Afterwar[ds,] the Messiah of Israel [shall str]etch out his hands toward the bread.* [And afterwards, they shall ble]ss all the congregation of the community, each [one according to] his dignity. And in accordance with this precept one shall act at each me[al, when] at least ten me[n are ga]thered. (*1QRule of the Congregation* [1QSa] 2:11-22)

Although scholars continue to debate whether this text describes one messiah or two, there can be no doubt that the banquet it describes is messianic.[31] As James VanderKam states: "The meal is messianic in the most literal sense because it is eaten in the presence of the messiah of Israel. . . . It is also explicitly eschatological, as the first words state: 'This is the Rule for all the congregation of Israel in the last days.'"[32] Moreover, it is also a cultic banquet: the meal is

31. See esp. Lawrence H. Schiffman, "Rule of the Congregation," in *Encyclopedia of the Dead Sea Scrolls* (2 vols.; ed. Lawrence H. Schiffman and James C. VanderKam; Oxford: Oxford University Press, 2000), 2:797-98; J. F. Priest, "The Messiah and the Meal in IQSa," *JBL* 82 (1953): 95-100.

32. James VanderKam, *The Dead Sea Scrolls Today* (Grand Rapids: Eerdmans, 1994), 175; see also Philip S. Alexander, "Rules," in Schiffman and Vanderkam, eds., *Encyclopedia of the Dead Sea Scrolls,* 2:801.

carried out in the presence of the sons of Aaron, the priests of the assembly, and no one is to begin eating until "the priest" — presumably the chief priest — first blesses the bread and wine.[33] Indeed, some scholars have even suggested that it is based on Ezekiel's vision of the priestly "prince" eating "bread" in the eschatological Temple (Ezek 44:3).[34] Significantly, although the meal is eschatological, there is a realized element. As Frank Moore Cross suggests, "the meal must be understood as a liturgical anticipation of the Messianic Banquet."[35] Finally, note too that the meal also appears to be tied to the restoration of the tribes of Israel: before the messiah sit the "heads of [the thousands of Israel," in a manner that suggests that the heads of the tribes have been somehow reestablished and are now present at the banquet.

Given our overall interest in the Passover, it is worth pointing out here that the messianic banquet in this Dead Sea Scroll consists of bread and wine. Why is this? One possible explanation is that, elsewhere in the Dead Sea Scrolls, the future priestly messiah is identified with Melchizedek, the "priest-king" of the book of Genesis, who was known for his sacrificial offering of "bread and wine" (Gen 14:18; cf. *11QMelchizedek* 2). Another possibility is that the meal described in the Scroll is a messianic Passover meal. Not only does the meal consist of "bread" and "wine," but the Scroll also explicitly requires "at least ten men" to be present for every meal celebrated in anticipation of the messianic banquet. This dovetails perfectly with other first-century evidence that it was necessary that "a fraternity of not fewer than ten persons" be present at a Jewish Passover meal, in contrast to an ordinary meal (Josephus, *Jewish War* 6.423).[36] Whether the meal in question is a Passover or not, this particular Dead Sea Scroll leaves little room for doubt that the expectation of a messianic banquet was alive and well in Jesus' day.

33. Schiffman, *The Eschatological Community of the Dead Sea Scrolls*, 56.

34. Schürer, *The History of the Jewish People*, 2:554; Russell, *The Method and Message of Jewish Apocalyptic*, 322; Black, *The Scrolls and Christian Origins*, 146.

35. Frank Moore Cross, *The Ancient Library at Qumran* (3rd ed.; Minneapolis: Fortress, 1995), 168. Following David E. Aune, *The Cultic Setting of Realized Eschatology in Early Christianity* (NovTSup 28; Leiden: E. J. Brill, 1972), one could speak here of the cultic or liturgical setting of a partially realized eschatology. See also Michael A. Knibb, *The Qumran Community* (Cambridge: Cambridge University Press, 1987), 154, on the meal in 1QSa as "an anticipation of the common meal of the messianic age."

36. In later Jewish tradition, this minimum requirement for ten men to be present, known in Hebrew as a *minyan*, would be applied to public synagogue service, the praying of the Eighteen Benedictions, and the recitation of nuptial blessings at a wedding (*m. Meg.* 4:3; *b. Ber.* 21b; *Meg.* 23b). See Cecil Roth, "Minyan," *Encyclopedia Judaica* (16 vols.; 1st ed.; Jerusalem: Ktav, 1971), 12:68.

When we turn to the Jewish Pseudepigrapha from the Second Temple period, the concept of the eschatological feast is also attested. For example, *1 Enoch* describes the age of salvation as a time when the righteous will be allowed to dine in the heavenly Temple on the fruit of the Tree of Life:

> And (as for) this fragrant tree, no flesh has the right to touch it until the great judgment, in which there will be vengeance on all and a consummation forever. *Then it will be given to the righteous and the pious, and its fruit will be food for the chosen. And it [the Tree of Life] will be transplanted to the Holy Place, by the house of God, the King of eternity. There they will rejoice greatly and be glad and they will enter into the sanctuary.* Its fragrances will be in their bones, and they will live a long life on earth, such as your father lived also in their days, and torments and plagues and suffering will not touch them. (*1 En.* 25:4-6)[37]

This is a remarkable description of the eschatological feast, bearing several significant aspects. In terms of locale, the banquet is heavenly, insofar as it takes place within the heavenly Temple of God, the "sanctuary" of God in the other-worldly realm.[38] In terms of character, the feast is also cultic, insofar as it is directly associated with the righteous (dead?) being able to enter the heavenly "sanctuary" in order to partake of the celestial food. From a Jewish perspective, this implies the participation in a sacrificial banquet of some sort, such as when the priests in the Temple ate the bread of the presence (cf. Lev 24:1-9). Intriguingly, the banquet appears to be both protological and eschatological in character. It is protological, in that the righteous are able to return to Paradise and partake of the prelapsarian fruit of the Tree of Life (cf. Gen 3:22). It is eschatological, in that partaking of its fruits is restricted until the time of the final judgment and, apparently, the bodily resurrection of the dead.[39] Finally, the banquet also appears to be miraculous or supernatural, in that partaking of the fruit communicates not merely natural sustenance but supernatural blessing, in the form of freedom from suffering.[40] Indeed, the banquet has the same effect as in Isaiah: those who partake of it will no longer taste the fruit of Adam's sin: suffering and death. Not only will God "wipe

37. Trans. in George W. E. Nickelsburg, *1 Enoch 1* (Hermeneia; Minneapolis: Fortress, 2001).

38. See Nickelsburg, *1 Enoch 1*, 313-15, on the "present inaccessible location" of the tree in the place where "God's throne" is (cf. *1 En.* 25:3; cf. 18:8).

39. Nickelsburg, *1 Enoch 1*, 315.

40. Priest, "A Note on the Messianic Banquet," 223.

every tear from their eyes," but the divine power will reside in "their bones," so that no "suffering" will touch them. In the words of Genesis: they will "eat, and live for ever" (Gen 3:22).

Elsewhere in *1 Enoch,* in the section referred to by modern scholars as "the Similitudes" (or Parables) of Enoch (chs. 37–71) — regarded by recent scholarship as originating later than the first part of the book, sometime in the first century around the turn of the era[41] — we find a second description of the eschatological banquet.[42] In this text, the future banquet is explicitly messianic:

> And the righteous and the chosen will be saved on that day; and the faces of the sinners and the unrighteous they will henceforth not see. And the Lord of Spirits will abide over them, and *with that Son of Man they will eat, and they will lie down and rise up forever and ever.* And the righteous and the chosen will have arisen from the earth, and have ceased to cast down their faces, and have put on the garment of glory. And this will be your garment, the garment of life from the Lord of Spirits; and your garments will not wear out, and your glory will not fade in the presence of the Lord of Spirits. (*1 En.* 62:13-16)[43]

In this text, the eschatological character of the feast is on full display: it is linked with the salvation of the righteous elect; it is hosted by the "Son of Man," who is elsewhere explicitly identified as the messiah (*1 En.* 48:6-10; 49:3-4; 52:4); and it is directly tied to the resurrection of the dead. Moreover, the imagery of "garments" of "glory" suggests that "the locus of everlasting life is heaven rather than earth,"[44] where the "Lord of Spirits abide[s] over" the righteous, or on a supernaturally renewed earth, in which the two spheres somehow meet.

Perhaps the most elaborate description of the messianic banquet comes to us from *2 Baruch,* which is commonly dated to the late first century A.D. Although the text is long, it is worth quoting in full, as it is perhaps the most full-blown expectation of the messianic feast from the period:

41. On first-century dating of *1 Enoch* 37–71, see now George W. E. Nickelsburg and James C. VanderKam, *1 Enoch 2* (Hermeneia; Minneapolis: Fortress, 2012), 58-64 (with full bibliography).

42. Smith, "Messianic Banquet," 789.

43. Trans. in Nickelsburg and VanderKam, *1 Enoch 2.*

44. Nickelsburg and VanderKam, *1 Enoch 2,* 266-68.

> And it will happen that when all that which should come to pass in these parts has been accomplished, *the Messiah will begin to be revealed.* And Behemoth will reveal itself from its place, and Leviathan will come from the sea, the two great monsters which I created on the fifth day of creation and which I shall have kept until that time. *And they will be nourishment for all who are left.* The earth will also yield fruits ten thousandfold. And on one vine will be a thousand branches, and one branch will produce a thousand clusters, and one cluster will produce a thousand grapes, and one grape will produce a cor of wine. *And those who are hungry will enjoy themselves and they will, moreover, see marvels every day.* For winds will go out in front of me every morning to bring the fragrance of aromatic fruits and clouds at the end of the day to distill the dew of health. *And it will happen at that time that the treasury of manna will come down again from on high, and they will eat of it in those years because these are they who will have arrived at the consummation of time.* And it will happen after these things when the time of the appearance of the Anointed One has been fulfilled and he returns with glory, that then all who sleep in hope of him will rise. And it will happen at that time that those treasuries will be opened in which the number of the souls of the righteous were kept, and they will go out and the multitudes of the souls will appear together, in one assemblage, of one mind. And the first ones will enjoy themselves and the last ones will not be sad. For they know that the time has come of which it is said that it is the end of times. (2 *Bar.* 29:1–30:4)

Several aspects of this grand vision are worth highlighting. First, the banquet is both eschatological and explicitly messianic, directly tied both to the coming of the "Anointed One" and the "end of times."[45] Second, it is important to stress that "eating in the messianic age takes place not on a single occasion, but 'every day.'"[46] Hence "the messianic banquet not only marks the beginning of the eschatological age but is a feature of it in perpetuity."[47] Third, the banquet is described in terms evocative of the exodus from Egypt. Its commencement will be marked by the return of the manna from heaven. It will take place alongside the return of the heavenly "dew" that brought the manna in the first place (Exod 16:13-14). Even the image of superabundant wine and enormous clusters

45. For comment, see R. H. Charles, *The Apocalypse of Baruch* (Ancient Texts and Translations; Eugene: Wipf & Stock, 2005 [orig. 1896]), 52-53.

46. Priest, "A Note on the Messianic Banquet," 224.

47. Priest, "A Note on the Messianic Banquet," 224.

of grapes harks back to the gathering of the grapes in the land of Canaan by the emissaries of Joshua at the end of the exodus (Num 13:21-24). Fourth, and quite memorably, the righteous can also expect to feed on the flesh of Leviathan and Behemoth. It is not clear whether this image is hyperbolic and figurative or is intended as a literal description of the viands of the banquet. Either way, it seems to represent the triumph of the righteous over the destructive powers of this world. Lastly, but by no means least significantly, the inauguration of the messianic banquet directly precedes the return of the messiah to heaven and the resurrection of the righteous dead.[48] The reason this is significant is that it suggests that while the banquet begins to be celebrated on earth during the days of the messiah, it finds its ultimate fulfillment in the return of the pre-existent messiah — apparently along with the resurrected righteous — to heaven. This suggests that *the banquet has both an earthly component and a heavenly component:* just as the righteous on earth "enjoy themselves" during the days of the messiah by eating the manna (2 *Bar.* 29:6), so too those who are raised from the dead will "enjoy themselves" in the heavenly "assemblage" of the exalted messiah (2 *Bar.* 30:2).

Finally, although debate continues about the provenance of the *Testaments of the Twelve Patriarchs,* it is worth noting that one of the arguably early Jewish testaments also links the eschatological feast to the coming of a priestly messiah, who will likewise take the saints into the heavenly paradise, in this case so that they can eat the fruit of the protological Tree of Life:

> *And he [the priestly Messiah] shall open the gates of paradise;* he shall remove the sword that has threatened since Adam, and *he will grant the saints to eat of the tree of life.* (*T. Levi* 18:10-11)

In light of such evidence from the Scrolls and Pseudepigrapha, it seems clear that a vibrant awareness of a coming banquet that was not just eschatological but also heavenly was part of Jewish speculation on the age of salvation in the Second Temple period.

With this information in mind, we can now turn to those texts in the Gospels that appear to be rooted in the Jewish hope for the messianic banquet and see what light they might throw on Jesus' own vision of the coming kingdom of God.

48. Charles, *The Apocalypse of Baruch,* 56 n. XXX.1. So too Klausner, *The Messianic Idea in Israel,* 343.

Eating and Drinking with Abraham, Isaac, and Jacob[49]

Arguably the most explicit description of the eschatological banquet in the Gospels is Jesus' teaching about a coming feast in "the kingdom" at which the patriarchs themselves will be present:

49. For discussion, see Gerhard Lohfink, *Jesus of Nazareth: What He Wanted, Who He Was* (trans. Linda M. Maloney; Collegeville: Liturgical Press, 2012), 70-71; Maurice Casey, *Jesus of Nazareth: An Independent Historian's Account of His Life and Teaching* (London: T. & T. Clark, 2010), 222; Dale C. Allison Jr., *Constructing Jesus: Memory, Imagination, and History* (Grand Rapids: Baker Academic, 2010), 178-79, 186; Craig S. Keener, *The Historical Jesus of the Gospels* (Grand Rapids: Eerdmans, 2009), 390-91; Scot McKnight, "Jesus and the Twelve," in *Key Events in the Life of the Historical Jesus* (ed. Darrell L. Bock and Robert L. Webb; WUNT 247; Tübingen: Mohr Siebeck, 2009), 181-214 (here 204-5); Karen J. Wenell, *Jesus and Land: Sacred and Social Space in Second Temple Judaism* (LNTS 334; London: T. & T. Clark, 2007), 128-35; Michael F. Bird, *Jesus and the Origins of the Gentile Mission* (LNTS 331; London: T. & T. Clark, 2007), 83-93; James D. G. Dunn, *Jesus Remembered* (*Christianity in the Making*, vol. 1; Grand Rapids: Eerdmans, 2003), 426-27; Gerd S. Lüdemann, *Jesus after 2000 Years: What He Really Did and Said* (trans. John Bowden; London: SCM; Amherst: Prometheus, 2001), 155-56; Ulrich Luz, *Matthew 8–20* (trans. James E. Crouch; Hermeneia; Minneapolis: Fortress, 2001), 8-12; Bart D. Erhman, *Jesus: Apocalpytic Prophet of the New Millennium* (Oxford: Oxford University Press, 1999), 142-43; Dale C. Allison Jr., *Jesus of Nazareth: Millenarian Prophet* (Minneapolis: Fortress, 1998), 143-44; Gerd Theissen and Annette Merz, *The Historical Jesus: A Comprehensive Guide* (trans. John Bowden; Minneapolis: Fortress, 1998), 254; Jürgen Becker, *Jesus of Nazareth* (trans. James E. Crouch; New York and Berlin: Walter de Gruyter, 1998), 66-68; Dale C. Allison Jr., *The Jesus Tradition in Q* (Harrisburg: Trinity Press International, 1997), 176-91; Marius Reiser, *Jesus and Judgment: The Eschatological Proclamation in Its Jewish Context* (trans. Linda M. Maloney; Minneapolis: Fortress, 1997), 230-41; Joachim Gnilka, *Jesus of Nazareth: Message and History* (trans. Siegfried S. Schatzmann; Peabody: Hendrickson, 1997), 195-98; N. T. Wright, *Jesus and the Victory of God* (Minneapolis: Fortress, 1996), 308-9, 328-29; John P. Meier, *A Marginal Jew: Rethinking the Historical Jesus* (4 vols. [5th vol. forthcoming]; Anchor Yale Bible Reference Library; New Haven and London: Yale University Press, 1991, 1994, 2001, 2009), 2:309-17; W. D. Davies and Dale C. Allison Jr., *A Critical and Exegetical Commentary on the Gospel According to Saint Matthew*, 3 vols. (Edinburgh: T. & T. Clark, 1988, 1991, 1997), 2:25-32; Gerd Theissen, *The Gospels in Context* (trans. Linda M. Maloney; Minneapolis: Fortress, 1991), 45 (suggesting both Diaspora Jews and Gentiles being gathered in); G. R. Beasley-Murray, *Jesus and the Kingdom of God* (Grand Rapids: Eerdmans, 1986), 169-74; E. P. Sanders, *Jesus and Judaism* (Philadelphia: Fortress, 1985), 219-20, 394; Joseph Fitzmyer, *The Gospel according to Luke* (2 vols.; AB; New York: Doubleday, 1983, 1985), 2:1020-27; Dieter Zeller, "Das Logion Mt 8,11f/Lk 13,28f und das Motive der Völkerwallfahrt," *BZ* 15 (1971): 222-37 and 16 (1972): 84-93; Joachim Jeremias, *New Testament Theology* (trans. John Bowden; London: SCM, 1971), 245-47; Norman Perrin, *Rediscovering the Teaching of Jesus* (New York: Harper & Row, 1967), 161-64; Günther Bornkamm, *Jesus of Nazareth* (Minneapolis: Fortress, 1995 [orig. 1960]), 78; Joachim Jeremias, *Jesus' Promise to the Nations* (trans. S. H. Hooke; London: SCM, 1958), 55-63.

> I tell you, many will come from east and west and sit at table with Abraham, Isaac, and Jacob in the kingdom of heaven, while the sons of the kingdom will be thrown into the outer darkness; there men will weep and gnash their teeth. (Matt 8:11-12)

> There you will weep and gnash your teeth, when you see Abraham and Isaac and Jacob and all the prophets in the kingdom of God and you yourselves thrust out. And men will come from east and west, and from north and south, and sit at table in the kingdom of God. (Luke 13:28-29)

As is widely known, these sayings appear in different contexts in their respective Gospels: the first appears in the account of Jesus and the centurion in Capernaum (Matt 8:5-13); the second appears in Jesus' instructions given during his journey to Jerusalem (Luke 13:22-30).[50] In keeping with our method of proceeding, we will focus our attention on the substance of the sayings, which is much the same.[51] In both texts, Jesus clearly envisions a future time when people will come to dine with the patriarchs in the kingdom of God. Yet several questions immediately arise: Who is this multitude coming from "east" and "west"? Where are they coming from, and to where are they being gathered? In both texts, Jesus describes the goal of their pilgrimage as a great banquet with the patriarchs. When and where will this banquet take place? And how will the patriarchs be present, when they are long dead? In both texts, Jesus contrasts the joy of the banquet with the weeping and gnashing of teeth of those outside the banquet. What then does this imagery reveal about the nature of the kingdom and the restoration envisaged? Who are those who are excluded from the banquet, and why are they excluded?

Who Will Come "from East and West"?

Out of all the interpretive issues raised by this passage, the most debated continues to be the question of the identity of those who come from east and west to dine at the banquet. Answers to this question can be roughly divided into three camps.

First, most interpreters identify the ingathering multitudes without qual-

50. For discussion, see Davies and Allison, *Saint Matthew*, 2:25-32; Fitzmyer, *The Gospel according to Luke*, 2:1020-27.

51. Beasley-Murray, *Jesus and the Kingdom of God*, 169.

ification as the Gentile nations.[52] From this perspective, the divide in Jesus' saying falls along ethnic lines, with the Gentiles being gathered in to the banquet, while the Israelites are cast out. Within this perspective, interpreters can be more or less exclusive in the way interpretation is formulated. For some, the divide envisioned in the saying consists of a complete acceptance of the nations and a complete rejection of the Israelites.[53]

A second viewpoint argues instead that the multitudes coming from east and west do not refer to pagan peoples, but to the Jews of the Diaspora, who are being gathered into the holy land.[54] From this perspective, Jesus' words only refer to the geographical ingathering of the Jewish Diaspora — those Jews scattered throughout the Gentile world; there is no pilgrimage of the Gentile nations in view.

Finally, there are still others who argue that both the scattered Israelites and the righteous Gentiles are in view.[55] From this perspective, the dividing line lies not along geography or ethnicity but stands in accord with one's response to the proclamation of the kingdom. Though in some ways a minority position, this last view is the best explanation of the evidence, for several reasons.

For one thing, the idea of both the scattered children of Israel and the Gentiles being gathered to the eschatological banquet coheres perfectly with the image of the eschatological feast in Jewish Scripture. Look once again at the primary text:

> On this mountain the LORD of hosts will make *for all peoples a feast* of fat things, a feast of wine on the lees, of fat things full of marrow, of wine on the lees well refined. And he will destroy on this mountain the covering that is cast over all peoples, the veil that is spread over *all nations.* He will swallow up death for ever, and the Lord GOD will wipe away tears from

52. E.g., Becker, *Jesus of Nazareth,* 67-68; Gnilka, *Jesus of Nazareth,* 195-97; Reiser, *Jesus and Judgment,* 230, 240; Wright, *Jesus and the Victory of God,* 308-10; Meyer, *The Aims of Jesus,* 167-68, 247; Bornkamm, *Jesus of Nazareth,* 78-79; Perrin, *Rediscovering the Teaching of Jesus,* 163; Jeremias, *Jesus' Promise to the Nations,* 63.

53. Lüdemann, *Jesus After 2000 Years,* 155-56, cf. 356; Zeller, "Das Logion," 87-88.

54. E.g., Wenell, *Jesus and Land,* 132; Allison, *Jesus of Nazareth,* 141-44; idem, *The Jesus Tradition in Q,* 176-91; Davies and Allison, *Saint Matthew,* 2:27-29; Sanders, *Jesus and Judaism,* 219-20; Buchanan, *Jesus,* 34-35, 114.

55. E.g., Bird, *Jesus and the Origins of the Gentile Mission,* 89-93; Theissen, *The Gospels in Context,* 45. Cf. Reiser, *Jesus and Judgment,* 234, on only the "righteous" Gentiles being gathered, not all Gentiles without discrimination.

> all faces, and *the reproach of his people he will take away* from all the earth, for the LORD has spoken. (Isa 25:6-8)

Clearly, according to this description of the eschatological banquet in Jewish Scripture itself, the presence of both Israel ("his people") and the Gentile nations ("all nations") is explicit. The banquet is expressly designated as a feast for "all peoples" *(kol hāʿamîm)* (Isa 25:6). To the extent that Jesus' oracle is drawing on the Isaianic vision of the eschatological banquet — and this is strongly suggested by the fact that both Jesus' teaching and the prophecy of Isaiah seem to envision the overthrow of death — this fact weighs against the view that the multitude coming to the banquet is either exclusively Gentile or exclusively Israelite.[56]

Moreover, the idea of the lost tribes and the Gentiles being gathered in finds support from other prophecies in Jewish Scripture of many coming from east and west.[57] Although some scholars have argued that the Jewish Scripture does not use the image of being gathered "from east and west" to refer to the Gentile nations, this is in fact not true.[58] In at least two places, we find that the ingathering of the scattered tribes of Israel and the ingathering of the Gentile nations are inextricably intertwined with one another:

> "Fear not, for I am with you; *I will bring your offspring from the east, and from the west I will gather you;* I will say to the north, Give up, and to the south, Do not withhold; *bring my sons from afar and my daughters from the end of the earth,* every one who is called by my name, whom I created for my glory, whom I formed and made." Bring forth the people who are blind, yet have eyes, who are deaf, yet have ears! *Let all the nations gather together, and let the peoples assemble.* (Isa 43:5-9)

> Thus says the LORD of hosts: Behold, *I will save my people from the east country and from the west country; and I will bring them to dwell in the midst of Jerusalem;* and they shall be my people and I will be their God, in faithfulness and in righteousness. . . . Thus says the LORD of hosts: Peoples yet shall come, even the inhabitants of many cities. . . . Many peoples and strong nations shall come to seek the LORD of hosts in Jerusalem, and to

56. Cf. Beasley-Murray, *Jesus and the Kingdom of God,* 170, 174; Jeremias, *New Testament Theology,* 247.

57. See Jeremias, *Jesus' Promise to the Nations,* 58-59.

58. *Contra* Davies and Allison, *Saint Matthew,* 2:27; Beasley-Murray, *Jesus and the Kingdom of God,* 170; see Pitre, *Jesus, the Tribulation, and the End of the Exile,* 281 n. 149.

> entreat the favor of the LORD. Thus says the LORD of hosts: *In those days ten men from the Gentiles of every tongue shall take hold of the robe of a Jew,* saying, "Let us go with you, for we have heard that God is with you." (Zech 8:7-8, 20-23)

It is texts such as these, I would suggest, that also inform the biblical background of Jesus' words.[59] When interpreted in the light of the oracles of the Old Testament prophets, the gathering of the multitude "from east and west" to dine in the kingdom refers neither to the exclusive ingathering of the Gentiles (and the concomitant rejection of all Israel) nor to the exclusive gathering of the Jewish Diaspora (and the concomitant rejection or neglect of the Gentiles). Instead, Jesus seems to be describing both the eschatological restoration of the scattered tribes of Israel and the ingathering of the Gentiles. As Michael Bird concludes: "the inter-textual echoes of the phrase 'east and west' evoke a larger narrative in Israel's sacred traditions which connotes the salvation of the Gentiles as an immediate consequence of the eschatological regathering of Israel."[60]

In support of this interpretation, it is crucial to point out that the idea that both Israel and the Gentiles are gathered to the banquet is the only position that corresponds to the biblical history of the Assyrian and Babylonian exiles.[61] Although the point is often overlooked, those who argue that Jesus is referring to the ingathering of the Jewish "Diaspora" fail to make a proper distinction between (1) the Jews living throughout the Roman Empire, a population whose location was easily verified and referred to as the "Diaspora"; and (2) the lost tribes of the northern kingdom of Israel and their descendants, whose numbers were incalculable and whose whereabouts were unknown.[62] In this regard, the first-century description of the continuing exile by Josephus is instructive:

> In this way it has come about that there are *two tribes in Asia and Europe* subject to the Romans, while until now there have been *ten tribes beyond the Euphrates* — countless myriads whose number cannot be ascertained. (Josephus, *Antiquities* 11.133)

Notice in the above quotation that Josephus is quite clear on the fact that the imperial Diaspora consists of descendants of the southern kingdom of

59. So too Wenell, *Jesus and Land*, 130-31, who sees the "close associations between the gathering of Israel and the gathering of the nations." See also *Ps. Sol.* 11:2-3; 17:26-32.

60. Bird, *Jesus and the Origins of the Gentile Mission*, 84.

61. See Pitre, *Jesus, the Tribulation, and the End of the Exile*, 279-83, cf. 31-40.

62. E.g., Sanders, *Jesus and Judaism*, 220.

Judah whereas the lost ten tribes of the northern kingdom of Israel consist of an innumerable multitude whose number cannot be ascertained.[63] In other words, the lost tribes are not part of the visible Diaspora, since they have been intermingled with the Gentile nations for centuries.

The reason this distinction is so crucial for our purposes is that it shows that those who argue that Jesus envisions the geographical ingathering of the Jewish Diaspora are failing to recognize that *the ingathering of the contemporary Diaspora, even if it could be accomplished, would not actually bring about the restoration of all Israel.* It is difficult to overstress the point, so I will repeat it: the geographical ingathering of Jews from the Diaspora — which would include figures such as Saul (Paul) of Tarsus, a Diaspora Benjamite and descendant of the southern kingdom (Phil 3:4-5; Acts 22:3) — simply does not solve the problem of the ingathering of the twelve tribes of Israel. For the Diaspora consisted primarily of descendants of only two tribes: Judah and Benjamin. However, as we saw above, in Isaiah, Jeremiah, Ezekiel, and other biblical descriptions of the restoration of Israel, it is all twelve tribes that are restored and gathered, including the ten northern tribes — Reuben, Simeon, Zebulun, Gad, Issachar, Dan, Asher, Naphtali, Ephraim, Manasseh — whose descendants are indistinguishably intermingled with the Gentile nations.

Once this point is clear, it simultaneously becomes evident why the restoration of the lost tribes of Israel and the ingathering of the Gentile nations are inextricably bound up with one another.[64] Because the countless multitude of descendants of the northern kingdom are scattered among the Gentiles, then it makes sense that the ingathering of the lost tribes should be closely tied to the ingathering of the Gentiles among whom they were scattered. Although the point is frequently overlooked, this is, of course, exactly how the book of Isaiah ends:

> [Thus says the LORD:] For I know their works and their thoughts, and I am coming *to gather all nations and tongues; they shall come and see my glory,* and I will set a sign among them. And from them I will send

63. See Scott, "Exile and Restoration," 254-55; see also James M. Scott, *Restoration: Old Testament, Jewish, and Christian Perspectives* (JSJSup 72; Leiden: E. J. Brill, 2001); idem, *Exile: Old Testament, Jewish, and Christian Conceptions* (JSJSup 56; Leiden: E. J. Brill, 1997); Allison, *Jesus of Nazareth,* 141-45. See also David C. Greenwood, "On Jewish Hopes for a Restored Northern Kingdom," *ZAW* 88 (1976): 376-85; Stephen D. Ricks, "The Prophetic Literality of Tribal Reconstruction," in *Israel's Apostasy and Restoration* (ed. Avraham Gileadi; Grand Rapids: Baker, 1988), 273-81.

64. Cf. Wright, *Jesus and the Victory of God,* 308.

> survivors to the nations, to Tarshish, Put, and Lud, who draw the bow, to Tubal and Javan, to the coastlands afar off, that have not heard my fame or seen my glory; and they shall declare my glory among the nations. *And they shall bring all your brethren from all the nations as an offering to the* LORD, upon horses, and in chariots, and in litters, and upon mules, and upon dromedaries, to my holy mountain in Jerusalem, says the LORD, just as the Israelites bring their cereal offering in a clean vessel to the house of the LORD. (Isa 66:18-20)

As Joachim Gnilka rightly points out, this text clearly envisions some kind of "mission to the nations."[65] Hence, the eschatological ingathering of both Israel and the Gentiles is not only presupposed in the biblical description of the eschatological feast (Isa 25:6-8), but explicitly described in the climactic ending of the book of Isaiah. In Isaiah 66, the salvation of the Gentiles is closely bound up with the regathering of Israel because the vast multitude of the descendants of the twelve tribes of Jacob (ten-twelfths of Israel, to be exact) have been scattered among the Gentile nations. In other words, *it is precisely by gathering the Gentile nations that God will bring home the scattered "brethren" of Israel with them.* This is the vision of the prophet Isaiah, and this is the vision I am suggesting is present in Jesus' words about the multitude coming from east and west to dine with the patriarchs in the banquet of the kingdom.

Who Is Cast Out of the Banquet?

Once the identity of those being gathered to the banquet is clarified, we can then answer the question of who is being cast out of the banquet. Although the precise terminology is different, both sayings speak of invitees who are thrown out of the banquet, whether it is the "sons of the kingdom" who are thrown into the "outer darkness" where they will "weep and gnash their teeth" (Matt 8:12), or a less clearly defined group (addressed simply as "you") who are likewise "thrust out" of the "kingdom of God" into an unspecified place where they will "weep and gnash your teeth" (Luke 13:28).

Again, interpreters are divided. On the one hand, commentators who are convinced that the many gathered from east and west are exclusively Gentiles

65. Gnilka, *Jesus of Nazareth,* 196 n. 19. *Contra* Jeremias, *Jesus' Promise to the Nations,* 60: "The Gentiles will not be evangelized where they dwell, but will be summoned to the holy Mount by the divine epiphany." See also Jeremias, *New Testament Theology,* 247.

tend to identify those cast out as Jews, who have been rejected. For example, Joachim Jeremias considers Jesus' statements about the banquet with the patriarchs to be one of the most "severe" and "devoid of hope for Israel," since "in the final judgment Gentiles will take the place of the sons of the Kingdom."[66] On the other hand, commentators who argue that Jesus envisioned the geographical ingathering of the Diaspora take one of two approaches. Either they argue that Jesus envisions "Palestinian Jews" being cast out of the kingdom,[67] or they attempt to soften the force of declaration of judgment, either by stressing that there is no indication that all of the Jews of the land would be cast out or by denying that Jesus said the negative part of the saying.[68]

However, the weakness of both of these interpretations is manifest in their inability to plausibly identify the group being cast out of the banquet. By contrast, once we identify the multitude gathered from east and west as consisting of both Israelites and Gentiles who respond to the proclamation of the kingdom, the identity of the group being cast out becomes quite clear. Both groups consist of some Israelites and some Gentiles, and the dividing line falls not along ethnic boundaries but according to the manner of response to the invitation to the kingdom.[69] From this view, those who are excluded from the banquet are simply those who reject Jesus' proclamation of the kingdom, whether through their lack of faith in his works and presumption about inheriting the kingdom (Matthew) or their commission of evil doings and presumption about being close to the leader of the kingdom (Luke).[70]

Indeed, upon closer inspection of the saying as a whole, the idea that Jesus' saying envisions the rejection of the Jews as a whole is nonsensical. In the words of John Meier:

> They [those cast out of the kingdom banquet] are certainly not "all Israel," since the patriarchs, no doubt representing all the righteous of the OT, are at the banquet, and presumably Jesus would include at the table his

66. Jeremias, *Jesus' Promise to the Nations,* 51. Likewise, Reiser, *Jesus and Judgment,* 233-35.

67. Buchanan, *Jesus,* 34-35, 114, is largely alone in this, though it is the logical implication of his position.

68. E.g., Davies and Allison, *Saint Matthew,* 2:30-31; cf. Sanders, *Jesus and Judaism,* 219-20, who suggests that only the positive part of the saying is authentic, without giving a clear interpretation of the negative element.

69. Casey, *Jesus of Nazareth,* 222.

70. Lohfink, *Jesus of Nazareth,* 71; Gnilka, *Jesus of Nazareth,* 195-98; Beasley-Murray, *Jesus and the Kingdom of God,* 172. Cf. Fitzmyer, *The Gospel according to Luke,* 2:1026.

> own disciples (especially the Twelve, representing the reconstituted tribes) as well as the tax collectors, sinners, and other assorted Israelites who heeded his message. The "you" [i.e., those cast out] must be those among his contemporaries in Israel who made a point of rejecting his mission.[71]

In light of such consideration, the common interpretation of this saying as a rejection of all Israel should itself be rejected. Once again, Meier rightly concludes:

> [T]here are no grounds for speaking of "the rejection of all Israel." Nothing in the saying indicates that *all* Israel is involved, only some unspecified group of Israelites who oppose or reject Jesus' message.[72]

Hence, when Jesus' words are situated in the context of Jewish Scripture and ancient Jewish eschatology, the oracle about many coming to dine in the kingdom constitutes neither a wholesale rejection of Israel nor an exclusively Israelite vision of salvation.

The Heavenly Banquet with the Patriarchs

With the identity of the multitude established, the final interpretive question is: To where are the multitudes being gathered? Or, to put the question another way: Where is the banquet with the patriarchs? Does Jesus' language of the ingathering of a multitude from "east and west" and "north and south" presuppose an earthly pilgrimage to the land of Israel? Should we think of the banquet of the kingdom as taking place inside the borders of Israel? Or do Jesus' words envisage something else? In contrast to the attention given to the identity of the gathering multitude, commentators are sometimes less exact (or less certain) in their answers to this question.

On the one hand, many scholars hold that Jesus is speaking about a geographical return of the Diaspora Jews from out of exile to the promised land. From this perspective, Jesus is speaking of the lost tribes being gathered "to Palestine and Zion."[73] Or, as Dale Allison avers: "When Matthew and Luke

71. Meier, *A Marginal Jew,* 2:316.

72. Meier, *A Marginal Jew,* 2:316.

73. Wenell, *Jesus and Land,* 129; Allison, *Jesus of Nazareth,* 144; cf. McKnight, "Jesus and the Twelve," 205; Jeremias, *Jesus' Promise to the Nations,* 58.

have Jesus foretell the ingathering of people from east and west (Matt 8:11-12; Luke 13:28-29), the presumed destination of their centripetal movement must be Palestine and its chief city, which Jews imagined as the *axis mundi*."[74] From this perspective, however eschatological Jesus' vision is, it is also decidedly this-worldly, and has nothing to do with the heavenly realm. As Bart Ehrman asserts: "[W]hen Jesus talks about the Kingdom, he appears to refer principally to something here on earth."[75]

On the other hand, a remarkable number of scholars have argued that Jesus' vision of the restoration of Israel and the ingathering of the Gentiles here is "in some way discontinuous with this present world."[76] James Dunn puts it strongly:

> Here should also be mentioned the positive hope expressed in terms of hunger satisfied and the eschatological banquet. . . . The many coming from east and west will recline in the kingdom of heaven/God with Abraham, Isaac, and Jacob (Matt 8.11/Luke 13.28-29). *Here the kingdom seems to be equivalent to heaven* or at least to *the idealized future state following the final consummation.*[77]

From this point of view, the kingdom being described is "a truly transcendent reality."[78] Far from being a simple mundane restoration, it appears in some way to be a heavenly reality, in keeping with the transcendent emphasis of apocalyptic literature and the apocalyptic worldview in general.[79]

With this in mind, three considerations argue strongly against a merely geographical restoration from exile and in favor of Dunn's view of some kind of ingathering into a kingdom that is both heavenly and eschatological.

First, while some interpreters assume that Jesus is speaking of the ingathering of the exiles to the earthly city of Jerusalem as the "presumed des-

74. Allison, *Constructing Jesus*, 51. See also Casey, *Jesus of Nazareth*, 222.

75. Ehrman, *Jesus*, 142. So too Reiser, *Jesus and Judgment*, 236-39.

76. Meier, *A Marginal Jew*, 2:317.

77. Dunn, *Jesus Remembered*, 427 (emphasis added).

78. Jacques Schlosser, *La Règne de Dieu dans les Dits de Jésus* (2 vols.; Paris: Gabalda, 1980), 2:641; cited in Reiser, *Jesus and Judgment*, 238 n. 137.

79. Early Jewish apocalypticism is known for its emphasis on transcendent realms such as heaven, hell (or Hades), Gehenna, Abraham's bosom, Paradise, etc. (e.g., *1 En.* 14–16; 17–36; *Apoc. Abr.* 15-17; *T. Lev.* 2-5; *2 En.* 1-9, etc.). See Brant Pitre, "Apocalypticism and Apocalyptic Teaching," in *Dictionary of Jesus and the Gospels* (2nd ed.; ed. Joel B. Green, Jeannine K. Brown, and Nicholas Perrin; Downers Grove: IVP Academic, 2013), 25-26; Martha Himmelfarb, *Ascent to Heaven in Jewish and Christian Apocalypses* (Oxford: Oxford University Press, 1993).

tination,"[80] it is important to emphasize that *Jesus does not explicitly mention Jerusalem, the Temple, or Mount Zion.*[81] Like many other of Jesus' sayings in the Gospels, the focus of any "centripetal movement" is not the city of Jerusalem, but the kingdom of God. Moreover, to the extent that Jesus is speaking of the Danielic "kingdom" of God, as described in Daniel 7, it is an essentially heavenly reality, though it manifests itself on earth as well in mysterious ways (cf. Dan 2:44-45).

Second — and this is very significant — in both versions of Jesus' saying, two opposing realms are in view, which mutually illuminate one another: the realm of the kingdom where the banquet with the patriarchs is celebrated is contrasted with the realm of the damned, where "there is weeping and the gnashing of teeth" *(ho klauthmos kai ho brygmos tōn odontōn)* (Matt 8:12; Luke 13:28).[82] This imagery is a very Jewish way of describing the spiritual place of damnation and punishment, commonly known as "hell":[83]

> Their names will be erased from the book of life and from the books of the holy ones, and their seed will perish forever; their spirits will be slaughtered, and they will cry out and groan in a desolate unseen place, and in fire they will burn, for there is no earth there. (*1 En.* 108:3)

Although sometimes overlooked, this contrast between the destination of the gathering multitudes and the place into which the damned are cast is extremely significant. For it strongly suggests that the place to which the lost tribes and the Gentiles are gathered is not the earthly Jerusalem or the earthly promised land. Rather, *in Jesus' vision of the ingathering of Israel and the Gentiles, the realm of the kingdom stands in direct contrast to the realm of the damned.* From this perspective, the kingdom itself is implicitly depicted as a heavenly realm, which is contrasted with its opposite: the spiritual (but abysmal) realm of the damned.[84]

Third and finally, but by no means least significant, the presence of "Abraham, Isaac, and Jacob" at the banquet provides a critical clue to the nature of the ingathering envisaged (Matt 8:11; Luke 13:28). It should go without saying that in the first century, these patriarchs had been dead and buried for centuries. Hence, in speaking of Israel and the nations coming to dine with

80. Allison, *Constructing Jesus,* 51.

81. Meier, *A Marginal Jew,* 2:314; this is admitted by Reiser, *Jesus and Judgment,* 238.

82. Reiser, *Jesus and Judgment,* 237.

83. See Nickelsburg, *1 Enoch 1,* 556.

84. Fitzmyer, *The Gospel according to Luke,* 2:1026: the kingdom has a "spatial sense" here.

the forefathers, Jesus is clearly indicating something more than a mere geographical return from exile. In the words of John Meier:

> With the affirmation that the Gentiles will join the long-dead patriarchs of Israel at the banquet, Jesus indicates that this fully realized kingdom of God is not only future but also in some way discontinuous with this present world. Whether Jesus is thinking in this logion more of the resurrection of the dead or of the souls of the saved in heaven is not clear. How "transcendent" or "earthly" the kingdom exactly is in Jesus' mind is not illumined by this prophecy, which obviously operates in the realm of religious symbols. But the idea of the Gentiles streaming into the kingdom of God to be joined by the long-dead but now obviously living patriarchs of Israel surely brings us beyond any political kingdom of this present world. . . . *In particular, the depiction of the three great patriarchs as alive and participating in a heavenly banquet implies both the transcendence of death and the regathering of the people of Israel not only from all places but also from all times.*[85]

In this last line, Meier has put his finger on the key point missed by so many: in order for the restoration envisaged in Jesus' prophecy to be a complete realization of the kingdom, it must involve the regathering of Israel and the nations not only from all places but also from all times. This all but demands that the kingdom in question (and the ingathering that leads to it) be far more than a purely earthly return from exile; rather, Jesus' vision of salvation appears to depict a heavenly and/or eschatological banquet in which the living and the dead will somehow participate, in a realm that is somehow "discontinuous with this present world."[86]

In sum, when interpreted in light of its Old Testament background

85. Meier, *A Marginal Jew,* 2:317 (emphasis added).

86. So too Dunn, *Jesus Remembered,* 427; Davies and Allison, *Saint Matthew,* 2:29: "Should one then think of a literal pilgrimage by Jews or Gentiles to Palestine? While this cannot be excluded . . . one is inclined to think that . . . the eschatological promises are to find their realization not in this world as it is but in a re-created world, an old world made new, in which the boundaries between heaven and earth will begin to disappear. If so, any mundane or literal interpretation. . . . would seem to be excluded." Cf. John J. Collins, "Apocalyptic Eschatology as the Transcendence of Death," *CBQ* 36 (1974): 21-43. See also Wenell, *Jesus and Land,* 137, who, despite her insistence on "a firmly 'earthed' kingdom," recognizes that in an apocalyptic framework, attention is shifted to the "heavenly world" in Jesus' description of the kingdom. She is following John J. Collins, *Apocalypticism in the Dead Sea Scrolls* (London: Routledge, 1997), 130.

and situated in the broader context of the history of Israel's two exiles, Jesus' prophecy of people coming from the corners of the globe to dine with the patriarchs in the banquet of the kingdom provides us with a powerful vision of the age of salvation. According to this vision, the scattered tribes of Israel and the Gentiles will one day be gathered in to dine with the long-dead figures of Abraham, Isaac, and Jacob, in the long-awaited banquet of the kingdom. Although (apparently) all will be invited to this banquet, not everybody will be able to enter, and those who reject the proclamation of the kingdom or presume upon entry thereunto — even those who by descent belong to the family of Abraham — will be cast out of the banquet into the realm of the damned, where they will weep and gnash their teeth. Although some interpreters have taken Jesus' words as describing a geographical ingathering of the Gentiles or the Diaspora into the earthly land of Israel, when due attention is given to the fact that the realm of the kingdom is juxtaposed with the imagery of being cast into the realm of the damned, it is hard to avoid the conclusion that Jesus envisioned an other-worldly banquet, whether of the resurrected dead in a world made new and/or of the souls of the righteous into a heavenly kingdom. In striking contrast to some other visions of salvation, it is the banquet of the kingdom, and not the earthly Jerusalem or the land, that stands at the center of the centripetal movement being described in Jesus' vision of salvation.

With this in mind, the question now before us is whether there are good reasons for thinking that the substance of the vision in Matthew 8:11-12 and Luke 13:28-29 is in fact historically plausible on the lips of Jesus.

Arguments against Historical Plausibility

On the one hand, a minority of scholars hold that most or all of the material in Matthew 8:11-12 and Luke 13:28-29 is historically implausible on the lips of Jesus. Three major arguments are given in support of this position.

First and foremost, scholars who interpret the saying as a wholesale exclusion of the Jewish people from the kingdom of God argue that the saying is implausible in an ancient Jewish context. Gerd Lüdemann sums up this position succinctly when he writes: "The sayings are inauthentic, as they presuppose anti-Judaism which only arose after Easter."[87]

Second, other scholars argue that the saying does not cohere with Jesus' mission to his fellow Israelites or his tendency to mercy. Rudolf Bultmann, for

87. Lüdemann, *Jesus after 2000 Years*, 156.

example, rejects its authenticity as "a warning which has no reference to the Person of Jesus."[88] More directly, the Jesus Seminar contends that "the Fellows of the Seminar do not think that such wholesale condemnations are typical of Jesus, even though they cut against the social grain."[89] Finally, splitting the saying in twain, E. P. Sanders accepts the positive image of the gathering from east and west (which he interprets as a reference to the Jewish Diaspora) as historically plausible, but rejects the image of some being "thrown out" of the kingdom into the realm of the damned as an inauthentic reference to the rejection of the Jews.[90]

Third and finally, when this interpretation of the rejection of all Jews is combined with the identification of the multitude coming from east and west as all Gentiles, some scholars add that the saying is too continuous with the practices and beliefs of the early church. From this point of view, the relation of Jews and Gentiles envisaged in the sayings "may reflect much more of the early community's preoccupation with it than Jesus' own."[91] Along similar lines, the Jesus Seminar concludes that the text reflects "the emerging new movement [that] was separating from the newly emerging form of Judean religion."[92] In other words, the saying about the banquet does not square with Jesus' restriction of his mission to "the lost sheep of the house of Israel" (Matt 10:5-6) but appears to presuppose the later development of the early Christian mission to the Gentiles (e.g., Acts 10).

Perhaps more than any other episode we have studied thus far, this material demonstrates just how crucial a role exegesis plays in the question of evaluating historical plausibility.[93]

Context: The Ingathering, the Heavenly Kingdom, and the Banquet with the Patriarchs

In addition to these considerations, there are several other arguments that make a strong case for the historical plausibility of this oracle on the lips of Jesus.

88. Bultmann, *The History of the Synoptic Tradition,* 116.

89. Robert W. Funk, Roy Hoover, and the Jesus Seminar, *The Five Gospels: The Search for the Authentic Words of Jesus* (New York: Macmillan, 1993), 348.

90. Sanders, *Jesus and Judaism,* 219-20, 394 n. 38.

91. Fitzmyer, *The Gospel according to Luke,* 2:1023.

92. Funk, Hoover, and the Jesus Seminar, *The Five Gospels,* 348.

93. Pitre, *Jesus, the Tribulation, and the End of the Exile,* 279.

First and foremost, the saying fits quite squarely into an ancient Jewish context.[94] For one thing, as we saw above, Jesus' vision of many being gathered from east and west, when interpreted in the light of the ingathering of the scattered tribes of Israel, fits quite squarely into the biblical hope for the restoration of the twelve tribes of Israel (e.g., Isa 11:10-12; Jer 23:2-6; Ezek 37:15-24).[95] It coheres solidly with the widespread hope for the restoration of all Israel that continued during the Second Temple period and on through into early rabbinic Judaism (e.g., Sir 36:11; 11QTemple[a] 57:1-14; *Ps. Sol.* 17:21-32; *4 Ezra* 13:32-47; *t. Sanh.* 13:12). Along the same lines, although there are positive and negative depictions of the fate of the Gentiles in Jewish Scripture, the basic expectation of many Gentiles being gathered into the kingdom along with the children of Israel is quite plausible in an ancient Jewish context. Not only is the ingathering of the nations a regular hope expressed by the biblical prophets (e.g., Isa 11:6-10; 42:1-12; 56:6-8; 66:23; Mic 4:1-3; Zech 8:21; 14:16), and, in various forms, in the Second Temple period (e.g., *Jub.* 2:28; *4 Ezra* 3:36; *2 Bar.* 42:5; 68:5; 72:2-6; *Sib. Or.* 4:493-500; 7:702-75), and some rabbinic texts (e.g., *t. Sanh.* 13:2). Above all, the prophet Isaiah explicitly states that the eschatological feast will be both for God's "people" (Israel) and "for all peoples" (the Gentiles) (Isa 25:6-8). Those who would argue that it is historically implausible that Jesus could have envisioned the ingathering of the nations to the banquet of the kingdom are forced into the rather absurd position of asserting that Jesus could not have envisioned what is explicitly described in Jewish Scripture.

Second, even Jesus' warning that some people will be cast out of the kingdom — including Israelites who presume that their status as "sons of the kingdom" will by itself secure them a place in the banquet, regardless of whether they are "workers of iniquity" (cf. Matt 8:12; Luke 13:27) — fits squarely into his Jewish context, especially his relationship with John the Baptist.[96] Think here of John the Baptist's warning to the scribes and Pharisees not to presume that descent from Abraham, in the absence of repentance and good deeds, is a sufficient condition for securing the eschatological reward (Matt 3:7-10; Luke 3:7-9). In the words of Dale Allison:

> One simply cannot come away from the Gospels or even from a very critical sifting of them with the impression that good Israelites are saved

94. Perrin, *Rediscovering the Teaching of Jesus,* 162-63.

95. So Sanders, *Jesus and Judaism,* 219-20 (who accepts the image of ingathering as historical).

96. Becker, *Jesus of Nazareth,* 67-68.

> just because they are in the covenant. The question of who is "in" is completely open, for a decision is required of everybody. In line with this, one of the notes most frequently sounded in the synoptic tradition is that of judgment. Jesus declares again and again that a harsh divine judgment is coming and that it will fall upon the people in Israel (Mt. 7.13-14, 15-20, 21-23, 24-27; 10.15, 32-33; 11:20-23, etc.). If in this respect the Gospels are not reliable, then as sources for the teaching of Jesus they must be utterly unyielding land. But if they are accurate in this matter, Jesus could not but have believed that all Israel would be winnowed and indeed that many would suffer damnation (cf. Mt 13:24-30, 47-50). The proclamation of judgment did not take salvation for granted but presupposed that people were in peril. Descent from Abraham and obedience to the Law were not by themselves going to get anyone through the gates. Why not? Because the one thing needful was recognition of God's eschatological viceroy.[97]

In other words, the warnings of judgment in Jesus' vision of many being gathered to the banquet and some being cast out cohere quite well with the teaching of his predecessor, John the Baptist, not to mention other sayings of his in the Gospels. Hence, even the warnings in Matthew 8:11-12 and Luke 13:28-29, which seem to call into question covenantal presumption, are quite historically plausible. Therefore, although Gentiles are certainly included in the multitude that come from east and west to dine at the banquet, this by no means implies the rejection of all Israel or some kind of anti-Jewish polemic.[98] To the contrary, as I showed above, the imagery of a multitude being gathered from east and west is biblical imagery for the restoration of the twelve tribes of Israel — not its rejection — from among the Gentile nations. Far from being a case of anti-Jewish polemic then, the saying is drawing on Isaiah's vision of the eschatological banquet in which "the reproach of his people" — i.e., Israel — will be "taken away" (Isa 25:8).

Third, even Dunn and Meier's suggestion that the "kingdom" in which Abraham, Isaac, and Jacob dine is somehow transcendent or discontinuous with the present world is also contextually plausible. As Dale Allison has demonstrated in a recent *tour de force* on the subject, despite the popular contention that the kingdom of God in the Gospels refers to a "reign" (dynamic sense) and not a "realm" (spatial sense), there is in fact Jewish evidence in

97. Dale C. Allison Jr., "Jesus and the Covenant: A Response to E. P. Sanders," *JSNT* 29 (1987): 57-78 (here 73).

98. Bird, *Jesus and the Origins of the Gentile Mission,* 85-86.

which the kingdom is described as the heavenly realm over which God already reigns, into which the righteous can enter:[99]

> These are the Princes of those marvelously clothed for service, the Princes of the kingdom, *the kingdom of the holy ones of the king of holiness in all the heights of the sanctuaries of his glorious kingdom.* (4QSongs of Sabbath Sacrifice[f] [4Q405] frg. 23, col. II 10-12)[100]

> [Your] lofty kingdom . . . heavens . . . *the beauty of your kingdom . . . by the gates of the lofty heavens.* (4QSongs of Sabbath Sacrifice[a] [4Q400] frg. 1 col. II 1-4)[101]

> When a righteous man [Jacob] fled from his brother's wrath, she [wisdom] guided him on straight paths; she showed him *the kingdom of God.* (Wis 10:10; cf. Gen 28:10-21)

> Blessed are you *in the temple of your holy glory,*
> and to be extolled and highly glorified forever;
> Blessed are you upon *the throne of your kingdom. . . .*
> Blessed are you *in the firmament* [of heaven]. (Dan 3:53-54, 56 [Theod.])

> [Job said to his friends:] "Quiet! Now I will show you my throne with the splendor of its majesty, which is among the holy ones. *My throne is in the upper world,* and its splendor and majesty come from the right hand of the Father. The whole world shall pass away and its splendor shall fade. . . . But *my throne is in the holy land,* and its splendor is in *the world of the changeless one.* Rivers will dry up, and the arrogance of their waves goes down into the depths of the abyss. But the rivers of *my land, where my throne is,* do not dry up nor will they disappear, but they will exist forever. These kings will pass away, and rulers come and go. . . . But *my kingdom* is forever and ever, and its splendor and majesty are in the chariots of the Father." (*T. Job* 33:1-9)

99. See the brilliant excursus on "The Kingdom of God and the World to Come" in Allison, *Constructing Jesus,* 164-203.

100. Trans. Geza Vermes, *The Complete Dead Sea Scrolls in English* (New York: Penguin, 1997), 329, cited in Allison, *Constructing Jesus,* 171.

101. Trans. Carol Newsom, *Songs of the Sabbath Sacrifice: A Critical Edition* (HSS; Atlanta: Scholars Press, 1985), 94; cited in Allison, *Constructing Jesus,* 171.

In light of such evidence, Allison reasonably concludes that in ancient Jewish literature, the kingdom of God (and its conceptual parallel, "the world to come") are ways of referring to "the upper world"[102] or "the heavenly realm"[103] or "the realm known as 'heaven.'"[104] If we may put it so, the kingdom of God and the world to come are thus not only eschatological; they are also anagogical — they exist in heaven now, and, in some texts, will be fully manifest at the end of the age.

Fourth and finally, it is worth noting that even Jesus' explicit emphasis on the patriarchs — Abraham, Isaac, and Jacob — participating in the banquet of the kingdom finds several remarkable parallels in a trajectory of texts from the Second Temple period to the rabbinic literature.[105] These traditions likewise depict the age of salvation as a transcendent banquet with the resurrected patriarchs:

> And he [the "new priest"] shall open *the gates of paradise;* he shall remove the sword that has threatened since Adam, and *he will grant to the saints to eat of the tree of life. . . . Then Abraham, Isaac, and Jacob will rejoice,* and I [Levi] shall be glad, and all the saints shall be clothed in righteousness. (*T. Levi* 18:10, 14)

> Another explanation of "He shall dwell *on high*" [Isa 33:16]. It is written, "For the Lord thy God bringeth thee into *a good land*" [Deut 8:7] — to see *the table that is prepared in Paradise,* as it says, "I shall walk before the Lord in the lands of the living" [Ps 116:9]. *He [God] as it were sits above the patriarchs, and the patriarchs and all the righteous sit in his midst,* as it says, "And they sit down at Thy feet" [Deut 33:3], *and He distributes portions to them.* Should you wonder at this, then recall how even in this world He placed Himself between the two cherubim for their sake . . . then how much more will this be so in Paradise! *He will bring them the fruit from*

102. Allison, *Constructing Jesus,* 172.

103. Allison, *Constructing Jesus,* 173.

104. Allison, *Constructing Jesus,* 173.

105. Perrin, *Rediscovering the Teaching of Jesus,* 162. One ancient Jewish text describes Adam and the patriarchs dining at the banquet in "the Paradise of Eden" (2 *En.* 42:3-5). Another describes Jacob being invited to "the feast of redemption" (*Midrash on Psalms* 14:7). Still another says that the prophet Elijah had a vision of "Abraham, Isaac, and Jacob, and all the pious" sitting and eating "delicacies" in "the middle of the Garden of Eden" at a banquet prepared by God himself. (*Sefer Eliahu,* in *Bet haMidrash* 3:67). See Johannes Behm, "*deipnon, deipneō,*" *TDNT* 2:34-35.

> *the Garden of Eden and will feed them from the Tree of Life.* Who will be the first to say Grace? All will respectfully request God to order one to say Grace; He will bid Michael say it; and he will bid Gabriel, and Gabriel *the patriarchs,* and they will give the honour to David, saying, "It befits an earthly king to bless the Heavenly King." They will hand over the cup to David, who will say, "I will lift up the cup of salvation and call upon the name of the Lord." . . . Hence "For the LORD thy God bringeth thee into a good land," and for this reason does it say, "He shall dwell on high." (*Exod. Rab.* 25.8)[106]

Although this rabbinic tradition dates from centuries after the time of Jesus, its similarity with the oracle about dining with the patriarchs at the kingdom banquet is remarkable. First, it explicitly describes the banquet of salvation as taking place with the patriarchs (Abraham, Isaac, and Jacob). Second, it situates the banquet with the patriarchs in Paradise, which exists "on high" — i.e., in heaven. At this heavenly feast, the long-dead patriarchs dine on the fruit of the Tree of Life and drink wine from the fruit from the Garden of Eden. Third, it identifies the promised land with the heavenly realm: Paradise is the true "good land" to which Israel will be gathered and in which the patriarchs and the people of God will feast forever. In short, if ancient Jewish sources such as these could describe the banquet with the patriarchs as both eschatological and heavenly, it seems reasonable to conclude that Jesus could have done likewise, especially when the Gospels provide us concrete evidence that he did.

Coherence: The Kingdom, the Twelve Tribes, and Losing Salvation

A second argument in favor of the historical plausibility of Matthew 8:11-12 and Luke 13:28-29 is that the substance of these sayings coheres perfectly with a wide array of other data about Jesus given us in the Gospels.[107]

For one thing, it should go without saying that the saying coheres with Jesus' characteristic focus on the "kingdom" of God, as well as the evidence that Jesus depicted the kingdom using the imagery of a banquet (Matt 22:1-14; Luke 14:15-24; Matt 26:29; Mark 14:25; Luke 22:15-18, 28-30; cf. Luke 12:35-40).[108] In

106. Trans. in Maurice Simon, *Midrash Rabbah* (10 vols.; London/New York: Soncino Press, 1983), 3:309-10.

107. Beasley-Murray, *Jesus and the Kingdom of God*, 172.

108. Perrin, *Rediscovering the Teaching of Jesus*, 163.

light of such evidence E. P. Sanders once concluded that it is "almost beyond the shadow of doubt" that Jesus "depicted the kingdom in metaphorical terms, including that of a banquet."[109] As we will see momentarily, the joining together of the hope for the eschatological banquet and the imagery of the kingdom of God is also congruent with Jesus' promise not to drink of the fruit of the vine at the Last Supper until the advent (in some form) of the kingdom (Matt 26:29; Mark 14:25; Luke 22:15-18).[110]

Moreover, the saying coheres perfectly with Jesus' selection of the Twelve disciples as a prophetic sign of the eschatological restoration of Israel (e.g., Matt 19:28; Luke 22:28-30). If, as I suggested above, the multitudes coming from east and west do in fact include the so-called "lost tribes of Israel" scattered among the Gentile nations, then Jesus' gathering of the Twelve around him is a perfect complement to the imagery of the many coming from east and west to the kingdom banquet. In the words of N. T. Wright:

> From the historian's point of view, one would strongly expect that anyone announcing the kingdom, and offering this critique of his contemporaries, would envisage that part of the result of his work would be the ingathering of the nations of which the prophets had spoken.[111]

Indeed, when the fact that the restoration of Israel is tied to the conversion of the nations is kept in mind, there is nothing historically implausible about Jesus uttering a saying that positively envisions the eschatological ingathering of both Israel and the Gentiles. As we saw above, the ingathering of the Gentiles, although described with different emphases in different places, is repeatedly spoken of by the prophets in Jewish Scripture (e.g., Isaiah 43, 66; Zechariah 8, 14, etc.).[112] Hence, the vision of the conversion and ingathering of the Gentiles into the kingdom is completely plausible on the lips of a first-century Jewish eschatological prophet like Jesus, who was deeply rooted in Jewish Scripture.[113] As a result, those who argue that the vision of salvation for the nations is too continuous with the early church fail to see that to the extent that Jesus aimed at the restoration of all twelve tribes of Israel, the ingathering of the Gentiles was but a logical extension of this.

109. Sanders, *Jesus and Judaism,* 307.

110. Meier, *A Marginal Jew,* 2:316.

111. Wright, *Jesus and the Victory of God,* 309.

112. For many more texts, see Bird, *Jesus and the Origins of the Gentile Mission,* 25-29; Jeremias, *Jesus' Promise to the Nations,* 57-62.

113. See esp. Bird, *Jesus and the Origins of the Gentile Mission,* 26-45, et passim.

Finally, with reference to its more negative dimensions, the oracle is also congruent with other sayings of Jesus that strongly criticize any presumption of salvation based on (apparent) membership in the covenant family of Abraham.[114] He frequently speaks of the salvation of one group that heeds his message and then opposes them to another group, which rejects the invitation, and, as a result, loses its salvation: think here of the parable of the royal wedding feast (Matt 22:1-14) and the parable of the great banquet (Luke 14:15-24), as well the parable of the wicked tenants (Matt 21:33-46; Mark 12:1-12; Luke 20:9-19).[115] Indeed, such warning is consistent with "many similar utterances" attributed to Jesus in which those who reject his message lose their place in the kingdom of salvation.[116] For example, Jesus condemns his generation by comparing them to unruly children who reject both his message and the message of John the Baptist (Matt 11:16-18; Luke 7:31-35). He condemns the cities of Chorazin, Bethsaida, and Capernaum for failing to respond to his message of salvation, and declares that wicked Gentile cities such as Sodom, Tyre, and Sidon would have responded more positively to his preaching of the kingdom (Matt 11:21-24; Luke 10:13-15). Perhaps most significant, he even declares that the wicked among his own generation of fellow Israelites will be judged by both penitent and pious Gentiles such as the Ninevites or the Queen of Sheba on judgment day (Matt 12:41-42; Luke 11:31-32). In short, a host of sayings of Jesus strewn throughout the Gospels are animated by precisely the same logic we find in the description of the kingdom banquet with the patriarchs. Hence, despite the objections of some scholars, there are ample data to suggest that the material in Matthew 8:11-12 and Luke 13:28-29 coheres quite well with what we know about Jesus from elsewhere.

Effects: The Gentile Mission and the Eucharistic Kingdom of God

Third and finally, Jesus' vision of the many coming from east and west to dine in the kingdom also displays a consequential continuity with the practice and belief of early Christianity, in at least two ways.

114. Bird, *Jesus and the Origins of the Gentile Mission,* 86; Becker, *Jesus of Nazareth,* 67-68; Bornkamm, *Jesus of Nazareth,* 78.

115. See Brant Pitre, "Jesus, the Messianic Wedding Banquet, and the Restoration of Israel," *Letter & Spirit* 8 (2013): 35-54, for a discussion of Matt 22:1-14 in this regard.

116. Reiser, *Jesus and Judgment,* 240-41; see also Bird, *Jesus and the Origins of the Gentile Mission,* 8, citing Dunn, *Jesus Remembered,* 415 n. 173; Becker, *Jesus of Nazareth,* 68; Wright, *Jesus and the Victory of God,* 183, 328; Beasley-Murray, *Jesus and the Kingdom of God,* 172-73.

First, the vision of Israel and the Gentiles dining with the resurrected patriarchs in the kingdom of God provides a plausible explanation for both the origin of the Gentile mission in the early church as well as the lack of clarity about exactly when and how such a mission should be carried out. As E. P. Sanders has noted in his discussion of Jesus' teachings about the banquet:

> As far as we can see from Galatians, as I have pointed out before, no Christian group objected to the Gentile mission; they disagreed only as to its terms and conditions. Matt 10.5f could conceivably show that there was a hard-line group not mentioned in Galatians, one which positively opposed the Gentile mission. *But the overwhelming impression is that Jesus started a movement which came to see the Gentile mission as a logical extension of itself.*[117]

This is an important observation when considering the plausibility of the effects of Jesus' teaching about both Israelites and Gentiles being gathered into the banquet of the kingdom. Jesus' oracle about the banquet with the patriarchs, when interpreted in the light of its Old Testament background, clearly presupposes that some Gentiles will have a place in the eschatological kingdom of God. However, it leaves quite open the question of *when* those Gentiles will come in, as well as *how* they will be admitted into the kingdom. Will their inclusion only take place at the end of history, when the kingdom comes in its fullness, as some commentators have assumed?[118] Or does the saying presuppose a mission to the Gentiles, in which they will come to the banquet of the kingdom because they have been invited to the banquet, as described in the book of Isaiah (Isa 66:18-21) or in other parables of the kingdom (Matt 22:1-14; Luke 14:15-24)? In other words, the teaching of Jesus in Matthew 8:11-12 and Luke 13:28-30 is clear enough about the presence of the Gentiles to explain why the early church ultimately included the nations in its proclamation of the kingdom but vague enough to explain how it was that the earliest Jewish Christians seemed a bit unsure about the when and how of Gentile entry into the assembly of Jesus' disciples. Hence, the passage passes what Theissen and Winter refer to as the "criterion of plausibility of effects" with flying colors, giving us a very important piece of the historical puzzle that sheds light on the early Christian Gentile mission.

117. Sanders, *Jesus and Judaism,* 220 (emphasis added).

118. So Meier, *A Marginal Jew,* 2:315.

Second, Jesus' teaching about the banquet with the patriarchs may also provide a plausible historical explanation for the relationship between the eschatological banquet and the kingdom of God in first-century Christianity. Consider the following first-century eucharistic prayer:

> *Just as this broken bread was scattered upon the mountains*
> *And then was gathered together and became one,*
> *So may your church be gathered together*
> *from the ends of the earth into your kingdom;*
> for yours is the glory and the power through Jesus Christ forever.
> But let no one eat or drink of your Eucharist except those who have been baptized into the name of the Lord, for the Lord has also spoken concerning this: "Do not give what is holy to dogs." (*Didache* 9.4-5)[119]

Notice both the continuity and development that take place. What begins as a very Jewish teaching of Jesus about many being gathered from east and west to dine with the patriarchs, becomes a very Christian affirmation of the ingathering of "the church" *(hē ekklēsia)* in the context of "your eucharist" *(eucharistias hymōn)*. And the bridge between these two is the concept of the banquet of the "kingdom" *(basileia)*. This is precisely the kind of subtle combination of continuity and development that we have seen before, which can be reasonably explained by positing that Jesus himself spoke about the ingathering of God's people into the kingdom in a way that was centered on the eschatological banquet and which impacted later, more developed Christian belief.

In sum, Jesus' teaching about the banquet of the patriarchs is contextually plausible within a Jewish setting, coherent with other evidence of his words and deeds, and continuous with certain aspects of early Christian faith and practice. In light of such considerations, we can conclude, along with the majority of scholars, there are good reasons to conclude that the substance of the teaching in Matthew 8:11-12 and Luke 13:28-29 has its historical origin with Jesus himself.[120]

119. Trans. in Michael W. Holmes, *The Apostolic Fathers: Greek Texts and English Translations* (3rd ed.; Grand Rapids: Baker Academic, 2007).

120. Meier, *A Marginal Jew,* 2:316.

Jesus' Vow at the Last Supper[121]

In chapter 5, I argued at some length that, by means of the words of institution, Jesus revealed to the twelve disciples that he saw himself as the eschatological Passover lamb whose death would inaugurate the eschatological exodus spoken of by the prophets and anticipated in early Jewish eschatology. However, we reserved our examination of his declaration that he would not partake of the Passover again until doing so in the kingdom of God for this chapter. Now that we have had a chance to explore Jewish ideas about the messianic banquet, as well as two of Jesus' parables of the banquet of the kingdom, we can now turn to the evidence in the Gospels in which Jesus forges a link between the

121. See Nicholas Perrin, "The Last Supper," in *Dictionary of Jesus and the Gospels* (2nd ed.; ed. Joel B. Green, Jeannine K. Brown, and Nicholas Perrin; Downers Grove: IVP Academic, 2013); Lohfink, *Jesus of Nazareth,* 255-56; Casey, *Jesus of Nazareth,* 221, 435; Allison, *Constructing Jesus,* 146 n. 518, 178, 193; Keener, *The Historical Jesus of the Gospels,* 300; Joel Marcus, *Mark* (2 vols.; AYB 27-27A; New Haven: Yale University Press, 2000, 2009), 2:967-68; R. T. France, *The Gospel of Matthew* (NICNT; Grand Rapids: Eerdmans, 2007), 995-96; Jens Schröter, *Das Abendmahl: Frühchristliche Deutungen und Impulse für die Gegenwart* (SBS 210; Stuttgart: Katholisches Bibelwerk, 2006), 25-52, 132-34; McKnight, *Jesus and His Death,* 328-34; Dunn, *Jesus Remembered,* 427-28; Lüdemann, *Jesus after 2000 Years,* 97; Theissen and Merz, *The Historical Jesus,* 254; Gnilka, *Jesus of Nazareth,* 138-39, 282-83; Becker, *Jesus of Nazareth,* 341; Davies and Allison, *Saint Matthew,* 3:475-77; Marinus de Jonge, "Mark 14:25 among Jesus' Words about the Kingdom of God," in *Sayings of Jesus: Canonical and Non-Canonical: Essays in Honour of Tjitze Baarda* (NovTSup 89; Leiden: Brill, 1997), 123-35; Wright, *Jesus and the Victory of God,* 561; Darrell L. Bock, *Luke* (2 vols.; BECNT; Grand Rapids; Baker, 1994), 2:1718-24; Meier, *A Marginal Jew,* 2:302-9; Geza Vermes, *The Religion of Jesus the Jew* (Minneapolis: Fortress, 1993), 141, 146-47; Xavier Léon-Dufour, *Sharing the Eucharistic Bread: The Witness of the New Testament* (trans. Matthew J. O'Connell; New York/Mahwah: Paulist, 1987 [orig. 1982]), 165-68; Fitzmyer, *The Gospel according to Luke,* 2:1395-98; H. F. Bayer, *Jesus' Predictions of Vindication and Resurrection* (WUNT 2:20; Tübingen: Mohr Siebeck, 1986), 42-53; Beasley-Murray, *Jesus and the Kingdom of God,* 261-63; Sanders, *Jesus and Judaism,* 147-48; I. Howard Marshall, *Last Supper and Lord's Supper* (London: Paternoster, 1980), 81-82; Martin Hengel, *The Atonement: The Origins of the Doctrine in the New Testament* (trans. John Bowden; Minneapolis: Fortress, 1984), 72ff.; Jeremias, *New Testament Theology,* 137, 290; C. H. Dodd, *The Parables of the Kingdom* (rev. ed.; London: Nisbet; New York: Scribner's, 1961), 39-40; Bornkamm, *Jesus of Nazareth,* 160-61; John A. T. Robinson, *Jesus and His Coming* (Philadelphia: Westminster, 1957), 42-43; Bultmann, *History of the Synoptic Tradition,* 265; Vincent Taylor, *The Gospel According to St Mark* (2nd ed.; London: Macmillan, 1966), 547; A. J. B. Higgins, *The Lord's Supper in the New Testament* (Chicago: Alec R. Allenson; Alva: Robert Cunningham & Sons, 1952), 47-49; Jeremias, *The Eucharistic Words of Jesus,* 207-18; Vincent Taylor, *Jesus and His Sacrifice: A Study of the Passion Sayings in the Gospels* (London: Macmillan, 1959), 139-42, 183-86. See also L. Goppelt, *"pinō," TDNT* 6:135-60.

Jewish Passover meal, his own impending death and restoration to life, and the kingdom of God:

> I say to you, I shall never drink from now on of this fruit of the vine until that day when I drink it new with you in the kingdom of my Father. (Matt 26:29)[122]

> Amen I say to you that I shall never again drink from the fruit of the vine until that day when I drink it new in the kingdom of God. (Mark 14:25)

> And when the hour came, he reclined at table and the apostles with him. And he said to them, "With desire I have desired to eat this Passover with you before I suffer. For I say to you that I shall never eat it [again][123] until it is fulfilled in the kingdom of God." And he took a cup, and when he had given thanks he said, "Take this and divide it among yourselves; for I say to you, from now on I shall not drink from the fruit of the vine until the kingdom of God comes." (Luke 22:14-18)

These data give us a prime example of why I have chosen in this study to resist the temptation to offer a hypothetical reconstruction of the *ipsissima verba Jesu* and to focus rather, to the extent that it is possible, on the *substantia verba Jesu*. Even a cursory reading of this evidence reveals several noteworthy differences in detail.

The most significant differences are as follows: In Matthew's and Mark's accounts, only one vow of Jesus is recorded, whereas in Luke's Gospel, Jesus utters one vow over the food of the Passover meal, and the other over the wine. Moreover, in Matthew's and Mark's accounts, Jesus' vow appears to be uttered at the end of the meal, just before singing the Passover hymn, whereas in Luke's accounts, Jesus' vow over the wine is pronounced over an earlier cup in the meal, and before any mention of his blood. In addition, in Luke's account, multiple cups of wine are blessed and drunk, whereas in Matthew and Mark, only one cup is explicitly mentioned (though a final cup is perhaps implied).[124] Finally, on the level of exact wording, in Mark, Jesus speaks of

122. Author's translations.

123. Some manuscripts lack here the word "again."

124. Given our limited focus on the basic substance of Jesus' words, an exact reconstruction of the sequence of cups at the Last Supper is beyond the bounds of this project. However, it is worth noting the scholarly debate about exactly which two cups Luke describes. With regard to the earlier cup, scholars are divided on whether the references should be correlated to the

drinking the wine new in the kingdom; in Matthew, he speaks of drinking it new with the disciples; and in Luke, he speaks of eating the Passover with the disciples and conjoins the language of partaking in the kingdom with the (apparently synonymous) image of the kingdom coming.

In light of such differences, twentieth-century research abounds in attempts to reconstruct the exact original form of Jesus' words, or to choose one form of the words of institution, whether the so-called Markan/Matthean version or the so-called Lukan/Pauline versions as original.[125] The particularly

---

"first cup" *(kôs ri'shon)* of the Jewish Passover, which was mixed and drunk at the very beginning of the service, just before the eating of the "appetizers" (*m. Pes.* 10:2), or whether it should be correlated with the "second cup" *(kôs shēnî)* of wine, which was mixed after the serving of the meal, but before its consumption, at the point in the meal in which the son would ask the father to explain the significance of Passover night (*m. Pes.* 10:4). I am inclined to accept the view that Jesus' vow not to drink again is pronounced over the second cup, since Jesus' parallel vow not to eat "this Passover" seems to imply that the main course — the Passover lamb — has already been served (Luke 22:14-16). Of course, one cannot be certain in this instance, given Luke's lack of specificity and the brief nature of the Last Supper account. The situation is different when it comes to the later cup, the one that Jesus identifies with the blood of the covenant. In this instance, there are reasons for correlating this cup with the third cup of the Jewish Passover meal. For one thing, Luke (and Paul, for that matter) make very explicit that the cup in question was the cup "after supper." This corresponds to the "third cup" *(kôs sh^{e}lîshî)* of the Jewish Passover meal, which was mixed before the blessing of the meal but not drunk until after the meal was completed. As the Mishnah states, "After they have mixed for him the third cup he says the Benediction over his meal" (*m. Pes.* 10:7). Furthermore, in later rabbinic tradition, this third cup came to be referred to as "the cup of blessing" *(kôs shel b^{e}rākāh)* (*b. Ber.* 51a). This rabbinic terminology finds an exact parallel in Paul's reference to the eucharistic cup of wine as "the cup of blessing" (1 Cor 10:16). Taken together, the evidence in both Luke and Paul makes a very strong case for the "cup of consecration" as being the third cup of the Jewish Passover meal. This view has led a number of scholars to suggest that Jesus' vow (at least in its Matthean and Markan versions) can be linked specifically with the fourth and final Passover cup. See, e.g., Calum Carmichael, "The Passover Haggadah," in *The Historical Jesus in Context* (ed. Amy-Jill Levine, Dale C. Allison Jr., and John Dominic Crossan; Princeton and Oxford: Princeton University Press, 2006), 343; Gillian Feeley-Harnik, *The Lord's Table: Eucharist and Passover in Early Christianity* (Philadelphia: University of Pennsylvania, 1981), 145; William Lane, *The Gospel according to Mark* (NICNT 2; Grand Rapids: Eerdmans, 1974), 508-9; Daube, *The New Testament and Rabbinic Judaism,* 330. On the entire subject of the cups, see Fitzmyer, *The Gospel of Luke,* 2:1390-91; Beasley-Murray, *Jesus and the Kingdom of God,* 262; Patsch, *Abendmahl und historischer Jesus,* 90-100.

125. For a reconstruction of an original form, see Meier, *A Marginal Jew,* 2:303. For the contention that Luke's form is most original, see Heinz Schürmann, *Der Einsetzungsbericht, Lk 22, 19-20;* Part II: *Einer quellenkritischen Untersuchung des lukanischen Abendmahlsberichtes, Lk 22,7-38* (NTAbh 20.4; Münster: Aschendorff, 1955), 82-132. For the contention that the Markan form is oldest, see Jeremias, *The Eucharistic Words of Jesus,* 189-91.

strong urge to do so seems to stem from the fact that in the case of Jesus' words at the Last Supper, if they are historical, there must have been a single original form, since by their very nature they are not the kind of sayings Jesus could have uttered on multiple occasions. Instead, they have as their context the singular setting of Jesus' Last Supper.

Nevertheless, in my opinion, such attempts to reconstruct the exact original are ultimately futile.[126] As John Meier points out, Jesus' vow over the wine is "a prime example of being fairly certain about the *general content* and structure of a logion, while not being completely sure about the *exact wording*."[127] Thankfully, we are not interested in exact wording, but in the general content, and in this regard, as W. D. Davies and Dale Allison point out, the differences in detail between the Synoptic accounts "amount to little: the sense is the same."[128] Indeed, when we focus our attention on the basic substance of the evidence we find important common ground. In all three accounts, Jesus announces that he will not partake of the elements of the Passover meal — whether the food, the drink, or both — until doing so "in the kingdom" *(en tē basileia)* (Matt 26:29; Mark 14:25; Luke 22:14-18).[129] Hence, given the fact that in this study, it is only the gist in which I am interested and not the exact wording, we will focus our attention only on the general content of Jesus' pronouncement that is common to all three Synoptics: namely, that he will not partake of the Passover meal again until he does so in the kingdom of God.

The Final Passover and the Death of Jesus

In all three versions of Jesus' vow not to partake of the Passover again until doing so in the kingdom, there are both a negative and a positive aspect. We will examine each of these in turn.

The negative aspect of Jesus' words is his declaration of future abstention from the elements of the Passover meal. Although the exact wording and order of this declaration differ in the Synoptic accounts, in all three testimonies Jesus expresses this negative resolve over the paschal cup of wine:

126. Becker, *Jesus of Nazareth,* 341. Perrin, "The Last Supper," 492 notes that interest in this kind of exact reconstruction of an original has "waned" in recent years.

127. Meier, *A Marginal Jew,* 2:305 (emphasis added). This admission does not prevent Meier, in accordance with his method, from offering his own reconstruction of the most primitive form.

128. Davies and Allison, *Saint Matthew,* 3:476.

129. Evans, *Mark,* 395.

> "I say to you, I shall never *(ou mē)* drink from now on *(ap' arti)* of this fruit of the vine. . . ." (Matt 26:29)

> "Amen, I say to you that I shall never again *(ouketi ou mē)* drink from the fruit of the vine. . . ." (Mark 14:25)

> "For I say to you, [that] from now on *(apo tou nun)* I shall not drink from the fruit of the vine. . . ." (Luke 22:18)

In Luke's account, we have additional evidence that Jesus uttered a similarly negative declaration over the paschal food, which, in context, refers primarily to the lamb:[130]

> "With desire I have desired to eat this Passover with you *(meth' hymōn)* before I suffer. For I say to you that I shall never *(ou mē)* eat it [again]. . . . (Luke 22:15-16a)

Leaving the differences of exact wording and order aside, we can conclude that the basic thrust of this evidence is that Jesus is solemnly declaring that he will not partake of the elements of the Passover again, whether of its wine (as in all three Synoptics) or of the meal as a whole (as in Luke). What is the meaning of this solemn declaration?

The first thing that should be said is that the point of Jesus' declaration does not seem to be that he himself abstains from the elements of the Last Supper. To be sure, the Gospel evidence is admittedly ambiguous enough that commentators have debated for centuries whether or not Jesus partakes of the Last Supper, with most supporting the idea that Jesus does eat and drink, and some supporting the idea he abstains entirely.[131] On closer inspection, several considerations favor the conclusion that he partakes of the meal. For one thing, Jesus' declaration in Luke that "I have greatly desired to eat this Passover with

130. Fitzmyer, *The Gospel according to Luke*, 2:1396.

131. For arguments that Jesus partook, see, e.g., Keener, *The Historical Jesus of the Gospels*, 300; Bock, *Luke*, 2:1723; Fitzmyer, *The Gospel according to Luke*, 2:1396; Marshall, *Last Supper and Lord's Supper*, 82; Patsch, *Abendmahl und historischer Jesus*, 131-39; Taylor, *The Gospel according to St Mark*, 547. Intriguingly, the point was debated in the patristic era and Middle Ages. See Thomas Aquinas, *Summa Theologica* III, Q. 81, Art. 1; John Chrysostom, *Homilies on Matthew* 82.1; Jerome, *Epistle* 30; Irenaeus, *Against Heresies* 5.33.1. For arguments that Jesus abstained, see, e.g., McKnight, *Jesus and His Death*, 287; Dodd, *The Parables of Jesus*, 60; Jeremias, *The Eucharistic Words of Jesus*, 208-12; Dalman, *Jesus-Jeshua*, 140.

you before I suffer" (Luke 22:15), when taken in context, probably should not be interpreted as an unfulfilled wish.[132] On linguistic grounds, this reading suffers from the fact that *epithymein* does not suffice to connote an unfulfilled wish without being accompanied by an explicit negative statement.[133] Indeed, when read in context, Jesus' statements suggest the opposite conclusion: it is his express intention to partake of this Passover with his disciples. Recall, as we saw in chapter 3, that in Jesus' instructions to the disciples to go into the city to prepare the Passover, he explicitly states that his purpose is to "keep the Passover with my disciples" (Matt 26:18), or to "eat the Passover with my disciples" (Mark 14:14; Luke 22:11, also 22:8). It seems reasonable to suggest that Jesus' declaration of desire to eat the Last Supper should be interpreted in this broader context, which clearly suggests his intention to actually partake of the Passover feast. Finally, despite their differences in form and vocabulary, in all three accounts of Jesus' declaration, the adverbs used emphasize future abstention, and in no way state that he does not partake of the present meal. He declares that he will not drink "from now on *(ap' arti)*" (Matt 26:29) or "never again *(ouketi ou mē)*" (Mark 14:25) or "from now on *(apo tou nun)*" (Luke 22:18). As various commentators point out, the most natural interpretation of this evidence is that Jesus is stating that, while he has just partaken of the wine of the Last Supper, he will not do so again.[134] Finally, on the level of history, it is worth noting that it is doubtful that Jesus would have deliberately broken the Mosaic Torah by abstaining completely from the celebration of the Jewish Passover.[135]

With that said, Jesus' negative declaration also does not appear to be a formal vow of complete abstinence from food and drink (cf. Num 30:2). In his study of the Last Supper, Joachim Jeremias famously interpreted Jesus' declaration as a "vow of abstinence," suggesting that the primary meaning of Jesus' words is that he was fasting from all food or drink on behalf of the unbelieving Jewish people.[136] Against this suggestion stand several

132. Fitzmyer, *The Gospel according to Luke,* 2:1396.

133. See A. M. Ambrozic, *The Hidden Kingdom: A Redaction-Critical Study of the References to the Kingdom of God in Mark's Gospel* (CBQMS 2; Washington, DC: Catholic Biblical Association, 1972), 192.

134. Marcus, *Mark,* 2:959; Fitzmyer, *The Gospel of Luke,* 2:1396; Davies and Allison, *Saint Matthew,* 3:475 n. 144, consider Matthew's account ambiguous. However, this ambiguity diminishes when Jesus' words at the Supper are interpreted in light of his previous intentions to keep the Passover (Matt 26:18).

135. Ambrozic, *The Hidden Kingdom,* 193.

136. Jeremias, *The Eucharistic Words of Jesus,* 207-18, and followed by W. G. Kümmel, *Promise and Fulfillment* (London: SCM, 1961), 31; R. H. Fuller, *The Mission and Achievement of Jesus* (London: SCM, 1954), 76-77.

points.[137] First, Jeremias's description of Jesus' words as a vow of abstinence is ultimately rooted in his contention that Jesus abstained from the Last Supper entirely. If, however, Jesus actually partook of the Last Supper, then Jeremias's proposal falls apart. Second, as John Meier points out, Jesus does not employ "the technical formula of a vow," and no mention is made of him cutting his hair or engaging in other acts that attended such vows (cf. Judg 13:5-7; Acts 18:18).[138] Third and finally, in order to support this interpretation, Jeremias is forced to import the notion of fasting for the Jewish people completely into the text.[139] By contrast, in the actual accounts of the Last Supper, all of the emphasis falls on the fact that Jesus is dying for others, not fasting for others (Matt 26:28; Mark 14:24). Jesus' declaration is focused on not partaking of the passover meal again, not on a complete vow of abstinence from food and drink.[140]

With these two implausible interpretations aside, we can say rather that Jesus' solemn declaration that he will not partake from now on of the Passover does appear to be identifying the Last Supper as *his final Passover meal* on earth. As John Meier states:

> For Jesus to affirm that he would never again drink wine (the sign of a special festive meal) until he does so in the kingdom of God is to affirm *ipso facto* that this is the last festive meal of his life in this present world.[141]

Along similar lines, Jürgen Becker writes:

> Admittedly, a comparison of Mark 14:25 with Luke 22:18 reveals that it is next to impossible to reconstruct the earliest form of the saying. What is certain is that the saying from the beginning reveals Jesus' certainty that he is going to die.[142]

Again, in Luke's account, this implicit passion prophecy is made explicit when Jesus says "I have greatly desired to eat this Passover with you *before I suffer*"

137. See esp. Patsch, *Abendmahl und historischer Jesus*, 133-39.

138. Meier, *A Marginal Jew*, 2:369 n. 66, and Evans, *Mark*, 395.

139. Marshall, *Last Supper and Lord's Supper*, 82.

140. Marshall, *Last Supper and Lord's Supper*, 82; Patsch, *Abendmahl und historischer Jesus*, 131-39; Strauss, *The Life of Jesus*, 634.

141. Meier, *A Marginal Jew*, 2:303 (though it should be noted that Meier does not believe this "festive meal" to be a Passover; see chapter 4).

142. Becker, *Jesus of Nazareth*, 341.

(Luke 22:15).[143] Here Jesus is clearly identifying the meal as his *last* supper. He, in contrast to the disciples, will not partake of the Passover again, because he is going to die. When seen in this light, the negative aspect of Jesus' declaration functions as an oblique and implicit prophecy of his imminent death.[144]

The New Passover and the Kingdom of God

In addition to the negative aspect of Jesus' declaration, there is the positive prospect of resuming the Passover banquet in the kingdom of God. Again, although the exact wording and order of Jesus' words differ in the Synoptic accounts, in all three testimonies he expresses this positive prospect:

> . . . until that day when I drink it new with you *(meth' hymōn)* in the kingdom of my Father *(en tē basileia tou patros mou).* (Matt 26:29)

> . . . until that day when I drink it new in the kingdom of God *(en tē basileia tou theou).* (Mark 14:25)

> . . . until the kingdom of God comes *(heōs hou hē basileia tou theou elthē).* (Luke 22:18)

Once again, in Luke's account, we have additional evidence that Jesus utters a similarly positive declaration over the Passover food:

> . . . until it [i.e., the Passover] is fulfilled in the kingdom of God *(hotou plērōthē en tē basileia tou theou).* (Luke 22:16)

As mentioned above, the differences in the exact wording of these positive statements are obvious. Nevertheless, given our interest in the *substantia verba* rather than the *ipsissima verba,* it is important to emphasize that in all three Synoptic testimonies to Jesus' words over the wine, there are two common elements: despite the temporary abstention because of his death, (1) Jesus will

143. See Fitzmyer, *The Gospel according to Luke,* 2:1396; Higgins, *The Lord's Supper in the New Testament,* 47.

144. Pesch, *Das Abendmahl und Jesu Todesverständnis,* 101-2. Along similar lines, see McKnight, *Jesus and His Death,* 331; Theissen and Merz, *The Historical Jesus,* 254; Gnilka, *Jesus of Nazareth,* 138; Davies and Allison, *Saint Matthew,* 3:475; A. Y. Collins, *Mark,* 567; Marcus, *Mark,* 2:967, etc.

partake of the Passover again; (2) but he will do so in the Passover banquet of the kingdom of God. If we leave aside the differences in detail, and focus on these two common elements, there are several important implications.

First and foremost, Jesus' promise of future resumption of the Passover implies that his life, though soon to be taken by suffering and death, will ultimately be restored, so that he will once again be able to partake of the feast. Hence, at its most basic level, Jesus' declaration of not drinking again is both an intimation of death and a prophecy of restoration to life.[145] As Rudolf Pesch says regarding Jesus' words over the wine: "Jesus' prophecy of his death [in Mark 14:25] has its apex in his knowledge of his resurrection."[146]

Second, when Jesus is restored to life, he will partake of the Passover banquet again, but not in its ordinary earthly mode. Rather, he looks forward to participating in the eschatological banquet of Jewish expectation. This connection between the Last Supper and the messianic banquet is made particularly clear when we focus on Jesus' emphasis on drinking again of the "fruit of the vine" (Matt 26:29; Mark 14:25; Luke 22:18). In the Bible and later Jewish literature, wine is not only a symbol of joyful celebration; it is also consistently identified as the drink of the eschatological banquet:[147]

> On this mountain the LORD of hosts will make for all peoples a feast of fat things, *a feast of wine on the lees,* of fat things full of marrow, *of wine on the lees well refined.* (Isa 25:6)

> And *in that day the mountains shall drip sweet wine,* and the hills shall flow with milk . . . and a fountain shall come forth from the house of the LORD to water the valley of Shittim. (Joel 3:18)

> As for you also, because of *the blood of my covenant* with you, I will set your captives free from the waterless pit. . . . On that day the LORD their God will save them for they are the flock of his people; for like the jewels of a crown they shall shine on his land. Yea how good and how fair it shall be! *Grain shall make the young men flourish and new wine the maidens.* (Zech 9:11, 16-17)

145. McKnight, *Jesus and His Death,* 331; Davies and Allison, *Saint Matthew,* 3:475; Evans, *Mark,* 395; Taylor, *The Gospel According to St Mark,* 547. See H. F. Bayer, *Jesus' Predictions of Vindication and Resurrection* (WUNT 2:20; Tübingen: Mohr Siebeck, 1986), 42-53.

146. Pesch, *Das Abendmahl und Jesu Todesverständnis,* 101 (author's translation).

147. Marcus, *Mark,* 2:957; cf. Gen 27:28; Deut 33:28; Prov 3:10; Ps 104:15.

> *After, [the Mess]iah of Israel shall [enter]* and before him shall sit the heads of the th[ousands of Israel, each] one according to his dignity. . . . *And [when] they gather [at the tab]le of community [or to drink the n]ew wine,* and the table of the community is prepared [and *the*] *new wine [is mixed] for drinking,* [no-one should stretch out] his hand to the first-fruit of the bread and of [the new wine] before the priest, for [he is the one who bl]esses the first-fruit of the bread and of *the new win*[*e* and stretches out] his hand towards the bread before them. (*1QRule of the Congregation* [1QSa] 2:14-15, 17-20)

In light of such parallels, Jesus' emphasis on drinking the fruit of the vine again undoubtedly should be interpreted as a reference to his participation in the eschatological banquet, and it sets his future participation in stark contrast to the foreboding prophecy of his death.[148]

Third and finally — and this is important — Jesus is not only linking the Last Supper to the messianic banquet. By promising his disciples that he will partake of the Passover in the kingdom of God, he is also identifying the messianic banquet itself as an eschatological Passover meal. I. Howard Marshall puts this well when he writes:

> We may also presume that Jesus looked forward to the future act of redemption in which God would again act as he had done at the exodus from Egypt. . . . [T]he fact that Jesus himself shared this hope is evident from his own words at the meal. He spoke of eating the Passover again when "it is fulfilled in the kingdom of God" (Luke 22:16). Similarly, we are told that Jesus took a cup of wine and spoke of drinking it again when "the kingdom of God comes" (Luke 22:18), or, if we follow Mark's version, he spoke of the day when he would "drink it new in the kingdom of God" (Mark 14:25). Whichever version of these words we regard as original, common to them all is the hope of a future celebration of the Passover in a new way. Thus there is a strong emphasis on the element of future expectation, or rather of certain hope, in the sayings of Jesus. Jesus, however, introduces a fresh element into the hope by speaking of the new Passover in the context of the kingdom of God.[149]

Along similar lines, Joseph Fitzmyer has this to say about Luke's account:

148. Davies and Allison, *Saint Matthew,* 3:476.

149. Marshall, *Last Supper and Lord's Supper,* 79.

> Jesus thus gives a new eschatological dimension to the Passover meal being taken with his apostles. The Passover meal was not merely a commemoration of the deliverance of the Hebrews from Egyptian bondage, but one which also looked for deliverance of a new sort (in messianic expectation). The connection that is now made by Jesus between the newly interpreted Passover and the kingdom of God introduces a different eschatological dimension. . . .[150]

This "different eschatological dimension" is that in Jesus' words, the messianic banquet of the kingdom is not just any kind of feast. It is a new Passover. Again, Jesus' words indicate that the banquet is not merely a general symbol of future joy, but the ultimate fulfillment of the Jewish Passover. *In other words, for Jesus, "new Passover" and "banquet of the kingdom of God" are two ways of saying the same thing.* His promise of partaking of the fruit of the vine in the kingdom forges an unbreakable bond between three realities: the Last Supper, the new Passover, and the eschatological kingdom of God. This connection both presumes and implies that the banquet of the kingdom will bring to fruition in an ultimate way the "transition from bondage to freedom" and the exodus of the people of God signified by the Jewish Passover.[151]

All of these connections with the Passover will prove important momentarily, when we attempt to integrate our conclusions about how the Last Supper fits into the overall portrait of Jesus' eschatological expectations.

What Does Jesus Mean by Partaking "in the Kingdom"?

Before doing so, however, we have to take up one last question: In all three accounts, Jesus declares that he will not partake of the Passover again until he does so in the coming kingdom:

> . . . until that day when I drink it new with you in the kingdom of my Father *(en tē basileia tou patros mou)*. (Matt 26:29)

> . . . until that day when I drink it new in the kingdom of God *(en tē basileia tou theou)*. (Mark 14:25)

150. Fitzmyer, *The Gospel according to Luke*, 2:1397.

151. Higgins, *The Lord's Supper in the New Testament*, 48; Dalman, *Jesus-Jeshua*, 130.

> . . . until it [i.e., the Passover] is fulfilled in the kingdom of God *(en tē basileia tou theou).* (Luke 22:16)

Several key questions arise here. What is the meaning of the phrase "in the kingdom"? Specifically, when does Jesus expect to partake of the Passover again? And where does Jesus expect to partake of the Passover again? The answer to these questions — which of course depends almost entirely upon how one understands Jesus' view of the kingdom of God — has given rise to a fascinating and revealing array of scholarly proposals.

With regard to *when* Jesus expects to partake again of the Passover, the answers could not be more diverse. Some scholars are vague about their answers, stating only that Jesus will resume the feast "later"[152] or "when God has completed his liberation and restoration of Israel," whenever that is.[153] Others suggest that Jesus may even expect for the kingdom to come "so soon that it will spare him the way through death."[154] More common is the view that Jesus expects the advent of the kingdom to coincide with his death, so that he will resume the feast "in the immediate future"[155] or "in the next few days."[156] Others contend that Jesus expects to resume the banquet immediately after his "present situation of distress": that is, just after his resurrection and exaltation into heaven as Son of Man.[157] Strauss famously argued that Jesus expected to wait a bit longer: his words only suggest that he would die "within the space of a year."[158] Still other scholars hold out for an interim period of an extended period of time, from decades to centuries. Jesus' resumption of the Passover would be "imminent," but would not take place until after his predictions of the period of tribulation culminating in Jerusalem's destruction were fulfilled.[159] Jesus' reference to drinking wine in the kingdom refers to a time after Jesus' final "return" at the end of time, when the Temple — after having been destroyed — will be restored and animal sacrifices reinstituted, though not as sacrifices for sin.[160]

152. Witherington, *The Christology of Jesus,* 206.

153. Evans, *Mark,* 396.

154. Theissen and Merz, *The Historical Jesus,* 254.

155. Bultmann, *History of the Synoptic Tradition,* 266; Jeremias, *New Testament Theology,* 137.

156. Allison, *Constructing Jesus,* 146.

157. Robinson, *Jesus and His Coming,* 42-43; cf. Casey, *Jesus of Nazareth,* 435.

158. Strauss, *The Life of Jesus,* 634.

159. McKnight, *Jesus and His Death,* 331.

160. Bock, *Luke,* 2:1721.

With regard to *where* Jesus expects to resume the Passover banquet, commentators (ancient and modern) are likewise strongly divided.[161] A remarkable number of scholars apparently feel no need to explain what "in the kingdom" means, despite its obvious significance. They simply repeat the expression without elaboration.[162] Others contend that Jesus expects to resume the Passover meal on earth. He will drink again when "God brings the divine dominion to earth,"[163] or when "God would set up his kingdom finally on earth."[164] Others insist that Jesus speaks of partaking of the Passover banquet in the heavenly kingdom. From this perspective, "the images of eating and drinking in the kingdom do not necessarily imply a messianic kingdom on earth,"[165] but rather "a hope for life beyond death (kingdom=heaven)."[166] The kingdom is a "heavenly feast"[167] or "the heavenly authority into which Jesus is so soon to enter, 'sitting at the right hand of Power.' "[168] Still others insist on a kind of middle ground: Jesus will indeed drink wine again on earth, but only when heaven and earth are wed to one another and transfigured in the eschaton. In this view, Jesus will drink of the fruit of the vine again in "the Messianic meal on a transformed earth."[169]

In light of such a vast array of proposals, it seems incontrovertible that how one interprets Jesus' promise of partaking of the Passover in the kingdom of God will depend almost entirely on how one conceives of Jesus' eschatological scenario of the future (when) and how one understands Jesus' concept of the kingdom of God (where). Taken in isolation, the words of Jesus themselves do not clarify these points. As E. P. Sanders writes:

161. It should be noted here that some scholars deny that "in the kingdom" should be taken in the spatial sense at all. For these, it has rather a temporal or instrumental meaning. E.g., Meier, *A Marginal Jew,* 2:307; Fitzmyer, *The Gospel according to Luke,* 2:1397. Dale Allison rightly critiques these views as based on the widespread (but erroneous) idea that the kingdom is a "reign" rather than a "realm" and points out that the imagery of a banquet adverts to both "a time and place not yet arrived . . . a place with a central location." Allison, *Constructing Jesus,* 178.

162. E.g., Keener, *The Historical Jesus of the Gospels,* 300; Theissen and Merz, *The Historical Jesus,* 254; France, *The Gospel of Mark,* 572; Evans, *Mark,* 395; Wright, *Jesus and the Victory of God,* 438; Fitzmyer, *The Gospel according to Luke,* 2:1397.

163. Marcus, *Mark,* 2:967-68.

164. Casey, *Jesus of Nazareth,* 221.

165. A. Y. Collins, *Mark,* 657.

166. Dunn, *Jesus Remembered,* 427.

167. Dodd, *The Parables of the Kingdom,* 39.

168. France, *The Gospel of Mark,* 572.

169. Jeremias, *The Eucharistic Words of Jesus,* 218.

> Does [his declaration over the wine] indicate that Jesus thought that the disciples would constitute a group which would survive his death and endure until the eschaton, or that the kingdom would arrive immediately, with no interval? Is the kingdom this-worldly or other-worldly? We find here the uncertainty which generally characterizes discussions which attempt to specify the precise meaning of the sayings material.[170]

Without conceding to Sanders's overall skepticism towards the sayings of Jesus (which I think unwarranted), it seems to me that Sanders is correct in claiming that Jesus' promise of partaking again of the Passover simply does not clarify when he expects to partake of the Passover of the kingdom.[171]

However, given everything we have learned so far in this chapter about the Jewish concept of the messianic banquet and Jesus' view of the kingdom of God, I would contend that we can offer a solid answer to the question of *where* Jesus expects to partake of the kingdom feast, if we recall two basic points. First, Jesus is speaking of the eschatological banquet. As we saw in our survey of the Jewish hope for the messianic banquet in Jewish sources, this banquet is sometimes depicted as a transcendent feast, one that takes place in Paradise, the heavenly Temple, the invisible realm of the angels, or with the risen dead (*1 En.* 25:4-6; 62:13-16; *2 Bar.* 29:1–30:1-2; *T. Levi* 18:10-11; *Exod. Rab.* 25:8).

Second, and even more important, as we saw in this and earlier chapters, when Jesus speaks of the banquet of the kingdom of God, he consistently uses the image of the banquet to depict the heavenly kingdom of God. For example, as we saw in chapter 5, when Jesus speaks about eating and drinking with the long-dead patriarchs Abraham, Isaac, and Jacob, he depicts the kingdom banquet as the antithesis to the invisible realm of the damned (Matt 8:11-12; Luke 13:28-29). This implies that the banquet takes place in the invisible realm of the righteous dead, or, as James Dunn puts it, in a place that seems to be "equivalent to heaven."[172] Along similar lines, in the parable of the Royal Wedding Banquet, a man is thrown *out* of the banquet and *into* the realm of the damned (Matt 22:1-14; cf. *1 En.* 108:12-15). Once again, the obvious implication of this contrast between the banquet and Gehenna is that the feast of the kingdom is otherworldly, and not merely eschatological (unless one is to imagine Gehenna simply as the earthly valley of Hinnom, south-southwest of the kingdom of God!). Finally, in the Parable of the Great Banquet, the invitees are excluded from the

170. Sanders, *Jesus and Judaism,* 148.

171. So too Meier, *A Marginal Jew,* 3:370 n. 72.

172. Dunn, *Jesus Remembered,* 427; see chapter 5.

kingdom not because they are evildoers, but because they choose the things of this world — property, possessions, a family — over the kingdom banquet (Luke 14:15-24). When Jesus' statements about partaking of the Passover are interpreted in light of Jewish ideas about a heavenly feast and other evidence in the Gospels for the heavenly kingdom banquet, the primary meaning of his words seems to be that he expects to die, be restored to life, and be exalted to participate in the heavenly banquet of the coming kingdom of God.

Third and finally, as C. H. Dodd pointed out, the combination of banquet imagery with the implication of an interim period points us to the heavenly kingdom:

> The figure of the heavenly kingdom determines the symbolism [in Mark 14:25 and par.]. Jesus is about to die. He will never again partake of wine at any earthly meal, but he will drink wine of a new sort, "in the Kingdom of God." The form of expression suggests something of a pause or interval before this comes about. Are we to think of the Kingdom of God as something yet to come? If so, it is not to come in this world, for the "new wine" belongs to the "new heaven and new earth" of apocalyptic thought, that is, to the transcendent order beyond space and time.[173]

If Dodd is right, and it seems to me that he is, then Jesus' declaration that he will be restored to life seems to presuppose that, after death, he will be exalted into the glory of the heavenly kingdom, where he will partake of the ultimate fulfillment of the Passover banquet in the kingdom of God. This interpretation is especially cogent when we recall, as we saw in chapter 2, that Jesus' command to the disciples to repeat his actions in remembrance of him presupposes an interval during which he will be visibly absent from the disciples (Luke 22:19; 1 Cor 11:24-25). To use Dodd's language, Jesus' words appear to imply that he expects to enter into the heavenly paradise that will only come in its fullness at the end of the interval of visible separation between himself and the disciples. Indeed, the heavenly nature of the kingdom banquet is suggested by the fact that Jesus' words seem to presuppose this interim period, distinguishing his fate from that of the Twelve disciples. He does not say "we" will not partake of the Passover again until doing so in the kingdom, but "I" will not partake until doing so in the kingdom. Despite his impending death which will make this meal his final Passover on earth, in a singular way he will partake of the ultimate fulfillment of the Passover meal in the glorious banquet of the heavenly kingdom of God.

173. Dodd, *The Parables of the Kingdom*, 39-40.

In other words, for Jesus, the kingdom is nothing less than the heavenly fulfillment of the earthly Passover meal, and the Last Supper as his final Passover is an anticipation of this heavenly and eschatological kingdom. In sum: while recognizing that the words of Jesus themselves leave the question of timetable unanswered, given everything we have seen so far in this chapter, I would argue that the most natural interpretation of what Jesus means by partaking of the Passover in the kingdom is that he expects, after dying and being restored to life, to enter into the eschatological banquet of the heavenly kingdom. The Last Supper is thus both a kind of anticipation and antedonation of the heavenly and eschatological kingdom of God.

Arguments against Historical Plausibility

With this interpretation in mind, we can now briefly take up the question of whether Jesus' declaration over the elements of the Passover meal is historically plausible on the lips of Jesus. With the reminder that we are not looking here for the *ipsissima verba Jesu,* but the *substantia verba Jesu,* we can briefly examine the question. Thankfully, in this case, there is relatively little debate among scholars, with the vast majority favoring the basic historicity of Jesus' vow.

On the one hand, a small number of scholars do argue against the historical plausibility of the basic substance of Jesus' vow.[174] These arguments, which are usually given with extreme brevity, can be boiled down to three.

First, some scholars appear to hold that Jesus' declaration does not cohere with other evidence about Jesus in which he showed no intentions of starting a new "cult." For example, according to Geza Vermes:

> Jesus' supposed mention at the last supper of not drinking wine again until doing so "in the Kingdom of God" (Mark 14.25; cf. Matt. 26.29; Luke 22.16), strikes the reader straightaway as an unhistorical "cult legend," to use once more Bultmann's terminology.[175]

174. I leave aside here those scholars who reject certain details of the various forms of the vow as redactional, since we are not seeking the exact words. E.g., Meier, *A Marginal Jew,* 303-5, in dialogue with Schlosser, *Le règne de Dieu,* 1:376-89. Others reject both the evidence in Luke and the evidence in Matthew that Jesus spoke of drinking wine "with" the disciples. E.g., Dodd, *The Parables of the Kingdom,* 39 n. 2.

175. Vermes, *The Religion of Jesus the Jew,* 141, cf. 159; cf. Bultmann, *History of the Synoptic Tradition,* 265. For further objections, see also Marxsen, *The Lord's Supper,* 22.

Second, other scholars reject Jesus' declaration of abstention in the course of rejecting the accounts of the Last Supper as a whole, because the entire event is too continuous with the practices and beliefs of the early church:

> The supper tradition has been so overlaid with Christianizing elements and interpretation that it is impossible to recover anything of an original event, much less any of the original words spoken by Jesus.[176]

Third and finally, and perhaps most striking of all, there is the argument that Jesus could not have celebrated a foretaste of the messianic banquet that was so focused on himself. Dennis Smith, an expert on the banquet in Jewish literature, formulates the argument this way:

> One might also ask how a messianic banquet can be envisioned to take place in real life. That is to say *such a meal requires the presence of a messiah,* a "real" messiah who has *full access to heavenly blessings,* not a messianic pretender or someone in the process of becoming a messiah. I do not find it plausible that the historical Jesus could have added that dimension to a meal simply by being present. *Indeed, I find it highly unlikely that any historical figure could celebrate such a meal centered on himself.* The messianic banquet is in its essence a mythological meal, *a meal that takes place on a divine level* with the participation of divine characters. . . . Such a meal takes its form from its ritual character within the context of an eschatological community. These factors were not present at the meals of Jesus.[177]

For Smith, then, in order for the Last Supper to have historically been celebrated as the inauguration of the messianic banquet, the Messiah himself would have to be present, the meal would have to be centered on Jesus himself as Messiah, it would have to entail some kind of "participation" in "divine" realities, and it would need to take place within the context of an eschatological community. At the risk of getting ahead of ourselves here (see further arguments below), it is remarkable just how well Smith has summed up the historical reasons for regarding the Last Supper as historical: namely, that Jesus saw himself as the messianic king of the kingdom of God, spoke of the immi-

176. Funk and Hoover, *The Five Gospels,* 118, and 388 (on Luke 22:14-18): the account "is so overlaid with Christianizing elements that it is difficult — if not impossible — to recover the actual event; the words Jesus spoke on that occasion are beyond recovery." So too Ehrman, *Jesus: Apocalyptic Prophet,* 215.

177. Smith, *From Symposium to Eucharist,* 235 (emphasis added).

nent inauguration of the banquet of the kingdom, centered the Last Supper on his redemptive death, established the Twelve disciples as the nucleus of the eschatological community of a renewed Israel, and saw his death as giving them access to the fullness of the heavenly blessings of the kingdom of God.

Given the weakness of these arguments, it is not surprising that the vast majority of scholars conclude that Jesus' declaration is substantially historical.[178] Joachim Gnilka goes so far as to say that its "authenticity has never been seriously contested."[179] However, as Meier notes, the reasons for this positive verdict are not always articulated, so it will be helpful to do so here, using our triple-context approach.[180]

Context: The Messianic Passover, the Liturgical Restoration of Israel, and the Hallel Psalms

First, it should go without saying that, given everything we have seen so far in this chapter, Jesus' image of eating and drinking in the banquet of the kingdom is historically congruent with his ancient Jewish context. Two additional points should be added here.

First, as a number of scholars have pointed out, Jesus' intimations of a future Passover seem to reflect an idea similar to that found in other ancient Jewish texts from the Septuagint to the rabbis.[181] In such texts, the Jewish Passover not only looks back in time to Israel's deliverance from bondage in

178. Casey, *Jesus of Nazareth,* 435; Keener, *The Historical Jesus of the Gospels,* 300; Schröter, *Das Abendmahl,* 133; Lüdemann, *Jesus after 2000 Years,* 97; Dunn, *Jesus Remembered,* 427-28; Davies and Allison, *Saint Matthew,* 3:477 n. 158, citing Bayer, *Jesus' Predictions,* 29-53 (here 41); Becker, *Jesus of Nazareth,* 341; Wright, *Jesus and the Victory of God,* 561; Gnilka, *Jesus of Nazareth,* 283; some members of the Jesus Seminar, see Funk and Hoover, *The Five Gospels,* 118; Witherington, *The Christology of Jesus,* 206; Sanders, *Jesus and Judaism,* 147-48 (with characteristic circumspection); Schlosser, *Le règne de Dieu,* 398; Ambrozic, *The Hidden Kingdom,* 196; Jeremias, *New Testament Theology,* 137; Bornkamm, *Jesus of Nazareth,* 160-61; Higgins, *The Lord's Supper in the New Testament,* 41.

179. Gnilka, *Jesus of Nazareth,* 283.

180. Meier, *A Marginal Jew,* 2:303.

181. E.g., Marcus, *Mark,* 2:920; Wright, *Jesus and the Victory of God,* 559; Jeremias, *The Eucharistic Words of Jesus,* 206-7; Le Déaut, *La Nuit Paschale,* 253. Cf. *Tg. Lam.* 2:22. Contra McKnight, *Jesus and His Death,* 334, such evidence is pertinent to Jesus' statements. As anyone familiar with contemporary Jewish Passover customs knows, this eschatological prospect remains a central feature of the Jewish Passover meal to this day. See the modern Passover Haggadah, which includes the declaration: "Next year in Jerusalem!"

Egypt at the time of Moses, but forward to the final redemption. For example, consider the following:

> In that day, says the Lord, I will break the yoke off their neck, and will burst their bonds, and they shall no longer serve strangers; but they shall serve the Lord their God, *and I will raise up for them David their king.* . . . For thus says the Lord to Jacob: Rejoice, and exult over the head of the nations: make proclamation and praise, saying, the Lord has delivered his people, the remnant of Israel. Behold, I bring them from the north, and will gather them from the end of the earth *during the feast of Passover.* (Jer 37:8-9; 38:7-8 LXX)

> *This is the night of the Passover* to the name of the LORD: *it is a night reserved and set aside for the redemption of all Israel,* throughout their generations. (*Targum Neofiti* on Exod 12:42)[182]

Once again, as I argued above, given the eschatological expectation of a new exodus in the prophets, it makes sense that some ancient Jews would also expect there to be a new (or eschatological) Passover that would inaugurate the age of salvation, just as the first exodus was inaugurated by the Passover of Egypt.

Second, the idea that Jesus sought to restore the twelve tribes of Israel by celebrating the Passover with representatives of the Twelve tribes is also plausible within a first-century Jewish context, since in the Old Testament, it is the Passover feast that King Hezekiah uses as the mechanism in his attempt to restore the twelve tribes of Israel and the unity of the Davidic kingdom.[183] Although the passage is lengthy, it is worth quoting in full:

182. Translation in Martin McNamara, *The Aramaic Bible: Targum Neofiti I and Pseudo-Jonathan: Exodus* (Collegeville: Liturgical Press, 1994), 52-53, slightly adapted. Cf. Jeremias, *The Eucharistic Words of Jesus,* 206. In the rabbinic tradition, note the following: "A night of watching to the Lord" [Exod 12:42]. "In that night they were redeemed and in that night they will be redeemed" (*Mekilta* on Exod 12:42). "Rabbi Joshua says, 'In Nisan [the month of Passover] they were delivered, and in Nisan they will be delivered in the time to come.' Whence do we know this? Scripture calls [the Passover] 'a night of watchings'" (Exod 12:42) . . . (Babylonian Talmud, *Rosh Hashanah* 11b). "Messiah is called 'first,' for it says: 'The first unto Zion I will give: Behold, behold them' [Isa 41:27]. God who is called 'the first' will come and build the Temple which is also called 'first,' and will exact retribution from Esau, also called 'first.' Then will Messiah who is called 'first' come in the first month, as it is said: 'This month shall be unto you the beginning of months'" (Exod 12:1) (*Exod. Rab.* 15:1).

183. See Brant Pitre, "Jesus, the Messianic Wedding Banquet, and the Restoration of Israel," *Letter & Spirit* 8 (2013): 35-54.

> *Hezekiah sent to all Israel and Judah, and wrote letters also to Ephraim and Manasseh that they should come to the house of the LORD at Jerusalem, to keep the Passover* to the LORD the God of Israel. . . . So they decreed to make a proclamation throughout all Israel, from Beer-sheba to Dan, that the people should come and keep the Passover to the LORD the God of Israel, at Jerusalem; for they had not kept it in great numbers as prescribed. *So couriers went throughout all Israel and Judah with letters from the king and his princes, as the king had commanded, saying, "O people of Israel, return to the LORD*, the God of Abraham, Isaac, and Israel, that he may turn again to the remnant of you who have escaped from the hand of the kings of Assyria. Do not be like your fathers and your brethren, who were faithless to the LORD God of their fathers, so that he made them a desolation, as you see. Do not now be stiff-necked as your fathers were, but yield yourselves to the LORD, and come to his sanctuary, which he has sanctified forever, and worship the LORD your God, that his fierce anger may turn away from you. For if you return to the LORD, your brethren and your children will find compassion with their captors, and return to this land. For the LORD your God is gracious and merciful, and will not turn away his face from you, if you return to him." So the couriers went from city to city through the country of Ephraim and Manasseh, and as far as Zebulun; but they laughed them to scorn, and mocked them. Only a few men of Asher, of Manasseh, and of Zebulun humbled themselves and came to Jerusalem. The hand of God was also upon Judah to give them one heart to do what the king and the princes commanded by the word of the LORD. *And many people came together in Jerusalem to keep the feast of Unleavened Bread, in the second month, a very great assembly.* . . . Then the whole assembly agreed together to keep the feast another seven days; so they kept it for another seven days with gladness. . . . *The whole assembly of Judah, and the priests and the Levites, and the whole assembly that came out of Israel, and the sojourners who came out of the land of Israel, and the sojourners who dwelt in Judah, rejoiced.* So there was great joy in Jerusalem, for since the time of Solomon the son of David king of Israel there had been nothing like this in Jerusalem. (2 Chron 30:1, 5-13, 23, 25-26)

Notice three key parallels with Jesus' action at the Last Supper. First, just as King Hezekiah specifically invites representatives from both "Israel" (the ten northern tribes) and "Judah" (the two southern tribes), so too Jesus celebrates his final Passover with the twelve disciples, who symbolize all the tribes of Israel. Second, just as King Hezekiah attempts to unite the twelve tribes by means of the Passover banquet — and not, for example, through military action — so too Jesus performs a sign of the unified kingdom at a Passover banquet. In the words of Scott Hahn: "The Chronicler presents Hezekiah's Passover as a kind of sacrament of the united kingdom intended by God. It is a sign of the unity of all the tribes under the Davidic king as well as the efficacious means or instrument by which their unity is brought about."[184] In other words, just as Hezekiah attempted the historical restoration of Israel through the celebration of the Passover in Jerusalem, so too Jesus performs a sign of the eschatological restoration of Israel through the eschatological Passover set in motion by the Last Supper. If this inference is correct, the third parallel is obvious, but consequential: just as King Hezekiah the Davidide takes the initiative in celebrating the Passover of the kingdom of Israel, so too Jesus — acting in the role of the messianic king — takes the initiative in celebrating the new Passover of the kingdom of God.

Third, if the "hymn" sung by Jesus and the disciples at the Last Supper (Matt 26:30; Mark 14:26) does, as many scholars believe, correspond to the Passover songs later known as the Hallel psalms (see Psalms 113–118), then this would provide a powerful support to the contention that Jesus united his own imminent suffering, death, and vindication with the Passover sacrifice and meal. For these psalms describe the suffering "servant" *('ebed)* of YHWH, who offers a sacrifice of thanksgiving for deliverance from death. Imagine Jesus singing the following psalms at the Last Supper:

> *The snares of death encompassed me;*
> *the pangs of Sheol laid hold on me;*
> I suffered distress and anguish.
> Then I called on the name of the LORD:
> "O LORD, I beseech you, save my life!" . . .
> You have delivered my soul from death,
> my eyes from tears, my feet from stumbling;
> I walk before the LORD in the land of the living. . . .
> What shall I render to the LORD for all his bounty to me?
> *I shall lift up the cup of salvation*
> *and call on the name of the LORD. . . .*
> Precious in the sight of the LORD
> is the death of his holy ones.

184. Scott W. Hahn, *The Kingdom of God as Liturgical Empire: A Theological Commentary on 1-2 Chronicles* (Grand Rapids: Baker Academic, 2012), 181.

O L*ORD*, *I am your servant;*
I am your servant; the son of your handmaid.
You have loosed my bonds;
I will offer you *the sacrifice of thanksgiving,*
and call on the name of the LORD. (Ps 116:3-4, 8-9, 12-13, 15-17)

Out of my distress I called to the L*ORD;*
the L*ORD answered me and set me free. . . .*
I shall not die, but I shall live,
and recount the deeds of the LORD.
The LORD has chastened me sorely,
but he has not given me over to death.
Open to me the gates of righteousness,
that I may enter through them and give thanks to the LORD.
This is the gate of the LORD;
the righteous shall enter through it.
I thank you because you have answered me and become my salvation.
The stone which the builders rejected has become the head of the corner.
This is the LORD's doing; it is marvelous in our eyes. (Ps 118:5, 17-23)

It is beyond the boundaries of this study to trace out the possible connections between this passage and evidence elsewhere in the Gospels that Jesus saw himself as the "stone" rejected by the builders (Matt 21:33-43; Mark 12:1-12; Luke 20:9-18).[185] For now, the only point I wish to make is that Psalms 116 and 118, if sung at Passover in the first century — and even scholars who are skeptical of a pre-70 "Seder" meal accept the singing of the Hallel psalms as early[186] — constitute almost a kind of "script" for the servant of God who offers a sacrifice of thanksgiving for deliverance from suffering and death. If Jesus sang these Jewish hymns at the Last Supper, it would have been easy for him

185. See Barber, "The Historical Jesus and Cultic Restoration Eschatology," 354-409; Bird, *Jesus and the Origins of the Gentile Mission,* 158-59; Wright, *Jesus and the Victory of God,* 497-501; Evans, *Jesus and His Contemporaries,* 397-401; Seyoon Kim, "Jesus — The Son of God, the Stone, the Son of Man, and the Servant: The Role of Zechariah in the Self-Identification of Jesus," *Tradition and Interpretation in the New Testament: Essays in Honor of E. Earle Ellis* (ed. G. F. Hawthorne and O. Betz; Tübingen: Mohr-Siebeck; Grand Rapids: Eerdmans, 1987), 134-38.

186. E.g., I. J. Yuval, "Easter and Passover," in *Passover and Easter: Origin and History to Modern Times* (ed. Paul F. Bradshaw and Lawrence A. Hoffman; Notre Dame: University of Notre Dame, 2000), 117: "During the time of the Temple the celebration of Passover included two main components, the sacrificial meal and the *Hallel.*"

to see his own fate outlined in the words of the suffering servant described in the Psalter.[187]

If these psalms were sung during the first-century Jewish Passover, they would provide a contextually plausible background for the eschatological scenario I have been arguing for throughout this book: Jesus not only expected to die in the eschatological Passover as the suffering Servant and eschatological Passover lamb, he also expected to be raised from the dead and to enter into the heavenly promised land in his own personal exodus. Though he would presumably descend into "Sheol" like the other dead, he would do so as the messianic deliverer of the dead. He would bring about the end of their exile from the heavenly promised land, so that they too might "walk in the land of the living" and lift up "the cup of salvation" in the heavenly kingdom of God (Ps 116:3, 9, 13). In this light, it is no wonder that Jesus and his disciples sang the Passover hymns at the institution of the new Passover. Amazingly, the script for this scenario was laid out for him in the Passover psalms, and buttressed by their eschatological interpretation in ancient Jewish tradition.

Coherence: The Kingdom, Eschatology, and the Ascension of the Son of Man

Jesus' declaration that he will not partake of the Passover until doing so in the kingdom of God also strongly coheres with other words and deeds of Jesus.[188]

187. In this regard, it is fascinating to note that later rabbinic tradition explicitly connects the singing of the Passover Hallel psalms (Psalms 113–118) with both the tribulation of the Messiah and the resurrection of the dead: "Why do we recite this [the Passover Hallel]? Because it includes the following five things: The exodus from Egypt, the dividing of the Red Sea, the giving of the Torah, *the resurrection of the dead, and the pangs of Messiah.* The exodus from Egypt, as it is written, 'When Israel came forth out of Egypt' (Ps 114:1); the dividing of the Red Sea: 'The sea saw it, and fled' (Ps 114:3); the giving of the Torah: 'The mountains skipped like rams' (Ps 114:4); resurrection of the dead: 'I shall walk before the LORD' (Ps 116:9); the pangs of the Messiah: 'Not unto us, O LORD, not unto us'" (Ps 115:1) (Babylonian Talmud, *Pesaḥim* 118a). From this point of view, just as Jesus associates his final Passover meal with his own death and resurrection, so too this rabbinic tradition directly associates the Passover Hallel psalms with the future suffering of the Messiah and the eschatological resurrection of the dead. As I have argued elsewhere, Jesus saw himself as undergoing the tribulation of the messiah in his own person; see Pitre, *Jesus, the Tribulation, and the End of the Exile,* 381-504 (though I was unaware of this connection with the Passover psalms when I wrote that book).

188. Although I have repeatedly urged that the exact wording of the vow is impossible

First, it should go without saying that Jesus' declaration about the eating and drinking in the kingdom of God coheres perfectly with his overall emphasis on the coming "kingdom of God" (e.g., Matt 8:11-12; 12:28; Luke 13:28-29; Mark 9:1; 10:23; Luke 11:20; 17:20-21; John 3:3, 5, etc.). Indeed, it is precisely because of this case of coherence that scholars otherwise disposed to regard the words of institution as largely unhistorical nevertheless conclude that the vow goes back to him.[189]

Second, his language of the kingdom banquet at the Last Supper dovetails perfectly with his apparently common practice of table-fellowship as a sign of the coming age of salvation.[190] As John Meier states:

> The Last Supper does not stand in splendid isolation. It is instead quite literally the "last" of a whole series of meals symbolizing the final feast in the kingdom of God. There is therefore nothing strange about Jesus' holding a special symbolic meal with his disciples (especially if he sensed his approaching arrest or death) or about his connecting the meal with the coming of the kingdom of God.[191]

Along these lines, Jesus' reference to the kingdom banquet at the Last Supper would constitute a kind of climax to his characteristic acts of dining with others as a sign of the impending fellowship of the kingdom (e.g., Mark 2:15-16; Matt 9:9-13; Luke 5:27-32; Matt 11:18-19; Luke 7:33-34).

Third, the eschatological thrust of Jesus' words over the Passover elements meshes nicely with his overall eschatological outlook, in a couple of key ways.[192] As we just saw above, depiction of the coming kingdom as a banquet

---

to reconstruct, it is worth noting that the words "I say to you" *(legō de hymin),* present in all three Synoptic accounts of Jesus' vow (Matt 26:29; Mark 14:25; Luke 22:16, 18), undoubtedly seems to have been Jesus' distinctive way of speaking (see Meier, *A Marginal Jew,* 2:305). In the four Gospels, Jesus uses the phrase "I say to you," usually accompanied by the prefatory "amen," at least sixty-eight times. Jeremias, *New Testament Theology,* 35, provides a remarkable list of examples: Matt 5:18, 26; 8:10; 10:15; 11:11; 13:17; 18:13; 23:36; 24:47; Mark 3:28; 8:12; 9:1, 41; 10:15, 29; 11:23; 12:43; 13:30; 14:9, 18, 25, 30; Luke 10:12, 24; 11:51; 12:44; John 1:51; 3:3, 11; 5:19, 24, 25; 6:26, 32, 47, 53; 8:34, 51, 58, 10:1, 7; 12:24; 13:16, 20, 21, 38; 14:12; 16:20, 23; 21:18. For those interested in the *vox Jesu,* if there is any statement that "sounds like Jesus" in the Gospels, it is the expression "I say to you."

189. E.g., Schröter, *Das Abendmahl,* 133.

190. Meier, *A Marginal Jew,* 2:303. Cf. Sanders, *Jesus and Judaism,* 20; Joachim Jeremias, *New Testament Theology,* 116.

191. Meier, *A Marginal Jew,* 2:303.

192. Meier, *A Marginal Jew,* 2:309; cf. Casey, *Jesus of Nazareth,* 435, 221.

in his declaration of abstinence dovetails perfectly with the other banquet teachings we have examined, such as the saying about eating and drinking with Abraham, Isaac, and Jacob (Matt 8:11-12; Luke 13:28-29), not to mention the parables of the Great Banquet (Luke 14:15-24) and the parable of the Royal Wedding Feast (Matt 22:1-14).[193] Moreover, even the lack of an exact eschatological timetable for the resumption of Passover fellowship in the kingdom, however frustrating it may be for exegetes, also seems to fall in line with Jesus' reluctance in other places to be exact about the timing of the coming of the kingdom of God: "Of that day or hour no one knows, not even the angels in heaven, nor the son, but only the Father" (Matt 24:35-36; Mark 13:32). Similarly, in Jesus' words at the Last Supper, the timing is left unspecified: "Its nearness, while intimated, remains indistinct; no timetable is given."[194]

Fourth and finally, but by no means least significant, Jesus' implicit promise of an imminent restoration to life after death, so that he will be able to partake of the banquet in the heavenly kingdom, also presents a striking case of coherence with his momentous response to the high priest Caiaphas during his trial. After the high priest demands that Jesus answer the question of whether he is indeed the Messiah, Jesus responds:

> Jesus said to him: "You have said so. But I say to you, from now on you will see the Son of man seated at the right hand of Power and coming on the clouds of heaven." (Matt 26:64)
>
> And Jesus said, "I am; and you will see the Son of man sitting at the right hand of Power, and coming with the clouds of heaven." (Mark 14:62)
>
> "But from now on the Son of man will be seated at the right hand of the power of God." (Luke 22:69)

Although it is widely recognized that Jesus' words here allude to the famous vision of "one like a son of man" in Daniel 7, what is sometimes overlooked is the direction the Son of Man is traveling in the vision of Daniel. Although many readers assume that Jesus is speaking about the Son of Man coming *from* heaven to earth, both his words and Daniel's vision describe the "son of man" *ascending* to the throne of God to receive the heavenly kingdom:

193. On these, see esp. Long, *Jesus the Bridegroom,* 210-19, 231-37. Cf. A. Y. Collins, *Mark,* 657; Meier, *A Marginal Jew,* 2:303.

194. Meier, *A Marginal Jew,* 2:308.

> I saw in the night visions, and *behold, with the clouds of heaven there came one like a son of man,* and *he came to the Ancient of Days and was presented before him.* And to him was given dominion and glory and *kingdom,* that all peoples, nations, and languages should serve him; his dominion is an everlasting dominion, which shall not pass away, and *his kingdom* one that shall not be destroyed. (Dan 7:13-14)

As James Dunn and others have pointed out, the Danielic oracle that Jesus alludes to before Caiaphas describes "a coming *to* the Ancient of Days" — i.e., the exaltation of the Son of Man into the heavenly throne room.[195] Likewise, N. T. Wright states: "The 'son of man' figure 'comes' to the Ancient of Days. He comes *from* earth *to* heaven, vindicated after suffering."[196] The reason for the ascension of the son of man is simple: it is so that he too might be seated on a heavenly throne, in order to rule over the everlasting kingdom.[197]

Now, if this interpretation is correct, then it dovetails perfectly with the interpretation of Jesus' vow at the Last Supper that I am suggesting.[198] Both Jesus' vow at the Last Supper and his declaration to Caiaphas appear to presuppose his exaltation into the heavenly kingdom. Both Jesus' vow at the Last Supper and his declaration to Caiaphas also imply that his entry into the heavenly glory will be imminent. In other words, in both exchanges, Jesus declares his own imminent exaltation into the glory of the heavenly kingdom, whether through the image of the banquet (as with the Twelve disciples) or with the language of enthronement (as with Caiaphas). In support of this

195. Dunn, *Jesus Remembered,* 750.

196. Wright, *Jesus and the Victory of God,* 361. It is worth noting here that no less an expert on Daniel than John Collins likewise sees the son of man as being enthroned: "The 'one like a human being' who appears in v 13 is given a kingdom, so it is reasonable to assume that he is enthroned, even though his enthronement is not actually described" (Collins, *Daniel,* 301). For similar interpretations of the ascension of the son of man, see Geza Vermes, *Jesus the Jew,* 186-88; Jeremias, *New Testament Theology,* 273-74; T. F. Glasson, "The Reply to Caiaphas (Mark xiv.62)," *NTS* 7 (1960-61): 88-93, who argues that "exaltation rather than return was envisaged" both in Daniel and in Jesus' remarks to Caiaphas (the latter cited in Dunn, *Jesus Remembered,* 750).

197. See James D. G. Dunn, "Ascension," in *The Routledge Encyclopedia of the Historical Jesus* (ed. Craig A. Evans; London: Routledge, 2008), 41-43; see also idem, "The Ascension of Jesus: A Test Case for Hermeneutics," in *Auferstehung — Resurrection* (ed. F. Avemarie and H. Lichtenberger; WUNT 135; Tübingen: Mohr Siebeck, 2001), 301-22.

198. For a full discussion with bibliography, see Darrell L. Bock, "Blasphemy and the Jewish Examination of Jesus," in *Key Events in the Life of the Historical Jesus* (ed. Darrell L. Bock and Robert L. Webb; WUNT 247; Tübingen: Mohr Siebeck, 2009), 589-668.

interpretation of these two declarations, recall that according to the Gospel of Luke, Jesus intertwines heavenly enthronement and banqueting imagery in another saying at the Last Supper.

> You are those who have stood by me in my trials. As my Father covenanted a kingdom to me, so do I covenant to you, that you may *eat and drink at my table in my kingdom,* and *sit on thrones* judging the twelve tribes of Israel. (Luke 22:28-30)

Here we have it: suffering (trials), exaltation to thrones (as in Daniel 7), and banqueting "in the kingdom" (as in his vow). The prophetic sign of the Last Supper, like the prophetic oracle before Caiaphas and the Sanhedrin, presupposes the exaltation and enthronement of Jesus in the heavenly kingdom of God.

Effects: The Eucharist, Eschatology, and the Ingathering in the Early Church

Finally, Jesus' words over the Passover meal at the Last Supper also present an important case of continuity with early Christian beliefs about the eucharist, especially its connections with heavenly glory and eschatology.[199] In several early Christian texts regarding the Eucharist, we see elements of both continuity and development that are in line with the interpretation of Jesus' declaration we have traced out here.

First is the classic case of Paul's eschatological interpretation of the Lord's Supper. After relaying the eucharistic words of Jesus to the church at Corinth, Paul adds:

> For as often as you eat this bread and drink the cup, *you proclaim the Lord's death until he comes.* (1 Cor 11:26)

Why does Paul associate the Christian eucharist both with the death of Jesus and with future eschatology?[200] One plausible explanation is that Jesus himself

199. For discussion of texts, see Geoffrey Wainwright, *Eucharist and Eschatology* (2nd ed.; Nashville: Order of St Luke, 2002).

200. Jeremias, *The Eucharistic Words of Jesus,* 253-54. A third element is not demonstrable, but still worth noting: Paul's statement that "you proclaim" *(katangellete)* the Lord's death in the eucharist may reflect technical Jewish Passover language, which draws of "proclaiming"

had done so, in his words to the disciples at the Last Supper. If this is correct, then it would fit nicely with the development that takes place between Jesus and Paul: whereas Jesus' vow is focused on his entry into and/or the coming of the kingdom, Paul places the emphasis on the future advent of Jesus himself as "the Lord." The emphasis has thus shifted from Jesus' entry into the kingdom after his death to the coming of Christ in the glory of the *parousia.*[201]

A second early Christian text that may be of significance comes from the book of Revelation, in which the risen Christ says to the church at Laodicea:

> Behold, I stand at the door and knock; *if any one hears my voice and opens the door, I will come in and eat with him, and him with me.* He who conquers, *I will grant him to sit with me on my throne,* as I myself conquered and sat down with my Father on his throne. (Rev 3:20-21)

Once again, notice the connection between possible eucharistic language ("eating" with Christ) and the enthronement of Jesus as Messiah. Just as Jesus promises the disciples that he will be restored to life after death at the Last Supper, so too does the risen Christ promise that those who conquer — i.e., faithfully endure eschatological tribulation (cf. Rev 3:10) — will be exalted and enthroned in heaven (cf. Dan 7:14-25). And just as Jesus describes his own exaltation into glory at the Last Supper in terms of participating in the Passover in the kingdom, so too does the risen Christ in Revelation describe salvation in terms of "eat[ing]" with him. As the angel declares later in the book to John: "Blessed are those who are called to the marriage supper of the Lamb" (Rev 19:9). How do we explain this combination of eucharistic language and eschatological enthronement? Once again, they make good historical sense if Jesus himself linked the two at the Last Supper. This is an especially plausible trajectory of effects when we notice that development has once again taken place, for Revelation is focused on the present participation of Christians in the heavenly banquet and their future exaltation after tribulation, rather than with the fate of Jesus himself.

---

or "declaring" *(haggad)* what God has done for his people in the deliverance wrought for his people in the exodus from Egypt and the entry into the promised land (see Deut 26:1-11, esp. v. 3). Remarkably, this language of "proclamation" would later go on to so determine the celebration of the Jewish feast known as the Passover *Haggadah* (see Mishnah, *Pesaḥim* 10:5-6). See, e.g., S. Safrai and Z. Safrai, *The Haggadah of the Sages* (repr.; Jerusalem: Carta, 2009 [orig. 1999]). Paul's use of proclamation language here may therefore constitute a first-century witness to the connection between the celebration of the Passover and proclamation.

201. McKnight, *Jesus and His Death,* 328.

Finally, there is once again the imagery of ingathering in the *Didache*'s description of the Christian eucharist:

> Just as this broken bread was scattered upon the mountains
> And then was gathered together and became one,
> *So may your church be gathered together*
> *from the ends of the earth into your kingdom;*
> for yours is the glory and the power through Jesus Christ forever.
> (*Didache* 9.4-5)[202]

Note again the combination of both continuity and development. Just as Jesus identifies the Last Supper with the idea of eating and drinking "in the kingdom" (Matt 26:29; Mark 14:25; Luke 22:18, 29-30), so too the *Didache* links the eucharist with entering into God's "kingdom." On the other hand, Jesus' enigmatic references to offering his life for the "many" (Matt 26:28; Mark 14:24) are not present; instead we find a clear reference to the gathering in of "the church *(ekklēsia)*" into the kingdom. What begins as Jesus' very Jewish hope for the ingathering of the twelve tribes of Israel and the nations has become an explicitly Christian hope for the ingathering of the church into the heavenly kingdom in a way that is directly connected to the celebration of the eucharist.

In sum, we once again find ourselves with strong examples of early Christian continuity with Jesus' words at the Last Supper. Although there are other ways one could explain the origins of these early Christian traditions, I have sketched here what seems to be a plausible history of effects. If Jesus did associate the Last Supper with the Passover banquet in the kingdom of God, as well as his own death, resurrection, and exaltation into that heavenly kingdom, it would provide a reasonable explanation for why certain early Christian writers could conceptualize the Christian eucharist as both a participation in the heavenly banquet and a foretaste of the eschatological consummation, in which they too would share after having faithfully endured the trials of this world. In short, if Jesus did indeed connect his own actions at the Last Supper with the eschatological Passover meal and the coming of the kingdom of God, it would provide a sound historical explanation for why early Christians sometimes associated the eucharist not only with Passover and the death of Jesus, but also with eschatology and the gathering of God's people into the heavenly kingdom.[203]

202. Trans. Michael W. Holmes.

203. Cf. McKnight, *Jesus and His Death*, 328.

In light of such considerations, it seems reasonable to conclude that the basic substance of Jesus' declaration that he would not partake of the Passover meal until doing so in the kingdom of God is historically plausible on his lips. By means of his actions at the Last Supper, Jesus was doing nothing less than inextricably tying together the Jewish Passover, his own suffering, death, and restoration to life, and the coming of the kingdom of God.

It is hard to overestimate the significance of this insight for grasping the "new eschatological dimension" of Jesus' vow of abstinence.[204] When this vow is interpreted in the context of the biblical prophecies of a new exodus, the Jewish expectation of an eschatological Passover, and other sayings of Jesus about the coming of the kingdom of God, it becomes perhaps one of the most revealing passages in all the Gospels for understanding exactly how Jesus may have envisaged the coming of the kingdom of God. For it suggests that, *by means of the Last Supper, Jesus is not only symbolizing but actually setting in motion the new exodus spoken of by the prophets, and, therefore, the coming of the kingdom.* That, after all, is what prophetic signs do: they effect what they signify. Just as the first exodus was set in motion by the Passover sacrifice, so too the new exodus, which will usher in the kingdom, is set in motion by a new Passover — an eschatological Passover — that is accomplished by means of his own suffering, death, and restoration to life "in the kingdom." This is, of course, not to say that the two Passovers are identical. The old exodus is set in motion by the sacrifice of ordinary lambs; the new exodus will be set in motion by the suffering and death of Jesus. Likewise, in the old exodus of Moses, Egypt was the point of departure and the mountain of God (= Jerusalem) the ultimate destination (Exod 15:17); *in the new exodus of Jesus, Jerusalem is the point of departure and the kingdom of God is the ultimate destination.*

In short, the evidence also suggests that Jesus reconfigured this hope for the restoration of Israel around himself and his disciples in several key ways. Above all, he seems to have centered his vision of the eschatological restoration of Israel on the kingdom of God as its telos rather than the geographical return of current-day exiles to the earthly land of Israel or the city of Jerusalem. Indeed, Jesus seems to have connected the ingathering of the twelve tribes of Israel into the heavenly kingdom of God with his words and deeds at the Last Supper. Indeed, to the extent that the envisioned restoration is a covenantal action, the mechanism by which he expected present-day Israel to be reconstituted and made partakers of the heavenly kingdom was through the disciples' repetition of his cultic actions at the Last Supper (cf. Luke 22:14-

204. Cf. Fitzmyer, *The Gospel according to Luke*, 2:1397.

23). If correct, then a case can be made that Jesus envisioned what we might call the eucharistic restoration of Israel, which would take place through the mission and ministry of his disciples after his death. The Last Supper of Jesus is also the last Passover meal he will celebrate before the kingdom comes. The next time he celebrates the Passover, it will be the new Passover in the heavenly kingdom of God, which is nothing other than the messianic banquet of Jewish expectation. In other words, Jesus' vow is transposing the earthly Passover into a heavenly and eschatological key: not "next year in Jerusalem," but "next time, in the kingdom of God."

Finally, if everything we've said about the Last Supper is correct, then the Last Supper is not only an anticipation of the messianic banquet, it is also a foretaste of the power of the kingdom of God. In particular, it gives the disciples a share in the redemptive power of the kingdom, which will be unleashed in Jesus' death on the cross and fulfilled by Jesus' restoration to life and entry into the joyful banquet of the heavenly kingdom. In sum, by means of this vow, Jesus is tying the Last Supper to his own death and to the eschatological Passover, and tying the Last Supper to the messianic banquet of the heavenly kingdom. The upshot of these multiple connections is that *the Last Supper is both the inauguration of the eschatological Passover and the antedonation of the messianic kingdom banquet.* Seen in this light, it may be described — to adjust the words of C. H. Dodd slightly — as "the sacrament of inaugurated eschatology."

CHAPTER 7

Conclusion

In order to bring our study to a close, let us gather up some of the more significant results of our study and apply them to the original four questions of Jesus research with which we began.

First, there is the question of Jesus' relationship to Judaism. In this regard, this study has confirmed, over and over again, the importance contemporary Jesus research places on Jesus' Jewish context. In every single chapter, our study has pointed up how deeply embedded the words and deeds of Jesus at the Last Supper are in their ancient Jewish context. The feeding of the multitude, the Lord's Prayer, the discourse in the synagogue at Capernaum, the teachings on the banquet with the patriarchs, the words and deeds of Jesus at the Last Supper — not to mention the question of whether or not it was a Passover meal — all have shown themselves to be thoroughly immersed in Jewish Scripture and traditions about Moses, the blood of Mount Sinai, the manna, the resurrection of the dead, the eschatological banquet, the messiah, the Jerusalem Temple, and the hope for the world to come. Any attempt to understand these words and deeds of Jesus apart from this Jewish matrix of meaning and their ancient parallels is doomed to failure from the outset. The Jewish Jesus and the eucharistic Jesus are inextricably bound up with one another. That I hope to have confirmed beyond refutation.

On the other hand, despite its emphasis on Jesus' Jewish context, as I suggested in chapter 1 and hope to have shown over the course of the book, contemporary Jesus research has sometimes failed to bring to bear on the Last Supper all that can be learned from ancient Judaism. However, it is precisely this Jewish context that often enables us to make sense of otherwise difficult, obscure, or seemingly incomprehensible aspects of Jesus' words and deeds in the Upper Room. Above all, we discovered that Jesus' identification of the bread and wine of the Last Supper with his own body and blood, and his command for his disciples to consume these elements, far from being impossible in his Jewish context, flowed directly out of a deeply Jewish understanding of the covenant at Mount Sinai and the hope for a new exodus. Just as the flesh of the Passover lamb had to be eaten in order for the sacrifice to be completed, so too the flesh of the new Passover lamb, given under the form of bread, had to be consumed by the disciples in order that they might participate in the eschatological Passover set in motion by Jesus' prophetic sign. And just as the Jewish Torah prohibited the consumption of animal blood because the "life" was in the blood, so too, for this very reason, Jesus commanded his disciples to consume his blood, so that they might be partakers of the life of the world to come, through the eschatological banquet of the kingdom of God. Far from being impossible in a Jewish context, it is precisely Jewish beliefs about the blood, bread, covenant, manna, and Passover lamb that enable us to make any sense of why Jesus of Nazareth could have ever spoken as he did about his body and blood.

Then there is the issue of his self-understanding. Again, standing on the shoulders of much of the work done on Jesus in the last forty years or so, this study has confirmed the suggestion of recent studies that contend that Jesus saw himself as more than just an eschatological prophet. When his words and deeds are situated carefully against the backdrop of Jewish Scripture, the Temple cult, and eschatological hopes for the future, a strong case can be made that he implicitly but repeatedly (and often shockingly) identified himself as the eschatological Moses, whose prophetic signs would not only signify the new exodus spoken of by the prophets, but actually set it in motion. Moreover, his teachings in both the Synagogue at Capernaum and the Last Supper confirm recent scholarship that concludes that Jesus spoke of himself as not just *a* son of man, but as *the* Danielic Son of Man, the mysterious royal figure who is set over and against the kings and kingdoms of this world and who was from our earliest Jewish sources (including the Gospels) identified as none other than the messiah.

With that said, this study added certain elements to the portrait of Jesus' self-understanding. Namely, Jesus not only spoke and acted as if he were the prophet like Moses of Jewish expectation, but as one greater than Moses. Moses poured out the blood of bulls and goats to seal the covenant between God and Israel. Jesus speaks of his own blood being poured out to seal the eschatological covenant. Moses fed the multitudes in the desert with heavenly bread that gave physical life; in the Lord's Prayer, Jesus instructs his disciples to pray for the manna of the kingdom of God, and in the synagogue at Capernaum he promises to give the eschatological manna of the Son of Man, which will give those who receive a share in the bodily resurrection of the dead. Moses instituted the bread and wine of the presence in the Tabernacle as a sign of the everlasting covenant established at Mount Sinai and the heavenly banquet in which Moses and the priests participated; at the Last Supper, Jesus institutes the bread and wine of his own presence as a sign of the eschatological covenant in his blood, and thereby establishes his disciples as a kind of eschatological priesthood. The most plausible historical explanation for the apparent audacity of such acts — especially within a Jewish context — is that Jesus saw himself as both the new and greater Mosaic prophet and the heavenly Son of Man from the book of Daniel, whose coming would bring about a new exodus, the final unleashing of the heavenly kingdom of God in this world, and the ingathering of the new Israel, centered on himself and his disciples, to the banquet of that kingdom.

Which brings us to the question of Jesus' eschatological expectations. It goes without saying, as the quotation from Albert Schweitzer at the beginning of the book should make clear, that this study is irretrievably indebted to the twentieth-century hypothesis that Jesus must be understood within the context of Jewish eschatology. Jesus shared the hopes of the biblical prophets, and expressed those hopes in language and imagery stunningly akin to the apocalyptic literature circulating in the Second Temple period, in particular the book of Daniel. With the exception of chapter 4, on the date of the Last Supper, every chapter in this book is, in the final analysis, about the eschatology of Jesus. The new Moses, the new exodus, the hope for the manna of the Messiah, the prayer for the kingdom of God, the eschatological Passover, the messianic banquet, the ingathering of the exiles and the nations — all of it reveals that Jesus was, as Ben Meyer once put it, "bent on" the eschatological restoration of Israel.

However, to simply say "restoration eschatology" is not enough. It does not answer certain pressing questions. In particular: *How* did Jesus expect Israel to be restored? By a geographical return from the Diaspora? If so, then what about the generations of those Israelites who had died over the centuries? Would they too share in the life of the world to come? *When* did he expect this restoration to take place? Immediately after his death? After an interim period? In the distant future? As I suggested in chapter 1, at least since Reimarus and definitely since Schweitzer, scholars have tried all too often to answer these questions without taking into account the eschatological implications of Jesus' words and deeds at the Last Supper. As I argued, Jesus' express declaration that he was inaugurating a covenant akin to that of Mount Sinai, one that was to be renewed by the disciples in his absence, provides a powerful challenge to those who would follow Schweitzer in holding that Jesus expected the cataclysmic "end of the world" to happen immediately after his death. That is of course why the words of institution were dismissed by Schweitzer's followers and continue to be ignored (or dismissed as insignificant) to this very day by those who argue for such a Jesus. By contrast, as I have tried to demonstrate, it is precisely Jesus' embrace of apocalyptic eschatology that enables us to explain how it is that he both expected the kingdom to be inaugurated by his passion and death and commanded his disciples to celebrate a ritual enactment of his redemptive death in his absence. As his teaching regarding the banquet with the patriarchs and his vow at the Last Supper show, for Jesus, as in Second Temple Jewish apocalyptic literature, the kingdom of God was not only an eschatological reality to be tasted at the "end of the world," but a heavenly reality that already existed in the invisible transcendent realm. Far too many studies of Jesus and Jewish apocalyptic have placed all of the emphasis on the eschatological and failed to take into account apocalyptic literature's concomitant (and sometimes greater) emphasis on heavenly realities. In this way, the Last Supper itself, as well as the remembrance of it to be celebrated by the disciples after his death, becomes the mechanism of the eschatological restoration of Israel. As the prophetic sign performed by Jesus with the Twelve disciples makes abundantly clear, it is not a geographical restoration Jesus envisaged (any more than it was a biological reunification of the twelve tribes), but a cultic restoration — we might even call it a "eucharistic" restoration — in which the scattered descendants of Israel and the nations spoken of by Isaiah are already beginning to be gathered into the banquet of the heavenly and eschatological kingdom by eating and drinking alongside the patriarchs and the Son of Man himself in the covenant meal instituted by Jesus.

Last, but certainly not least, there is the question of Jesus' intentions. It is only when we have sketched his relationship to Judaism, his self-understanding, and his eschatological outlook, that we can speak with any clarity at all about the contorted question of whether he intended to establish a community in the wake of his death. As we saw in chapter 1, even to ask the question of whether "Jesus intended to found a church" smacks of historical anachronism, and in no small part it has been discarded as a question unsuited to Jesus research and more fitted to systematic theology.

And yet, as we saw in our study, and as the burgeoning literature on the Jewish Temple, priesthood, cult, and sacrifices has begun to suggest, a close look at the Last Supper strongly suggests that the question needs to be revisited. There are sound historical reasons to conclude that Jesus did intend to establish the nucleus of a community that would not only endure in his absence, but be centered around and find its lifeblood in the blood of the covenant drunk at the Last Supper. In favor of such a conclusion, there stands above all the fact that Jesus not only celebrated the Last Supper with the Twelve, but that he did so as a kind of new Moses, inaugurating a new Sinai. If every other covenant in Jewish salvation history presupposed a period of covenant relationship and renewal, it is quite reasonable to presume that Jesus intended his own covenant community to do the same, even if the exact length of its duration (not to mention the day or hour when it would finally be consummated) remained unspecified and unknown. Indeed, if the Last Supper was indeed an eschatological Passover meal, in which Jesus identified himself as the eschatological Passover lamb, whose blood would be poured out and whose body would be eaten by the eschatological priests of a new cult, then the implication is that he intended to establish not only a new people, but a new cultus. This new act of "remembrance," however, would no longer look back to the exodus of the twelve tribes from Egypt, but forward to the eschatological ingathering of Israel and the nations into the heavenly and eschatological reality of God's kingdom, into which Jesus himself would enter in advance, in anticipation of the day when he would drink the fruit of the vine new with his disciples in the kingdom of God. A. J. B. Higgins was right: the cleavage of opinion over whether Jesus "founded the church" is inextricably bound up with the debate over the origin of the eucharist. If this study is correct, and Jesus the Jewish prophet saw himself as establishing the new sacrifice of a new cult — or, to put it another way, the new Passover of a new Temple — then the answer must be yes. For it is as impossible to isolate the church from the eucharist as it is to isolate Israel from the Passover. This is the community Jesus envisioned when he commanded the disciples to do what he did in remembrance of him. And this is the community he envisaged when he declared that many would come from east and west and dine at table with Abraham, Isaac, and Jacob in the kingdom of God.

Bibliography

Abbot, E. A. *Johannine Grammar.* London: A. & C. Black, 1906.

Abegg, Martin, Jr., Peter Flint, and Eugene Ulrich. *The Dead Sea Scrolls Bible.* San Francisco: HarperOne, 1999.

Abrahams, Israel. "Moses." Volume 12, pages 371-411 in *Encyclopedia Judaica.* 16 vols. Edited by Cecil Roth. Jerusalem: Keter, 1972.

Ådna, Jostein. "Jesus' Symbolic Act in the Temple (Mark 11:15-17): The Replacement of the Sacrificial Cult by His Atoning Death." Pages 461-75 in *Gemeinde ohne Tempel = Community without Temple: Zur Substituierung und Transformation des Jerusalemer Tempels und seines Kults im Alten Testament, antiken Judentum und frühen Christentum,* ed. B. Ego, A. Lange, and P. Pilhofer. Tübingen: Mohr-Siebeck, 1999.

———. *Jesu Stellung zum Tempel.* Wissenschaftliche Untersuchungen zum Neuen Testament 2.119. Tübingen: J. C. B. Mohr (Paul Siebeck), 2000.

Alexander, Philip S. "Rules." Pages 799-803 in *Encyclopedia of the Dead Sea Scrolls.* 2 vols. Edited by Lawrence H. Schiffman and James C. VanderKam. Oxford: Oxford University Press, 2000.

Allison, Dale C., Jr. "The Allusive Jesus." Pages 238-48 in *The Historical Jesus in Recent Research,* ed. James D. G. Dunn and Scot McKnight. Winona Lake: Eisenbrauns, 2005.

———. *Constructing Jesus: Memory, Imagination, and History.* Grand Rapids; Baker Academic, 2010.

———. "The Eschatology of Jesus." Pages 267-302 in *The Encyclopedia of Apocalypticism.* Volume 1: *The Origins of Apocalypticism in Judaism and Christianity,* ed. J. J. Collins. New York: Continuum, 1998.

———. "How to Marginalize the Traditional Criteria of Authenticity." Pages 3-30 in *The Handbook for the Study of the Historical Jesus,* ed. Tom Holmén and Stanley E. Porter. 4 vols. Leiden: Brill, 2009.

———. *The Intertextual Jesus: Scripture in Q.* Harrisburg: Trinity Press International, 2000.

———. "Jesus and the Covenant: A Response to E. P. Sanders," *Journal for the Study of the New Testament* 29 (1987): 57-78.

———. *Jesus of Nazareth: Millenarian Prophet.* Minneapolis: Fortress, 1998.

———. *The Jesus Tradition in Q.* Harrisburg: Trinity Press International, 1997.

———. *The New Moses: A Matthean Typology.* Minneapolis: Fortress, 1993.

———. "Q's New Exodus and the Historical Jesus." Pages 395-428 in *The Sayings Source Q and the Historical Jesus.* Bibliotheca Ephemeridum theologicarum Lovaniensium 158. Edited by A. Lindemann. Leuven: Leuven University, 2001.

Ambrozic, A. M. *The Hidden Kingdom: A Redaction-Critical Study of the References to the Kingdom of God in Mark's Gospel.* Catholic Biblical Quarterly Monograph Series 2. Washington, DC: Catholic Biblical Association, 1972.

Anders, Paul N., Felix Just, and Tom Thatcher, eds. *John, Jesus and History,* Volume 1: *Critical Appraisals of Critical Views.* Society of Biblical Literature Symposium Series 44. Atlanta: Society of Biblical Literature, 2007.

Anderson, Bernhard. "Exodus Typology in Second Isaiah." Pages 177-95 in *Israel's Prophetic Heritage: Essays in Honor of James Muilenberg.* New York: Harper, 1962.

Anderson, Gary. "Sacrifice and Sacrificial Offerings (OT)." Pages 881-82 in volume 5 of *Anchor Bible Dictionary,* ed. D. N. Freedman. 6 vols. Anchor Bible Reference Library. New York: Doubleday, 1992.

———. *Sin: A History.* New Haven: Yale University Press, 2010.

Anderson, Paul N. *The Christology of the Fourth Gospel: Its Unity and Disunity in the Light of John 6.* Reprint. Eugene: Wipf & Stock, 2010.

———. *The Fourth Gospel and the Quest for Jesus: Modern Foundations Reconsidered.* Library of New Testament Studies 321. New York: T. & T. Clark, 2006.

———, Felix Just, S.J., and Tom Thatcher, eds. *John, Jesus, and History,* Volume 1: *Critical Appraisals of Critical Views.* Atlanta: Society of Biblical Literature, 2007.

———, Felix Just, S.J., and Tom Thatcher, eds. *John, Jesus, and History,* Volume 2: *Aspects of Historicity in the Fourth Gospel.* Atlanta: Society of Biblical Literature, 2009.

Arnal, William. *The Symbolic Jesus: Historical Scholarship, Judaism and the Construction of Contemporary Identity.* Sheffield: Equinox, 2005.

Aune, David E. *The Cultic Setting of Realized Eschatology in Early Christianity.* Novum Testamentum Supplements 28. Leiden: Brill, 1972.

———. *The New Testament in Its Literary Environment,* ed. W. A. Meeks. Philadelphia: Westminster, 1987.

———. "A Note on Jesus' Messianic Consciousness and 11Q Melchizedek," *Evangelical Quarterly* 45 (1973): 161-65.

———. "The Phenomenon of Early Christian 'Anti-Sacramentalism.'" Pages 194-214 in *Studies in the New Testament and Early Christian Literature: Essays in Honor of A. P. Wikgren,* ed. D. E. Aune. Leiden: Brill, 1972.

———. *Prophecy in Early Christianity and the Ancient Mediterranean World.* Grand Rapids: Eerdmans, 1983.

———. "Restoration in Jewish Apocalyptic Literature." Pages 147-77 in *Restoration: Old Testament, Jewish, and Christian Perspectives,* ed. James H. Scott. Supplements to the Journal for the Study of Judaism. Leiden: Brill, 2001.

———. *Revelation.* 3 vols. Word Biblical Commentary 52a-c. Dallas: Word, 1997.

Baasland, Ernst. "Fourth Quest? What Did Jesus Really Want?" Pages 31-56 in *Handbook for the Study of the Historical Jesus*, ed. Tom Holmén and Stanley E. Porter. 4 vols. Leiden: Brill, 2011.

Backhaus, K. "Hat Jesus vom Gottesbund gesprochen?" *Theologie und Glaube* 86 (1996): 343-56.

Bahr, Gordon J. "The Seder of the Passover and the Eucharistic Words," *Novum Testamentum* 12 (1970): 181-202.

———. "The Use of the Lord's Prayer in the Primitive Church." Pages 149-55 in *The Lord's Prayer and Jewish Liturgy*, ed. Jakob J. Petuchowski and Michael Brocke. New York: Seabury, 1978.

Balla, Peter. "What Did Jesus Think about His Approaching Death?" Pages 239-58 in *Jesus, Mark and Q: The Teaching of Jesus and Its Earliest Records*, ed. M. Labahn and A. Schmidt. London: T. & T. Clark, 2001.

Barber, Michael. "The Historical Jesus and Cultic Restoration Eschatology: the New Temple, the New Priesthood, and the New Cult." Ph.D. Dissertation. Fuller Theological Seminary, 2010.

Barnett, P. W. "The Feeding of the Multitude in Mark 6/John 6." Pages 273-93 in *Gospel Perspectives: The Miracles of Jesus.* Volume 6, ed. David Wenham and Craig Blomberg. Sheffield: JSOT, 1986.

———. "The Jewish Sign Prophets — A.D. 40-70 — Their Intentions and Origin," *NTS* 27 (1981): 679-97.

Barrett, C. K. *The Gospel according to St. John.* 2nd ed. Philadelphia: Westminster, 1978.

———. "Luke XXII.15: To Eat the Passover," *Journal of Theological Studies* 9 (1958): 305-7.

Barstad, H. M. *A Way in the Wilderness: The 'Second Exodus' in the Message of Second Isaiah.* Manchester: University of Manchester Press, 1989.

Bauckham, Richard. "Eyewitnesses and Critical History: A Response to Jens Schröter and Craig Evans," *Journal for the Study of the New Testament* 31 (2008): 221-35.

———. *Jesus and the Eyewitnesses: The Gospels as Eyewitness Testimony.* Grand Rapids: Eerdmans, 2006.

———. "Jesus' Demonstration in the Temple." Pages 197-202 in *Law and Religion: Essays on the Place of Law in Israel and Early Christianity*, ed. B. Lindars. Cambridge: Clarke, 1988.

———. *The Testimony of the Beloved Disciple: Narrative, History, and Theology in the Gospel of John.* Grand Rapids: Baker Academic, 2007.

Bayer, H. F. *Jesus' Predictions of Vindication and Resurrection: The Provenance, Meaning and Correlation of the Synoptic Predictions.* Wissenschaftliche Untersuchungen zum Neuen Testament 2.20. Tübingen: Mohr-Siebeck, 1986.

Beasley-Murray, George R. *Jesus and the Kingdom of God.* Grand Rapids: Eerdmans, 1986.

———. *Jesus and the Last Days: The Interpretation of the Olivet Discourse.* Peabody: Hendrickson, 1993.

Beck, N. A. "The Last Supper as an Efficacious Symbolic Act," *Journal of Biblical Literature* 89 (1970): 192-98.

Becker, Jürgen. *Jesus of Nazareth.* Translated by James E. Crouch. New York and Berlin: Walter de Gruyter, 1998.

Beckwith, Roger T. *Calendar and Chronology, Jewish and Christian: Biblical, Intertestamental and Patristic Studies.* Leiden: Brill, 2001.

———. "The Date of the Crucifixion: The Misuse of Calendars and Astronomy to Determine the Chronology of the Passion." Pages 276-96 in *Calendar and Chronology, Jewish and Christian: Biblical, Intertestamental, and Patristic Studies.* Leiden: Brill, 2001.

Behm, Johannes. *"deipnon."* Volume 2, pages 34-35 in *Theological Dictionary of the New Testament,* ed. G. Kittel and G. Friedrich. Translated by G. W. Bromiley. 10 vols. Grand Rapids: Eerdmans, 1964-1976.

———. *"diathēkē."* Volume 2, pages 104-34 in *Theological Dictionary of the New Testament,* ed. G. Kittel and G. Friedrich. Translated by G. W. Bromiley. 10 vols. Grand Rapids: Eerdmans, 1964-1976.

Bellinger, William H., and William F. Farmer, eds. *Jesus and the Suffering Servant: Isaiah 53 and Christian Origins.* Harrisburg: Trinity Press International, 1998.

Bellizoni, A. J. *The Sayings of Jesus in the Writings of Justin Martyr.* Leiden: Brill, 1967.

Berger, Klaus. "Kriterien für echte Jesuworte?" *Zeitschrift für Neues Testament* 1 (1998): 52-58.

Bergsma, John S. *The Jubilee from Leviticus to Qumran: A History of Interpretation.* Supplements to Vetus Testamentum. Leiden: E. J. Brill, 2006.

Bernard, J. H. *The Gospel according to St. John.* Edinburgh: T. & T. Clark, 1953.

Betz, Otto. "Jesus and Isaiah 53." Pages 70-87 in *Jesus and the Suffering Servant: Isaiah 53 and Christian Origins,* ed. William R. Farmer and William H. Bellinger Jr. Harrisburg: Trinity Press International, 1998.

Bietenhard, Hans. *Die himmlische Welt im Urchristentum and Spätjudentum.* Wissenschaftliche Untersuchungen zum Neuen Testament 2. Tübingen: Mohr-Siebeck, 1991.

Billings, Bradly S. *Do This in Remembrance of Me: The Disputed Words in the Lukan Institution Narrative (Luke 22.19b-20): An Historico-Exegetical, Theological and Sociological Analysis.* Library of New Testament Studies 314. London: T. & T. Clark, 2006.

Bird, Michael F. *Are You the One Who Is to Come? The Historical Jesus and the Messianic Question.* Grand Rapids: Baker Academic, 2009.

———. *Jesus and the Origins of the Gentile Mission.* Library of Historical Jesus Studies 331. New York: T. & T. Clark, 2007.

Black, Matthew. "The Messianism of the Parables of Enoch: Their Date and Contribution to Christological Origins." Pages 145-68 in *The Messiah: Developments in Earliest Judaism and Christianity,* ed. J. H. Charlesworth. Minneapolis: Fortress, 1992.

———. *The Scrolls and Christian Origins: Studies in the Jewish Background of the New Testament.* New York: Charles Scribner's Sons, 1961.

Black, Matthew, with James C. VanderKam. *The Book of Enoch or First Enoch: A New English Edition with Commentary and Textual Notes.* Studia in Veteris Testamenti Pseudepigrapha 7. Leiden: Brill, 1985.

Blackman, Philip. *Mishnayoth.* 6 vols. New York: Judaica, 1963.

Blinzler, Josef. *The Trial of Jesus.* Translated by Isabel McHugh and Florence McHugh. Westminster: Newman, 1959.

Blomberg, Craig L. "The Authenticity and Significance of Jesus' Table Fellowship with Sinners." Pages 215-50 in *Key Events in the Life of the Historical Jesus,* ed. Darrell L. Bock and Robert L. Webb. Wissenschaftliche Untersuchungen zum Neuen Testament 247. Tübingen: Mohr Siebeck, 2009.

———. *The Historical Reliability of John's Gospel: Issues and Commentary.* Downers Grove: IVP, 2001.

———. *The Historical Reliability of the Gospels.* 2nd ed. Downers Grove: IVP Academic, 2007.

———. "John and Jesus." Pages 209-26 in *The Face of New Testament Studies: A Survey of Recent Research,* ed. Scot McKnight and Grant R. Osborne. Grand Rapids: Baker Academic, 2004.

Boccachini, Gabrielle. *Middle Judaism: Jewish Thought 300 B.C.E. to 200 C.E.* Minneapolis: Fortress, 1991.

Bock, Darrell L. "Blasphemy and the Jewish Examination of Jesus." Pages 589-668 in *Key Events in the Life of the Historical Jesus,* ed. Darrell L. Bock and Robert L. Webb. Wissenschaftliche Untersuchungen zum Neuen Testament 247. Tübingen: Mohr Siebeck, 2009.

———. *Jesus according to Scripture.* Grand Rapids: Baker Academic, 2002.

———. *Luke.* Baker Exegetical Commentary on the New Testament. 2 vols. Grand Rapids: Baker Books, 1994, 1996.

———. "The Son of Man Seated at God's Right Hand and the Debate over Jesus' 'Blasphemy.'" Pages 181-91 in *Jesus of Nazareth Lord and Christ: Essays on the Historical Jesus and New Testament Christology,* ed. J. B. Green and M. Turner. Grand Rapids: Eerdmans, 1994.

———, and Michael Glaser, eds. *The Gospel According to Isaiah 53: Encountering the Suffering Servant in Jewish and Christian Theology.* Grand Rapids: Kregel Academic, 2012.

Bockmuehl, Markus. *This Jesus: Martyr, Lord, Messiah.* Edinburgh: T. & T. Clark, 1994.

Bokser, Baruch M. *The Origins of the Seder.* Berkeley: University of California Press, 1984.

———. "Unleavened Bread and Passover, Feasts of." Volume 6, pages 755-65 in *Anchor Bible Dictionary.* 6 vols. Edited by David Noel Freedman. New York: Doubleday, 1992.

———. "Was the Last Supper a Passover Seder?" *Bible Review* 3 (1987): 24-33.

Borg, Marcus. "A Temperate Case for a Non-Eschatological Jesus," *Forum* 2 (1986): 81-102. Reprinted in Marcus Borg, *Jesus in Contemporary Scholarship.* Valley Forge: Trinity Press International, 1994.

———, and John Dominic Crossan. *The Last Week: The Day-by-Day Account of Jesus's Final Week in Jerusalem.* San Francisco: HarperCollins, 2006.

Bornkamm, Günther. "Die eucharistische Rede im Johannesevangelium," *Zeitschrift für die neutestamentliche Wissenschaft* 47 (1956): 161-69.

———. *Jesus of Nazareth.* Translated by Irene and Fraser McLuskey with James M. Robinson. New York: Harper, 1960.

Bovon, François. *Luke 3.* Translated by James Crouch. Hermeneia; Minneapolis: Fortress, 2012.

Bowley, J. "Moses in the Dead Sea Scrolls: Living in the Shadow of God's Anointed." Pages

159-81 in *The Bible at Qumran: Text, Shape, and Interpretation.* Grand Rapids: Eerdmans, 2001.

Bradshaw, Paul F. *Eucharistic Origins.* Oxford: Oxford University Press, 2004.

———. *The Search for the Origins of Christian Worship.* Oxford: Oxford University Press, 1992.

Braun, H. *Qumran und das Neue Testament.* Tübingen: Mohr, 1966.

Brooke, George J. *Exegesis at Qumran: 4QFlorilegium in Its Jewish Context.* Journal for the Study of the Old Testament: Supplement Series 29. Sheffield: JSOT, 1985.

Brown, Francis, S. R. Driver, and Charles A. Briggs. *The Brown-Driver-Briggs Hebrew and English Lexicon.* Reprint. Peabody: Hendrickson, 1996 (orig. 1906).

Brown, Raymond E. *The Death of the Messiah: From Gethsemane to the Grave: A Commentary on the Passion Narratives in the Four Gospels.* Anchor Bible Reference Library. 2 vols. New York: Doubleday, 1994.

———. *The Gospel According to John.* 2 vols. Anchor Bible 29-29A. New York: Doubleday, 1966, 1970.

———. "The Pater Noster as an Eschatological Prayer." Pages 279-323 in *New Testament Essays.* New York: Doubleday, 2010 (orig. 1968).

Bruce, F. F. "The Book of Zechariah and the Passion Narrative," *Bulletin of the John Rylands University Library of Manchester* 43 (1960-61): 336-53.

Bryan, Steven M. *Jesus and Israel's Traditions of Judgment and Restoration.* Society for New Testament Studies Monograph Series 117. Cambridge: Cambridge University Press, 2002.

Buchanan, George Gray. *Sacrifice in the Old Testament: Its Theory and Practice.* New York: Ktav, 1971 (orig. 1925).

Buchanan, George Wesley. *Jesus: The King and His Kingdom.* Macon: Mercer University Press, 1984.

Bultmann, Rudolf. *The Gospel of John.* Translated by G. R. Beasley-Murray. Philadelphia: Westminster, 1971 (orig. 1964).

———. *History of the Synoptic Tradition.* Translated by John Marsh. Rev. ed. Oxford: Basil Blackwell, 1963.

———. *Jesus and the Word.* Translated by L. P. Smith and E. H. Lantero. New York: Charles Scribner's Sons, 1958.

———. "The Primitive Christian Kerygma and the Historical Jesus." Pages 15-42 in *The Historical Jesus and the Kerygmatic Christ: Essays on the New Quest for the Historical Jesus,* ed. Carl E. Braaten and Roy A. Harrisville. Nashville: Abingdon, 1964.

———. *Theology of the New Testament.* 2 vols. New York: Charles Scribner's Sons, 1951-55.

Burchard, Christoph. "The Importance of Joseph and Aseneth for the Study of the New Testament: A Fresh Look at the Lord's Supper," *NTS* 33 (1987): 102-34.

Burkett, Delbert. *The Son of Man Debate: A History and Evaluation.* Society for New Testament Studies Monograph Series 107. Cambridge: Cambridge University Press, 1999.

———. *The Son of Man in the Gospel of John.* Journal for the Study of the New Testament Supplements 56. Sheffield: Sheffield Academic Press, 1991.

Burridge, Richard A. "Gospel: Genre." Pages 335-42 in *Dictionary of Jesus and the Gospels.*

2nd ed. Edited by Joel B. Green, Jeannine K. Brown, and Nicholas Perrin. Downers Grove: IVP Academic, 2013.

———. *What Are the Gospels? A Comparison with Graeco-Roman Biography.* 2nd ed. Grand Rapids: Eerdmans, 2004.

Byrskog, Samuel. *Story as History — History as Story: The Gospel Tradition in the Context of Ancient Oral History.* Boston/Leiden: Brill, 2002.

Cantalamessa, Raniero. *Easter in the Early Church: An Anthology of Jewish and Early Christian Texts.* Translated by James M. Quigley, S.J. and Joseph T. Lienhard, S.J. Collegeville: Liturgical Press, 1993.

Carmichael, C. B. "David Daube on the Eucharist and the Passover Seder," *Journal for the Study of the New Testament* 42 (1991): 45-67.

———. "The Passover Haggadah." Pages 343-56 in *The Historical Jesus in Context,* ed. Amy-Jill Levine, Dale C. Allison Jr., and John Dominic Crossan. Princeton and Oxford: Princeton University Press, 2006.

Carmignac, Jean. *Recherches sur le "Notre Père."* Paris: Letouzey & Ané, 1969.

Carson, D. A. *The Gospel According to John.* Grand Rapids: Eerdmans, 1991.

Casey, Maurice. *Is John's Gospel True?* London and New York: Routledge, 1996.

———. *Jesus of Nazareth: An Independent Historian's Account of His Life and Teaching.* London: T. & T. Clark, 2010.

———. "The Original Aramaic Form of Jesus' Interpretation of the Cup," *Journal of Theological Studies* 41 (1990): 1-12.

Casey, P. M. "Culture and Historicity: The Plucking of the Grain (Mark 2.23-8)," *NTS* 34 (1988): 1-23.

Cassuto, Umberto. *A Commentary on the Book of Exodus.* Translated by Israel Abrahams. Jerusalem: Magnes, 1967.

Chapman, David W. *Ancient Jewish and Christian Perceptions of Crucifixion.* Wissenschaftliche Untersuchungen zum Neuen Testament 2.244. Tübingen: Mohr Siebeck, 2008; Grand Rapids: Baker Academic, 2010.

Charles, R. H. *The Apocalypse of Baruch.* Ancient Texts and Translations. Eugene: Wipf & Stock, 2005 (orig. 1896).

———. *The Book of Enoch or 1 Enoch.* Oxford: Clarendon, 1912.

Charlesworth, James H. *Jesus within Judaism: New Light from Exciting Archaeological Discoveries.* Anchor Bible Reference Library. New York: Doubleday, 1988.

———. "Solomon and Jesus: The Son of David in the Ante-Markan Traditions (Mark 10:47)." Pages 125-51 in *Biblical and Humane,* ed. L. B. Elder, D. L. Barr, and E. S. Malbon. Atlanta: Scholars Press, 1996.

———, ed. *Jesus and the Dead Sea Scrolls.* Anchor Bible Reference Library. New York: Doubleday, 1992.

———, ed. *John and Qumran.* London: Geoffery Chapman, 1972.

Charlesworth, James H., and Loren L. Johns, eds. *Hillel and Jesus: Comparisons of Two Major Religious Leaders.* Minneapolis: Fortress, 1997.

Chenderlin, Fritz. *"Do This as My Memorial": The Semantic and Conceptual Background and Value of Anamnēsis in 1 Corinthians.* Analecta Biblica 99. Rome: Biblical Institute, 1982.

Chester, Andrew. *Messiah and Exaltation.* Wissenschaftliche Untersuchungen zum Neuen Testament 207. Tübingen: Mohr Siebeck, 2007.

Chilton, Bruce. *A Feast of Meanings: Eucharistic Theologies from Jesus through Johannine Circles.* Leiden: Brill, 1994.

———. *The Temple of Jesus: His Sacrificial Program within a Cultural History of Sacrifice.* University Park: Pennsylvania State University Press, 1992.

Choi, J. D. *Jesus' Teaching on Repentance.* Binghamton: Binghampton University Press, 2000.

Clancy, Robert A. D. "The Old Testament Roots of Remembrance in the Lord's Supper," *Concordia Journal* 19, no. 1 (1993): 35-50.

Clements, R. E. "Isaiah 53 and the Restoration of Israel." Pages 47-54 in *Jesus and the Suffering Servant: Isaiah 53 and Christian Origins,* ed. William H. Bellinger Jr. and William R. Farmer. Harrisburg: Trinity Press International, 1998.

Colautti, Federico M. *Passover in the Works of Josephus.* Supplements to the Journal for the Study of Judaism 75. Leiden: Brill, 2002.

Collins, Adela Yarbro. *Mark.* Hermeneia; Philadelphia: Fortress, 2007.

Collins, Adela Yarbro, and John J. Collins. *King Messiah as Son of God: Divine, Human, and Angelic Messianic Figures in Biblical and Related Literature.* Grand Rapids: Eerdmans, 2008.

Collins, C. John. "The Eucharist as Christian Sacrifice: How Patristic Authors Can Help Us Read the Bible," *Westminster Theological Journal* (2004): 1-23.

Collins, John J. "Apocalyptic Eschatology as the Transcendence of Death," *Catholic Biblical Quarterly* 36 (1974): 21-43.

———. *The Apocalyptic Imagination: An Introduction to Jewish Apocalyptic Literature.* 2nd ed. Grand Rapids: Eerdmans, 1998.

———. *Apocalypticism in the Dead Sea Scrolls.* London: Routledge, 1997.

———. *Daniel: A Commentary on the Book of Daniel,* ed. Frank Moore Cross. Hermeneia. Minneapolis: Fortress, 1993.

———. "Joseph and Aseneth: Jewish or Christian?" *Journal for the Study of the Pseudepigrapha* 14, no. 2 (2005): 97-112.

———. *The Scepter and the Star: The Messiahs of the Dead Sea Scrolls and Other Ancient Literature.* Anchor Bible Reference Library. New York: Doubleday, 1995.

———. "The Son of Man in Ancient Judaism." Pages 154-68 in *Handbook for the Study of the Historical Jesus.* 4 vols. Edited by Tom Holmén and Stanley E. Porter. Leiden: Brill, 2011.

Collins, Raymond F. *First Corinthians.* Sacra Pagina 7. Collegeville: Liturgical Press, 1999.

Coloe, Mary L., and Tom Thatcher, eds. *John, Qumran, and the Dead Sea Scrolls: Sixty Years of Discovery and Debate.* Atlanta: Society of Biblical Literature, 2011.

Cooke, Bernard. "Synoptic Presentation of the Eucharist as Covenant Sacrifice," *Theological Studies* 21, no. 1 (1960): 1-44.

Cross, Frank Moore. *The Ancient Library of Qumran.* 3rd ed. Minneapolis: Fortress, 1995.

Crossan, John Dominic. *The Historical Jesus: The Life of a Mediterranean Jewish Peasant.* San Francisco: HarperCollins, 1991.

———. *Jesus: A Revolutionary Biography.* San Francisco: HarperCollins, 1994.

Cullmann, Oscar. *Early Christian Worship.* Translated by A. S. Todd and J. B. Torrance. London: SCM, 1953.

Cyster, R. F. "The Lord's Prayer and the Exodus Tradition," *Theology* 64 (1961): 377-81.

Daaph, D. S. *The Relationship between John the Baptist and Jesus of Nazareth: A Critical Study.* Lanham: University Press of America, 2005.

Daise, Michael A. *Feasts in John: Jewish Festivals and Jesus' "Hour" in the Gospel of John.* Wissenschaftliche Untersuchungen zum Neuen Testament 2.229. Tübingen: Mohr Siebeck, 2007.

Dalman, Gustaf. *Jesus-Jeshua: Studies in the Gospels.* Translated by P. P. Levertoff. New York: Macmillan, 1929.

Daly, R. "The Eucharist and Redemption: The Last Supper and Jesus' Understanding of His Death," *Biblical Theology Bulletin* 11 (1981): 21-27.

Daly, R. J. "Eucharistic Origins: From the New Testament to the Liturgies of the Golden Age," *Theological Studies* 66 (2005): 3-22.

Danby, Herbert. *The Mishnah.* Oxford: Oxford University Press, 1933.

Danker, Frederick William. *A Greek-English Lexicon of the New Testament and Other Early Christian Literature.* 3rd ed. Chicago and London: University of Chicago Press, 2000.

Daube, David. *He That Cometh.* St. Paul's Cathedral Lecture. London: Diocesan Council, 1966.

———. *The New Testament and Rabbinic Judaism: Jordan Lectures in Comparative Religion.* London: Athlone Press, 1956.

———. *Wine in the Bible.* St. Paul's Lecture 13; London: London Diocesan Council for Christian-Jewish Understanding, 1974.

Davies, W. D. *Paul and Rabbinic Judaism: Some Rabbinic Elements in Pauline Theology.* London: SPCK, 1968.

———, and Dale C. Allison Jr. *A Critical and Exegetical Commentary on the Gospel According to Saint Matthew.* 3 vols. International Critical Commentary. Edinburgh: T. & T. Clark, 1988, 1991, 1997.

De Boer, H. "An Aspect of Sacrifice." Pages 27-47 in *Studies in the Religion of Israel,* ed. G. W. Anderson et al. Vetus Testamentum Supplements. Leiden: Brill, 1972.

de Jonge, Marinus. "Jesus' Death for Others and the Death of the Maccabean Martyrs." Pages 142-51 in *Text and Testimony,* ed. T. J. Baarda et al. Kampen: Kok, 1988.

———. "Mark 14:25 among Jesus' Words about the Kingdom of God." Pages 123-35 in *Sayings of Jesus: Canonical and Non-Canonical: Essays in Honour of Tjitze Baarda.* Novum Testamentum Supplements 89. Leiden: Brill, 1997.

de Vaux, Roland. *Ancient Israel: Its Life and Institutions.* Reprint. Grand Rapids: Eerdmans, 1997.

den Heyer, C. J. *Jesus and the Doctrine of the Atonement: Biblical Notes on Controversial Topic.* Translated by John Bowden. Harrisburg: Trinity Press International, 1998.

Dibelius, Martin. *From Tradition to Gospel.* London: Ivor Nicholson and Watson, 1934.

Dodd, C. H. *The Founder of Christianity.* London: Macmillan, 1970.

———. *Historical Tradition in the Fourth Gospel.* Cambridge: Cambridge University Press, 1963.

———. *The Interpretation of the Fourth Gospel.* Cambridge: Cambridge University Press, 1953.

———. *The Parables of the Kingdom.* Rev. ed. London: Nisbet; New York: Scribner's, 1961.

Douglas, Mary. "The Eucharist: Its Continuity with the Bread Sacrifice of Leviticus," *Modern Theology* 15, no. 2 (1999): 209-24.

Downing, F. Gerald. *The Church and Jesus: A Study in History, Philosophy, and Theology.* London: SCM, 1968.

Driver, G. R. *The Judean Scrolls.* Oxford: Oxford University Press, 1965.

Du Toit, David S. "Redefining Jesus: Current Trends in Jesus Research." Pages 82-124 in *Jesus, Mark and Q: The Teaching of Jesus and Its Earliest Records,* ed. M. Labahn and A. Schmidt. Sheffield: Sheffield Academic Press, 2001.

Dumoulin, P. *Entre la Manne et l'Eucharistie: Étude de Sg 16,15–17,1a.* Analecta Biblica. Rome: Pontifical Biblical Institute, 1994.

Dunn, James D. G. "Ascension." Pages 41-43 in *The Routledge Encyclopedia of the Historical Jesus,* ed. Craig A. Evans. London: Routledge, 2008.

———. "The Ascension of Jesus: A Test Case for Hermeneutics." Pages 301-22 in *Auferstehung — Resurrection,* ed. F. Avemarie and H. Lichtenberger. Wissenschaftliche Untersuchungen zum Neuen Testament 135. Tübingen: Mohr Siebeck, 2001.

———. *Baptism in the Holy Spirit.* Studies in Biblical Theology 2:15. London: SCM, 1970.

———. "Did Jesus Attend the Synagogue?" Pages 206-22 in *Jesus and Archaeology,* ed. James H. Charlesworth. Grand Rapids: Eerdmans, 2006.

———. *Jesus Remembered.* Christianity in the Making, Volume 1. Grand Rapids: Eerdmans, 2003.

———. "Jesus, Table Fellowship and Qumran." Pages 254-72 in *Jesus and the Dead Sea Scrolls,* ed. J. H. Charlesworth. Anchor Bible Reference Library. New York: Doubleday, 1992.

———. "John VI — A Eucharistic Discourse?" *New Testament Studies* 17 (1970-71): 328-38.

Dunnill, John. *Covenant and Sacrifice in the Letter to the Hebrews.* Society for New Testament Studies Monograph Series 75. New York: Cambridge University Press, 1992.

Eddy, Paul Rhodes, and Gregory A. Boyd. *The Jesus Legend: A Case for the Historical Reliability of the Synoptic Jesus Tradition.* Grand Rapids: Baker Academic, 2007.

Edwards, James R. *The Hebrew Gospel & the Development of the Synoptic Tradition.* Grand Rapids: Eerdmans, 2009.

Ehrman, Bart D. *Jesus: Apocalyptic Prophet of the New Millennium.* Oxford: Oxford University Press, 1999.

Epp, Eldon Jay. "The Disputed Words of the Eucharistic Institution (Luke 22,19b-20): The Long and Short of the Matter," *Biblica* 90 (2009): 407-16.

Evans, Craig A. "Aspects of Exile and Restoration in the Proclamation of Jesus and the Gospels." Pages 263-93 in *Jesus in Context: Temple, Purity, and Restoration,* ed. Bruce Chilton and Craig A. Evans. Arbeiten zur Geschichte des antiken Judentums und des Urchristentums 39. Leiden: Brill, 1997.

———. "Did Jesus Predict His Death and Resurrection?" Pages 82-97 in *Resurrection.* Journal for the Study of the New Testament Supplement 186, ed. S. E. Porter, M. A. Hayes, and D. Tombs. Sheffield: Sheffield Academic Press, 1999.

———. "From 'House of Prayer' to 'Cave of Robbers': Jesus' Prophetic Criticism of the Temple Establishment." Pages 417-22 in *The Quest for Context and Meaning: Studies in Biblical Intertextuality in Honor of James A. Sanders,* ed. C. A. Evans and S. Talmon. Leiden: Brill, 1997.

———. "Jesus' Action in the Temple: Cleansing or Portent of Destruction?" Pages 395-439 in *Jesus in Context: Temple, Purity, and Restoration.* Arbeiten zur Geschichte des antiken Judentums und des Urchristentums 39. Leiden: Brill, 1997.

———. *Jesus and His Contemporaries: Comparative Studies.* Arbeiten zur Geschichte des antiken Judentums und des Urchristentums 25. Leiden: E. J. Brill, 1995.

———. "Jesus and the Continuing Exile of Israel." Pages 77-100 in *Jesus and the Restoration of Israel: A Critical Assessment of N. T. Wright's* Jesus and the Victory of God. Edited by Carey C. Newman. Downers Grove: IVP, 1999.

———. "Jesus and Zechariah's Messianic Hope." Pages 373-88 in *Authenticating the Activities of Jesus,* ed. B. Chilton and C. A. Evans. New Testament Tools and Studies 28.2. Leiden: Brill, 1999.

———. "Jesus' Dissimilarity from Second Temple Judaism and the Early Church." Pages 145-58 in *Memories of Jesus: A Critical Appraisal of James D. G. Dunn's* Jesus Remembered. Edited by Robert B. Stewart and Gary R. Habermas. Nashville: B&H Academic, 2010.

———. *Mark 8:27–16:20.* Word Biblical Commentary 34b. Nashville: Thomas Nelson, 2001.

———. "Messiahs." Pages 537-42 in *Encyclopedia of the Dead Sea Scrolls,* ed. L. H. Schiffman and J. C. VanderKam. 2 vols. Oxford: Oxford University Press, 2000.

———. *Noncanonical Writings and New Testament Interpretation.* Peabody: Hendrickson, 1992.

———. "Opposition to the Temple: Jesus and the Dead Sea Scrolls." Pages 235-53 in *The Bible and the Dead Sea Scrolls: Scripture and the Scrolls.* The Princeton Symposium on the Dead Sea Scrolls. Edited by J. H. Charlesworth. Waco: Baylor University Press, 2006.

———. "Predictions of the Destruction of the Herodian Temple in the Pseudepigrapha, Qumran Scrolls, and Related Texts," *Journal for the Study of the Pseudepigrapha* 10 (1992): 89-147.

———. "Prophet, Sage, Healer, Messiah, and Martyr: Types and Identities of Jesus." Pages 1217-44 in *Handbook for the Study of the Historical Jesus.* 4 vols. Edited by Tom Holmén and Stanley E. Porter. Leiden: Brill, 2011.

———. "Sitting on Twelve Thrones of Israel: Scripture and Politics in Luke 22:24-30." Pages 455-79 in *Jesus in Context: Temple, Purity, and Restoration,* ed. Bruce Chilton and Craig A. Evans. Arbeiten zur Geschichte des antiken Judentums und des Urchristentums 39. Leiden: Brill, 1997.

———, ed. *The Routledge Encyclopedia of the Historical Jesus.* London: Routledge, 2008.

Evans, Craig A., and L. Novakovic. "Typology." Pages 986-90 in *Dictionary of Jesus and the Gospels.* 2nd ed. Edited by Joel B. Green, Jeannine K. Brown, and Nicholas Perrin. Downers Grove: IVP Academic, 2013.

Eve, Eric. *The Jewish Context of Jesus' Miracles.* Journal for the Study of the New Testament Supplement Series 231. London: Sheffield Academic Press, 2002.

Fabry, H.-J. "*leḥem.*" Volume 7, pages 525-27 in *Theological Dictionary of the Old Testament.* 15 vols. Edited by G. Johannes Botterweck et al. Grand Rapids: Eerdmans, 1974-2006.

Falk, Daniel K. *Daily, Sabbath, and Festival Prayers in the Dead Sea Scrolls.* Leiden: Brill, 1998.

———. "Festivals and Holy Days." Pages 636-45 in *The Eerdmans Dictionary of Early Judaism,* ed. John J. Collins and Daniel C. Harlow. Grand Rapids: Eerdmans, 2010.

———. "Moses." Pages 576-77 in *Encyclopedia of the Dead Sea Scrolls.* 2 vols. Edited by Lawrence H. Schiffman and James C. VanderKam. Oxford: Oxford University Press, 2000.

———. "Moses." Pages 967-70 in *The Eerdmans Dictionary of Early Judaism,* ed. John J. Collins and Daniel C. Harlow. Grand Rapids: Eerdmans, 2010.

Fanous, Daniel. *Taught by God: Making Sense of the Difficult Sayings of Jesus.* Rollinsford, NH: Orthodox Research Institute, 2010.

Farmer, William. "Reflections on Isaiah 53 and Christian Origins." Pages 260-80 in *Jesus and the Suffering Servant: Isaiah 53 and Christian Origins,* ed. William Farmer and William Bellinger. Harrisburg: Trinity Press International, 1998.

Fee, Gordon. *1 Corinthians.* New International Commentary on the New Testament. Grand Rapids: Eerdmans, 1987.

Feeley-Harnik, Gillian. *The Lord's Table: Eucharist and Passover in Early Christianity.* Philadelphia: University of Pennsylvania, 1981.

Feldman, Louis H. *Flavius Josephus: Translation and Commentary: Judean Antiquities 1-4,* ed. Steve Mason. Leiden: Brill, 1999.

———. *Philo's Portrayal of Moses in the Context of Ancient Judaism.* Notre Dame: University of Notre Dame Press, 2007.

———. "Restoration in Josephus." Pages 223-63 in *Restoration: Old Testament, Jewish, and Christian Perspectives,* ed. James H. Scott. Supplements to the Journal for the Study of Judaism 72. Leiden: Brill, 2001.

Feneberg, Rupert. *Christliche Passafeier und Abendmahl. Eine biblisch-hermeneutische Untersuchung der neutestamentlichen Einsetzungsbericht.* Studien zum Alten und Neuen Testaments 27. Munich: Kösel, 1971.

Feuillet, André. *Johannine Studies.* Translated by Thomas E. Crane. New York: Alba House, 1965.

Finegan, Jack. *Handbook of Biblical Chronology.* Princeton: Princeton University Press, 1964.

Finlan, Stephen. *The Background and Context of Paul's Cultic Atonement Metaphors.* Atlanta: Society of Biblical Literature, 2004.

Fitzmyer, Joseph A. *First Corinthians: A New Translation with Introduction and Commentary.* Anchor Yale Bible 32. New Haven: Yale University Press, 2008.

———. *The Gospel according to Luke.* 2 vols. Anchor Bible 28-28A. New York: Doubleday, 1983, 1985.

———. *The One Who Is to Come.* Grand Rapids: Eerdmans, 2007.

———. "The Priority of Mark and the 'Q' Source in Luke." Pages 131-70 in *Jesus and Man's Hope*. Pittsburgh: Pittsburgh Theological Seminary, 1970.

Flesher, Paul V. M. "Bread of the Presence." Volume 1, pages 780-81 in *Anchor Bible Dictionary*. 6 vols. Edited by David Noel Freedman et al. New York: Doubleday, 1992.

Fletcher-Louis, Crispin H. T. "Jesus as the High Priestly Messiah: Part 1," *Journal for the Study of the Historical Jesus* 4, no. 2 (2006): 155-75.

———. "Jesus as the High Priestly Messiah: Part 2," *Journal for the Study of the Historical Jesus* 5, no. 1 (2006): 57-79.

Flew, R. Newton. *Jesus and His Church*. London: Epworth, 1938.

Flusser, David. "The Last Supper and the Essenes." Pages 202-6 in *Judaism and the Origins of Christianity*. Jerusalem: Magnes, 1988.

———. *The Sage from Galilee: Rediscovering Jesus' Genius*. Translated by R. S. Notley, with J. H. Charlesworth. Grand Rapids: Eerdmans, 2007. Translation of *Jesus in Selbstzeugnissen und Bilddokumenten*. Hamburg: Rowohlt, 1968.

Foerster, W. "*epiousios*." Volume 2, pages 590-99 in *Theological Dictionary of the New Testament*, ed. G. Kittel and G. Friedrich. Translated by G. W. Bromiley. 10 vols. Grand Rapids: Eerdmans, 1964-1976.

Foster, Paul. "Memory, Orality, and the Fourth Gospel: Three Dead Ends in Historical Jesus Research," *Journal for the Study of the Historical Jesus* 10 (2012): 191-227.

Foster, Paul, A. Gregory, J. S. Kloppenborg, and J. Verheyden, eds. *New Studies in the Synoptic Problem: Oxford Conference, April 2008; Essays in Honor of Christopher M. Tuckett*. Bibliotheca Ephemeridum Theologicarum Lovaniensium 239. Leuven: Peeters, 2011.

France, R. T. *The Gospel of Mark*. New York: Doubleday, 1968.

———. *The Gospel of Matthew*. New International Commentary on the New Testament. Grand Rapids: Eerdmans, 2007.

———. *Jesus and the Old Testament*. Downers Grove: InterVarsity, 1971.

Fredriksen, Paula. *Jesus of Nazareth, King of the Jews*. New York: Vintage Books, 1999.

Freedman, David Noel, and David Miano. "People of the New Covenant." Pages 7-26 in *The Concept of the Covenant in the Second Temple Period*. Journal for the Study of Judaism Supplements 71. Edited by S. E. Porter and J. C. R. De Roo. Leiden: Brill, 2003.

Freyne, Sean. *Jesus, a Jewish Galilean: A New Reading of the Jesus-Story*. London: T. & T. Clark, 2005.

Frickenschmidt, Dirk. *Evangelium als Biographie: Die vier Evangelien im Rahmen antiker Erzählkunst*. Texte und Arbeiten zum neutestamentlichen Zeitalter 22. Tübingen: Francke, 1997.

Fuller, Michael E. *The Restoration of Israel: Israel's Re-gathering and the Fate of the Nations in Early Jewish Literature and Luke-Acts*. Berlin: Walter de Gruyter, 2006.

Fuller, R. H. *The Mission and Achievement of Jesus*. London: SCM, 1954.

Funk, Robert W., and the Jesus Seminar. *The Acts of Jesus: The Search for the Authentic Deeds of Jesus*. San Francisco: HarperSanFrancisco/Polebridge, 1998.

Funk, Robert W., Roy Hoover, and the Jesus Seminar. *The Five Gospels: The Search for the Authentic Words of Jesus*. New York: Macmillan, 1993.

Galavaris, George. *Bread and the Liturgy: The Symbolism of Early Christian and Byzantine Bread Stamps.* Madison: University of Wisconsin Press, 1970.

Gane, Roy. "'Bread of the Presence' and Creator in Residence," *Vetus Testamentum* 42, no. 2 (1992): 179-203.

García Martínez, Florentino. "New Jerusalem." Pages 606-10 in *Encyclopedia of the Dead Sea Scrolls.* 2 vols. Edited by Lawrence H. Schiffman and James C. VanderKam. Oxford: Oxford University Press, 2000.

García Martínez, Florentino, and Eibert J. C. Tigchelaar. *The Dead Sea Scrolls Study Edition.* 2 vols. Grand Rapids: Eerdmans, 2000.

Garnet, Paul. *Salvation and Atonement in the Qumran Scrolls.* Wissenschaftliche Untersuchungen zum Neuen Testament 3. Tübingen: Mohr Siebeck, 1977.

Gärtner, Bertil. *John 6 and the Jewish Passover.* Coniectanea neotestamentica 17. Lund: Gleerup, 1959.

———. *The Temple and the Community in Qumran and the New Testament: A Comparative Study of the Symbolism of the Qumran Texts and the New Testament.* Cambridge: Cambridge University Press, 1965.

Geldenhuys, Norval. *Commentary on the Gospel of Luke.* New International Commentary on the New Testament. Grand Rapids: Eerdmans, 1951.

Gibson, Jeffrey B. "Matthew 6:9-13//Luke 11:2-4: An Eschatological Prayer?" *Biblical Theology Bulletin* 31 (2001): 961-1005.

Ginzberg, Louis. *The Legends of the Jews.* 7 vols. Reprint. Translated by Henrietta Szold. Baltimore and London: Johns Hopkins University Press, 1998.

Glasson, T. F. *Jesus and the End of the World.* Edinburgh: St. Andrew, 1980.

———. *Moses in the Fourth Gospel.* Studies in Biblical Theology 40. London: SCM, 1963.

———. "The Reply to Caiaphas (Mark xiv.62)," *New Testament Studies* 7 (1960-61): 88-93.

———. "Schweitzer's Influence — Blessing or Bane?" Pages 107-20 in *The Kingdom of God in the Teaching of Jesus,* ed. Bruce Chilton. Philadelphia: Fortress, 1984.

———. "What Is Apocalyptic?" *New Testament Studies* 27 (1980): 98-105.

Gnilka, Joachim. *Jesus of Nazareth: Message and History.* Translated by Siegfried S. Schatzmann. Peabody: Hendrickson, 1997.

Goodacre, Marc. *The Case Against Q: Studies in Markan Priority and the Synoptic Problem.* Harrisburg: Trinity Press International, 2002.

———, and Nicholas Perrin, eds. *Questioning Q: A Multidimensional Critique.* Downers Grove: IVP, 2005.

Goppelt, L. "*pinō.*" Volume 6, pages 135-60 in *Theological Dictionary of the New Testament,* ed. G. Kittel and G. Friedrich. Translated by G. W. Bromiley. 10 vols. Grand Rapids: Eerdmans, 1964-1976.

Gorman, Frank H. "Passover, Feast of." Pages 1013-14 in *Eerdmans Dictionary of the Bible,* ed. David Noel Freedman. Grand Rapids: Eerdmans, 2000.

Graupner, Axel, and Michael Wolpner, eds. *Moses in Biblical and Extrabiblical Traditions.* Beihefte zur Zeitschrift für die alttestamentliche Wissenschaft 372. Berlin: De Gruyter, 2007.

Gray, George Buchanan *Sacrifice in the Old Testament: Its Theory and Practice.* Oxford: Clarendon, 1925.

Gray, Rebecca. *Prophetic Figures in Late Second Temple Jewish Palestine: The Evidence from Josephus.* New York: Oxford University Press, 1993.

Greenwood, David C. "On Jewish Hopes for a Restored Northern Kingdom," *Zeitschrift für die Alttestamentliche Wissenschaft* 88 (1976): 376-85.

Gregg, David W. A. *Anamnesis in the Eucharist.* Grove Liturgical Study 5. Bramcote: Grove Books, 1976.

———. "Hebraic Antecedents to the Eucharistic ΑΝΑΜΝΗΣΙΣ Formula," *Tyndale Bulletin* 30 (1979): 165-68.

Grossfeld, Bernard. *The Targum Onqelos to Deuteronomy.* Aramaic Bible 9. Wilmington: Michael Glazier, 1988.

———. *The Targum Onqelos to Exodus.* Aramaic Bible 7. Wilmington: Michael Glazier, 1988.

Groves, J. Alan "Atonement in Isaiah 53: 'For He Bore the Sins of Many.'" Pages 61-89 in *The Glory of the Atonement,* ed. C. E. Hill and Frank A. James III. Downers Grove: IVP, 2004.

Guilding, Aileen. *The Fourth Gospel and Jewish Worship: A Study of the Relation of St. John's Gospel to the Ancient Jewish Lectionary System.* Oxford: Clarendon, 1960.

Haacker, Klaus. "What Must I Do to Inherit Eternal Life? Implicit Christology in Jesus' Sayings about Life and the Kingdom." Pages 140-53 in *Jesus Research: An International Perspective,* ed. James H. Charlesworth and Petr Pokorný. Grand Rapids: Eerdmans, 2009.

Haenchen, Ernst. *John.* 2 vols. Translated by E. Haenchen. Hermeneia; Philadelphia: Fortress, 1984.

Häfner, Gerd. "Das Ende der Kriterien? Jesusforschung angesichts der geschichtstheoretischen Diskussion." Pages 97-103 in *Historiographie und fiktionales Erzählen: Zur Konstrucktivität in Geschichtstheorie und Exegese,* ed. Knut Backhaus and Gerd Häfner. Neukirchen-Vluyn: Neukirchener Verlag, 2008.

Hahn, Scott W. *The Kingdom of God as Liturgical Empire: A Theological Commentary on 1-2 Chronicles.* Grand Rapids: Baker Academic, 2012.

———. *Kinship by Covenant: A Canonical Approach to the Fulfillment of God's Saving Promises.* Anchor Yale Bible Reference Library. New Haven/London: Yale University Press, 2009.

Ham, C. "The Last Supper in Matthew," *Bulletin of Biblical Research* 10 (2000): 53-69.

Hamilton, Victor. *Exodus: An Exegetical Commentary.* Grand Rapids: Baker Academic, 2011.

———. *Handbook on the Pentateuch.* Grand Rapids: Baker Academic, 2005.

Hampel, Volker. *Menschensohn und historischer Jesus: Ein Rätselwort als Schlüssel zum messianischen Selbstverständnis Jesu.* Neukirchen-Vluyn: Neukirchener Verlag, 1990.

Haran, Menahem. "Shewbread." Volume 14, pages 1394-95 in *Encyclopedia Judaica.* 16 vols. Edited by Cecil Roth. Jerusalem: Keter, 1979.

———. *Temples and Temple Service in Ancient Israel.* Oxford: Clarendon, 1978.

Hartley, John F. *Leviticus.* Word Biblical Commentary 4. Dallas: Word Books, 1991.

Hatina, Thomas R. "Moses." Pages 420-21 in *The Routledge Encyclopedia of the Historical Jesus,* ed. Craig A. Evans. London: Routledge, 2008.

Hayward, C. T. R. *The Jewish Temple: A Non-Biblical Sourcebook.* London: Routledge, 1996.

Heawood, P. J. "The Time of the Last Supper," *Jewish Quarterly Review* 42 (1951): 37-44.

Heinemann, Joseph. "Amidah." Volume 2, pages 838-45 in *Encyclopedia Judaica.* 16 vols. Edited by Cecil Roth. Jerusalem: Keter, 1972.

———. "The Background of Jesus' Prayer in the Jewish Liturgical Tradition." Pages 81-89 in *The Lord's Prayer and Jewish Liturgy,* ed. Jakob J. Petuchowski and Michael Brocke. New York: Seabury, 1978.

Hengel, Martin. *The Atonement: The Origins of the Doctrine in the New Testament.* Translated by John Bowden. Minneapolis: Fortress, 1984.

———. "Eye-witness Memory and the Writing of the Gospels: Form Criticism, Community Tradition, and the Authority of the Authors." Pages 70-96 in *The Written Gospel,* ed. Markus Bockmuehl and Donald Hagner. Cambridge: Cambridge University Press, 2005.

———. "Jesus, the Messiah of Israel: The Debate about the 'Messianic Mission' of Jesus." Pages 323-49 in *Authenticating the Activities of Jesus,* ed. Bruce Chilton and Craig A. Evans. New Testament Tools and Studies 28.2. Leiden: Brill, 1999.

———. *Studies in Early Christology.* Edinburgh: T. & T. Clark, 1995.

Hengel, Martin, with Daniel P. Bailey, "The Effective History of Isaiah 53 in the Pre-Christian Period." Pages 75-146 in *Jesus and the Suffering Servant: Isaiah 53 and Christian Origins,* ed. P. Stuhlmacher and B. Janowski. Harrisburg: Trinity Press International, 1998.

Hengel, Martin, and Anna Maria Schwemer. *Der messianische Anspruch Jesu und die Anfange der Christologie: Vier Studien.* Wissenschaftliche Untersuchungen zum Neuen Testament 138. Tübingen: Mohr Siebeck, 2003.

Hengel, Martin, and Anna Maria Schwemer. *Jesus und das Judentum.* Geschichte des frühen Christentums, Vol. 1. Tübingen: Mohr-Siebeck, 2007.

Hennecke, E., and W. H. Schneemelcher. *New Testament Apocrypha.* 2 vols. Philadelphia: Westminster, 1963, 1965.

Hennig, John. "Our Daily Bread," *Theological Studies* (1943): 445-54.

Herzog, W. R., II. *Prophet and Teacher: An Introduction to the Historical Jesus.* Louisville: Westminster John Knox, 2005.

Hibbard, James Todd. *Intertextuality in Isaiah 24–27: The Reuse and Evocation of Earlier Texts and Traditions.* Forschungen zum Alten Testament 2/16. Tübingen: Mohr-Siebeck, 2006.

Hiers, R. H. *The Historical Jesus and the Kingdom of God: Present and Future in the Message and Ministry of Jesus.* Gainesville: University of Florida, 1973.

Higgins, A. J. B. *The Lord's Supper in the New Testament.* Chicago: Alec R. Allenson; Alva: Robert Cunningham and Sons, 1952.

Himmelfarb, Martha. *Ascent to Heaven in Jewish and Christian Apocalypses.* Oxford: Oxford University Press, 1993.

Hirsch, Emil G. "Showbread." Volume 11, pages 312-13 in *The Jewish Encyclopedia*. 12 vols. Edited by Isidore Singer. New York: Ktav, 1901.

Hoehner, Harold W. *Chronological Aspects of the Life of Christ.* Grand Rapids: Zondervan, 1977.

———. "The Chronology of Jesus." Pages 2315-59 in *The Handbook for the Study of the Historical Jesus,* ed. Tom Holmén and Stanley E. Porter. 4 vols. Leiden: Brill, 2011.

Hofius, Otfried. "The Lord's Supper and the Lord's Supper Tradition." In *One Loaf, One Cup: Ecumenical Studies of 1 Cor 11 and Other Eucharistic Texts.* New Gospel Studies 6. Edited by B. F. Meyer. Macon: Mercer University Press, 1993.

Holmén, Tom. "Authenticity Criteria." Pages 43-54 in *Encyclopedia of the Historical Jesus,* ed. C. A. Evans. New York/London: Routledge, 2008.

———. "Doubts About Double Dissimilarity: Restructuring the Main Criterion of Jesus-of-History Research." Pages 47-80 in *Authenticating the Words of Jesus,* ed. Bruce Chilton and Craig A. Evans. New Testament Tools and Studies 28. Leiden: E. J. Brill, 1999.

———. "An Introduction to the Continuum Approach." Pages 1-16 in *Jesus from Judaism to Christianity: Continuum Approaches to the Historical Jesus,* ed. Tom Holmén. Library of New Testament Studies 352. Edinburgh: T. & T. Clark, 2007.

———. *Jesus and Jewish Covenant Thinking.* Biblical Interpretation 55. Leiden: Brill, 2001.

———. "Jesus and the Purity Paradigm." Pages 2709-44 in *The Handbook for the Study of the Historical Jesus,* ed. Tom Holmén and Stanley E. Porter. 4 vols. Leiden: Brill, 2011.

———. "Jesus, Judaism, and the Covenant," *Journal for the Study of the Historical Jesus* 2, no. 1 (2004): 3-27.

———. "The Jewishness of Jesus in the 'Third Quest.'" Pages 143-62 in *Jesus, Mark and Q: The Teaching of Jesus and Its Earliest Records,* ed. M. Labahn and A. Schmidt. Sheffield: Sheffield Academic Press, 2001.

Holmén, Tom, ed. *Jesus from Judaism to Christianity: Continuum Approaches to the Historical Jesus.* Library of New Testament Studies 352. Edinburgh: T. & T. Clark, 2007.

———, and Stanley E. Porter, eds. *Handbook for the Study of the Historical Jesus.* 4 vols. Leiden: Brill, 2011.

Holmes, Michael W. *The Apostolic Fathers: Greek Texts and English Translations.* 3rd ed. Grand Rapids: Baker Academic, 2007.

Hooker, Morna D. "Did the Use of Isaiah 53 to Interpret His Mission Begin with Jesus?" Pages 125-51 in *Jesus and the Suffering Servant: Isaiah 53 and Christian Origins,* ed. William H. Bellinger Jr. and William R. Farmer. Harrisburg: Trinity Press International, 1998.

———. *Jesus and the Servant.* London: SPCK, 1959.

———. "On Using the Wrong Tool," *Theology* 75 (1972): 570-81.

———. *The Signs of a Prophet: The Prophetic Actions of Jesus.* London: SCM, 1997.

Horbury, William. *Jewish Messianism and the Cult of Christ.* London: SCM, 1998.

———. "The Messianic Associations of the 'Son of Man,'" *Journal of Theological Studies* 36 (1985): 34-55.

———. "The Twelve and the Phylarchs," *New Testament Studies* (1986): 503-27.

Horsley, Richard A. "The Dead Sea Scrolls and the Historical Jesus." Pages 36-60 in *The Bible and the Dead Sea Scrolls,* Volume Three: *The Scrolls and Christian Origins,* ed. James H. Charlesworth. Waco: Baylor University Press, 2006.

———. "'Messianic' Figures and Movements in First Century Palestine." Pages 276-95 in *The Messiah: Developments in Earliest Judaism and Christianity,* ed. James H. Charlesworth. Minneapolis: Fortress, 1992.

———, and Tom Thatcher. *John, Jesus, and the Renewal of Israel.* Grand Rapids: Eerdmans, 2013.

Hoskyns, E. C. *The Fourth Gospel.* London: Faber & Faber, 1947.

Houk, C. B. "*PEIRASMOS,* The Lord's Prayer, and the Massah Tradition," *Scottish Journal of Theology* 19 (1966): 216-25.

Howard, George. *Hebrew Gospel of Matthew.* Macon: Mercer University Press, 1995.

Howard, V. "Did Jesus Speak about His Own Death?" *Catholic Biblical Quarterly* 39 (1977): 515-27.

Huber, Wolfgang. *Passa und Ostern: Untersuchungen zur Osterfeier der alten Kirche.* Beihefte zur Zeitschrift für die neutestamentliche Wissenschaft. Berlin: Walter de Gruyter, 2011.

Hugenberger, H. P. "The Servant of the Lord in the 'Servant Songs' of Isaiah: A Second Moses Figure." Pages 105-40 in *The Lord's Anointed,* ed. P. E. Satterthwaite, R. S. Hess, and G. J. Wenham. Grand Rapids: Baker, 1995.

Humphreys, Colin J. *The Mystery of the Last Supper: Reconstructing the Final Days of Jesus.* Cambridge: Cambridge University Press, 2011.

Humphreys, Colin J., and W. G. Waddington. "Astronomy and the Date of the Crucifixion." Pages 165-81 in *Chronos, Kairos, Christos: Nativity and Chronological Studies Presented to Jack Finegan,* ed. Jerry Vardaman and Edwin Yamauchi. Winona Lake: Eisenbrauns, 1989.

Humphreys, Colin J., and W. G. Waddington. "Dating the Crucifixion," *Nature* 306 (1983): 743-46.

Hunter, Archibald M. *The Gospel according to John.* Cambridge Bible Commentary. Cambridge: Cambridge University Press, 1965.

Instone-Brewer, David. *Feasts and Sabbaths: Passover and Atonement.* Traditions of the Rabbis in the Era of the New Testament 2A. Grand Rapids: Eerdmans, 2011.

———. "Jesus' Last Supper: the Synoptics and John," *Expository Times* 112 (2001): 122-23.

Janowski, Bernd, and Peter Stuhlmacher, eds. *The Suffering Servant: Isaiah 53 in Jewish and Christian Sources.* Translated by Daniel P. Bailey. Grand Rapids: Eerdmans, 2004.

Jaros, Karl. *Jesus von Nazareth: Geschichte und Deutung.* Mainz: Verlag Philipp von Zabern, 2000.

Jastrow, Marcus. *Dictionary of the Targumim, Talmud Babli, Yerushalmi and Midrashic Literature.* 2 vols. New York: Judaica Press, 1971.

Jaubert, Annie. *The Date of the Last Supper.* Translated by I. Rafferty. Staten Island: Alba House, 1965 (orig. 1957).

Jeremias, Jeremias. *The Eucharistic Words of Jesus.* Translated by Norman Perrin. Philadelphia: Fortress, 1977.

———. *Jesus' Promise to the Nations.* Translated by S. H. Hooke. London: SCM, 1958.

———. "*Mōüsēs.*" Volume 4, pages 848-73 in *Theological Dictionary of the New Testament,* ed. G. Kittel and G. Friedrich. Translated by G. W. Bromiley. 10 vols. Grand Rapids: Eerdmans, 1964-1976.

———. *New Testament Theology,* vol. 1: *The Proclamation of Jesus.* Translated by John Bowden. New York: Charles Scribner's Sons, 1971.

———. "*pascha.*" Volume 5, pages 896-904 in *Theological Dictionary of the New Testament,* ed. G. Kittel and G. Friedrich. Translated by G. W. Bromiley. 10 vols. Grand Rapids: Eerdmans, 1964-1976.

———. *The Prayers of Jesus.* London: SCM; Philadelphia: Fortress, 1967.

———, with Walter Zimmerli. *The Servant of God.* London: SCM, 1957, rev. 1965.

Jerome. *Commentary on Matthew.* Translated by Thomas P. Scheck. Washington, DC: Catholic University of America Press, 2008.

Johnson, Brian D. "The Jewish Feasts and Questions of Historicity in John 5–12." Pages 117-29 in *John, Jesus, and History,* Volume 2: *Aspects of Historicity in the Fourth Gospel,* ed. Paul N. Anderson, Felix Just, S.J., and Tom Thatcher. Atlanta: Society of Biblical Literature, 2009.

Joyce, P. M. "King and Messiah in Ezekiel." Pages 323-37 in *King and Messiah in Israel and the Ancient Near East,* ed. J. Day. Journal for the Study of the Old Testament Supplements 270. Sheffield: Sheffield Academic Press, 1998.

Just, Arthur A., Jr. *Luke.* St. Louis: Concordia, 1996.

Kaiser, Otto. *Isaiah 13–39: A Commentary.* Old Testament Library. Philadelphia: Westminster, 1974.

Kaiser, Walter. *The Messiah in the Old Testament.* Studies in Old Testament Biblical Theology. Grand Rapids: Zondervan, 1995.

Kanof, Abram. "Passover." Volume 13, pages 163-73 in *Encyclopedia Judaica.* 16 vols. Edited by Cecil Roth. Jerusalem: Keter, 1972.

Kattenbusch, F. "Der Quellort der Kirchenidee." Pages 143-72 in *Festgabe von Fachgenossen und Freunden A. von Harnack zum siebzigsten geburtstag dargebracht.* Tübingen: Mohr-Siebeck, 1921.

Keener, Craig S. *Acts: An Exegetical Commentary.* 3 vols. Grand Rapids: Baker Academic, 2012, 2013.

———. *A Commentary on the Gospel of Matthew.* Grand Rapids: Eerdmans, 1999.

———. *The Gospel of John: A Commentary.* 2 vols. Peabody: Hendrickson, 2003.

———. *The Historical Jesus of the Gospels.* Grand Rapids: Eerdmans, 2009.

———. *Miracles: The Credibility of the New Testament Accounts.* 2 vols. Grand Rapids: Baker Academic, 2011.

Keith, Chris. "The Indebtedness of the Criteria Approach to Form Criticism and Recent Attempts to Rehabilitate the Search for an Authentic Jesus." Pages 25-48 in *Jesus, Criteria, and the Demise of Authenticity,* ed. Chris Keith and Anthony Le Donne. London: T. & T. Clark, 2012.

———. *Jesus' Literacy: Scribal Culture and the Teacher from Galilee.* Library of New Testament Studies 413. Library of Historical Jesus Studies 8. London: Bloomsbury T. & T. Clark, 2011.

———, and Anthony Le Donne, eds. *Jesus, Criteria, and the Demise of Authenticity.* London: T. & T. Clark, 2012.

Kim, Seyoon. "Jesus — The Son of God, the Stone, the Son of Man, and the Servant: The Role of Zechariah in the Self-Identification of Jesus." Pages 134-48 in *Tradition and Interpretation in the New Testament: Essays in Honor of E. Earle Ellis for His 60th Birthday,* ed. G. F. Hawthorne and O. Betz. Tübingen: Mohr-Siebeck; Grand Rapids: Eerdmans, 1987.

———. *The 'Son of Man' as the Son of God.* Wissenschaftliche Untersuchungen zum Neuen Testament 30. Tübingen: J. C. B. Mohr (Paul Siebeck), 1983.

Kirk, Alan. "Memory Theory and Jesus Research." Pages 809-43 in *Handbook for the Study of the Historical Jesus.* 4 vols. Edited by Tom Holmén and Stanley E. Porter. Leiden: Brill, 2011.

Kirk, Alan, and Tom Thatcher, eds. *Memory, Tradition, and Text: Use of the Past in Early Christianity.* Society of Biblical Literature Symposium Series. Atlanta: Society of Biblical Literature, 2005.

Kittel, G., and G. Friedrich, eds. *Theological Dictionary of the New Testament.* Translated by G. W. Bromiley. 10 vols. Grand Rapids: Eerdmans, 1964-1976.

Klauck, Hans-Josef. "Presence in the Lord's Supper: 1 Corinthians 11:23-26 in the Context of Hellenistic Religious History." Pages 57-74 in *One Loaf, One Cup: Ecumenical Studies of 1 Cor 11 and Other Eucharistic Texts.* The Cambridge Conference on the Eucharist, August 1988. New Gospel Studies 6. Edited by B. F. Meyer. Macon: Mercer University Press, 1993.

Klausner, Joseph. *Jesus of Nazareth: His Life, Times, and Teaching.* Translated by Herbert Danby. New York: Macmillan, 1925.

———. *The Messianic Idea in Israel from Its Beginnings to the Completion of the Mishnah.* Translated by W. F. Stinespring. New York: Macmillan, 1955.

Klawans, Jonathan. "Interpreting the Last Supper: Sacrifice, Spiritualization, and Anti-Sacrifice," *New Testament Studies* 48 (2002): 1-17.

———. *Purity, Sacrifice, and the Temple: Symbolism and Supersessionism in the Study of Ancient Judaism.* Oxford: Oxford University Press, 2006.

———. "Was Jesus' Last Supper a Seder?" *Bible Review* 17 (2001): 24-33.

Klink, E. W. *The Audience of the Gospels: The Origin and Function of the Gospels in Early Christianity.* Library of New Testament Studies 353. London: T. & T. Clark, 2010.

Knibb, Michael A. *The Qumran Community.* Cambridge Commentaries on Writings of the Jewish and Christian World 200 BC to AD 200 2. Cambridge: Cambridge University Press, 1987.

Knoch, Otto. "'Do This in Memory of Me!' (Luke 22:20; 1 Corinthians 11:24ff.): The Celebration of the Eucharist in the Primitive Christian Communities." Pages 1-10 in *One Loaf, One Cup: Ecumenical Studies of 1 Cor 11 and Other Eucharistic Texts.* The Cambridge Conference on the Eucharist, August 1988. New Gospel Studies 6. Edited by B. F. Meyer. Macon: Mercer University Press, 1993.

Kodell, Jerome. *The Eucharist in the New Testament.* Collegeville: Michael Glazier/Liturgical Press, 1988.

Koenig, John. *The Feast of the World's Redemption: Eucharistic Origins and Christian Mission.* Harrisburg: Trinity Press International, 2000.

Köhler, Kaufmann. "Eschatology." Pages 211-12 in volume 5 of *The Jewish Encylopedia,* ed. Isidore Singer. 12 vols. New York: Ktav, 1964.

Köstenberger, Andreas J. "John." Pages 415-512 in *Commentary on the New Testament Use of the Old Testament,* ed. G. K. Beale and D. A. Carson. Grand Rapids: Baker Academic, 2007.

———. "Was the Last Supper a Passover Meal?" Pages 1-25 in *The Lord's Supper: Remembering and Proclaiming Christ Until He Comes,* ed. T. R. Schreiner and M. R. Crawford. NAC Studies in Bible and Theology 10. Nashville: B&H Academic, 2011.

Krause, H. J. *Worship in Israel: A Cultic History of the Old Testament.* Oxford: Basil Blackwell, 1966.

Kuhn, Heinz-Wolfgang. "Jesus im Licht der Qumrangemeinde." Pages 1245-86 in *Handbook for the Study of the Historical Jesus.* 4 vols. Edited by Tom Holmén and Stanley E. Porter. Leiden: Brill, 2011.

Kuhn, K. G. "The Lord's Supper and the Communal Meal at Qumran." Pages 65-93 in *The Scrolls and the New Testament,* ed. K. Stendahl. London: SCM, 1958.

Kümmel, Werner Georg. *Promise and Fulfillment.* London: SCM, 1961.

Lagrange, Marie-Joseph. *Le Judaïsme avant Jésus-Christ.* Paris: Gabalda, 1931.

Lane, William L. *The Gospel According to Mark.* New International Commentary on the New Testament. Grand Rapids: Eerdmans, 1974.

Lang, Friedrich. "Abendmahl und Bundesgedanke im Neuen Testament," *Evangelische Theologie* 35 (1975): 524-38.

Latourelle, René. *The Miracles of Jesus and the Theology of Miracles.* Translated by Matthew J. O'Connell. New York: Paulist, 1988.

Laporte, Jean. *Eucharistia in Philo.* Lewiston: Edwin Mellen, 1984.

LaVerdiere, Eugene. *The Eucharist in the New Testament and the Early Church.* Collegeville: Liturgical Press, 1996.

Lebeau, Paul. *Le vin nouveau du royaume: Étude exégétique et patristique sur la parole eschatologique de Jésus à la Céne.* Bruges: Desclée de Brouwer, 1966.

Le Déaut, Roger C.S.Sp. *La Nuit Paschale: Essai sur la signification de la Pâque juive à partir du Targum d'Exode XII 42.* Rome: Institut Biblique Pontifical, 1963.

Le Donne, Anthony. "The Criterion of Coherence: Its Development, Inevitability, and Historiographical Limitations." Pages 95-114 in *Jesus, Criteria, and the Demise of Authenticity,* ed. Chris Keith and Anthony Le Donne. London: T. & T. Clark, 2012.

———. *The Historiographical Jesus: Memory, Typology, and the Son of David.* Waco: Baylor University Press, 2009.

Le Donne, Anthony, and Tom Thatcher, eds. *The Fourth Gospel in First-Century Media Culture.* Library of New Testament Studies 426. London: T. & T. Clark, 2011.

Leenhardt, F. J. "This Is My Body." Pages 24-31 in *Essays on the Lord's Supper,* ed. O. Cullmann and F. J. Leenhardt. London: Lutterworth, 1958. Reprint. Cambridge: James Clark & Co., 2004.

Léon-Dufour, Xavier. *Sharing the Eucharistic Bread: The Witness of the New Testament.* Translated by Matthew J. O'Connell. New York/Mahwah: Paulist, 1987.

Leonhard, C. "Das alttestamentlich und das jüdische Pesachfest." Pages 14-31 in *Die Osterfeier in der alten Kirche,* ed. H. auf der Maur, R. Messner, and W. G. Schöpf. Liturgica Oeninpontana 2. Münster: Lit, 2003.

———. *The Jewish Pesach and the Origins of the Christian Easter: Open Questions in Current Research.* Studia Judaica 35; Berlin and New York: De Gruyter, 2006.

Leonhardt, Jutta. *Jewish Worship in Philo of Alexandria.* Texts and Studies in Ancient Judaism 84. Tübingen: Mohr-Siebeck, 2001.

Levine, Amy-Jill. *The Misunderstood Jew: The Church and the Scandal of the Jewish Jesus.* San Francisco: HarperCollins, 2006.

Levine, Baruch A. *Leviticus.* JPS Torah Commentary; Philadelphia: Jewish Publication Society, 1989.

Lichtenberger, H. "'Bund' in Abendmahlüberlieferung." Pages 217-28 in *Bund und Tora: Zur theologischen Begriffsgeschichte in alttestamentlicher, frühjüdischer und urchristlicher Tradition.* Wissenschaftliche Untersuchungen zum Neuen Testament 92. Edited by F. Avemarie and H. Lichtenberger. Tübingen: Mohr-Siebeck, 1996.

Lierman, John.*The New Testament Moses: Christian Perceptions of Moses and Israel in the Setting of Jewish Religion.* Wissenschaftliche Untersuchungen zum Neuen Testament 2.173. Tübingen: Mohr Siebeck 2004.

Lietzmann, Hans. *Mass and Lord's Supper: A Study in the History of the Liturgy.* Translated by D. H. G. Reeves. Leiden: Brill, 1953-79.

Lightfoot, J. B. *Saint Paul's Epistles to the Colossians and Philemon.* London: Macmillan, 1879.

Lim, Timothy H. "11 QMelch, Luke 4 and the Dying Messiah," *Journal of Jewish Studies* 43 (1992): 90-92.

Lindars, Barnabas. *John.* Sheffield: Sheffield Academic Press, 1990.

Lindsay, D. R. "*Todah* and Eucharist: The Celebration of the Lord's Supper as a 'Thank Offering' in the Early Church," *Restoration Quarterly* 39 (1997): 83-100.

Lohfink, Gerhard. *Jesus and Community.* Translated by John P. Galvin. Philadelphia: Fortress; New York: Paulist, 1984.

———. *Jesus of Nazareth: What He Wanted, Who He Was.* Translated by Linda M. Maloney. Collegeville: Liturgical Press, 2012.

Lohmeyer, Ernst. *"Our Father": An Introduction to the Lord's Prayer.* Translated by John Bowden. New York: Harper & Row, 1965 (orig. 1952).

Loisy, Alfred. *The Gospel and the Church.* Translated by Christopher Home. London: Isbister & Co., 1903.

Long, Philip J. *Jesus the Bridegroom: The Origin of the Eschatological Feast as a Wedding Banquet in the Synoptic Gospels.* Eugene: Pickwick, 2013.

Longenecker, Richard N. "Literary Criteria in Life of Jesus Research: An Evaluation and Proposal." Pages 217-29 in *Current Issues in Biblical and Patristic Interpretation,* ed. M. C. Tenney. Grand Rapids: Eerdmans, 1975.

Lourié, B., M. Petit, and A. Orlov. *L'Eglise des deux Alliances: Mémorial Annie Jaubert (1912-1980).* Orientalia Judaica Christianica 1. Piscataway: Gorgias, 2008.

Lövestam, Evald. *Jesus and 'This Generation': A New Testament Study.* Coniectanea neotestamentica 25. Stockholm: Almqvist & Wiksell, 1995.

Lüdemann, Gerd. *Jesus after Two Thousand Years: What He Really Said and Did.* Translated by John Bowden. London: SCM; Amherst: Prometheus Books, 2001.

Lust, J., E. Eynikel, and K. Hauspie. *A Greek-English Lexicon of the Septuagint.* 2 vols. Stuttgart: Deutsche Bibelgesellschaft, 1992.

Luz, Ulrich. *Matthew 8–20.* Translated by James E. Crouch. Hermeneia; Minneapolis: Fortress, 2001.

Maiberger, P. *Das Manna.* Ägypten und Altes Testament 6. Wiesbaden: Harrassowitz, 1983.

Maier, Johann. *Jesus von Nazareth in der talmudischen Überlieferung.* Erträge der Forschung 82. Darmstadt: Wissenschaftliche Buchgesellschaft, 1978.

———. "Temple." Pages 921-27 in *Encyclopedia of the Dead Sea Scrolls,* ed. L. H. Schiffman and J. C. VanderKam. 2 vols. Oxford: Oxford University Press, 2000.

Malina, Bruce J. *The Palestinian Manna Tradition: The Manna Tradition in the Palestinian Targums and Its Relationship to the New Testament Writings.* Leiden: E. J. Brill, 1968.

Mann, C. S. "The Chronology of the Passion and the Qumran Calendar," *Church Quarterly Review* 160 (1959): 446-56 (here 451).

Manson, T. W. *The Sayings of Jesus.* London: SCM, 1949.

———. *The Teaching of Jesus.* Cambridge: Cambridge University Press, 1963.

Marcus, Joel. *Mark.* 2 vols. Anchor Yale Bible 27-27A. New Haven: Yale University Press, 2000, 2009.

———. "Passover and Last Supper Revisited," *New Testament Studies* 59 (2013): 303-24.

Marshall, I. Howard. "The Last Supper." Pages 529-641 in *Key Events in the Life of the Historical Jesus,* ed. Darrell L. Bock and Robert L. Webb. Wissenschaftliche Untersuchungen zum Neuen Testament 247. Tübingen: Mohr Siebeck, 2009.

———. *Last Supper and Lord's Supper.* London: Paternoster, 1980.

Marxsen, Willi. *The Beginnings of Christology: Together with the Lord's Supper.* Philadelphia: Fortress, 1979.

———. *The Lord's Supper as a Christological Problem.* Philadelphia: Fortress, 1970.

Matson, Mark A. "The Historical Plausibility of John's Passion Dating." Pages 291-312 in *John, Jesus, and History,* Volume 2: *Aspects of Historicity in the Fourth Gospel,* ed. Paul N. Anderson, Felix Just, S.J., and Tom Thatcher. Atlanta: Society of Biblical Literature, 2009.

Mburu, Elizabeth W. *Qumran and the Origins of Johannine Language and Symbolism.* Jewish and Christian Texts 8. London: T. & T. Clark, 2008.

McGowan, Andrew. *Ascetic Eucharists: Food and Drink in Early Christian Ritual Meals.* New York: Oxford University Press, 1999.

———. "'Is There a Liturgical Text in This Gospel?': The Institution Narratives and Their Early Interpretive Communities," *Journal of Biblical Literature* 118, no. 1 (1999): 73-87.

McGuckin, John A. "Sacrifice and Atonement: An Investigation into the Attitude of Jesus of Nazareth towards Cultic Atonement." Pages 648-61 in *Remembering for the Future,* vol. 1. Oxford: Pergamon Press, 1988.

McKelvey, R. J. *The New Temple: The Church in the New Testament.* Oxford: Oxford University Press, 1969.

McKiver, Robert. *Jesus, Memory, and the Synoptic Gospels.* Atlanta: Society of Biblical Literature, 2011.

McKnight, Scot. *Jesus and His Death: Historiography, the Historical Jesus, and Atonement Theory.* Waco: Baylor University Press, 2005.

———. "Jesus and Prophetic Actions," *Bulletin for Biblical Research* 10 (2000): 197-232.

———. "Jesus and the Twelve." Pages 181-214 in *Key Events in the Life of the Historical Jesus,* ed. Darrell L. Bock and Robert L. Webb. Wissenschaftliche Untersuchungen zum Neuen Testament 247. Tübingen: Mohr Siebeck, 2009.

———. "Jesus and the Twelve," *Bulletin of Biblical Research* 11 (2001): 203-31.

McNamara, Martin. *The Aramaic Bible: Targum Neofiti I and Pseudo-Jonathan: Exodus.* Collegeville: Liturgical Press, 1994.

———. *Targum and Testament.* Grand Rapids: Eerdmans, 1972.

McNamara, Martin, M.S.C., and Michael Maher, M.S.C. *Targum Neofiti 1: Exodus and Targum Pseudo-Jonathan: Exodus.* ArBib 2. Collegeville: Liturgical Press, 1994.

Meeks, Wayne A. *The Prophet King: Moses Traditions and the Johannine Christology.* Novum Testament Supplements 14. Leiden: Brill, 1967.

Meier, John P. "Basic Methodology in the Quest for the Historical Jesus." Pages 291-331 in *Handbook for the Study of the Historical Jesus.* 4 vols. Edited by Tom Holmén and Stanley E. Porter. Leiden: Brill, 2011.

———. "The Eucharist at the Last Supper: Did It Happen?" *Theology Digest* (1995-96): 1-17.

———. "Jesus, the Twelve, and the Restoration of Israel." Pages 365-404 in *Restoration: Old Testament, Jewish, and Christian Perspectives,* ed. James M. Scott. Supplements to the Journal for the Study of Judaism 72. Leiden: Brill, 2001.

———. *A Marginal Jew. Rethinking the Historical Jesus.* Volume One: *The Roots of the Problem and the Person.* Anchor Bible Reference Library. New York: Doubleday, 1991.

———. *A Marginal Jew. Rethinking the Historical Jesus.* Volume Two: *Mentor, Message, and Miracles.* Anchor Bible Reference Library. New York: Doubleday, 1994.

———. *A Marginal Jew. Rethinking the Historical Jesus.* Volume Three: *Companions and Competitors.* Anchor Bible Reference Library. New York: Doubleday, 2001.

———. *A Marginal Jew. Rethinking the Historical Jesus.* Volume Four: *Law and Love.* New Haven: Yale University Press, 2009.

Metzger, Bruce M. "Seventy or Seventy-Two Disciples?" *NTS* 5 (1958-59): 299-306.

———. *A Textual Commentary on the Greek New Testament: A Companion Volume to the United Bible Societies' Greek New Testament.* 2nd ed. Stuttgart: Deutsche Bibelgesellschaft, 1994.

Meye, R. P. *Jesus and the Twelve.* Grand Rapids: Eerdmans, 1968.

Meyer, Ben F. *The Aims of Jesus.* London: SCM, 1979.

———. "Appointed Deed, Appointed Doer: Jesus and the Scriptures." Pages 155-76 in *Authenticating the Activities of Jesus,* ed. Bruce Chilton and Craig A. Evans. New Testament Tools and Studies 28.2. Leiden: Brill, 1999.

———. "The Expiation Motif and the Eucharistic Words: A Key to the History of Jesus?" *Gregorianum* 69 (1988): 461-87.

Meyer, R. "Manna." Volume 4, pages 462-66 in *Theological Dictionary of the New Testament,* ed. G. Kittel and G. Friedrich. Translated by G. W. Bromiley. 10 vols. Grand Rapids: Eerdmans, 1964-1976.

Meyers, Carol L., and Eric M. Meyers. *Zechariah 9–14.* Anchor Bible 25C. New York: Doubleday, 1993.

Milgrom, Jacob. *Leviticus: A New Translation with Introduction and Commentary.* 3 vols. Anchor Bible 3, 3A, 3B. New York: Doubleday, 1991, 2000, 2001.

Milik, J. T. *Ten Years of Discovery in the Wilderness of Judea.* London: SCM, 1959.

Millar, Robert J. "The (A)Historicity of Jesus' Temple Demonstration: A Test Case in Methodology." Pages 235-52 in *Society of Biblical Literature 1991 Seminar Papers.* Society of Biblical Literature Seminar Papers 30. Edited by E. Lovering. Atlanta: Scholars Press, 1991.

———, ed., *The Apocalyptic Jesus: A Debate.* Santa Rosa: Polebridge, 2001.

Moloney, Francis J. *The Gospel of John.* Sacra Pagina 4. Collegeville: Liturgical Press, 1998.

———. *The Gospel of Mark: A Commentary.* Peabody: Hendrickson, 2002.

Montefiore, H. W. "Revolt in the Desert," *New Testament Studies* 8 (1962): 135-41.

Moore, George Foot. *Judaism in the First Centuries of the Christian Era: The Age of the Tannaim.* 3 vols. Cambridge, MA: Harvard University Press, 1927.

Mowinckel, Sigmund. *He That Cometh: The Messiah Concept in the Old Testament and Later Judaism.* Translated by G. W. Anderson. New York: Abingdon, 1956. Reprint. Grand Rapids: Eerdmans, 2005.

Nakamura, Catherine Lynn. "Monarch, Mountain, and Meal: The Eschatological Banquet of Isaiah 24:21-23; 25:6-10a." Ph.D. Dissertation. Princeton Theological Seminary, 1992.

Neusner, Jacob. *The Babylonian Talmud: A Translation and Commentary.* 22 vols. Reprint. Peabody: Hendrickson, 2005.

———. *The Mishnah: A New Translation.* New Haven: Yale University Press, 1988.

———. "Money-Changers in the Temple: The Mishnah's Explanation," *New Testament Studies* 35 (1989): 287-90.

Newman, Carey C., ed. *Jesus and the Restoration of Israel: A Critical Assessment of N. T. Wright's* Jesus and the Victory of God. Downers Grove: IVP; Carlisle: Paternoster, 1999.

Newsom, Carol A. "Songs of Sabbath Sacrifice." Pages 887-89 in volume 2 of *Encyclopedia of the Dead Sea Scrolls.* 2 vols. Edited by L. Schiffman and J. C. VanderKam. Oxford: Oxford University Press, 2002.

———. *Songs of the Sabbath Sacrifice: A Critical Edition.* Harvard Semitic Studies. Atlanta: Scholars Press, 1985.

Nickelsburg, George W. E. "Apocalyptic Ascent and the Heavenly Temple." Pages 210-17 in *Society of Biblical Literature Seminar Papers.* Atlanta: Scholars Press, 1987.

———. *1 Enoch 1: A Commentary on the Book of 1 Enoch, Chapters 1–36; 81–108.* Hermeneia. Minneapolis: Fortress, 2001.

———, and James C. VanderKam. *1 Enoch: A New Translation.* Minneapolis: Fortress, 2004.

———, and James C. VanderKam. *1 Enoch 2.* Hermeneia. Minneapolis: Fortress, 2012.

Niederwimmer, Kurt, and Linda M. Maloney. *The Didache.* Hermeneia. Minneapolis: Fortress, 1998.

Ninow, N. *Indicators of Typology within the Old Testament: The Exodus Motif.* New York: Peter Lang, 2001.

Nodet, E. "On Jesus' Last Supper," *Biblica* 91 (2010): 348-69.

North, C. R. *The Second Isaiah.* Oxford: Clarendon, 1964.

Nusca, A. R. *Heavenly Worship, Ecclesial Worship: A 'Liturgical Approach' to the Hymns of the Apocalypse of St. John.* Rome: Pontificia Universitas Gregoriana, 1998.

Oakman, Douglas E. "The Lord's Prayer in Social Perspective," in *Authenticating the Words of Jesus,* ed. C. A. Evans and B. Chilton. Leiden: Brill, 2002.

O'Connor, James T. *The Hidden Manna: A Theology of the Eucharist.* 2nd ed. San Francisco: Ignatius Press, 2010.

O'Connor, Jerome Murphy. "Jesus and the Money Changers (Mark 11:15-17; John 2:13-17)," *Revue biblique* 107 (2000): 42-55.

Oegema, Gerben S. *The Anointed and His People: Messianic Expectations from the Maccabees to Bar Kochba.* Journal for the Study of the Pseudepigrapha Supplement 27. Sheffield: Sheffield Academic Press, 1998.

Ogg, George. "The Chronology of the Last Supper." Pages 75-96 in *Historicity and Chronology in the New Testament,* ed. D. E. Nineham et al. London: SPCK, 1965.

O'Neill, J. C. "Did Jesus Teach That His Death Would Be Vicarious as Well as Typical?" Pages 9-27 in *Suffering and Martyrdom in the New Testament: Studies Presented to G. M. Styler by the Cambridge New Testament Seminar,* ed. William Horbury and Brian McNeil. Cambridge: Cambridge University Press, 1981.

Oswalt, John N. *The Book of Isaiah Chapters 1–39.* New International Commentary on the Old Testament. Grand Rapids: Eerdmans, 1986.

O'Toole, R. F. "The Parallels between Jesus and Moses," *Biblical Theology Bulletin* 20 (1990): 22-29.

Page, Sydney T. "The Authenticity of the Ransom Logion (Mark 10:45b)." Pages 137-61 in *Gospel Perspectives: Studies of History and Tradition in the Four Gospels,* ed. R. T. France and D. Wenham. Sheffield: JSOT Press, 1980.

Pao, David W. *Acts and the Isaianic New Exodus.* Wissenschaftliche Untersuchungen zum Neuen Testament 2:130. Tübingen: Mohr Siebeck: 2000.

Patrick, Dale A. "Epiphanic Imagery in Second Isaiah's Portrayal of a New Exodus," *Hebrew Annual Review* 8 (1984): 125-41.

Patsch, H. *Abendmahl und historischer Jesus.* Calwer theologische Monographien 1. Stuttgart: Calwer, 1972.

Paulus, Heinrich Eberhard Gottlieb. *Das Leben Jesu als Grundlage einer reinen Geschichte des Urchristentums.* 2 vols. Heidelberg: C. F. Winter, 1828.

Perrin, Nicholas. *Jesus the Temple.* Grand Rapids: Baker Academic, 2010.

———. "Last Supper." Pages 492-501 in *Dictionary of Jesus and the Gospels.* 2nd ed. Edited by Joel B. Green, Jeannine K. Brown, and Nicholas Perrin. Downers Grove: IVP Academic, 2013.

Perrin, Norman. *The Kingdom of God in the Teaching of Jesus.* New Testament Library. Philadelphia: Westminster, 1963.

———. *Rediscovering the Teaching of Jesus.* London/New York: SCM/Harper & Row, 1967.

Pesch, Rudolf. *Das Abendmahl und Jesu Todesverständnis.* Quaestiones disputatae 80. Freiburg: Herder, 1978.

———. *Das Markusevangelium.* 2 vols. Herders theologischer Kommentar zum Neuen Testament. Freiburg: Herder, 1977.

———. "The Gospel in Jerusalem: Mark 14:12-26 as the Oldest Tradition of the Early Church." Pages 106-48 in *The Gospel and the Gospels,* ed. Peter Stuhlmacher. Grand Rapids: Eerdmans, 1991.

Peterson, Silke. *Brot, Licht und Weinstock: Intertextuelle Analysen johanneischer Ich-bin-Worte.* Novum Testamentum Supplements 127. Leiden: Brill, 2008.

Petuchowski, Jakob J., and Michael Brocke, eds. *The Lord's Prayer and Jewish Liturgy.* New York: Seabury, 1978.

Pitre, Brant J. "Apocalypticism and Apocalyptic Teaching." Pages 22-33 in *Dictionary of Jesus and the Gospels.* 2nd ed. Edited by Joel B. Green, Jeannine K. Brown, and Nicholas Perrin. Downers Grove: IVP Academic, 2013.

———. "Jesus, the Messianic Wedding Banquet, and the Restoration of Israel," *Letter & Spirit* 8 (2013): 35-54.

———. "Jesus, the New Temple, and the New Priesthood," *Letter & Spirit* 4 (2008): 47-83.

———. *Jesus, the Tribulation, and the End of Exile.* WUNT 2.204. Tübingen: Mohr-Siebeck; Grand Rapids: Baker Academic, 2005.

———. "The Lord's Prayer and the New Exodus," *Letter & Spirit* 2 (2006): 69-96.

Pixner, Bargil. "An Essene Quarter on Mount Zion?" Pages 245-86 in *Studia Hierosolymitana in onore del P. Belarmino Bagatti,* vol. 1, *Studi archeologici.* SBFCMa 22. Jerusalem: Franciscan, 1976.

———. "The History of the 'Essene Gate' Area," *Zeitschrift des Deutschen Palästina-Vereins* 105 (1989): 96-104.

———. "Mount Zion, Jesus, and Archaeology." Pages 309-22 in *Jesus and Archaeology,* ed. James H. Charlesworth. Grand Rapids: Eerdmans, 2006.

———. *Paths of the Messiah: Jesus and Jewish Christianity in Light of Archaeological Discoveries.* San Francisco: Ignatius Press, 2010.

Pixner, Bargil, D. Chen, and S. Margalit. "Mount Zion: The 'Gate of the Essenes' Reexcavated," *Zeitschrift des Deutschen Palästina-Vereins* 105 (1989): 85-95 and plates 6-16.

Porter, Stanley E. *The Criteria for Authenticity in Historical-Jesus Research: Previous Discussion and New Proposals.* Journal for the Study of the New Testament Supplement Series 191. Sheffield: Sheffield Academic Press, 2000.

Porter, Stanley E., and Jacqueline C. R. de Roo, eds. *The Concept of the Covenant in the Second Temple Period.* Journal for the Study of Judaism in the Persian, Hellenistic, and Roman Periods Supplement 71. Leiden: Brill, 2003.

Powell, Mark Alan. "The De-Johannification of Jesus: The Twentieth Century and Beyond." Pages 121-32 in *John, Jesus, and History, Volume 1: Critical Appraisals of Critical Views,* ed. Paul N. Anderson, Felix Just, S.J., and Tom Thatcher. Atlanta: Society of Biblical Literature, 2007.

———. "Table Fellowship." Pages 925-31 in *Dictionary of Jesus and the Gospels.* 2nd ed.

Edited by Joel B. Green, Jeannine K. Brown, and Nicholas Perrin. Downers Grove: IVP Academic, 2013.

Priest, J. "The Messiah and the Meal in 1QSa," *Journal of Biblical Literature* 82 (1963): 95-100.

———. "A Note on the Messianic Banquet." Pages 222-38 in *The Messiah: Developments in Earliest Judaism and Christianity,* ed. James H. Charlesworth. Minneapolis: Fortress, 1992.

Propp, William H. C. *Exodus 1–18.* Anchor Bible 2. New York: Doubleday, 1998.

Ratzinger, Joseph (Pope Benedict XVI). *Jesus of Nazareth, Part Two: Holy Week, From the Entrance into Jerusalem to the Resurrection.* San Francisco: Ignatius Press, 2011.

Reich, R. "*Mishnah Sheqalim* 8:3 and the Archaeological Evidence." [Modern Hebrew]. Pages 225-56 in *Jerusalem in the Second Temple Period: Abraham Schalit Memorial Volume,* ed. A. Oppenheimer, U. Rappaport, and M. Stern. Jerusalem: Magnes, 1980.

Reimarus, Hermann Samuel. *Fragments.* Edited by Charles H. Talbert. Translated by Ralph Fraser. Philadelphia: Fortress, 1970 (orig. 1774-78).

Reiser, Marius. *Jesus and Judgment: The Eschatological Proclamation in Its Jewish Context.* Translated by Linda M. Maloney. Minneapolis: Fortress, 1997.

Reumann, J. H. "The Problem of the Lord's Supper as Matrix for Albert Schweitzer's 'Quest of the Historical Jesus,'" *New Testament Studies* 27 (1980-81): 475-87.

Reynolds, Benjamin E. *The Apocalyptic Son of Man in the Gospel of John.* Wissenschaftliche Untersuchungen zum Neuen Testament 2.249. Tübingen: Mohr-Siebeck, 2008.

Ricks, Stephen D. "The Prophetic Literality of Tribal Reconstruction." Pages 273-81 in *Israel's Apostasy and Restoration,* ed. Avraham Gileadi. Grand Rapids: Baker, 1988.

Riesner, Rainer. "Das Jerusalemer Essenerquartie und die Urgemeinde." Pages 1175-1222 in *Aufstieg und Niedergang der Römischen Welt* 26.2, ed. H. Temporini and W. Haase. Berlin: De Gruyter, 1995.

———. "Jesus, the Primitive Community, and the Essene Quarter of Jerusalem." Pages 198-234 in *Jesus and the Dead Sea Scrolls,* ed. James H. Charlesworth. New York: Doubleday, 1992.

———. "Josephus' 'Gate of the Essenes' in Modern Discussion," *Zeitschrift des Deutschen Palästina-Vereins* 105 (1989): 105-9.

Roberts, Alexander, and James Donaldson. *The Ante-Nicene Fathers.* 10 vols. Reprint. Peabody: Hendrickson, 1994.

Robinson, John A. T. "The Destination and Purpose of St John's Gospel," *New Testament Studies* 6 (1960): 117-31.

———. *Jesus and His Coming.* Philadelphia: Westminster, 1957.

———. "The Lord's Prayer." Pages 44-64 in *Twelve More New Testament Studies.* London: SCM, 1984.

———. *The Priority of John.* London: SCM, 1985.

Rodríguez, Rafael. "Authenticating Criteria: The Use and Misuse of a Critical Method," *Journal for the Study of the Historical Jesus* 7 (2009): 152-67.

Roth, Cecil. "Kaddish." Volume 10, pages 660-61 in *Encyclopedia Judaica.* 16 vols. Edited by Cecil Roth. Jerusalem: Keter, 1972.

———. "Manna." Volume 11, pages 884-85 in *Encyclopedia Judaica.* 16 vols. Jerusalem: Keter, 1971.

———. "Minyan." Volume 12, page 68 in *Encyclopedia Judaica.* 16 vols. 1st ed. Jerusalem: Ktav, 1971.

Routledge, R. "Passover and Last Supper," *Tyndale Bulletin* 53 (2002): 203-21.

Rowland, Christian. *The Open Heaven: A Study of Apocalyptic in Judaism and Early Christianity.* New York: Crossroad, 1982.

Rowley, H. H. *Worship in Ancient Israel: Its Forms and Meaning.* London: SPCK, 1967.

Rubenstein, Jeffrey L. *The History of Sukkot in the Second Temple and Rabbinic Periods.* Atlanta: Scholars Press, 1995.

Ruckstuhl, Eugen. *Chronology of the Last Days of Jesus: A Critical Study.* Translated by Victor J. Drapela. New York: Desclée, 1965.

———. *Die literarische Einheit des Johannes-Evangeliums.* Freiburg: Paulus, 1951.

Russell, D. S. *The Method and Message of Jewish Apocalyptic.* Philadelphia: Westminster, 1964.

Safrai, S., and Menahem Stern, eds., with David Flusser and W. C. van Unnik. *The Jewish People in the First Century: Historical Geography, Political History, Social, Cultural, and Religious Life and Institutions.* 2 vols. Compendia rerum iudaicarum ad Novum Testamentum, Section 1. Assen: Van Gorcum, 1974-76.

Safrai, S., and Z. Safrai. *The Haggadah of the Sages.* Reprint. Jerusalem: Carta, 2009 (orig. 1999).

Saldarini, Anthony J. *Jesus and Passover.* New York: Paulist, 1984.

Sanders, E. P. *The Historical Figure of Jesus.* London: Penguin, 1993.

———. *Jesus and Judaism.* Minneapolis: Fortress, 1985.

———. *Jewish Law from Jesus to the Mishnah: Five Studies.* London: SCM; Philadelphia: Trinity Press International, 1990.

———. *Judaism: Practice and Belief 63 BCE–66 CE.* London: SCM; Philadelphia: Trinity Press International, 1992.

Sanders, E. P., and Margaret Davies. *Studying the Synoptic Gospels.* London: SCM; Philadelphia: Trinity Press International, 1989.

Saulnier, Stéphane. *Calendrical Variations in Second Temple Judaism: New Perspectives on the 'Date of the Last Supper' Debate.* Journal for the Study of Judaism Supplements 159. Leiden: Brill, 2012.

Schäfer, Peter. *Jesus in the Talmud.* Princeton and Oxford: Princeton University Press, 2007.

Schaff, Philip, and Henry Wace, eds. *Nicene and Post-Nicene Fathers: Second Series.* 14 volumes. Reprint. Peabody: Hendrickson, 1994.

Schapdick, S. "Moses." Pages 610-15 in *Dictionary of Jesus and the Gospels.* 2nd ed. Edited by Joel B. Green, Jeannine K. Brown, and Nicholas Perrin. Downers Grove: IVP Academic, 2013.

Schiffman, Lawrence H. *The Eschatological Community of the Dead Sea Scrolls.* Society of Biblical Literature Monograph Series 38. Atlanta: Scholars Press, 1989.

Schlosser, Jacques D. *Le Règne de Dieu dans les Dits de Jésus.* 2 vols. Paris: Gabalda, 1980.

Schnackenburg, Rudolf. *The Gospel according to St. John.* Volume 2. Translated by Cecily Hastings et al. New York: Crossroad, 1990.

Schneemelcher, Wilhelm. *New Testament Apocrypha.* 2 vols. Translated by R. McL. Wilson. Louisville: Westminster John Knox, 1991, 1992.

Schröter, Jens. *Das Abendmahl: Frühchristliche Deutungen und Impulse für die Gegenwart.* Stuttgarter Bibelstudien 210. Stuttgart: Katholisches Bibelwerk, 2006.

Schürer, Emil. *The History of the Jewish People in the Age of Jesus Christ (175 B.C.–A.D. 135).* Revised and edited by Geza Vermes et al. 4 vols. Edinburgh: T. & T. Clark, 1973, 1979, 1986, 1987.

Schürmann, Heinz. *Der Einsetzungsbericht, Lk 22, 19-20.* Part II: *Einer quellenkritischen Untersuchung des lukanischen Abendmahlsberichtes, Lk 22,7-38.* Neutestamentliche Abhandlungen 20.4. Münster: Aschendorff, 1955.

Schweitzer, Albert. *The Mystery of the Kingdom of God.* Translated by Walter Lowrie. London: A. & C. Black, 1925 (orig. 1901).

———. *The Mysticism of Paul the Apostle.* Translated by William Montgomery. 2nd ed. London: A. & C. Black, 1953.

———. *The Problem of the Lord's Supper.* Translated by A. J. Mattill Jr. Edited by John Reumann. Macon: Mercer University Press, 1982 (orig. 1901).

———. *The Quest of the Historical Jesus. First Complete Edition.* Translated by William Montgomery, J. R. Coates, Susan Cupitt, and John Bowden. Minneapolis: Fortress, 2001.

———. *The Quest of the Historical Jesus: A Critical Study of Its Progress from Reimarus to Wrede.* Translated by William Montgomery. Rev. ed. New York: Macmillan, 1968.

Schweizer, Eduard. *The Lord's Supper according to the New Testament.* Translated by James M. Davis. Facet Books, Biblical Series 18. Philadelphia: Fortress, 1967.

Scott, James M. "Exile and Restoration." Pages 251-58 in *Dictionary of Jesus and the Gospels.* 2nd ed. Edited by Joel B. Green, Jeannine K. Brown, and Nicholas Perrin. Downers Grove: IVP Academic, 2013.

———, ed. *Exile: Old Testament, Jewish, and Christian Conceptions.* Journal for the Study of Judaism Supplements 56. Leiden: E. J. Brill, 1997.

———, ed. *Restoration: Old Testament, Jewish, and Christian Perspectives.* Journal for the Study of Judaism Supplements 72. Leiden: E. J. Brill, 2001.

Segal, J. B. *The Hebrew Passover from the Earliest Times to A.D. 70.* London Oriental Studies 12. London: Oxford University Press, 1963.

Simon, Maurice, ed. *Midrash Rabbah.* 10 vols. London/New York: Soncino Press, 1983.

Simonetti, Manlio. *Matthew.* 2 vols. Ancient Christian Commentary on Scripture. Downers Grove: IVP, 2001, 2002.

Skehan, Patrick W. "The Date of the Last Supper," *Catholic Biblical Quarterly* 20 (1958): 192-99.

Slayton, Joel C. "Manna." Volume 4, page 511 in *Anchor Bible Dictionary,* ed. D. N. Freedman. 6 vols. Anchor Bible Reference Library. New York: Doubleday, 1992.

Smit, Peter-Ben. *Fellowship and Food in the Kingdom.* Wissenschaftliche Untersuchungen zum Neuen Testament 2/234; Tübingen: Mohr-Siebeck, 2008.

Smith, Barry D. "The Chronology of the Last Supper," *Westminster Theological Journal* 53, no. 1 (1991): 29-45.

———. *Jesus' Last Passover Meal.* Lewiston: Edwin Mellen, 1993.

———. "Last Supper, Words of Institution." Pages 365-68 in *Encyclopedia of the Historical Jesus,* ed. Craig A. Evans. London: Routledge, 2008.

———. "The More Original Form of the Words of Institution," *Zeitschrift für die neutestamentliche Wissenschaft und die Kunde der älteren Kirche* 83 (1992): 166-86.

Smith, Dennis E. *From Symposium to Eucharist: The Banquet in the Early Christian World.* Minneapolis: Fortress, 2003.

———. "Meals." Pages 530-32 in *Encyclopedia of the Dead Sea Scrolls.* 2 vols. Edited by L. Schiffman and J. C. VanderKam. Oxford: Oxford University Press, 2002.

———. "Messianic Banquet." Volume 4, pages 787-91 in *Anchor Bible Dictionary,* ed. D. N. Freedman. 6 vols. Anchor Bible Reference Library. New York: Doubleday, 1992.

———. "The Messianic Banquet Reconsidered." Pages 64-73 in *The Future of Early Christianity: Essays in Honor of Helmut Koester,* ed. B. A. Pearson. Minneapolis: Fortress, 1991.

Smith, Dwight Moody. "Jesus Tradition in the Gospel of John." Pages 1997-2039 in *Handbook for the Study of the Historical Jesus,* ed. Tom Holmén and Stanley E. Porter. 4 vols. Leiden: Brill, 2011.

Smith, Morton. *Jesus the Magician.* San Francisco: Harper & Row, 1978.

Snodgrass, Klyne R. *Stories with Intent: A Comprehensive Guide to the Parables of Jesus.* Grand Rapids: Eerdmans, 2008.

———. "The Temple Incident." Pages 636-40 in *Key Events in the Life of the Historical Jesus,* ed. Darrell L. Bock and Robert L. Webb. Wissenschaftliche Untersuchungen zum Neuen Testament 247. Tübingen: Mohr Siebeck, 2009.

Stacey, W. David. "Appendix: The Lord's Supper as Prophetic Drama." Pages 80-95 in Morna D. Hooker, *The Signs of a Prophet: The Prophetic Actions of Jesus.* London: SCM, 1997.

———. "The Lord's Supper as Prophetic Drama," *Epworth Review* 21 (1994): 65-74.

Stanton, Graham. *The Gospels and Jesus.* 2nd ed. Oxford: Oxford University Press, 2002.

———. *Jesus and Gospel.* Cambridge: Cambridge University Press, 2004.

Stein, Robert H. "The Criteria of Authenticity." In *Gospel Perspectives: Studies of History and Tradition in the Four Gospels,* vol. 1. Edited by R. T. France and D. Wenham. Sheffield: JSOT, 1980.

Stemberger, Günter. "Pesachhaggada und Abendmahlsberichte des Neuen Testaments." In idem, *Studien zum rabbinischen Judentum.* Stuttgarter biblische Aufsatzbände 10. Stuttgart: Katholisches Bibelwerk, 1990.

Stern, Sacha. *Calendar and Community: A History of the Jewish Calendar, 2nd Century* BCE *to 10th Century* CE. Oxford: Oxford University Press, 2001.

Stewart, Robert B., and Gary R. Habermas, eds. *Memories of Jesus: A Critical Appraisal of James D. G. Dunn's* Jesus Remembered. Nashville: B&H Academic, 2010.

Story, Cullen I. K. "The Bearing of Old Testament Terminology on the Johannine Chronology of the Final Passover of Jesus," *Novum Testamentum* 31 (1989): 316-24.

Strack, Hermann L., and Paul Billerbeck. *Kommentar zum Neuen Testament aus Talmud und Midrasch.* 4 volumes. 3rd ed. Munich: C. H. Beck, 1961.

Strauss, David Friedrich. *The Life of Jesus Critically Examined.* Translated by G. Eliot. Philadelphia: Fortress, 1972 (orig. 1840).

Stuhlmacher, Peter. *Biblische Theologie des Neuen Testaments.* 2 vols. Göttingen: Vandenhoeck und Ruprecht, 1992.

———. "Isaiah 53 in the Gospels and Acts." Pages 147-62 in *The Suffering Servant: Isaiah 53 in Jewish and Christian Sources,* ed. Bernd Janowski and Peter Stuhlmacher. Translated by Daniel P. Bailey. Grand Rapids: Eerdmans, 2004.

———. *Jesus of Nazareth — Christ of Faith.* Translated by Siegfried S. Schatzmann. Peabody: Hendrickson, 1993.

Stuhlmueller, Carroll. *Creative Redemption in Deutero-Isaiah.* Rome: Pontifical Biblical Institute, 1970.

Swetnam, James. "Hallowed Be Thy Name," *Bib* 52 (1972): 556-63.

Tabory, Joseph. *Jewish Festivals in the Time of the Mishna and Talmud.* Jerusalem: Magnes, 1995.

———. "Towards a History of the Passover Meal." In *Passover and Easter: Origin and History to Modern Times,* ed. Paul F. Bradshaw and L. A. Hoffman. Notre Dame: University of Notre Dame, 1999.

Tan, Kim Huat. *The Zion Traditions and the Aims of Jesus.* Society for New Testament Studies Monograph Series 91. Cambridge: Cambridge University Press, 1997.

Taylor, Joan E. *The Immerser: John the Baptist within Second Temple Judaism.* Studying the Historical Jesus. Grand Rapids: Eerdmans, 1997.

———. *Jewish Women Philosophers of First-Century Alexandria: Philo's "Therapeutae" Reconsidered.* Oxford: Oxford University Press, 2004.

———. "John the Baptist." Pages 819-21 in *The Eerdmans Dictionary of Early Judaism,* ed. John J. Collins and Daniel C. Harlow. Grand Rapids: Eerdmans, 2010.

Taylor, Vincent. *The Gospel according to St. Mark.* 2nd ed. London: Macmillan, 1966.

———. *Jesus and His Sacrifice: A Study of the Passion Sayings in the Gospels.* London: Macmillan, 1959.

Teeple, Howard M. *The Mosaic Eschatological Prophet.* Society of Biblical Literature Manuscript Series 10. Philadelphia: Society of Biblical Literature, 1957.

Thatcher, Tom. *Jesus the Riddler: The Power of Ambiguity in the Gospels.* Westminster: John Knox, 2006.

Theissen, Gerd. *The Gospels in Context: Social and Political History of the Synoptic Tradition.* Translated by Linda M. Maloney. Minneapolis: Fortress, 1991.

Theissen, Gerd, and Annette Merz. "The Delay of the Parousia as a Test Case for the Criterion of Coherence," *Louvain Studies* 32 (2007): 49-66 (here 54).

Theissen, Gerd, and Annette Merz. *The Historical Jesus: A Comprehensive Guide.* Translated by John Bowden. Minneapolis: Fortress, 1998.

Theissen, Gerd, and Dagmar Winter. *The Quest for the Plausible Jesus: The Question of Criteria.* Translated by M. Eugene Boring. Louisville: Westminster John Knox, 2002.

Thiselton, Anthony. *The First Epistle to the Corinthians: A Commentary on the Greek Text.* New International Greek Testament Commentary. Grand Rapids: Eerdmans, 2000.

Thompson, Marianne Meye. *The Promise of the Father: Jesus and God in the New Testament.* Louisville: Westminster John Knox, 2000.

Tilling, Chris. "Tribes of Israel." Pages 662-63 in *The Routledge Encyclopedia of the Historical Jesus,* ed. Craig A. Evans. London: Routledge, 2008.

Torrey, C. C. "The Date of the Crucifixion according to the Fourth Gospel," *Journal of Biblical Literature* 50 (1931): 227-41.

———. "In the Fourth Gospel the Last Supper Was a Passover Meal," *Jewish Quarterly Review* 42 (1951-52): 237-50.

Twelftree, Graham H. "Jesus and the Synagogue." Pages 3105-34 in *Handbook for the Study of the Historical Jesus.* 4 vols. Edited by Tom Holmén and Stanley E. Porter. Leiden: Brill, 2011.

———. *Jesus the Miracle Worker: A Historical & Theological Study.* Downers Grove: IVP, 1999.

Ulrich, Eugene C., and James C. VanderKam, eds. *The Community of the Renewed Covenant: The Notre Dame Symposium on the Dead Sea Scrolls.* Notre Dame: University of Notre Dame Press, 1994.

VanderKam, James C. *Calendars in the Dead Sea Scrolls: Measuring Time* (London: Routledge, 1998).

———. *The Dead Sea Scrolls Today.* Grand Rapids: Eerdmans, 1994.

———. "Exile in Jewish Apocalyptic Literature." Pages 90-108 in *Exile: Old Testament, Jewish, and Christian Conceptions,* ed. James Scott. Supplements to the Journal for the Study of Judaism 56. Leiden: Brill, 1997.

———. "Isaac's Blessing of Levi and His Descendants in *Jubilees* 31." Pages 497-519 in *The Provo International Conference on the Dead Sea Scrolls: Technological Innovations, New Texts, and Reformulated Issues,* ed. D. W. Parry and Eugene Ulrich. Studies on the Texts of the Desert of Judah 30. Leiden: E. J. Brill, 1999.

———. "Passover." Volume 2, pages 637-38 in *Encyclopedia of the Dead Sea Scrolls.* 2 vols. Edited by Lawrence H. Schiffman and James C. VanderKam. Oxford: Oxford University Press, 2000.

———. "Righteous One, Messiah, Chosen One, and Son of Man in 1 Enoch 37–71." Pages 169-91 in *The Messiah: Developments in Earliest Judaism and Christianity,* ed. James H. Charlesworth. Minneapolis: Fortress, 1992.

VanderKam, James C., and Peter Flint. *The Meaning of the Dead Sea Scrolls.* San Francisco: HarperCollins, 2002.

van der Loos, H. *The Miracles of Jesus.* Novum Testamentum Supplements 9. Leiden: E. J. Brill, 1965.

van der Wahl, A. "Themes from Exodus in Jeremiah 30–31." Pages 559-67 in *Studies in the Book of Exodus.* Bibliotheca ephemeridum theologicarum lovaniensum. Edited by M. Vervenne. Leuven: Leuven University Press, 1996.

Vanhoye, Albert. *Old Testament Priests and the New Priest According to the New Testament.* Petersham, MA: St. Bede's Publications, 1986.

Van Tilborg, S. "A Form-Criticism of the Lord's Prayer." *Novum Testamentum* 14 (1972): 94-105.

Vermes, Geza. *The Changing Faces of Jesus.* New York: Viking Compass, 2000.

———. *The Complete Dead Sea Scrolls in English.* New York: Penguin, 1997.

———. *Jesus and the World of Judaism.* London: SCM, 1983.

———. *Jesus the Jew: A Historian's Readings of the Gospels.* London: Collins, 1973.
———. *The Religion of Jesus the Jew.* Minneapolis: Fortress, 1993.
von Rad, Gerhard. *Old Testament Theology.* 2 vols. Translated by D. M. G. Stalker. New York: Harper & Row, 1965.
Wainwright, Geoffrey. *Eucharist and Eschatology.* 2nd ed. Nashville: Order of St Luke, 2002.
Walther, Georg. *Jesus, das Passalamm des Neuen Bundes: Der Zentralgedanke des Herrenmahles.* Gütersloh: Bertelsmann, 1950.
Watts, Rikki E. *Isaiah's New Exodus and Mark.* Wissenschaftliche Untersuchungen zum Neuen Testament 2:88. Tübingen: Mohr Siebeck, 1997.
———. "Jesus' Death, Isaiah 53, and Mark 10:45: A Crux Revisited." Pages 125-51 in *Jesus and the Suffering Servant: Isaiah 53 and Christian Origins,* ed. William R. Farmer and William H. Bellinger Jr. Harrisburg: Trinity Press International, 1998.
Webb, Robert L. "The Historical Enterprise and Historical Jesus Research." Pages 54-75 in *Key Events in the Life of the Historical Jesus,* ed. Darrell L. Bock and Robert L. Webb. Wissenschaftliche Untersuchungen zum Neuen Testament 247. Tübingen: Mohr Siebeck, 2009.
———. *John the Baptizer and Prophet: A Sociohistorical Study.* Reprint. Eugene: Wipf & Stock, 2006.
Webster, J. *Ingesting Jesus: Eating and Drinking in the Gospel of John.* Society of Biblical Literature Archaeology and Biblical Studies 6. Atlanta: Society of Biblical Literature, 2003.
Weiss, Johannes. *Jesus' Proclamation of the Kingdom of God.* Translated by Richard Hyde Hiers and David Larrimore Holland. Philadelphia: Fortress, 1971 (1892 orig.).
Wellhausen, Julius. *Das Evangelium Johannis.* Berlin: Georg Reimer, 1908.
Wenell, Karen J. *Jesus and Land: Sacred and Social Space in Second Temple Judaism.* Library of New Testament Studies 334. London: T. & T. Clark, 2007.
Wenham, David. "How Jesus Understood the Last Supper: A Parable in Action," *Themelios* 20, no. 2 (1995): 11-15.
Westcott, B. F. *The Gospel according to St. John.* Grand Rapids: Eerdmans, 1953.
Whiston, William. *The Works of Josephus: Complete and Unabridged.* Rev. ed. Peabody: Hendrickson, 1987.
Wilkins, Michael J. "Peter's Declaration concerning Jesus' Identity at Caesarea Philippi." Pages 292-381 in *Key Events in the Life of the Historical Jesus,* ed. Darrell L. Bock and Robert L. Webb. Wissenschaftliche Untersuchungen zum Neuen Testament 247. Tübingen: Mohr Siebeck, 2009.
Williams, S. K. *Jesus' Death as a Saving Event: The Background and Origin of a Concept.* Harvard Dissertations in Religion 2. Missoula: Scholars Press, 1975.
Willitts, Joel. "Presuppositions and Procedures in the Study of the 'Historical Jesus': Or, Why I Decided Not to Be a 'Historical Jesus' Scholar," *Journal for the Study of the Historical Jesus* 3, no. 1 (2005): 61-108.
Wills, L. M. *The Quest of the Historical Gospel: Mark, John, and the Origins of the Gospel Genre.* London: Routledge, 1997.
Winter, Dagmar. "Saving the Quest for Authenticity from the Criterion of Dissimilarity:

History and Plausibility." Pages 115-31 in *Jesus, Criteria, and the Demise of Authenticity,* ed. Chris Keith and Anthony Le Donne. London: T. & T. Clark, 2012.

Winter, Paul. *On the Trial of Jesus.* Berlin: Walter de Gruyter, 1961.

Wise, Michael, Martin Abegg Jr., and Edward Cook. *The Dead Sea Scrolls: A New Translation.* San Francisco: HarperCollins, 1996.

Witherington, Ben, III. *The Christology of Jesus.* Minneapolis: Fortress, 1990.

———. *Jesus the Seer: The Progress of Prophecy.* Peabody: Hendrickson, 1999.

———. *Making a Meal of It: Rethinking the Theology of the Lord's Supper.* Waco: Baylor University Press, 2007.

Wright, N. T. "In Grateful Dialogue." Pages 244-77 in *Jesus and the Restoration of Israel: A Critical Assessment of N. T. Wright's* Jesus and the Victory of God, ed. Carey C. Newman. Downers Grove: IVP, 1999.

———. *Jesus and the Victory of God.* Minneapolis: Fortress, 1996.

———. "The Lord's Prayer as a Paradigm for Christian Prayer." Pages 132-54 in *Into God's Presence: Prayer in the New Testament,* ed. Richard N. Longenecker. Grand Rapids: Eerdmans, 2001.

———. *The New Testament and the People of God.* Minneapolis: Fortress, 1992.

———. *The Resurrection of the Son of God.* Minneapolis: Fortress, 2003.

———. "The Servant and Jesus: The Relevance of the Colloquy." Pages 281-97 in *Jesus and the Suffering Servant: Isaiah 53 and Christian Origins,* ed. W. H. Bellinger and William R. Farmer. Harrisburg: Trinity Press International, 1998.

Yee, Gale A. *Jewish Feasts and the Gospel of John.* Wilmington: Michael Glazier, 1989.

Yofre, Simian. *"panîm."* Volume 11, pages 589-615 in *Theological Dictionary of the Old Testament.* 15 vols. Edited by G. Johannes Botterweck et al. Grand Rapids: Eerdmans, 1974-2006.

Yuval, I. J. "Easter and Passover," in *Passover and Easter: Origin and History to Modern Times,* ed. Paul F. Bradshaw and Lawrence A. Hoffman. Notre Dame: University of Notre Dame, 2000.

Zahn, Theodor. *Introduction to the New Testament.* Translated by J. M. Trout et al. 3 vols. London: T. & T. Clark, 1909.

Zeitlin, Solomon. "The Date of the Crucifixion according to the Fourth Gospel," *Journal of Biblical Literature* 51 (1932): 263-71.

———. "The Last Supper as an Ordinary Meal in the Fourth Gospel," *Jewish Quarterly Review* 42 (1951-52): 251-60.

Zeller, Dieter. "Das Logion Mt 8,11f/Lk 13,28f und das Motive der Völkerwallfahrt," *Biblische Zeitschrift* 15 (1971): 222-37 and 16 (1972): 84-93.

Index of Authors

Index of Subjects

Index of Biblical and Other Ancient Literature